❧ Marking Evil ☙

MAKING SENSE OF HISTORY
Studies in Historical Cultures
General Editor: Stefan Berger
Founding Editor: Jörn Rüsen

Bridging the gap between historical theory and the study of historical memory, this series crosses the boundaries between both academic disciplines and cultural, social, political and historical contexts. In an age of rapid globalization, which tends to manifest itself on an economic and political level, locating the cultural practices involved in generating its underlying historical sense is an increasingly urgent task.

Volume 1
Western Historical Thinking: An Intercultural Debate
 Edited by Jörn Rüsen

Volume 2
Identities: Time, Difference, and Boundaries
 Edited by Heidrun Friese

Volume 3
Narration, Identity, and Historical Consciousness
 Edited by Jürgen Straub

Volume 4
Thinking Utopia: Steps into Other Worlds
 Edited by Jörn Rüsen, Michael Fehr, and Thomas W. Rieger

Volume 5
History: Narration, Interpretation, Orientation
 Jörn Rüsen

Volume 6
The Dynamics of German Industry: Germany's Path toward the New Economy and the American Challenge
 Werner Abelshauser

Volume 7
Meaning and Representation in History
 Edited by Jörn Rüsen

Volume 8
Remapping Knowledge: Intercultural Studies for a Global Age
 Mihai Spariosu

Volume 9
Cultures of Technology and the Quest for Innovation
 Edited by Helga Nowotny

Volume 10
Time and History: The Variety of Cultures
 Edited by Jörn Rüsen

Volume 11
Narrating the Nation: Representations in History, Media and the Arts
 Edited by Stefan Berger, Linas Eriksonas, and Andrew Mycock

Volume 12
Historical Memory in Africa: Dealing with the Past, Reaching for the Future in an Intercultural Context
 Edited by Mamadou Diawara, Bernard Lategan, and Jörn Rüsen

Volume 13
New Dangerous Liaisons: Discourses on Europe and Love in the Twentieth Century
 Edited by Luisa Passerini, Liliana Ellena, and Alexander C. T. Geppert

Volume 14
Dark Traces of the Past: Psychoanalysis and Historical Thinking
 Edited by Jürgen Straub and Jörn Rüsen

Volume 15
A Lover's Quarrel with the Past: Romance, Representation, Reading
 Ranjan Ghosh

Volume 16
The Holocaust and Historical Methodology
 Edited by Dan Stone

Volume 17
What is History For? Johann Gustav Droysen and the Functions of Historiography
 Arthur Alfaix Assis

Volume 18
Vanished History: The Holocaust in Czech and Slovak Historical Culture
 Tomas Sniegon

Volume 19
Jewish Histories of the Holocaust: New Transnational Approaches
 Edited by Norman J. W. Goda

Volume 20
Helmut Kohl's Quest for Normality: His Representation of the German Nation and Himself
 Christian Wicke

Volume 21
Marking Evil: Holocaust Memory in the Global Age
 Edited by Amos Goldberg and Haim Hazan

MARKING EVIL

Holocaust Memory in the Global Age

Edited by
Amos Goldberg and Haim Hazan

Published in 2015 by
Berghahn Books
www.berghahnbooks.com

© 2015, 2019 Amos Goldberg and Haim Hazan
First paperback edition published in 2019

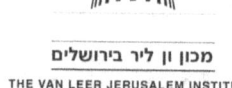

מכון ון ליר בירושלים
THE VAN LEER JERUSALEM INSTITUTE
معهد فان لير في القدس

All rights reserved. Except for the quotation of short passages
for the purposes of criticism and review, no part of this book
may be reproduced in any form or by any means, electronic or
mechanical, including photocopying, recording, or any information
storage and retrieval system now known or to be invented,
without written permission of the publisher.

Library of Congress Cataloging-in-Publication Data

Marking evil : Holocaust memory in the global age / edited by Amos Goldberg
and Haim Hazan.
  pages cm — (Making sense of history ; volume 21)
  Includes index.
  ISBN 978-1-78238-619-3 (hardback) — ISBN 978-1-78238-620-9 (ebook)
 1. Holocaust, Jewish (1939–1945)—Historiography—Congresses.
2. Holocaust, Jewish (1939–1945)—Moral and ethical aspects—Congresses.
3. Collective memory—Congresses. I. Goldberg, Amos, editor. II. Hazan, Haim,
editor.
 D804.348.M35 2015
 940.53'18—dc23

2014033537

British Library Cataloguing in Publication Data

A catalogue record for this book is available from the British Library

ISBN 978-1-78238-619-3 hardback
ISBN 978-1-78920-056-0 paperback
ISBN 978-1-78238-620-9 ebook

Contents

List of Figures — viii

Preface — x
    Amos Goldberg and Haim Hazan

Section I. Introductions

Chapter 1. Ethics, Identity, and Antifundamental Fundamentalism: Holocaust Memory in the Global Age (a Cultural-Political Introduction) — 3
    Amos Goldberg

Chapter 2. Globalization versus Holocaust: An Anthropological Conundrum — 30
    Haim Hazan

Section II. How Global Is Holocaust Memory?

Chapter 3. The Holocaust Is Not—and Is Not Likely to Become—a Global Memory — 47
    Peter Novick

Chapter 4. The Holocaust as a Symbolic Manual: The French Revolution, the Holocaust, and Global Memories — 56
    Alon Confino

Chapter 5. "After Auschwitz": A Constitutive Turning Point in Moral Philosophy — 70
    Ronit Peleg

Chapter 6. Cosmopolitan Body: The Holocaust as Route to the
Globally Human   99
Nigel Rapport

Section III. Memory, Trauma, and Testimony: The Holocaust and Non-Western Memories

Chapter 7. Holocaust Memories and Cosmopolitan Practices: Humanitarian Witnessing between Emergencies and the Catastrophe   121
Michal Givoni

Chapter 8. The Global Semiotics of Trauma and Testimony: A Comparative Study of Jewish Israeli, Cambodian Canadian, and Cambodian Genocide Descendant Legacies   146
Carol A. Kidron

Chapter 9. Genres of Identification: Holocaust Testimony and Postcolonial Witness   171
Louise Bethlehem

Chapter 10. Commemorating the Twentieth Century: The Holocaust and Nonviolent Struggle in Global Discourse   193
Tamar Katriel

Chapter 11. Rethinking the Politics of the Past: Multidirectional Memory in the Archives of Implication   211
Michael Rothberg

Section IV. The Poetics of the Global Event: A Critical View

Chapter 12. Pain and Pleasure in Poetic Representations of the Holocaust   233
Rina Dudai

Chapter 13. Auschwitz: George Tabori's Short Joke   266
Shulamith Lev-Aladgem

Chapter 14. The Law of Dispersion: A Reading of W. G. Sebald's Prose   284
Jakob Hessing

Chapter 15. Holocaust Envy: Globalization of the Holocaust in
Israeli Discourse 296
Batya Shimony

Section V. Closure

Chapter 16. Messages from a Present Past: The Kristallnacht as
Symbolic Turning Point in Nazi Rule 319
Emanuel Marx

Chapter 17. A Personal Postscript 345
Sidra DeKoven Ezrahi

Notes on Contributors 354

Index 358

Figures

Figure 1.1. Participants at the ceremony marking the inauguration of the new museum for commemoration of the Holocaust at Yad Vashem, Jerusalem, March 2005 — 4

Figure 6.1. The iron gates of Auschwitz: "Arbeit Macht Frei" — 111

Figure 12.1. Spielberg's *Schindler's List*: deportees moving over the bridge into the ghetto — 242

Figure 12.2. Spielberg's *Schindler's List*: the camera pans from the anonymous crowd on the bridge to a single Jewish child — 242

Figure 12.3. Spielberg's *Schindler's List*: Amon Göth with Ellen in the cellar — 244

Figure 12.4. Spielberg's *Schindler's List*: the singer with Schindler on the first floor — 244

Figure 12.5. Spielberg's *Schindler's List*: Amon Göth with Ellen again in the cellar — 245

Figure 12.6. Spielberg's *Schindler's List*: the singer with Schindler again on the first floor — 245

Figure 12.7. Spielberg's *Schindler's List*: the gas chamber turns into a shower — 246

Figure 12.8. Fast's *Spielberg's List*: the train station in Krakow in 2003 on the right, and the opening sequence of Spielberg's *Schindler's List* on the left — 250

Figure 12.9. Fast's *Spielberg's List*: the contemporary bridge, created by juxtaposing the two screens — 251

Figure 12.10. Fast's *Spielberg's List*: the bridge on the left screen starts to change its angle and approach the viewer — 252

Figure 12.11. Fast's *Spielberg's List*: on the left screen the figure in red under the bridge — 252

Figure 12.12. Fast's *Spielberg's List*: two screens are showing simultaneously a segment from *Schindler's List* people marching on the bridge — 253

Figure 12.13. Fast's *Spielberg's List*: the fragmented bridge seen from the tourist's van — 253

Figure 12.14. Fast's *Spielberg's List*: second-order testimony with camera — 255

Preface

Amos Goldberg and Haim Hazan

Let us begin with a timely cultural puzzle, one that throws into relief the built-in historical, political, linguistic, and cosmopolitan contradictions of viewing the Holocaust as a global property.

The October 2013 conference of the Association of Holocaust Organizations (AHO) was held in Harbin and Shanghai, China. At first glance this might seem a bit strange; what does the Holocaust have to do with China? The Chinese were unquestionably not involved in the Holocaust and apparently are not affected by it. They have their own history and their own genocidal tragedies to remember. Why would they be interested in the Holocaust so much so that they would establish an institution to commemorate it by? And why is this institution affiliated with an international organization to the extent that it hosts this organization's conference?

Is this what we mean when we talk about the globalization of Holocaust memory? Let us take a closer look at the umbrella organization, the AHO. Perhaps it could teach us something else about this alleged global Holocaust memory.

First the date that it was established: 1985. Why then? What happened in those years that encouraged the founding of such an international organization for Holocaust education? Let us recall that in the same year *Shoah* was released by Claude Lanzmann and the Bitburg affair erupted. One year later David Grossman's *See Under: Love* was first published in Hebrew (to be translated in the coming years into many other languages) and the *Historikerstreit* erupted in West Germany. This does not seem to be accidental. What happened in those years that made the world so concerned with the Holocaust?

Now let us also consider the capacity of this organization. In 2011 the AHO included 250 worldwide organizations that were linked in one way or

---

Notes for this section begin on page xiv.

another to Holocaust education.¹ By February 2013 the website had already listed over 300 of them, located in 33 countries.² Quite a lot! One can certainly doubt that there is anything of this kind in relation to any other event in history. Moreover, this does not show the full magnitude of the picture. South Africa, for example, is represented in the list by only one organization, the South African Holocaust and Genocide Foundation, whereas in fact there are three Holocaust centers in the country—in Cape Town, Durban, and Johannesburg³—each of which houses its own museum.

So there seems to be a rapidly growing worldwide interest in the Holocaust, amplified and institutionalized on an international scale. But does that make Holocaust memory global? Let us peruse the AHO directory list. This could offer some more hints as to the character of this phenomenon.

Of the more than 300 institutions included, more than 200 (which constitute approximately two-thirds) are based in the United States (in 42 states) and only one in Africa. None of these Holocaust centers are situated in Arab or Muslim countries, and only three Asian countries are represented—Israel, China, and Japan. Only eight of the institutions are located in Latin America (in Argentina, Chile, Brazil, and Uruguay).

So how global, actually, is this memory? Are we not conflating "global" with "Western" or perhaps even "American"? And what is the content of this allegedly global memory? If we go back to the Harbin and Shanghai seven-day conference program, we realize that the first session after the keynote address was dedicated to "The Jews in China—Introduction of Jews in Kafeng, Harbin, Tianjin & Shanghai," while the second session was about the "Japanese Genocide in China." Neither of these two issues, as with most of the other topics of this conference, directly addressed the Holocaust. They gave the impression that the "Holocaust" stands for something else, perhaps many other things, which are all beyond the scope of the historical event that struck the Jews in Europe between 1939 and 1945. Therefore, it was taken as a trigger for local Jewish history and a local genocide. Nonetheless, there seemed to be local political sponsorship for this event, as the evening of Sunday 13 October was dedicated to a "Welcome dinner by Shanghai Government." So we may ask, is the global Holocaust memory about Jews? Is it about Jewish history? Would it concern other genocides? And how political and politicized is this "global memory"?

One item, however, was very much missing in this program—there was no mention of "human rights." On the one hand, this is hardly surprising, given the place of the conference, but on the other hand, "human rights" is a signifier often connected to the "global memory of the Holocaust." It is clearly stated, for example, in the UN General Assembly resolution on Holocaust remembrance that was adopted on 1 November 2005, which, among other things, announced 27 January as an International Holocaust Remembrance Day. The resolution begins by explicitly "[r]eaffirming the Universal Declaration of Human Rights, which proclaims that everyone is entitled to all the rights and freedoms set forth therein, without distinction of any kind, such as race, religion or other status."

So, is this global memory really about "human rights"? According to Levy and Sznaider, who offer the first thorough and comprehensive analysis of Holocaust memory as a global memory,[4] the answer is in the affirmative, as they argue that the Holocaust lies at the foundation of the postwar human rights regime. Their thesis is that in light of the collapse and breakdown of the great ideological narratives and the destabilization of national narratives, a new mythology organized around the Holocaust has emerged suggesting a basis for a fresh political ethic. Levi and Sznaider celebrate this as a new diasporic, humanistic moral order signaling a better world.

Following the questions broached above, this volume endeavors to critically explore these and other notions of the alleged "global Holocaust memory" as articulated by Levy and Sznaider and many others. Is it so prevalent? What does it actually mean? How does it function on various social, cultural, and political grounds? How is it related to other memories? What does its vocabulary consist of? To what extent is it truly global, and how does it encounter local traditions? How is it globally reproduced, and how is it formulated, compromised, negotiated, or subverted? And what are its moral, political, and cultural roots and ramifications?

These questions and their like were explored during the years 2008–9 by a research group composed of Israeli scholars coming from various academic fields under the auspices of the Van Leer Jerusalem Institute. The group also invited four renowned guest scholars to participate in a conference held in Jerusalem in 2009 on these issues. This volume is the outcome of this joint scholarly project. We would like to pay special tribute to one of those scholars—Peter Novick, whose contribution to the debate was invaluable, but, to our great sorrow, who passed away in February 2012. The volume is dedicated to his memory.

The volume is divided into five sections. The first is an introduction consisting of two chapters. The first of these is a chapter oriented in cultural studies by cultural historian Amos Goldberg, who unravels the tensions between the Holocaust global memory's ethicopolitical dimensions and its "Western" identity formation consequences. The second, by social anthropologist Haim Hazan, presents the inherent theoretical aporia that is at the heart of this implausible juxtaposition of "Holocaust" and "globalization." These two chapters propose an overview of the phenomenon at stake and its basic problematizations.

The second section critically explores the validity, the meaning, and the capacity of the global memory of the Holocaust. Historian Peter Novick refutes the very existence of such a global or even American memory. He claims that this is an optical illusion caused by the predominance of individual Jews in American cultural institutions and particularly in the film industry. Historian Alon Confino, on the other hand, suggests that the Holocaust is an event that replaced the French Revolution as the West's "foundational past," as he coins it. Philosopher Ronit Peleg follows Confino to see the theme of "after Auschwitz" as a turning point in moral Continental philosophy, which she explores through Lyotard's and Blanchot's philosophical writings. While Peleg's chapter is very much poststructuralist oriented, social anthropologist Nigel Rapport's chapter is existential in nature. Rapport contends that, functioning as a trope, the Holocaust serves as a global fund of knowledge, or a memory bank, that is large, ominous, awful, ambiguous, and conflicted enough to hold all that we know of being human, including and most significantly its contradictoriness.

The third section considers some key words in the commonplace vocabulary making up the language of the globalized Holocaust, such as testimony, trauma, human rights, and collective memory. These are examined vis-à-vis other, mostly non-Western, cultural expressions and memories. Political theorist Michal Givoni studies the ethics of witnessing the French section of the now multinational humanitarian movement Médecins Sans Frontières (Doctors Without Borders) to conclude that not only does its genealogy have very little to do with the Holocaust, but that "for testimony to go global and become the practical infrastructure of a new cosmopolitics ... the ethical legacy of the Holocaust had, in many respects, to be bypassed." Anthropologist Carol A. Kidron compares patterns of intergenerational transmission of the genocide legacy in Jewish Israeli and Cambodian second generations. She concludes that though very different from each other, both are very much culturally constructed and hence deviate from the globally disseminated reductionist profile of pathologically captivated trauma descendants. Louise Bethlehem, a postcolonial literary scholar, discusses some dimensions of postcolonial theory and its unacknowledged or even denied debt to Holocaust studies. She advocates a closer exchange between the two mutually inclusive fields that will enrich both. In the next chapter the communication scholar Tamar Katriel compares the establishment of two events on the UN ceremonial calendar: the International Holocaust Remembrance Day and the International Day of Non-Violence commemorating Mahatma Gandhi. In the closing chapter of this section, cultural historian Michael Rothberg addresses anew his extremely influential concept of "multidirectional memory," which powerfully resonates in many of this volume's chapters. In the second part of his chapter, Rothberg investigates the political repercussions of his concept through the analysis of Sebald's writings and the works of the British Israeli visual artist Alan Schechner.

The fourth section is about the poetics of the Holocaust as a global event. It portrays some of the major global Holocaust artists—none of whom is a Holocaust survivor, but all of whom are seeking new poetic avenues in their critical exploration of the nonrepresentational grand traumatic event. The literature scholar Rina Dudai disentangles the nexus of pain and pleasure in Spielberg's famous film *Schindler's List,* which evolves, according to Dudai, into a tangle of kitsch and simulacra. She does this by following the critical video artwork

Spielberg's List by the video artist Omer Fast. The theater scholar Shulamith Lev-Aladgem takes a different track. She analyzes the work of the controversial British Jewish playwright George Tabori on the Holocaust. Appreciating his bent to universalize the Holocaust and to break every possible taboo of its memory, she nonetheless acknowledges and respects, as a descendant of Holocaust survivors, those who object to such artistic manifestations. If there is a writer who stands in stark opposition to Tabori, it is W. G. Sebald, who is preoccupied with issues of unresolved trauma and melancholia. In his analysis, the German literature scholar Jakob Hessing maintains that Sebald's poetics are indeed universal and diasporic, but at a price: the law of dispersion drives Sebald's characters beyond the point of no return, and his prose brings to us the voices of the dead. The literature scholar Batya Shimony takes us back to the Israeli local scale, where the tension of the global and the local are manifested and dismantled. Shimony investigates Israeli Mizrahi writers who adopt and emulate various poetic strategies in coming to terms with an omnipresent memory turned major Jewish symbolic capital from which they are excluded.

The fifth and last section is a closure. Social anthropologist Emanuel Marx turns his gaze back to the November 1938 *Kristallnacht,* to which he was a witness. In his chapter Marx upholds that this event was a crucial symbolic turning point on the twisted road to the Holocaust and to other genocides that the Nazis perpetrated. His chapter oscillates between the personal and the universal meanings of this event. Sidra DeKoven Ezrahi, the group's senior Holocaust scholar, who has written extensively on Holocaust literature since the 1970s, brings us in her postscript back to the place where this project started—to Jerusalem. She distinguishes between an open and creative centrifugal memory, defined as the "comic," and a melancholic dead-end centripetal memory, regarded as sacrificial in nature. She warns us of the catastrophic political and ethical consequences of the latter, especially when it is conflated with another Jewish sacrificial myth—that of the Temple Mount. Hence, the gamut of chapters in this volume ranges from the assumed global to the essential local, thereby propounding a vicious circle interlocking a perpetual momentum of universal and particular, centrifugal and centripetal, quiddity and liquidity, engraving and deleting, inculcating and denying. These dialectics imprint the reverberations of the Holocaust as an increasingly cultural text.

This volume owes much to many who cannot all be mentioned. However we wish to extend special gratitude to the anonymous readers for their helpful comments and to the extremely professional Berghahn team. We would also like to thank Prof. Gabriel Motzkin, the Director of the Van Leer Jerusalem Institute and Dr. Tal Kohavi the Executive Editor and Director of Publications at the VLJI for her encouragement and generous support without which this volume would not have materialized.

Notes

1. Alvin Rosenfeld, *The End of the Holocaust* (Bloomington and Indianapolis: Indiana University Press, 2011), 11. Rosenfeld does not state when his counting actually took place.
2. See http://www.ahoinfo.org.
3. An extremely interesting one is the museum currently being built in Johannesburg, which will be dedicated the Holocaust as well as to the Rwandan genocide. Its opening is scheduled for the mid–2015.
4. Daniel Levy and Natan Sznaider, *The Holocaust and Memory in the Global Age* (2001; repr., Philadelphia: Temple University Press, 2006).

Bibliography

Levy, Daniel, and Natan Sznaider. *The Holocaust and Memory in the Global Age*. Philadelphia: Temple University Press, 2006. First published 2001.

Rosenfeld, Alvin. *The End of the Holocaust*. Bloomington and Indianapolis: Indiana University Press, 2011.

Section I

INTRODUCTIONS

CHAPTER 1

Ethics, Identity, and Antifundamental Fundamentalism
*Holocaust Memory in the Global Age
(a Cultural-Political Introduction)*

AMOS GOLDBERG

Globalization of Memory

On 15 March 2005 some forty distinguished representatives of states and international organizations gathered at Yad Vashem in Jerusalem, Israel's national Holocaust Martyrs' and Heroes' Remembrance Authority, to mark the inauguration of the new museum for commemoration of the Holocaust. Among the participants were the UN Secretary-General Kofi Annan, sixteen state presidents and prime ministers, including French Prime Minister Jean-Pierre Raffarin, Polish President Aleksander Kwaśniewsk, and Prime Minister of Holland Dr. Jan Pieter Balkenende, and foreign ministers, other senior ministers, influential political figures, and Israel's most prominent political leaders, including Prime Minister Ariel Sharon.[1]

During the ceremony all the participants posed for a group photograph (figure 1.1). The upper part of the museum building appears in the background, built as a prism-like triangular structure penetrating the hillside. This multiparticipant photo closely resembles others taken at symbolic and celebratory events of international politics, such as the traditional group photo of all the world leaders published annually at the opening of the UN General Assembly or at other important international conventions such as the G20. By means of this joint photo the leaders of the world's nations reaffirm each year their commitment to and partnership in international institutions, and in particular the United Nations. Such joint photos seem to signify that there is a dimension of global international institutional partnership that exists alongside and in some

---

Notes for this section begin on page 21.

Figure 1.1. Participants at the ceremony marking the inauguration of the new museum for commemoration of the Holocaust at Yad Vashem, Jerusalem, March 2005 (courtesy of Yad Vashem)

respects transcends the internal politics of each of the nations and even the bilateral relations between them.

It would appear that the photo of the many participants at Yad Vashem, which visually or even ichnographically belongs to the same genre, likewise symbolizes something similar. It indicates that many of the world's leaders, and certainly those of the Western world, are unified in regarding the commemoration of the Holocaust as a defining and important memory, and in their support of the Israeli Yad Vashem institution, which is to a large extent perceived as the representative and the mouthpiece of the victims. This is, as it were, a most lofty public declaration, proclaiming that the Holocaust has become an event of international political and cultural importance, the memory of which extends far beyond its direct major historical agents—namely, the Jews and the Germans. This photo indicates that the Holocaust has undergone a form of globalization and that its memory has become a supreme ethical imperative for many societies in the world, particularly the Western world, which is inherently linked, so it appears, to other processes of globalization characteristic of the turn of the century in the transition from what the sociologist Ulrich Beck termed early modernity to late modernity.[2] It seems as though almost the entire world, or at least the Western world, is "talking Holocaust" in one form or another.

In this respect, as Levy and Sznaider depicted,[3] the memory of the Holocaust perhaps symbolizes a highly significant process of definition of collective identities that cross the traditional boundaries of nations or ethnicity.

Traditionally, after all, collective memory is linked to the consciousness of relatively highly cohesive political and social groupings such as nations and ethnic groups.[4] Such groups form their common identity through an imagined common past that shapes their present and facilitates a horizon of an imagined hope for the future.[5] In the nation-state, collective memory is traditionally largely constructed around what Pierre Nora termed "lieu de mémoire,"[6] which constitute a locus of pilgrimage and signify a nexus between a common consciousness and territory. Holocaust memory, however, seemingly generates a form of common identity or common awareness of belonging that creates a very large kind of imagined community of the "global village," or at least the Western global village.[7]

The global distribution of Holocaust memory as a fundamental ethical-political and cultural memory, as well as the dramatic shift in the structure and function of this memory, is likewise evident in the nature of the major "sites of remembrance" of Holocaust commemoration, namely, Yad Vashem in Jerusalem, the United States Holocaust Memorial Museum in Washington DC, the monument to the memory of the Holocaust and the Jewish Museum in Berlin, and the commemoration site at Auschwitz.[8] In their role as global shrines of memory, they mark a shift in the manner in which they relate to national territory, since they do not function merely as geographically delimited shrines of a national civilian religion but are also taking their place as global shrines of memory that attract pilgrims from a multitude of nations. They serve as centers of testimony, as recognized authorities that dictate a new ethics, as centers that generate knowledge about the Holocaust, and as role models for other centers. They have furthermore created among themselves tightly knit networks of professional and economic cooperation, and their distribution roughly delineates the current boundaries of the areas of intensive presence of Holocaust memory—Israel, North America, and Western and Eastern Europe.

The Holocaust's role as perhaps today's central Western identity-generating symbol, shared in one way or another by the Jews and the entire Western world, may be best validated through its margins and that which lies beyond it. Apart from the few European and North American Holocaust deniers who are rejected and ostracized by their societies,[9] the most dominant voice in this context belongs to Iran's former president Mahmoud Ahmadinejad, who raises the standard of Holocaust denial in loud and clear tones. As a representative of a militant political Islamist alternative antithetical to "Europe," "America," and the West, Ahmadinejad attacks and attempts to undermine the validity of that major symbol, the Holocaust. Some of the other Islamist and Arab circles engaged in bitter struggle against Israel and the Western world tend to make similar assertions.[10] It is thus unsurprising that those intellectual circles in the Arab and Muslim world who identify with the values of the French Revolution, as Gilbert Achcar put it, strenuously renounce denial of the Holocaust or attempts to play down its significance.[11]

Yet what is the nature of this "globalization" of Holocaust memory?

Levy and Sznaider's book, *The Holocaust and Memory in the Global Age*,[12] is the first comprehensive attempt to formulate the memory of the Holocaust as a sort of global memory, which they celebrate as part of a diasporic, cosmopolitan ethic. They argue that the Holocaust forms part of and to some extent has even constituted a cosmopolitan "politics of human rights" that has gradually been adopted by the West since World War II, which circumscribes the authority and curbs the sovereignty of the nation-state in favor of international institutions of law and justice. This global process that breaches the boundaries of the nation-state began in the immediate postwar years at the Nuremberg trials and thereafter with the signing of the Convention on the Prevention and Punishment of the Crime of Genocide and in particular the Universal Declaration of Human Rights adopted by the UN in 1948.[13] Yet its breakthrough into consciousness as a significant new force on the international arena occurred mainly following the fall of the Communist bloc in the late 1980s and early 1990s, when the West lost its common interests and values and needed to adopt fresh symbols. Holocaust memory constituted one of the foremost of these.[14]

These processes, contend Levy and Sznaider, should be viewed within the broad context of fundamental changes in the basic concepts of international politics, namely, the transition from international relations to global relations: "While the 'old Internationalism' regulated the relations between nation-states and sanctified their sovereignty, the 'new cosmopolitanism' challenges the primacy of the nation-state and emphasizes the underlying interdependence in a global age."[15] Memory of the Holocaust, however, does not flow in only one direction, according to Levy and Sznaider. Like all global processes, it too is dialectical in nature. They borrow the concept "glocalization" coined by Ronald Robertson[16] to express the ongoing dialogue between the universal and cosmopolitan element of memory and the local context into which it is woven: "We argue that this dual process of particularization and universalization has produced a transnational symbol that is based on a cosmopolitanized memory—one that does not replace national memories but exists as their horizon."[17]

These processes occur also at the institutional level. Memory becomes increasingly fixed and established within international institutions and organizations or global cooperative networks. The two best-known examples are, first, UN Resolution 60/7 of 1 November 2005, adopted unanimously by the General Assembly to designate 27 January, the day on which the Auschwitz extermination camp was liberated by the Soviet army in 1945, as the International Holocaust Remembrance Day. The resolution specifically mentions the Jewish people, one-third of which perished during the Holocaust, as well as the Universal Declaration of Human Rights and the Convention on the Prevention and Punishment of the Crime of Genocide adopted in 1948 in the wake of the atrocities committed during World War II. A second example that symbolizes the institutional globalization of Holocaust memory is the Taskforce for International Cooperation on Holocaust Education, Remembrance, and Research (ITF), established in 1998 through the initiative of then Swedish Prime Minister Göran Persson, which was renamed International Holocaust Remembrance Alliance (IHRA) in 2013.[18] Its current thirty-one member states are all European or North American, apart from Israel and Argentina.[19]

Since Levy and Sznaider adopt a predominantly ethical approach, they view the global Holocaust memory as a commendable emergence of a cosmopolitan memory. Yet there is no consensus on this matter among scholars. Alvin Rosenfeld, for example, laments these processes, which he calls "the end of the Holocaust":

> What happens in the light of such developments is fairly predictable: as the mass murder of millions of innocent people is trivialized and vulgarized, a catastrophic history, bloody to its core is lightened of its historical burden and gives up the sense of scandal that necessarily should attend it. The very success of the Holocaust wide dissemination in the public sphere can work to undermine its gravity ... made increasingly familiar through repetition, it becomes normalized.[20]

Others emphasize the political aspect of these processes. The book *Universalisierung des Holocaust?*[21] (The Universalization of the Holocaust?), edited by Jan Eckel and Claudia Moisel, examines precisely these issues by means of an empirical study conducted in six Western countries and in Hungary. The editors regard the UN declaration establishing the 27th of January as International Holocaust Remembrance Day as an indication of the international recognition of the Holocaust as a global symbol that emerged following the Cold War and view the work of the ITF as an example of the manner in which the memory of the Holocaust operates at the European level as a common symbol that serves to shape a new European identity in the era of the European Union. They agree with Levy and Sznaider that this memory reduces the power of each particular national narrative as it transcends them. But unlike Levy and Sznaider, several of the authors of the book's chapters do not celebrate this newly created memory as an enlightened and progressive cosmopolitan memory that sensitively draws particular attention to the victims of political cruelty. They regard it rather as a construct essential to the strengthening of the still weak all-European identity. As the book's title suggests, there remain serious doubts as to the contents, the nature, the benefits, and even the actual existence of this universalization.

The late Peter Novik sounds a similar note of ironic skepticism when he describes the Americanization of the Holocaust as a result of the activism of the United States' Jewish community and its relations with the administration as well as the dominance of many individual Jews in American culture, academia, and politics. Novik asserts that, when all is said and done, the Holocaust is not an authentic American memory, but largely an optical illusion resulting from Jews' (as individuals) dominance in academia, culture, and the media.[22]

Yet even if we are to accept Novik's assertions regarding agents of culture who promote Holocaust memory, it would appear that it is of far greater significance to Europe and the Western world. As Dan Diner, for example, argues:

> As the twentieth century has drawn to a close, the Holocaust appears to be assuming the character of an icon of a now-past saeculum—something like the ultimate core event of "our" time.... Although the conspicuous presence of the Holocaust in public discourse may be easily traced from the late 1970s onwards, and its impact became particularly manifest in the 1980s, its significance for universal historical consciousness and moral standards became irrevocable only after 1989.[23]

Following Diner, Alon Confino goes even further in contending that the Holocaust has become a "foundational event": "By 'foundational past' I mean an event that represents an age because it embodies a historical novum that serves as a moral and historical yardstick, as a measure of things human."[24] He believes that, as such, Holocaust memory has replaced the memory of the French Revolution for the West.

Ethics, Politics, and Identity

The comparison Confino makes between these two foundational memories—the French Revolution and the Holocaust—is most instructive and points to some of the problems and tensions addressed in this book. The place of these two events in historical consciousness is, after all, very different. The status of the French Revolution as a foundational event for the world did not stem from its commemoration by remembrance institutions but rather from a commitment to its political and moral heritage embodied in its values—equality, liberty, and fraternity—which was partly manifested in a commitment to democracy and to human and civil rights. The institutions of memory merely bolstered this political aspect of the historic event epitomized in The Declaration of the Rights of Man and of the Citizen. The French Revolution was and is far less a historical memory than a political legacy. The Holocaust, on the other hand, is primarily a memory that, as Peter Novik has shown, can convey virtually any political message.[25] It would appear that if Confino is correct in stating that Holocaust memory is replacing the French Revolution as the West's defining myth, then this entails the replication of public symbols from the sphere of politics and political ethics to the realm of memory and collective identity.

This distinction regarding Holocaust memory between questions of political ethics and questions of the politics of identity is of major significance in assessing the ubiquitous character of this memory. The unresolved issue is whether the global Holocaust memory generates an ethical standard that establishes a new form of normative legitimacy according to which individuals and societies are enabled to regulate their relations in a more equitable and moral manner. Is it, in other words, a political project stemming from an acknowledgment of the catastrophic faults of modern European history and politics? Or is it rather primarily a sort of global mirror before which individuals and societies define themselves as belonging to the society of decent people and thereby accordingly define those located outside that society, namely, the "barbarians" of our generation?[26] These are two questions, not completely disconnected but nonetheless of a completely different order—one is about law, political ethics, and political thought while the other is mostly about identity formation or, in Lacanian terms, the "Imaginary."[27] These two options compose two different discourses that express different and at times opposite trends with regard to the global Holocaust memory and the various debates concerning it. Obviously they are mostly bound together, but the question is which is more dominant and primary in contemporary global Holocaust memory?

Holocaust Legal-Ethical-Political Discourse

One aspect of the Holocaust legacy that is very much about progressive politics is the legal one, which generates critical discussion of a dual nature. On the one hand, legal systems have sought to broaden their concepts in order to contend with extreme crimes of the kind exposed by Nazism, World War II, and in particular the Holocaust. These gave rise to juridical and political discourses that sought to deal with the catastrophic event on three planes. First, individuals were brought to trial and punished for the commission of extreme and perhaps unprecedented crimes. This was done at the Nuremberg trials[28] and subsequently in a series of further trials of Nazis and other criminals involved in genocide or other mass political crimes held both in local courts and international tribunals. Second, political discourses and legislative processes were initiated that sought to minimize the likelihood that crimes of this sort would be committed in the future. These placed anti-Semitism, racism, and racial thinking, so popular even within the scientific sphere prior to World War II, beyond the pale, and in various ways anchored human and civil rights and deterred potential transgressors.[29] Third, attention was drawn to the suffering of the victims of crimes of mass violence and their subsequent rights, and cultural and legal mechanisms were produced by which their voices might be heard and in which they could demand some compensation for the evil done to them. This threefold course of action was a complex process, and a prolonged effort was required to create a conceptual world sufficiently broad to grapple with these phenomena.

At the same time, however, the Holocaust contributed to the postmodern suspicions of the universal law. It drew awareness that there is always some "otherness" that transcends the universal law conceived by the Enlightenment and that underlies the liberal discourse on rights. This figure of the "other" in its various forms constantly challenges and expands the cultural, political, and juridical systems so that they can include it.[30] Thus, the "ethics of catastrophe," for which the Holocaust serves as its major trope and symbol, is mainly premised on the "the rejection of the metaphysics of comprehension."[31]

Discussion of Holocaust memory within the realm of juridical, political, and ethical thought therefore inevitably involves questions of universal moral laws and the relations of inclusion and exclusion that necessarily arise. Within this conceptual frame and aware of its intrinsic limitations, this discussion seeks, in the words of Adi Ofir, to minimize "superfluous evils,"[32] or, as Dominick LaCapra puts it within the framework of trauma theory: "Memory of this sort is important for an attempt to acknowledge and relate to the past in a manner that helps to make possible a legitimate democratic polity in the present and future."[33] The ethical-political discourse on the Holocaust is therefore preoccupied with the continual extension of "universal" political systems and legal discourses in order to establish a "safe haven" for all people while fully acknowledging the particularity of the "otherness" that continues to challenge and undermine that very universality. This kind of tension, inherent in the symbolic discourse of laws and legality, of social and cultural structures, and of ethics, seems to be a very productive one.[34] It endeavors to counter basic structures, norms, and tendencies inherent to modernity and the modern nation-state which brought about many of the big catastrophes of the twentieth century for which Auschwitz stands as a symbol.

Holocaust Identity Discourse

The discourse of identity regarding the Holocaust is completely different. Its characteristic questions do not address universal laws and ethics and the breaching of them, nor do they address issues of dangerous political tendencies and structures, but rather discuss identities and images. In Lacanian terms, these are considered issues of the dimension of the "Imaginary." And since according to Lacan, the "Imaginary" is very much connected to narcissistic aspects in the structure of subjectivity, it inevitably contains a potential of aggressiveness. The "Imaginary's" fundamental metaphor is the gaze looking at the mirror, where one seeks to receive from the reflected image reassurance of one's unity, coherency, sovereignty, and beauty—or in other words, one's identity.[35] The subject finds solace from the nightmarish "human condition" of plurality and inner cleavage by looking into the mirror and identifying with the image reflected in it. The problem with such a gaze is that it tends to violently deny or oppress that "otherness"—from within or from without—which disrupts its comforting image. We always expect the mirror of identity to reflect an affirmative and attractive image, just as Narcissus did upon gazing into the water of the lake. And as the story of Snow White relates, when the mirror refuses to comply, violence immediately erupts.

One can thus, albeit somewhat simplistically, conclude that while the discourse of law, politics and ethics is from the outset required to address questions of "otherness," identity discourse tends to erase or conceal the problem of "otherness" (or plurality, in Arendt's political thought[36]) inherent to the human condition, since this "otherness" tends always to detract from the comforting and harmonious reflection that we expect to meet upon gazing into the mirror of identities. In this sense this discourse carries within it an inherent potential of destructiveness and violence.

Ethics versus Identity

An area already mentioned in which Holocaust memory plays a very active part is the juridical sphere and its perception of the concepts of justice that have undergone considerable transformation, largely following the Holocaust and World War II (or at least mythically anchored in their memories). I would like now to further discuss these issues at greater length.

Since the 1990s, a new dictionary of terms has aggressively entered dominant arenas in the public sphere, where it has proposed a reshaping and even a new perception of the past. Among these terms are "crimes against humanity," "war crimes," "genocide," "ethnic cleansing," "testimony," "trauma," "victims," "compensation," "restitution," "human rights." And while none of these are new, their dominance and the way they have overshadowed other cultural and political concepts mark a fundamental change in our perception of the past. As we have seen, some link this change to cosmopolitanism, others to multicultural ethics, and at the philosophical level even to postmodernism itself.[37]

A clear example is provided by the change in the manner in which local and international legal systems relate to the victims of radical political violence that occurred in the wake of the Holocaust and World War II. These systems increasingly accept the need for official recognition of the crimes committed as well as the need to apologize for them, to compensate the victims, and to return their property.

These issues were initially raised during the final stages of World War II and immediately thereafter as the Jews returned home while the Nazis were gradually defeated. In many cases both in Eastern and in Western Europe they were received with reservation, sometimes hostility, and on occasion even violence. Their struggle to win back their property was waged in the public and legal spheres and was not always successful. On occasion, it gave rise to new waves of violence directed against them.[38]

From the 1950s onward, however, a series of agreements and compensation claims were concluded in which both sovereign nations and financial institutions were involved, resulting in the transfer of relatively large amounts of compensation money and/or the return of property to the state of Israel, international Jewish organizations, local Jewish communities, and individual victims. In the wake of these processes the international norms governing issues of restitution and compensation for the victims of war crimes and mass political crimes underwent fundamental change.[39]

The first major step was taken by Konrad Adenauer's West Germany, which, in order to facilitate its acceptance into the fold of decent nations in the historical context of the beginning of the Cold War, concluded a restitution agreement with the government of Israel in 1952 (which did not, however, prevent Adenauer from employing close aides with proven Nazi pasts). During the 1990s, a series of further claims involving forced laborers, Swiss banks, insurance companies, and so forth were investigated. These were in many cases heard in US courts.[40]

As John Torpey and Elazar Barkan[41] have shown, these issues were quickly reproduced in other historical contexts in which the regulations and precedents established in the context of the Holocaust were put to juridical and public use. Demands for apology,[42] reparations, and return of property were made by black people in the United States with regard to the slave trade and years of slavery; by African and other "third world" nations for the years of colonial exploitation; and in Eastern Europe for the years of Communist oppression. It is noteworthy that the Holocaust thus indeed served as a standard for claims to justice, recognition, and monetary compensation not only in the "Euro-Atlantic" space, as Torpey defined it, but also far beyond it.

These discussions should be located within the broader context addressed above in discussing the observations of Levy and Sznaider on the growing power of nonstate organizations such as international judicial tribunals (and nations' willingness to conduct trials involving war crimes and human rights perpetrated beyond their borders) and the activity of international human rights organizations over large areas of the globe. What Torpey terms the "global spread of 'reparations politics'"[43] developed in these contexts, constituting "part of a broader challenge to state power and sovereignty that has been one of the major consequences of the post-Holocaust era."[44]

These aspects indeed demonstrate to what extent the Holocaust has become a sort of global yardstick for understanding the past and the duties it casts in the present. Torpey and Levy and Sznaider celebrate this development, whereas others are more skeptical. They believe it is the "Imaginary" and problematic dimensions of the creation of a European or Western identity based on the Holocaust that constitute the major global step—or to put it a bit differently, it is less about politics of justice and law and more about identity politics. Tony Judt concludes his book on the postwar period with a chapter on Holocaust memory in which he writes: "Those who would become full Europeans in the dawn of the 21st century must first assume a new and far more oppressive heritage. Today the pertinent European reference ... is extermination. Holocaust recognition is our contemporary European entry ticket. ... To deny or belittle the Shoah—the Holocaust—is to place yourself beyond the pale of civilized cultured public discourse."[45]

This was not a unidirectional or a linear process and has not necessarily come to a conclusion everywhere in Europe. This process reached its climax in France, for example, when, in 1995, then French president Jacques Chirac recognized France's responsibility for the crimes of Vichy and the deportation of the Jews to the camps, saying "we owe them an ineradicable debt." Additional European countries followed this process, among them countries in Eastern Europe that regarded such a form of apology as a means of entering the fold of the "West" and as an admission test. In many of these countries, such as Poland and, in a very different manner, Lithuania, a public debate continues to this day as to the way in which the national past during the war is perceived, the collaboration with the Nazis, and the extent of involvement in the persecution and extermination of the Jews.[46]

These processes, however, Judt maintains, generate a new order of problems, particularly for many of the Eastern European nations. Poland and the Czech Republic, for example, have indeed adopted the memory of the Holocaust as part of their national identity, and Poland has even engaged over the past decade in a thorough reappraisal of its citizens' involvement in the persecution and extermination of Jews during the Holocaust, as have many Western European nations in the two preceding decades. This does not mean of course that there are not loud objections in these countries to such tendencies. However, in general terms and on the level of state policy, Poland and the Czech Republic seem to adapt themselves to Western Holocaust memory norms. Yet in Hungary, for example, and certainly in the Ukraine and the Baltic states, things are more complex. Many there seek to divert attention from the Holocaust and to focus on the oppression and murderous crimes that they suffered during the Communist period.[47] In the introduction to the *Black Book of Communism* describing Communist crimes, editor Stéphane Courtois controversially explains why to his mind the crimes of communism have been leniently judged:

> After 1945 the Jewish genocide became a byword for modern barbarism, the epitome of twentieth-century mass terror ... a single minded focus on the Jewish genocide in an attempt to characterize the Holocaust as a unique atrocity has also prevented an assessment of other episodes of comparable magnitude in the Communist world.[48]

Finally, since it is so divisive a memory that it generates endless rivalry over the position of victim (clear questions of narcissistic identity[49]) and emphasizes to such an extent dimensions of guilt, Judt proposes and hopes that Europe will transform the memory of catastrophe as a unifying memory for other more constructive ones. Once the peoples of Europe have recognized their catastrophic history and their individual involvement and responsibility for this past, the time has come for some forgetfulness: "[S]ome measure of neglect and even forgetting is the necessary condition for civil health,"[50] asserts Judt, his words reverberating with Freud's basic distinction between mourning and melancholy.[51] It appears that Judt is calling upon us to complete the processes of mourning the Holocaust and the extermination of the Jews and to refrain from sinking into endless processes of melancholy, which are deeply linked in Freud's work to narcissistic aspects that Lacan associates with the "Imaginary" order. I believe Judt indeed points here to some problematic aspects of European Holocaust memory and its driven identity. And while one can certainly disagree with his call of forgetting, an investigation of some of these problematic aspects might indeed be useful.

A Reassuring Narrative?

According to Charles Maier, two narratives compete in explaining the twentieth century—the Holocaust narrative and the anti- and then postcolonial narrative.[52] Broadly speaking, one may say that during the 1950s and early 1960s these two narratives served as political narratives and were closely bound up with each other. This is clearly apparent in the work of Franz Fanon, Hannah Arendt, Alain Renais, Jean-Paul Sartre, Charlot Delbo, and many others.[53] These two accounts, however, have parted company, and while the postcolonial narrative has sustained its criticism of Western societies and their liberal democracies for their ongoing historical involvement in acts of domination, racism, extreme violence, and criminality, the Holocaust seem to become a reassuring narrative. It was the "bad guys"—the Nazis—who messed it all up, and as long as we stick to our democratic values and strengthen our civic society while moderating radical ideological trends, we can protect ourselves from slipping into criminality, thereby reinforcing our identity as the "good guys," the upholders of democracy and freedom.

Hence it might very well be that Ross Poole was right when he asserted in regard to Holocaust memory: "Though we feel horror at the images, we can comfort ourselves with the secret satisfaction deriving from our own sense of moral goodness in recognizing that horror. The cultural circulation of Holocaust horrors can all too easily become moral kitsch."[54] It therefore took thinkers who observed European history from a peripheral position to put things more accurately. The Nigerian Nobel Prize winner and writer Wole Soyinka, for example, states:

> I have railed against the thesis that it was the Jewish Holocaust that placed the first question mark on all claims of European humanism—from the Renaissance through the Enlightenment to the present-day multicultural orientation. Insistence on that thesis, we must continue to maintain, merely provides further proof that the European mind has yet to come into full cognition of the African world as an equal sector of a universal humanity, for, if it had, its historic recollection would

have placed the failure of European humanism centuries earlier—and that would be at the very inception of the Atlantic slave trade.[55]

In this respect, Holocaust memory, by contrast perhaps to the memories of which Soyinka speaks, might be a sort of reaffirming memory, certainly for the peoples of Europe. It is perhaps a mirror of memory that as it contaminates the past it also polishes and purifies the present. As the peoples of Europe stand before it they indeed accept their problematic past, but at the same time they join the rest of the Western countries in observing their shared current image as attractive and moral. They are, after all, remembering the Holocaust together and expressing remorse over it, combating anti-Semitism and outlawing Holocaust denial. This is a mirror that enables affirmation of a renewed European identity that rests upon sharing the guilt of the past but also on the establishment of a contemporary liberal-democratic identity that constitutes a kind of powerful self-affirmation and validation in face of the atrocities of the Holocaust now cast back into the past. As fragile as it may be, this identity is growing stronger in the face of its undermining with regard to the treatment by Europe of the peoples formerly under colonial rule and of non-European migrants and in particular Muslims within Europe.

Political Consequences

It thus transpires that Holocaust memory as a global memory moves between these two (not completely disconnected) planes—the ethical-political and the identificational (the "Imaginary"). Between human rights politics and identity politics of self-affirmation. And it is this that creates the tension whose various aspects are addressed in this book. I shall now try to elaborate on the nature of this tension, since one must eventually inquire which of these two aspects is the more dominant: "cosmopolitan" questions about a more refined and just regime of human and civil rights that creates new identities that are subordinate to it, as Levy and Sznaider approvingly see things; or a type of melancholic memory that creates narcissistic identities that have perhaps internalized the Jews as part of the "collective Western self" but find it increasingly difficult to contain other "otherness." So the question is whether this global memory perhaps still functions primarily as a mechanism of exclusion that may indeed dismantle the old iniquitous structures but that builds others that might be no less problematic in their stead.

Let us now return to the photograph with which we began. As already noted, the leaders of the Western world are standing in front of Yad Vashem in a photo that brings to mind international political events such as the assembly at the annual opening of the UN General Assembly. Yet there is nevertheless a difference. The United Nations, an international political organization of varying effectiveness, is a political institution. It grew and gained its validity following two world wars and particularly after the second of these in order to prevent the outbreak of a third such war. Yad Vashem is not a political institution. It is a cultural institution devoted to commemoration, which contains a museum, a library, an archive, an educational wing, a research institute, and so forth. Why, then, is its opening event marked by a convention of leading politicians rather than one of intellectuals and people of culture who are supposed to preserve the memory of the Holocaust within culture? Why did the event feel far more political than cultural given the roles of its participants?

It would appear that this is a common case of politics disguised as memory. Or perhaps to be more precise, this is a symptom of a kind of politics that seeks its major symbols in a memory that is overly engrossed with the past rather than engaging in the establishment of institutions devoted to organizing our future life in a better and more just manner. And perhaps this manifests something alluded to above when mentioning Confino's assertion that the Holocaust has replaced the French Revolution as the founding memory of the West: that the political field itself has been transformed from a sphere that organizes social life in an equitable manner to one engaged in a struggle of identities. The historian Charles Maier alluded to this in 1993. In an article that sparked considerable discussion, he contended that the exaggerated engagement with memory in general and Holocaust memory in particular marks to a large degree a crisis of the political sphere:

> My own belief is that at the end of the twentieth century, Western societies have come to an end of a massive collective project. It is not just the project of the communist or even the socialist Left or even the Left *tout court*.... It is also the end or at least the interruption of the capacity to found collective institutions that rest on aspirations for the future.[56]

Maier contends that memory has appropriated the place occupied by the kind of politics that establishes institutions engaged in building a future based on common agreement. Following him, Manuela Consoni makes the more radical assertion that at the turn of the millennium Europe is tending ever more toward an ethnic politics at the expense of the civil politics of the classic liberal nation-state. Since it is essentially ethnic rather than political in nature, Holocaust memory well serves this trend, which, while turning the Jews into part of the European "self," tends to exclude migrants and Muslims and gives rise to Islamophobic feelings. While foreigners can, at least theoretically, be absorbed into the traditional nation-states of Europe based on secular citizenship, now, with the increasing ethnification of Europe of which Holocaust memory constitutes a part, this option is becoming progressively unrealistic, not merely practically but also ideologically, given the constitutional character and political atmosphere of European countries.[57]

This state of affairs naturally has political repercussions within and beyond Europe. Identification with Holocaust victims, for example, has rendered support for Israel a fundamental and defining component of contemporary European and Western identity. If in the past the Jews were perceived as the "other" of the European Christian world, nowadays European mainstream culture and identity is increasingly perceived to be a product of "the Judeo-Christian tradition,"[58] which Muslims might find hard to share. Thus, claims Jonathan Boyarin, the empathy toward the Jewish victims of the Holocaust resembles the fact that "we can only empathize with, feel ourselves into, those we can imagine as ourselves."[59] Or as Steven Aschheim put it: "[I]n the post-Holocaust era we have extended our moral, ethnic and empathic boundaries to include, rather than outlaw, the Jews," who are part of the Eurocentric "we." At the same time, he continues, "we are less likely to be taken aback by atrocities removed from the imagined Western 'core.'" He therefore concludes that "this tendency to empathize with those with whom we identify, who are closest to us, is most natural and cannot be considered a particularly ethical achievement."[60] Indeed, this empathy seems to be more related to mirrors of identity than to ethics. These mirroring processes of identity and identification generate intriguing dynamics in Europe—between European states and their Jewish and Muslim communities[61]—and also outside of Europe. One can also assert that this kind of empathy might be very fragile, as the current rise of anti-Semitism in France, Hungry, and other Eastern and Western European countries, for example, indicate.

Let us return now one last time to the photograph and inspect it more closely.

Not only are all the figures in the photograph politicians, but as we have already stressed, they are all "Western" politicians. As the Israeli genocide scholar Yair Auron has noted on several occasions, not even one representative of peoples that have been victims of genocide during the twentieth century was invited to the ceremony. Not Armenians, not Tutsis, not Cambodians, not Congolese, and not Namibians. The only African in the photo is the Nigerian Kofi Annan, who was invited because of his position as UN Secretary-General. Moreover, the photo was taken in March 2005 in Jerusalem, at the end of the Palestinian intifada and during the debate on Ariel Sharon's plan of disengagement from the Gaza strip (which actually took place in August of that year). As the Israeli press took pains to note, a diplomatic event on such a scale had never taken place in the country other than at the funeral of Prime Minister Yitzhak Rabin, who was murdered eleven years previously against the backdrop of his signing of the Oslo accords with the Palestinians. The photograph thus bears witness to a form of exclusion within the political milieu of Holocaust memory on the one hand, and to a privileged status translated into very concrete political terms on the other.

The event captured in the photograph occurred, therefore, in its own time and place. It did not occur on some ahistorical and universal plane. What, then, is the significance of holding such a politically colored ceremony for global Holocaust memory? What does this tell us about the tension between questions of identity and those of justice? Between the ethical and the imaginary? Is this a particular or a universal event?

As A. Dirk Moses has noted, the particular and the universal tend to become confused with regard to the global memory of the Holocaust. After all, on the one hand, as we have seen, the Holocaust is becoming a kind of defining metaphor for global human rights regimes, while at the same time it is intimately linked to a very particular historical agent, namely, its Jewish victim. Is the Holocaust a universal metaphor that is becoming detached from its historical bearers? Or is it rather a concrete event that bestows special privileges on those perceived to be its primary victim, namely, the Jews, thereby placing an obligation on the historical victimizers—first and foremost Germany—to compensate and support, and then spreading the circle wider to include first Europe and then the entire world that merely stood by?

As Moses has noted with regard to the state of Israel, these two regimes of memory—the universal and the particular, the ethical and the identical—collide and reach a state of open conflict with the oppression of the Palestinians, the depravation of their civic and national rights, and the violation of their basic human rights.[62] He exemplifies this in the case of Elie Wiesel. On the one hand, "Wiesel has written regularly on the theme of hate as the human scourge, a phenomenon he now tends to equate with Islam, coding it, like many others today, as the modern Nazism."[63] But on the other, "Wiesel recently condemned Human Rights Watch—in a letter to the *New York Times* co-signed with Alan Dershowitz—for supposedly picking on Israel without mentioning the occupation of the Palestinian West Bank or siege of and attack on Gaza, which, according to anyone who has studied and visited the region, accounts in large measure for the hate he fears and deplores." The reason for that, according to Moses, is "[h]e genuinely cannot see his own blindness because it is constitutive of his subjectivity as a universal particular."[64]

The two societies in which this tension noted by Moses between the particular and the universal and between questions of identity and those of ethics have evolved into open contradiction are the German and Israeli societies. In contemporary Germany, so it would seem (and in fact to a large degree also in the whole of Europe's elites), identification with the victim of the Holocaust, the imperative to resist every instance of what might be seem as anti-Semitism, and the obligation to support Israel are so entrenched in the German identity that when these collide with ethical principles in the context of the Israeli-Palestinian conflict they often take precedence. For Germany, the issue of its relations with Israel rest first and foremost on principles of identity and identification with the Jewish victim, also and perhaps precisely at those moments that it ceases to be a victim.[65] In the case of Germany's official and traditional policy, there is a consistent preference for dealing with narcissistic issues of guilt, identity, and identification directed toward the entity perceived to be the direct descendant and representative of the victims, namely, the state of Israel, while Germany is much more reluctant to engage with the burning ethical issues of racism and exclusion directed toward the current "others" of Europe—namely, Muslims and migrants, and to support the Palestinian struggle against the Israeli colonial occupation. It is no wonder, then, that Gilbert Achkar complains that if in German and European public discourse "the word 'Islam' were replaced by 'Judaism' [it] would provoke an uproar and in Europe lead to legal prosecution."[66]

But there is also an ironic twist to this story. The universalization of Holocaust memory as a global metaphor for human rights proved to be very successful. In one way or another, these two terms ("Holocaust" and "human rights") became very much bound together in European and Western discourse. Hence, for example, the 2005 UN General Assembly's resolution on the International Holocaust Remembrance Day, which was initiated and promoted, as Tamar Katriel shows in this volume, by the Israeli ministry of Foreign Affairs, is completely about human rights. It seems that in this case Israel was willing to universalize the Holocaust as long as it acknowledged particularly the Jews as the major victims of Nazi crimes. But the irony is that this human rights discourse became so powerful and ubiquitous to the extent that it is the main discourse by which Israel is criticized as a state that brutally violates human rights norms in of the Palestinians. One must add, though, that such critique almost never alludes explicitly to the Holocaust. In large segments of the Israeli political spectrum, on the other hand, and in many organized pro-Israeli circles, "human rights" became a synonym for "delegitimization of the state of Israel," and Israeli human rights groups such as Betzelm and Breaking the Silence are perceived as traitors.[67]

A Fundamental Foundation of Western Antifundamentalism

Yet the question of the paradoxical tension between the universal and the particular, the metaphorical and the concrete, the ethical and issues of identity, surfaces not only in European and Israeli identity discourse, but also at the heart of the human rights regimes that established the cosmopolitan global ethics supported by Holocaust memory.

Thus, as previously noted, as an ethical symbol adopted by the West, the Holocaust generally underpins a liberal, cosmopolitan position that extols the individual and their rights to an extreme degree.[68] Paradoxically, however, the Holocaust at the same time delineates a clear-cut boundary to those same rights. It is the only event whose denial constitutes an unthinkable infringement of a taboo. This is, moreover, a criminal offence in twelve countries and carries a severe penalty.[69] These countries thereby limit freedom of speech to an unprecedented degree, bearing in mind that this is one of the most fundamental individual freedoms that is generally curtailed only in cases of a substantiated suspicion of an immediate, direct, and imminent threat to public security. Precisely because the Holocaust as a memory constitutes for many a liberal, ethical, and perhaps even multicultural or cosmopolitan commitment, it has itself become a fundamentalist pillar of belief that is not, under any circumstances, to be destabilized or questioned. It enjoys the status of what Slavoj Žižek terms, in another context, "absolute meaning."[70] And indeed, the European Court for Human Rights ruled on 17 December 2013 that denying the Armenian genocide is not a crime as it falls within the rights of the freedom of speech, while denying the Holocaust is a crime that transcends this freedom.[71]

A similar dynamic occurs with regard to the issue of restitution discussed above following Torpey and Barkan. In the wake and context of the Holocaust, the obligation to recompense victims of political crimes is universal. Nevertheless, here too the status of Holocaust victims and the obligation to compensate them is of a completely different order of meaning, as Debórah Dwork and Robert Jan Van Pelt assert: "Unlike any refugee group in the modern era … the survivor of the Holocaust … won a measure of material restitution."[72] But there is something further. Reparations have a different function in regard to the Holocaust.

Regularly, as Charles Maier has pointed out, processes of reparation in the wake of political crimes possess the power to erase memory. They shift the hallowed sense of suffering to the mundane plane of negotiation. Discussion of recompense has a diluting effect, transforming even the most terrible occurrence into something worldly and subject to negotiation.[73] This is not the case regarding Holocaust reparations, which seem to follow a different logic. Reparation in this case does not return the crime to the sphere of the worldly and the mundane. On the contrary, its cultural meaning is gained by affirming the sanctity of the event as one that almost any claim emanating from it is justified, but at the same time cannot even begin to compensate for suffering that is inconvertible, even at the symbolic level, to the monetary plane. In the case of the Holocaust, reparation is always justified and, at the same time, marks the infinite nature of the crime that therefore justifies far-reaching claims compared to other crimes.[74]

A similar process with regard to the Holocaust is discernible in postmodern discourses as manifested, for example, in the historian Saul Friedländer's influential book *Probing the Limits of Representation* and in his writing in general. On the one hand, he states: "It is precisely the 'Final Solution' which allows postmodernist thinking to question the validity of any totalizing view of history, of any reference to a definable metadiscourse, thus opening the way for a multiplicity of equally valid approaches."[75] And Friedländer continues by elucidating the position taken by Lyotard, the prophet of postmodernism, who wrote extensively on the Holocaust: "The striving for totality and consensus is, in Lyotard's view, the very basis of the fascist enterprise."[76] At the same time, the history and discussion of the Holocaust are immune from being fully historicized. In his essay "The Unease of Historical Interpretation," Friedländer characterizes the Holocaust as a historical event that, owing to its singular force, stands beyond historical comprehension. Nothing in the "final solution" can, after all, teach us anything about life or about our existence in this world. In this respect it is an event without significance. And because of its nonrelevance, as he puts it, "the final solution embodies an implied relation to a certain kind of 'exemplary' category ... it is precisely from this perspective that the 'final solution' appears exceptional in its opaqueness [to historical comprehension]."[77] Here too the Holocaust constitutes a postmodern-like discourse that is completely impervious to the effects of postmodernism's historical relativizing insights.

The Holocaust thus establishes or at least supports discourses identified above all with cosmopolitan late modernism. These are discourses of recompense to victims, of multiculturalism, of human rights, and of postmodernist (at least partial) relativism. In this respect the Holocaust has become a sort of ethical, historical, and cultural metaphor detached from its bearers and from its concrete historical context in order to lay down universal cosmopolitan rules. And all the while the Holocaust as a historical event and its historical victims are largely immune from the relativizing effect of these very discourses. They somehow occupy a different and fundamentalist status in relation to them. Holocaust discourse thus undergoes a metaphorical abstraction while at the same time maintaining its links to its bearers and victims on a different, almost sanctified plane. Paradoxically, this comes about within discourses that not only present themselves as an alternative to what is perceived to be religious (primarily Islamic) fundamentalism, but also inherently undermine the idea of fundamentalism itself. One may thus refer to Holocaust discourse as the fundamental foundation of Western antifundamentalism. It seems to stand beyond the discourse that it itself constitutes. It is as though the Holocaust generates a liberal cosmopolitan discourse that cannot be applied to it and its carriers, since the entire discourse would collapse were this essential belief to be cracked. Should the Holocaust lose its sanctity and become "just another" political or historical event, how would it be possible to justify the commitment to a cosmopolitan discourse of rights linked to its memory as a global ethical imperative? In this respect, the global Holocaust memory is cosmopolitan in its ethics but confers a privileged status divorced from this ethics on its victims. While it belongs to the ethical order, it is forever shackled to the imaginary discourse of European and Western politics of identity that limits it and, as we have seen, at times even overshadows it.

Notes

I wish to thank Alon Confino, Donald Bloxham, and Sidra DeKoven Ezrahi and especially A. Dirk Moses for their extremely useful comments.

1. For further information on the inauguration events, see the Yad Vashem website at http://www1.yadvashem.org/yv/en/about/events/2005/inaugurating_the_new_museum.asp. On Yad Vashem as a global museum, see Amos Goldberg, "The 'Jewish Narrative' in the Yad Vashem Global Holocaust Museum," *Journal of Genocide Research* 14, no. 2 (June 2012): 187–213.

2. See, e.g., Ulrich Beck, *Risk Society: Towards a New Modernity* (London: Sage, 1992); also very relevant to our discussion is Ulrich Beck, *Cosmopolitan Vision* (Cambridge: Polity Press, 2006), though here Beck uses the term "postmodernity" and he wishes to go beyond it.

3. Daniel Levy and Natan Sznaider, *The Holocaust and Memory in the Global Age* (Philadelphia: Temple University Press, 2006).

4. Maurice Halbwachs, *On Collective Memory* (Chicago: University of Chicago Press, 1992).

5. Benedict Anderson, *Imagined Communities: Reflections on the Origin and Spread of Nationalism* (London: Verso, 1983).

6. Pierre Nora, *Realms of Memory*, vol. 1, *Conflicts and Divisions* (New York: Columbia University Press, 1996).

7. See also Tvetan Todorov, "The Uses and Abuses of Memory," in *What Happens to History: The Renewal of Ethics in Contemporary Thought*, ed. Howard Marchitello (London and New York: Routledge, 2001), 11–22. Todorov distinguishes between "literal memory," which is more local, and "exemplar memory," which becomes more global.

8. One should mention the entry of the Auschwitz concentration camp on the World Heritage List in 1979 as an expression of the universalization of Holocaust memory that had occurred already in the late 1970s. In the very same year the Jewish-Christian controversy over the nature of the site rose to one of its peaks during the pope's visit to Auschwitz. For this important controversy, see Debórah Dwork and Robert Jan Van Pelt, *Auschwitz: 1270 to the Present* (New York and London: Norton, 1996), 354–78. Today, I think there is no doubt that Auschwitz is associated first and foremost with the Jewish Holocaust worldwide.

9. See, e.g., the famous Irving trial case. Deborah Lipstadt, *History on Trial: My Day in Court with David Irving* (New York: Ecco, 2005).

10. Gilbert Achcar, *The Arabs and the Holocaust: The Arab-Israeli War of Narratives* (New York: Metropolitan Books, 2010); Meir Litvak and Esther Webman, *From Empathy to Denial: Arab Responses to the Holocaust* (New York: Columbia University Press, 2009). It is, of course, not the only and perhaps not even the dominant attitude toward the Holocaust in the Arab world. See books for different references, especially the former.

11. See Achcar, *The Arabs and the Holocaust*. Very famous for their fierce rejection of Holocaust denial are, among others, Elias Khuri, Eduard Said, and Azmi Bishar.

12. Levy and Sznaider, *The Holocaust and Memory*. See also, of uttermost importance, Jeffrey C. Alexander, "On the Social Construction of Moral Universals: The 'Holocaust' from Mass Murder to Trauma Drama," *European Journal of Social Theory* 5, no. 1 (2002): 5–86; and the follow-up debate, Jeffrey C. Alexander, *Remembering the Holocaust: A Debate* (Oxford and New York: Oxford University Press, 2009).

13. According to Samuel Moyn, this description is complete myth, since there was no historical linkage between the rise of the "human rights utopia" and the Holocaust. See Samuel Moyn, *The Last Utopia: Human Rights in History* (Cambridge, MA, and London: Harvard University Press, 2010). See also Marco Duranti, "The Holocaust, the Legacy of 1789 and the Birth of International Human Rights Law: Revisiting the Foundation Myth," *Journal of Genocide Research* 14, no. 2 (June 2012): 159–86.

14. Others locate this turn toward the globalization of Holocaust memory in the late 1970s. See, e.g., Peter Novick, *The Holocaust in American Life* (Boston: Houghton Mifflin, 1999).

15. Levy and Sznaider, *The Holocaust and Memory*, 19. For a critique of Levy and Sznaider, see Ross Poole, "Misremembering the Holocaust: Universal Symbol, Nationalist Icon or Moral Kitsch?," in *Memory and the Future: Transnational Politics, Ethics and Society*, ed. Yifat Gutman, Adam Brown, and Amy Sodaro (Houndmills, UK: Palgrave MacMillan, 2010), 31–49; Aleida Assmann, "The Holocaust—a Global Memory? Extensions and Limits of a New Memory Community," in

Memory in a Global Age: Discourses, Practices and Trajectories, Society, ed. Aleida Assmann and Sebastian Conrad (New York: Palgrave MacMillan, 2010), 97–118.

16. Roland Robertson, "Glocalization: Time-Space and Homogeneity-Heterogeneity," in *Global Modernities*, ed. Mike Featherstone, Scott Lash, and Roland Robertson (London: Sage, 1995), 25–44.

17. Levy and Sznaider, *The Holocaust and Memory*, 13.

18. On this organization, see Larissa Allwork, *Holocaust Remembrance between the National and the Transnational*. London: Bloomsbury, forthcoming.

19. See IHRA's website, https://www.holocaustremembrance.com/member-countries/ (accessed 15 January 2015).

20. Alvin Rosenfeld, *The End of the Holocaust* (Bloomington and Indianapolis: Indiana University Press, 2011), 11.

21. Jan Eckel and Claudia Moisel, eds., *Universalisierung des Holocaust? Erinnerungskultur und Gesschictspolitik in Internationaler Perspective*, Beiträge zur Geschichte des Nationalsozialismus 24 (Göttingen: Wallstein, 2008).

22. Peter Novick, "The American National Narrative of the Holocaust: There Isn't Any," *New German Critique*, no. 90 (Autumn 2003): 27–35. See also his essay in this volume.

23. Dan Diner, "The Destruction of Narrativity: The Holocaust in Historical Discourse," in *Catastrophe and Meaning: The Holocaust and the Twentieth Century*, ed. Moishe Postone and Eric Santner (Chicago: University of Chicago Press, 2003), 67.

24. Alon Confino, *Foundational Pasts: The Holocaust as Historical Understanding* (Cambridge: Cambridge University Press, 2012), 5.

25. Peter Novick, *The Holocaust in American Life*, chap. 11.

26. On this, see Sidra DeKoven Ezrahi, "From Auschwitz to the Temple Mount: Binding and Unbinding the Israeli Narrative," in *After Testimony: The Ethics and Aesthetics of Holocaust Narrative for the Future*, ed. Jakob Lothe et al. (Columbus: Ohio University Press, 2012), 291–313; See also her very relevant distinction between centrifugal imagination and the centripetal imagination: Sidra DeKoven Ezrahi, "Representing Auschwitz," *History and Memory* 7, no. 2 (1996): 121–54.

27. Very generally speaking, the "Imaginary" is distinguished from the "Symbolic." The latter is about structure, law, and language, while the former is about one's narcissistic fascination with one's self-image, which is always also delusionary, seductive, and unavoidably accompanied by aggressiveness.

28. On two different treatments of the Nuremberg trials and their legacies, see Donald Bloxham, *Genocide on Trial* (Oxford: Oxford University Press, 2001); Norbert Ehrenfreund, *The Nuremberg Legacy* (New York: Palgrave Macmillan, 2007).

29. On these processes, see Alexander, "On the Social Construction," esp. 49–51. Moyn's critique that the emergence of a "human rights utopia" had almost nothing to do with the Holocaust is very convincing. For this, see Moyn, *The Last Utopia*. However, this new "utopia" is nonetheless morally anchored in the "lessons" of the Holocaust. See, e.g., the UN resolution adopted by the General Assembly on the International Holocaust Remembrance Day (A/RES/60/7, 1 November 2005), which begins with the reaffirmation of the 1948 Universal Declaration of Human Rights.

30. Hence, the victim's voice becomes essential to the procedure in order to make justice. See, e.g., Shoshana Felman, "Theaters of Justice: Arendt in Jerusalem, the Eichmann Trial, and the Redefinition of Legal Meaning in the Wake of the Holocaust," *Critical Inquiry* 27, no. 2 (2001): 201–38; Leora Bilsky, *Transformative Justice: Israeli Identity on Trial* (Ann Arbor: University of Michigan Press, 2004), 105–13, 250–52.

31. Robert Eaglestone, *The Holocaust and the Postmodern* (Oxford: Oxford University Press, 2004), 3.

32. Adi Ophir, *The Order of Evils: Towards an Ontology of Morals* (New York: Zone Books, 2005).

33. Dominick LaCapra, *Writing History, Writing Trauma* (Baltimore, MD: Johns Hopkins University Press, 2001), 91.

34. For a very useful philosophical discussion of the universal vs. particular problematics vis-à-vis the Holocaust and the legacy of the Enlightenment, see Berl Lang, *Act and Idea in the Nazi Genocide* (Chicago: University of Chicago Press), chap. 7.

35. Jacques Lacan, "The Mirror Stage as Formative of the Function of the I as Revealed in Psychoanalytic Experience," in *Ecrits: A Selection* (New York: W.W. Norton, 1977), 1–7.

36. Hannah Arendt, *The Human Condition* (Chicago: University of Chicago Press, 1958). Denying plurality as the essence of the human is, according to Arendt, the core of the totalitarian state.

37. This was, as is well-known, Lyotard's view. On this, see Eaglestone, *The Holocaust and the Postmodern*. See also Gabrielle Spiegel, "Previsioning the Past/Previsioning the Present: How Change Happens in Historiography," *History and Theory* 46 (2007): 1–19. For a problematization of this view, see Berl Lang, *Holocaust Representation* (Baltimore, MD and London: Johns Hopkins University Press, 2000), 140–57.

38. The story of the 1946 pogrom in Kielce, Poland, is the most well-known but far from the only one. See Jan Gross, *Fear: Anti-Semitism in Poland after Auschwitz—an Essay in Historical Interpretation* (New York: Random House, 2005).

39. Elazar Barkan, *The Guilt of Nations: Restitution and Negotiating Historical Injustices* (Baltimore, MD: Johns Hopkins University Press, 2000). See also in this regard the Nigerian writer Wole Soyinka's book *The Burden of Memory, the Muse of Forgiveness* (New York and Oxford: Oxford University Press, 1999), 23–92.

40. Michael Marrus, *Some Measure of Justice: The Holocaust Era Restitution Campaign of the 1990s* (Madison: University of Wisconsin Press, 2009).

41. John Torpey, "Making Whole What Has Been Smashed: Reflections on Reparations," *The Journal of Modern History* 73, no. 2 (2007): 333–58; Barkan, *The Guilt of Nations*.

42. See Roy Brooks, ed., *When Sorry Isn't Enough: The Controversy over Apologies and Reparations for Human Rights Injustices* (New York: New York University Press, 1999).

43. Torpey, *Making Whole*, 334.

44. Ibid., 335.

45. Tony Judt, *Postwar: A History of Europe since 1945* (London: Vintage, 2010), 803–4.

46. For the memory wars in Europe, see Dan Stone, "Memory Wars in the 'New Europe,'" in *Oxford Handbook for Post War European History*, ed. Dan Stone (Oxford: Oxford University Press, 2012), 714–32.

47. Stéphane Courtois et al. (eds.), *Black Book of Communism: Crimes, Terror, Repression*, trans. Jonathan Murphy and Mark Kramer (Cambridge, MA: Harvard University Press, 1999).

48. Ibid., 23. See also Annegret Ehmann, "Is the Holocaust a Unique and Unprecedented Tragedy? On Holocaust Politics and Genocide," *Dapim: Studies on the Holocaust* 25 (2011): 347–57.

49. See Amos Goldberg, "The Victim's Voice and Melodramatic Aesthetics in History," *History and Theory* 48, no. 3 (2009): 220–37.

50. Judt, *Postwar*, 829.

51. Sigmund Freud, "Mourning and Melancholia," in *The Standard Edition of the Complete Psychological Work of Sigmund Freud*, vol. 14 (Translated from the German under the general editorship of James Strachey) (London: Hogarth Press, 1957), 243–58.

52. See Charles S. Maier, "Consigning the Twentieth Century to History: Alternative Narratives for the Modern Era," *American Historical Review* 165, no. 3 (June 2000): 807–31.

53. Michael Rothberg, "Multidirectional Memory and the Universalization of the Holocaust Memory," in *Remembering the Holocaust: A Debate*, by Jeffrey C. Alexander (Oxford: Oxford University Press, 2009), chap. 4; Michael Rothberg, "Between Auschwitz and Algeria: Multidirectional Memory and the Counterpublic Witness," *Critical Inquiry* 33, no. 1 (Autumn 2006): 158–84.

54. Ross Poole, "Misremembering the Holocaust," 38.

55. Soyinka, *The Burden of Memory*, 38–39.

56. Charles S. Maier, "A Surfeit of Memory? Reflections on History Melancholy and Denial," *History and Memory* 5, no. 2 (Fall/Winter 1993), p. 147.

57. Manuella Consonni "The New Grammar of Otherness: Europe, the Shoah, and the Jews," *Jewish History* 24, no. 2 (2010): 105–26. For an opposite analysis though with very similar conclusions, see Matti Bunzl, "Between Anti-Semitism and Islamophobia: Some Thoughts on the New Europe," *American Ethnologist* 32, no. 4 (November 2005): 499–508. Bunzl contends that anti-Semitism was invented in the late nineteenth century to police the ethnically pure nation-state; Islamophobia, by contrast, is a formation of the present, marshaled to safeguard a supranational Europe. Whereas traditional anti-Semitism has run its historical course with the supersession of the nation-state, Islamophobia threatens to become the defining condition of the new Europe.

58. As German Chancellor Angela Merkel, representing the presidency of the European Union, declared in a press conference in March 2007 to mark the signature of the Declaration of Berlin commemorating the fiftieth anniversary of the founding of the European Economic Community, "the Judeo-Christian values ... sustain the EU ... we are marked by this Judeo-Christian past." Quoted in Hakan Yilmaz, "Turkish Identity on the Road to the EU: Basic Elements of French and German Oppositional Discourses," *Journal of Southern Europe and the Balkans* 9, no. 3 (2007): 296.

59. Quoted in Carolyn Dean, *The Fragility of Empathy after the Holocaust* (Ithaca, NY, and London: Cornell University Press, 2004), 9.

60. Steven Aschheim, *At the Edges of Liberalism: Junctions of European, German and Jewish History* (Basingstoke, UK: Palgrave Macmillan, 2012), chap. 11, "The (Ambiguous) Political Economy of Empathy," 133–44. Quotes are from pp. 137, 140.

61. See, e.g., in the context of Germany, Gökçe Yurdakul and Y. Michael Bodemann, "We Don't Want to Be the Jews of Tomorrow: Jews and Turks in Germany after 9/11," *German Politics & Society* 24, no. 2 (Summer 2006): 44–67.

62. On the constant use and abuse of the Holocaust by Israel in the Arab-Israeli conflict, see Idith Zertal, *Israel's Holocaust and the Politics of Nationhood* (Cambridge: Cambridge University Press, 2005). See also Avraham Burg, *The Holocaust Is Over: We Must Rise From Its Ashes* (New York: Palgrave Macmillan, 2009).

63. See, e.g., Jeffrey Herf, "Antisemitism in Comparative Historical Perspective," *Dapim: Studies on the Holocaust* 25 (2011): 331–35.

64. A. Dirk Moses, "The Holocaust and World History," paper presented at the Genocide, Memory, Justice: The Holocaust in Comparative Contexts conference, University of Illinois Urbana-Champaign, 5–6 November 2009. A version of the paper will be published in Moses's forthcoming Cambridge University Press 2016 *Genocide and the Terror of History*.

65. The scholar of culture Frank Stern has pointed out with regard to the patterns according to which post-1967 Israel is presented: "In the West German media, Israeli military prowess was glorified and Israelis now came to be seen as the 'Prussians of the Orient.' An Israeli military victory was celebrated by segments of the West German press as an indication of the success of the *Blitzkrieg*." Frank Stern, *The Whitewashing of the Yellow Badge: Antisemitism and Philosemitism in Postwar Germany,* trans. William Templer (Oxford: Pergamon Press, 1992), 430; see also Martin Braach-Maksvytis, "Germany, Palestine, Israel and the (Post) Colonial Imagination," in *German Colonialism: Race, the Holocaust, and Postwar Germany,* ed. Volker Langbehn and Mohammad Salama (New York: Columbia University Press, 2011), 294–314; Achcar, *The Arabs and the Holocaust*, 279–82.

66. Achcar, *The Arabs and the Holocaust*, 283.

67. I thank Alon Confino for articulating this irony.

68. Levy and Sznaider, *Holocaust and Memory*. Regarding claims for restitution and the return of property, see Barkan, *The Guilt of Nations*.

69. See Deborah Lipstadt's book on the prosecution of Holocaust denier David Irving: Lipstadt, *History on Trial*.

70. Slavoj Žižek, *Tarrying with the Negative: Kant, Hegel, and the Critique of Ideology* (Durham, NC: Duke University Press, 1993), chap. 4. In the political context of the riots that took place in UK in summer 2011, see "Shoplifters of the World Unite," *London Review of Books,* 19 August

2011, http://www.lrb.co.uk/2011/08/19/slavoj-zizek/shoplifters-of-the-world-unite (accessed 14 January 2014).

71. Ofer Aderet and Reuters, "European Court: Denying Armenian 'Genocide' Is No Crime," *Haaretz*, 18 December 2013, http://www.haaretz.com/news/world/1.564226.

72. Debórah Dwork and Robert Jan Van Pelt, *Flight from the Reich: Refugee Jews 1933–1946* (New York and London: Norton, 2009), xiv. For the inequality in standards of compensation and restitution compared to the African case, see Soyinka, *The Burden of Memory*, 92; in the case of South Africa postapartheid processes, see Antjie Keog, *The Country of My Skull* (New York: Three Rivers Press, 1999), 171.

73. Charles S. Maier, "Overcoming the Past? Narrative and Negotiation, Remembering and Reparations: Issues at the Interface of History and Law," in *Politics and the Past*, ed. John Torpey (Lanham, MD: Rowan and Littlefield, 2003), 297.

74. This is very evident in José Brunner, Constantin Goschler, and Norbert Frei (ed), *Die Globalisierung der Wiedergutmachung: Politic, Moral, Moralpolitic*, Göttingen: Wallstein, 2013 (and especially the editors introduction pp. 7–33).

75. Saul Friedländer, "Introduction," in *Probing the Limits of Representation*, ed. Saul Friedländer (Cambridge, MA: Harvard University Press, 1992), 5.

76. Ibid.

77. Saul Friedländer, *Memory, History and the Extermination of the Jews* (Bloomington: Indiana University Press, 1993), 112–13. For more on the difficulty of weaving the Holocaust into modern European history, see the chapters by Anson Rabinbach, Dan Diner, and Moishe Postone in the second volume of Moishe Postone and Eric Santner, eds., *Catastrophe and Meaning: The Holocaust and the Twentieth Century* (Chicago: University of Chicago Press, 2003), 51–114.

Bibliography

Achcar, Gilbert. *The Arabs and the Holocaust: The Arab-Israeli War of Narratives.* New York: Metropolitan Books, 2010.

Aderet, Ofer, and Reuters. "European Court: Denying Armenian 'Genocide' Is No Crime." *Haaretz*, 18 December 2013. http://www.haaretz.com/news/world/1.564226 (accessed 14 January, 2014).

Alexander, Jeffrey C. "On the Social Construction of Moral Universals: The 'Holocaust' from Mass Murder to Trauma Drama." *European Journal of Social Theory* 5, no. 1 (2002): 5–85.

———. *Remembering the Holocaust: A Debate.* Oxford and New York: Oxford University Press, 2009.

Allwork, Larissa. *Holocaust Remembrance between the National and the Transnational.* London: Bloomsbury, forthcoming.

Anderson, Benedict. *Imagined Communities: Reflections on the Origin and Spread of Nationalism.* London: Verso, 1983.

Arendt, Hannah. *The Human Condition.* Chicago: University of Chicago Press, 1958.

Aschheim, Steven, *At the Edges of Liberalism: Junctions of European, German and Jewish History* (Basingstoke, UK: Palgrave Macmillan, 2012), chap. 11, "The (Ambiguous) Political Economy of Empathy," 133–44. Quotes are from pp. 137, 140.

Assmann, Aleida. "The Holocaust—a Global Memory? Extensions and Limits of a New Memory Community." In *Memory in a Global Age: Discourses, Practices and Trajectories, Society,* ed. Aleida Assmann and Sebastian Conrad, 97–118. New York: Palgrave MacMillan, 2010.

Barkan, Elazar. *The Guilt of Nations: Restitution and Negotiating Historical Injustices.* Baltimore, MD: Johns Hopkins University Press, 2000.

Beck, Ulrich. *Cosmopolitan Vision.* Cambridge: Polity Press, 2006.

———. *Risk Society: Towards a New Modernity.* London: Sage, 1992.

Bilsky, Leora. *Transformative Justice: Israeli Identity on Trial*. Ann Arbor: University of Michigan Press, 2004.

Bloxham, Donald. *Genocide on Trial*. Oxford: Oxford University Press, 2001.

Braach-Maksvytis, Martin. "Germany, Palestine, Israel and the (Post) Colonial Imagination." In *German Colonialism: Race, the Holocaust, and Postwar Germany*, ed. Volker Langbehn and Mohammad Salama, 294–314. New York: Columbia University Press, 2011.

Brooks, Roy, ed. *When Sorry Isn't Enough:* The Controversy over Apologies and Reparations for Human Rights Injustices. New York: New York University Press, 1999.

Brunner, José, Goschler Constantin, and Frei Norbert (ed). *Die Globalisierung der Wiedergutmachung: Politic, Moral, Moralpolitic*. Göttingen: Wallstein, 2013.

Bunzl, Matti. "Between Anti-Semitism and Islamophobia: Some Thoughts on the New Europe." *American Ethnologist* 32, no. 4 (November 2005): 499–508.

Burg, Avraham. *The Holocaust Is Over: We Must Rise From Its Ashes*. New York: Palgrave Macmillan, 2009.

Confino, Alon. *Foundational Pasts: The Holocaust as Historical Understanding*. Cambridge: Cambridge University Press, 2012.

Consonni, Manuela. "The New Grammar of Otherness: Europe, the Shoah, and the Jews." *Jewish History* 24, no. 2 (2010): 105–26.

Courtois, Stéphane, Nicolas Werth, Jean-Louis Panné, Andrzej Paczkowsk, Karel Bartošek, and Jean-Louis Margolineds. *Black Book of Communism: Crimes, Terror, Repression*. Translated by Jonathan Murphy and Mark Kramer. Cambridge, MA: Harvard University Press, 1999.

Dean, Carolyn. *The Fragility of Empathy after the Holocaust*. Ithaca, NY, and London: Cornell University Press, 2004.

Diner, Dan. "The Destruction of Narrativity: The Holocaust in Historical Discourse." In *Catastrophe and Meaning: The Holocaust and the Twentieth Century*, ed. Moishe Postone and Eric Santner, 67–80. Chicago: University of Chicago Press, 2003.

Duranti, Marco. "The Holocaust, the Legacy of 1789 and the Birth of International Human Rights Law: Revisiting the Foundation Myth." *Journal of Genocide Research* 14, no. 2 (June 2012): 159–86.

Dwork, Debórah, and Robert Jan Van Pelt. *Auschwitz: 1270 to the Present*. New York and London: Norton, 1996.

———. *Flight from the Reich: Refugee Jews 1933–1946*. New York and London: Norton, 2009.

Eaglestone, Robert. *The Holocaust and the Postmodern*. Oxford: Oxford University Press, 2004.

Eckel, Jan, and Claudia Moisel, eds. *Universalisierung des Holocaust? Erinnerungskultur und Gesschictspolitik in Internationaler Perspective*. Beiträge zur Geschichte des Nationalsozialismus 24. Göttingen: Wallstein, 2008.

Ehmann, Annegret. "Is the Holocaust a Unique and Unprecedented Tragedy? On Holocaust Politics and Genocide." *Dapim: Studies on the Holocaust* 25 (2011): 347–57.

Ehrenfreund, Norbert. *The Nuremberg Legacy*. New York: Palgrave Macmillan, 2007.

Ezrahi, Sidra DeKoven. "From Auschwitz to the Temple Mount: Binding and Unbinding the Israeli Narrative." In *After Testimony: The Ethics and Aesthetics of Holocaust Narrative for the Future*, ed. Jakob Lothe, Susan Rubin Suleiman, and James Phelan, 291–313. Columbus: Ohio University Press, 2012.

Ezrahi, Sidra DeKoven. "Representing Auschwitz." *History and Memory* 7, no. 2 (1995). 121–54.

Felman, Shoshana. "Theaters of Justice: Arendt in Jerusalem, the Eichmann Trial, and the Redefinition of Legal Meaning in the Wake of the Holocaust." *Critical Inquiry* 27, no. 2 (2001).

Freud, Sigmund. "Mourning and Melancholia." In *The Standard Edition of the Complete Psychological Work of Sigmund Freud*, vol. 14 (translated from the German under the general editorship of James Strachey), 243–58. London: Hogarth Press, 1957.

Friedländer, Saul. "Introduction." In *Probing the Limits of Representation: Nazism and the "Final Solution,"* ed. Saul Friedländer, 1–21. Cambridge, MA: Harvard University Press, 1992.

———. *Memory, History and the Extermination of the Jews of Europe*. Bloomington: Indiana University Press, 1993.

———. *Nazi Germany and the Jews*. Vol. 1, *The Years of Persecution: 1933–1939*. New York: HarperCollins, 1997.

———. *Nazi Germany and the Jews*. Vol. 2, *The Years of Extermination*. New York: HarperCollins, 2007.

Goldberg, Amos. "The Victim's Voice and Melodramatic Aesthetics in History." *History and Theory* 48, no. 3 (2009): 220–37.

———. "The 'Jewish Narrative' in the Yad Vashem Global Holocaust Museum," *Journal of Genocide Research* 14, no. 2 (June 2012): 187–213.

Gross, Jan. *Fear: Anti-Semitism in Poland after Auschwitz—an Essay in Historical Interpretation*. New York: Random House, 2005.

Halbwachs, Maurice. *On Collective Memory*. Chicago: University of Chicago Press, 1992.

Herf, Jeffrey. "Antisemitism in Comparative Historical Perspective." *Dapim: Studies on the Holocaust* 25 (2011): 331–35.

Judt, Tony. *Postwar: A History of Europe since 1945*. London: Vintage, 2010.

Keog, Antjie. *The Country of My Skull*. New York: Three Rivers Press, 1999.

Lacan, Jacques. "The Mirror Stage as Formative of the Function of the I as Revealed in Psychoanalytic Experience." In *Ecrits: A Selection* (translated by Bruce Fink in collaboration with Héloise Fink and Russell Grigg), 1–7. New York: W.W. Norton, 1977.

LaCapra, Dominick. *Writing History, Writing Trauma*. Baltimore, MD: Johns Hopkins University Press, 2001.

Lang, Berl. *Act and Idea in the Nazi Genocide*. Chicago: University of Chicago Press, 1990.

———. *Holocaust Representation*. Baltimore, MD and London: Johns Hopkins University Press, 2000.

Levy, Daniel, and Natan Sznaider. *The Holocaust and Memory in the Global Age*. Philadelphia: Temple University Press, 2006.

Lipstadt, Deborah. *History on Trial: My Day in Court with David Irving*. New York: Ecco, 2005.

Litvak, Meir, and Esther Webman. *From Empathy to Denial: Arab Responses to the Holocaust*. New York: Columbia University Press, 2009.

London Review of Books. "Shoplifters of the World Unite." 19 August 2011. http://www.lrb.co.uk/2011/08/19/slavoj-zizek/shoplifters-of-the-world-unite (accessed 14 January, 2014).

Maier, Charles S. "Consigning the Twentieth Century to History: Alternative Narratives for the Modern Era." *American Historical Review* 105, no. 3 (June 2000): 807–31.

———. "Overcoming the Past? Narrative and Negotiation, Remembering and Reparations: Issues at the Interface of History and Law." In *Politics and the Past,* ed. John Torpey, 295–304. Lanham, MD: Rowan and Littlefield, 2003.

———. "A Surfeit of Memory? Reflections on History Melancholy and Denial." *History and Memory* 5, no. 2 (Fall/Winter 1993): 136–52.

Marrus, Michael R. *Some Measure of Justice: The Holocaust Era Restitution Campaign of the 1990s*. Madison: University of Wisconsin Press, 2009.

Moses, A. Dirk. "The Holocaust and World History." Paper presented at the Genocide, Memory, Justice: The Holocaust in Comparative Contexts conference, University of Illinois Urbana-Champaign, 5–6 November 2009.

Moyn, Samuel. *The Last Utopia: Human Rights in History*. Cambridge, MA, and London: Harvard University Press, 2010.

Nora, Pierre. *Realms of Memory*. Vol. 1, *Conflicts and Divisions*. New York: Columbia University Press, 1996.

Novick, Peter. "The American National Narrative of the Holocaust: There Isn't Any." *New German Critique*, no. 90 (Autumn 2003): 27–35.

———. *The Holocaust in American Life*. Boston: Houghton Mifflin, 1999.

Ophir, Adi. *The Order of Evils: Towards an Ontology of Morals*. New York: Zone Books, 2005.

Poole, Ross. "Misremembering the Holocaust: Universal Symbol, Nationalist Icon or Moral Kitsch?" In *Memory and the Future: Transnational Politics, Ethics and Society,* ed. Yifat Gutman, Adam Brown, and Amy Sodaro, 31–49. Houndmills: Palgrave MacMillan, 2010.

Robertson, Roland. "Glocalization: Time-Space and Homogeneity-Heterogeneity." In *Global Modernities,* ed. Mike Featherstone, Scott Lash, and Roland Robertson, 25–44. London: Sage, 1995.
Rosenfeld, Alvin. *The End of the Holocaust.* Bloomington and Indianapolis: Indiana University Press, 2011.
Rothberg, Michael. "Between Auschwitz and Algeria: Multidirectional Memory and the Counterpublic Witness." *Critical Inquiry* 33, no. 1 (Autumn 2006): 158–84.
———. "Multidirectional Memory and the Universalization of the Holocaust Memory." In *Remembering the Holocaust: A Debate,* by Jeffrey C. Alexander, 123–34. Oxford: Oxford University Press, 2009.
Soyinka, Wole. *The Burden of Memory, the Muse of Forgiveness.* New York and Oxford: Oxford University Press, 1999.
Spiegel, Gabrielle. "Previsioning the Past/Previsioning the Present: How Change Happens in Historiography." *History and Theory* 46 (2007): 1–19.
Stern, Frank. *The Whitewashing of the Yellow Badge: Antisemitism and Philosemitism in Postwar Germany.* Translated by William Templer. Oxford: Pergamon Press, 1992.
Stone, Dan. "Memory Wars in the 'New Europe.'" In *Oxford Handbook for Post War European History,* ed. Dan Stone. Oxford: Oxford University Press, 2012: 714–31.
Todorov, Tvetan. "The Uses and Abuses of Memory." In *What Happens to History: The Renewal of Ethics in Contemporary Thought,* ed. Howard Marchitello, 11–22. London and New York: Routledge, 2001.
Torpey, John. "Making Whole What Has Been Smashed: Reflections on Reparations." *The Journal of Modern History* 73, no. 2 (2007): 333–58.
Yilmaz, Hakan. "Turkish Identity on the Road to the EU: Basic Elements of French and German Oppositional Discourses." *Journal of Southern Europe and the Balkans* 9, no. 3 (2007): 293–305..
Yurdakul, Gökçe, and Y. Michael Bodemann. "We Don't Want to Be the Jews of Tomorrow: Jews and Turks in Germany after 9/11." *German Politics & Society* 24, no. 2 (Summer 2006): 44–67.
Zertal, Idith. *Israel's Holocaust and the Politics of Nationhood.* Cambridge: Cambridge University Press, 2005.
Žižek, Slavoj. *Tarrying with the Negative: Kant, Hegel, and the Critique of Ideology.* Durham, NC: Duke University Press, 1993.

CHAPTER 2

Globalization versus Holocaust
An Anthropological Conundrum

HAIM HAZAN

The Dilemma

This book is set to reveal an implausible narrative of the momentous presence and potency of the Holocaust as a global idiom. It is composed of cross-nationally recounted and enacted stories that draw on the uniqueness of the Holocaust and at the same time render it ubiquitous. These globally sanctified tales[1]—woven from historical evidence, political interests, philosophical deliberations, and moral teachings—offer their captivated, at times captive,[2] listeners a quasi-theological and pedagogical dogma of recognizing truth, evil, guilt, confession, judgment, retribution, and penance. On the other hand, although complementarily, therapeutic nomenclature, such as trauma, posttrauma, psychological identification,[3] depression, resilience, and rehabilitation, is indicated to suggest an ego-based discourse summoning all survivors to a supposedly universal fold of theory and practice of managing Holocaust repercussions. However, the immensity of this all-embracing grand project only stresses its inbuilt improbability, as it is our belief that the two intertwined components—globalization[4] and the trope of the Holocaust—are starkly and inherently opposed. Hopefully it will be shown that it is the dynamics generated by this gulf that furnish the ever-increasing circles of the unfulfilled globalized preoccupation with Holocaust resonance. Unfulfilled, for accrediting global attributes to the assumed quiddity of the Holocaust implies contradiction in expressive terms. This is a contrast that emerges from the divergence in the descriptive practices commonly and academically employed to articulate both constructs. There-

---

Notes for this section begin on page 40.

fore, ineffability, silence, and unintelligibility are often enlisted to circumvent areas of incommunicability with and among survivors, thus marking them as dwelling in impervious, closed self-referential systems of a metonymic nature whose perfidious understanding could be executed through staged testimonies and induced reminiscing.[5] Conversely, the meandering or direct discourses concerning the Holocaust follow the rules of communicating by way of metaphoric channels of speech and action that are capable of attributing shared modes of understanding and meaning to the unspoken and inexpressible. The logic of global codification is decidedly and without reservation dedicated to that end of silencing the cacophonic sound of the singular for the sake of the orchestrated general.

So compelling is the globalized appropriation and co-optation of the Holocaust as an intelligible omnipresent phenomenon that even a trace of a claim to its unprecedented exceptional standing is culturally cleansed. Therefore, framing the Holocaust within a graded index of genocide events or concealing any occurrence of anticipated discontent in Holocaust terms are both tacit suggestions of denying the uniqueness of the Holocaust.[6] The ubiquity of this form of renunciation is far more effective than blunt and conspicuous declarations negating the very incidence or great degree of the Holocaust. What follows is intended to trace a few impulses in the reasoning of the globalized Holocaust to the extent that, except for the word, hardly any similarity remains between the two Holocausts. Like in the Cartesian wax argument,[7] transformations of form and matter divorce the authentic Holocaust from its globally perplexing manifestations. The thrust of that transformation, however, is not unhinged on one specific case of wax or Holocaust, but on a move from one cultural state of matter to another—namely, from quiddity to liquidity. The understanding of that critical change would facilitate an acquittal of the debate on the Holocaust as a unique human condition peculiar to World War II European Jews while not abandoning the gist of it, which is the quest for a general rule of telling the original from its representations.

Let us begin with the proverbially quoted title of Primo Levy's 1947 book *If This Is a Man*, which has become an aphorism signifying the puzzlement instilled in any discourse of the Holocaust, namely, the cogency of some given assumptions referring to the nature of mankind. Levy's Auschwitz experience challenges the very notion of civilization both as a process and a product of socialization and humanization.

Universal knowledge and conceptions of culture, humanity, and morality are therefore stretched to the limits of conception, and the soundness of translating experience into communicable language is as a result put into question. This much-debated epistemological rupture brings out conceptual gaps in the public sphere, as well as in academia, where it figures as an active and potent digressive agent of beating about the bush of the inexolicable phenomenon, thereby standing accountable for the disconcerted cosmologies that make up the discursive universe of the Holocaust. The cultural devices with which these spaces decivilized are rendered uncivilized and yet become negotiable and, culturally reformed, constitute the essence of the following. As with any intellectually divergent discourse, the line of the argument is spurned by recognizing a contradiction, which in this case is the apparent inconsistency between the two leading themes of our ongoing discussion—namely, the imputed centripetal authority of the existentially essential category, "Holocaust," as against the centrifugal diffusing forces associated with the process of globalization. Juxtaposing the two concepts is in all probability a necessary oxymoronic exercise of bringing to light some inconsistencies ingrained in late modernity, as addressed by sociologists who identified the duality of the pursuit of atavistic tribalism as a counterforce to the supremacy of engulfing constructionism.[8] Such a constructivist standpoint is glaringly attested to in the ways the Holocaust is appropriated, processed, represented, and disciplined by academic discourses to which global presence and viability are the final justifications.[9]

Falling back on a Foucauldian assumption regarding the surveillance properties of any discourse,[10] it could be recognized that forms of talk and performance surrounding the Holocaust are definitional acts of disciplining the uncontrolled reverberations of what is thought to be its muted essence. The discipline of anthropology is not an exception, and yet it presents an outstanding example for that dictum. As such it could be a case study for other disciplines caught up between a politically incorrect fervor for authentic essentialism and a socially mandated production of infinite interpretations. It, therefore, seems apt to tackle the problem of reluctantly suppressed discourses of the Holocaust through some fundamental references to that particular form of talk whose claim to fame is its open-minded partiality to anything human.

Anthropology at the Core

Of all sciences of memory, as Hacking coined it[11]—that is, sociology, history, political science, et cetera—only sociocultural anthropology seems to have eluded an extensive intellectual engagement with issues related to the Holocaust.[12] Despite preoccupation with genocide, testimony, authentic witnessing, commemoration, taboo, humanness, and moral order—all possible offshoots of grappling with the meanings of the Holocaust—anthropology has not taken advantage of its theoretical faculties and comparative capacities in such deliberations.[13] Challenged from both within and without, anthropology seems indisposed to rise to that discursive occasion and to develop its own interpretive versions of accounting for the unaccountable.[14] Notwithstanding the interdisciplinary, often unanswered calls for invoking post-Holocaust consequences as templates for revisiting and reframing anthropological interests in the understanding of violence, stratagems of exclusion, systems of classification, and boundary maintenance, it is fascinating to observe that scholarly pleas by nonanthropologists for anthropological involvement in deciphering the Holocaust by and large remain ignored. For example, there is Dan Diner's assertion, made in 2008, as to the respective intellectual claim by and commitment of history and anthropology to fathom and appropriate certain aspects of the Holocaust:

> The phenomenon of the crime against humanity experienced by the Jews ... can be split and regarded from ... two opposing perspectives: one that argues historically and that is above all adopted by the victims, while the other is an anthropologically inclined perception of the events which rather reaches further into a universal domain. The latter focuses on the significance of the events for the species as such. These perspectives are necessarily unequal. They may even work against each other.[15]

The assignation of "the universal domain" to the world of anthropology reflects a conventional image of the discipline as the study of humanity, and as such it suits anthropologists to adopt a cross-cultural view of human comportment, a perspective very appropriate to comment on the global effects of a worldwide cataclysm. Nonetheless, rather than converting the Holocaust into a reference point for assessing and testing the limits of culture, attention has been mainly directed to instances of ethnic cleansing, colonial oppression, and racial discrimination to the exclusion of the Holocaust from any comparative scale. Holocaust-based implications for the anthropology of memory, cohorts, and cosmopolitanism are rare in the discipline. How can these, seemingly deliberate, lacunae of anthropological knowledge be expounded, and in what way do they suggest the imminent presence of other such cultural voids? Three complementary heuristic explanations might be presented to deal with this dilemma.

The first draws on the moral motto based on the anthropological ethos, namely, the relativistic credo that foils any hierarchical order of suffering, victimization, and malevolence, thus resisting all suggested epigenetically propelled essentials.[16] Globally marked off as inflicted by ultimate, indivisible evil, the Holocaust opposes any idea of contingent moralities and context-bound rationalities. Acquiescing to these sorts of presumptions would imply unsubscribing to cross-cultural research agendas. It also suggests the redundancy of ethnographic fieldwork, as it is a priori debunked of any serendipitous moments. Such a prospect arguably amounts to the eventual collapse of most timely anthropological discourses.

The second filtering device responsible for illuminating anthropological knowledge of the Holocaust is found in the temporal constitution of the discipline. Formulated within the concept and precept of the ethnographic authenticity set in fieldwork time, anthropological accountability is bound to the present. Discussing the disengagement between history and anthropology, anthropologist Michel-Rolph Trouillot comments in his seminal book *Silencing the Past: Power and the Production of History* on contemporary cultural products designed to represent the Holocaust: "The illuminating value of the Holocaust Museum in Washington may be as much tied to the current situation of American Jews as to the real bodies in and around Auschwitz. Indeed, many Holocaust survivors are not sure that such a museum would be illuminating as Auschwitz itself. The crux of the matter is the here and now, the relations between the events described and their public representation in specific historical context."[17] Consequently, the proliferation of ethnographic studies of commemoration ceremonies, simulated performances of past events, memorial monuments, designated sites, and artifacts associated with the Holocaust to the desertion of direct encounters with uncultivated personal testimonies anchored in the past. The crisis of witnessing in anthropology, therefore, happens when faithfulness to context positions survivors' dismembered subjectivities on two temporally different planes—past and present—of which only the latter could be discursively managed by the discipline. Otherwise, psychological and phenomenological conceptual props ought to be pitched to assist temporally interconnected selves on an uninterrupted continuum.[18] Thus, presupposed theoretical conceptions of trauma, posttrauma, life story, being in the world, and other continuity-stipulated terms of reference could be cited to thread together fragments of time on a string of a meaningfully embroidered life review.

These two constitutive axes of anthropological activity are interwoven into a third, which is the grist of the discipline's methodology of doing fieldwork—namely, participant observation. This oxymoronic practice confounding subject and object, inside and outside gazes, and self and other engenders continual fluency and interchangeability, thus breaking down such apparent binary oppositions. The rationale that catalyzes this diversion of set positions in the research arena is the innate anthropological commitment to knowledge based on cross-cultural translation, including the common language established between the professional stranger and the proverbial native. This rule of disciplinary self-justification assumes transformability of both protagonists of the ethnographic project—researcher and native—to the extent of role reversal and mutual identification under the façade of shared inseparable experience to the extent of invalidating otherness. As a result, anthropological discourse more often than not reflects the other's image as communicable, transient, and amenable to disciplinary domestication as a natural narrator of local knowledge.

Anthropological Savagery

This anthropologically uncultured native no longer falls under the category of a "savage"[19] who is, by nature, irrevocably untamable and undisciplined. This form of savagery is presumed inherently indestructible and as a result is beyond human discourse, bordering, as it were, on barbarism and even bestiality. This extracultural position does not offer negotiating terms of coexistence, thus consigning the uncontrolled savage to an uncivilized space where real or imaginary beings with whom no measure of mutual understanding could be struck are placed. The other type of other, however, the one that could be colonized, educated, enchanted, and beguiled, is expected to uphold an entirely different anthropological transaction. Persuaded to reveal a personal life story, this homely other, prototyped on the imagery of the "noble savage," lets anthropologists process their shared dialogue as an account of indigenous authenticity while lamenting the "crisis of representation"[20] supposedly aborting such claims. An argument could be made that testimonies by Holocaust survivors contain something of the first category of savage-like otherness insomuch as their hard core is often culturally rendered foreboding, inexplicable, and hence untranslatable. Additionally, such socially provoked reported memories could be publicly displayed as self-declared experience of "another planet," like the dramatic court appearance, during the Eichmann trial, of Auschwitz survivor Yehiel Dinur (Ka-Tzetnik), who lost consciousness while trying to relate his present ordeal of being hounded by the past ghosts that flooded his life. This class of embodied evidence is difficult to negotiate by anthropologists, whose critical discourse is set to give precedence to the present over the past and not the other way around, as manifested in that courtroom drama. Possessed by the spirit of the unexpected, unrestrained, unruly savage, the tormented witness for the prosecution disengaged from the orderly codex of giving testimony, as he was returning to an anthropologically unexplored terrain, an area devoid of any scholarly recognizable cultural regulation and of the presence of reversible, reclaimed others.

The distinction between the two diametrically opposed anthropological others cannot be counted as just a yardstick for testing the limits of anthropological perception. However, as anthropology is, by nature of its scope and ambition, a globally geared, undisciplined discipline,[21] it could provide an explanation for the management of the constraints of translation and some key properties of the process of globalization in general, for savages still prowl its every nook and cranny. Regardless of the heated debate on approaches to conceptualizing the phenomenon of globalization, it would be just to observe the prevalence of the assertion of transformability, transience, liquidity, and hence boundless translatability in a late capitalistic epoch of converting almost all relationships, goods, services, and moralities into fiscal matters. Thus, the trope of money as the ultimate converter of anything to anything else and vice versa spells a transformative mechanism detached from mores and morals.[22]

The agent of that conviction in the universal rationality of exchangeability, *homo economicus,* infiltrates the fabric of globalization as an open-ended civil society transcending and transmuting symbolic and territorial boundaries. Inherent in this model is the presumption of hybridity as the paramount cultural logic of globalization, facilitating its constant dynamics of mixing, fusing, and converting. In that sense the hybrid has changed its cultural position from the menacing territory of the witch, the monster, the impure, the stranger, the unhomely,[23] the abjection,[24] and the taboo to the home space of everyday cinematic and other media imagery of transsexuality, hyphenated cultures,[25] mixed races, humanized animals, cyborgs, and aliens—all legitimate and welcomed sojourns of the postmodern. The once feared, hence marginalized, hybrid, the perpetrator of moral panic and disorder, has moved to the legitimate core of social action. Consequently, formerly disdained domains of deemed irrationality, savagery, and arbitrary unpredictability are transformed into a naturalized order of culture.

The Global Turn in the Construction of Otherness

This inversion could be described as a globalization-generated reversal of cultural fortunes. The previously prohibited haunted house of despicable ghoulish ghosts of abomination and horror[26] now renders itself as a desirable temple of consumerism and mass media, while the hallowed ground—the pure, primordial, unadulterated—becomes a forbidden land of unmanageable extracultural demons whose immutable presence is against the grain of liquidized life in a global age. An informative example for this kind of conversion is the Agambenian concept of *homo sacer*,[27] that outcast sacred whose excommunicated bare life denies his killing from being credited with propitiatory sacrificial value. Accordingly, whole populations of peoples , such as the Jews, could be liable to be marked as belonging to the state of exception of bare life. Thus, under the guise of such imputed emergency situations, such populations could be mass murdered with impunity. However, to deter dire consequences of possible extermination, culturally engineered methods of handling such threats to the momentum of ever-increasing transactional circles are made available in the form of normalizing therapeutic practices or humanizing institutional decisions. These are intended to displace the singularly enduring essential from being transfixed in an ahistorical point of time into a negotiable construction conforming to the effervescence of globalized temporality and rationality. Therefore, the Holocaust could be framed as genocide, which, in turn, is construed in terms of the logic of modernity,[28] colonial conflicts, or the boom of psychoanalytic forces—all subject to reasoning, understanding, and sometimes to condoning forgiveness or forgetfulness leading to redemptive therapy.[29]

A few examples of the operation of that corrective practice turning clearly uncivilized voids into civilized, globally incorporable spaces could be taken from all walks of daily living in today's world. One such example is the changing case of contemporary definitions of the condition of autism. What was once regarded as a socially vacuous discrete mental disorder, more often than not dubbed in nonhuman metaphoric terms such as "feral" or "fairy children," is today placed on a behavioral continuum labeled "the autistic spectrum," along which most usual suspects of cognitive-cum-emotional aberration could move forward or backward, thus humanizing all its socially approved actors.[30] Another example is the predicament of encountering the ultimate extracultural state of old age in a secular society, where no promise of immortality is offered. For as long as the illusion of still time can be supported through the so-called antiaging maintenance of aging bodies, ageless selves are credited with conditional social inclusion. However, when in the throes of final irreversible decrepitude, symbolic and territorial barriers are erected to avoid any contamination by the doomed.[31]

Uncivilized Spaces

The assumption of irreversibility as the turning point after which communication and interaction become defunct also guides attitudes toward situations of conceived cultural totality, as in religious fundamentalism, racist persuasions, and uncompromising political ideologies. Thus, confrontations with unglobalized cultural units are usually described in terms of mutual exclusivity resulting in imminent warfare and possible elimination through extermination. As the dwellers of such uncivilized spaces are contaminated by the overall dehumanized nature of that category, the fate of the consequently depersonalized is of no consequence to those who act in the name of belonging to another category, one that is potentially hybridized and therefore does not resist globalization.

The identification between cultural categories and people effaces the latter for the former; thus, the elimination of an uncivilized space would mean that the same destiny is shared by both. Being branded as a member of a categorically irreversible as well as nontransactional population subverts the sense of a natural, assumed certainty in the ability to negotiate terms of survival. Following the realization that structural constraints completely override agency is the daunting awareness that globally sanctified notions of choice and subjectivity are shown to be impertinent in effecting the category's destination. The logic of globalization, in itself, gives no rule or indication as to the possible circumstances of inclusion in an uncivilized space, hence the arbitrariness of falling under such a category. Random existential chances, therefore, could not be predicted and prepared for, and since life-and-death matters are sometimes at stake, the apprehension, if not dread, of being exiled to an extracultural desert is a cause for deep concern. The argument is that the dread of nonnegotiable arbitrariness is neither irrational, assuming the undercurrent work of a murky, outlandish mythical power, nor is it the necessary upshot of processes of rationalized modernity. It is, in fact, the disturbing recognition of the arational character of a history devoid of story. It is that unaccountable happening and course of events that breeds the prevalence of the common stance toward cultural voids in general and that of the Holocaust in particular as inimitable realities, but nevertheless of a shared character. This line of argument safeguards the proverbially held view of the uniqueness of the Holocaust as a quintessentially unprecedented event, while offering an ahistorical level of comparison analogizing culturally comparable phenomena on the merit of their structural qualities rather than on the basis of their phenomenological characteristics.

Articulating these spaces might suggest a contradiction in terms, for uttering the indescribable, while being faithful to the meaninglessness of the extracultural, could prove an incommunicable speech act. Accordingly, silence is a favored choice among those who are reluctant to bear witness to the unfathomable. Holocaust talk is enabled, however, by circumventing the presupposition of the nonrepresentational. This is done through surrounding descriptive and conceptual Holocaust-related discourses by the logic of globalization. Subscribing to constructionist principles of an unequivocal translation, leaving no space for cultural idiosyncrasy, is one way of avoiding the experience of uncivilized spaces by civilizing it in global terms. In addition, the centrifugal forces of transformation and transcendence are liable to distance and as a result assuage untainted suffering, victimization, and sense of futility, thereby losing sight of the authentic origin of witnessing and conceding to the debate centered around its supposed crisis.

The attenuation and dissemination of witnessing incomparable anguish originate from the logic of globalization insofar as it is not meant to contain and tolerate insoluble totalities. These, when inescapably thrown into relief, are restricted and sequestrated in heterotopic camp-like enclaves for modern untouchables, such as institutions for the mentally sick, retirement homes, and the darkened enclosures of theater and cinema. However, when totalities like the undifferentiated totality of a cultural void are exposed, the reaction to that insufferable presence in the midst of a highly differentiated society would unfailingly be an attempt at decomposing the phenomenon into discrete constituents. These could make themselves be amenable to being trivialized, compared to, and assimilated into even remotely similar events, as is the case with the conceptualized articulation of the Holocaust. Therefore, the component of evil becomes banal, the camp is colonized, the extermination is industrialized, and the bare life is rendered nonsacrificial. As a result of globalizing different aspects of the inseparable total whole, three of its defining dimensions are forfeited: categorical boundedness, arbitrariness, and nonnegotiable irreversibility. The abstract, yet compelling, idea of reducing an assumed collectivity to some attributed categorical properties that in turn subject it to possible obliteration is despicable to the quest of ever-expanding cosmologies of universally inclusive cosmopolitanism. Thus, inimitability is replaced by an unbounded and unconditional conception of humanity as globally manifested in the rise of social, political, and legal concerns with the preservation and safeguarding of human rights.

The Holocaust as an Uncivilized Space

Present-bound arbitrariness, which renders memory superfluous while forestalling action, interaction, and planning, is extricated from that arational, paralyzing state by rationalizing and mobilizing it at all intellectual costs, even at the expense of contemplating other existential options such as life depleted of making sense, such as in some Holocaust-based literature, art, and discourses. The very idea of nonnegotiability as identified with the unpredictability of stumbling into a randomized practice of fateful categorization is not acceptable to any vision of global communication. Unfurled communicability, therefore, is revered as a promised guarantee for sharing discourses of understanding and cooperation.

All these cover-ups for cultural voids qualify as their denial, and the Holocaust is no exception. Any discursive deconstruction of its distilled, untranslatable residuals would put into question the very feasibility of turning it global. Indeed, the usual Holocaust deniers who repudiate the empirical or logical contingency of the event conform to viewing the phenomenon as humanly implausible, hence acknowledging its objectionable quiddity. Tacitly inherent in both implicit and explicit modes of denial is today's growing assertion that perpetrators and victims alike should be construed in human terms, as inconceivable as that was in the past. Looking at that welded, humanly dubious, joint space from the angle of the relations between the two categories partaking in its creation, it becomes clear why anthropology gives up a singular opportunity to harness the Holocaust in the service of unraveling some of its principal concerns; a war of taxonomies goes beyond the limits of disciplinary mandate.

However, given the intellectual transgressions intrinsic to the encounter with Holocaust matters, it would seem that Agamben's philosophical concept of "the anthropological machine" could be of compelling interest to those committed to "the science of man." This epistemological mechanism is utilized to identify and signify such transgressions, in particular those fording the crossing between the human and the inhuman. In Agamben's book *The Open,* he writes that "the anthropological machine of humanism is an ironic apparatus that verifies the absence of a nature proper to Homo, holding him suspended between a celestial and a terrestrial nature, between animal and human—and, thus, his being always less and more of himself."[32] This intracategorical exploration of the open limits of humanity has been pursued by a number of anthropologists but seldom, if ever, in reference to the very issue of the humanity or otherwise of the state of betweenness of the beings populating uncivilized spaces.[33] Not only might the study of the Holocaust gain from such academic entrepreneurship, but the discourse of anthropology itself could be reinherited as a contact zone between various domains of the human and inhuman conditions. Should this challenge be left unmet, the propositions propounded by titles such as *Eternal Treblinka: Our Treatment of Animals and the Holocaust*[34] might surf the waves of globalization to further obscure the boundaries between the category of humans and that of animals. Based on a phrase by Bashevis Singer suggesting that "for the animals it is an eternal Treblinka,"[35] Holocaust scholar Charles Patterson's book likens the industrialized slaughtering of animals to that of the Jews. This would seem a mandatory conclusion of an anthropologically uncritical approach to the conceptual fusion binding the oxymoron Holocaust and globalization: a union of opposites that might be the precursor of the ultimate form of an acceptable transcultural form of denial,[36] one that calls for no apology, documentation, or even malice.

Notes

1. For example, the International Holocaust Remembrance Day held on 27 January, declared by the General Assembly of the United Nations in 2005.

2. Such as in Israeli state-sponsored school tours to Auschwitz. For an ethnographic study of the tours, see Jackie Feldman, *Above the Death Pits, Beneath the Flag* (New York: Berghahn Books, 2008).

3. For example, in Alexander's work on the universalization of the Holocaust; see Jeffrey C. Alexander, *Remembering the Holocaust: A Debate* (Oxford: Oxford University Press, 2009).

4. Drawing on a myriad of literature and broadly and uncritically put, "globalization" is a commonly used catchphrase relating to the unhindered spread and interconnectedness of production, communication, and technologies across the globe. Among the many studies of the interrelation between Holocaust and globalization see, e.g., Daniel Levy and Natan Sznaider, *The Holocaust and Memory in a Global Age* (Philadelphia: Temple University Press, 2006), in which the role of the Holocaust as a cue to the spreading of human rights in a global age is emphasized.

5. See, e.g., Shoshana Felman and Dori Laub, *Testimony* (London: Routledge, 1992) on testimony; Hannah Arendt, *Eichmann in Jerusalem* (1963; repr., New York: Penguin Books, 1992) on the staging of Eichmann's trial.

6. An example for this growing trend of framing the Holocaust within a postcolonial context and nomenclature is A. Dirk Moses, *Empire, Colony, Genocide: Conquest, Occupation, and Subaltern Resistance in World History* (New York: Berghahn Books, 2008).

7. In Descartes's "Second Meditation"; see Roger Ariew and Eric Watkins, eds., *Modern Philosophy: An Anthology of Primary Sources* (Boston: Hackett, 1998).

8. Zygmunt Bauman, *Modernity and Ambivilence* (Cambridge: Polity Press, 1991).

9. Zygmunt Bauman, *Modernity and the Holocaust* (Cambridge: Polity Press, 1991); Giles B. Gunn, *Beyond Solidarity: Pragmatism and Difference in a Globalized World* (Chicago: University of Chicago Press, 2001); David Bruce MacDonald, *Identity Politics in the Age of Genocide: The Holocaust in Historical Representation* (London: Taylor and Francis, 2007).

10. Foucault's writing is rife with references to this relationship. See, e.g., Michel Foucault, *Discipline and Punish: The Birth of the Prison* (1975; repr., Harmondsworth, UK: Penguin, 1997).

11. Ian Hacking, *Rewriting the Soul: Multiple Personality and the Science of Memory* (Princeton, NJ: Princeton University Press, 1998).

12. For laments on the neglect of the Holocaust in anthropological research, see Carroll McC. Lewin, "The Holocaust: Anthropological Possibilities and the Dilemma of Representation," *American Anthropologist* 94, no. 1 (1992): 161–66; Erika Bourguignon, "Memory in an Amnestic World: Holocaust, Exile, and the Return of the Suppressed," *Anthropological Quarterly* 78, no. 1 (2005): 63–88.

13. Holocaust issues are sometimes marginalized as topics on the general agenda of anthropological interest in genocide—see Alexander Laban Hinton, ed., *Annihilating Difference: The Anthropology of Genocide* (Berkeley: University of California Press, 2002)—or militarism—see Hugh Gusterson, "Anthropology and Militarism," *Annual Review of Anthropology* 36 (2007): 155–75.

14. Some studies of intergenerational transmission of genocidal memories with an emphasis on the Holocaust could be noted as an exception, particularly those with a comparative frame of reference. See, e.g., Carol A. Kidron, "Alterity and the Particular Limits of Universalism: Comparing Jewish-Israeli Holocaust and Canadian-Cambodian Genocide Legacies," *Current Anthropology* 53, no. 6 (2012): 725–54.

15. Dan Diner, "Epistemics of the Holocaust Considering the Question of 'Why?' and 'How?,'" *Naharayim* 1, no. 2 (2008): 195.

16. For a discussion of the anthropological discourses of cultural relativism, see Michael F. Brown, "Cultural Relativism 2.0," *Current Anthropology* 49 (2008): 363–83.

17. Michel-Rolph Trouillot, *Silencing the Past: Power and the Production of History* (Boston: Beacon, 1995), 26.

18. Postcolonial notions of exile, dispossession, and displacement attest to the current anthropological preoccupation with the temporal interconnectedness of cultural selves.

19. For a discussion of the anthropological discourse of the idea of the savage, see Michel-Rolph Trouillot, "Anthropology and the Savage Slot: The Poetics and Politics of Otherness," in *Recapturing Anthropology: Working in the Present*, ed. Richard G. Fox, 17–44 (Santa Fe, NM: School of American Research Press, 1991).

20. A term referring to the inadequacy of anthropology to represent reality (a phrase coined by anthropologists). George E. Marcus and Michael M. J. Fischer, *Anthropology as Cultural Critique: An Experimental Moment in the Human Sciences* (Chicago: University of Chicago Press, 1986).

21. Anna Lowenhaupt Tsing, *Friction: An Ethnography of Global Connection* (Princeton, NJ: Princeton University Press, 2005).

22. See Georg Simmel's classic work on the philosophy of money, *The Philosophy of Money*, ed. David Frisby, trans. Tom Bottomore and David Frisby (1900; repr., London: Routledge, 2004).

23. Homi K. Bhabha, "The World and the Home," *Social Text* 31–32 (1992): 141–53.

24. Julia Kristeva, *Powers of Horror* (New York: Columbia University Press, 1982).

25. Smadar Lavie, "Between and Among the Boundaries of Culture: Bridging Texts and Experience in the Third Timespace," *Cultural Studies* 10, no. 1 (1996): 154–79.

26. Mary Douglas, *Purity and Danger: An Analysis of Concepts of Pollution and Taboo* (London: Penguin, 1966); Mary Douglas, *Risk and Blame: Essays in Cultural Theory* (London: Routledge, 1992).

27. Giorgio Agamben, *Homo Sacer: Sovereign Power and Bare Life*, trans. Daniel Heller-Rozen (Stanford, CA: Stanford University Press, 1998).

28. Bauman, *Modernity and the Holocaust*.

29. A cue to this process could be found in Illouz's analysis of the works of therapeutic culture in modernity. See Eva Illouz, *Saving the Modern Soul: Therapy, Emotions, and the Culture of Self-Help* (Berkeley: University of California Press, 2008).

30. For the two poles of this epistemological spectrum, see Ian Hacking, "Humans, Aliens and Autism," *Dædalus* 138, no. 3 (2009): 44–59 on "aliens" and Gil Eyal, Brendan Hart, Emine Onculer, Neta Oren and Natasha Rossi et al., *The Autism Matrix* (Cambridge: Polity, 2010) on the growing inclusive taxonomy of autism.

31. Haim Hazan, "Gerontological Autism: Terms of Accountability in the Cultural Study of the Category of the Fourth Age," *Ageing and Society* 3, no. 7 (2011): 1125–140.

32. Giorgio Agamben, *The Open: Man and Animal* (Stanford, CA: Stanford University Press, 2004), 37.

33. As examples for such states of dubious humanity, see Victor W. Turner, *The Ritual Process: Structure and Anti-Structure* (Chicago: Aldine, 1969) on novices in the stage of liminality in the course of rites of passage; Andrea Sankar, "The Living Dead: Cultural Aspects of the Oldest Old," in *The Elderly as Modern Pioneers*, ed. Philip Silverman (Bloomington: Indiana University Press,

1987), 345–56, on the "living dead" elderly; John L. Comaroff and Jean Comaroff, "Alien-Nation: Zombies, Immigrants, and Millennial Capitalism," *CODESRIA Bulletin* 1999, nos. 3–4 (1999): 17–28 on the sighted "zombies" in postcolonial South Africa.

34. Charles Patterson, *Eternal Treblinka: Our Treatment of Animals and the Holocaust* (New York: Lantern Books, 2002).

35. Quoted from the epigraph of Patterson's book, ibid., 1.

36. This is unlike other forms of denial critiqued from a historical point of view—see Deborah E. Lipstadt, *Denying the Holocaust: The Growing Assault on Truth and Memory* (New York: Plume, 1993)—or a philosophical point of view—see Alain Finkielkraut, *The Future of Negation: Reflections on the Question of Genocide*, trans. Mary Byrd Kelly (Lincoln: University of Nebraska Press, 1998); Elhanan Yakira, *Post-Zionism, Post-Holocaust: Three Essays on Denial, Forgetting, and the Delegitimation of Israel* (Cambridge: Cambridge University Press, 2009).

Bibliography

Agamben, Giorgio. *Homo Sacer: Sovereign Power and Bare Life*. Translated by Daniel Heller-Rozen. Stanford, CA: Stanford University Press, 1998.

———. *The Open: Man and Animal*. Stanford, CA: Stanford University Press, 2004.

Alexander, Jeffrey C. *Remembering the Holocaust: A Debate*. Oxford: Oxford University Press, 2009.

Arendt, Hannah. *Eichman in Jerusalem*. New York: Penguin Books, 1992. First published 1963.

Ariew, Roger, and Eric Watkins, eds. *Modern Philosophy: An Anthology of Primary Sources*. Boston: Hackett, 1998.

Bauman, Zygmunt. *Modernity and Ambivalence*. Cambridge: Polity Press, 1991.

———. *Modernity and the Holocaust*. Cambridge: Polity Press, 1991.

Bhabha, Homi K. "The World and the Home." *Social Text* 31–32 (1992): 141–53.

Bourguignon, Erika. "Memory in an Amnesic World: Holocaust, Exile and the Return of the Suppressed." *Anthropological Quarterly* 78 (2005): 63–88.

Brown, Michael F. "Cultural Relativism 2.0." *Current Anthropology* 49 (2008): 363–83.

Comaroff, John L., and Jean Comaroff. "Alien-Nation: Zombies, Immigrants, and Millennial Capitalism." *CODESRIA Bulletin* 1999, nos. 3–4 (1999): 17–28.

Diner, Dan. "Epistemics of the Holocaust Considering the Question of 'Why?' and 'How?'" *Naharayim* 1, no. 2 (2008): 195.

Douglas, Mary. *Purity and Danger: An Analysis of Concepts of Pollution and Taboo*. London: Penguin, 1966.

———. *Risk and Blame: Essays in Cultural Theory*. London: Routledge, 1992.

Eyal, Gil, Brendan Hart, mine Onculer, Neta Oren, and Natasha Rossi. *The Autism Matrix*. Cambridge: Polity, 2010.

Feldman, Jackie. *Above the Death Pits, Beneath the Flag*. New York: Berghahn Books, 2008.

Felman, Shoshana, and Dori Laub. *Testimony*. London: Routledge, 1992.

Finkielkraut, Alain. *The Future of Negation: Reflections on the Question of Genocide*. Translated by Mary Byrd Kelly. Lincoln: University of Nebraska Press, 1998.

Foucault, Michel. *Discipline and Punish: The Birth of the Prison*. Harmondsworth, UK: Penguin, 1997. First published 1975.

Gunn, Giles B. *Beyond Solidarity: Pragmatism and Difference in a Globalized World*. Chicago: University of Chicago Press, 2001.

Gusterson, Hugh. "Anthropology and Militarism." *Annual Review of Anthropology* 36 (2007): 155–75.

Hacking, Ian. "Humans, Aliens and Autism." *Dædalus* 138, no. 3 (2009): 44–59.

———. *Rewriting the Soul: Multiple Personality and the Science of Memory*. Princeton, NJ: Princeton University Press, 1998.

Hazan, Haim. "Gerontological Autism: Terms of Accountability in the Cultural Study of the Category of the Fourth Age." *Ageing and Society* 31, no. 7 (2011): 1125–140.

Hinton, Alexander Laban, ed. *Annihilating Difference: The Anthropology of Genocide.* Berkeley: University of California Press, 2002.

Illouz, Eva. *Saving the Modern Soul: Therapy, Emotions, and the Culture of Self-Help.* Berkeley: University of California Press, 2008.

Kidron, Carol A. "Alterity and the Particular Limits of Universalism: Comparing Jewish-Israeli Holocaust and Canadian-Cambodian Genocide Legacies." *Current Anthropology* 53, no. 6 (2012): 725–54.

Kristeva, Julia. *Powers of Horror.* New York: Columbia University Press, 1982.

Lavie, Smadar. "Between and Among the Boundaries of Culture: Bridging Texts and Experience in the Third Timespace." *Cultural Studies* 10, no. 1 (1996): 154–79.

Levy, Daniel, and Natan Sznaider. *The Holocaust and Memory in a Global Age.* Philadelphia: Temple University Press, 2006.

Lewin, Caroll McC. "The Holocaust: Anthropological Possibilities and the Dilemma of Representation." *American Anthropologist* 94, no. 1 (1992): 161–66.

Lipstadt, Deborah E. *Denying the Holocaust: The Growing Assault on Truth and Memory.* New York: Plume, 1993.

MacDonald, David Bruce. *Identity Politics in the Age of Genocide: The Holocaust in Historical Representation.* London: Taylor and Francis, 2007.

Marcus, George E., and Michael M. J. Fischer. *Anthropology as Cultural Critique: An Experimental Moment in the Human Sciences.* Chicago: University of Chicago Press, 1986.

Moses, A. Dirk. *Empire, Colony, Genocide: Conquest, Occupation, and Subaltern Resistance in World History.* New York: Berghahn Books, 2008.

Patterson, Charles. *Eternal Treblinka: Our Treatment of Animals and the Holocaust.* New York: Lantern Books, 2002.

Sankar, Andrea. "The Living Dead: Cultural Aspects of the Oldest Old." In *The Elderly as Modern Pioneers,* ed. Philip Silverman, 345–56. Bloomington: Indiana University Press, 1987.

Simmel, Georg. *The Philosophy of Money.* Edited by David Frisby. Translated by Tom Bottomore and David Frisby. London: Routledge, 2004. First published 1900.

Trouillot, Michel-Rolph. "Anthropology and the Savage Slot: The Poetics and Politics of Otherness." In *Recapturing Anthropology: Working in the Present,* ed. Richard G. Fox. Santa Fe, NM: School of American Research, 1991: 17–44.

———. *Silencing the Past: Power and the Production of History.* Boston: Beacon, 1995.

Tsing, Anna Lowenhaupt. *Friction: An Ethnography of Global Connection.* Princeton, NJ: Princeton University Press, 2005.

Turner, Victor W. *The Ritual Process: Structure and Anti-Structure.* Chicago: Aldine, 1969.

Yakira, Elhanan. *Post-Zionism, Post-Holocaust: Three Essays on Denial, Forgetting, and the Delegitimation of Israel.* Cambridge: Cambridge University Press, 2009.

Section II

How Global Is Holocaust Memory?

CHAPTER 3

The Holocaust Is Not—
and Is Not Likely to Become—
a Global Memory

PETER NOVICK

In this chapter I am going to make some remarks about how I believe collective memory operates, and about how I see the current reach of Holocaust memory. It is my hope that what I have to say on those subjects will make clear why I believe that the idea of a consequential "global memory of the Holocaust" is chimerical.

Collective memories that do real work in the world, that make a difference, are taken to express essential and enduring truths: they tell members of a community who they are, what to expect, and what to do. As Alon Confino wrote a decade ago, a collective memory of this kind speaks to "a shared identity that unites a social group; [it] ... steer[s] emotions, motivate[s] people to act ... become[s] a socio-cultural mode of action."[1]

We surely want to be able to distinguish between this kind of collective memory and those that are relatively inconsequential. If we want to know whether an individual has a rich and coherent memory of his or her high school days or one that's thin and fragmentary, we interrogate the individual and evaluate what we find. In the case of a society's collective memories, it is not practical to interrogate the members of society about the extent and degree to which they share a historical memory. Instead, what we almost always do is look not at "memories"—properly so-called—but at what Pierre Nora called "sites of memory,"[2] which, functionally, are not memories but mnemonics: practices or artifacts designed to assist or promote memory. This displacement of our vision might be acceptable if we accurately described what we are doing ... but we do not. Instead, we misdescribe these mnemonics as memory itself.

Notes for this section begin on page 54.

The literature on collective memory of the Holocaust is filled with titles like "When a Day Remembers"[3] (about a commemorative practice), or describing how a particular monument or museum or movie "remembers." We probably all know the story of the man who is looking under the street lamp for car keys that he dropped halfway down the block. Asked why he's conducting his search under the street lamp, he answers that "the light's better here." What happens with "looking for collective memory" is rather worse, because while the man in the story is unlikely to confuse the pebbles and chewing gum wrappers he finds under the street lamp with his car keys, students of "memory" do precisely that when they look at mnemonics and call them memory.

There is probably some relationship between the prevalence of mnemonic institutions or practices in a society and the prevalence of the memory to which they point—but the relationship is surely far from straightforward. In American cities and towns there are more monuments dedicated to the American dead of World War I than to anything else: all cities, and all but the smallest or most recently founded towns, have such monuments. Millions of people pass by them every day, but as Robert Musil once observed, "nothing is as invisible as a monument."[4] Probably some of the millions who daily pass by these monuments give a thought to World War I. But how many? And what kind of index to the breadth and depth of American memory of World War I is the prevalence of these monuments?

What is most misleading about confusing mnemonics with memory is that it obfuscates agency. Mnemonics (museums, memorials, artistic representations, and commemorative practices) are initiated, or carried to fruition, by particular individuals and groups, acting out of various particular motives. When we treat the aggregate of these mnemonics as an index to how, and how much, a society "remembers," the result is pure mystification. This is a subject to which I will have occasion to return.

Let me now turn to the present distribution of "Holocaust memory," the point of departure for predictions of its future spatial expansion. One can describe the reach of Holocaust memory as a series of concentric circles. In the innermost circle are Israel, a country whose population—or much of it—has a special relationship to the victims of the crime, and Germany, the country of the criminals and their descendants. The next circle is made up of the countries of Europe that were occupied by Germany during World War II, which were the scene of the deportation to death (or the actual murder) of their Jewish citizens. Once we leave Europe we move to countries without any such "organic" connection to the Holocaust. Those who see the Holocaust as on the way to becoming a "global memory"—one in which "organic connections" to the crime are increasingly irrelevant—make far-reaching claims for the extent to which the Holocaust has become an American memory. In their view the American case is the bellwether example, pointing the way to Holocaust memory becoming global. So far as the current distribution of Holocaust memory is concerned, beyond the circle occupied by the United States, and countries that in many ways resemble it like Canada and Australia, there is, effectively, nothing.

First, Israel and Germany. Symbolically, Israel insists that it is the "legatee of" and "spokesman for" those who died in the Holocaust. Materially, it is home to the largest number of Holocaust survivors, who, together with their descendants, are a substantial portion of the population, and a much larger portion of the politically and culturally dominant Ashkenazi segment of the Jewish population. Particularly (but not exclusively) on the right, Israeli Holocaust memory, like that of so many traditional powerful memories, is that of a grievance, and of a "victim identity." Though in many ways the strongest power in the Middle East, the fact of being a very small state surrounded by much larger, mostly hostile states has surely given many Israelis a sense of the contemporary relevance of the Holocaust. It is my impression that, while still powerful, Holocaust memory in Israel has, over recent decades, receded a bit. I doubt that anyone would describe Israel today, as the *New York Times*' Thomas Friedman did in the 1980s, as "Yad Vashem with an Air Force."[5]

The German case is complicated by the fact that for more than forty years after the war, there were two very different Germanies. Because the scope of this chapter is limited, I am going to ignore the East German experience. Postwar West Germany, apart from the immediate task of rebuilding the devastated country, suffered under a double burden in which moral and "public relations" concerns were inextricably entangled. Though for various reasons a sustained German encounter with the scope of Nazi crimes was postponed for several years, the fiction that those crimes were the work of a handful of Nazi zealots who imposed their will on the German population was too absurd to be sustained. In part, the rejection of this alibi and the acceptance of moral responsibility for the Holocaust, as well as for the Nazi regime's other crimes, was purely a matter of conscience. I am filled with admiration for the moral seriousness with which many German historians have undertaken the work of "confronting" the memory of the Holocaust. At the same time, the breadth and depth of anti-German sentiment in the neighboring countries occupied by Germany during the war made it something of a patriotic duty to respond to this antipathy by offering continuing evidence of German shame and repentance. In principle, and sometimes in the case of individuals, one can separate purely moral from prudential considerations in Germany's shouldering the burden of the memory of the Holocaust. I have remarked that significant collective memories tell members of a community "who they are"—speak to a community's essential and enduring identity. In the case of Germany, "identity" is also the focus, but, uniquely in this instance, the act of remembrance is intended to underline the great distance between who Germans were then and who they are now.

If we are speaking of nations that have an "organic" sense of connectedness to the Holocaust, it is appropriate to name Israel and Germany. But if what is at issue is the division between those with "organic" ties to the protagonists and those with no such ties, one should discuss, alongside Germans, both Jews in Israel and Jews in the Diaspora. In some important respects, American Jews, whose families left Europe relatively recently, have more organic ties to the victims of the Holocaust than Mizrahim in Israel, whose ties with Europe, if any, were severed centuries ago. One might illustrate what Jews and Germans share, and others do not, with reference to the well-known photograph of the terrified Jewish boy in the Warsaw ghetto, his arms raised as a German soldier points a rifle at him. I am sure that I have lots and lots of company among other Jews, particularly those whose families emigrated from Europe relatively recently, in seeing the accident of emigration as all that saved me from being that boy. I am also sure that there are many Germans who were sickened at the realization that but for contingent circumstances, they might have been the one holding the rifle. I am not suggesting that Jews and Germans are the only ones for whom the Holocaust has been, or will be in the future, a personally meaningful memory. But it seems to me manifestly the case that the sort of relationship to the great crime that is shared by Jews and Germans makes their sense of connection to the Holocaust so much greater than that of others as to constitute a difference in kind, rather than just one of degree.

A more difficult question—one I will not attempt to answer here but that should be asked—is whether the behavior of Israel and Germany in the world has been much influenced by their memories of the Holocaust. As concerns Israel's relations with the Palestinians and their Arab neighbors, would those relations have been different absent the Holocaust, or were they broadly consistent with what might have been predicted on the basis of the pre-Holocaust views of Labor and Revisionist Zionists? In Germany's case, was the centering of Holocaust memory from the 1970s onward important in refiguring German political culture, or was that refiguration already well established by that time? The way I have framed the questions probably points to my own hunch—but it is no more than a hunch.

Europeans whose countries were occupied by Germany during the war occupy the next circle with respect to the "immediacy" of the Holocaust experience. Some unknowable fraction of the minority of today's Europeans who lived through World War II were, in some sense, "witnesses" to the Holocaust—though not usually having any direct involvement with the crime. Europeans' experiences with German occupation differed greatly, and their postwar experiences differed even more. In Western Europe (things were different in the East) the entirety of the wartime experience, including but by no means centering on the Holocaust, was a sort of "negative creation myth" after 1945. As Zionists sought to "negate the Diaspora" in Israel, so the liberated countries in the West constructed their postwar polities as the negation of Nazism, of the German occupation, and of the antiparliamentary domestic political forces that had collaborated with the Germans. There is so much variety in how the nations of Europe have dealt with the memory of the Holocaust in recent years that I find it impossible to generalize. Many times the remarks of statesmen at the Stockholm Holocaust Conference in the year 2000 are offered as evidence for the breadth and depth of Holocaust memory around the world—and particularly in Europe.[6] When I consulted those texts, I found the variety that I have mentioned. There were, to be sure, some that appeared to reflect a thoughtful encounter with the Holocaust. Other texts were exculpatory and self-congratulatory. National spokesmen competed as to which of their countries was the most philo-Semitic; which one's citizens had labored most tirelessly during the war to save Jews. Who knew how beloved Jews were in Ukraine?

Let us cross the Atlantic. As I remarked above, what is described as Americans' wholehearted embrace of Holocaust memory is repeatedly presented as the bellwether of "global Holocaust memory": incontrovertible proof that one need not have the direct relationship to the Holocaust shared by Jews and Germans, or the indirect relationship characteristic of Europeans, for the Holocaust to take hold of a nation's consciousness.

Earlier I pointed out the conflation, in contemporary discourse, of "sites of memory"—mnemonic aides to memory like films and museums—with memory itself. And I noted that one of the ways in which this conflation can systematically mislead is by obscuring agency: treating these mnemonic devices—created by particular individuals and groups for various particular purposes—as if they were spontaneous emanations of the society as a whole. Nowhere is this mystification more egregious than in inflated claims concerning "American Holocaust memory"; in the assertion that Holocaust memory in the United States illustrates how, in the "global media village," collective memory no longer depends on the kinds of organic connections between a population and the event being remembered that have previously grounded memory.

The facts are quite clear and the evidence is unambiguous. With the most trivial exceptions, every "site of Holocaust memory" in the United States—the museums, large and small; representations of the Holocaust in every imaginable media; Holocaust curricula at all educational levels; commemorative practices, from the local to the national; and every other genre of Holocaust mnemonic—is the result of initiatives coming from the 2 percent of the American population that is Jewish.

I am absolutely not saying that this is the result of any coordinated effort by organized American Jewry. From time to time, particularly back in the 1970s, major Jewish organizations worked to promote "general American" Holocaust consciousness, both to mobilize support for Israel and because they believed that the only way to promote American Jewish awareness of the Holocaust, for purposes of communal solidarity, was to make that awareness general throughout American society. But in the great majority of cases, the production of

Holocaust mnemonics were the result of private initiatives by American Jews, acting independently of the organized Jewish community. We are not just "the people of the book," but the people of the Hollywood film and the television miniseries, of the magazine article and the newspaper column, of the comic book and the academic symposium. When a high level of concern with the Holocaust came to be widespread within American Jewry, it was, given the extraordinarily important role that Jews play in American media and opinion-making elites, not only natural but virtually inevitable that it would diffuse widely through the culture at large.

And none of this is to say that non-Jewish Americans are "insincere" when, as decent people, they express sorrow and dismay when their Jewish fellow citizens set before them images of the Holocaust. But that is a long way from Americans feeling that the Holocaust is their memory—that it speaks to who they are—which is what consequential collective memories do for the collectivity involved.

It is said that as the Holocaust became "Americanized" it was also "universalized"—made to teach "Brotherhood Week" lessons rather than, as frequently in Israel, to illustrate that "Esau hates Jacob."[7] This is another sense in which the American experience is made an augury of future developments. It is true that as compared with Israel—and, in a different way, as compared with Germany—the Holocaust was often "universalized" in the United States, but this was not the work of gentile Americans, but of Jews. The symbolic protagonists in the discursive struggles between "particularism" and "universalism" were two Holocaust survivors: Elie Wiesel, a religious mystic of Hasidic background, and Simon Wiesenthal, a secular and cosmopolitan Jew. It is no doubt true that reluctance to parade a "particularist" sensibility before their gentile fellow citizens was among the reasons for promoting a more "universal" interpretation of the Holocaust and its meaning. But more to the point, most American Jews had a greater attachment to secular liberalism than to the "Esau hates Jacob" of traditional Judaism—were more at home with "universalism" than with "particularism." As a practical matter, formulae that fudge the differences have taken over.

It is worth remarking that the most commonly invoked "universalist" lesson of the Holocaust—the "imperative to intervene," the dialectical response to the "crime of indifference"—originated as a very "particularist" lesson—though its reach came to transcend its origins. "Holocaust memory" was first pressed by American Jews in the aftermath of the near-catastrophic Yom Kippur War, when Israel was increasingly isolated in the world and there was fear that Americans might, in the next crisis, abandon Israel to its fate. Though the theme of "the abandonment of the Jews" by the United States was not completely new, it was at this moment that it became a central theme in American Holocaust memory—and that it eventually became mandatory for American presidential candidates to pledge, invoking the Holocaust, that this time the Jews would not be abandoned. Barack Obama did this very effusively in addressing the American Israeli Public Affairs Committee (AIPAC) in 2008, sweetening the pot with references to the indivisibility of Jerusalem.

As I have said, assessing the depth and breadth of the hold of a memory on that elusive entity, "national consciousness," is all but impossible. Assessing a memory's consequences ought to be easier, but since controlled experiments are impossible, there is a lot of guesswork involved in weighing Holocaust memory against other considerations in shaping American policy. I dissent from the claim by my friends John Mearsheimer and Steve Walt that Jewish neoconservatives—all of whom regularly invoked the Holocaust—were decisive in the decision for war in Iraq.[8] Nor would I give much causal weight to the influence of Elie Wiesel, still the Holocaust's most authoritative interpreter in the United States, who argued in 2003 that the memory of the Holocaust mandated the invasion of Iraq.[9] As in the earlier, very ginger interventions in Bosnia and Kosovo—interventions whose scope was quite limited because Americans would not tolerate the casualties that a meaningful intervention would have brought—I find it impossible to weigh the influence, if any, of invocations of the Holocaust as compared with other considerations.

It is notoriously difficult to "prove a negative," and in any case the question of the Holocaust becoming a "global memory" is not one that admits of proof. By sketching where, and how, and why the Holocaust has or has not become a consequential memory in the West, I have, by indirection, suggested why I think it is unlikely that its reach—such as it is—will extend to the non-West. Does the experience of that majority of the world's people who are part of the non-West—and particularly their experience with the West—make it likely that they will embrace the memory of this quintessentially "Western" event as their own? Are the concerns that the "lessons of the Holocaust" address the ones most likely to be near the top of their communal agendas? These are not rhetorical questions, but are matters worthy of discussion.

Let me conclude by saying that because the claim that the Holocaust is on its way to becoming, and ought to become, a "global memory" seems implausible to me, I am inevitably led to some speculations about why it seems otherwise to many learned and highly intelligent people.

The first speculation can be stated quite briefly. It seems to be a widespread belief that an encounter with the memory of the Holocaust will have morally uplifting consequences for the person who has the encounter. Manifestly, anyone who shares this belief will want Holocaust memory to have the widest possible reach. To be sure, I do not know that this belief in the therapeutic power of encounters with the Holocaust is wrong, but neither am I aware of any evidence that it is right.

My other speculations have to do with the idea, which saturates discussions of the Holocaust, that it was a "world-transforming" event. In my own view, while the Holocaust was clearly a catastrophe of unprecedented dimensions for the Jewish people, and had various other consequences, the notion of it as "world transforming" makes implicitly empirical and comparative claims that are debatable.

There are events that are "world transforming" independently of what is believed about them: World War II would be one example. There are events that are "world transforming" both because of what we may call their "material" consequences and because of what is believed about them: the French Revolution both transformed Europe in its time and generated myths that had even greater transformative effects thereafter. Then there are events that are only "transformative" because of what is believed about them. For non-Christians like myself, the putative life, crucifixion, and resurrection of Jesus were "transformative"—as they clearly were—only because millions of people came to believe that they were.

All of which leads me to two related speculations. One is that among the many people who believe that the Holocaust *is*, unambiguously, a "world-transforming" event, some have apparently concluded that it is therefore natural, desirable, and perhaps inevitable that this fact be acknowledged around the world by the Holocaust becoming a "global memory."

The final speculation—neither wholly consistent nor wholly inconsistent with the one just offered—is that to the extent that the Holocaust's potential to be "world transforming" depends on its being acknowledged as such, the drive to make it a "global memory" is an attempt to accomplish this, and perhaps, to some extent, to thus pluck something positive out of the horror.

As I said, just speculations.

Notes

1. Alon Confino, "Collective Memory and Cultural History: Problems of Method," *The American Historical Review* 102, no. 5 (1997): 1390.

2. Pierre Nora, "Between Memory and History: Les Lieux de Mémoire," in "Memory and Counter-Memory," special issue, *Representations*, no. 26 (Spring 1989): 7–24.

3. See, e.g., James Young, "When a Day Remembers: A Performative History of Yom Hashoah," *History and Memory* 2 (Winter 1990): 54–75.

4. Robert Musil, *Nachlaß zu Lebzeiten* (Hamburg: Rowohlt, 1957), 59. All translations are the author's.

5. Thomas Friedman, *From Beirut to Jerusalem* (New York: Farrar, Straus and Girouz, 1989), 281.

6. See http://www.government.se/content/1/c6/06/66/96/52af23bc.pdf (accessed 18 January 2015).

7. A known rabbinic phrase expressing eternal hatred of the Christian world to Jews. Its source is Rashi's commentary on Genesis 33:4.

8. John Mearsheimer and Steve Walt, *The Israel Lobby and U.S. Foreign Policy* (New York: Farrar, Straus, and Giroux, 2007).

9. Elie Wiesel, "Peace Isn't Possible in Evil's Face," *Los Angeles Times*, 11 March 2003.

Bibliography

Confino, Alon. "Collective Memory and Cultural History: Problems of Method." *The American Historical Review* 102, no. 5: 1386–403.

Friedman, Thomas. *From Beirut to Jerusalem.* New York: Farrar, Straus and Girouz, 1989.

Mearsheimer, John, and Steve Walt. *The Israel Lobby and U.S. Foreign Policy.* New York: Farrar, Straus, and Giroux, 2007.

Musil, Robert. *Nachlaß zu Lebzeiten.* Hamburg: Rowohlt, 1957.

Nora, Pierre. "Between Memory and History: Les Lieux de Mémoire." In "Memory and Counter-Memory," special issue, *Representations,* no. 26 (Spring 1989): 7–24.

Wiesel, Elie. "Peace Isn't Possible in Evil's Face." *Los Angeles Times,* 11 March 2003.

Young, James. "When a Day Remembers: A Performative History of Yom Hashoah," *History and Memory* 2 (Winter 1990): 54–75.

CHAPTER 4

The Holocaust as a Symbolic Manual
The French Revolution, the Holocaust, and Global Memories

Alon Confino

The first thing we note when attempting to link the words "global" and "memory" and "Holocaust" is how tenuous and imprecise the connection is. These are big words, too big: they invoke monumentality and imply exceptionality. That alone should provoke doubt and demand critical reflection. On the most basic level, the notion of "the global memory of Holocaust" is simply inaccurate. In most parts of the world the memory of the extermination of the Jews lacks the powerful emotional content it possesses in Europe, Israel, and the United States. In China, the Holocaust has no real resonance; what does resonate is the association of Japan with Germany and the comparison of the Holocaust to the Nanjing Massacre of 1937, which some refer to as "China's Holocaust."[1] In India, public discourse about morality and genocide centers on the partition in 1947, not the Jewish Holocaust. And in Latin America as well as Africa, the Holocaust is barely a subject that reverberates dominantly. And yet, there is plenty of evidence that the extermination of the Jews has turned into an emblem of morality and human rights. The Chinese *do* use the Holocaust as a marker of evil. At question is how to make sense of these overlapping relations.

The notion of "the global memory of the Holocaust" is misleading because it potentially assumes straightforward relations. The implication of "the" is that this memory is clearly defined and can be isolated, held apart from everything else. The word "memory" implies a uniformity of meaning. "Global" evokes improbable worldwide diffusion. And the words "the Holocaust" suggest an event unparalleled and incomparable. We need a series of small ques-

---

Notes for this section begin on page 67.

tions interrogating the terms and their relations, while at the same time a sense of perspective, that is, thinking of the meaning of Holocaust memory together with another memory of similar impact in modern history.

I would like to raise in this chapter some thoughts on the issue at hand by asking three defined questions and associating two big memories. The three specific questions are: Is the worldwide diffusion of a shared foundational past particular to the Holocaust? How hegemonic has Holocaust memory been, and can we conceive of the relations between it and other cultural, political, and intellectual trends (such as the interest in genocide and human rights) in terms of the reciprocal circulation of ideas rather than in terms of hegemony? What is actually remembered, and where, in the diffusion of Holocaust memory? The two memories I associate are those of the Holocaust and the French Revolution.

★ ★ ★ ★ ★

In the discussions about the diffusion of Holocaust memory in the global age there is a vague though persistent notion that this presents a particular case. The new conditions of our era, it is argued, have been characterized by new technologies that have collapsed space and time and fostered international interdependency, which created the need for a shared universal symbol, namely, the Holocaust. My emphasis here is on the claim that our era is unique in its global reach and in the production of a memory that transcends national boundaries.

This is the implicit argument of Daniel Levy and Natan Sznaider in their book *The Holocaust and Memory in the Global Age*.[2] Globalization, they argue, has changed the status of memory, for societies are no longer defined by their national and ethnic belonging. The fall of communism, the end of the Cold War, and the need for new international values and cooperation made the Holocaust in the 1990s a touchtone for moral and political debate the world over. They ask, "Can an event defined by many people as a watershed in European history be remembered outside the ethnic and national boundaries of the Jewish victims and the German perpetrators?"[3] This rhetorical question implies two answers: yes, it can be remembered outside its immediate context; and no, it did not quite happen this way before.

But this argument places Holocaust memory in a particular narrative. It implies that the memory of the Nazi genocide is the first memory to have escaped its national confines to assume a new global form embraced worldwide. It severs whatever we understand under the term "Holocaust memory in a global age" from previous trends in memory, politics, and morality. And by implying that the global reach of this memory has no antecedents, it comes close to characterizing Holocaust memory as sui generis, and perhaps also the Holocaust itself. In some sense, I read the interpretation of Levi and Sznaider as taking the argument of the uniqueness of the Holocaust—which has usually been made with respect to Germans and Jews in their specific European context—and making it global. Though I should say I do not think that this was the intention of the authors.

I would like to propose a different narrative by thinking of another foundational event that was remembered the world over: the French Revolution.[4] Like the Holocaust, the Revolution was a historical *novum*: the Declaration of the Rights of Man and of the Citizen and the Reign of Terror redefined politics and morality. The Revolution gave birth to ideas and practices that determined modern European and world history from 1789 on: we can think of liberalism, socialism, feminism, human rights, *levée en masse* (mass conscription), the Terror, and the idea of revolution itself. It was the first modern experience of democracy and of state-orchestrated terror, a model to be avoided—we can think of the British philosopher Edmund Burke—or to be emulated—we can think of Lenin. It saw itself as breaking all historical patterns. For generations after 1789, the Revolution was a compass that organized questions of history and morality. And it had universal meaning: first, in the intention of its makers, and second, in the spread and impact of its ideas for liberty and justice. The Chinese Communist leader Zhou Enlai perhaps captured best this enormous political and symbolic influence in the modern age: when he was asked in the 1960s about the impact of the Revolution, he famously replied that it was still too early to tell.

The Revolution created a symbolic manual, forcefully used until not long ago, with which to understand political action and redemption in the modern world. It is not dissimilar to the Holocaust that has become, as Levi and Sznaider observed, a "decontexualized" symbol, "dislocated from space and time," used by different people in different ways to articulate local experiences in shared global images. Similarly, the symbolic manual of the Revolution was multifaceted; no one had a copyright on its ideas. It was appropriate for different political and social causes, and inspired in the nineteenth and twentieth centuries national, revolutionary, and anticolonial struggles, be it by Giuseppe Mazzini, Vladimir Lenin, Rosa Luxemburg, Simón Bolívar, or Jawaharlal Nehru.

My point is, to go back to where this discussion began, that the global aspect of current Holocaust memory is not at all particular and in itself does not reveal enough about the phenomenon under investigation. The ideas of the French Revolution circled the globe without the Internet and in a world largely defined by national and ethnic belonging. It should be asked, how useful is the term "global" in the notion "the global memory of the Holocaust," and what does it actually mean? If by "global" we mean wide diffusion of ideas beyond their immediate geographical and cultural context, then we explain too little. If we mean the inherent conditions of our time, and possibly the inherent character of the Holocaust, which produced the first worldwide memory—then we explain too much.

It is intriguing, therefore, to place the Holocaust within a narrative of (what are to my mind) the two foundational pasts of modern European history, the French Revolution and the Holocaust. After being a foundational past for generations and deep into the twentieth century, the importance of the Revolution as a cornerstone for political, moral, and historiographical thinking seemed to have ebbed around the 1970s. François Furet famously declared in 1978 that the French Revolution was over.[5] He argued for a recognition that the passing of time, of memories, and of histories petered out the political and symbolic passions that dominated the memory of the Revolution since 1789. At exactly the same time, interestingly, the Holocaust began to take its place as a foundational event of our time. It is not the wide diffusion of Holocaust memory that is particular, but the meaning of the transformation from one foundational past to another.

Placing Holocaust memory in this narrative is good to think with. It gives us a necessary perspective by thinking of Holocaust memory with a foundational memory of its degree. My point here is not to compare but to think in association, thus hopefully raising new questions and providing new insights for old ones. I would like, therefore, to turn to the next topic, the hegemony of Holocaust memory.

★ ★ ★ ★ ★

In the scholarly and public discussions the emergence of Holocaust memory has been interpreted as the motor for a whole host of legal, cultural, intellectual, and political trends such as public debates about slavery and colonialism, interest in the topics of genocide and human rights, and the growing importance of the ideas of testimony, survivor, trauma, genocide, and ethnic cleansing. This argument implies the hegemonic symbolic role of Holocaust memory in the making of these trends. This is implied in the book of Levi and Sznaider, and, I should add, in some of my own writing in the past.

I now see things differently. The importance of Holocaust memory to the making of these trends and ideas is clear, but the view described above has a hegemonic view of hegemony. Holocaust memory rose after the war as one among many cultural memories and political causes that sought renewal, if symbolically it was the leading one. The rise of Holocaust memory was dependent on a multidimensional memory universe, which was in turn shaped by the symbolic importance of the Holocaust.

I would like to illustrate this by pointing out the different chronological trajectory of the French Revolution and the Holocaust to be perceived as a rupture in historical time. The Revolution saw itself as creating a new world, breaking all known historical patterns, and it was instantly perceived as such by contemporaries. Evaluation of this state of affairs varied, but the condition was acutely sensed. Edmund Burke lamented at the beginning of *Reflections on the Revolution in France* that "everything seems out of nature," while the English poet William Wordsworth felt in contrast ecstasy that nothing needed to be accepted anymore as set in the nature of things.[6]

The perceptions of the Holocaust as a foundational event, in contrast, took several decades to form. This is especially significant because if both events were earth-shattering, the metaphor of earthquake also captures the particular earthquake that was the Holocaust. The French Revolution was likened by the German Romantic Friedrich Schlegel (1772–1829) to "the greatest and most remarkable phenomenon in the history of states … an almost universal earthquake, an immeasurable inundation in the political world." But the Holocaust was compared by Jean-François Lyotard to an "earthquake [that] destroys not only lives, buildings, and objects but also the instruments used to measure earthquakes directly and indirectly."[7] The extermination of the Jews has called into question the very relations between the things that happened and their narration. And still, several decades went by before this perception became widespread. There is perhaps no other case in history in which people first rather ignored a contemporary event, only thereafter coming to view it as the moral signifier of their age.

It is precisely the interval between the extermination of the Jews and the rise of Holocaust memory in public consciousness that complicates the narrative of the hegemonic symbolic role of the Holocaust. The idea that Holocaust memory burst into public consciousness in the late 1970s and 1980s like Minerva, the goddess of knowledge, bursting from Zeus's head is too neat; it isolates Holocaust memory from contemporary trends, and it cannot explain the interval of several decades. The Revolution was considered foundational immediately by revolutionaries and counterrevolutionaries, Frenchmen and foreigners. The sheer immediate shock provoked by the events in Paris—the fall of the Bastille, the execution of Louis XVI, the Terror—served as a motor to recast things. But the importance of the Holocaust was discovered several decades after the event, and this can be explained much better by placing Holocaust memory within the myriad of intellectual and political trends that also became prominent in the 1950s, 1960s, 1970s, and beyond. These may include, for example, the growing public and scholarly interest in issues of memory and identity, the growing legal and international awareness of human rights and genocide, and the impact of decolonization.

Viewing the Holocaust as a hegemonic memory is too crude: it conceives of the relations between the Holocaust and other memories as opposing, contradicting, or canceling each other out, instead of as overlapping and commingling in a universe made of circulating ideas moving in all directions. In fact, Holocaust memory was multifaceted, mobile, and not at all fixed and stable. Thus, Charlotte Delbo, the non-Jewish French resister, linked in the 1950s her Auschwitz experience with the Franco-Algerian war; in her work, Holocaust testimony and decolonization went hand in hand.[8] Different memory strands commingled and influenced each other in the postwar era; this view challenges the perceived hierarchy of testimony and memory as moving linearly from the private to the public sphere. Holocaust memory shaped attitudes toward decolonization as much as it was shaped by it. It was not constructed by survivors and perpetrators in Germany, Israel, and the United States in isolation, but was all along culturally intertwined with some main themes of the period.

Similarly, we should question the hierarchy of spaces whereby Holocaust memory started at the local level (that is, in Germany, Israel, and the United States) and proceeded in turn to spread worldwide. It seems instead a spasmodic and unmethodical process whereby specific Holocaust memories molded and were molded by global issues such as human rights and the interest in genocide. Differently put, notions and practices of human rights, testimony, survivor, trauma, genocide, ethnic cleansing, and others would have become important without the Holocaust. Their emergence is connected but is not determined by it. We should know much more about how they influenced Holocaust memory, and not only about how Holocaust memory influenced them.

Of course, one must be blind not to see the importance of the Holocaust to the construction of these terms and their meanings. They cannot be reduced to the idea of Auschwitz, but they would not have developed the same without it. Holocaust memory rose after the war as one among many cultural memories and political causes that sought renewal, if symbolically the leading one. I would like to turn now to discuss briefly this symbolic meaning, the Jew, in the memory of the Holocaust in a global age.

★ ★ ★ ★ ★

What do people actually remember, when they remember the Holocaust? I would like to open again with a reflection on the memory of the Revolution and of the Holocaust. The core meaning of Holocaust memory as a moral tale about good and evil comes into sharp focus when we think of it in association with the memory of the Revolution. The core memory of the Revolution was political: its ideas were to be emulated and implemented. The memory of the Holocaust is, of course, political in the sense that every memory is used and appropriated for political purposes. But as a moral-historical compass, Holocaust memory is about an abstract sense of ultimate evil, not about charting specific political plans of action. Marx and Lenin found in the course of the Revolution a specific political blueprint uncovering the laws of history on the way to redemption. The memory of the Holocaust is about the breakdown of historical laws, of reason, of the belief in human improvement. (Of course, this perceived breakdown did not start with the Holocaust, which continued a process that had started earlier at least from World War I).

Because the core memory of the Holocaust is moral, it is allergic to raising doubts about its validity. As a moral compass, the Revolution pointed to diametrically opposed ideological routes. It was viewed by the revolutionaries as well as by successive Marxist and liberal historians as an agent of progress. But right from the beginning, there developed a rich tradition among those who viewed the Revolution as unnecessary and indeed morally wicked: one can think of Edmund Burke or Hippolyte Taine (1828–93), a major thinker of the Revolution in the nineteenth century who, admiring the empirical thinking and gradual historical development of England, observed in his monumental study *The Origins of Contemporary France* that "the best qualified, most judicious and profoundest observer of the Revolution will find nothing to compare to it but the invasion [by the barbarians] of the Roman Empire in the fourth century."[9] Most recently, opponents of the Revolution from the right, such as Pierre Chaunu, compared it to Nazism and the Wars of the Vendée to genocide, while feminists and historians of gender have almost unanimously condemned the Revolution as bad for women's rights.[10]

But if the Revolution was embraced as well as rejected, the idea of someone minimizing, justifying, or denying the Holocaust or parts thereof imposes enormous strain on public, historical, and political discourse. Such cases occur, but they provoke revulsion and are seen as a result of deep moral and human failure. They function as exceptions that prove the moral rule. The memory of the Revolution called for political divisiveness, while that of the Holocaust is about a moral taboo that calls for sacredness. In this sense, for societies in Europe the taboo of Holocaust denial serves as a marker of the limits of freedom of speech and of academic freedom in a context that is not about state security but ultimately about morality.

It is this sense of vague moral value that may have traveled the world over. In China, India, and other places, as I said at the outset of this chapter, the Holocaust is not a central element of identity, and is referred to, if at all, with different sensibility than in the West. It seems that the farthest the Holocaust reaches from its core areas of Europe, Israel, and the United States, the less specific it is about its core events. It is less about Jews, Germans, and Judeo-Christian civilization in Europe and more about an abstract moral invocation. This is not surprising. When symbols circulate within and between societies they change, are appropriated and negotiated to fit local needs, cultures, politics, and fantasies.

Is "global" the right word to describe it? I doubt it. The word is too expansive and ambiguous. More revealing would be to explore whether the Holocaust created a symbolic manual with which societies imagine, think, and talk about morality, genocide, human rights, and other issues. This symbolic manual is not a duplication of the actual events of the extermination of the Jews and their lessons (as they are understood by Jews, Germans, and other Europeans). It is not a memory of the Holocaust that reproduces the intentions of Jews and Germans during the event. It is an abstract, in a sense empty, image suitable to fit different needs of different people, while keeping a symbolic backbone about morality and evil. The symbolic manual can be used in societies that do not remember, strictly speaking, the Holocaust at all. The question is not simply whether in India the Holocaust is remembered, but whether partition, the traumatic event in modern Indian history, has been constructed in the last twenty-five years using symbolic elements (such as images and terms) from Holocaust scholarship and remembrance. It is possible that people use these symbols while not connecting them at all to the historical Holocaust. This is a worthwhile working hypothesis, although we need much more detailed research on this. (In this sense, it is not so much that the Holocaust—understood as the extermination of the Jews—has become global as much as that the Holocaust—understood as a network of symbols—has been attached to causes that are global, such as human rights, genocide, and ethnic cleansing.)

★ ★ ★ ★ ★

Let us take a step back from our topic of the global memory of the Holocaust, and ask about the viability of associating the extermination of the Jews with the French Revolution. Where did it come from, if at all, or is this simply my arbitrary choice? There has been a tradition of thinking about the French Revolution and Nazism in tandem, because from 1933 it was a useful way of articulating meanings and values of modern history.

For contemporaries who lived in the 1930s and 1940s it was obvious to measure 1933 against 1789, whether the new world created by the Nazis as an alternative to the values of the French Revolution generated a sense of foreboding or of hope. Nazism measured itself against the Revolution, which was the measure of all things in the modern world. Joseph Goebbels, the Nazi minister of propaganda, proclaimed this in a radio broadcast on 1 April 1933: with the Nazi revolution "the year 1789 has been expunged from the records of history … we want to eradicate the ideology of liberalism and the freedom of the individual and replace it with a new sense of community" in which human equality and free will will give way to a racial order.[11]

Nazi scholars and ideologues predicted that 30 January 1933, when Hitler was appointed chancellor, would eclipse 14 July, the fall of the Bastille, as a historical turning point.[12] The historical importance of 1789 was the idea of democracy, wrote Alfred Rosenberg, the self-designated ideologue of the Nazi Party, in a special issue of *School Letters* (*Der Schulungsbrief*) dedicated to the topic "From the French to the Ethnic Revolution": "Today we stand, however, in front of a similarly important historical fact … that millions and millions forsake the altar of democracy" and join the racial revolution.[13] Welcoming the Nazi nationwide book burning of 10 May 1933, Ernst Bertram, professor of German at the University of Cologne, spoke "against the enemy of life—rationality, against destructive Enlightenment … against every kind of the 'ideas of 1789,' against all anti-German tendencies."[14] Hitler himself drew on the Revolution as a source of repulsion and admiration. Repulsion—because the Jew was the "midwife" of this Revolution, attaining equal rights in order to subjugate Aryans and others. But even Hitler could not remain indifferent to the pull of the event. The celebration of 14 July, he said with a tinge of envy in 1929, "evokes the memory of historical passion." In spite of the Jews it was a "heroic" age that gave rise to Napoleon and his empire. Hitler the empire builder thus found a Revolutionary legacy to embrace.[15]

Victor Klemperer made the association between the French Revolution and Nazism into a minor but recurring theme in his celebrated diary. As a scholar of modern French literature working on a major study on Voltaire and Rousseau, he was especially sensitive to the historical and linguistic affinities between the two periods. He planned on writing a comparative study of the language of the French Revolution and of Nazism. With Rousseau, the Third Reich is "going through my mind," he wrote in his diary, "whole passages could be from Hitler's speeches…. [His] political model (no matter whether the Führer has read it or not) is the *Contrat social.*"[16] Klemperer compared the Nazi leaders to Robespierre, and the Nazi attempt to build a new society by giving German names to the months to the revolutionaries' creation of a new calendar.[17]

Historians outside Germany interpreted contemporary events as the passing of historical eras. A paper read at the December 1940 meeting of the American Historical Association by Beatrice Hyslop of Hunter College and published in April 1942 in the *American Historical Review* begins with the following paragraph:

> A little over two years ago the one hundred and fiftieth anniversary of the beginning of the French Revolution was being celebrated. No one, even among skeptics and detractors of that movement, could have predicted the events of the following twelve months. It is possible that the era dominated by the concepts initiated by the French Revolution, embodied in the trinity of words, 'Liberty, Equality, Fraternity,' has passed forever or that a different emphasis and meaning will be given to each of the words.[18]

In 1948, Hyslop began an essay on the Revolution, published in the *Journal of Modern History,* with a tone that not so much celebrated the victory over Nazism as it recorded the terror, still felt several years after 1945, occasioned by contemplating the possible consequences of its triumph: "The greatest challenge to the 'principles of 1789' since 1815 culminated in September 1939…. Had the Nazis and their allies won the war, there is little doubt that the French Revolution and its principles could have sunk into historical oblivion."[19]

Implicit and explicit analogies between the Revolution and Nazism came up regularly in post-1945 art and history. When Peter Brook staged Peter Weiss's *Marat/Sade* in 1964, Susan Sontag observed that "the heart of the play is a running debate between Sade, in his chair, and Marat, in his bath, on the meaning of the French Revolution, that is on the psychological and political premises of modern history, but seen through a very modern sensibility, one equipped with the hindsight afforded by the Nazi concentration camps."[20] In 1982, François Furet, one of the greatest scholars of the Revolution in the twentieth century, chaired with Raymond Aron a conference on the Holocaust at the École des hautes études en sciences sociales in Paris; among the participants were Saul Friedländer, Christopher Browning, Raul Hilberg, Amos Funkenstein, and Pierre Vidal-Naquet.[21]

I view my work as part of this intellectual tradition. I seek in the association between the French Revolution and the Holocaust a tool to evaluate the current state of Holocaust memory. Scholars know how difficult it is to talk about the Holocaust while keeping a sense of historical perspective: that is, preserving the important historical aspects of the Holocaust while not making the event into a unique, central point of history.[22] One way of addressing this difficulty, as I have tried to do in this chapter, is to think of Holocaust consciousness and historiography in tandem with the consciousness and historiography of the French Revolution.

★ ★ ★ ★ ★

Exploring the symbolic manual of the Holocaust, I have argued, may illuminate a query posed at the outset of this chapter, that is, why in China the Jewish Holocaust is not an important topic, while at the same time an abstract Holocaust is used as a measure of evil. To make sense of this symbolic manual, scholars should explore the meaning and use of the Holocaust in places such as China, but also the continuous production of Holocaust symbols in the core countries of Germany, Israel, and lately also the United States. And in this sense, we need not go as far as China to understand the symbolic manual of the Holocaust as an abstract, open-ended image of moral travesty. One's backyard might just suffice.

In 2005 Israel pulled out of the Gaza Strip, withdrew its army to the 1967 borders, and evacuated the Jews that had settled there in previous decades. The Gaza Strip was in 2005 home to about eight thousand settlers, who lived in sixteen settlements, and 1.4 million Palestinians. It is a piece of land twenty-seven miles long and seven miles across at its widest point. Over the years, Israel had taken control of some 15 percent of the Gaza Strip's land (54 square kilometers out of total of 365) allocated for the use of the settlers; this area was not accessible to the Palestinian population. The Palestinian areas had been some of the poorest and most densely populated in the world.

While most Israelis supported the disengagement plan, the settlers fervently opposed it on religious, national, and historical grounds. They evoked symbols of the Holocaust in a move that partly reflected a public relations strategy to attract attention but also a deep-seated belief in the historical analogy. The symbol of the opposition was an orange star worn on the clothing. Settlers tattooed their Israeli identity number on their forearm and dressed in a striped concentration camp uniform. Graffiti was scrawled labeling Ariel Sharon, the prime minister behind the disengagement plan, the heir of the Pharaoh, Titus (who destroyed the Temple in 70 CE), and Hitler. Settlers created minidramas, barricading themselves in their houses and calling soldiers "Nazis." They entered at night the Valley of the Communities in Yad Vashem in Jerusalem and wrote graffiti commemorating the "destroyed communities of the Katif Block" (the name of the Jewish settled area). Finally, they created a museum for their communities modeled after a Holocaust museum.

One of the initiators of the plan to use Holocaust symbols, Roni Bakshi from the settlement of Neveh Dekalim, explained in December 2004: "I would not dare to do this if I did not have the bad feeling that the plan here is to expel Jews."[23] Moshe Freiman, a son of a Holocaust survivor who is buried in a settlement, said he would wear the star on his shirt: "We, the second generation of Holocaust survivors, always complained to those who were there—why did they not rise up, why did they not cry out and do something? Today, justifiably, this is said about us—why are we not doing anything against this plan?"[24] And 75-year-old Ruth Matar observed: "As an eight-year-old girl, the Nazi storm troopers came and kicked down the door of my home in Austria and beat my mother because she wanted to go back into the house to get warm jackets for the children. Well there is no difference now, except it's Jewish police coming into a home and dragging unwilling people out."[25]

This use of Holocaust symbols caused an outpouring of anger in Israel from across the political and cultural spectrum, including members of the settler movement, political figures, journalists, and various Holocaust organizations of survivors and their offspring. Yad Vashem condemned "using in political debates terms and expressions from the Holocaust."[26] But the Israeli historian of the Holocaust Hanna Yablonka was correct when she identified in this event deeper trends of Holocaust memory in Israeli culture. She lamented the everyday ideological use of Holocaust memory as well as the widespread ignorance about the Holocaust among young Israelis, who are taught "lessons" of the Holocaust but not its history. According to this lesson, "it is always the Jewish people that is in the right and is the accuser. The people of the world are obligated to stand before it abashed and ashamed." In light of this, wrote Yablonka, in the debate over the "results of the Six Days' War, it is very convenient to invoke an event in which we were only right and the world was only guilty."[27]

Indeed, the symbolic manual of the Holocaust could work for any cause.[28] In well-choreographed scenes, children were instructed to leave their homes with their hands raised and their orange Star of David visible with the writing "Jude." The analogy to a specific, famous photograph from the Holocaust was clear.[29] This was quite a radical transformation of Holocaust symbols: Jews who for years lived by denying their Palestinian neighbors basic human rights accused other Jews of being Nazis. The memory of the Holocaust became a justification for an ongoing, brutal, and inhuman occupation. But, in principle, this case was not very different from other cases where Holocaust symbols were used to fit local politics, memories, cultures, and fantasies, however morally repulsive they may be. Indeed, in the Israeli case, the clearer the immorality of the occupation is, the stronger is the embrace of Holocaust memory, as a shield against guilty feelings and bad consciences, and as a justification for innumerable injustices.

For ultimately, the symbolic manual of Holocaust remembrance is used everywhere. And in this sense, to understand the global memory of the Holocaust we should look as far as China but also right at home.

Notes

I am indebted to Amos Goldberg and Haim Hazan, as well as to the members of the research group on the Holocaust in global perspective, for their fellowship, scholarship, and lively discussions.

1. Recently, scholars in China began showing interest in the Holocaust and extended an invitation to Yehuda Bauer, the renowned Holocaust historian, and other scholars at Yad Vashem to visit China and speak about the topic.

2. Daniel Levy and Natan Sznaider, *The Holocaust and Memory in the Global Age* (Philadelphia: Temple University Press, 2006).

3. Ibid., 4.

4. For the interpretative benefits for Holocaust historiography of associating these two foundational events, see my *Foundational Pasts: The Holocaust as Historical Understanding* (New York: Cambridge University Press, 2012).

5. François Furet, *Interpreting the French Revolution* (Cambridge: Cambridge University Press, 1981). The original title was *La Révolution française est terminée*. Since the publication of Furet's essay there have been arguments against the pastness of the Revolution. Most recently, see Vincent Peillon, *La Révolution française n'est pas terminée* (Paris: Seuil, 2008).

6. For Burke, see Peter Fritzsche, "How Nostalgia Narrates Modernity," in *The Work of Memory: New Directions in the Study of German Society and Culture*, ed. Alon Confino and Peter Fritzsche (Urbana: University of Illinois Press, 2002), 66. See also Peter Fritzsche, *Stranded in the Present: Modern Time and the Melancholy of History* (Cambridge, MA: Harvard University Press, 2004). For Woodsworth, see William Doyle, *The French Revolution: A Very Short Introduction* (Oxford: Oxford University Press, 2001), 75.

7. Schlegel, *Athenäum*, fragment 424 (1798), cited in Ehrhard Bahr and Thomas Saine, eds., *The Internalized Revolution: German Reactions to the French Revolution, 1789–1989* (New York: Garland, 1992), 3; Jean-François Lyotard, *The Differend: Phrases in Dispute* (Manchester: Manchester University Press, 1988), 56.

8. Michael Rothberg, *Multidirectional Memory: Remembering the Holocaust in the Age of Decolonization* (Stanford, CA: Stanford University Press, 2009).

9. Hippolyte Taine, *The Origins of Contemporary France*, ed. Edward Gargan (Chicago: University of Chicago Press, 1974), 124.

10. On the comparison of the Revolution to Nazism, see Steven Kaplan, *Farewell Revolution: Disputed Legacies* (Ithaca, NY: Cornell University Press, 1995), 91–97. On feminism and the Revolution, see Lynn Hunt, "Forgetting and Remembering: The French Revolution Then and Now," *American Historical Review* 100, no. 4 (October 1995): 1131. For a balanced discussion of the differences between the Wars of the Vendée and genocide, see David Bell, *The First Total War: Napoleon's Europe and the Birth of Warfare as We Know It* (Boston: Houghton Mifflin, 2007), 157–61.

11. The speech is available in Wolfgang von Hippel, ed., *Freiheit, Gleichheit, Brüderlichkeit? Die Französische Revolution im deutschen Urteil von 1789 bis 1945* (Munich: DTV, 1989), 344–45. All translations are the author's.

12. Claudia Koonz, *The Nazi Conscience* (Cambridge, MA: Harvard University Press, 2003), 205.

13. *Das Schulungsbrief* 6 (1939): 220–21. This was a journal of the Nazi party and the German Labor Front (Deutsche Arbeitsfront).

14. Gerhard Sauder, "Akademischer 'Frühlingssturm': Germanisten als Redner bei der Bücherverbrennung," in *10. Mai 1933: Bücherverbrennung in Deutschland und die Folgen*, ed. Ulrich Walberer (Frankfurt: Fischer Verlag, 1983), 143.

15. A speech of 13 July 1929, cited in Klaus Lankheit, ed., *Hitler: Reden, Schriften, Anordnungen—Februar 1925 bis Januar 1933*, vol. 3, no. 2 (Munich: K. G. Saur, 1994), 297. See also the speech of 29 August 1930, cited in ibid., 371; Norman Baynes, ed., *The Speeches of Adolf Hitler: April 1922–August 1939* (London: Oxford University Press, 1942), 210.

16. Victor Klemperer, *I Will Bear Witness, 1933–1941*, vol. 1 (New York: Random House, 1998), 180, 208, 404. At the beginning of the diary Klemperer viewed Hitler as the direct offspring of Rousseau, but as the years went by he learned to appreciate the differences between them. He meant to change his chapter on Rousseau because "the men of the French Revolution speak to an assembly of the people, which is present," while Hitler speaks in front of a silent mass (404).

17. Ibid., 114, 117.

18. Beatrice Hyslop, "Recent Work on the French Revolution," *American Historical Review* 47, no. 3 (April 1942): 488.

19. Beatrice Hyslop, "Historical Publication since 1939 on the French Revolution," *Journal of Modern History* 20, no. 3 (September 1948): 232.

20. For the history of this linkage in theater, see Freddie Rokem, *Performing History: Theatrical Representations of the Past in Contemporary Theater* (Iowa City: University of Iowa Press, 2000). The book examines theater performances after 1945 that present the French Revolution and the Holocaust, focusing on the efforts to bring together the historical past and the theatrical present in two extreme historical events that called into question issues of witnessing. I am indebted to Freddie Rokem for our conversations on the topic.

21. François Furet, ed., *Unanswered Questions: Nazi Germany and the Genocide of the Jews* (New York: Schocken Books, 1989).

22. The discussion among historians about the uniqueness of the Holocaust raged especially in the 1980s and 1990s, at a period during which Holocaust representations assumed a growing public role. It is noteworthy that the claim that the Holocaust was unique has lost its intellectual and emotional power, at least among scholars. For an example of the old trend, see Alan Rosenbaum, ed., *Is the Holocaust Unique? Perspectives on Comparative Genocide* (Boulder, CO: Westview Press, 1996). In general, see Steven Aschheim, *In Times of Crisis: Essays on European Culture, Germans, and Jews* (University of Wisconsin Press, 2001), chaps. 4 and 10.

23. Conal Urquhart, "Settlers Fight Back with Symbol of the Holocaust," *The Guardian*, 22 December 2004, http://www.guardian.co.uk/world/2004/dec/22/israel (accessed 13 September 2014).

24. Ibid.

25. Harry De Quetteville, "Settlers Evoke Images of Holocaust in Gaza," *The Age* (Australia), 16 August 2005, http://www.theage.com.au/articles/2005/08/15/1123958007019.html (accessed 13 September 2014).

26. *Yediot Aharonot*, 2 September 2005 (accessed 13 September 2014).

27. Hanna Yablonka, "Verging on Holocaust Denial," *Haaretz*, 23 July 2005.

28. On this topic, see the article by Peter Novick in this volume.

29. See Dan Porat, *The Boy: A Holocaust Story* (New York: Hill and Wang, 2010).

Bibliography

Aschheim, Steven. *In Times of Crisis: Essays on European Culture, Germans, and Jews*. Madison: University of Wisconsin Press, 2001.

Bahr, Ehrhard, and Thomas Saine, eds. *The Internalized Revolution: German Reactions to the French Revolution, 1789–1989*. New York: Garland, 1992.

Baynes, Norman, ed. *The Speeches of Adolf Hitler: April 1922–August 1939*. London: Oxford University Press, 1942.

Bell, David. *The First Total War: Napoleon's Europe and the Birth of Warfare as We Know It*. Boston: Houghton Mifflin, 2007.
Confino, Alon. *Foundational Pasts: The Holocaust as Historical Understanding*. New York: Cambridge University Press, 2012.
Doyle, William. *The French Revolution: A Very Short Introduction*. Oxford: Oxford University Press, 2001.
Fritzsche, Peter. "How Nostalgia Narrates Modernity." In *The Work of Memory: New Directions in the Study of German Society and Culture*, ed. Alon Confino and Peter Fritzsche. Urbana: University of Illinois Press, 2002: 62–85.
———. *Stranded in the Present: Modern Time and the Melancholy of History*. Cambridge, MA: Harvard University Press, 2004.
Furet, François. *Interpreting the French Revolution*. Cambridge: Cambridge University Press, 1981.
———, ed. *Unanswered Questions: Nazi Germany and the Genocide of the Jews*. New York: Schocken Books, 1989.
Hippel, Wolfgang von, ed. *Freiheit, Gleichheit, Brüderlichkeit? Die Französische Revolution im deutschen Urteil von 1789 bis 1945*. Munich: DTV, 1989.
Hunt, Lynn. "Forgetting and Remembering: The French Revolution Then and Now." *American Historical Review* 100, no. 4 (October 1995): 1119–135.
Hyslop, Beatrice. "Historical Publication since 1939 on the French Revolution." *Journal of Modern History* 20, no. 3 (September 1948): 232–51.
———. "Recent Work on the French Revolution." *American Historical Review* 47, no. 3 (April 1942): 488–517.
Kaplan, Steven. *Farewell Revolution: Disputed Legacies*. Ithaca, NY: Cornell University Press, 1995.
Klemperer, Victor. *I Will Bear Witness, 1933–1941*. Vol. 1. New York: Random House, 1998.
Koonz, Claudia. *The Nazi Conscience*. Cambridge, MA: Harvard University Press, 2003.
Lankheit, Klaus, ed. *Hitler: Reden, Schriften, Anordnungen—Februar 1925 bis Januar 1933*. Vol. 3, no. 2. Munich: K. G. Saur, 1994.
Levy, Daniel, and Natan Sznaider. *The Holocaust and Memory in the Global Age*. Philadelphia: Temple University Press, 2006.
Lyotard, Jean-François. *The Differend: Phrases in Dispute*. Manchester: Manchester University Press, 1988.
Peillon, Vincent. *La Révolution française n'est pas terminée*. Paris: Seuil, 2008.
Porat, Dan. *The Boy: A Holocaust Story*. New York: Hill and Wang, 2010.
Quetteville, Harry De. "Settlers Evoke Images of Holocaust in Gaza." *The Age* (Australia), 16 August 2005. http://www.theage.com.au/articles/2005/08/15/1123958007019.html (accessed 13 September 2014).
Rokem, Freddie. *Performing History: Theatrical Representations of the Past in Contemporary Theater*. Iowa City: University of Iowa Press, 2000.
Rosenbaum, Alan, ed. *Is the Holocaust Unique? Perspectives on Comparative Genocide*. Boulder, CO: Westview Press, 1996.
Rothberg, Michael. *Multidirectional Memory: Remembering the Holocaust in the Age of Decolonization*. Stanford, CA: Stanford University Press, 2009.
Sauder, Gerhard. 1983. "Akademischer 'Frühlingssturm': Germanisten als Redner bei der Bücherverbrennung." In *10. Mai 1933: Bücherverbrennung in Deutschland und die Folgen*, ed. Ulrich Walberer. Frankfurt: Fischer Verlag, 1983, 140-59.
Das Schulungsbrief 6 (1939): 220–21.
Taine, Hippolyte. *The Origins of Contemporary France*. Edited and with an introduction by Edward Gargan. University of Chicago Press, 1974.
Urquhart, Conal. "Settlers Fight Back with Symbol of the Holocaust." *The Guardian*, 22 December 2004. http://www.guardian.co.uk/world/2004/dec/22/israel (accessed 13 September 2014).
Yablonka, Hanna. "Verging on Holocaust Denial." *Haaretz*, 23 July 2005.

CHAPTER 5

"After Auschwitz"
A Constitutive Turning Point in Moral Philosophy

RONIT PELEG

> How can thought be made the keeper of the Holocaust where all was lost, including guardian thought? In mortal intensity, the fleeing silence of the countless cry.
> —Maurice Blanchot, *The Writing of the Disaster*

> Auschwitz does not lend itself to commemoration. There can be no Er-innerung when the Innere of ear has been destroyed. It is not the "presence" of the voice that must be honored, it is more appropriate to mediate upon its disappearance in the abandonment of a dark night.
> —Jean-François Lyotard and Eberhard Gruber, *The Hyphen*

Introduction

The following discussion asks why it is that the notion of "after Auschwitz"—as coined by Theodor Adorno—has become the central theme in contemporary Continental philosophy. I shall argue that, from the perspective of Continental philosophy, this may be a constitutive turning point for Western moral philosophy—a moment that, first and foremost, requires philosophy to give a comprehensive moral-philosophical account of all that was brought to its end in "Auschwitz," and to reorganize the moral discursive field in light of these (philosophical) "ends." I argue that this moment is primarily related to the moral

Notes for this section begin on page 95.

duty of moral philosophy—a duty that has always been there—to detach itself from Hegelian speculative thinking—the type of thinking that came to its end at "Auschwitz," as argued by Adorno—and from its main concepts, its foundational distinctions, and its philosophical and moral operations.

In the following discussion, I shall expand upon the philosophical and moral consequences of this obligation. It is my aim to establish that this is a radical turning point in moral philosophy, whose shock waves have spread to the republican political discourse of the West. From the perspective of contemporary Continental philosophy, this does not involve merely reevaluating the central concepts of moral philosophy in light of the event called "Auschwitz," but rather knocking the discourse of Western moral philosophy off its axis due to the unprecedented schism in Western thought brought about by that event. According to Continental philosophers, herein lies the justification for the globalization of the Shoah and the moral-philosophical interest in it.

I focus on the philosophy of Jean-François Lyotard, though every now and then my scope will be broadened to include Maurice Blanchot, Emmanuel Levinas, and Jacques Derrida as well. Three main (and interrelated) issues are at stake: first, the kinds of responses offered by moral philosophy to disaster—any disaster, not only that of "Auschwitz"; second, the question of what constitutes the "we" of a group, a community, or a nation, or the test of membership (*commonium*) in a (or any) community; and third, a possible outline for an ethics "after Auschwitz," and most importantly, after the end of the Hegelian speculative discourse at "Auschwitz."

I shall develop these outlines in light of Lyotard's philosophy, which, I shall argue, is an ethical thought that detached itself from Hegelian speculative thought such that the latter cannot reincorporate the former again; it cannot incorporate the philosophical-moral gestures of that ethical thought: not the ethical concepts at its center, and not its ethical figures. It is thus an ethical thought that cannot be the continuation of Hegelian speculative thought "after Auschwitz," or the speculative result of "Auschwitz."[1]

In his book *Negative Dialectics,* Adorno asserts that "Auschwitz" is the event that signifies the absolute failure of speculative dialectics, or its final breakdown. "After Auschwitz" thus is a sense of refusal to derive any meaning whatsoever from the victims' fate, or to extract any kind of affirmation from existence. Philosophy experienced a shock—the fear that it was distancing us from things as they are. The fact that the event that bears the name "Auschwitz" is held up to the philosopher in such a way as to dismantle speculative thought, argues Adorno, creates a new condition for philosophical thought. *"After Auschwitz,"* he says, *"there is no word tinged from on high, not even a theological one, that has any right unless it underwent a transformation."*[2]

Lyotard and Blanchot continue this line of thought. In *The Differend,* Lyotard transcribes (*transcrire*) Adorno's argument into the linguistic discussion he presents in that book. There, Lyotard establishes the claim that "Auschwitz" signifies a linguistic experience that brings the Hegelian speculative discourse to a complete and utter halt. "After Auschwitz" one can no longer strive for that discourse.[3] Similarly, Blanchot argues that the disaster called the Holocaust is an absolute signifier that ruptures history; an absolute conflagration, in which all of history went up in flames, the movement of meaning came to a halt, and time was knocked off its axis. In *The Writing of the Disaster,* Blanchot expands on these arguments and asserts that nothing is more foreign to a disaster—any disaster—than dialectics, even if reduced only to its destructive moment. The disaster cannot be contained within a notion of totality; the disaster has no future, just as there is no time and space for its completion.[4]

However, if Adorno characterizes the end of Hegelian speculative thought at "Auschwitz" as an experience of shock for philosophy, then, I argue, Lyotard and Blanchot establish philosophy's duty to continue to detach itself morally from the speculative dialectic "after Auschwitz"—to morally refuse to revive (speculatively) that which came to its end. In contrast to Adorno, the issue is not only the impossibility that philosophy will continue to adhere to a discourse that was forced to its end (in Auschwitz), but also that its moral duty—a duty that has always been there—is to detach itself totally from speculative thought.

It should be stressed that what is at stake here is not the refutation of dialectical thinking or its temporary rupture; nor is this an attempt to reinterpret Hegel against himself—attempts that are all doomed to be trapped once more in the net of Hegelian speculative philosophy. Rather, it is a moral rejection of Hegelian speculative thinking—an absolute moral refusal of dialectics.

I argue that this refusal first and foremost touches on moral philosophy's obligation to detach itself from the speculative economics of life and death and from the central concept that supports and drives it, the notion of the "speculative death" (or the "beautiful death")—the form of death that stands at the foundations of the Western republican discourse—and from the (constant) temptation to develop a speculative response to the disaster (that which has happened and that which may yet happen)—to speculatively calculate life and death. When faced with the disaster (any disaster), philosophy is required to desist from rehabilitating, mediating, consoling, reconciling, uniting, or reconstructing thought—to detach itself from the attachment between disaster and promise. Also at issue here is the moral obligation to rethink the republican concept of "we," which affords the "beautiful death" its moral and political legitimacy.

(It would appear unnecessary to make it clear that this questioning of the concept of the "beautiful/speculative death" and the speculative economy of life and death seeks to sanctify life, or at least not to provide the next disaster with a soft or comforting and, retrospectively, justificatory platform. Similarly, the call for detachment from the speculative economics of life and death does not pertain to the decision of individuals to bestow the disaster that befell them with meaning and purpose that go beyond it, but rather to the communal and public use of this economics, and to the philosophical, religious, and political discourse of the concept of the "beautiful death.")

This is, first and foremost, a moral agenda. Therefore, our detachment from Hegelian speculative logic and from the (constant) temptation to develop a speculative response to the disaster must strive to be absolute and final.[5]

I argue that this detachment radically alters the discursive field of moral philosophy. It obliges those philosophers who claim to be thinking about moral obligation "after Auschwitz" to detach themselves from the central notions, or "tools," of philosophy, such as the concepts of the "speculative death" or the "beautiful death," the speculative self, the speculative result (Result), the speculative community, and the concepts of reconciliation, overcoming, and completion. As I shall show, this is a radical turning point in moral philosophy.[6]

I maintain that the success of this detachment is primarily dependent on placing "Auschwitz" at the beginning of any moral discussion of obligation, and not as the signifier of the end of such a discussion. If the death called "Auschwitz" is the name of the event that signifies the halting point of the Hegelian speculative discourse, as argued by Adorno and Lyotard, because of the unprecedented schism in Western thought brought about by this death—an argument that I shall try to establish and develop further in the first part of my discussion—then any discussion of obligation "after Auschwitz" must first and foremost include the form of that death, and constitute it, or the types of philosophical, linguistic, and moral "ending" that it implies, as the necessary and only starting point for thinking about moral obligation (in the world "after Auschwitz").

It is my contention that this process stands at the foundations of Lyotard's ethical thought and illuminates its image; it sheds light on the concerns of this thought, its language, its central ethical concepts, and its ethical figures—those that take the place of the (Hegelian) speculative subject.

My argument develops in two stages. In its first stage, following Lyotard, who develops Adorno's argument, I shall establish the claim that the death called "Auschwitz" signifies the halting point of the Hegelian speculative discourse. I shall also elaborate on the moral, linguistic, political, and philosophical meanings of this breakdown. Then, I shall seek to justify my claim that not only is it impossible for philosophy to continue to adhere to a discourse whose end was forced on it by the death called "Auschwitz," but also that philosophy has a moral duty to continue to detach itself from dialectical speculative thought "after Auschwitz," and to establish this (moral) detachment as a necessary starting point for any moral discussion of obligation.

In this regard, I shall try to untangle the complex and tense status of "Auschwitz" in the current discussion.[7] First of all, this discussion signifies the uniqueness of Auschwitz, of that specific disaster, in the sense of an event that brought the Hegelian speculative discourse to its halting point. Second, and simultaneously, "Auschwitz" also serves as a model (in Adorno's sense). As Adorno explains, it is of the essence of a model—as opposed to an example—

that it cannot be replaced by other examples, because the affinity between the particular and the universal in a model is essential to it and cannot serve as an example that refers to another universal. Nor can the model be part of a system; it does not illustrate anything: rather, things are measured in relation to it.[8]

Therefore, everything that came to its end or disintegrated "there" becomes a model of failure. As such, it not only applies to this specific disaster, but to all disasters—those before "Auschwitz" and those that have happened or will happen "after Auschwitz." ("Auschwitz" always appears in quote marks, and the theme, "after Auschwitz," does not have temporal connotations.)

Third, and simultaneously, "Auschwitz" is also the most extreme, abhorrent, and distant edge of the conceptual, epistemological, and ontological continuities that are stretched between "there" and "here." In this regard, "Auschwitz" is not only an event that brought the Hegelian speculative discourse to a halt, but also an event that, as I shall argue, demands that we reexamine the morality of the central concepts of the republican discourse, primarily among them the concept of the republican "we," and that we reconsider the status of the concept of the "beautiful death" in republican political discourse.

In the second stage of my argument, I shall briefly sketch out the possible outlines of a philosophical-ethical discourse following detachment from the Hegelian speculative discourse, and I shall develop the ethical and philosophical-political potential inherent in that discourse. Inter alia, I shall ask what might follow the speculative concept of self and what might replace the concept of the "speculative death" or the "beautiful death," as well as what might come after the concepts of (speculative) result and speculative community. In this regard I shall try to clarify what kinds of new ethical sensitivity and ethical attentiveness are now required. As mentioned, I shall do this in light of Lyotard's ethical thinking, though I shall occasionally broaden my scope to include Levinas, Blanchot, and Derrida as well.

I should note that what Adorno saw as an experience of shock in philosophy, I prefer to characterize as its constitutive turning point.[9]

The Final Breakdown of Hegelian Speculative Thought in "Auschwitz"

The death called "Auschwitz" determines the final breakdown of Hegelian speculative thought. The uniqueness and extremity of the death we have named "Auschwitz" emerge clearly when held up against the concept of the "speculative death," or what Lyotard (following Plato) called the "beautiful death" (*belle mort*) or the "magical death" (*magique mort*), a death that met its final end at "Auschwitz."

The "beautiful death" is a death that can be justified, explained, and elevated (*Aufhebung*) philosophically; a death that preserves and supports speculative movement. Within the speculative economics of life and death, as Derrida calls it, there is nothing that cannot be made to have meaning, including, or maybe above all else, death. Death must be productive. It has to work, to produce speculative "profits," or to instigate what Blanchot calls "the step beyond." It cannot be an absolute and irreversible loss—an end that serves no meaning at all.[10]

The greed of the speculative discourse forbids absolute wastage, that is, sacrifice, destruction, and death that leave no reserve. The dialectical process requires a remnant in order to carry on. For this reason, the possibility of working with death must always be sustained. Death cannot be seen as a simple end. It must be reappropriated and seen as part of the work of the negation that is necessary for the dialectical process, work that can never lead to simple destruction, but rather generates Being at a higher level.

Through the central operation of the speculative discourse—the operation of *Aufhebung,* the operation of negation/preservation/sublation (to a higher level of knowledge of Being in its totality, and thus of "the truth")—or the way in which Derrida causes the term to write itself anew—*relèver,* preservation, elevation, quieting, easing, and replacing—risks become investments, negation becomes a resource. Thus, the continuous progress of the speculative movement is ensured. As Hegel puts it:

> Death, if that is what we want to call this nonactuality, is of all things the most dreadful, and to hold fast what is dead requires the greatest strength. Lacking strength, Beauty hates the Understanding, for asking of her what it cannot do. But the life of Spirit is not the life that shrinks from death and keeps itself untouched by devastation, but rather the life that endures it and maintains itself in it. It wins its truth only when, in utter dismemberment, it finds itself. It is this power, not as something positive, which closes its eyes to the negative, as when we say of something that it is nothing or is false, and then, having done with that, turn away and passes on to something else; on the contrary, Spirit is this power only by looking the negative in the face, and tarrying with it. This tarrying with the negative is the magical power that converts it into being.[11]

Speculative death is thus a death that has "movement"—the movement of death—and is always working. This is not a pure and absolute nothingness or a simple border, but rather a dialectical overcoming that discards while at the same time preserving and elevating. Just as reality is constructed from the negative, so Spirit is constructed out of its confronting the negative, death, suffering, and destruction, while "looking the negative in the face," dealing with it, and "tarrying with it"; thus, the negative becomes a positive force, a power that constructs reality. In this way the human being evades his own death, dialectically, and puts an end to its finiteness—a surplus right reserved for human beings.[12]

In Lyotardian terms, the speculative death, or the "beautiful death" (in quote marks, of course), is a death that gives its intended victim (such as the soldier sent into battle) an "opportunity" to convert his finiteness (as a mortal being), through his death, into infinity (as someone who belongs to the collective name—of the nation, or the group—which is immortal). The speculative economics of life and death presents one's preparedness to sacrifice one's life as the ultimate expression of obligation of the individual to the community, of his participation (communion) in it and membership of it—a "surplus right" that is not preserved for "others" who do not belong to the group.[13] The preparedness to pay off this debt of sacrifice—a debt that stands at the foundations of the definition of community in its speculative (and republican) sense—provides the individual with an entrance pass into the eternal life of the collective name (with your death you enter the Pantheon of the names of the heroes, which is eternal). In this way the victim is meant to escape the miserable fate of a "regular" death, and to gain—in return for his death—eternal life. As Lyotard puts it: "Such is the Athenian 'beautiful death,' the exchange of the finite for the infinite, of the eschaton for the telos: the Die in order not to die."[14] Lyotard expands on the meaning of the concept of the "beautiful death" and develops the (political and moral) dimension of its "beauty" as it emerges from the West's republican discourse (from Plato to the present day).

According to Lyotard, the "beauty" of the "beautiful death" also derives from the fact that it always allows the victim to join the collective name of the legislative authority, which orders the individual to defend or fight to the death … and constructs this order as a normative law of the community/nation. Lyotard explains that this joining depends, first and foremost, on modalizing the order "Die" (rather than escape, be defeated, be enslaved), and on giving the victim of the prescription a choice: to fulfill the obligation that calls for his possible death, or to choose another obligation (to flee, to betray, to surrender, to refuse).[15] This choice enables him to identify himself with two roles: he who is carrying out the prescription, or the obligation, and as he who legislates it as a normative law of the community. The use of the Western republican political discourse (from Plato through to the current day) in constructing the pronoun "we"—"we the Athenians," "we the French nation," "we the Israelis," and so on—is what makes this double identification possible. This is because it unites the addressee of the prescription and the addressor of the law into a single entity and forges symmetrical and mutually convertible relations between them, at least in principle. The normative law and its subsequent prescription both talk in terms of "we." This ensures that whoever determines the norm that one's preparedness to sacrifice one's life is the ultimate expression of obligation cannot exclude himself from the duty that he constructs as a norm.[16]

A "beautiful" death indeed….

This raises the following questions: How does the specific death called "Auschwitz" cause the death of the "beautiful death," or put an end to the possibility of death being "beautiful" (in quote marks)? Why Auschwitz in particular? And what are the moral and philosophical consequences of this?

The Hegelian speculative dialectic falls apart when faced with the death called "Auschwitz" because it cannot incorporate the logic of that death, or more precisely, the cleft introduced into Western thought by that death. The logic on which "Auschwitz" is based is designed from the outset to rule out any possibility of the "beautiful death" (this argument refers to the Jews and other victims, that is, those who were sent to their deaths in the camps, and not to the soldiers). Instead of the dialectical movement to negate-preserve-sublate death, in "Auschwitz" death tried to comprehensively eradicate not only the physical victims, or its possible witnesses, but also any traces of the eradication, any traces of the witnesses (the third party), the victims' names (their private names but also their collective name), death itself, and any kind of discourse that might have been able to talk about that death, to bear witness to it, to commemorate it, or to exclude, preserve, elevate, relieve, or alleviate it.

As Adorno put it, "Auschwitz" constitutes a model of absolute eradication, the eradication even of evil and suffering. In terms of the Aryan discourse, this was a model of a "final solution." What is at stake here is the total detachment between the logic of the "beautiful death," or the speculative death, and the logic of the death named the "final solution," or the "nonbeautiful death," the same logic that aspires to finality in the sense of total eradication—traceless eradication. It should be noted that this total detachment does not relate to the gap between the cruelty of the death called "Auschwitz" and that of the "beautiful death"; after all, the cruelty and meaningless of death has also been described in relation to other atrocities throughout history (and certainly in relation to World War I). What is being discussed here is the new and exceptional aspect of death at "Auschwitz": the aspiration to finiteness in the sense of total eradication, including of evil and suffering, and total loss, including the loss of the ability to lose.[17] The detachment is between a logic that aspires to final and absolute death and a logic that aspires to extract a remnant, or a positive result, from death.

In terms of Lyotard's linguistic discussion, "Auschwitz" is the name of the radical and unprecedented dispersion of phrases—a dispersal worse than exile. It is my argument that this is a threefold set of phrasal detachment that destroys any possibility of constructing any kind of shared "we" (the axis that is necessary for the movement of the speculative dialectic): not between those who send others to their death and those who are sent to their death (that is, the "we" of the political-republican community); not between all those who were sent to their death (that is, the "we" of the victims); and not between those who remain in the world "after Auschwitz" and the victims who were "there" (that is, the "we" of the speculative community—that which conjoins the living and the dead of the community). These detachments establish the impossibility that those who were sent to their death at "Auschwitz" could have died a "beautiful death" as well as the fact that the space of death at "Auschwitz" was not one of sacrifice. They also establish the impossibility that death could ever be "beautiful" again in a world "after Auschwitz."

The philosophical, political, and moral implications of this set of detachments are, in my view, radical. What is at stake here is, first of all, the debt that stands at the foundation of the (republican) definition of community and the test of membership (*communium*) in the community.

Following Lyotard, let us develop these notions and examine their implications. From a Lyotardian point of view, the death called "Auschwitz" is enfolded within a minimal discursive situation that expresses two phrases of ultimate obligation that are radically detached from one another (or cannot be linked dialectically with one another): the Nazi phrase, or the prescriptive phrase of those sending others to their death, that commands: "He must die—it is my law"; and the Jewish phrase, or the prescriptive phrase of the deportee, which prescribes: "I must die—it is his law." Given this situation of detachment, it was impossible to construct a "we" that was shared by those who sent to death (the Aryans) and those who were sent to their death (the Jews), nor a "we" that was shared by the victims (the eradication of the collective name, "Jews"). In the lack of such a shared "we," those who were sent to their death at "Auschwitz" could not move from their position as the referents of the order to die to that of addressor/legislator of the normative phrase so as to construct the order "Die" as a normative law, thereby "winning" a "beautiful death." This is because death at "Auschwitz" totally detached the possibility of linkage between the (non-Aryan) deportee and the (Aryan) law that ordered his death. In "Auschwitz" there was no mutual conversion between the addressor of the normative law and its addressee (the Jews were not the addressees of the Aryan law that sent them to death, but rather the referents of that law)—a conversion that, as noted, forms the basis of the concept of the "beautiful death," and, more broadly, is foundational to the republican political model of the West.

Therefore, a situation was created in which those who issued the death order at "Auschwitz" and constructed it as law excluded themselves from the duty both to justify it to its victims and to actually carry it out. Those who took that duty on themselves were excluded from the boundaries of legitimation. "That is what is marked by the shattering of the prescriptive phrase and of its legitimation into two phrases issuing from that fissure.... Dispersion is at its height."[18] In other words, the "Auschwitzian" discourse of death was not a discourse of obligation and sacrifice, and the space of death called "Auschwitz" denied such a discourse to the deportees. (In the framework of the Aryan discourse, a closed community of names was created that enabled only its members, who had Aryan names, to die a "beautiful death." The boundaries of this world of names were sealed off against any attempt to penetrate it from the "outside" by anyone who was not Aryan.)[19]

The deportee at "Auschwitz," therefore, was sentenced to a final death, lacking all justification or meaning, to be totally forgotten. As argued by Jean-Luc Nancy, the death camps were the sites of a death lacking ceremonies and sacrificial altars. The deportee at the death camp (the Jewish victim)—unlike the Aryan—is a figure of the unsacrificeable, according to Nancy. There is nothing about him to preserve or to appropriate from him; he is only to be eradicated, or to be got rid of and detached from totally and finally. (In this sense, excluding the Jews from society, or annulling their membership to the "we"—which was redefined as a solely Aryan "we"—before sending them to the camps was the beginning of the same logic of death that did not allow them to sacrifice themselves [for the community] or to die as martyrs, and part of the evolving process of the "nonbeautiful death," or part of the logic of the "final solution").[20]

The speculative dialectic, therefore, encounters an event whose logic of eradication is thoroughly foreign and exceptional to the Hegelian speculative logic. We should recall that this is not a temporary halting of the speculative dialectic, but rather the absolute cessation of its primary engine in light of a death that strives for the total nullification not only of its subjects, but also of nullification itself—death with no traces or remnants. From the perspective of the speculative enterprise, this is a death that one cannot work with, that cannot be elevated (*Aufhebung*); a death that has no movement and that freezes or engulfs everything. As Lyotard puts it, this is a death that creates an unprecedented schism in Western thought.

"Auschwitz" is thus the name of a new type of death that also inspires a new type of fear of death: "Since 'Auschwitz,'" says Adorno, "fearing death means fearing worse than death." This is the fear of the insight that death itself can be killed, and the horrifying knowledge that there is something worse than death: an irreversible death that does not serve any meaning, that has no productivity or movement, the end as such, including the end of the eternal.

However, at this point in the discussion one wonders: is the end of the speculative or the "beautiful death" at "Auschwitz" really "worse than death," as Adorno put it? Broadly speaking, I would like to claim that the breakdown of the Hegelian speculative discourse in light of the disaster of "Auschwitz" is not an expression of the radical evil of that death, which did not even allow its victims to die a "beautiful death," but an expression of the radical and new logic of that death.

I would like to elaborate the possible linguistic, philosophical, moral, and political implications of this breakdown, and to establish the moral duty of philosophy to continue detaching from the Hegelian speculative discourse "after Auschwitz." (I should emphasize once again that what is at stake here is not the cruelty of the death called "Auschwitz" vis-à-vis the cruelty of other wars, as troubling as they may be, but rather the radical logic of the "Auschwitzian" "nonbeautiful death," or of the "final solution," which strove to eradicate everything, including the traces of the eradication itself.)

The moral duty of philosophy to continue detaching from the Hegelian speculative discourse, and not to try and rehabilitate or resuscitate it "after Auschwitz," implies that it is no longer possible ("after Auschwitz") "to work" publicly with death; to "calculate" it, "to get over it" or its finiteness; to give it meaning and a purpose that transcend it, thus infusing it with the value of sacrifice, either in the eyes of those who were sent to their possible death (or to fight to the death), or those who sent others to their possible death. In other words, the end of the possibility of death being "beautiful" implies the end of the possibility of transcribing the prescriptions that send people to their possible death (or that instruct them to fight to the death) into the language of obligation (into some kind of abstract concept, or to the eternal collective name of the group or the nation), and to portray them as the ultimate expression of obligation (to the community/nation).

The absolute halt of the Hegelian speculative discourse also determines the impossibility of religiously, philosophically, or politically elevating death (*Aufhebung*), thereby putting an end to the possibility of any trade between the finite and the infinite. The final detachment from the concept of the "beautiful death," or the "magical death," means that we can no longer "be saved" after the disaster by a speculative process. Nothing "magical" will happen after the disaster. Because there is no "beautiful death," therefore (as argued by Blanchot), it is impossible to let the painful thought be consoled, because there really is no way of referring to the loss by means of any mediating notions whatsoever.

Moreover, I argue that the (moral) duty of moral philosophy to continue to detach itself from the concept of the "beautiful death," even "after Auschwitz," not only refers to the duty to put an end to the speculative economics of life and death and the concept of the (speculative) "we" on which it is based. There is also a moral duty to reexamine and rethink the concept of the republican "we" (which supports this economics and affords the "beautiful death" its moral and political legitimacy). "Auschwitz" reinforces the urgency of doing this, as, in this context, it is positioned as an extreme example (and as a horrifying reminder) of the (moral and political) structural failures (potentially) incorporated within the concept of "we" on which the Western republican political model is based.

This conclusion emerges from Lyotard's linguistic analysis in *The Differend* regarding the mechanisms that legitimate prescriptions in the modern republican political discourse and turn them into obligating norms or laws. The problem here is the very effort made by the republican modern discourse to publicly ratify prescriptive phrases and afford them the status of obligatory law, including, or above all, prescriptions that send to defend or fight to the death, as an expression of ultimate obligation to the community. In fact, what follows is a broad and principled contestation of the source of legitimacy of this political model and an attempt to expose its moral failings. This exposure strives to detach the question of obligation from the question of its public affirmation or justification and to maintain it as a distinct moral issue that must be privately and individually settled. This decision has to be made by the obligated "I," and by him alone (even when the decision touches on the willingness to defend the nation or the group). (This issue is central to the discussion in the second part of the text.)

It is important to stress that this is not the moral problematic of the individual's private decision to sacrifice his life to save another, or to protect his community or any other group. Rather, the moral problem lies with the public prescriptions that send people to fight until their possible death (including the prescriptions of the republican discourse), or, more precisely, with the republican philosophical and political apparatus, which elevates such prescriptions to the status of a normative and obligatory law, and positions the willingness to choose it (and not other possible obligations) as the expression of the individual's ultimate obligation to his community and his belonging to its "we." The question that emerges from Lyotard's linguistic analysis is whether there is necessarily a total overlap between those who are sent to die a "beautiful death" (or to fight to the death), and those who issue these prescriptions and legislate them as normative laws, as implied by the philosophical and political façade of the republican discourse (as mentioned, such an overlap would contribute to the "beauty" of that death). In this regard, "Auschwitz" is positioned as the most severe, extreme, and terrifying model of the (total) nonconvergence between the prescription and the norm, or between the legislator sending others to their possible death and those sent to a possible death—a nonconvergence that is also potentially included in the concept of the "beautiful death."

Let us proceed gradually. As mentioned, the central axis of the republican legitimating discourse of prescriptions is the use of the pronoun "we" in the first-person plural. This is because the assumption at the foundation of the republican model, which constitutes the source of its legitimacy, is that whoever determines the norm or the law must also obey it (and vice versa). This is the notion of autonomy, in its moral and political sense.

However, Lyotard's linguistic analysis of the legitimating mechanism of prescriptions in the republican discourse seeks to mark out the potential gap between the legislators (of the norms or the laws) and the addressees of the prescriptions, and hence to question the assumption of overlap. The analysis of the structure of the linguistic positions of the prescriptive phrase (which in this regard says: "We ought to defend our country to the death") and of the normative or legal phrase (which in this context asserts: "We hereby rule that it is an obligatory norm to defend the nation/country to the death, and we see the preparedness to die as the ultimate expression of this commitment") exposes a false presentation of homogeneity that camouflages the linguistic fact that the "we" of the prescriptive phrase is not necessarily the same "we" of the normative phrase. There is no necessary unification or overlap between the components of the "we," as they subsist in different linguistic positions. In the prescriptive or obligatory phrase, the "we" of the prescription will always occupy the position of the addressee, and in the normative phrase it is "we" that occupies the position of the addressor.

The rhetoric of political discourse that talks in terms of "we" erases this heterogeneity and violently imposes homogeneity at the very moment that it unites that which is actually "us" (the legislators—those who propagate the law) and "you" (the addressees of the prescription, or those to whom the law is applied) into a single, shared entity of "we." In this way it creates (among all of us) a (nearly automatic) false assumption that the people determining the normative law are the same as those who adhere to it. The moral problematic broadens given the possibility (in principle) that the republican "we" also incorporates the position of a third party (that is, the "we" is comprised of "I," "you," and "him")—a position that is also blurred and repressed through being named in the first-person plural.

To reverse this formulation, the immediate assumption of overlap that is encouraged by the rhetoric of the republican philosophical and political discourse that talks in terms of "we" sees whoever questions the "we," or is not prepared to be included within it, or whoever challenges the definition of community on which the "we" is based, as exceptional, and as outside society and its normative consensus. This position also determines the political and moral attitude to him. This attitude—and most certainly when it relates to the question of whether one is willing to sacrifice one's life as the ultimate expression of his obligation to the community—ranges between discomfort and seeing such views as constituting a threat to the very existence of the community.

Lyotard's linguistic analysis of the process of the legitimating mechanism of prescriptions in the republican discourse is primarily aimed at exacting its formulation and marking out the potential gap between the addressors of the law and the addressees of the prescriptions, thereby undermining the assumption of overlap. The process of authorization is actually comprised of the following two statements: "I declare and determine as an obligatory law that you must ..." and "You must ..." A third phrase is also potentially latent here: "The prescription that obliges me derives from their law."

The meaning of the linguistic gap between the legislating "I" and the "you" of the prescriptive phrase—a gap that is not only a linguistic-philosophical gap, of course, but rather a political and moral fact as well—is that the linkage used by the modern republican discourse to ratify prescriptions that send others to their possible deaths, and to present those prescriptions as the ultimate expression of obligation to the group or the nation, is morally problematic from the very outset. This is because it fundamentally incorporates a threatening and hidden potential nonconvergence or gap between components of the "we"—a gap that also potentially dwells within the concept of the "beautiful death." This problematic is pertinent not only to these prescriptions, of course, but also to the entire republican political model. However, it becomes more acute (in the current case) when it serves to legitimate prescriptions that send people to fight to their possible death. The extremity of the price only highlights the overhastiness of its construction.

The principled (yet camouflaged) moral problematic of the concept of the "beautiful death" and the possible fictiveness of the axis of "we" that would seem to ensure the process whereby all of the possible addressors and addressees agree to this death (thereby embodying the "beauty" of this death) establish, first and foremost, the lack of moral legitimacy of the attempt to transcribe the prescriptions that send others to their death (or to fight to the death) into a language of obligation to the community's normative laws. It also most certainly establishes the impossibility of presenting it as the expression of the citizen's ultimate obligation to the communal "we."

From this perspective, the "Auschwitzian" situation of death—which has been radically detached from those phrasal mechanisms, and which blocks any possibility of constructing a speculative "we" that (allegedly) unites those who sent others to a possible death with those who were sent to it, and those who died with those who live—is a (radically) extremized and horrifying testimony of the possible essence of all the prescriptions that send others to their possible death: of the possibility that they lack the moral legitimacy on which they purport to rest; of the possibility that they are sending others to a "nonbeautiful death" (in the speculative sense of the term). In Derridean terms, what is at stake here is the possible (and permanent) danger that the "beautiful death" is contaminated by the "nonbeautiful death."[21]

Accepting these conclusions implies a moral obligation, "after Auschwitz," to treat all prescriptions that send others to a possible death (or to fight to the death) as prescriptions that send them to a finite and private death and therefore to a "nonbeautiful death." It also implies a moral obligation to treat all those who are sent to a possible death (or to fight to the death) as the possible victims of prescriptions that send them to their finite and illegitimate death.[22]

Contrariwise, it might be argued that it is possible to carry on speculatively "working" with death and to create speculative linkages between the living and the dead, but only at the cost of ignoring that which reaches its total cessation in the face of the death of "Auschwitz," namely, at the cost of ignoring the radical consequences of that event.

From this perspective it could be argued that only the death called "Auschwitz," or, more precisely, the logic behind that death, could succeed in uprooting the conception—which is almost automatic among republican political communities—that sees the implementation of those prescriptions as the expression of maximal obligation to the community. In this sense, death at "Auschwitz" has created a constitutive turning point in moral philosophy.

Within the context of the present discussion, therefore, we could see in "Auschwitz," or, more precisely, the radical logic behind the "final solution," that which obliges us to reevaluate our thinking about issues of sacrifice, obligation, and community (here and now). It makes it possible to wonder whether obligation and belonging to the community must ultimately, or at their extremity, be based on the linkage between responsibility (toward the state, the community, or the individual) and the idea of the "gift of death" (*donner la mort*)—a view that sees the given death as the ultimate expression of the responsibility of the "I," as explained by Derrida.[23] It also means we can examine whether it is impossible to think about another principle that could define belonging to a community/nation and form the bond of the "we." Here, in my view, lies a crucial turning point, from a philosophical and moral point of view.

As a very initial attempt to think about this, it would appear that moral and political philosophy now stands at a new junction: it must rethink that tense linkage, or anxious proximity, that we find throughout the history of philosophy, as argued by Derrida, via different modalities, between the concept of responsibility (or obligation, in Lyotardian terms) and the idea of "letting yourself die." Throughout philosophy, this linkage—which Jean-Luc Nancy sees as the cornerstone of the West—has given rise to different figures of "given death," which are also different figures of responsibility, each of which contains a different understanding of death, a different concern for death, and a different experience of death. Despite the differences between Plato's view of death and that of Heidegger, or Bataille, or Levinas, and between various concerns about death (mine, or that of the other), they are all rooted in the same permanent philosophical attentiveness to the fundamental and foundational possibility of sacrifice, as Derrida would say, or its enchantment with that possibility, as Nancy would add.[24]

Perhaps the absolute end of the idea of the "beautiful death" at "Auschwitz," and the unsurpassable obstacle placed by death at "Auschwitz" in the path of Hegelian speculative philosophy, obliges moral philosophy to stop watching over death; to stop trying to access its space, to stop "looking it directly in the eye," as Hegel said, and "practicing it," as Plato said. Maybe here there is an "opportunity" to untie the (Gordian) knot between the concept of responsibility (or obligation) and the culture of death, to put an end to the fundamental and foundational understanding of responsibility as modalities of "giving death to myself" (*se-donner la mort*).

However, it should be stressed that in this regard there is a structural and essential difference between ethical responsibility and political responsibility, despite the fact that they are both involved in the economics of sacrifice. Ethical sacrifice, as Levinas understands it, for instance, is always for a specific other, and not for an abstract collective, and it is always the outcome of a sense of obligation toward the other who has been scandalously abandoned, or the feeling that "the other's death is a scandal," in Levinas's words. While ethical responsibility is also inextricably involved in the economics of sacrifice, as Derrida puts it (for instance, when we choose to fulfill an absolute obligation toward a certain other and therefore at the same time unavoidably sacrifice all others, who are also absolute others), ethical responsibility is always a space of aporia, which does not accept that sacrifice as a given but rather is constantly disturbed by it.[25] This is not the case with political responsibility. In the political economics of life and death, the logic of sacrifice is not rejected or questioned.[26]

Either way, the philosophical linkage between the concept of responsibility and the concept of "letting yourself die" is, in my view, a troubling one. One might think of continuities between the ethical and the political discourses. Sacrifice, even if it is for the sake of an absolute or specific other, must be an event or action that cannot be commanded—no one has the right to do so, not even the moral philosopher (as, for example, Levinas does).[27] There need not be an obligation "to die for the other," not even an ethical one. Each person must reach this decision by himself and take unique responsibility for it. Sacrifice cannot and should not have a public language (not political, nor religious, nor moral-philosophical). The language of sacrifice should always be secret and silenced.

In my view, at this turning point, moral and political philosophy must think of another principle for defining belonging to a community or nation, thereby involving the community in a different kind of experience of belonging, and in a different type of political logic, to borrow from Derrida.[28]

This moral obligation also reaches philosophy's moral obligation to put an end to the constitutive linkage in speculative thought between disaster and promise. This is not only the end of the "speculative death" at "Auschwitz" and the moral obligation to continue to establish this end "after Auschwitz," but also the end of the concept of the speculative result (Result) at "Auschwitz," as discussed by Lyotard—which also signifies the very same turning point in moral philosophy. In what follows I shall elaborate on the moral and political consequences of this.

As mentioned, "Auschwitz" places an insurmountable object in the path of Hegelian speculative thought. Dialectical logic has to incorporate an event such as "Auschwitz" within itself, to extract some positive outcome from it, and to make it into a moment in a broader process. It cannot simply ignore it and place it to one side as a unique event, or as a "different planet."

However, the (Hegelian) speculative discourse is incapable of doing this, because "Auschwitz" lacks a (speculative) outcome. It is an event whose logic is entirely foreign to that of speculative logic—an event constructed on the principle of exclusion, distancing, pest control, sanitation, and total eradication with no positive outcome, with no witnesses, with no "we" (as third party) who can testify to the disaster, close the rupture, and create a transition to the next stage.

In consequence, there is no possible way of thinking about the disaster, explaining it, or justifying it speculatively, that is, of analyzing it as a disaster that immanently and necessarily resulted from earlier stages, or as an inevitable moment in a broader process. Nor is there any way of locating the disaster in any framework of totality, of representing it as part of a history of meaning that is developing itself, creating itself, and realizing itself in a linear, progressive, regressive, tragic, or circular fashion. To reverse this formulation, the Hegelian speculative discourse can only treat "Auschwitz" in a speculative manner and make it into just another disaster in a chain of disasters that preceded it and that will follow it at the cost of erasing the uniqueness of "Auschwitz" and failing to understand the radical logic on which it was based.

"Auschwitz" is therefore the name of the total disintegration of the concept of the (speculative) "we," or its radical dispersion, as well as of the inability to create any kind of shared "we": not the "we" of the republican community; not the "we" of the community of victims; and not the "we" that can (in retrospect) reconstruct the disaster, heal the rift, and create a transition to the next stage.

This impossibility dismantles the idea of the speculative community (the idea that, through the concept of the "we," conjoins the community's dead and living, those who died in the disaster and those who live in the world "after the disaster") once and for all. It also dismantles the practices of participation and belonging that stand at the basis of the idea and reinforce it.[29] The impossibility of speculatively crossing the death named "Auschwitz," of closing the rupture and creating a transition to the next stage, finally halts the operation of *Aufhebung,* which, as mentioned, ensures the ongoing movement of the dialectic. Like a black hole, the death named "Auschwitz" swallows up the Hegelian speculative dialectic. This total blockage, I argue, also creates a constitutive turning point in moral philosophy.

The end of the possibility of thinking about and reacting to "Auschwitz" in terms of its speculative result means that we have to find new ways of thinking about the disaster, and new ways of responding to it. The breakdown of the concept of the speculative result first and foremost forces philosophy to desist from rehabilitating, mediating, consoling, reconciling, uniting, or reconstructing thought. This is not only an obligation to desist from thinking that responds to the disaster—which is a private name and a concrete and singular event—and clarifies its meaning by (ultimately) assimilating it as a moment within a narrative of a developing totality (of the kind of large historical story told by Marx, Hegel, or Kant) and by internalizing it as a concept. What we actually have here is an opportunity, or rather an obligation, for philosophy to rid itself of its desire for meaning and recognize the fact that this desire actually discretely collaborates with the disaster. It might even be an accomplice to the crime.

Philosophy must therefore stand up to the disaster and think about its attitude to the disaster—every disaster—while refusing absolutely to make the particular into a way station, thereby healing the rupture and coming to terms with the death and suffering for the sake of a reconciliation that takes place in thought. Philosophy must protect the absent meaning of the disaster, and see death only for what it is: negation without remainder, and not as a negation within a process.

Only then will philosophy be able to face up to the "disasterousness" of the disaster, to the absolute loss, or the "nonbeautiful death," that it forever creates, and to the silences that it leaves behind—"Silences, instead of a Result (speculative result)", in Lyotard's words.

"The disaster," says Blanchot, "*exposes us to a certain idea of passivity, a passivity that is not simple receptivity, but rather a task in another language—a language of non-dialectical drive.*"[30] This primarily requires a philosophy with patience, a philosophy that dissuades itself—a philosophy that has foregone the power of wakefulness, a clear view of the world, the superiority of sharp perceptions, the form of logos. This requires a philosophy without passion, without desire, a philosophy that does not take pleasure in itself, that does not calculate. Another language is called for—not one of craving, or of arguments and counterarguments, verification and negation, silence and speech. Not everything should be overcome; not everything can be, or should be, mended.

The Possible Outlines of a Philosophical-Ethical Discourse

What then, is the role of moral philosophy at this point, after everything has been said, or maybe more precisely, before everything has started to be said, before words and concepts, and given the silences that surround the disaster (any disaster)? What happens to philosophical thinking when it has lost the mechanism that enables it to reap "speculative gain" from "what happened"—the peak of pleasure of speculative philosophy—and its ability to alleviate, to uplift, to soften, to reconcile, to release from pain, all in one movement of thought? How does one respond to a disaster without making *relèver*, as Derrida puts it? How do we move forward after the loss of the guiding star (*des-astre,* as Blanchot elegantly deconstructs the concept), without any philosophical horizons extending above us, in the dark, starless night?

I would like to offer a possible answer to these questions, based on the philosophy of Lyotard, and to outline an ethical discourse that takes place in the discursive and philosophical conditions after the breakdown of Hegelian speculative philosophy—conditions that, according to the moral interpretation put forward here, embody the world "after Auschwitz."[31]

Lyotard's attempt to think about obligation in a world "after Auschwitz"— along with his endeavor to detach himself from Hegelian speculative thought— from its economics, its territories, its desires, its arrogance—is, I argue, an essential platform for shaping an ethics of moral attentiveness and response, an ethics that positions sentiments as the necessary criteria for both moral evaluation and action.

When philosophical thinking encounters silences instead of speculative results, and there is a moral requirement not to try and think conceptually about those silences, to withdraw—"to know not to know," as Derrida puts it—and when it arrives, or is led to the verge of nonpaths—abysses, lacunae, antinomies, and tears—and comes up against the boundaries of its possibility, Lyotard, following Levinas, invites philosophy to listen. His ethical thought is first and foremost an exercise in listening. What is at stake is the theme of being an ethical addressee.

In a world where silences replace (speculative) results, obligation, from a Lyotardian perspective, is a matter both of being affected by quasi-phrases of feelings and sentiments, whose occurrence produces a special situation of attentiveness that demands listening, and of a moral obligation toward them. This listening is the only way not to reproduce speculative logic, and the only way that does not deal with the disaster speculatively.[32]

I argue that Lyotard deals with obligation "after Auschwitz" from within this situation of listening. He constantly feels that the signs are leaving their mark on him, that he is required to listen, and that he is affected. Out of his concern with "Auschwitz," a moral axis is forged in his ethical thought that connects silence, voice, hostage, listening, sign, sentiment, and obligation. These concepts are central components of a Lyotardian ethics.

This platform of sensitivity sheds light on the emergence and the status of the Voice in Lyotard's discussion of obligation, and constructs the moral agenda of Lyotard's philosophy. This agenda revolves around issues that relate to the comprehension of and listening to the ethical call, and to the distinction between the ethical voice (the Voice) and other voices that also demand their addressee's obligation, from the voice that commanded Abraham to sacrifice his son to the voice that commanded the Nazi to send the Jew to his death. It also relates to an analysis of the linguistic-ethical characteristics that enable these voices to be distinguished from one another.

In keeping with Lyotard's thinking, the ethical distinctions gradually emerge from his linguistic-ethical analysis of the occurrence of the prescriptive phrase—an analysis that focuses on understanding the linguistic structure of the experience of being called to obligation, and on mapping the linguistic-ethical boundaries of that experience. The aim of this is to locate the signs that might indicate the constitution of an ethical attitude to the Voice (as opposed to other possible modes of attitude to the voice), or of an ethical grasp by the Voice; to make the structure of attentiveness incorporated with the ethical experience of the Voice more accurate; and mainly, to try to refine the Voice's language—that which the Voice cannot say, the powers and abilities that it cannot arouse in its addressee, the overcomings or abstentions that it cannot demand of him, the authorizations that it cannot ratify. What is at stake here is the integrity and the rectitude of listening to the Voice. Slowly, the conditions for being addressed ethically are beginning to emerge, along with the figure of the Lyotardian obligated "I"—that which follows the collapse of the speculative self.

At the very beginning of the discussion of "obligation" in *The Differend*—a chapter that in many ways is the culmination of the book's ethical discussion—Lyotard asserts, following Levinas, that the ethical obligated "I" is the addressee of a call that includes a prescription, or a figure of a "you" that is being called, which finds itself held—like a hostage—in a heteroautonomous Voice that he cannot fully understand or answer, but which he cannot fully exempt himself from either—a Voice that calls for his obligation to it and demands that he be affected by it.

The whispering of the Voice is empty; it does not indicate what the obligation is, but only that the "I" must respond, that he is indebted. The debt that is at stake in the situation of obligation is not only the obligation to remember and to testify to what was "there," or the obligation "to there".

> The voice, which cannot even be heard, demands that your actions be honest and that your judgment be just. You hear it without hearing it, you cannot understand it, it says nothing clear, apart from that "you must" and that "you must listen." To listen means: to tell yourself what the voice wants to say, to transcribe it and to make it public in just judgments and honest actions.[33]

This constitutive emptiness of the Voice emerges from the linguistic analysis of the experience of being called by the Voice, or of the occurrence of the prescriptive phrase. This analysis suggests that at the point of being called to obligation, the obligated "I" finds itself thrown to the instance of the "you" of the prescriptive phrase. The position of the addressor of that phrase is left totally empty.[34]

As Lyotard emphasizes, these linguistic-structural conditions are the distinguishing conditions of the ethical situation, in contrast to the cognitive situation. As such, they are the first signs that are able to signal to the ethical addressee of the voice that the situation of obligation is being opened up. The ethical addressee cannot therefore ratify his ethical decision as to whether to answer the Voice or to seal himself off from it, from the source of the Voice—after all, the position of the addressor is empty—or from its content—after all, the Voice's empty whisper says only to its addressee: "You must …" "You must listen …" "You are indebted …"

Unlike the Hegelian subject, who is gradually filled through the movement of the Spirit's journey and expands until he reaches full totality, the Lyotardian ethical addressee, similarly to that of Levinas, is a figure that is being positioned, at the moment of the ethical summons, as someone who lacks all attributes and predicates—only as a "you"—bereft, in Lyotard's terms, of any of the radiance of its culture, and detached or deprived of all its property, its intellectual abilities and positions of power and authority, and of all its purposes "for itself," with its defenses dismantled—expelled from itself, as Levinas puts it.[35] From an ethical point of view, this situation of dismantling and laying bare in the face of the ethical summons is crucial, as it constructs the ethical addressee as a platform of defenseless exposure to the Voice that demands his obligation and as being able to be affected by the Voice.

The Lyotardian ethical addressee (similarly to the Levinasian one) is here called upon to make a different kind of effort from that of conscious control and conceptual acknowledgment. It is not about more focused attention; what is required is preparedness for another (nonspeculative) mode, not of ability or power or causality. He must approach the Voice ascetically, and, first and foremost, to strip himself of his concepts—to strip himself as one enters a monastic order—to be passible (beyond the contradiction of passive-active), and to allow himself to be touched and guided by signs of emotion.

This is not a situation of freedom, and it is certainly not a situation that one can gain speculative profit from. It is a situation that creates an unrelenting sentiment of debt, of obligation. Speculators would no doubt remove themselves from this situation. To reverse this formulation, we might say that these modes of the Lyotardian obligated "I" embody and establish the final halt of the Hegelian speculative dialectic at "Auschwitz." My argument is that this is an ethical thought that Hegelian speculative thought cannot reincorporate within itself; in Hegelian speculative thought there is not, and cannot be, a "we" comprised of "hostages" who reach up to voices that they cannot totally understand, reach, or reconcile; there is not, and cannot be, room in this thought for an ethical prescription that demands unending listening on the part of its addressee and that forbids him from thinking that he has deciphered its sense and fulfilled his obligation to it; there is not, and cannot be, room in this thought for an ethical addressee whose relationship with the Voice is not one of understanding, but rather one of subjugation to expropriation and ownership by the Voice (whose characteristics are those of total otherness).

The speculative dialectic also cannot preserve, cancel, or sublate that which lacks all attributes and predicates, that which does not allow itself to be conjugated in the first or the third person (singular or plural), because it has to be left only at the touchable pole of the address of the ethical call. In this condition, the ethical "I" (and the philosopher) has no (linguistic, philosophical, and moral) means of rediverting the direction of the ethical movement, or, at most, of turning it into a moment of loss—for a moment—and recovery and growth (*Aufhebung*) of the self. This is an ethical philosophy that cannot, therefore, be the speculative result of "Auschwitz."

In contradistinction to the Hegelian etymology of *Aufhebung* (negation-preservation-sublation)—an etymology that may represent the final depletion of modern philosophy—a different kind of etymology might be taking shape: emptying/being touched (by the Voice)/listening. It should be noted that this does not imply foregoing thought or the passing of judgment but rather, or so I argue, the (Lyotardian) formulation of the conditions of possibility of ethical thinking and judgment.

Therefore, what follows the (speculative) subject is first and foremost an affected, emptied, touched, held, passible, and receptive figure that is constituted in certain conditions of attentiveness. It is a figure of (sentimental) "you," and not one of an "I" that thinks, holds, appropriates, accumulates, cancels-preserves-elevates, softens, reconciles, and eases. This figure stands in front of the Voice in a state of unfathomable (ethical) loneliness, and not as a member of a community of presignified addressees and addressors, or of a presignified "we."

The call of the Voice reaches him alone through an enigmatic sense of "you must," without being able to share this feeling with other moral addressees. The uniqueness of the ethical address prevents it from lingering in the bosom of an ethical community, or from trying to create such a community, and to appropriate the asymmetrical relationship of the "I-you" within a "we" that is comprised of a community of those who make others obligated and those who are obligated, who can be replaced by one another (moving from "me" to "we"). The price of doing so is to transgress the ethical relationship. The address, says Derrida, is always singular and unique, idiomatic.

Herein lies the constitutive gap between the ethical phrase and the political phrase, or between the idiomatic (ethical) prescription and the "normed" (political) prescription—which is formulated as a normative law—and between ethical responsibility and political responsibility. As the addressee of the normative law, the obligated "I" can belong to a political community, but not to an ethical community—as there is no such community. As Lyotard puts it: "However, the Voice that says simply: 'be just' abandons you to the desert, throws you into a cruel anguish."[36]

The Lyotardian ethical addressee thus remains the only witness of the event. He must judge his obligation to the Voice in solitude, "from nowhere and in nobody's name," and he must know that every linkage of the Voice to a certain source, to a specific addressor, or to certain content, is his interpretation of the voice (which is entirely his responsibility)—it is his ethical decision about how he should respond to the Voice.

However, and precisely because of that, the experience of being called to obligation requires the "I's" ethical watchfulness and judgment; that is, not every call to obligation is an ethical call, not every prescriptive phrase is an ethical phrase, not every feeling of obligation is an ethical feeling. Just as the ethical addressee finds himself in the grasp of a voice instructing him, "You must," so Abraham hears a voice telling him, "You must" (sacrifice your son), and the Nazi/executioner hears a voice telling him, "You must" (kill the Jew).

As an ethical addressee, the "I" that finds itself in the grasp of the Voice demanding its obligation must thus suspend the immediacy of its response to that Voice and first of all confront the evasive and deceptive nature of the Voice. No one can do that in its place, or at its side (not even the moral philosopher writing about that relationship), for he is the sole addressee of the Voice that grasps him.[37]

If the obligated "I" wishes to find itself in the ethical space of the Voice, it must withstand the temptation to make the Voice itself talk directly and visibly. It must also withstand the temptation to give the Voice an image. The Voice has no embodiment or incarnation, not in the form of God, and not in the form of any kind of messenger. It must also know that it cannot pass from the "you must" of the prescriptive phrase to the "I know" of the knowledge phrase without transgressing the ethical phrase and turning it into a cognitive one.

Listening is not about knowing—there is no way of knowing how to listen correctly to the Voice (nor is there any way of instructing others as to how to listen to it).[38] The Voice forbids—and even prevents—its addressee from identifying with it or even gaining from it. In the ethical space of the Voice there can be no occupation, no empire can be built, no Third Reich will arise, there can be no homeland from the sea to the River Jordan.

The ethical addressee can thus only hear that the Voice wants something from him—to experience its intransigence. Ethics is possible for as long as the strangeness of the Voice is preserved, and at the cost of that preservation. "'Listen' aims at an attitude of the one who is addressed rather some signification. What must be done, thought, and so forth thus remains to be invented."[39] So many dangers, so many temptations, so many concerns.

From the moment that an ethical relationship to the Voice is constituted, it tears the biography of the obligated "I" into two—before listening and afterward. While the Voice's empty whispering, or its constituting withdrawal, offers a large number of varied ways to fulfill the obligation, or to respond to the voice it simultaneously ties the response—whatever that may be—to an immanent doubt, or to a penetrative uncertainty: the addressee can never know whether he still has an ethical obligation to the Voice. This doubt forces him to try and answer its call over and over again, but he must never think that he has succeeded. This sense of failure, which is not a deficiency in attentiveness but rather its integrity, is immanent to the Lyotardian experience of being ethically obligated.

From this point on, the Lyotardian ethical addressee becomes a hostage to the Voice. He is constantly subject to its grasp, and to the possibility that it will demand that he redeem the remainder of his debt; his existence (as a debtor) is haunted by his obsession with the Voice. Even if the addressee thinks that he has eradicated that debt, or that it has been wiped clean, the Voice will draw back from its besieging grasp and will whisper its empty but troubling whisper over and again: "You will not be able, you will not know, you will not conquer, you will not overcome, you will not reach reconciliation and acceptance, you cannot, but you must (*tu es oblige*) try to listen." Thus, the Voice will come back and subject him once more to its jurisdiction.

This implies that what we have here is the existential connection of the Lyotardian ethical addressee to the voices. The moral test of the obligated "I" primarily concerns its ability to take upon itself the "facticity" of the moral debt, on its "power" to bear and preserve his situation as having a debt that can never be paid off, or on his moral preparedness to preserve a constant affinity with the debt in its life and to repel any temptation of emancipation from the voice. The Lyotardian moral debt (like that of Levinas) thus becomes a lifelong debt. This lifelong debt is not only a debt in relation to "Auschwitz," but also an ethical debt under present conditions: a debt to those wrongs that can still be prevented (through just deeds and judgments), to sufferings that can still be alleviated, to those who can still be saved.

It is my contention that these outlines of Lyotardian ethics embody a profound turning point in ethical thought "after Auschwitz"; in its concerns, its gestures, its central ethical concepts, and its ethical-linguistic figures. They also embody the depth of the detachment of Lyotard's ethical thought from Hegelian speculative thought and Lyotard's attempt to establish its final stopping point in a world "after Auschwitz." This is an ethical thought that speculative thought cannot contain. In speculative thought based in Hegel, there are not, nor can there be, addressees who are "hostages," chained to voices that cannot be fully understood, attained, or reconciled with; in this thought there is not, nor can there be, a place for ethical phrases that demand of their addressees unending listening and forbid them from thinking that they have succeeded in deciphering their meaning and repaying their debt; also, there is not, and there cannot be, room for ethical addressees whose attitude to the Voice is not one of understanding but rather of being able to be expropriated, to be passible (affectivity), and to be owned by it (a voice that has the characteristics of total otherness).

Moral philosophy thus finds itself at a constitutive turning point whose shock waves must necessarily reach the republican political discourse. Therefore, we should also discuss the moral obligation to rethink the political "we" that lives in the world "after Auschwitz," and mostly, I argue, the more cautious, alert, and fragile use of the term "we." We must think about a "we" that is constantly and unrelentingly aware of its potential instability and of its being potentially divided. Such a "we" will identify itself based on the lack of identity between the legislator and the obligated, or based on the potential gap between them, and will strive to defend this lack of identity and will not try to overcome or erase it (by including those who prefer to remain in the standpoint of the third party and not be part of this "we," or by distancing them). It is not only a "we" that accepts the constant uncertainty surrounding all aspects of its possible identity (because of this potential gap), but also a "we" that sees it as a constitutive (and worthy) part of its identity.

An Ending

Lyotard's efforts at thinking about obligation in a world "after Auschwitz," along with his endeavors to detach himself from Hegelian speculative thought—from its greed, its self-enjoyment, its power, and its occupations—can elucidate the figure of Lyotardian ethical thought. More broadly, it can clarify the figure of contemporary Continental thought—its philosophical gestures, its concerns, its language, and the ethical concepts at its center. These efforts lead Lyotard's philosophy to take the shape of an ethics of moral attentiveness and moral response—an ethics that places at its center the themes of being the ethical addressee of the Voice demanding our obligation, and of the infinite debt to that Voice.

The radical and heteronymous nature of the Lyotardian ethical call (similarly to that of Levinas) and the impossibility of fully and finally answering it explains the image of this ethics, which is in principle alert, anxious, and trembling. It is perpetually in a state of unrest, it can never attain completion, reach its end, a Result. It also explains the ethical figures of this ethics, those that take the place of the speculative subject—sentimental figures, lonely, passible, held, touched, haunted, hesitant, concerned and restless figures, figures of addressees that are being called—aimed at a life of perpetually listening to Voices that cannot be understood, or to be prepared for them, as they demand their obligation to them.

It is important to emphasize that this is not a paralyzing anxiety. Instead, the ethical dimension lies precisely in the hesitation or doubt that will always be etched into every decision that the "I" makes about how it responds to the Voice, or in the philosophy that will always tremble—trembling as a philosophical-moral horizon. From a speculative point of view, which strives to utterly clarify philosophy to itself, this is a negative paralysis. From the point of view of Lyotardian (and Levinasian) philosophy, this troublesomeness is an expression of probity, of honesty, of modesty, and of preparedness. As Lyotard would say, this is the strength of the weak.

To conclude, I would like to return to the summons that, I argue, has been opened up to moral (and political) philosophy by the absolute end of the "beautiful death" at "Auschwitz"—the summons to rethink the reason that constructs the linkage of the "we" of the group, the community, the nation, or the test of membership (*commonium*) in a (or any) community. I would like to ask: Who is the "we" that follows the breakdown of the speculative concept of "we" in "Auschwitz"? Who is the "we" that lives in the world "after the disaster"?

Each in their own way, and each with their own terminology, Lyotard, Levinas, and Derrida all try to offer a possible answer to that question. I shall offer my answer using words from Paul Celan's poem "Vast, Glowing Vault,"[40] and in the spirit of contemporary French philosophy.

After the most "pronounced interruption," or "abyssal duration of a blank silence, like a disjointed aphorism," as Derrida elegantly puts it,[41] one single sentence, "isolated, islanded," dissociated and separated from all the verses before, "supports itself, carries itself all alone" and concludes the poem like its last breath, "the expiration of the poem," at the end of the world—where "no world can any longer support us, serve as mediation, as ground, as earth, as foundation or as alibi"—"pronounced like a sentence, in the form of a sigh or a verdict" of another time:

"The World is gone, I must carry you."

Notes

1. We must distinguish between a result and a speculative result (Result). The implications of this distinction will become clear in the course of the following discussion.

2. Theodor Adorno, *Negative Dialectics*, trans. E. B. Ashton (London: Routledge, 1973), 361.

3. Jean-François Lyotard, *The Differend: Phrases in Dispute*, trans. Georges Van Den Abbeele (Minneapolis: University of Minnesota Press, 1988), 88.

4. Maurice Blanchot, *The Writing of the Disaster*, trans. Ann Smock (Lincoln: University of Nebraska Press, 1986), 2, 36.

5. It should be stressed that not everybody who declares "the end of speculation" actually succeeds in throwing off its shackles, and, in the context of the current discussion, succeeds in thinking about obligation while philosophically, morally, and linguistically detaching himself from any linkage with the speculative dialectic. The mechanisms of the speculative discourse are widespread in everyday language and hold on to it by means of a multitude of hidden strings, and the speculative logic is also implicitly bedded in non-Hegelian thought, even that which seeks to negate and disprove it, and thus extract itself from it. This grasp on language and thought is especially notable in the reactions of (philosophical, social, religious, and political) thought to a disaster—any disaster at all.

6. If, as Levinas argued, for the philosopher, determining his position in relation to Hegel is parallel to the relationship between the weaver and his loom before he starts his work, what then happens to philosophy when it loses its primary tool? Lyotard adds to Levinas's question and wonders, what might philosophy look like when it has lost its most significant (modern) gesture—the speculative phrase?

7. This, I argue, is also the complex status of "Auschwitz" in Lyotard's *Differend*.

8. Adorno, *Negative Dialectics*, 29.

9. In her text "Lyotard's and Derrida's 'Catastrophist Phenomenology,'" Michal Ben-Naftali follows Dominick LaCapra, who recognized the mourning sensibility that pervades several postmodernist writings, and suggests that they indicate a posttraumatic fixation, which prevents these thinkers from moving on with life, as if compelling them to repeat the trauma they experienced, directly or indirectly. Following LaCapra, Ben-Naftali asks: Why indeed were Lyotard (and Derrida) so determined to mourn? To whom is their mourning addressed? What are the ethical implications of the melancholic mournful subjectivity that they constitute? Ben-Naftali develops further LaCapra's criticism. She connects the notion of "catastrophe" and "mourning" and discusses what she calls the "catastrophist phenomenology" of Lyotard and Derrida.

The current discussion aims to suggest a different interpretation of the complex and tensed status of "Auschwitz" in Lyotard's ethical thought and a different elaboration of the ways it carries upon itself the burden of the disaster named "Auschwitz." Though "Auschwitz" is the paradigm of the differend, Lyotard posits "Auschwitz" within and in continuation of discussions analyzing everyday discursive situations, and within and in continuation of discussions dealing with philosophical texts, all the while examining it in light of the "essential and current concerns" of his discourse, such as the problem of linguistic representation, the limits of the speculative discourse, the problematics of procedures for proving reality and judgmental procedures of the cognitive discourse, the problem of sacrifice, the question regarding the authority of the phrase of the norm, and the status of the concept of "beautiful death" in current republican discourse. The discussion of "Auschwitz" makes constant reference to problems of suffering, injustice, evil, and victimization that become constituted in the linguistic practices of everyday reality. As Lyotard emphasizes, the question of "Auschwitz" is immediately the question of "after Auschwitz." The second part of this chapter will question Ben-Naftali's interpretation of Lyotard's ethical thought as a "catastrophist phenomenology" and as a work of mourning. The discussion will try to establish the claim that although Lyotard's ethical thought is constituted under the heavy shadow of the trauma of the past, it orients itself—not only as a work of testimony and mourning—to the conditions of the present. Alongside such work of mourning that focuses on a disaster that already took place, and on the debt of memory and testimony to its victims, such an ethics seeks to direct its eyes and ears toward the future, striving to answer a Voice that comes from the future. "Auschwitz" would be a crucial reference point for such a Lyotardian ethics, although certainly not its only or even final point of reference. See Michal Ben-Naftali, "Lyotard's and Derrida's 'Catastrophist Phenomenology,'" in *Theoretical Interpretations of the Holocaust,* ed. Dan Stone (Amsterdam and Atlanta, GA: Rodopi, 2001), 169–204.

10. See Jacques Derrida, "From Restricted to General Economy: A Hegelianism without Reserve," in *Writing and Difference,* trans. Alan Bass (Chicago: University of Chicago Press, 1978), 327–28.

11. G. W. Hegel, *Preface to the Phenomenology of Spirit* [in Hebrew] (Jerusalem: Magness Press, 1996), 19.

12. We should clarify that Hegel also acknowledges the existence of the purposeless and arbitrary death that lacks all meaning—an empty negativity with nothing positive in it, with nothing that fills it with content. In *Phenomenology of Spirit* he describes this death as the coldest and cruelest death of all (a death which, according to the prevalent interpretation, refers to the horrors and the terror of the French Revolution). However, Hegelian logic dialectically annuls the purposeless and superfluousness of this death and promises the continuity of the spirit and its development into a higher stage (in the moral sense): that of the Moral Spirit. See G. W. Hegel, *Phenomenology of Spirit,* trans. A. V. Miller (Oxford: Clarendon Press, 1977), § 595, p. 363.

13. In Christianity, the concept of "communion" has a number of valued meanings. First and foremost it is associated with the Christian ceremony in which believers commune in order to remember Jesus's sacrifice and to examine their own hearts. The same principled connection between participation, community, and sacrifice can also be found in the Western republican discourse's perception of political obligation. Or to reverse this formulation: the republican notion of participation and community has a perpetual debt to sacrifice.

14. Lyotard, *The Differend,* 100. It should be stressed that the "beautiful death," as an idea that defines the ultimate test of belonging and commitment to a community (in its speculative sense), is not an idea that derives from Hegel or Hegelian speculative philosophy. In the Platonic dialogue *Menexos,* for instance, Plato would appear to be writing a satire of the concept of the "beautiful death," as represented in the exalting funeral orations to heroes who fell in battle. Actually, though, he wishes to further reinforce the concept and its standing as the exclusive determinant of belonging to the community of "fine" Athenian citizens. The speech delivered by Socrates in the dialogue *Phaedon* is also a canonical example of a "beautiful death." See Plato, *Menexos,* in *Plato's Writings* [in Hebrew], vol. 1, trans. Yosef G. Liebes (Tel Aviv: Schocken, 1969), 397; Plato, *Phaedo, Plato's Writings* [in Hebrew], vol. 2, trans. Yosef G. Liebes (Tel Aviv: Schocken, 1979), 16, 20–23.

15. In the republican discourse, death is prescribed as an alternative to another obligation (civic duty, military glory, freedom) if the latter is revealed to be impracticable.

16. This "we" also makes it possible for one to die both on command and "freely" or "knowingly."

17. This is not similar to the death of millions of soldiers in the trenches.

18. Lyotard, *The Differend,* 101.

19. The word "Holocaust" is precisely a speculative attempt to reappropriate that death, to give it meaning and a purpose, to turn it into a "beautiful death." However, as Lyotard and Agamben argue, because there is no element of sacrifice in that disaster, it is absurd to use the word "Holocaust" for what the Jews call the Shoah. "What was burnt in the ovens of extermination was not any kind of good (some possession) to be given up to God." See Jean-François Lyotard and Eberhard Gruber, *The Hyphen: Between Judaism and Christianity,* trans. Pascale-Anne Brault (New York: Humanity Books, 1999), 10, 83.

20. Primo Levi's concept of the "gray area," as symbolizing the arena of death in the world of the camps, illuminates another aspect of the argument that the death called "Auschwitz" gave its victims no way of dying a "beautiful death." I am referring here to the disintegration of the possibility of creating a shared and stable "we," even among the victims—a "we" that the victims could have sacrificed their lives for in order to protect its name—and, first and foremost, the disintegration of the possibility to distinguish between the human—that which is capable of sac-

rifice—and the inhuman. See Primo Levi, *The Drowned and the Saved* [in Hebrew] (Tel Aviv: Am Oved, 1997), 27–53.

21. This does not imply disproving the concept of the "beautiful death"—a move that can be easily incorporated within the Hegelian speculative discourse—but rather the permanent danger of contamination of the concept of the "beautiful death."

22. Recall that the name "Auschwitz" appears here in quote marks because the collapse of the concept of the "beautiful death" is a model of the failure of this concept in principle. As such, it does not refer to, or is not limited to, the specific disaster of Auschwitz (as a historical event).

23. Jacques Derrida, *The Gift of Death* [in Hebrew] (Tel Aviv: Resling, 2008), 19.

24. Ibid., 19, 50; Jean-Luc Nancy, "The Unsacrificeable," *Yale French Studies* 79 (1991): 20–38.

25. This disturbance lies at the focal point of Derrida's discussion in *The Gift of Death* and, in other senses, is also central to Lyotard's discussion of "obligation" in *The Differend*.

26. I thank Michal Givoni for sharpening this point for me in her important comments on this text.

27. "Does not the relationship to the other in sacrifice, in which the death of the other preoccupies the human being-there before his own death, indicates precisely a beyond ontology—or a before ontology—while at the same time also determining—or revealing—a responsibility for the other, and through that responsibility a human 'I' that is neither the substantial identity of the subject nor the Eigntlichkeit in the 'mineness' of being? ... A uniqueness of the choseness!" Emmanuel Levinas, "Dying for ... ," in *Entre nous: Thinking-of-the-Other*, trans. Michael B. Smith and Barbara Harshav (New York: Columbia University Press, 1998), 217.

28. Jacques Derrida, *Monolingualism of the Other, or the Prosthesis of Origin,* trans. Patrick Mensah (Stanford, CA: Stanford University Press, 1998), 14–15.

29. "In the concentration camps, there would have been no subject in the first-person plural. In the absence of such a subject, there would remain 'after Auschwitz' no subject, no Selbst which would prevail upon itself to name itself in naming 'Auschwitz.' No phrase inflected in this person would be possible: we did this, we felt that." Lyotard, *The Differend*, 97–98.

30. Maurice Blanchot, *The Writing of the Disaster.* Trans. Ann Smock (Lincoln: University of Nebraska Press, 1986), 27.

31. In his own distinct way, Levinas also strives to detach himself from speculative thinking, or to think about the "I's" responsibility to "the other" in a way that is totally disconnected from the speculative discourse. This endeavor stands at the center of Levinas's discussion in *Otherwise than Being or Beyond Essence* (Dordrecht: Kluwer Academic Publishers, 1991), 112.

32. Lyotard also establishes the status of sentiments as phrases in a text that complements *The Differend*. In this discussion, Lyotard deals with the linguistic-moral-philosophical status of sentiments that cannot be articulated at all, that are not directed to any specific address, and that cannot be deciphered or authoritatively said to have one meaning or another—sentiments that indicate an affective situation of the "I," or a feeling of being touched and held by an internal voice of heteroautonomous origins, a voice that cannot be understood in advance, that one cannot be ready for, or prepare oneself for with a conceptual scheme. The question here is of the moral obligation toward these nonexpressed voices, where the silences that signify them are not silences waiting to be formulated in a phrase, when the right idiom is found, and every attempt at attributing meaning to them, and to impose argumentation on them, creates radical evil, according to Lyotard. See Lyotard, *The Differend*, 57; Jean-François Lyotard, "La Phrase-affect (D'un supplement au Differend)," in *Misere de La Philosophie* (Paris: Galilee, 2000), 43–55.

33. Jean-François Lyotard, "Anamnesis of the Visible" [in Hebrew], *Studio*, no. 99 (December–January 1998–99): 30. All translations are the author's.

34. Lyotard, *The Differend*, 115.

35. Levinas, *Otherwise than Being or Beyond Essence*, 48–49.

36. The creation of symmetry between the addressor and the addressee creates a political (republican) community, but not an ethical one. See Lyotard, "Anamnesis of the Visible," 32.

37. Because of the limitations of this discussion, I shall briefly note that at this point a significant gap opens up between the ethical thought of Lyotard and Levinas. Unlike Levinas, Lyotard

does not attribute an immediate moral value to the experience of being called by the Voice, and he does not attribute the source of the Voice to an other. I maintain that the Lyotardian ethical addressee, unlike the Levinasian one, is called upon to repay (over and over again) his debt to the Voice of the ethical law, which takes the place of the Levinasian other. This voice thus takes on the attributes of the Levinasian other.

38. Lyotard and Gruber, *The Hyphen*, 79.
39. Ibid., 80.
40. Paul Celan, "Vast, Glowing Vault", in: Jacques Derrida, "Rams: Uninterrupted Dialogues—Between Two Infinities, the Poem," in *Sovereignties in Question: The Poetics of Paul Celan* (New York: Fordham University Press, 2005), 141.
41. Jacques Derrida, "Rams: Uninterrupted Dialogues—Between Two Infinities, the Poem," in *Sovereignties in Question: The Poetics of Paul Celan* (New York: Fordham University Press, 2005), 148, 158.

Bibliography

Adorno, Theodor. *Negative Dialectics*. Translated by E. B. Ashton. London and New York: Routledge, 2006.
Ben-Naftali, Michal. "Lyotard's and Derrida's 'Catastrophist Phenomenology.'" In *Theoretical Interpretations of the Holocaust,* ed. Dan Stone, 169–204. Amsterdam and Atlanta, GA: Rodopi, 2001.
Blanchot, Maurice. *The Writing of the Disaster*. Translated by Ann Smock. Lincoln: University of Nebraska Press, 1986.
Derrida, Jacques. "From Restricted to General Economy: A Hegelianism without Reserve." In *Writing and Difference,* trans. Alan Bass, 251–341. Chicago: University of Chicago Press, 1978.
———. *The Gift of Death* [in Hebrew]. Tel Aviv: Resling, 2008.
———. *Monolingualism of the Other, or the Prosthesis of Origin*. Translated by Patrick Mensah. Stanford, CA: Stanford University Press, 1998.
———. "Rams: Uninterrupted Dialogues—Between Two Infinities, the Poem." In *Sovereignties in Question: The Poetics of Paul Celan,* ed. Thomas Dutoit and Outi Pasanen, 135–64. New York: Fordham University Press, 2005.
Hegel, G. W. *Phenomenology of Spirit*. Translated by A. V. Miller. Oxford: Clarendon Press, 1977.
———. *Preface to the Phenomenology of Spirit* [in Hebrew]. Jerusalem: Magness Press, 1996.
Levi, Primo. *The Drowned and the Saved* [in Hebrew]. Tel Aviv: Am Oved, 1997.
Levinas, Emmanuel. "Dying for …" In *Entre nous: Thinking-of-the-Other,* trans. Michael B. Smith and Barbara Harshav, 207–17. New York: Columbia University Press, 1998.
———. *Otherwise than Being or Beyond Essence*. Translated by Alphonso Lingis. Dordrecht: Kluwer Academic Publishers, 1991.
Lyotard, Jean-François. "Anamnesis of the Visible" [in Hebrew]. *Studio,* no. 99 (December–January 1998–99): 26–35.
———. *The Differend: Phrases in Dispute*. Translated by Georges Van Den Abbeele. Minneapolis: University of Minnesota Press, 1988.
———. "La Phrase-affect (D'un supplement au Differend)." In *Misere de La Philosophie,* 43–55. Paris: Galilee, 2000.
Lyotard, Jean-François, and Eberhard Gruber. *The Hyphen: Between Judaism and Christianity*. Translated by Pascale-Anne Brault. New York: Humanity Books, 1999.
Nancy, Jean-Luc. "The Unsacrificeable." *Yale French Studies* 79 (1991): 20–38.
Plato. *Menexos*. In *Plato's Writings* [in Hebrew], vol. 1, trans. Yosef G. Liebes. Tel Aviv: Schocken, 1969.
———. *Phaedo*. In *Plato's Writings* [in Hebrew], vol. 2, trans. Yosef G. Liebes. Tel Aviv: Schocken, 1979.

CHAPTER 6

Cosmopolitan Body
The Holocaust as Route to the Globally Human

NIGEL RAPPORT

Introduction: Memory, Body, Symbol

My approach is a phenomenological one. Memory is an embodied phenomenon, individual, personal. There can be no collective or shared memory any more than there can be a collective or shared experience, or a collective or shared interpretation of symbolic phenomena such as words in a conversation or a musical performance or a behavioral gesture. Perception, interpretation, and recollection are properties of bodies. The distinction between bodies and languages is a fundamental one: the ontological and atomistic nature of the former as distinct from the fictional (constructed) and mediatory qualities of the latter. When my wife tells me that my memory is erroneous—that it was our daughter and not our son who accompanied us to Israel in 1999—she intervenes in an ongoing meditation that I have with myself. I might admit that she is correct, but nevertheless her intervention is dependent on the weight I afford it, whereas the personal (and possibly unreliable) complex of my consciousness is continuous and unavoidable. I might endeavor to balance the evanescence of her words, their lightness, against the intrinsic ground of my memory-feelings. It is not that bodies and languages do not connect, but rather that the connection is epiphenomenal. The language that connects my wife's memory with my own has no being, no will of its own, and is dependent on the significance I accord to its symbolic forms. At the same time, however, I can assume that a commensurate ground is being occupied by my wife: her body, with its obvious physical presence and its hidden conscious processes, abuts my own. The

Notes for this section begin on page 115.

bodiliness of memory is a human universal, I conclude: we are united in our bodily separations.

What is it to posit a widespread, globalizing memory of the Holocaust? This must be largely vicarious, fictional. There may be widespread written histories of the Holocaust, and built memorials to it and spoken declarations concerning it, but there can be no universal memories. One does not remember something one did not experience, while experience, even of the apparently "same" event, will remain inevitably individual and personal. The only universality possibly possessed by the Holocaust concerns its symbolic usage. As a figure of speech, a ritual performance, a storied account, it reaches global extents. What may be the value of such universal symbolization? What connection might we endeavor to effect between a bodily knowing of the Holocaust as experience and memory and its deployment as a symbol in conversational exchange? These are the questions I treat.

The material I centrally address in search of answers is Imre Kertesz's novel *Fateless*, the story of a teenaged boy, György Köves, whose incarceration in the Nazi concentration camps of Zeitz, Auschwitz, and Buchenwald loosely follows Kertesz's own remembered experiences. Against this I set brief accounts of experiences of my own of visiting contemporary Holocaust memorials, including the site of Auschwitz itself in present-day Oświęcim, Poland. I have in the past been exercised by the imagination of retracing Kertesz's steps through a walking of my own, interrogating my right to make a Holocaust "testimonial."[1] In this chapter I revisit Kertesz's writing and my own walking with a different end in mind.

I have been aware, in Britain, of the public distaste of singling out the "Jewish" experience of the Holocaust as being something either especially relevant or (paradoxically) especially unique. (Is not continuing discourse on the Holocaust a poor excuse for the existence of Israel—an obfuscation of colonialism, past and present?) As a "widespread globalizing memory," the Holocaust must be said to assume the character of a floating signifier, devoid of essence, so disparate and contested is its current meaning—including contestation of its very historical existence. It represents a paradoxical object: supposedly global yet divorced from its direct subjects, international and transnational; a cataclysm yet affording a certain cachet or cultural capital to its surviving victims; a global singularity in an age of "postmodern" aversion to universalizing claims and grand narrative; a teleological site in which human behavior may be subjected to an all-encompassing standard of evaluation; a sourcebook or manual of "politically correct" responses. My argument will be that the very elusiveness and ambiguity of "the Holocaust" as a symbol may be a virtue. There is an immensity here with which we may perform "cosmopolitan" work: lodge human diversity, disparateness, and contrariety in an inclusive fashion. Humanity meets here. Hopes and fears, arguments over history and futurity, selfhood and otherness: all are variously contained, "remembered," their contradictoriness intact. "The

Holocaust" can serve as a symbol in whose terms a global conversation may be conducted. The meetings may not be of opinions or experiences or memories, or even meanings, so much as a mere "form of life," in Wittgenstein's terms;[2] but it is a singular, inclusive form all the same.

"Everything human resolves itself finally into contradictions"

In 1985 the novelist Milan Kundera received the Jerusalem Prize and delivered a lecture entitled "The Novel and Europe" at the Hebrew University. "Exiled from their land of origin and thus lifted above nationalist passions," Kundera began, "the great Jewish figures have always shown an exceptional feeling for ... a Europe conceived not as territory but as culture"; it is thus that Israel, the little Jewish homeland finally regained, feels to Kundera like "the true heart of Europe—a peculiar heart located outside the body."[3]

Warming to his theme, however, it becomes clear that the "soul" of Europe is the true treasure for Kundera, and this was to be found in the art form of the novel. In *Don Quixote,* its earliest classic exemplar, Cervantes has his eponymous hero set forth into a world from which God was departing as arbiter of values and meaning and order. It was a fearsome world of ambiguous, myriad, contingent truths—our post-Enlightenment world of the modern era—where the only certain wisdom concerned uncertainty. The novel was image and model of this world, embodying the ambiguities of truth: an "ironic art," undeclaring absolute truth. The creation of this amoral terrain was a European invention of enormous significance, Kundera elaborates. In its history, the novel has ensured that we do not forget the situatedness of being, while exhibiting a continuing, existential passion for knowledge and claiming for itself a radical autonomy to say all it might know about the human condition. As a social institution or procedure, the novel insisted on eschewing final moral judgment: it insisted on describing and expressing over and against a conventional evaluation. Moreover, fictional characters appeared in the novel conceived of not as the function of a preexistent truth or even representatives of objective laws, but as autonomous beings grounded in their own moral universes, as individuals. Indeed:

> The novel is the imaginary paradise of individuals. It is the territory where no-one possess the truth ... but where everyone has the right to be understood.... That imaginative realm of tolerance was born with modern Europe, it is the very image of Europe—or at least our dream of Europe, a dream many times betrayed but nonetheless strong enough to unite us all in the fraternity that stretches far beyond the little European continent.[4]

It is the case, however—and has been since Cervantes—that this world of tolerance is fragile and perishable, Kundera asserts. "European culture" is under threat today from within and without, emblemized by attacks on what is most precious about it: its novel respect for the individual, for original thought and expression, for the right to an inviolable personal preserve. Theocracy goes to war against the modern era as fascism did before it, targeting its most representative creation—freedom of expression—and putting in its place a fixed, closed, institutionalized world that is overseen by dogmatic and doctrinal supreme judgments. But no peace is possible between the world of the novel, Kundera concludes, and a totalized, totalitarian universe of those who are certain that they know, and that one human truth is necessarily universal. A single truth could never accommodate the questioning, doubting spirit of the novel, the spirit of complexity, of difficulty, and of elusiveness with which it is imbued.

I begin with Kundera, and the valued connections he discovers between the post-Holocaust state of Israel, European culture, uncertainty, ambiguity, individuality, and the discerning of a personal truth, because it provides an introduction to an argument I wish to make concerning the nature of the Holocaust as a symbolic entity. There is value in the latter that I would discover—akin to Kundera—in a capacity to encompass contradiction. "Everything human resolves itself finally into contradictions," as the existentialist philosophy of Søren Kierkegaard concluded.[5] I find the conclusion too in Imre Kertesz's individual account of existence in Nazi concentration camps. My intention is to revisit *Fateless* as an instantiation of the Holocaust as symbolic memory in which one is encouraged to recognize the contrariety of human experience as irreducible. But first let me return to Kierkegaard and his exposition of human contradictoriness.

Contradiction for Kierkegaard, the inexplicable, inconsistent, and paradoxical in human experience, was a category of its own, part of the mysteriousness of consciousness. There must be a relationship between human cognition and eternal truths, Kierkegaard reckoned, but the connection was fated to remain mysterious, albeit "God" might be expected to know the solution. Kierkegaard wrote: "One ought to be a mystery, not only to others but also to oneself. I study myself. When I am weary of this, then for a pastime I light a cigar and think: 'The Lord only knows what He meant by me, or what He would make out of me.'"[6] In this vein, the admission by Franz Kafka is also resonant: "What have I in common with Jews? I have hardly anything in common with myself and should stand very quietly in a corner, content that I can breathe."[7] Kierkegaard was content to situate the mystery of experience, the contrariety of consciousness, in the lap of God. Faith in the divine—an offense to rationality, an absurdity in itself—effected a leap over contradictions that human cognitions could not further reduce or resolve, and so provided an existential resting point. My intuition would be that in a Godless age, a world of the novel from which God has departed as final arbiter of values, meaning, and practical necessity and as ultimate judge of knowledge, as Kundera described it, also a world of globalizing social, economic, and political processes where erstwhile absolute values, meanings, and judgments clash and contradict, in this contemporary world, the Holocaust is a large enough phenomenon—imposing itself on consciousness and yet ambiguous, myriad, incomprehensible—to be the container and maintainer of our contradictions. The Holocaust as a trope offers a kind of global treasury, large, ominous, awful, and awesome, in which to lodge all we know of the human, all we "remember," including its contradictoriness, perhaps most significantly its contradictoriness. The ambiguity of the Holocaust, and at the same time its singular presence, provides it with a status as a global signifier.

This proposition is a variant of an argument of Leo Strauss's: what he dubs "reductio ad Hitlerum."[8] As absolutes and universalizing claims are threatened by relativism on a shrinking globe of multicultural ontologies, the Holocaust seems to maintain its imaginative grasp not only as pivotal event but as telos: as a site of ultimate truths by which human experience can be subjected to an all-encompassing standard, a "moral marker of absolute evil." Strauss was highly critical of this reduction: perceiving the world through the prism of this worst of happenings, constantly comparing contemporary events to the Holocaust as baseline of catastrophe and evil. My interpretation would be more neutral, even positive. As Michael Bernstein also observes, to employ the Holocaust as the extreme or primal or limiting case in a context of everyday globalism is to provide humanity *as a singularity* with a home.[9] It is a *cosmopolitan* application. The Holocaust becomes a site at which we engage in a critical examination of the human condition, admitting its overwhelming complexities, its contrarieties and diversities, without finding resolution but also without losing sight of a holism. The Holocaust as global trope is a site at which the all too human is universally accessible and universally accessed.

In identifying the novel as the genre of an ambiguous human wholeness, Milan Kundera spoke in Jerusalem about the Jewish recognition of civilized values ("European culture") that attached to time and not space. Jewishness, he said, was above nationalist passion. The irony, of course, was that he was delivering his address in Israel, where Jews had been involved in wars over territory for decades and had come to occupy a state where the balance between civic and ethnic citizenship was far from clear. His entire talk could be said to take the form of a novel, but a resolution of sorts is brought about by an unstated event: the Holocaust. It is the Holocaust that causes Israel, "the heart of Europe," to be located outside the body; it is the Holocaust that resolves the contradiction between Jewishness and Israeliness. But it is not an easy resolution, or even a satisfying one: praising the ideally open-ended novel in a necessarily militarized state would seem a contradiction in terms. The Holocaust as a discourse of human immensity, we might say, is a container but also a work in progress.

I would continue this work, deploying the Holocaust as a means to talk about, assert, know, value, and judge the human as a universal. This is part of a cosmopolitan program, combining science, morality, and politics.[10] The human is a necessary moral figure; it is a possible political figure occupying a domain of global human rights law. The human is also an existential figure: our humanity is a species-wide, inclusive ontology. This latter is my main focus in what follows: how I might deploy "the Holocaust" as symbolic means to come to terms with the human being as a universal individual actor, recognizable across time and space. I expect this to be a contradictory figure, full of weaknesses and strengths, admirable and despicable, but I also expect to recognize myself. The central material of my research, as I have said, will be a novelistic depiction of the Holocaust, a subgenre that Primo Levi regarded as paradigmatically revealing of a universal human ambiguity, a "grayness," compromised, with "ill-defined outlines" separating one human being, one human body, from all others.[11]

The Holocaust as Tragedy?

According to Dwight Macdonald, the Nazi death camps should be accorded a status as "horrors beyond tragedy."[12] While tragedy was a genre of thought and representation that dealt with the consequences of *human* action (and inaction), there was an inhumanity to Auschwitz-Birkenau and Bergen-Belsen that took them beyond the bounds of such generic, conventional, and normative discourse. "The victims were helpless before a catastrophe that had no more relation to their characters, motives or actions than an earthquake."[13] Auschwitz was not a "tragedy" for those incarcerated and killed because of its intrinsic meaninglessness relative to their lives—a gratuitous or random event, an "act of God."[14]

Macdonald's conclusion—recall too Theodor Adorno's of 1949 that after Auschwitz there can be no "poetry," no celebration of human creativity, poiesis, and its capacity to overcome—finds extensive treatment in Primo Levi's writings, where the effect of the Nazis is always to conjure up the image of a kind of supernatural force, beyond human accounting.[15] Even when, some thirty years after penning his classic testament *If This Is a Man,* Levi returned to recount the stories of a few individuals who had found the strength in Auschwitz to achieve some kind of meaning for their actions within the regime of the camp, *Moments of Reprieve* ends with a kind of fatalism. Do not forget, he writes, "that all of us are in the ghetto, that the ghetto is fenced in, that beyond the fence stand the lords of death, and not far away the train is waiting."[16] Levi published this a year before (apparently) committing suicide. Reprieve is momentary, he seems to say, however dazzled we might become by power and material success, and there remains an essential human fragility before a fate, whether institutionally orchestrated or "divinely," that assigns human beings a life and a death beyond reckoning.

Imre Kertesz's *Fateless* is as scrupulous as is Levi in conveying the ambiguities of camp life, the effort to find meaning. Were the death camps a (tragic) arena of human action? Amid a form of life that was apparently random and murderous and would consign the individual willy-nilly to oblivion (first social and then physical), Kertesz determines nevertheless that even here human beings *must* be considered "fateless": "we ourselves are fate."[17] If there is such a thing as fate, then there is no freedom, while if there is freedom, there is no fate; even in the most total of social institutions it is not true to say that there is no such thing as freedom, the space of a tragic will.

If Auschwitz is to be conceived of as tragedy—something meaningful in human and individual terms, in distinction to a natural or "divine," impersonal, cataclysm—then Kertesz recognizes that this was only as a result of enormous efforts of will on the parts of inmates, fighting to connect random happenstance in the camps with a continuing personal life course.[18] Most pertinently, Kertesz describes what he terms three kinds of everyday "escape" from Auschwitz. First, the imagination. Seemingly mired in the camp, Kertesz describes his main character, György Köves, as frequently absenting himself. The easiest was for György to imagine himself "modestly" away, conducting a perfect day at home in Budapest; but even Florida was within reach: "I can attest to its truth: narrow prison walls cannot set limits to the flight of our imagination."[19] The imagination is asserted to be a human being's inalienable resource. A second escape is stubbornness, which appeared in Auschwitz in a variety of styles: a stubborn talk about the past, the future, about freedom; stubbornly indulging in word play, jokes, and teasing; a stubborn and tearful clinging to life when the rational thing was to wish for senselessness and death.[20] Most important for my purposes here is the third kind of escape that Kertesz asserts: an escape born out of what might be termed (borrowing a phrase from Foucault, but reversing his views on cause, on fate) "disciplinary detail."[21] One parcels out time and space into idiosyncratic and fussy particulars. The more gradations there are to concentrate on, negotiate, and overcome, the greater the sense of achievement: the more life becomes a matter of one's own symbolic classification and the more an encompassing capriciousness, meaninglessness, void, is eschewed. Concentrating physically, for instance, on taking one step after another, self-consciously making oneself cognizant of the minutiae of the terrain of one's life, or concocting temporal minischedules for oneself, however ephemeral, afforded the sanity of attending to life in the present moment—achieving life—rather than (the chasm of) giving way to death. "You live, you act, you move, you fulfil the new requirements of every new step of development."[22] Waiting in queues in Auschwitz, for instance, and roll calls that condemned the selected to death, György took one step forward at a time: "The point is in the steps. *Everyone stepped forward as long as they could.*"[23] Fetishizing the forward steps, the many minigradations they traverse, it becomes as if one may never stop, never arrive at the point of fatal selection: at worst one arrives in one's own time and on one's own itinerary. In Kertesz's portrayal, in short, disciplinary detail that is personally, continually evoked is to be appreciated as a kind of imaginative, liberating, and idiosyncratic fetish. One walks without arriving—or not arriving at a "fated" place. One disciplines oneself into seeing one's time and space in the camp as constituted by minute particulars of a personal stamp to which one willfully attends.[24]

There is one thing, however, that Kertesz describes György as able to secure no escape from: his body, and the growing alterity of its needs. Hunger made György a voracious void that he tried everything (sand, grass) to fill. His thought, action, and sight comes to be dominated by attempts to quell this body. It remains incomprehensible how such a body could alter so fast. From day to day György might observe his body rotting away. No longer in harmony with "him," each flaw, each atrocity of aging and decay, makes this body more an alien object: less an acquaintance, never mind a friend. There is a progression to the body that obeys its own schedule, seemingly beyond individual will and the Nazis alike. There is the "culture" of the Nazi camp, its institutionalism, its fetish for classification and symbolic cleanliness, there is the personal culture of György and his fellow inmates, endeavoring to make sense and find a way to escape Auschwitz's fatefulness, such as through a fetishistic attention to irrelevant detail (detail whose relevance escaped the attention of the Nazi regime), and there is the human body, its bodily nature standing apart from symbolization. The distance between symbolization and bodily experience in time, and of time, is what I turn to more specifically below.

The Limits of Symbolism?

Zeno's paradoxes were philosophical fragments, collected by Aristotle, which might be said to concern the appearance of control over time and space by means of logic. The "dichotomy" or "race course" paradox is briefly stated as follows: "That which is in locomotion must arrive at the half-way stage before it arrives at the goal."[25] Let us suppose Imre Kertesz, or his character György Köves, is considering the walk to a point of selection at Auschwitz. Before he reaches there, he knows he must get halfway there. But before he gets halfway there, he knows he must get a quarter of the way there. Before he travels a quarter way, he must travel an eighth; before an eighth, a sixteenth; and so on and so forth. Considered this way, his walk, although seemingly a finite distance, will comprise an infinitude of (increasingly small) portions. Covering finite distances, Zeno concluded, should logically be impossible and take an infinite time—which is to say, should never be completed. Indeed, not only could such a walk never be logically completed, it cannot ever be begun. For any possible first distance Kertesz or György decide to step must first be divided in half (and hence would not really be first at all). Before they can step a foot they must step half a foot; and before half a foot, a quarter; and so on. The possibly fatal walk to selection for death cannot either begin or end. The argument is called the "dichotomy" paradox because it concerns space repeatedly being split into two parts, with the paradoxical—yet seemingly logical—conclusion that all motion across finite space must be illusionary.

In the structural anthropology of Claude Lévi-Strauss, similar exploration was made into the paradoxical features of symbolic systems and the play that might be made with human cognition. According to Lévi-Strauss, for example, myths may be understood as "cognitive machines" to suppress a sense of passing of time and space, an argument Edmund Leach then extends to ritual performance in general.[26] A creation myth gives onto a fixed point from which the world *always* took and takes shape; a religious ceremony affords a constancy and normativity to human life in its conventional reiteration of form *irrespective* of time, place, situation, mood, and the possibly infinite changes of these. Both religious music and architecture are symbolic depictions of divine changelessness amid a changing human world; medieval European cathedrals embody a changelessness in stone, in stasis, while church music embodies a changelessness in pattern, in melody, and in rhythm. In the structure of the music and the architectural design alike, as again with myth, there is a circularity. There is a playing out of themes and variations whose patterning is finite and accords to a certain conventional grammar: the end is known in the beginning. In short, the symbolic iteration affords reiteration through the culture, and the members to which the symbolic systems belong might expect to overcome a linear, fateful, and fatal passage of time and of spatial distance.

The "Four Quartets" are a poem sequence of T. S. Eliot's said to represent both the four seasons and the four elements, and also a disquisition on the passage of time:[27] how the England of the Blitz of World War II was also the England of the fourteenth-century female Christian mystic Julian of Norwich, and the England from which Eliot's own ancestor had departed for the New World in 1669. Published during the war as a pamphlet, the poems enjoyed a wide readership; they were seen as a unifying force and also as conveying the fundamentals of a Christian faith and experience in a modern idiom. They also expressed what Eliot saw as the wasteland of European modernist culture and modernity. Eliot is diffident and pessimistic. What have the years between the Great War and the present one brought but waste, where, as Eliot writes in the final quartet, "Little Gidding," every attempt at trying to speak poetically is at once "a wholly new start, and a different kind of failure"? Have not Enlightenment notions of progress, of a forward-marching time, been thoroughly discredited? "Little Gidding" goes on:

> Every phrase and every sentence is an end and a beginning,
> Every poem an epitaph. And any action
> Is a step to the block, to the fire, down the sea's throat
> Or to an illegible stone: and that is where we start.
> We die with the dying:
> See, they depart, and we go with them.
> We are born with the dead:
> See, they return, and bring us with them.

> ... for history is a pattern
> Of timeless moments. So, while the light fails
> On a winter's afternoon, in a secluded chapel
> History is now and England.
>
> With the drawing of this Love and the voice of this Calling
>
> We shall not cease from exploration
> And the end of all our exploring
> Will be to arrive where we started
> And know the place for the first time.[28]

Eliot appears to reconcile himself, symbolically, to a kind of poetry and a kind of life that moves through time and space without progressing. The famous allusiveness of his poetic style makes otherness ever present. This might be seen to accord too to his chosen religiosity: the Roman Catholicism that offered an institutionalism and ceremonialism that disavowed reformation, insisting on certainty and continuity, even circularity.

Poetry, music and architecture, myth and ritual, logic: here seem to be comparable attempts, by way of different symbolic languages, to cognitively control, even overcome, movement through time and space and the fateful changes this might wreak. What are the overlaps between these academic or intellectual models (Eliot's, Leach's and Lévi-Strauss's, Zeno's) and the pragmatic modeling of Auschwitz that Kertesz has György Köves and his fellow inmates effect for their emotional survival? György Köves makes a symbolic fetish out of detail and so produces personal landscapes of movement that he can control: movement, possibly, he alone is able to perceive and measure. Auschwitz becomes a time and space of minute, personal particulars, and achieving routine in terms of continuing movement through this personal, "disciplined" grid, György gains a phenomenological leverage upon the discipline to which the Nazis would subject him. His temporal and spatial grids might undercut theirs: momentarily he might forget theirs. Their depersonalization of him is cognitively ameliorated by an imaginative transformation of their temporal and spatial designs: their moving him to points of possible selection for death is experientially overwritten and at least slowed. Concentrating, like Zeno, like the French structuralists and Eliot, on the patterned forms of his own symbolic classification, he might assure himself that arriving at a point coinciding with Nazi plans is less likely or can be obviated.

In short, there are resonances here concerning how time and space can be symbolically constructed: linearity being replaced by circularity (Eliot, Leach, Lévi-Strauss), progression becoming impossible (Zeno), a possible fatal terminus being obviated by imaginative deviations and diversions (Kertesz). Traversing time and space is risky, entropic, aging, even fatal, hence one travels in circles or refrains from starting, or stopping. "Man's greatest strength," Aldous Huxley observed, "lies in his capacities for irrelevance" (in the midst of pestilence, wars, and famines he builds cathedrals).[29] Faced by the possibility of a "horror beyond tragedy," the fateful and fatal foreshortening of the time and space of their lives, Kertesz has György Köves and his fellow inmates attend to moving, developing temporal routines, stepping forward, for as long as they can.

But what of "reality," of the human body and its nature, that which, as Huxley phrased it, it might be more "relevant" to treat? György Köves could not escape from his body, its demands and career, Kertesz concludes, however much he might construct a personal symbolic culture in opposition to that of the Nazis. No symbolic classification could circumvent the ontology, the brute thingness, of the human body and its ability to force itself on human attention. Its decay, its existence in time, amounted to a radical otherness to all symbolic fictions. ("Theory is all well and fine," Jean-Martin Charcot observed, "but it does not stop things from existing."[30]) The resonances between Zeno, the French structuralists, and Eliot on the one hand and Kertesz on the other break down, one can say, at the point where György Köves recognizes that his body is a material void that may neither be filled nor symbolically quelled. Kertesz allows us to glimpse the paradoxical nature of the human body: both the vehicle of a capacity to invent culture and symbolize—to variously classify and fetishize time and space—and also that which stops any such symbolic construction from becoming absolutely cognitively or emotionally effective as a world apart, a world in itself. The symbolic does not supervene upon the ontology of the body or the universal and stubborn foundation this provides to human experience. A memory of Auschwitz (Kertesz's) is not to be confused with its global symbolization, albeit the latter allows for all manner of poetic, mythic, even logical, work to be done with the Holocaust as a concept and its memorialization as a moral and political program.

My Body in Auschwitz?

On 20 June 2006, I accompanied Andrew Irving and a class of his students from Concordia University on a visit to the Montreal Holocaust Museum. The students were taking Irving's course, "Deathly Encounters: The Anthropology of Death, Consciousness and the Body," at the university.[31] As part of the course Irving had arranged for a guided tour of the museum exhibit, in particular for the class to hear the testimony of one of Montreal's large number of Holocaust survivors: an old man whose extraordinary experiences now elicited regular appearances and recitations.

Our progress around the museum was not fast. The class was large for the cramped and windowless space, and our route was made circuitous by the guide trying to infuse with personal and contemporary meaning the glass casements filled with fading artifacts dating from World War II. The class was polite, but I sensed a disconnection between visitors and guide. The latter's delivery was deliberate and precise and he was patient, but his experiences seemed distant, as did his age. Did not his person, his narrative, and his expression possess more the aura of ritual relic than of truth relevant to the everyday here and now? Did not the class of young Montrealers have its own experiences of discrimination, dislocation, diaspora, and migration? Its members included people who had journeyed from the instabilities of Colombia, Sudan, Eritrea, and Zimbabwe to relocate in Montreal. I sensed that both the Montreal setting of relative affluence and security and the class members' own challenges of selfhood, maturation, and personal relationships made the Holocaust into a cautionary tale as scripted and unreal, allegorical and distant—and also tired and clichéd—as a fable from the Bible or the Brothers Grimm.

I tried to animate my own experience of the exhibit by turning my attention to the casements. In one there were printed captions that recorded survivors' accounts of finally reaching Canada. One such account, reporting how, even immediately after the war, Holocaust experiences were not communicable to Montreal locals, I found could have been voiced by Kertesz's György Köves on his return to postwar Budapest: "'You suffered?' they would say, 'But we did too, our war was hard: we had no meat.'" In another caption, a survivor asked himself whether life could so easily carry on once one had experienced it being treated so cheaply and capriciously, and ended so arbitrarily. And his answer was yes. In the war, he went on, "it was as if the sky descended to the earth": the dimensions of one's world were radically foreshortened, one's options reduced, one's limits far more apparent. But one adapted. And afterward, wars still go on—the Balkans, Rwanda, Darfur, Iraq—where erstwhile neighbors murder each other. And you go on too. "You learn to avoid certain groups of people—Germans, say—and you avoid confrontation. You walk a distance around a possible conflagration, if necessary." In addition to the way in which these survivors learned to keep their memories to themselves, or only to share them with fellow survivors, I was struck by the survivors' imagery: war meant no meat, it meant a landscape without horizons, it meant walking away from fateful encounters wherever possible and whatever the distance.

The Montreal museum tour also reminded me of how I had myself felt as a visitor to the Auschwitz memorial site in present-day Oświęcim, Poland: the failure I had felt the experience to be.[32] This was five years earlier (July 2001), occasioned by my attending a conference in Krakow, "The Moral Fabric in Contemporary Societies."[33] I found I could book myself a day tour to Auschwitz through the conference administration. Following the coach journey to Oświęcim (how could people go on living in a town that still bore that name—the "anus of the universe," as the Nazis had dubbed it—and how could life proceed with the seeming normalcy that was displayed beyond the bus windows?), I and my fellow tourists alighted at the iron gates I had seen so often in photographs ("Arbeit Macht Frei" [figure 6.1]). It was a pleasantly warm summer's day.

Figure 6.1. The iron gates of Auschwitz: "Arbeit Macht Frei."

The blue-uniformed, young, female, Polish guides who greeted us and accompanied us through the site on the prescribed route were serious and knowledgeable and professional. But their very professionalism grated, as did the text that the tour represented, its symbolization in words and the particular sights we were offered. How did the enormity of the historical happening coincide with this encapsulated account? The task was impossible. I began to resent the institutionalism and to question the textual terms in which the tour was being conducted: Why *these* photographs on the walls? Why the word "Polish" not "Jewish," "political" not "ethnic" or "religious," used in this or that explanation? Why the number of hours the visitor was led to spend in the careful showcase that Auschwitz, the reconstructed prison camp, had become, compared to the meager minutes left at the end to wander unescorted the wasteland that Birkenau remained—the vast adjoining death camp, with its demolished wooden shacks, gas chambers, ovens, and chimneys—before we were quickly ushered back onto the coach for the drive back to Krakow?

The tour was a failure, for me, because of its particular symbolization, I would now say, how it was verbally and behaviorally constructed. The distance between memorialization and memory was not being sufficiently recognized or respected: the script was wrong. In his account of his experience of World War II, *A Farewell to Arms,* Ernest Hemingway described the "obscenity" he came to find in any of the words used to memorialize awful events barring the most concrete. "The names of places had dignity. Certain numbers [of roads, of regiments] were the same and certain dates[; these] were all you could say and have them mean anything." But not "glory," "honor," "courage," "hallow"; nothing abstract, pat, too rhetorical or rehearsed.[34] "Touring" Auschwitz was too reminiscent of being a voyeur, at a theme park, being titillated by an obscene event. When I photograph the gates of Auschwitz, or the railway tracks at Birkenau, or have myself photographed inside Birkenau facing the row of reconstructed wooden dormitories, I am on a film set—Lanzmann's *Shoah*, Spielberg's *Schindler's List*. When I suspect the terms of my Polish tour guides' scripts I am remembering Jonathan Webber's work on the controversy surrounding the contemporary symbolizing of Auschwitz: borrowing his anger at the heavy-handedness of the Polish government and the Catholic Church.[35] The emotions I conjure up and to which I lay claim are, at least partly, secondhand, the memories vicarious. Do I have a right to them?

Karl Marx advised that "dead generations weigh like a nightmare on the brains of the living," their circumstances becoming part of the historical conditions under which the living make their present.[36] But the situation is actually more complex, more ambivalent. A history must be admitted. Auschwitz as personal history (and tragedy) is something I have only gradually learned to wear, and with effort. It could be said to be quite remote from the terrain actually trod by me, also my family, in the United Kingdom and southern Wales. One of the signs displayed on the Auschwitz tour quoted George Santayana: "Those who cannot remember the past are condemned to repeat it."[37] It had resonated with me at the time—as part of a script somehow beyond my tour guides'. Equally, the enormous glass casements full of suitcases, of shoes, of eyeglasses, of human hair, of children's toys: at the time their muteness had resonated with me as testaments—the detritus of human lives ended in midstep—that were more true than the institutionalized tour and that I was somehow in a privileged position to appreciate. But now I would interrogate that claim of ownership, and the sentimental frisson that accompanied it. In what way is it "my" past that is being remembered here? The allocation of group identities and membership of cultural communities by virtue of birth alone, and according to someone else's classificatory schema, is something that I have always vehemently rejected as an anthropologist. I remember a virulent argument with a (religiously orthodox) cousin—we were both university students at the time—who demanded that I recognize my duties to "my people" who were being barred from leaving the Soviet Union, and my (Kafkaesque) reply that I felt more affinity to the Comanches than the Jews. But now, when I lay claim to a Jewish historical pain, do I not enjoy my resentments, grievances that are impossible to put right and that are so easy—leaving me with no present-day obligation except to feel indignation and feed a melancholic imagination? Walking the site of Auschwitz in the present day, along the route and at the pace that the tourist is allocated, holds nothing that I can construe as in any way an authentic memory. I am a privileged, British visitor. The sun shines, I dress casually, my fellow tourists bear cameras, baseball caps: we are holiday makers touring ruins. I am in holiday mood but trying to be appropriately sombre, and it is an act. The text recounted by the tour guides is a job of work, like any holiday couriers', but my resentment is another text, a claim to a historical victimhood that is vicarious. By what right do I expect the Polish tourist industry to live up to the version of the past in whose terms I choose vicariously to recollect and emote? I have no direct memory of the Holocaust, nor any direct means to approach the embodied experiences of Imre Kertesz (or Primo Levi).

Cosmopolitan Virtue?

In his mixing of symbolic genres for putting an account of the Holocaust on paper, W. G. Sebald concluded that it was not only epistemologically naïve to claim a direct approach to such tragic experiences but also ethically inappropriate. The official cultures of remembering and mourning that have grown up globally around the Holocaust claim a false intimacy with the dead, he suggested, and assume a "compromis[ing] moral position."[38] And yet this is perhaps not the end.

Imre Kertesz has György Köves recognize the "prize" he had won in being able to survive the Nazi death camps. Albeit that on returning to Budapest he was unable to make others understand what he had experienced, the passage of time always helped: "time changes everything."[39] A readiness to continue his life soon collected inside György; he would continue his stepping forward: "We can never start a new life. We can only continue the old one. I took my own steps. No one else did."[40] Nor did György's temperament turn morbid. "More than the terrors," he determined to try to remember "the happiness of the camps" and even that on first returning to Budapest he had felt "homesick" for them.[41] These are challenging statements, but I read them as attesting to the way in which Kertesz has György Köves feel he has come to own the time of his life. "Time changes everything" from impersonal to personal—including the personal phenomenology of a decaying body—and György knew that he had "taken his own steps forward and no one else's." (The tyranny of the Nazis felt itself most when there was no time, Kertesz elaborates at one point, when destruction came too randomly to make sense of, or when the passage of infernal events slowed down to nothing.) Time, we might guess, also works for Kertesz himself, turning experience into memory, and memory into story.

Time also allows me to draw the different strands of this chapter together: the memory of the Holocaust as against its memorialization; body as distinct from symbol; the globalization of Holocaust-as-symbol as a virtue. For the body-in-time, its aging and change, is an aspect of a universal human condition, as is too a capacity to symbolize time in ways that enable it to be imagined as under personal or social control, slowed, nonlinear, teleological, and so on. The novel is a "paradisiacal" space for individuals, Milan Kundera urged, because of the centrality the genre affords to accounting for individual consciousness. In Kertesz's novelistic treatment I meet an individual whose humanity I recognize. My walking Auschwitz is inevitably and only an experience of my own and I have no way of sharing Kertesz's memories, but through his symbolic account I have a means to imagine what it might have been like. Kertesz has György Köves imagine walking without stopping in Auschwitz, beyond the culture and institutionalism of the Nazis, in gradations of his own willful appreciation. Meanwhile, his body tyrannizes him with its need for sustenance. György can use his imagination to transcend both his body's needs and the regime of the camp, *to an extent,* but there is no ultimate escape from either: his hungry, apparently alien, body is the seat of his consciousness, and his personal disciplining of time and space cannot cancel out the Nazi selections. In György's imaginative transcending of time *and* his bodily inhabitation of time I meet a fictional account of a fellow human being, a fictional account of Kertesz's own experience. And I can empathize, both with the capabilities of the imagination and with bodily limits that may not be overcome. György Köves must fill the void of his starving body with sand and grass, and I cannot fill the temporal void between his/Kertesz's bodily walking of Auschwitz and my own. But then this is something that we do share: the present times of our different embodiments. *We are consciously present to ourselves, in time, in commensurate, human ways.* In short, Kertesz's novelistic account enables me to appreciate the individuality that differentiates us and to recognize the human embodiment that we share. "Everything is in consciousness, and everything in consciousness *is* together." I find this formulation of Benjamin Lee Whorf's preferable to Freudian divisions that posit unconsciousness as a more powerful other because of the stress it places on the conscious present.[42] If everything in consciousness *is* together, then while I do not and cannot share Kertesz's consciousness (or anyone else's), I *can* share an experience of presentism as a bodily condition. It is a *human* experience of consciousness in and of time.

This returns us finally to the issue of the Holocaust as global discourse. My argument would be that it can have the cosmopolitan virtue of making visible the individual body in time as a human universal: the common and precious presentism of our lives. It is the case that we are present to ourselves, our imagination, our memories, as no one else is present to us, and we are present to no one else. Yet in this difference we are the same. This insight bears a moral weight. If our temporal embodiment is a common, human condition, and limitation, then while I cannot overcome the distinct spatiality and temporality of individuality, I can expect a kind of universal, spatial, and temporal equality. Imre Kertesz has the right to make of his space and time what I can make of mine, far beyond the tragedy of dehumanization and war. The symbolic depiction of the Holocaust provides a warrant for a discourse of common human rights.

I have described an immensity to the Holocaust: as a global symbol it would appear to float without moorings, empty of essence. Imre Kertesz's "Holocaust" is not that of Primo Levi, never mind mine, or my orthodox cousin's, or Mahmoud Ahmadinejad's, or David Irving's, or the students' in Montreal. How can this be "virtuous"? Because that immensity is homologous with, and evidential of, the complexity of an individual human life, of individual consciousness-in-time. The play that is made with "the Holocaust" as symbol instantiates our agency to attend to the world, to interpret its nature, to make it meaningful, to remember and anticipate, to exist in time, in individual ways beyond limit.[43]

"The Holocaust" becomes a kind of treasury or bank of individual experience, of human existence: a banking of the complexity of the human condition. Its symbolic deployment offers a route to a global appreciation of our universal human nature, both our commonality and our irreducible individuality. Key to this virtuousness is a recognition of what a symbolic construction is: how it is a fiction, how it is distinct from the ontological realities of human bodies. "The Holocaust" as global symbol and trope expresses a human creative diversity. There is virtue in this globalism in that "the Holocaust" serves as a container of a universal exchange: an argument in which an increasing proportion of a global population partakes. "What was, what is, the Holocaust?" Yes, "the Holocaust" assumes very different and contradictory meanings: the global symbolic usage diversifies as it homogenizes. But it is an argument exemplificatory of the nature of the human, and instantiatory of a human conversation.

Milan Kundera saw in "Jewish" exile an encapsulation of the value that a European Enlightenment value had also come to place on truth that is divorced from territory: on truths that held universally. In the global spread of "the Holocaust," what is to be hoped for? In its symbolic ubiquity might be invested the valuable truth of the human as a singularity that supervenes upon territorial difference. Here is a site for an exploration of the human body-in-time, its commonalities and its individualities. The exploration can be both scientific and moral. Of what, in extremis, is the human body capable of suffering and of achieving? From what, without exception, should it be protected? "The Holocaust" as global trope thus carries a cosmopolitan mission.

Notes

1. See Nigel Rapport, "Walking Auschwitz, Walking Without Arriving," *Journeys* 9, no. 2 (2009): 32–54.
2. Ludwig Wittgenstein, *Philosophical Investigations* (Oxford: Blackwell, 1978), 241.
3. Milan Kundera, *The Art of the Novel* (London: Faber, 1990), 157.
4. Ibid., 159, 164–65.
5. Soren Kierkegaard, *The Journals of Kierkegaard 1834–1854* (Glasgow: Fontana, 1958), 117–18.
6. Soren Kierkegaard, *Either/Or* (Princeton, NJ: Princeton University Press, 1949), 21.
7. Franz Kafka, *The Diaries of Franz Kafka* (New York: Schocken, 1988), 252.

8. Cited in Steven Aschheim, "A Review of the *Journal of Genocide Research*," *Times Literary Supplement* 5145 (2001): 29.

9. See Michael Bernstein, "Homage to the Extreme: The Shoah and the Rhetoric of Catastrophe," *Times Literary Supplement* 4953 (1998): 6–8.

10. On cosmopolitanism, see Nigel Rapport, "Apprehending Anyone: The Non-Indexical, Post-Cultural and Cosmopolitan Human Actor," *Journal of the Royal Anthropological Institute* 16, no. 1 (2010): 84–101; Nigel Rapport, *Anyone: the Cosmopolitan Subject of Anthropology* (Oxford: Berghahn Books, 2012).

11. See Primo Levi, *The Drowned and the Saved* (London: Abacus, 1996), 27–33.

12. Cited in Geoffrey Wheatcroft, "Horrors beyond Tragedy," *Times Literary Supplement* 5071 (2000): 9–10.

13. Dwight Macdonald, cited in ibid., 9–10.

14. I suggest the term "nihilistic violence" for an act perpetrated deliberately on an individual with which the latter finds it impossible to come to terms or to find meaningful. Nigel Rapport, "'Criminals by Instinct': On the 'Tragedy' of Social Structure and the 'Violence' of Individual Creativity," in *Meanings of Violence*, ed. Goran Aijmer and Jan Abbink (Oxford: Berg, 2000), 39–54.

15. Cf. Nigel Rapport, "Society as a 'Morality-Silencing' Force: Primo Levi, Existential Power, and the Concentration Camp," in *The Moral Fabric in Contemporary Societies*, ed. Grazyna Skapska (Leiden: Brill, 2003), 309–34.

16. Primo Levi, *Moments of Reprieve* (London: Abacus, 1994), 172.

17. Imre Kertesz, *Fateless* (Evanston, IL: Northwestern University Press, 1992), 189.

18. For a reading of Kertesz's writings on the Nazi terror as emphatically affirming its coercive power, see Amos Goldberg, "Trauma, Narrative, and the Two Forms of Death," *Literature and Medicine* 25, no. 1 (2006): 122–40.

19. Imre Kertesz, *Fateless*, 116.

20. In Andrew Irving's terms, laughter entails an exhalation that symbolizes a confident exuberance or defiance in the face of death. "The Disembodiment of Knowledge: Laughter, Death and the Reclamation of Personhood," unpublished paper, University of Manchester.

21. See Michel Foucault, *Discipline and Punish* (New York: Pantheon, 1977).

22. Imre Kertesz, *Fateless*, 181.

23. Ibid., 188, emphasis added.

24. For further discussion of notions of disciplinary detail less as a (Foucauldian) epistemic imposition than a strategic resource of individual cognition, see Nigel Rapport, "A Policeman's Construction of 'the Truth': Sergeant Hibbs and the Lie-Detector Machine," *Anthropology Today* 4, no. 1 (1988): 7–11.

25. See Aristotle, *Physics* (Oxford: Oxford University Press, 1999), book VI, chap. 9, 239b10.

26. See Claude Lévi-Strauss, *The Raw and the Cooked* (New York: Harper Colophon, 1975), 14–30; Edmund Leach, *Culture and Communication* (Cambridge: Cambridge University Press, 1976), 44.

27. Thomas Stearns Eliot, *Complete Poems and Plays* (London: Faber, 1982). The series of poems was originally published in 1943.

28. Ibid., 197.

29. Aldous Huxley, *Antic Hay* (Harmondsworth, UK: Penguin, 1960), 151.

30. Cited in Sigmund Freud, *The Freud Reader*, ed. Peter Gay (New York: Norton, 1989), 50.

31. See Andrew Irving, "Ethnography, Art and Death," *Journal of the Royal Anthropological Institute*, n.s., 13, no. 1 (2007): 185–208.

32. See Nigel Rapport, "Walking Auschwitz."

33. In her preface to the published proceedings of the conference, Grazyna Skapska explained that its title, location, and timing were none of them accidental. The conference was held "at the beginning of a new millennium in a country that had experienced in the twentieth century the most atrocious crimes against humanity ['symbolized by nearby Auschwitz'] and two totalitarianisms" (vii). Surely, she went on, the lessons to be learned are that "history is neither the accomplice of utopia, nor does it necessarily evolve in a liberal direction." To make human history

"go anywhere," societies must have moral goals or visions and avoid any "decadent," postmodern notions that would reduce human identity and social exchange to mere language games (vii–viii). Grazyna Skapska, "Preface," in *The Moral Fabric in Contemporary Societies,* ed. Grazyna Skapska and Anna Orla-Bukowska (Leiden: Brill, 2003), vii–ix.

34. Ernest Hemingway, *A Farewell to Arms* (Harmondsworth, UK: Penguin, 1955), 144.

35. See Jonathan Webber, "Preface," in *The Battle for Auschwitz: Catholic-Jewish Relations under Strain,* by Emma Klein (London: Vallentine Mitchell, 2001).

36. Karl Marx, *The Eighteenth Brumaire of Louis Napoleon* (1852; repr., London: Lawrence and Wishart, 1985).

37. George Santayana, *Reason in Common Sense* (New York: Scribner's, 1905), 284.

38. Sebald, cited in Eric Homberger, "Obituary: W. G. Sebald," *Guardian,* 17 December 2001, http://www.guardian.co.uk/news/2001/dec/17/guardianobituaries.books1 (accessed 27 September 27).

39. Imre Kertesz, *Fateless,* 181.

40. Ibid., 188–89.

41. Ibid., 190–91.

42. See Benjamin Whorf, "The Relations of Habitual Thought and Behavior to Language," in *Language, Culture, and Personality,* ed. Leslie Spier (Menasha, WI: Sapir Memorial Publication Fund, 1941), 75–93.

43. See Nigel Rapport, *I Am Dynamite: An Alternative Anthropology of Power* (London: Routledge, 2003).

Bibliography

Aristotle. *Physics.* Oxford: Oxford University Press, 1999.

Aschheim, Steven. "A Review of the *Journal of Genocide Research.*" *Times Literary Supplement* 5145 (2001): 29–33.

Bernstein, Michael. "Homage to the Extreme: The Shoah and the Rhetoric of Catastrophe." *Times Literary Supplement* 4953 (1998): 6–8.

Eliot, Thomas. Stearns. *Complete Poems and Plays.* London: Faber, 1982.

Foucault, Michel. *Discipline and Punish.* New York: Pantheon, 1977.

Freud, Sigmund. *The Freud Reader.* Edited by Peter Gay. New York: Norton, 1989.

Goldberg, Amos. "Trauma, Narrative, and the Two Forms of Death." *Literature and Medicine* 25, no. 1 (2006): 122–40.

Hemingway, Ernest. *A Farewell to Arms.* Harmondsworth: Penguin, 1955.

Homberger, Eric. "Obituary: W. G. Sebald." *Guardian,* 17 December 2001. http://www.guardian.co.uk/news/2001/dec/17/guardianobituaries.books1 (accessed 27 September 2010).

Huxley, Aldous. *Antic Hay.* Harmondsworth: Penguin, 1960.

Irving, Andrew. "The Disembodiment of Knowledge: Laughter, Death and the Reclamation of Personhood." Unpublished paper, University of Manchester.

———. "Ethnography, Art and Death." *Journal of the Royal Anthropological Institute,* n.s., 13, no. 1 (2007): 185–208.

Kafka, Franz. *The Diaries of Franz Kafka.* New York: Schocken, 1988.

Kertesz, Imre. *Fateless.* Evanston, IL: Northwestern University Press, 1992.

Kierkegaard, Soren. *Either/Or.* Princeton, NJ: Princeton University Press, 1949.

———. *The Journals of Kierkegaard 1834–1854.* Glasgow: Fontana, 1958.

Kundera, Milan. *The Art of the Novel.* London: Faber, 1990.

Leach, Edmund. *Culture and Communication.* Cambridge: Cambridge University Press, 1976.

Levi, Primo. *The Drowned and the Saved.* London: Abacus, 1996.

———. *Moments of Reprieve.* London: Abacus, 1994.

Lévi-Strauss, Claude. *The Raw and the Cooked.* New York: Harper Colophon, 1975.

Marx, Karl. *The Eighteenth Brumaire of Louis Napoleon*. London: Lawrence and Wishart, 1985. First published 1852.

Rapport, Nigel. "A Policeman's Construction of 'the Truth': Sergeant Hibbs and the Lie-Detector Machine." *Anthropology Today* 4, no. 1 (1988): 7–11.

———. "'Criminals by Instinct': On the 'Tragedy' of Social Structure and the 'Violence' of Individual Creativity." In *Meanings of Violence*, ed. Goran Aijmer and Jan Abbink, 39–54. Oxford: Berg, 2000.

———. *I Am Dynamite: An Alternative Anthropology of Power*. London: Routledge, 2003.

———. "Society as a 'Morality-Silencing' Force: Primo Levi, Existential Power, and the Concentration Camp." In *The Moral Fabric in Contemporary Societies*, ed. Grazyna Skapska, 309–34. Leiden: Brill, 2003.

———. "Walking Auschwitz, Walking Without Arriving." *Journeys* 9, no. 2 (2009): 32–54.

———. "Apprehending Anyone: The Non-Indexical, Post-Cultural and Cosmopolitan Human Actor." *Journal of the Royal Anthropological Institute* 16, no. 1 (2010): 84–101.

———. *Anyone: The Cosmopolitan Subject of Anthropology*. Oxford: Berghahn Books, 2012.

Santayana, George. *Reason in Common Sense*. New York: Scribner's, 1905.

Skapska, Grazyna. "Preface." In *The Moral Fabric in Contemporary Societies*, ed. Grazyna Skapska and Anna Orla-Bukowska, vii–ix. Leiden: Brill, 2003.

Webber, Jonathan. "Preface." In *The Battle for Auschwitz: Catholic-Jewish Relations under Strain*, by Emma Klein. London: Vallentine Mitchell, 2001.

Wheatcroft, Geoffrey. "Horrors beyond Tragedy." *Times Literary Supplement* 5071 (2000): 9–10.

Whorf, Benjamin. "The Relations of Habitual Thought and Behavior to Language." In *Language, Culture, and Personality*, ed. Leslie Spier, 75–93. Menasha, WI: Sapir Memorial Publication Fund, 1941.

Wittgenstein, Ludwig. *Philosophical Investigations*. Oxford: Blackwell, 1978.

Section III

MEMORY, TRAUMA, AND TESTIMONY

The Holocaust and Non-Western Memories

CHAPTER 7

Holocaust Memories and Cosmopolitan Practices
Humanitarian Witnessing between Emergencies and the Catastrophe

MICHAL GIVONI

In its spring 2004 issue dedicated to humanitarian action, *Les temps modernes* reproduced a transcript of an interview conducted by Claude Lanzmann in 1979, when he was shooting his magnum opus, *Shoah*.[1] This was an interview with Dr. Maurice Rossel, a Swiss who was then in his sixties, who acted as a delegate of the International Committee of the Red Cross (ICRC) in Berlin during World War II. Rossel's testimony was not included in *Shoah* for what Lanzmann described as "reasons of length and structure."[2] It gravitated, however, around issues that were akin to the ones that Lanzmann set out to examine in his groundbreaking film. What made Rossel a "historical figure," in Lanzmann's words, was his visit to Theresienstadt, a showcase ghetto built by the Nazis to deceive international observers.[3] Rossel visited Theresienstadt in June 1944, and although Lanzmann makes a few polite inquiries about his experiences in Berlin, it is this and similar "inspections," namely, Rossel's unmediated encounters with the sealed off sites of extermination, that stand at the heart of the interview.

Lanzmann seems to be particularly interested in Rossel's failed attempts, in his own words, to "see beyond" what was staged for him by the Nazis. Although Rossel admits to having been aware of visiting a model ghetto, his laconic and approving report, which Lanzmann quotes at length, makes no reference to the fact. As in *Shoah,* in this interview Lanzmann seeks to lay bare the peculiar distributions of visibility and invisibility in the Holocaust and the puzzling relations between the possibility, the impossibility, the avoidance, and the engagement of witnessing the event. For this reason, it is not so much Ros-

---

Notes for this section begin on page 140.

sel's impressions as a privileged eyewitness that trigger Lanzmann's curiosity, as it is not elucidation or fuller knowledge of the mechanisms of extermination that he aims toward. Instead, the interview seeks to solicit a thick narration of witnessing that remains untarnished by Rossel's evasive memory and that his fading recollections actually cast in crude light. During the interview it is Lanzmann who acts as the authoritative source of information, often interrupting the flow of Rossel's testimony to supplement his account or underwrite his factual assertions. The act of witnessing that unfolds in the interview is thereby crafted as a live confrontation between the witness that Rossel was and the witness he now becomes. Rather than providing a standard eyewitness report, Rossel's dialogue with Lanzmann enacts the tormented process of becoming a witness to the Holocaust, and, as part of the same thing, the failure to witness atrocities in real time.

The main protagonist in *Shoah,* testimony undergoes an interesting twist in the interview with Rossel, which was edited in 1997 into an independent documentary entitled *Un vivant qui passe (A Visitor from the Living)*. In what became a canonical interpretation of Lanzmann's *Shoah* and an inaugural text in testimony theory, Shoshana Felman showed that this vast documentary project made exclusively of testimonies was not a standard reconstruction of atrocities but a "a film about witnessing" that sought to probe the limits of observation, memory, and understanding of the dreadful events.[4] Felman demonstrated that Lanzmann's interviews with victims, perpetrators, and bystanders staged both the crisis of witnessing that turned the Holocaust into a unique event in human history and the opportunity, provided by the act of witnessing, for a moral and emotional healing for its survivors. A similar displacement of testimony from its erstwhile status as documentary evidence and its similar recasting as a moral reenactment of subjectivity and responsibility are also manifest in *Un vivant qui passe*. In both cases, testimony is portrayed as a problematic performance whose lapses reveal more about the true nature of atrocities than the factual information it conveys. But over and beyond these similarities, Lanzmann's interview with Rossel seems to evince a distinctive problematization of witnessing, which cannot be easily assimilated into an ethics of testimony of the kind that is elaborated in *Shoah*.

According to Felman, *Shoah* portrays the Holocaust as an "event without a witness" by accentuating the irreconcilable restrictions that were placed upon the fields of vision of the various witnesses to the events.[5] *Shoah* shows, in her interpretation, how the Holocaust "precludes seeing and ... precludes the possibility of a *community of* seeing,"[6] associating both the success of the extermination and the failure to be a witness to the Holocaust with the incommensurable blind spots experienced by all those involved in the atrocious events. As his conversation with Lanzmann unfolds, however, the distinctive failure of Rossel's testimony turns out to be diametrically opposed to the crises of witnessing documented in *Shoah*. Unlike the other testimonies collected by Lanzmann, the story of Rossel's visit in Theresienstadt is a tragedy of unhindered witnessing: a witnessing whose flaws are not related to a fabricated blindness, but rather to a panoptic, all-encompassing, and universally sanctioned vantage point. The source of Rossel's fatal ignorance lies in his ability to see everything (to take as many photos as he liked, as he mentioned in his report), which was inseparable from his commitment to accommodate everybody. His role as an impartial inspector, a passing "visitor" whose moral authority was acknowledged by victims and perpetrators alike, generated its own biases and ultimately reduced witnessing to what he himself presented in retrospect as a purely "theatrical role."[7]

One can only speculate why it took Lanzmann almost twenty years to release the footage of his interview with Rossel. But I suspect that the resurrection and screening of *Un vivant qui passe* were at least partly indebted to the surge of interest in humanitarian action and its paradoxes; that, following the recent ordeals of nongovernmental humanitarianism and its failure to adequately respond to emergencies in Somalia, Rwanda, Zaire, and ex-Yugoslavia, among others, Rossel's ethical bankruptcy acquired a piercing relevance and a symbolic utility as a primal scene on which current dilemmas could be projected. The overwhelming discontent with transnational humanitarian action and the industry of humanitarian reflection and intellectual debate that it set in motion during the 1990s, which were particularly heightened in the French humanitarian scene, were the discursive climate in which Rossel could be invigorated as the prototype of the perplexed humanitarian witness. In this amalgamation of historical precedent and contemporary concerns exemplified by the special issue of *Les temps modernes,* the moral challenge of humanitarian witnessing was cast in terms that radically departed from what Felman referred to as the final solution's "historical assault on seeing."[8] In fact, the problematization of witnessing, which was one of the focal points of a broader interrogation of humanitarian responsibility that gained momentum since the end of the Cold War, was at odds with the repressive hypothesis on which relations between testimony and political power were predicated according to testimony theory. It tacitly acknowledged that evil regimes, governments, and paramilitaries that oppress or neglect the basic needs of civilians do not only hide and blur the traces of their shameful policies, but often stage spectacles of suffering and violence or have a vested interest in maintaining them. The problem with humanitarian action, according to this view, was that in the decades that followed World War II, international observers such as humanitarian practitioners, human rights activists, journalists, and photographers have become full-part actors and strategic nodes in the material and symbolic networks of political emergencies. To an ever-greater degree, their presence and unremitting inspection were anticipated and exploited by parties to the conflict. Embedded as humanitarian practitioners were in intricate webs of warfare, propaganda, and resources, their status as a neutral third party became extremely fragile. Their success turned out to be the source of their moral weakness, as the side effects of their intervention in the so-called complex political emergencies that mushroomed in the post–Cold War era made glaringly clear.

Hence the concern that fueled the debates that took place in the humanitarian community since the mid-1990s and stood behind its ethical engagement with buzz phrases like "humanitarian responsibility," "humanitarian dilemmas," and "the paradoxes of humanitarianism." How can humanitarian practitioners overcome the theatrical role ascribed to them not only by perpetrators but also often by victims and other international actors, abstain from maintaining the sham of moral intervention, and put together an independent representation of political emergencies? As an act that presupposes and reinforces a compassionate gaze that is both panoptic and telescopic, a gaze that audiovisual technologies have magnified into a global voyeurism, how can humanitarian testimony refrain from becoming a hollow reproduction of the immediately visible? Finally, in a time marked by a superabundance of images of distant suffering and by a growing institutionalization and professionalization of humanitarian action, what is the role that humanitarian representations should play in capturing and bringing to light the drifts of spectacular witnessing and of expert testimony?[9]

In what follows I would like to bring back these concerns of humanitarian witnessing into the critical discussion of testimony that has been heavily inspired by Holocaust survivors' accounts and self-proclaimingly haunted by the specter of the Jewish Holocaust. My aim in doing so is not to rectify a historical and theoretical negligence so much as to highlight the gaps that separate the self-reflective practices of witnessing elaborated in the humanitarian field more or less at the same period when testimony theory, and artistic practices related to it, have gained momentum from Holocaust memories and from the poststructuralist ethics of testimony invested with them. Holocaust memory and global humanitarian and human rights activism are usually considered as forming a historical and ethical continuum. The latter, which puts slogans such as "Never again!" and "That the world may know" on its banner, is depicted as a sort of mechanical reaction to the former. However, although links obviously do exist between contemporary humanitarian practice and its commitment to bear witness to political violence and the legacy of the Holocaust, I wish to argue that they only partially converge and do not form one seamless fabric of moral sensibility and ethical responsibility.

My argument is based on an examination of the ethics of witnessing of the French section of the now multinational humanitarian movement Médecins Sans Frontières (MSF, or Doctors Without Borders) as it evolved since the 1970s. MSF, recipient of the 1999 Nobel Peace Prize, was founded in 1971 and is well-known for its innovative medical and logistic techniques, its pioneering mobilization of public opinion as an agent of political leverage, and its commitment to *témoignage*—witnessing or bearing witness—which the group regards as "an inseparable supplement to the medical action."[10] Admittedly, the operational priorities and advocacy strategies of MSF-France are far from representative of humanitarian activity in general. Likewise, the organization's current ethics of witnessing—a combination of resounding acts of testimony and of systematic reflection on the role of public speech in humanitarian action—is probably unparalleled in other segments of the humanitarian community. Yet the singularity of MSF matches its notoriety as the actor that has revolutionized the humanitarian field, putting forward an alternative to the rule of the ICRC and its policy of confidentiality. According to its founding myth, MSF was born out of a rejection of the "guilty neutrality" of the ICRC, which kept silent during the Holocaust and refrained from denouncing the Nazi crimes in public. This nexus of a global mode of witnessing—in its aspirations if not in its actual scope—and Holocaust memory turns MSF into a particularly fitting case through which the impact of the Holocaust upon cosmopolitan practices—rather than simply upon ideas or sensibilities that affirm the global reach of moral concern—can be broached.

In what follows I seek to unpack MSF's morality of witnessing and chart how and to what extent Holocaust memories have been actually sedimented in it. I advance two interrelated claims. First, I show that even though Holocaust memories inspired humanitarian acts of witnessing, they did so in disparate, uneven, and even competing and controversial ways. There was no uniform conception of the Holocaust at work in humanitarian witnessing: throughout the years, humanitarian practitioners have activated Holocaust memories selectively, variably choosing from a diverse pool of moral and political sensibilities with which the Holocaust has been associated. Moreover, from the outset, the Holocaust memories invoked by MSF's practitioners have been interwoven with memories of other catastrophes and were part of a multidirectional formation of memory—to use Michael Rothberg's intriguing concept—in which the Jewish Holocaust occupied a central, but in no way exclusive, position.[11] In fact, rather than reacting to a fully formed legacy of past atrocities, humanitarian witnessing, which brought activists and publics into direct confrontation with political evil as it unfolded, has operated as a mnemonic site where the meanings of previous catastrophes were distilled, elaborated, and worked through.[12] What resulted was, to quote Rothberg, an "interplay between different pasts and a heterogeneous present," in which various political disasters—some of them now occurring in French ex-colonies—were juxtaposed and deciphered in light of one another, creating "a circulatory system of cross-reference."[13]

Second, in what follows I show that the ethics of witnessing exercised by MSF has largely outgrown the Holocaust memories that had partially inspired it and has been variably refashioned in new and shifting social and political contexts, serving as the primary means for the articulation of a distinctive humanitarian responsibility. In the next sections I trace the history and evolution of MSF's manifold ethics of witnessing in order to present a thicker account of this key humanitarian practice that questions its immediate association with acts of exposure, documentation, and truth telling. By pondering how the obligation to bear witness to political violence has been concretized, translated into practice, and rationalized, I wish to demonstrate that humanitarian witnessing, as Didier Fassin has argued in a slightly different context, is "much less homogeneous than is often suggested" and that it embraces multiple and even conflicting rationalities.[14] While witnessing has provided an ethical platform for humanitarian practices of documentation, reporting, storytelling, and denunciation, it involved more than the production and dissemination of what Peter Redfield has aptly described as "motivated truth" in states of emergency.[15] Formulated as an ethical action whose primary concern was to turn humanitarian actors into moral witnesses to emergencies, humanitarian witnessing has served other functions, engaged with a more varied set of problems, and has been animated by other concerns than those associated with the struggle against silence and indifference inherited from the Holocaust.

Daniel Levy and Natan Sznaider have argued that the Holocaust lies at the foundation of the postwar human rights regime. In their own words, "we understand the diffusion of human rights norms during the last six decades as the distillation of changing modes of Holocaust memory."[16] Levy and Sznaider claim that the Holocaust has exercised a formative influence on legal instruments such as the Universal Declaration of Human Rights and the UN Genocide Convention that were drafted in the immediate aftermath of World War II. Likewise, they show that Holocaust memory has been extremely patent in the post–Cold War period in calls for or justifications of military intervention to stop atrocities. However, what remains unexplored in their argument is the extent to which Holocaust memories have manifested themselves in more ordinary practices of humanitarian intervention or human rights activism, that is, in what practitioners normally do to put the legal obligations and opportunities enshrined in international human rights and humanitarian law into effect.

Bearing witness, as Fuyuki Kurasawa has shown, is one of the fundamental modes of practice through which the work of global justice is pursued and enacted today. It is one of the prominent patterns of social action in which human rights are embedded and that give flesh and traction to noble ideals of common humanity.[17] This form of ethical-political labor is sidestepped in most accounts of human rights and global justice that tend, as Kurasawa maintains, to "[reify] human rights by reducing them to things legally and institutionally allocated to subjects according to processes that seemingly operate above their heads."[18] Humanitarian and human rights politics and culture, according to this view, ultimately hinges on how practitioners and activists frame and execute moral and juridical obligations and on the overarching aims and meanings that structure and propel their actions.

In this vein, in what follows I will attempt to expand the empirical field in which the links between Holocaust memory and human rights regimes are currently pondered while giving due weight to the structured and structuring modes of collective action that constitute the backbone of humanitarian and human rights work. Such a focus on practices of humanitarian and human rights activism, which, by their very nature, are less hermetically structured than lofty treaties and declarations, may yield a twofold analytical gain. It is liable to provide a fuller and more nuanced portrait of our global moral-political culture, and also to highlight the original, creative, and often contentious work of interpretation involved in the transformation of Holocaust legacy into full-fledged ethical practices. Such a shift from juridical norms to moral and political actions and reflections may also have a direct bearing on broader questions that relate to how the globalization of moral responsibility actually unfolds. Specifically, it illustrates that in a globalized age moral responsibility is not simply extended and universalized but remodeled, as its underlining aims, modes of operation, mobilizing symbols, and intrinsic dilemmas are being recalibrated over and over again.

My aim in the rest of the chapter, then, is to look into the manifold constructions of MSF's ethics of witnessing and disentangle different understandings of how humanitarian witnessing is to be materialized, what turns it into a moral and political act, and in what ways an individual or a collective may turn into an authentic moral witness. I will examine both particular acts of witnessing or testimony and broader schemes of action and reflection that either give form to such acts or are prefigured and propelled by them. My argument will proceed along a chronological line, describing the various interpretations of witnessing in their order of appearance. It should be stressed, however, that the modes of witnessing that will be presented here cohabit in contemporary humanitarian practice and by no means can be taken to substitute one another.

The Seizing of Speech

The invention of humanitarian witnessing is usually attributed to a group of French physicians who volunteered in the ICRC's mission in Biafra in the fall of 1968, during the secession war between the Igbo southeastern provinces and the Nigerian federal government. According to the founding myth of French medical humanitarianism, those physicians were appalled by the destitution of the population in the enclave that was subjected to a protracted Nigerian siege and decided to speak out, thus violating and breaking with the ICRC's policy of confidentiality.[19] This inaugurating act of testimony was propelled by a condemnation of the silence of the ICRC during the Holocaust and its interpretation of the principle of neutrality. "It is impossible for us to keep quiet on what we saw and experienced," stated the physicians in an unsigned article published in January 1969; "the ambiguous approach of the Red Cross during the last war in relation to the massacres of the Jews was reproached to such an extent that a similar deed cannot repeat itself one more time."[20]

Bernard Kouchner, the most famous member of this group and a future founder of MSF, stated in retrospect that vociferous humanitarianism was "completely related" to the Holocaust, whose principal lesson was that "one should always be there and be a witness."[21] But although the silence of the ICRC and other bystanders during the Holocaust captured the imagination of Kouchner and his fellows, it was not the sole factor behind the introduction of testimony into the humanitarian repertoire. Kouchner and some of his colleagues had previously been members of radical leftists groups and were involved in the student protests in May 1968 as well as in the anticolonial struggle.[22] This political trajectory would ground their humanitarian engagement in a broad array of historical references, which did not limit itself to the Jewish Holocaust. As Kouchner later confessed, "I came to provide medical care in Biafra because I hadn't gone to Guernica, nor to Auschwitz, nor to Babi Yar, nor to Oradour-sur-Glane, nor to Sétif. In Biafra we were going to exorcise the nightmares of the grand massacres of Humanity, which were not reacted against sufficiently."[23] The legacy of the May 1968 events, which left their enduring mark on an entire generation of young French, played an important role in turning testimony into a conceivable and attractive political practice to start with. For contemporary observers, the liberation and the seizing of speech were among the most conspicuous features of the student uprising, in which language was foregrounded in playful and provocative speech acts.[24] "The event," as Pierre Nora has written, "became intimately related to its expression,"[25] designating speech as the primary arena of political action.

According to the standard history of the *sans frontières* movement, Biafra marked the liberation of humanitarian speech and inaugurated a brave new age of humanitarian engagement. The reality, however, was somewhat less unilinear. When MSF was founded in 1971 by Kouchner and his fellows together with a group of physicians formed around the medical newspaper *Tonus*, MSF's volunteers were prohibited from communicating their impressions in public.[26] Some of the founders accordingly declared that they will "go off on a mission as doctors, not as witnesses, and will come back the same."[27] "Silence," they stated, "is the condition of our efficacy," and the sole guarantee of access to theaters of war.[28] The injunction to refrain from testifying about disaster zones did not apply equally, however, to all forms of public speech. While in the first years of MSF's existence its executive committee took great pains to stifle denunciatory statements, first-person testimonies of volunteers who focused on their own personal experiences in far-flung emergencies were tolerated and sometimes even encouraged. By and large, at this embryonic stage the ethos of witnessing that animated the physicians' contentious proclamations in Biafra was overtaken by the ethos of medical secrecy and of medical neutrality, advanced by those founders and members associated with *Tonus*.

During the early years of its existence, MSF functioned largely as a placement agency, matching international development agencies and other humanitarian organizations with French physicians interested in working in developing countries. But as the organization grew and became more professionalized the view of testimony as the centerpiece of humanitarian action associated with Kouchner was marginalized to an even greater extent. In 1978, the executive board of MSF rejected Kouchner's proposal to man a ship—*l'Ile de lumière*—that would patrol the South China Sea taking on board refugees fleeing Communist Vietnam. While mainly grounded in operational reasons—the claim that a publicized tour in open sea would not succeed in recuperating the refugees, the observation that the latter needed a sustainable solution rather than sporadic acts of rescue, and the fear that such an operation would impel more refugees to risk the dangerous maritime flight[29]—MSF's decision also incarnated an opposition to the spectacular and self-justifying mode of witnessing advanced by Kouchner. Spokespersons for MSF responded to Kouchner's suggestion by reproaching it for its "lack of anonymity," hinting that the project was a means of self-promotion and, as such, carried out in violation of MSF's charter.[30] Likewise, they derided the members of the committee "A Boat for Vietnam" that initiated the project as "professional redressors of wrongs."[31]

Indeed, Kouchner's initiative sought to create new points of contact between intellectuals and celebrities—the traditional carriers of moral indignation—and humanitarian physicians.[32] Bringing their moral habitus together under the sign of emergency (*urgence*), or what Kouchner has called "the philosophy of the ambulance,"[33] it put forth a highly mediatized relief operation that merged witnessing with dramatic acts of rescue, casting them as mutually reinforcing gestures. The aid mission, which eventually took place without MSF's participation and under wide media coverage, was informed by what Kouchner would later call "the law of hype" (*le loi de tapage*). This particular alignment of humanitarian action and media representation was motivated by the recognition that, as Kouchner later put it, "speech protects" and testimony forms a "counterpower" to oppression.[34] Yet, it went even further than that in presupposing that the emergency was nonexistent if not adequately covered by the media and that "there is no indignation without an image."[35] Moreover, Kouchner's conception of testimony set vehement speech as a default response to political suffering, which had to take place notwithstanding its actual prospects of changing the course of disaster. "Since we're not done with the horror," he once stated, "it is better to shout, make a fuss, act as frenetic. There may remain something of it."[36]

The debate over *l'Ile de lumière,* which led Kouchner, along with other founding members, to quit MSF and found a new organization called Médecins du Monde that pursued his conception of witnessing, called into question the association of witnessing with passionate appeals that showcased individual conscience, put the figure of the witness to the fore, and celebrated the act of witnessing as the decisive response both to past and present atrocities. It triggered the crystallization of competing approaches to humanitarian witnessing that perceived it less as an assertion of a preexisting moral subjectivity and more as a means for humanitarian practitioners to cultivate an ethical personality and to craft themselves an autonomous moral position in political conflicts. Whereas Kouchner's model of witnessing reenacted preestablished models of intellectual indignation and conceived aid work primarily, in Ann Vallaeys's phrase, as "compassionate amplificator" of distant suffering, the alternative conceptions of witnessing that were consolidated in MSF since the end of the 1970s brought witnessing closer to the organization's increasingly professionalized medical and humanitarian aid practices and to the particular opportunities and challenges that they embodied.[37]

Direct Presence and Fact-Based Political Truth

The prohibition on testimony that was set in the first charter of MSF was perfectly in line with how witnessing was generally practiced by the group up until the mid-1980s. As Judith Soussan has shown, at this stage public statements were still made sporadically and witnessing mainly consisted of presence "where the others don't go," to quote one of MSF's most familiar slogans during the 1970s. A personal act that occurred far from the limelight of the public sphere, witnessing was associated, as one of its definitions in MSF's core principles would later put it, with "the direct presence of the volunteers next to people in danger in order to perform the medical gesture that combines proximity and listening."[38] "Going there" and "being there" emerged at this period as meaningful actions in their own right, as gestures that, however much they were entangled with the provision of medical assistance, produced their own beneficial consequences. Presence, according to Soussan, was "more than a neutral fact: in a world that is 'closing,' it [was] an act—an act considered protective (in the common sense of setting an obstacle to acts of violence) by its double aim of being '*close to*' and being a witness."[39]

The intrinsic ethical value that was attributed to presence in disaster zones was not only related to its interpretation as a protective act and as a sign of concern and solidarity. Concomitantly, direct witnessing was framed as an exceptional and even privileged experience that possessed the power to expand the physician's relations to others as well as his or her relations to him or herself. "Physicians returning from such missions," stated, for example, Xavier Emmanuelli, one of the founding members of MSF, "will no longer be entirely the same."[40] For physicians who took part in MSF's missions in the late 1970s and the beginning of the 1980s, the unmediated encounters with third world victims that were in immediate need of life-saving medical assistance were an opportunity to rediscover the true nature of medical practice and to retrieve the intimate dialogue with the patient, which was perceived to be under threat by the commercialization and technicalization of medicine in France.[41] Witnessing far-flung misery that was normally beyond the pale of Western physicians was construed as a gesture that lent a moral twist to standard medical practice and transformed physicians into better and more enlightened persons.[42]

Witnessing was therefore a mode of practice that was geared indistinguishably toward care for distant victims and toward care for Western selves. It was a form of ethical work (*ascesis*) that physicians performed upon themselves, and through which they could turn themselves simultaneously into humanitarian practitioners and more humane physicians.[43] The advent of this aspect of witnessing corresponded to the widespread feeling that the medical profession was in crisis and to the mounting critique leveled against the medicalization of society and the power of experts. This was reflected, for example, in the report on the founding of MSF published in the medical newspaper *Tonus*, which played a significant role in bringing the organization into being. Heralding MSF as "[t]he answer to all those who have doubted you," *Tonus* painted the physician as the "scapegoat of a certain society of consumption" and lauded those "[t]hree hundred among you and if necessary others more tomorrow" who "proved that disinterestedness, dedication, and a certain form of abnegation were the mark of this medical profession so much decried."[44] For *Tonus*, which first engaged with the organization of relief activities following the cyclone in Pakistan in 1970, direct, physical involvement of doctors in the plight of distant sufferers offered an opportunity to inspire physicians, who were growing increasingly frustrated with their medical practice, with a different perception of their profession. At the same time, a private, agile, and efficient relief dispensed by physicians who were not affiliated with any official or governmental body could reaffirm the virtues of the unique model of French liberal medicine, which *Tonus* strove to uphold against mounting fears of the socialization and technicalization of medical practice.

While direct presence has been the form of witnessing that most of MSF's aid workers engaged with throughout the years, it was not the sole nor the most influential version of witnessing that was consolidated in the *sans frontières* movement in the late 1970s. In what Rony Brauman later described as an attempt to appropriate the legacy of contentious testimony associated with the founding fathers of MSF, following the split in the organization its new leadership developed a new mode of witnessing that seemed to correspond more neatly with contemporary political concerns.[45] Influenced by the antitotalitarian sentiment that surged in France after the publication of Aleksandr Solzhenitsyn's *The Gulag Archipelago* and the discovery of the atrocities committed by the Khmer Rouge regime in Cambodia, MSF's newly elected management set out to erect witnessing as a counterweight to Marxist ideologies and as the pivot of an alternative model of political truth.

In 1979, in the wake of the fall of the Khmer Rouge dictatorship, MSF's general secretary, Claude Malhuret, and Brauman, who was hired as the first fully paid employee of the organization, initiated the organization's first public campaign, "The March for the Survival of Cambodia," to protest against what they perceived as the obstacles set by the Vietnamese army—which occupied parts of Cambodia after liberating the country from the Khmer Rouge dictatorship—to the humanitarian relief operation deployed after the fall of the regime. Arguably following a public relations briefing that recommended placing "the agony of the Khmer people in parallel to holocausts that no one can refute (without treating the problem on a political level but solely by employing the language of the heart),"[46] MSF leaders made abundant use of the genocide trope in their public appeals, relating not to the deeds of the now defunct Khmer Rouge regime but rather to the possible consequences of the Vietnamese occupation. In an article published in MSF's newsletter Malhuret proclaimed, for example, that as a result of the famine that raged in Cambodia and the limited access that international observers were afforded to its victims, "after that of the Armeniens and that of the Jews the third genocide of the 20th century is almost completed."[47]

These conjuring of genocides, in the plural, followed closely on a series of public affairs that cast Holocaust memory as a major issue in French public life, "plunging the country," in the words of Henry Rousso, "into lasting and bitter turmoil."[48] In a bit more than a year, and immediately preceding MSF's Cambodia campaign, the publication of the anti-Semitic statements of Louis Darquier, the former head of Vichy's office for Jewish affairs, the controversy around the screening of the American TV series *Holocaust*, the indictment of several Vichy officials who were previously exempted under the statute of limitations, and the negationist campaign of Robert Faurisson all contributed to making the Holocaust not just extremely present in French public discourses, but also more politically charged than ever before.[49] By insisting—against the reports of observers who visited Cambodia, among them physicians affiliated with the French Communist Party—that genocide was raging in the country as a result of the restrictive policies of Communist Vietnam, MSF was actually drawing on and prolonging these fresh controversies over Holocaust representation and political accountability to mass violence. The accusations made by the organization, which had considerable repercussions in France and managed to cast the condition of the Cambodian population in a cloud of incertitude, were both processing the same moral and political issues brought up in previous, Holocaust-related debates and instantiating them in a new context. What resulted was a merging of the politics of Holocaust memory—rather than of Holocaust memory per se—with the politics of a third world emergency.[50] In an effort to raise awareness of the Cambodian plight, MSF invited some two hundred public figures from France and elsewhere to join members of the organization in an action whose declared goal was to cross the border into Cambodia and "convince the Vietnamese occupier not to abandon the survivors of the Khmer Rouge genocide to their deaths."[51] "The simplest solution would have been to launch a campaign of petitions," wrote Brauman at the time, but "we preferred action that calls for the physical engagement, 'on the ground,' of public figures from all spheres of culture and politics, who may thus bear witness."[52] Keen on manifesting the impenetrability of the Cambodian territory, the tour that was organized by MSF included a symbolic protest on the border between Thailand and Cambodia, but also highly publicized visits of refugee camps where MSF's relief programs were under way.[53] By juxtaposing the refugee camp, a site of perfect visibility where the condition of remote victims could be attested to with certainty, to the shut-off state occupied by Communist Vietnam to which foreign observers had only limited access, the march positioned the camp and the humanitarian technologies that it harbored as an antithesis to Marxist politics.[54]

The refugee camp has been MSF's primary site of operation since the late 1970s. The Cambodian refugee camps in Thailand, where dozens of MSF volunteers operated in this period, were perceived, as the then president of MSF Xavier Emmanuelli later put it, as "virgin territory," providing a unique opportunity to conceive and develop standardized methods for operation in mass crises that would eventually become the hallmark of MSF.[55] It was in these camps in Thailand that the organization first endeavored to take full charge of planning and implementing large-scale aid operations and took the first steps toward their systematization.[56] The Cambodia campaign marked the intertwining of this emerging biopolitical apparatus, which conceived of the refugees as "bare life" devoid of political, cultural, and social identity markers,[57] with an apparatus of witnessing, which promoted the victims as the most legitimate foundation of political truth. It was the site that best materialized the dual ambition "to be actors who witness, or witnesses who act," which, according to Brauman, "imposed itself as self-evident" for the new leaders of the organization.[58]

The camp was a platform for the creation and public dissemination of truth claims about remote victims—a space where refugee testimonies could be collected, epidemiological data could be gathered and analyzed, and TV crews could produce compelling images of mass suffering. As such, it laid down the infrastructure for a mode of witnessing that was inseparable from the medical gaze and surveillance and shared their reduction of political evil to infallibly observed and documented distress. This affinity was borne out, for example, in several interviews given by MSF members around the event of the march in which they blended heart-rending descriptions of the plight of Cambodian refugees with detailed accounts of the medical and logistic techniques developed specifically for operating in camps.[59] In this context, to witness meant, essentially, to view politics from the perspective of "the ground" in which the raw facts of suffering were disclosed. It was perhaps no coincidence that in 1979, several months before the Cambodia campaign, Malhuret announced the intention to include mainly "informations, raw data or almost, and images" in MSF's newsletter, and to make more room for expression by its volunteers.[60]

Against the backdrop of the decline, but in no way the disappearance, of the Marxist worldview in France, the refugee camp operated as a "truth machine" that gave new impetus both to aid operations in the third world and to the antitotalitarian standpoint that was gaining momentum in France.[61] On the one hand, with the emergence of this specialized space for the care and protection of victims, the feeling that victims could no longer be discriminated against on the basis of their political affiliation could be embodied in standard techniques of observation, documentation, and narration, thus allowing for the rejection of ideologies to mount on an independent political trajectory. On the other hand, with the consolidation of a space of witnessing that provided perfect visibility of and unhindered access to the victims, a bridge was created between epidemiological techniques for the administration of life and the public sphere, thus allowing for medical gestures to be more easily translated into meaningful moral and political acts. MSF's reinvigoration of humanitarian factuality occurred on the crossroad between the medical gaze and the liberal opposition to Communist regimes, which was couched in an attempt to provide an alternative to the discourse of political enmity. It was fed both by the medicalization of humanitarian assistance and by the reconfiguration of the political field in France and elsewhere as the left-right dichotomy was wearing out.

Similar to Kouchner's parallel conception, MSF's new ethos of factual witnessing had its roots in a blend of holocausts memories (in the plural), acknowledgment of media power, and political remorse over previous Marxist convictions. Yet, it was guided by a very different idea of testimonial truth and of the means required to achieve it. In contradistinction to acts of witnessing that set the individual witness and his or her moral sentiments as their centerpiece and considered the value of testimony to be dependent upon the quality of the witness' performance, this mode of witnessing advanced by MSF since the end of the 1970s was shaped primarily as a collective enterprise. Unlike other examples of moral and political witnessing, it bracketed the subject of testimony and foregrounded instead the objective power of facts.[62] Witnessing was the name given to a political epistemology that sought to replace ideological loyalties. It pointed to an ongoing practice that was jointly carried out by a plurality of observers, who similarly deferred to the authority of unmediated suffering. Combining first-person narratives, often produced by relatively anonymous volunteers, and truth claims that were also, as Peter Redfield has shown, ethically engaged, this mode of witnessing remained prominent throughout the history of MSF.[63]

Speaking Out and the Consolidation of Humanitarian Concerns

Up until the mid-1980s, then, MSF's ethics of witnessing encompassed two complimentary models that incarnated different views as to the end of witnessing and its modus operandi: one that highlighted individual acts of presence in far-flung emergencies, which were considered as a medium both of assistance to and protection of people in danger and of subjective transformation of Western experts; and another that put emphasis on the collective production and dissemination of facts related to the human consequences of emergencies, regarded both as a prerequisite for other public actions and as a means for creating and securing a space for humanitarian sensibility in the political sphere. MSF's third formulation of witnessing, which would gain considerable weight in the 1990s, was in many ways an outgrowth of the previous two: a response to the blind spots of humanitarian empiricism, and an extension of the ethical labor needed in order to turn physicians into truly moral witnesses.

MSF's own conceptualization of witnessing as contentious speech germinated during its relief operations to the victims of the famine in Ethiopia in 1985, which provoked an unprecedented wave of public interest and donations. In what was since sacralized as a landmark in the evolution of humanitarian witnessing, the heads of the organization protested against the forced relocations conducted by the Marxist Ethiopian government and warned that humanitarian aid was being used as a bait to draw the civilian population to what were actually transit camps from which it was forcefully and violently transferred to the south of the country. As a consequence, MSF was expelled from Ethiopia and had to cease its aid programs. "What happened in Ethiopia returns us to several fundamental questions," stated Brauman, MSF's president at the time, at the general assembly of the organization held several months after the affair. "What is the limit beyond which it becomes legitimate to speak out, when we know that this means the expulsion of the medical teams? By what standard are we to measure the interest of the men and women whom we are going to aid? Under what circumstances does silence, a natural consort of the neutral operation on the ground, become blindness, if not collaboration?"[64]

The idea that aid could be unwittingly turned into collaboration and that the integrity of the humanitarian witness had to be reaffirmed by speaking out against his own implication in the workings of power was nourished by a variety of Holocaust memories. Brauman, who acted as MSF's president from 1982 until 1994 and was the living spirit behind the testimony on Ethiopia, revealed in retrospect that although still related to the "guilty silence" of the ICRC, this act was mainly inspired by Hannah Arendt's *Eichmann in Jerusalem*, which pointed to the duty to refuse to take part in oppressive actions of state.[65] As Brauman summarized this ethical position years later, "if you can't prevent a crime, you should at least avoid taking part in it."[66] Yet for its audience if not for its users, the trope of collaboration must have resonated with other historical references as well. In a special newsletter distributed to donors and to the press, Brauman invoked, for example, "the incredible passivity of Europeans when they were confronted with the deportations" to justify MSF's decision to speak out. This conjuring of the memories of the German occupation built upon, and probably also contributed to, the intensification of what Rousso has called "the Vichy syndrome," which since the late 1970s has become, according to Rousso, a matter of true obsession for the French society.[67] The testimony in Ethiopia inaugurated a new genre of humanitarian speech acts that was not concerned with the exposure of atrocities per se as with the cessation of the unwitting collaboration of humanitarian organizations with power and violence. As Brauman later remarked, "We did not want merely to denounce [Ethiopia's] policies. The main issue for us was that, as members of the humanitarian community, we found ourselves contributing to the destruction of the people we had come to help."[68] The moral and political crux of these acts of witnessing did not consist in the disclosure of hitherto unknown information—the forced relocations in Ethiopia were documented and published before MSF took a public stand on the matter[69]—nor was it exhausted by the simple occurrence of speech and the alleged dissipation of silence. What seemed to have turned these protests into acts of witnessing in the full, ethical sense of the term was the fact that they rescued the humanitarian witness from the grip of political power. By unraveling the adverse consequences of their actions and annunciating their exploitation by violent forces, humanitarian activists actually reaffirmed their autonomous moral position in conflicts and refashioned themselves as moral, rather than simply epistemic, witnesses.

The case of Ethiopia gave rise to the recognition that the physicians' presence in disaster zones was hardly sufficient for moral witnessing to be accomplished. As this presence was often manipulated by oppressive forces and turned against the victims that the humanitarian practitioners were striving to help, it could not perform as the unique channel either for the protection of victims or for the ethical self-cultivation of the aid workers. Against this backdrop, speaking out was therefore, and simultaneously, a way to care for the victims and to transform physicians into witnesses whose credibility relied both on medical expertise and the capacity to transgress it. Whereas one of the main preoccupations and effects of witnessing for Kouchner was to fill up, retrospectively, the empty place of the witness to catastrophe, this new mode of speaking out was more forward-looking in terms of its performativity, attempting to confront the political challenges of witnessing in the present and to generate both an individual and a collective figure of an independent witness that can tackle them efficiently. The point was not to fight an endless battle against indifference past and present, but rather to more thoughtfully address the power relations in current theaters of intervention.

The testimony against the forced relocations in Ethiopia left an enduring mark on the culture and ethics of witnessing of MSF-France. With the changing landscape of violence in the third world following the end of the Cold War and the withdrawal of superpower patronage and with the expansion of the mandate, fields of operation, and number of humanitarian organizations, reflexive testimonies acquired a new currency in the organization. The most paradigmatic and contentious testimony in what became a series of similar acts performed by MSF-France during the political disasters of the 1990s occurred in November 1994, a few months after the genocide in Rwanda. MSF publicly criticized the control of the Hutu *génocidaires* that found refuge in Congo (then Zaire) and Tanzania in the aftermath of the genocide over the refugee camps that were maintained and provided by humanitarian organizations, and declared its intention to cease its relief operation there. Explaining its stand in a newsletter for donors, MSF argued that "faced with a situation in which women and men are manipulated by a power guilty of genocide ... the responsibility of a humanitarian organization consists first and foremost in refusing in any way to vouch for this power through its actions."[70]

As in Ethiopia, the testimony on the Hutu refugee camps took shape for the most part in the headquarters of MSF-France, although the volunteers who were working in the camp took part in the deliberations that led to the decision to speak out and cease relief operations.[71] Far from being an eyewitness report detailing one's impressions of a specific episode, it was actually a proclamation that was nourished by the accumulated experience of the organization and issued after lengthy discussions and debates with volunteers and senior practitioners from several sections of the MSF international movement.[72] Like its predecessor in Ethiopia, MSF's statement embodied a shift, as Brauman has later suggested, from attestation to analysis, integrating and ethically framing available information rather than presenting new facts.[73] Going beyond the image, inherited from Kouchner, of humanitarian speaking out as a cry from the heart, this act was embedded in a sustained reflection on the political dynamics of crises and on the obstacles that prevented humanitarian action from attaining positive and efficient results.

The reciprocal links between acts of testimony and political analysis were already manifest in MSF's statement on the forced relocations in Ethiopia. The latter was produced shortly after the organization had established a controversial think tank, Liberté Sans Frontières, which initiated studies and conferences that sought to counter the dominant ideology of development known as third worldism while deflecting the blame for third world deprivation from the West to local regimes. In the mid-1990s, humanitarian reflection gained force and became both less provocative and more firmly institutionalized. In 1995, MSF-France turned an auxiliary organ called the MSF Foundation into a research department that supported the writing and publication of case studies and programmatic articles that dealt with the problematic linkages between humanitarian organizations and other actors in crisis zones and pondered the ethical dilemmas to which they gave rise. Together with the book series *Populations in Danger*, which discussed a number of acute emergencies at length, these internal studies formed an expanding corpus of humanitarian knowledge that applied analytical methods from such disciplines as international relations and political economy to what were increasingly coming to be seen as distinctively humanitarian problems.

Since the mid-1990s, MSF-France's acts of testimony increasingly converged with critical insights on the role of humanitarian action in emergencies that were elaborated by this apparatus of research and reflection, while forming one of their main breeding grounds. This coming together of acts of testimony and case-based knowledge on emergencies added up to a systematic ethical reflection on humanitarian action. In fact, MSF's efforts to disentangle and confront the quandaries of humanitarianism stood in sharp contrast to other ethical initiatives that mushroomed during the 1990s in response to what was perceived as the growing complexity of emergency zones, and mainly consisted of the codification of humanitarian principles. It brought forth an open-ended ethics that strove not to provide uniform solutions to humanitarian dilemmas but rather to tackle the quandaries of intervention in a casuistic manner, by systematically extricating the hard choices made in previous formative cases.

This ethical labor actually amounted to the construction of a new, multidirectional formation of humanitarian memory. The ethical connection forged between past, present, and future emergencies has increasingly reoriented the impetus to speak out and the justification to do so away from the shadow of the archetypal catastrophe and toward a series of emergencies in which similar pitfalls of aid were exhibited and either acted upon or ignored. Remarkably, there was hardly any direct reference to the Holocaust in the newsletter in which MSF sought to explain its withdrawal from the Hutu refugee camps, which did feature, conversely, "the precedents" in which the organization had to "put into question its founding principle [of] being at the side of the victims."[74]

The case of the Hutu refugees reflected the extent to which humanitarian judgment came to revolve around the issue of witnessing and its presumably harsh consequences. Moreover, it indicated the cleavages between the various ethos of witnessing that had been cultivated in MSF, which came to be seen more and more as conflicting. These disparities were staged most clearly when, following the case of the Hutu *génocidaires,* different sections of MSF's international federation diverged as to the appropriate action to take. Whether to maintain presence and to provide medical assistance on the ground or to speak out against abuses in a way that might endanger the continuation of the relief effort; whether to spread facts on the state of the victims or to point a finger toward their oppressors and complicit third parties—these options, which were each endorsed by different sections, were construed as the matrix of the humanitarian dilemmas.[75]

With varied sections of MSF's international federation embracing a different interpretation of witnessing, the decision between those interpretations figured not just as one of the most intense and unsettling humanitarian choices but also as a marker of one's humanitarian identity. In fact, in view of the growing internationalization of MSF's decision making on the one hand, and the appropriation of the humanitarian mission by more official and nongovernmental bodies on the other, acts of witnessing increasingly corresponded to needs and concerns that arose from within the humanitarian field. While enhancing the autonomy of the witnessing organization, speaking out also distinguished it from other agents that were veering for material and symbolic capital in a competitive humanitarian field. In this respect, it was a message addressed not just to governments, policy makers, and public opinion, but to other humanitarian agents as well.

Conclusion

In this brief, and undoubtedly incomplete, history of witnessing in one prominent humanitarian NGO, I sought to demonstrate that humanitarian witnessing has been far more than an expression and response to a moral obligation inherited from the Holocaust and other seminal catastrophes. However much it has been triggered by the "negative paradigm," to use a term put forward by Brauman, of the silence of the ICRC during the Holocaust, humanitarian witnessing followed its own courses of evolution, which corresponded to the contemporary political landscape of third world emergencies and Western public spheres.[76] It has grown to be the pivot of a sui generis humanitarian ethics, framing and grounding an ethical subjectivity, a truth regime, and a mode of moral reasoning that distinguished humanitarian engagement from other ethical and political ventures.

Interestingly, MSF's reflective ethics of witnessing had very little in common with poststructuralist insights that were elaborated around the same period by thinkers such as Jean-François Lyotard, Shoshana Felman and Dori Laub, and Giorgio Agamben, who construed witnessing as both an acting out and a working through of the ethical burden of Auschwitz.[77] While both conceptualizations shared an understanding of witnessing as an ethically problematic, and at the same time morally effectual, act, they gave rise to incommensurable paradigms of witnessing that were preoccupied with disparate moral quandaries. Indeed, both similarly assumed that the act of testimony was not simply the retrospective verbal reflection of the state of witnessing: both maintained that presence in the midst of events was not a sufficient condition of bearing witness and that it both validated and unsettled testimony. Accordingly, both held that witnessing did not solely hinge on one's proximity to the epicenter of disaster, and that its meaningful execution had to be thoughtfully constructed—by cultivating intuition, perception, and analytical skills in the case of humanitarian witnesses, or by creating conditions of emphatic conversation that will elicit and disseminate traumatic memories of the past in the case of Holocaust survivors and their secondary witnesses.

However, the poststructuralist "ethics of survivors," to use a term coined by Ronit Peleg, has been primarily concerned with the unfathomability of the catastrophe: it considered testimony as the moral reaction that corresponded to the unique, ongoing, and never-ending assault on witnessing that distinguished the final solution from other political disasters, and regarded individualized work of memory as a form of struggle against the always imminent realization of the catastrophe.[78] The humanitarian practices of reflexive witnessing, by contrast, principally sought to address the unruliness of the emergency: they construed witnessing and testimony as acts that have the power to restore the integrity of the humanitarian witness and assure some measure of morality in violent, lawless, and morally disorienting environments.

Whereas theories of testimony, which mainly drew on survivors' accounts of the Holocaust, considered witnessing as a philosophical laboratory in which relations between subjectivity and alterity, discourse and corporeality, were broached in their widest sense, humanitarian ethics was mainly interested in probing the meanings and implications of witnessing understood as a distinctive moral and political action. In fact, the ethics of witnessing that drew its impetus from the Holocaust and set the traumatic event as a philosophical, rather than as a political, model was incapable of conceiving, and let along addressing, the complexities and challenges involved in witnessing that was contemporaneous to the emergency and that faced not one singular catastrophe but a host of political disasters simultaneously. For testimony to go global and become the practical infrastructure of a new cosmopolitics, for witnessing to take root and to become a routinized expression of global citizenship, the ethical legacy of the Holocaust had, in many respects, to be bypassed.

Notes

1. Claude Lanzmann, "Un vivant qui passe," *Les Temps Modernes* 627 (April–June 2004): 160–88.
2. Ibid., 160. All translations are the author's.
3. Ibid., 161.
4. Shoshana Felman, "The Return of the Voice: Claude Lanzmann's *Shoah*," in *Testimony: Crises of Witnessing in Literature, Psychoanalysis and History*, by Shoshana Felman and Dori Laub (New York: Routledge, 1992), 205.
5. Ibid., 211.
6. Ibid.
7. Lanzmann, "Un vivant qui passe," 175.
8. Felman, "The Return of the Voice," 209.
9. The contemporary concerns of humanitarian witnessing were analyzed most notably in Thomas Keenan, "Publicity and Indifference," *PMLA* 117, no. 1 (January 2002): 104–16, and

James Dawes, *That the World May Know: Bearing Witness to Atrocities* (Cambridge, MA, and London: Harvard University Press, 2007).

10. MSF, "Principes de référence du mouvement Médecins Sans frontières (Document de Chantilly)," 1995.

11. See Michael Rothberg, "Between Auschwitz and Algeria: Multidirectional Memory and the Counterpublic Witness," *Critical Inquiry* 33 (2006): 158–84.

12. For a similar claim according to which "Holocaust memory and the new rights culture are … mutually constitutive," see Daniel Levy and Natan Sznaider, "The Institutionalization of Cosmopolitan Morality: The Holocaust and Human Rights," *Journal of Human Rights* 3, no. 2 (June 2004): 155.

13. Ibid., 162, 182.

14. Didier Fassin, "The Humanitarian Politics of Testimony: Subjectification through Trauma in the Israeli-Palestinian Conflict," *Cultural Anthropology* 23 (2008): 552.

15. Peter Redfield, "A Less Modest Witness: Collective Advocacy and Motivated Truth in a Medical Humanitarian Movement," *American Ethnologist* 33, no. 1 (2006): 3–26.

16. Levy and Sznaider, "The Institutionalization of Cosmopolitan Morality," 147. Levy and Sznaider's claim has been recently challenged by studies that showed that the Universal Declaration of Human Rights was not actually propelled by Holocaust memory, which is mythically considered to lie at its roots. See Samuel Moyn, *The Last Utopia: Human Rights in History* (Cambridge, MA, and London: Harvard University Press, 2010), 7; Marco Duranti, "The Holocaust, the Legacy of 1789 and the Birth of International Human Rights Law: Revisiting the Foundation Myth," *Journal of Genocide Research* 14, no. 2 (2012): 159–86.

17. Fuyuki Kurasawa, *The Work of Global Justice: Human Rights as Practices* (Cambridge: Cambridge University Press, 2007), intro. and chap. 1.

18. Ibid., 194.

19. Anne Vallaeys has recently shown that the story of the clash between the French physicians and the ICRC that supposedly resulted from this testimony was inflated. See Anne Vallaeys, *Médecins Sans Frontières: La biographie* (Paris: Fayard, 2004), 74–79.

20. "Attendre l'extermination?," *Concours médical,* January 1969.

21. Bernard Kouchner, "L'humanitaire a changé le monde," *Le Temps Modernes* 627 (April–June 2004): 12.

22. See Caroline Bollini, "La construction de la légitimité de Médecins sans frontières dans l'espace public" (master's thesis, Université de Nanterre–Paris X, 2001).

23. Bernard Kouchner, "La loi de l'oppression minimale," in *Le devoir d'ingérence: Peut-on les laisser mourir?,* ed. Mario Bettati and Bernard Kouchner (Paris: Denoël, 1987), 17–18.

24. See Jean-Pierre Le Goff, *Mai 68, l'héritage impossible* (Paris: La Découverte, 2002), chap. 5.

25. Cited in ibid., 73.

26. See MSF's first charter ("La Charte de Médecins sans Frontières," *Tonus,* 3 January 1972) and first statute (MSF, "Statuts de Médecins sans Frontières," 20 December 1971, art. 8).

27. Françoise Cordier, "Médecins sans Frontières," *Le Quotidien du Médecin,* 16 December 1971, 5.

28. François Jacquemont, "Le docteur Pigeon, 'La souffrance, partout, c'est l'ennemi,'" *L'est republicaine,* 26 December 1971; see also Vallaeys, *Médecins Sans Frontières,* 125.

29. These arguments are presented by Xavier Emmanuelli, MSF's vice president, in "Un bateau pour saint-germain-des-pres," *Quotidien du Médecin* (4 Septembre 1978).

30. Françoise Cordier, "'On peut pas toujours faire du spectaculaire,'" *Quotidien du Médecin,* 10 May 1979.

31. Emmanuelli, "Un bateau pour saint-germain-des-pres."

32. The appeal "A Boat for Vietnam" was endorsed by well-known French personalities affiliated both with the left and with the right, such as Raymond Aron, Alain Geismar, Bernard-Henri Lévy, Yves Montand, Roland Barth, Michel Foucault, Jean-Paul Sartre, and Simone Signoret. See Vallaeys, *Médecins Sans Frontières,* 280–81.

33. Andre Glucksmann and Bernard Kouchner, "Preuve par le Cambodge," *Le Nouvel Observateur*, 26 November 1979.
34. Kouchner, "La loi de l'oppression minimale," 18, 19.
35. Bernard Kouchner, "Le movement humanitaire," *Le Debat* 67 (November–December 1991): 30–40.
36. Glucksmann and Kouchner, "Preuve par le Cambodge."
37. Vallaeys, *Médecins Sans Frontières*, 248.
38. MSF, "Principes de référence du mouvement Médecins Sans Frontières."
39. Judith Soussan, *MSF et la protection: Une question réglée?* (Paris: MSF, 2008), 13 (emphasis in original).
40. Xavier Emmanuelli, "A quoi servons-nous?," *Bulletin Médecins Sans Frontières*, no. 2 (January–March 1975): 4. This argument is developed in greater length in Michal Givoni, "Humanitarian Governance and Ethical Cultivation: Médecins sans Frontières and the Advent of the Expert-Witness," *Millennium* 40, no. 1 (2011): 43–63.
41. These issues are repeatedly invoked in press interviews given by volunteer physicians after their return from their missions.
42. These arguments draw on a more detailed analysis of MSF's ethics of witnessing in the 1970s that I provide in my article "Humanitarian Governance and Ethical Cultivation."
43. On the notion of ethical work, see Michel Foucault, *The Use of Pleasure* (New York: Vintage Books, 1990), 28; Thomas Osborne, "Power and Persons: On Ethical Stylization and Person-Centered Medicine," *Sociology of Health and Illness* 16 (1994): 517. The interconnections between humanitarian work and ethical labor were analyzed, in relation to the historical case of the Quakers in the Gaza Strip in the wake of the Nakba, in Ilana Feldman, "The Quaker Way: Ethical Labor and Humanitarian Relief," *American Ethnologist* 34, no. 4 (2007): 689–705.
44. Philippe Bernier, "La reponse à tous ceux qui doutaient de vous," *Tonus*, 3 January 1972, 1, 3.
45. Rony Brauman, "Les liaisons dangereuses du témoignage humanitaire et des propagandes politiques: Biafra, Cambodge, les mythes fondateurs de Médecins Sans Frontières," in *Crises extrêmes: Face aux massacres, aux guerres civiles et aux génocides*, ed. Marc Le Pape, Johanna Siméant, and Claudine Vidal (Paris: La Découvert, 2006).
46. MSF, "Cambodge: Operation Marche pour la Survie," Paris, 7 January 1980, Archive MSF-France.
47. Claude Malhuret, "Agonies …," *Bulletin d'informations de médecins sans frontières* 3 (August–September 1979): 2.
48. Henry Rousso, *The Vichy Syndrom: History and Memory in France since 1944* (Cambridge, MA: Harvard University Press, 1994), 157.
49. For a detailed discussion of these affairs, see ibid., chap. 4.
50. Similar, though less explicit, interconnections were evinced in the polemics over François Ponchaud's *Cambodge année zéro*, a book that was published in France in 1977 and documented the Khmer Rouge's atrocities based on victims' testimonies. Serge Thion, an ultraleftist French sociologist who criticized the factual inaccuracies that accompanied the warm and remorseful endorsement of the book by French intellectuals who were now going back on their Marxist past, was also involved, around the same time, in the publication of negationist works. See Serge Thion, "Le Cambodge, la presse et ses bêtes noires," *Esprit* (September 1980), 95–111.
51. "'Médecins sans Frontières' accuse: L'aide humanitaire détournée au Cambodge," *Le Figaro*, 19 December 1979.
52. Rony Brauman, "Le moyen d'une 'prise de conscience,'" *Le Monde* (2 Février 1980).
53. See P.S., "Cambodge: Une 'marche' semée d'embuches," *Libération*, 1 February 1980. A detailed account of the march and the events that preceded it is available in Vallaeys, *Médecins Sans Frontières*, 307–60.
54. The subsequent discussion draws on a more detailed analysis of the march and the truth regime that it inaugurated provided in Michal Givoni, "Beyond the Humanitarian/Political

Divide: Witnessing and the Making of Humanitarian Ethics," *Journal of Human Rights* 10, no. 3 (2011): 55–75.

55. Xavier Emmanuelli, *Les prédateurs de l'action humanitaire* (Paris: Albin Michel, 1991), 215.

56. See Vallaeys, *Médecins Sans Frontières,* 327–36.

57. On biopolitical technologies and their production of "bare life," see Giorgio Agamben, *Homo Sacer: Sovereign Power and Bare Life* (Stanford, CA: Stanford University Press, 1998).

58. Rony Brauman, *Penser dans l'urgence: Parcours critique d'un humanitaire—Entretiens avec Catherine Portevin* (Paris: Editions du Seuil, 2006): 94.

59. See Xavier Emmanuelli, "Cambodge: Un Médecin Témoigne—un entretien avec Xavier Emmanuelli," *Le Nouvel Observateur,* 17 December 1979.

60. Claude Malhuret, "Pourquoi un journal?," *MSF: Bulletin d'informations de médecins sans frontières* 1 (January 1979): 1.

61. On the notion of truth machine, see Nicolas Rose, "Medicine, History and the Present," in *Reassessing Foucault: Power, Medicine and the Body,* ed. Colin Jones and Roy Porter (London and New York: Routledge, 1994), 59.

62. Redfield, "A Less Modest Witness," 16.

63. Ibid.

64. Rony Brauman, "Rapport moral," Assemblée Générale de Médecins Sans Frontières, 1986.

65. Brauman, *Penser dans l'urgence,* 147–48.

66. Rony Brauman, "Learning from Dilemmas: Interview with Rony Brauman," in *Nongovernmental Politics,* ed. Michel Feher, Gaëlle Krikorian, and Yates McKee (New York: Zone Books, 2007), 139.

67. Rousso, *The Vichy Syndrome,* chap. 4. Here again, MSF was invoking other catastrophes apart from the Holocaust to justify its controversial stand. In a press conference held in June 1986, for example, the organization compared the situation in Ethiopia to that of Cambodia under Pol Pot, stressing thereby the Marxist affiliations of the Ethiopian regime. See Laurence Binet, *Famine and Forced Relocations in Ethiopia 1984–1986* (MSF, 2005), 114.

68. Brauman, "Learning from Dilemmas," 138.

69. Reports and newspaper articles that preceded MSF's statement are mentioned in Binet, *Famine and Forced Relocations,* 41, 47–48, 58.

70. MSF-France, "Pourquoi nous quittons les camps de réfugiés rwandais," December 1994.

71. It is noteworthy that in the case of MSF's testimony on the forced relocations in Ethiopia, eyewitness accounts by volunteers who had been working in the camps were released, as a sort of supportive evidence, more than a month after Brauman's initial proclamation. See Binet, *Famine and Forced Relocations,* 90–91.

72. For a fascinating reconstruction of the discussions that preceded this testimony, see Laurence Binet, *Camps de Réfugiés Rwandais Zaïre-Tanzanie 1994–1995* (MSF, 2003). MSF-France was eventually accused by the other sections of acting unilaterally, without obtaining their due consent.

73. See Brauman, "Les liaisons dangereuses du témoignage humanitaire."

74. MSF-France, "Pourquoi nous quittons les camps de réfugiés rwandais."

75. The divergent views of the French, Belgian, and Dutch sections are documented in Binet, *Camps de Réfugiés rwandais Zaïre-Tanzanie.* On the disparities between notions of witnessing embraced by different sections of the MSF international movement, see also Redfield, "A Less Modest Witness," 9–10. To date, the international federation of MSF embraces twenty-four sections in various countries, five of them fully operational.

76. Brauman, "Learning from Dilemmas," 138.

77. Jean-François Lyotard, *The Differend: Phrases in Dispute* (Minneapolis: University of Minnesota Press, 1988); Shoshana Felman and Dori Laub, *Testimony: Crises of Witnessing in Literature, Psychoanalysis and History* (New York: Routledge, 1992); Giorgio Agamben, *Remnants of Auschwitz: The Witness and the Archive* (New York: Zone Books, 2002).

78. Ronit Peleg, "Language and Morality: *The Differend* by Jean-François Lyotard" (master's thesis, Tel Aviv University, 2006).

Bibliography

Agamben, Giorgio. *Homo Sacer: Sovereign Power and Bare Life*. Stanford, CA: Stanford University Press, 1998.

———. *Remnants of Auschwitz: The Witness and the Archive*. New York: Zone Books, 2002.

Bernier, Philippe. "La reponse à tous ceux qui doutaient de vous." *Tonus*, 3 January 1972, 1, 3.

Binet, Laurence. *Camps de Réfugiés Rwandais Zaïre-Tanzanie 1994–1995*. MSF, internal document, 2003.

———. *Famine and Forced Relocations in Ethiopia 1984–1986*. MSF, internal document, 2005.

Bollini, Caroline. "La construction de la légitimité de Médecins sans frontières dans l'espace public." Master's thesis, Université de Nanterre–Paris X, 2001.

Brauman, Rony. "Learning from Dilemmas: Interview with Rony Brauman." In *Nongovernmental Politics*, ed. Michel Feher, Gaëlle Krikorian, and Yates McKee, 131–47. New York: Zone Books, 2007.

———. "Les liaisons dangereuses du témoignage humanitaire et des propagandes politiques: Biafra, Cambodge, les mythes fondateurs de Médecins Sans Frontières." In *Crises extrêmes: Face aux massacres, aux guerres civiles et aux génocides*, ed. Marc Le Pape, Johanna Siméant, and Claudine Vidal, 188–204. Paris: La Découvert, 2006.

———. "Le moyen d'une 'prise de conscience.'" *Le Monde*, 2 February 1980.

———. *Penser dans l'urgence: Parcours critique d'un humanitaire—Entretiens avec Catherine Portevin*. Paris: Editions du Seuil, 2006.

———. "Rapport moral." Assemblée Générale de Médecins Sans Frontières, 1986.

Concours médical. "Attendre l'extermination?" January 1969.

Cordier, Françoise. "'On peut pas toujours faire du spectaculaire.'" *Quotidien du Médecin*, 10 May 1979.

———. "Médecins sans Frontières." *Le Quotidien du Médecin*, 16 December 1971, 5.

Dawes, James. *That the World May Know: Bearing Witness to Atrocities*. Cambridge, MA, and London: Harvard University Press, 2007.

Duranti, Marco. "The Holocaust, the Legacy of 1789 and the Birth of International Human Rights Law: Revisiting the Foundation Myth." *Journal of Genocide Research* 14, no. 2 (2012): 159–86.

Emmanuelli, Xavier. "A quoi servons-nous?" *Bulletin Médecins Sans Frontières*, no. 2 (January–March 1975): 4.

———. "Un bateau pour saint-germain-des-pres." *Quotidien du Médecin*, 4 September 1978.

———. "Cambodge: Un Médecin Témoigne—un entretien avec Xavier Emmanuelli." *Le Nouvel Observateur*, 17 December 1979.

———. *Les prédateurs de l'action humanitaire*. Paris: Albin Michel, 1991.

Fassin, Didier. "The Humanitarian Politics of Testimony: Subjectification through Trauma in the Israeli-Palestinian Conflict." *Cultural Anthropology* 23 (2008): 531–58.

Feldman, Ilana. "The Quaker Way: Ethical Labor and Humanitarian Relief." *American Ethnologist* 34, no. 4 (2007): 689–705.

Felman, Shoshana. "The Return of the Voice: Claude Lanzmann's *Shoah*." In *Testimony: Crises of Witnessing in Literature, Psychoanalysis and History*, by Shoshana Felman and Dori Laub, 204–83. New York: Routledge, 1992.

Felman, Shoshana, and Dori Laub. *Testimony: Crises of Witnessing in Literature, Psychoanalysis and History*. New York: Routledge, 1992.

Foucault, Michel. *The Use of Pleasure*. New York: Vintage Books, 1990.

Givoni, Michal. "Beyond the Humanitarian/Political Divide: Witnessing and the Making of Humanitarian Ethics." *Journal of Human Rights* 10, no. 3 (2011): 55–75.

———. "Humanitarian Governance and Ethical Cultivation: Médecins sans Frontières and the Advent of the Expert-Witness." *Millennium* 40, no. 1 (2011): 43–63.

Glucksmann, Andre, and Bernard Kouchner. "Preuve par le Cambodge." *Le Nouvel Observateur,* 26 November 1979.

Jacquemont, François. "Le docteur Pigeon, 'La souffrance, partout, c'est l'ennemi.'" *L'est republicaine,* 26 December 1971.

Keenan, Thomas. "Publicity and Indifference." *PMLA* 117, no. 1 (January 2002): 104–16.

Kouchner, Bernard. "L'humanitaire a changé le monde." *Le Temps Modernes* 627 (April–June 2004): 10–21.

———. "La loi de l'oppression minimale." In *Le devoir d'ingérence: Peut-on les laisser mourir?,* ed. Mario Bettati and Bernard Kouchner, 17–22. Paris: Denoël, 1987.

———. "Le movement humanitaire." *Le Debat* 67 (November–December 1991): 30–40.

Kurasawa, Fuyuki. *The Work of Global Justice: Human Rights as Practices.* Cambridge: Cambridge University Press, 2007.

Lanzmann, Claude. "Un vivant qui passé." *Les Temps Modernes* 627 (April–June 2004): 160–88.

Le Figaro. "'Médecins sans Frontières' accuse: L'aide humanitaire détournée au Cambodge." 19 December 1979.

Le Goff, Jean-Pierre. *Mai 68, l'héritage impossible.* Paris: La Découverte, 2002.

Levy, Daniel, and Natan Sznaider. "The Institutionalization of Cosmopolitan Morality: The Holocaust and Human Rights." *Journal of Human Rights* 3, no. 2 (June 2004): 143–57.

Lyotard, Jean-François. *The Differend: Phrases in Dispute.* Minneapolis: University of Minnesota Press, 1988.

Malhuret, Claude. "Agonies ..." *Bulletin d'informations de médecins sans frontières* 3 (August–September 1979): 1–2.

———. "Pourquoi un journal?" *MSF: Bulletin d'informations de médecins sans frontières* 1 (January 1979): 1.

Moyn, Samuel. *The Last Utopia: Human Rights in History.* Cambridge, MA, and London: Harvard University Press, 2010.

MSF. "Cambodge: Operation Marche pour la Survie." Paris, 7 January 1980. Archive MSF-France.

———. "Principes de référence du mouvement Médecins Sans frontières (Document de Chantilly)." 1995.

———. "Statuts de Médecins sans Frontières." 20 December 1971.

MSF-France. "Pourquoi nous quittons les camps de réfugiés rwandais." December 1994.

Osborne, Thomas. "Power and Persons: On Ethical Stylization and Person-Centered Medicine." *Sociology of Health and Illness* 16 (1994): 515–35.

Peleg, Ronit. "Language and Morality: *The Differend* by Jean-François Lyotard." PhD thesis, Tel Aviv University, 2006.

P.S. "Cambodge: Une 'marche' semée d'embuches." *Libération,* 1 February 1980.

Redfield, Peter. "A Less Modest Witness: Collective Advocacy and Motivated Truth in a Medical Humanitarian Movement." *American Ethnologist* 33, no. 1 (2006): 3–26.

Rose, Nicolas. "Medicine, History and the Present." In *Reassessing Foucault: Power, Medicine and the Body,* ed. Colin Jones and Roy Porter, 48–72. London and New York: Routledge, 1994.

Rothberg, Michael. "Between Auschwitz and Algeria: Multidirectional Memory and the Counterpublic Witness." *Critical Inquiry* 33 (2006): 158–84.

Rousso, Henry. *The Vichy Syndrom: History and Memory in France since 1944.* Cambridge, MA: Harvard University Press, 1994.

Soussan, Judith. *MSF et la protection: Une question réglée?* Paris: MSF, 2008.

Thion, Serge. "Le Cambodge, la presse et ses bêtes noires." *Esprit,* September 1980, 95–111.

Tonus. "La Charte de Médecins sans Frontières." 3 January 1972.

Vallaeys, Anne. *Médecins Sans Frontières: La biographie.* Paris: Fayard, 2004.

CHAPTER 8

The Global Semiotics of Trauma and Testimony
A Comparative Study of Jewish Israeli, Cambodian Canadian, and Cambodian Genocide Descendant Legacies

Carol A. Kidron

In recent decades Holocaust and genocide commemoration has taken great strides toward what Levy and Sznaider termed cosmopolitan memory.[1] Globalization has progressively constituted a more universal semiotics of genocide representation entailing common iconic media images of suffering, similar exhibits of death on display, recurrent narrative structures of testimony, and universal psychosocial profiles of wounded survivors and their descendants.[2] Although the emergence of a cosmopolitan semiotics appears to have transcended the potentially divisive parochiality of the particular, Rothberg asserts that a shift away from the entrenchment of particular national collective memories toward less exclusive versions of genocide-related cultural identity and representation does not necessarily silence the particular but rather allows for "multidirectional memory" that can both "cut across and bind diverse cultural pasts."[3]

Yet critiquing the earlier formulation of "cosmopolitan memory," Beck and Sznaider warn against the "homogenizing character of universal theories," asserting that "the particularity of others is sacrificed to an assumption of universal equality which denies its own context of emergence and its interests."[4] In the same critical vein, genocide scholars have noted that it remains to be determined if the proliferation of a "universal semiotics" of genocide suffering merely "binds" and translates diverse cultural pasts into a more common language of victimhood, or whether it has silenced particular cultural voices and idioms of suffering. According to Fassin, international agents of memory, be they mental health practitioners, international NGO workers, or genocide scholars, have globally disseminated a Euro-Western model of trauma-related

Notes for this section begin on page 163.

victimhood often incompatible with and thereby eliding sociopolitical and cultural realities on the ground.[5] In order to explore the potential tension between the universal semiotics of genocide suffering and divergent particular genocide legacies, this chapter presents an ethnographic comparative study of the lived experience of familial trauma and testimonial voice of Jewish Israeli Holocaust descendants, Cambodian Canadian descendants of the Cambodian genocide living in Canada, and Cambodian descendants living in Cambodia. It will be asserted that culturally specific Cambodian and Jewish Israeli paradigms and practices of memory deviate from the globally disseminated reductionist profile of the pathologized and enlisted trauma descendant and therefore problematize therapeutic and sociopolitical interventionist practices that "treat" genocide legacies as universal.

Trauma Theory and the Emergence of Universal Axioms of Suffering

Therapeutic discourse in general and trauma theory in particular has emerged as the main discursive arsenal of agents of memory, where the common denominator framing the understanding of diverse forms of genocide experience is the therapeutic and spiritually redemptive role of the testimonial voice.[6] According to psychological research, trauma survivors may suffer from a multitude of emotional and behavioral symptoms diagnosed as post-traumatic stress disorder (PTSD).[7] In studies of Holocaust victims, the disorder was found to impair survivor/veteran parenting, whereby the effects of PTSD may potentially be transmitted to their children.[8] Although nonclinical findings have failed to show evidence of psychopathology, both clinical and nonclinical studies have found that descendants of Holocaust victims and Vietnam veterans may suffer from maladaptive behavioral patterns and a damaged sense of self.[9] According to the logic of the PTSD paradigm, if left untreated, the long-term psychosocial effects of survivor and/or shell shock trauma could be transmitted from generation to generation. A familial "conspiracy" or "wall of silence" is said to often shroud the history of parental suffering in oppressive silence. The metaphor of the "wall of silence," thought to be ominously poised between psychically damaged survivors and their children, signifies the absence of the genocide past.[10] At once pathologizing and eliding the possibility of the lived experience of silent embodied forms of presence of the past, the majority of scholars of memory, mental health practitioners, and humanitarian workers worldwide have encouraged trauma survivors and their descendants to verbally articulate their repressed and silenced past of personal suffering and/or familial maladaptive relations.[11] Talk therapy in therapeutic settings and public forms of testimony and commemoration aim to liberate the silenced past, put forth as not only individually healing but also sociopolitically redemptive for the collective.[12]

Intergenerational Transmission of the Burden of Memory

According to the literature, as survivors repress their traumatic pasts and often resist testimonial voice, descendants have taken it upon themselves to work through the silenced past and act as surrogates for their parents, testifying to their own childhood memories in the shadow of genocide suffering or to their recollections of fragmentary accounts of genocide suffering.[13] The scholarship has traced the descendants' transition from silence to voice in Israel and around the world, documenting multiple forms of representation ranging from political activism challenging the silencing of survivors in national hegemonic narratives, therapeutic practices, heritage tourism, the documentation of the parental tale, or artistic representation of the traumatic past.[14] As in the case of the descendant's psychosocial profile, the scholarship rarely questions the assumption that descendants wish to seek out the survivor's tale and undertake public forms of representation and that they would experience commemoration as liberating.

Universalizing the PTSD Construct

The above research on Holocaust survivors and their descendants has served as a prototypical model for more recent psychological studies on collective traumatic events worldwide.[15] Cambodian genocide trauma has attracted extensive scholarly attention.[16] Research has focused both on first- and second-generation traumatization.[17] These studies conclude that survivors of the Cambodian genocide continue to suffer from PTSD-related emotional scars and somatized bodily distress while their children—be they in Cambodia, or Cambodian American, Canadian, or Australian young adults—have been found to exhibit increased symptomology causally related to their parents' traumatic experiences.[18] According to Rubin and Rhodes, as witnesses of their parents' traumatic fragmentary narrative reenactments, descendants mirror parental PTSD and ultimately suffer from their own intrusive memories of parental trauma.[19] Even findings regarding the positive adjustment of Cambodian youth have been interpreted as signifying overcompensation and psychically burdensome trauma-related intergenerational dynamics.[20] Although the above studies emerge from totally diverse sociocultural and national contexts, these studies utilize standardized psychological models and measures focusing solely on interfamily psychosocial dynamics. We may ask, do Cambodian youth perceive themselves as suffering from the scars of transmitted PTSD? Do they wish to work through and articulate the familial past, or does Cambodian culture present alternative meaning systems that differentially make sense of genocide memory and constitute different forms of familial interaction and intergenerational transmission of the past?[21]

Enlisting the Wounded Genocide Witness

Building upon the axioms of trauma theory yet concerned with the macro processes of the politics of silenced or curtailed collective memory, culture studies and human rights discourse also call for the voicing of silenced narratives of victimization and subjugation.[22] From this perspective, the narrativization of survivor and descendant legacies facilitates the civic and moral act of public testimony.[23] As genocide historians have asserted, pathos-filled and cathartic testimonies at "truth tribunals" not only document the violent past and contribute to the collective stock of memory, but also ideally facilitate restitution, reconciliation, and coexistence.[24] For example, the Turkish activist Munyas has called Cambodians to narratively work through their scarred past via public testimony.[25] The enlisted witnesses must adopt a humanist moral frame that would allow them to understand and empathize with the complex sociopolitical context that shaped genocide events, enabling reconciliation with the Khmer Rouge and a morally and emotionally healthy Cambodia. No less interventionist, scholars of ethnicity and immigrant studies promote the working through of the Cambodian diaspora and public testimony to the genocide past. Community-based scholars believe that knowledge and intergenerational dialogue surrounding the genocide will close the generation gap and empower the socioeconomically challenged and marginalized ethnic minority. Organizations are established enabling education and commemoration, to be managed by a Khmer youth "vanguard."[26]

However, do descendants wish to access verbal accounts of their legacies and publicly commemorate violent histories, or are there other channels of "remembrance," other forms of silent transmission of the past interwoven in the social milieu of everyday life?[27] When globally exporting Eurocentric models of traumatic suffering and resistant testimonial voice to victims around the world, to what degree has interventionist discourse and practice taken culture-specific conceptions of suffering, healing, and memory work into account?[28] Has Eurocentric psychosocial and politicized memory work weakened the survivor's link to traditional culture-specific forms of healing and remembrance rather than liberating them from the yoke of subjugation?[29]

The holistic and emic ("native's point of view") perspectives of anthropology enable a grounded and culturally sensitive exploration of the descendant's phenomenological experience of transmitted PTSD and enlistment in public memory work, allowing descendants to articulate their "lived experience" of suffering and voice.[30] There have, however, been few attempts to apply this approach to genocide descendant experiences. The subfield of the anthropology of genocide, particularly Hinton's work on Cambodia and Argenti and Schramm's volume on transmitted genocide legacies, have presented a culture-sensitive portrayal of the impact of trauma and alternative forms of commemoration.[31] Nevertheless, the ethnographic moral-political mission liberating victims from the "shadows of silence" has often elided the way apolitical everyday taken-for-granted practices are sustained and transmitted to create the lived presence of the past.[32]

Exploring the "everyday lived presence" of the Holocaust past, I undertook an ethnographic study of Holocaust descendants in Israel entailing seventy-five interviews with second- and third-generation descendants and participant observation at multiple mesopublic sites of memory.[33] Contrary to the literature (and vocal descendants in Israeli literary circles and popular culture), the majority rejected or critiqued the pathologizing construct of PTSD, although many did feel they were emotionally impacted by the Holocaust past. While asserting that survivors, the third generation, and other nonsurvivors must participate in all important commemorative projects, second generation descendants expressed little or no desire to participate in collective monumental commemoration as carriers of Holocaust memory. Instead, they presented accounts of (a) the silent nonpathological presence of the past in embodied person-person and person-object interaction in the everyday life of the family and fragmentary tales of survival that transmitted an enriching genocide-related meaning world, and (b) survivor-specific nonmonumental communal practices of Holocaust memory in voluntary mesopublic organizations that simulated intimate family silent memory.[34] The minority who chose to participate in monumental forms of commemoration referred to Jewish paradigms of memory to account for their obligation to act as public carriers of memory, and described themselves as suffering from transmitted PTSD.

We might ask, do descendants in other cultural/sociopolitical contexts accept the pathologizing construct? Do they retain alternative culture-specific responses to traumatic suffering, other forms of remembering or forgetting? Have activists successfully recruited descendants to communal or national organizations, where they are providing testimony to their own or their parents' past? If not, how may we explain differential legacies and responses?

The Comparative Case Study and Methodology

Building on the above study of Israeli Holocaust descendants, two comparative ethnographic studies of descendant genocide legacies were undertaken: one of Cambodian Canadian descendants (2005–6) and the other of Cambodian descendants living in Cambodia (2010).[35] Accessing the sample using the snowball method, I conducted fifty-five interviews with children of Holocaust survivors. Israeli descendant respondents ranged in age between thirty-five and fifty-five, with equal gender representation.[36] In-depth interviews were conducted using a semistructured and thematic format. Interviewees were asked open-ended questions about themselves and their families, allowing them to narrate and present the self as they saw fit. The great majority were born in

Israel, to survivor parents who had emigrated to Israel from Europe in the late 1940s and 1950s after surviving Nazi extermination camps, forced labor camps, ghetto incarceration, or extended periods of hiding. After an initial period of economic hardship, the majority achieved middle- to upper-middle-class status and the majority of descendants had some form of higher education.

Twenty-three in-depth ethnographic interviews were undertaken with Cambodian Canadian descendants, between the ages of seventeen and twenty-six, residing in Montreal, Quebec, and Toronto, Ontario. Participant observation was also undertaken at the Cambodian-Canadian Association of Ontario (from which initial respondents were accessed) and at a Buddhist pagoda (*wat*) in Montreal. In the case of the majority of descendants, their parents had emigrated to Canada in the mid- to late 1980s after surviving conditions of forced migration, forced labor, near starvation, and the loss of loved ones (see note for a brief history of the Cambodian genocide).[37] In Canada, survivor families experienced severe economic hardship, and nearly two decades later many families still live in inner-city, low-income housing, and at least 60 percent recounted some form of substance abuse and parental separation/divorce. Fifty-five percent of descendants attend or have attended a community college or a university.

Research in Cambodia entailed twenty-five in-depth ethnographic interviews with Cambodian descendants, between the ages of eighteen and thirty, residing in three different provinces. Respondents' parents had survived genocide conditions of forced migration, forced labor, near starvation, and the loss of loved ones. The great majority of the descendants' families are still experiencing extreme economic hardship, many still living in poor urban neighborhoods or the rural countryside, although the descendant generation has benefited from recent educational and economic opportunities. Thirty percent of the descendants had attended or are attending a vocational school, a community college, or a university. Participant observation was also undertaken at national and communal sites of commemoration and at Theravada Buddhist *wat*s. Interviews were undertaken with agents of genocide memory, including NGO officials, local genocide scholars, and Buddhist monks constituting the revival of a Buddhist religious/spiritual legacy.

The cross-cultural comparative study is challenging, as it entails very different socioeconomic and political contexts. Regarding the Israeli context, the Israeli legacy of the Holocaust involves the German other as perpetrator, while vocal national commemoration in the Israeli state is undertaken by a relatively privileged Jewish majority. In contrast, the Cambodian Canadian faces the more recent and ambiguous legacy of what has been most problematically termed "auto-genocide," remembered in silence in the Canadian diaspora by a poverty-ridden ethnic minority in a nation-state that takes pride in multicultural discourse and practice.[38] Descendants in Cambodia experience a still different sociopolitical reality characterized by the scars of French colonialism and feared subjugation by neighboring Vietnam, tense coexistence with Khmer Rouge perpetrators and their descendants, and until recently, collective silence regarding the genocide past.[39] Narratives of victimization and truth tribunals are now beginning to provide nationalist glue in this still conflict-ridden society. These important contextual differences most certainly alter particular dialectics between divergent contexts and the culturally framed experience of genocide legacies. Nevertheless, the present chapter aims to artificially disentangle the "braids" of context and culture to examine differential experiences of genocide legacies. It is asserted that it is precisely a close comparative examination of similarity and difference that will allow for the isolation and analysis of factors uniquely constituting particular descendant legacies. As noted by Gingrich and Fox, when comparing ethnographic findings, differences and similarities are utilized as stimulants for thinking about analytical axioms, and as will be seen below, important differences become particularly visible when set against similarities.[40]

Traumatic Legacies

Jewish Israeli Descendants

When asked about their parents' mental health, 70 percent of the Holocaust descendant sample stated that their parents did suffer from symptoms of post-trauma; however, 80 percent of this sample insisted that considering the intensity of their suffering, they were highly resilient and did not require therapy. Regarding their own mental health, the great majority of descendants asserted that they were not suffering from the transmitted effects of PTSD. The entire sample showed familiarity with popular cultural literature on transmitted PTSD and approximately 25 percent had experienced some form of short- or long-term psychosocial therapy or support group. Nevertheless, more than half of this "psychologically sophisticated" sample critiqued the transmitted PTSD construct and the efficacy of therapy, as did almost all of those who had not undergone therapy.[41]

A closer reading, however, discloses that descendants claim they were in fact *srutim,* a Hebrew slang expression literally translated as "scratched." Although parallel to the English slang "cracked," it also implies the superficiality of their wound. Descendants claimed that these scars were not markers of pathology, or even experienced as distressing, but were relatively benign emotive markers of difference. Hannah recounted: "There's no point to go to therapy. Of course we're *srutim,* how could we grow up with them [survivors] and not be different. But we're not sick, what happened to them just made us more sensitive, to our own pain and to the pain of others."[42] Echoing Hannah's reinterpretation of descendant transmitted scars as a mode of emotional being rather than as a psychological disorder, Leah added:

> I have had a very hard life. But I am proud of the fact that I know who I am and have worked on myself, dealing with all my emotional *sritot* [scratches] and I hope improving myself all the time. But this Holocaust thing ... its just too intense, part of our flesh ... you can't really "cure" it. It will always be there ... to remind us of what happened. Carrying it, is not only about us and our lives, but about something larger ... it's the kind of burden you have to carry.

Leah perceived herself as fulfilling a "larger" moral mission of collective Holocaust commemoration, by virtue of the emotional burden she carries. The accounts of the permanence of an emotional wound, and the disinterest in coping skills or disbelief in what Leah termed a "cure," is conceptualized as a form of descendent commemoration. The "scratch" appears to be a marker of a particular phenomenological experience incommensurable with the dichotomy of wellness or illness. If cultural meaning worlds differentially frame the moral order pertaining to the value of genocide memory and filial obligations, then descendant "scratches" or emotive markers such as recollections of intersubjective moments with traumatized parents might also be differentially experienced and conceptualized. Moreover, if the markers of emotional difference signify the semiotics of a morally valuable Holocaust presence, "essential to the exercise of virtue" and not merely a personal form of suffering, then treatment, healing, and closure are not only untenable but undesirable.[43] Collective meaning worlds may even be perpetuating individual scars as testimonial badges of honor. Interpreted as such, one cannot "diagnose" descendants as either solely vulnerable or resilient to distress, as they remain both vulnerable to and empowered by the scars of past "difference."

Cambodian Canadian Descendants

The great majority of Cambodian Canadians interviewed asserted that neither their parents nor they suffered from the psychosocial scars of genocide. In great contrast to the Holocaust sample, they also did not refer to any form of descendant emotional wound or unique emotional mode of being. A number of descendants attributed their parents' emotional crises not to the genocide, but to their economic adversity and difficult acclimation to Canadian life. Most surprising were the lengthy unsolicited references to Buddhist precepts. Ken explained: "Buddhism tells us that suffering is a part of life. This helped my father get over his traumatic experience. Belief systems like Buddhism are meant to strengthen people and help them succeed."[44] Sam outlined at length:

> I think the mentality, the way you live your life in general effects how you experience suffering. They believe in karma, so they believe the fact that it happened, your suffering, or death, is an effect of natural causes ... they accept what happened to them ... not being angry, bitter, or vengeful ... it's horrible but we must move on because it was just a matter of karma.

I asked Sam if it was possible that the Khmer may still have suffered the long-term effects of trauma despite what he describes as "Buddhist" acceptance.

He responded: "The nature of the strength that prevails above all else leads me to believe that the effects of trauma are negligible ... it's just the next fad." On the subject of intergenerationally transmitted trauma, Sam asserted: "[T]hey say things can affect you even in the womb ... these are just conjectures ... I was very young [in the refugee camp] and what affects you is the context where you grew up and for me that was Canada and I have no recollections of the early years, so it didn't affect me."

Although often ignored, religious canon as well as lay religious sensibilities act as critical mechanisms for the intergenerational transmission and preservation of cultural legacies, as these sensibilities embed normative modes of being, encapsulating the ideal moral order and schemas of selfhood.[45] In times of social transition and rupture, religion may become both an ideological resource with which to resist culture loss and assimilation, or a more resistant means to revive difference. In the diaspora, Khmer self-identity is strongly associated with Theravada Buddhism to the point where Christian converts are considered "traitors to Khmer culture."[46] Scholars highlight a number of key cosmological principles in the Khmer moral universe that have taken center stage in their lay interpretation of the genocide and its aftermath.[47] Echoing descendant accounts of "resilience" or immunity to trauma, memories of past suffering and victimhood must be accepted as one's karma, without undue attachment to the past, as all material existence is impermanent. Redemption is to be found through the long incremental process of samsara—death and rebirth, potentially endangered by cycles of violence and vengeance. Justice will be meted out through karma, while any individual attempt to dwell on evil and suffering will lead to individual illness and social distress. Like the cycle of reincarnation, even the difficult past can be "buried" and regenerated with the proper forward-looking attitudes.[48] Although one might assume a gap between Buddhist cannon and lay descendant knowledge of Buddhism, beyond the contention that the ethnographer should accept respondents' phenomenological lived experience as narrative truth, as Hinton notes, lay local religious idioms receive their force from ontological resonances of deeper cultural logics and cosmology, allowing the researcher to unpack how these deeper cosmological principals and related idioms structure descendant responses.[49]

It should also be noted that the above appeals to Buddhist readings of experience are most certainly impacted by the multicultural Canadian context. Hinting again at the dialectic between culture and context, the unique meaning world of karma might just be one more strategic cultural script in the politics of Canadian ethnic politics of identity and memory.

Cambodian Descendants in Cambodia

The accounts of Cambodian genocide descendants living in Cambodia regarding familial trauma are consistent with the Cambodian Canadian accounts above. The very great majority of Cambodian descendant respondents asserted that their parents were not suffering from the long-term effects of PTSD. As the therapeutic discourse and practice have yet to be widely disseminated in Cambodia, descendants were often not familiar with the construct of PTSD. Additional questions were therefore posed regarding "emotional well-being," to which the overwhelming response was, again, that their parents were not emotionally "sick" or "troubled."

However, a third question regarding parental responses to recollections of the genocide elicited references to "occasional sadness." Sophie recounted that "sometimes my mother would get sad, if she saw a film about the Khmer Rouge or if she heard about the trial [of a Khmer Rouge perpetrator], but this passes quickly, she is fine today, she has a loving family, plenty of rice, so no reason to be sad." Although Sophie's insistence upon her mother's wellness deviates from the pathologizing construct of PTSD, the Euro-Western mental health practitioner or trauma broker might translate Khmer "sadness" into a cultural-specific idiom of distress that may or may not require therapeutic care.[50] Yet if we were to appeal to lay Khmer understandings of their experience, descendants depict genocide-related "sadness" as a normative and normal emotional response that is not only fleeting but in no way endangers functioning or general well-being or requires treatment. More importantly, when examining the descendants' explanation for parental well-being, the majority of descendants interviewed, like Sophie, appeal to the palliative effect of present emotional and material conditions rather than the long-term impact of past traumatizing events. It may be concluded that from an ethnopsychological perspective, emotional well-being is dependent upon the present and not upon the haunting presence of the past.

When asked about the intergenerational transmission of trauma to the descendant generation, Cambodian descendants were perplexed by the question. When I rephrased the questions, asking if they were "emotionally sick" or "emotionally wounded" by their parents' genocide suffering, all descendants interviewed responded that they were not emotionally wounded by the genocide. Utilizing the above-mentioned Khmer idiom of sadness, I asked Pheakday if she too was sometimes sad when thinking about the genocide; she asserted that "I am sad for my father, but why would I be sad when I did not suffer." Echoing Pheakday, Rithy asked "how could I be hurt by something I did not experience, only they experienced that time [Khmer Rouge]." Consistent with Canadian Cambodians, here too the psychogenic dynamics of intergenerational transmission of distress or disorder appears to be incomprehensible to Cambodian descendants. Although empathizing with parental suffering, Khmer in Cambodia do not seem to vicariously identify as do Jewish descendants.[51]

Unlike the Canadian sample above, descendants in Cambodia did not appeal to Buddhism as a cultural source of immunity to PTSD. It might be tentatively suggested that in the more homogenous cultural context of Cambodia, as compared to the Western multicultural Canadian context, Buddhist meaning worlds may have remained taken-for-granted frames of experience. Nevertheless, as will be seen below, consistent with Canadian accounts, Buddhist cosmological or spiritual worldviews do in fact surface when accounting for Khmer descendant resistance to genocide commemoration in Cambodia.

Testimony and Commemoration

Jewish Israeli Descendants

The remembrance and reenactment of the past are key Jewish cultural tropes.[52] Reenactment takes place via ritual and liturgy, where perpetual narration of biblical mythic sequences guarantee that they remain culturally embedded as blueprints for interpretation. The imperative of personal remembrance encompasses the commemoration of communal and personal dead. The individual, perceived as the eternal witness embodying memory, and the community of which he/she is a part loop back to the past in order to make that past present and to create a meaningful "place" for the events and people on the continuum of history. Filial responsibility to the memory of one's parents and ancestors is of special importance and is deeply embedded in Jewish cosmology and praxis. The individual is also obliged to transmit the past to future generations. However, the Jewish witness need not have been an eyewitness to the past, as knowledge of the past is sufficient for testimony and transmission.[53] These deep structural Jewish paradigms of memory have found intense "revival" and transposition in the Israeli nation-state as state-sponsored memorial sites and ceremonies publicly glorify Holocaust survivors and fallen war heroes, collectively enlist survivors and bereaved families, and engineer pedagogic pilgrimages to Holocaust death worlds.[54] All these forms of memory work function to constitute the moral mission of those citizens prepared to carry the burden of collective and personal memory.[55]

In keeping with the above Jewish cultural tropes, the descendant sample unanimously expressed great concern with the future of Holocaust commemoration. Beyond the silent form of embodied-emotive commemoration of the transmitted "scratches" of the Holocaust past, the majority also recounted partaking in private votive practices of lighting candles in memory of the Holocaust dead, and those more religiously observant recounted participating in synagogue-based communal prayers commemorating both family members killed in the Holocaust and communities lost to the genocide.[56] However, when asked about the transmission of the Holocaust past to their children, or participation in public forms of commemorative testimony to the past, the majority of descendants explained that they preferred to remain silent and allow survivor grandparents and the education system to transmit personal and collective legacies. Others recounted that after exposure to practices of survival and Holocaust-related meaning worlds in their childhood, their children too would have to "learn to know and to feel" the wounds of the past "for all those who had died."[57] When further broaching the subject of descendant avoidance of public commemoration, respondents provided two recurring explanations. The first referred to the silent presence of the past in the parental home: "surviving through them in every breath we take." As walking testament to the Holocaust, this would obviate the need for public commemoration. The second expressed concern over the misrepresentation of their private memories, where historicity would usurp lived memory.

Cambodian Canadian Descendants

Cambodian Canadians voice complete rejection of almost all forms of commemorative practice. To explain their position, descendants appealed again to lay understandings of Buddhism. Ron explained that "time itself from a Buddhist perspective was in fact an illusion," making collective memory superfluous. The majority asserted that although it was important to know the history of the genocide, this event should not be considered more important than others in their past. When asking Seth if he would be interested in establishing a genocide memorial in Canada, he asserted: "I don't think we need one, everyone remembers their own dead privately at home. We could have a heritage and history museum though." When asked how much of the museum would be dedicated to the genocide, he appeared confused and responded, "Everything would be represented equally, the genocide is just one part of our history."

In contrast to the extensive commemorative practices and martyrology in Israel, Rachel more directly linked her view of commemoration to what she termed the "Khmer attitude" toward memorialization of the dead when she explained: "Khmer don't see any difference between remembering those who died a 'natural' death and those who died in the genocide—all of them visit us on Pchum Bon [Festival of the Dead] and we celebrate with all of them in the same way." If the genocide is only one of many events in history and descendants do not feel obliged to make that past publicly present in any distinctive manner, what of the transmission of the genocide past to future generations? When asking Rachel about transmission to her children, she replied, "Why burden them with this? We accept the past and look to the present."

Highlighting the one valorized function of transmission—namely, the perpetuation of key values or "meaning" embedded in survivor tales—Kevin asserted that "what is truly important is not the story … [but] the values that are under the surface of the story." Recalling the findings regarding intergenerational transmission of Holocaust survivor mythic tales, the one and only surviving form of presence of the past constituting future genocide legacies appears to be key moral values emergent from the genocide and the resultant ideal modes of forward-looking being.[58]

Although genocide engendered these key values, can their transmission sustain the commemorative presence of genocide, or will the event ultimately be forgotten? Sam asserted:

> Now if I have children who are as inquiring as me, then ... they will discover what happened in the past, but none of this is relevant to the situation they are in and also it does nothing in terms of making them better people. What we ought to do is learn to love them and ... pass down the virtues that were taken from our parents as it pertains to the situations related to the war. It is important for it to remain in history, but not to be reflected on in the future.

Sam critically asserted that only genocide-related "virtues" should be passed down to a third generation. The narrowing of descendant legacies is far from accidental, as it is aimed to serve an ethical function to "make them better people" while also meeting only "relevant" needs of the contemporary contextual "situation" of Canadian Cambodians. As for the transmission of the history of the genocide, Sam claimed it is important for it to "remain in history," yet as Nora insightfully noted, the historicity of commemorative documentation relegates the past to monumental sites of memory or to the archive preserving only "dead or duty memory."[59] This is apparent in Sam's contradictory statement that despite the importance of historicity, the past should not be "reflected upon in the future." Following Sam's rationale, other possible forms of re-presence of a commemorated genocide past such as reenactments or practices of survival would be both "irrelevant" to the Khmer situation and would not contribute to their moral careers.

Cambodian Descendants in Cambodia

The Khmer descendant sample in Cambodia expressed general disinterest in familial, communal, or national commemoration of the genocide past. Beginning with the national commemorative landscape, the national memorial day for the genocide or Day of Rage remains a grandiose performance of nationalist propaganda, tainted all the more by the fact that the ceremony was established by Vietnamese liberators perceived by Cambodians to be colonialists in disguise. Beyond schoolchildren in the capital forced to attend, the general population is indifferent to the ceremony. Regarding the National Genocide Museum at Tuol Sleng, previously a prison in which thousands of Khmer Rouge victims were tortured and killed, descendants interviewed assert that the site is of critical importance as it authenticates and documents the devastation of the Khmer Rouge period. In the same vein, descendants support the recent inclusion of genocide history as part of high school curricula.

Nevertheless, like the Canadian Khmer above, the very great majority assert that genocide history and ritual commemoration must be limited to these sites to allow for the Khmer people to "focus on the present and create a better future." Although the majority of descendants assert they have already visited or hope to visit Tuol Sleng one day, and that they will take their children to the site, they do not feel genocide history should be made present in Cambodian everyday life. Again, like the Canadian sample, Cambodian respondents highlight what they consider the sole purpose of recalling the difficult past—namely, the pedagogic role of genocide memory. As Kemrak explained: "We have to learn from our mistakes, and put the lessons of the past to good use in our work to become strong and productive and make sure we don't let hate destroy us again. Once we know this, there is no reason to dwell on the past." In great contrast to professional agents of memory in Israel, even agents of memory invested in the future contribution of the commemorative landscape in Cambodia insist on instrumentalizing and minimizing genocide memory solely in the service of a better future.[60] As one NGO worker proposed: "I want everyone to know our history, bad and good, but I don't want young people to carry the past on their backs, we need to build a new life now."

Regarding survivor testimony, descendants unanimously stated that they did not wish their parents to become enlisted in national or communal commemorative projects and saw no need to sadden them any further, as there is sufficient documentation to "prove that the Khmer Rouge period was real." As in the case of transmitted trauma, descendants were confused by references to the possibility that they too might provide testimony or enlist in communal or commemorative projects. Pich explained: "I was not there, I was not hungry like them, what would I tell?" When asking her if she would tell her parents' story to those who have not heard about the genocide, as do some descendants in Israel, she responded, "I cannot tell their story, there is enough of this in the museum, in the books."

Regarding familial commemoration, when asking descendants if they have a personal commitment to keep the genocide past interwoven in their everyday present lives, they are once again perplexed by the question, and ask how the past could be present in everyday life. Sophie went as far as to ask, "Why would anyone want the Khmer Rouge past to be present again?" When asking descendants about the future of familial genocide memory and the legacies to be transmitted to their children—the third generation—in contrast to Israeli descendants and parallel to Canadian Khmer, the great majority of Cambodian descendants insist that although their children must learn the history of this terrible time in school, they do not wish to burden their children with the few painful tales of suffering they heard from their parents. Consistent with the forward-looking themes embedded in the analysis above, Rithy explained that "they can learn from what happened to our parents—learn to appreciate their rice, hard work and family, but no need to talk about the evil, we want our children to have a good life."

Despite the recurring references to the apparent marginalization of genocide memory and the constitution of a solely forward-looking genocide legacy, like the Canadian sample before them, Cambodian Khmer respondents nevertheless recount tales of filial obligation to their ancestors, including those who perished in the genocide, which entails the daily or weekly practice of ancestor veneration at household altars and the yearly ritual veneration at the communal *wat* on the Festival of the Dead, Pchum Bon. Consistent again with the Canadian sample, these rituals sustain interaction with deceased relatives regardless of and without reference to the manner of their death. Thus, although individual relatives and the relations with those relatives are made perpetually present in the everyday domestic and communal social milieu, the genocide event as collective historical catastrophe in which an entire generation of ancestors found their death is not ritually represented.

Before making undue assumptions regarding the possible hegemonic silencing of individual and familial genocide memory in Cambodia (parallel to the silencing thought to characterize the first decades of the founding period of the Israeli state), it is important to note that the Cambodian government and provincial municipalities have for the past two decades been jointly constructing numerous communal sites of commemoration primarily located at Buddhist temple complexes throughout the country.[61] Architecturally identical, these sites include a stupa, or commemorative tower, containing the exhumed human skeletal remains of predominantly "unidentified" victims murdered in each particular province. They are clearly designed to simulate private stupas commemorating the familial dead located in the household and in communal *wats*. Despite their location in what is considered the heart of community social and religious life in both rural and urban Cambodia and their familiar form, these communal sites and their yearly ceremonies are all but ignored by the local population. Ceremonies are held yearly at these sites, officiated and paid for by local monks, municipal officials, and at times the rich elite, working closely with these officials, and prayers are recited to assist the dead in the passage to the next stage on their journey of samsara. Attempting to explain popular disinterest in communal sites of memory, and the gap between top-down hegemonic commemorative policies and the practices on the ground, I asked descendants why they do not attend the ceremonies at the communal genocide site or visit the site for private veneration of the genocide dead. Although many descendants responded that they might like to visit the stupa one day, Sopheap explained that "I don't know if my ancestors are there." Pich responded that "who would I ask merit from, they are not my family, I go to pray at my family stupa." It would appear from these brief accounts that collective forms of commemoration are incongruent with the basic precepts and practices of familial ancestor veneration, which as Langford has outlined sustains the daily personal engagement with ancestors and not the remembrance of communal or collective genocide suffering.[62]

Parallel to responses regarding traumatic legacies, and in contrast to the Canadian descendants above, the majority of descendants in Cambodia did not appeal to Khmer culture in general or Buddhist precepts in particular to account for their general disinterest in collective commemoration. Once again, the homogeneity of Cambodian society and the taken-for-granted nature of the way Buddhist meaning worlds frame lived experience appears to obviate the kind of reflexivity born of identity politics in Canada. Nevertheless, when directly asked whether Khmer culture could in any way explain popular disinterest in genocide commemoration, 65 percent of the descendants, many of whom had spent time at Buddhist temples during their youth, evoked Buddhist forward-looking values cited above in their responses to the question. Most interestingly, a number of descendants recounted the Buddhist taboo and resultant danger of displaying human remains, as the disgruntled spirit of the dead can haunt their family and the entire community.[63]

Discussion

This chapter set out to compare Cambodian Canadian, Cambodian, and Jewish Israeli genocide descendant legacies. The comparison yielded significant differences in the self-perceived experience of emotional wellness and future trajectory of commemoration of the genocide past. Despite the importance of divergent socioeconomic and political contexts, descendant accounts of their different experiences point to the constitutive role of culture in the shaping of particular descendant memory work. In keeping with Fassin's critique of the universal semiotics of suffering, findings pertaining to the culturally specific Cambodian and Jewish Israeli paradigms and practices of memory problematize the globally disseminated reductionist profile of the pathologized and enlisted trauma descendant and therapeutic and sociopolitical interventionist practices that "treat" genocide legacies as universal.[64]

Beginning with trauma-related legacies, Khmer respondents in Canada and Cambodia almost unanimously asserted they are not suffering from the intergenerational effects of PTSD, whereas the Israeli sample, albeit critical of the psychological construct, nevertheless describe the experience of an emotional wound that cannot be healed. Most interestingly, core religious Jewish and Buddhist paradigms of memory appear to have engendered these very different experiences of what has been conflated in the literature as a potentially universal trauma-related and intergenerationally transmitted experience of distress and suffering.

Although studies have begun to consider the long-term macro effect of trauma on the social fabric of nations and ethnic groups, survivor families and communities are still very much within the exclusive domain of the more person-centered psychological scholarship.[65] Psychological literature has in fact turned some attention to individual resilience and cultural-specific "protective layers," yet the great majority of academic and popular cultural accounts continue to present trauma victims and their descendants as psychosocially vulnerable, while ignoring more positive characteristics such as forward-looking strength of spirit, human endurance, and hope.[66] As Asad notes, different traditions deal differently with pain and suffering; not all cultural or religious traditions experience trauma as something "that cannot be lived with sanely."[67] The data analyzed here thus allows us to consider the ways in which microcultures with culture-specific values, practices, and modes of being have been conflated under the rubric of traumatic experience.

As mental health professionals begin to work with Khmer survivors and their descendants and memory workers establish commemorative projects, introducing Western forms of talk therapy and testimony, the findings here point once again to the importance of culturally sensitive conceptualizations of illness, healing, and memory work. Further comparative studies are called for so that lessons learned from victims of genocide may serve to sensitize those who seek to interpret, heal, historicize, and liberate wounded and silent voices of genocide.

Regarding memory, rejecting the role of carriers of collective and even familial memory, all three samples show little interest in providing public testimony to their parents' past and even have their doubts regarding the degree to which they will transmit the little historical knowledge they do have to future generations. Once again, culture-specific Jewish and Buddhist paradigms emerge as shaping the contours of these attitudes. Although Jewish paradigms promote the practice of intergenerational transmission of memory, the Israelis suffice in the existential status of their wounded commemorative role, preferring to relegate the role of transmission to their survivor parents and the education system. Alternatively, the Khmer appeal to Buddhist principles such as karma or taken-for-granted cosmological precepts regarding relations with the dead constitute forward-looking modes of being and obviate the need for collective memory.

As far as the future of public collective memory of the genocide, the samples express key differences regarding the centrality versus marginality of collective memory. Whereas the Israeli sample views the future of public Holocaust remembrance as very important, the Khmer appear relatively indifferent to future public or even communal-ethnic commemorative projects. This difference may very well be related to their very basic readings of their respective collective histories, with Israelis perceiving the Holocaust as one, if not the, major event in Jewish history, whereas the Khmer assert that the genocide is only one of many equally important events.

Narrowing the comparison to the findings in Cambodia and Canada, although the Khmer in both countries exhibit different degrees of reflexivity regarding the constitutive role of Buddhism in shaping the limits of private and collective memory, both selectively and strategically remember only empowering forward-looking lessons of the genocide, forgetting what would be damaging to the familial, collective, and national future.

The Cambodian findings provide a rare opportunity to observe the hegemonically orchestrated transition from private memory to communal and collective memory. Despite the obvious important differences, parallels may be drawn to the early decades of Israeli statehood and its nascent politics of memory. It will be interesting to see whether globalizing trauma brokers and interventionist NGOs or community activists will tip the balance in favor of Euro-Western trauma profiles and/or testimonial voice or if a unique syncretic culture-specific and context-specific "glocal" form of memory work will evolve.

One cannot ignore the fact that the discussion of trauma and memory work in this chapter has repeatedly highlighted the constitutive role of culture in descendant legacies. Despite the extensive ethnographic accounts of culture-bound illnesses, somatization, healing and related belief systems, and cross-cultural studies of collective memory, there have been few attempts to examine the way the core cultural conceptualizations of illness and memory work delegitimize or valorize remembering and forgetting or how and why they constitute unique mechanisms of transmission, be they verbal, embodied, or ideational.[68] Particular cultural sensibilities are deployed in references to Buddhist acceptance and the Jewish burden of memory. Culture-specific religious, cosmological, and spiritual worldviews also shape the very distinct contours of the Jewish and Khmer experiences of emotional well-being and moral rectitude. Cultural alterity in its own right still remains problematic in contemporary anthropological scholarship, evoking the scepter of essentialism or anxiety over the elision of macropolitical, historical, or socioeconomic interpretations.[69] Sociopolitical contextual analyses allow for the more comforting route of translation into a universal common language of suffering. Trauma theory is one such universalizing force, classifying and regulating the diverse lived experiences of suffering. The findings here call for renewed attention to the "particular" limits of universalizing axiomatic language, where translation of descendant accounts into the universal semiotics of suffering would have ultimately overshadowed subtly unique and multifaceted responses to genocide. It still remains to be seen if the proliferation of a "universal semiotics" of genocide suffering and multidirectional memories merely "binds" (in Rothberg's terms) diverse cultural pasts into a more common language of victimhood, or whether translation has silenced particular cultural voices and idioms of suffering.[70]

Notes

Research in Cambodia was made possible with the help of an Israel Science Foundation Grant (1323/09). I would also like to thank my informant and translator, Davith Bolin, without whom the majority of my interviews would not have been possible. Research in Canada (in

2005–6) was made possible thanks to a grant from the Halbert Association for Canadian Studies. I would like to finally thank Haim Hazan and Amos Goldberg and the other members of our forum for their insightful comments.

1. Daniel Levy and Natan Sznaider, "Memory Unbound: The Holocaust Formation of Cosmopolitan Memory," *European Journal of Social Theory* 5 (2002): 87–105.

2. James Edward Young, *Writing and Rewriting the Holocaust: Narrative and the Consequences of Interpretation* (Bloomington: Indiana University Press, 1988); Carol A. Kidron, "Toward an Ethnography of Silence: The Lived Presence of the Past in the Everyday Lives of Holocaust Trauma Descendants in Israel," *Current Anthropology* 50 (2009): 5–27.

3. Michael Rothberg, *Multidirectional Memory: Remembering the Holocaust in the Age of Decolonization* (Stanford, CA: Stanford University Press, 2009).

4. Ulrich Beck and Natan Sznaider, "Unpacking Cosmopolitanism for the Social Sciences: A Research Agenda," *British Journal of Sociology* 61 (2010): 381–403.

5. Didier Fassin, "Humanitarian Politics of Testimony: Subjectification through Trauma in the Israeli-Palestinian Conflict," *Cultural Anthropology* 23 (2009): 531–58.

6. Judith Lewis Herman, *Trauma and Recovery* (New York: Basic Books, 1992).

7. American Psychiatric Association. *Diagnostic and Statistical Manual of Mental Disorders (DSM-IV)* (Washington DC: American Psychiatric Association, 1994).

8. Harvey A. Barocas and Carol Barocas, "Manifestations of Concentration Camp Effects on the Second Generation," *American Journal of Psychiatry* 130, no. 7 (1973): 820–21.

9. Avraham Sagi-Schwartz et al., "Attachment and Traumatic Stress in Female Holocaust Child Survivors and Their Daughters," *American Journal of Psychiatry* 160, no. 6 (2003): 1086–92; Felice Zilberfein, "Children of Holocaust Survivors: Separation Obstacles, Attachments and Anxiety," in *A Global Perspective on Working with Holocaust Survivors and the Second Generation*, ed. J. Lemberger (Jerusalem: JDC-Brookdale Institute of Gerontology and Human Development, 1995), 413–22.

10. Dan Bar-On, "Israeli and German Students Encounter the Holocaust through a Group Process: 'Working Through' and 'Partial Relevance,'" *International Journal of Group Tensions* 22, no. 2 (1992): 81–118.

11. Kidron, "Toward an Ethnography of Silence," 5–27.

12. Herman, *Trauma and Recovery.*

13. Yael Danieli, "Introduction: History and Conceptual Foundations," in *International Handbook of Multigenerational Legacies of Trauma*, ed. Yael Danieli (New York: Plenum, 1998), 1–17.

14. Levy and Sznaider, "Memory Unbound," 87–105; Carol A. Kidron, "Surviving the Distant Past: A Case Study of the Cultural Construction of Trauma Descendant Identity," *Ethos* 31, no. 4 (2003): 1–32; Jackie Feldman, *Above the Death Pits, Beneath the Flag: Youth Voyages to Holocaust Poland and Israeli National Identity* (New York: Berghahn Books, 2008); Alisse Waterston and Barbara Rylko-Bauer, "Out of the Shadows of History and Memory: Personal Family Narratives in Ethnographies of Discovery," *American Ethnologist* 33 (2006): 397–412; Alan L. Berger, *Children of Job: American Second-Generation Witnesses to the Holocaust* (Albany, NY: SUNY Press, 1997).

15. Janine Altounian, "Putting into Words, Putting to Rest and Putting Aside the Ancestors: How an Analysand Who Was Heir to the Armenian Genocide of 1915 Worked Through Mourning," *International Journal of Psychoanalysis* 80, no. 3 (1999): 439–48; Donna J. Ida and Pahoua Young, "Southeast Asian Children and Adolescents," in *Children of Color: Psychological Interventions with Culturally Diverse Youth*, ed. Janine. T. Gibbs and Lorna. N. Huang (San Francisco: Jossey-Bass, 2003), 265–95.

16. J. David Kinzie et al., "Post-Traumatic Stress Disorder among Survivors of Cambodian Concentration Camps," *American Journal of Psychiatry* 141, no. 5 (1984): 645–50.

17. Larke Nahme Huang, "Southeast Asian Refugee Children and Adolescents," in *Children of Color: Psychological Interventions with Culturally Diverse Youth*, ed. Janine T. Gibbs and Lorna N. Huang (San Francisco: Jossey-Bass, 1998), 264–304; Cecile Rousseau, Aline Drapeau, and Robert Platt, "Family Trauma and its Association with Emotional and Behavioral Problems and Social Adjustment in Adolescent Cambodian Refugees," *Child Abuse and Neglect* 23, no. 12 (1999):

1263–73; Audrey Rubin and Lorna Rhodes, "Narrative and the Intergenerational Transmission of Trauma among Cambodian Refugees," in *Perspectives in Cross-Cultural Psychiatry*, ed. Anna M. Georgiopoulos and Jerrold F. Rosenbaum (Philadelphia: Lippincott Williams & Wilkins, 2005).

18. Christine A. Stevens, "Perspectives on the Meaning of Symptoms among Cambodian Refugees," *Journal of Sociology* 37, no. 1 (2001): 81–98.

19. Rubin and Rhodes, "Narrative and the Intergenerational Transmission of Trauma."

20. Rousseau, Drapeau, and Platt, "Family Trauma," 1263–73.

21. There have only been two attempts to explore the phenomenological experience of Cambodian descendants from the perspective of the child of the survivor. Both, however, generalize regarding the mental health of respondents (without psychological testing or descendant accounts on perceived health), and both samples are biased, one presenting the accounts of elite educated Cambodian youth, and the other a very small self-selected sample of those active in a community-based organization. See Rubin and Rhodes, "Narrative and the Intergenerational Transmission of Trauma"; Burcu Munyas, "Cambodian Youth: Transmitting (His)tories of Genocide to Second and Third Generation in Cambodia," *Journal of Genocide Studies* 10 (2008): 413–39.

22. Jeffrey C. Alexander, "Toward a Theory of Cultural Trauma," in *Cultural Trauma and Collective Identity*, ed. Jeffrey C. Alexander et al. (Berkeley: University of California Press, 2004), 1–30; Munyas, "Cambodian Youth," 413–39.

23. Kelly Mckinney, "'Breaking the Conspiracy of Silence': Testimony, Traumatic Memory and Psychotherapy with Survivors of Political Violence," *Ethos* 35 (2007): 265–99.

24. Ben Kiernan, *The Pol Pot Regime: Race, Power and Genocide in Cambodia under the Khmer Rouge* (New Haven, CT: Yale University Press, 1996).

25. Munyas, "Cambodian Youth," 413–39.

26. Judy Ledgerwood, May Ebihara, and Carol Mortland, "Introduction," in *Cambodian Culture since 1975: Homeland and Exile*, ed. M. M. Ebihara, C. A. Mortland, and J. Ledgerwood (Ithaca, NY: Cornell University Press, 1994), 1–26; Seok A. Kwon, "Ethnic Community Organizations: Fostering Cultural Identity among Cambodian and Mien Youth," paper for Project on South Asians and Visibility in Education, 2006.

27. Maurice Halbwachs, *The Collective Memory* (New York: Harper, 1980), 68–87.

28. Robert M. Hayden, "Moral Vision and Impaired Insight," *Current Anthropology* 48 (2007): 105–31.

29. Cecile Rousseau, Maria Morales, and Patricia Foxen, "Going Home: Giving Voice to Memory Strategies of Young Mayan Refugees who Returned to Gutamala as a Community," *Culture, Medicine and Psychiatry* 25 (2001): 135–68.

30. Michael Lambek and Paul Antze, "Introduction: Forecasting Memory," in *Tense Past: Cultural Essays in Trauma and Memory*, ed. Paul Antze and Michael Lambek (New York: Routledge, 1996), xi–xxxviii.

31. Alexander Laban Hinton, *Why Did They Kill: Cambodian in the Shadow of Genocide* (Berkeley, 2004); Nicolas Argenti and Katharina Schramm, *Remembering Violence: Anthropological Perspectives on Intergenerational Transmission* (New York: Berghahn Books, 2009).

32. Alisse Waterston and Barbara Rylko-Bauer, "Out of the Shadows of History and Memory," 397–412.

33. Carol Ann Kidron, "Children of Twilight: Deconstructing the Passage from Silence to Voice of Second and Third Generation Holocaust Descendants within the Private and Public Spheres in Israel" (PhD dissertation, Hebrew University, 2005).

34. Kidron, "Toward an Ethnography of Silence," 5–27.

35. Carol Ann Kidron, "Silent Legacies of Trauma: A Comparative Study of Cambodian Canadian and Israeli Holocaust Trauma Descendant Memory Work," in *Remembering Violence: Anthropological Perspectives on Intergenerational Transmission*, ed. Nicholas Argenti and Katharina Schramm (New York: Berghahn Books, 2009), 185–220.

36. Similar questions were used with both Holocaust and Cambodian descendants. These questions attempted to illicit responses along the following themes: parental past and present behavior and parent-child relationship; childhood memories of genocide-related dialogue or

storytelling and/or genocide-related practices in the home; past and present "consumption" of trauma-related discourse and cultural products; participation in genocide-related practices in the public domain; and finally, envisioned future of commemorative practices.

37. In 1970 General Lon Nol's military coup deposed Prince Shihanouk and allied with the United States, at which point the Cambodian monarchy was renamed the Khmer Republic. US and South Vietnamese forces entered Cambodia to block North Vietnamese incursion. Communist insurgency, aided by North Vietnamese support, culminated in 1975 in the downfall of the Khmer Republic and the rise of the Communist Party of Kampuchea (CPK) and Pol Pot's Khmer Rouge regime. The CPK instigated the evacuation of urban populations to the countryside to work as farmers. Beyond the brutal mass roundups and executions of intellectuals, bureaucrats, businessmen, educated Cambodians, and Buddhist monks, hundreds of thousands died of starvation and disease. The total death toll between 1975 and 1979 has been estimated at one to three million.

38. John B. Quigley "Introduction." In *Genocide in Cambodia: Documents from the Trial of Pol Pot and Leng Say*, ed. Howard J. De Nike, John Quigley, and Kenneth J. Robinson (Philadelphia: University of Pennsylvania Press, 2000), 1–18. The use of the term "genocide" to describe the massacre, starvation, and expulsion of the victims of the Khmer Rouge is problematic. As outlined by Quigley an expert in international law invited to attend the 1979 trial of Pol Pot and Leng Sary to determine whether they could be tried for crimes of genocide, the term "genocide" was defined by the UN Convention on the Prevention and Punishment of the Crime of Genocide in 1948. Genocide was defined by the convention as the intention to destroy a whole or part of a national, ethnic, racial, or religious group. Quigley (as do genocide scholars) explains that the controversy has arisen surrounding the use of the term "genocide" when applied to the case of Cambodia due to the fact that most of the victims, like the perpetrators, were Khmer—"so there was no racial animus behind the actions." Only a small minority of the victims could be classified as ethnic, religious, or national other (Chinese, Muslim Cham, and Vietnamese), and due to the political nature of Khmer Rouge motives, it is not clear that the perpetrators intended to kill these victims only due to their ethnic/religious status as other. Nevertheless, Quigley concluded that as the definition of genocide includes intention to kill a whole or part of a group, then the victimization of Khmer intellectuals or religious leaders would be considered a part of a national and ethnic group and would then be consistent with the UN definition. Genocide scholars, including those Khmer scholars working in Cambodia to document the events, have used the term "genocide," in some cases for lack of a better word, and in other cases due to the emergent genealogy of the term now used to classify a wide array of human loss and suffering. It might be claimed that considering the nature and scale of loss in Cambodia, the use of another term would raise no less difficult questions concerning global hierarchies of suffering.

39. Ledgerwood, Ebihara, and Mortland, "Introduction," 1–26.

40. Andre Gingrich and Richard Gabriel Fox, *Anthropology by Comparison* (New York: Routledge, 2002).

41. As clarified previously, the question posed to the descendants and in the chapter herein is not a diagnostic one as to whether they are or are not suffering from PTSD, but rather if and how the illness construct as cultural construction does or does not meaningfully frame their experience. As seen in the discussion that follows, descendants articulate emotive difference using an alternative cultural idiom, allowing for an analysis of the semiotics of their experience rather than a psychological diagnosis of their mental health.

42. All names were altered for the purpose of confidentiality. In Canada, Khmer names were Anglicized due to the very small, close-knit nature of the community.

43. Talal Asad, "Agency and Pain: An Exploration," *Culture and Religion* 1, no. 1 (2002): 29–60.

44. The great majority of interviews were in English. There were a number of interviews in French, translated by the author and one interview in Khmer translated by an informant.

45. Michael G. Wessels and Alison Strang, "Religion as Resource and Risk," in *World Turned Upside Down: Social Ecological Approaches to Children in War*, ed. N. Boothby, Alison Strang, and Michael G. Wessels (Bloomfield, 2008), 199–222.

46. Nichole. J. Smith-Hefner, "Ethnicity and the Force of Faith: Christian Conversion among Khmer Refugees," *Anthropological Quarterly* 67 (1994): 24–37.

47. Alexander Laban Hinton, "Truth Representation and Politics of Memory after Genocide," in *People of Virtue: Reconfiguring Religion, Power, and Moral Order in Cambodia,* ed. Alexandra Kent and David P. Chandler (Copenhagen: Nordic Inst of Asian Studies, 2008), 62–84.

48. Jean Langford, "Gifts Intercepted: Biopolitics and Spirit Debt," *Cultural Anthropology* 24 (2009): 681–711.

49. Kidron, "Toward an Ethnography of Silence," 5–27; D. Hinton et al., "Neck-Focused Panic Attack among Cambodian Refugees, a Logistic and Linear and Regression Analysis," *Journal of Anxiety Disorders* 20 (2006): 77.

50. Laurence J. Kirmayer, "Failures of Imagination: The Refugees Narrative in Psychiatry," *Anthropology and Medicine* 10 (2003): 167–86.

51. Kidron, "Toward an Ethnography of Silence," 5–27.

52. Yosef Hayim Yerushalmi, *Zakhor-Jewish History and Jewish Memory* (Seattle and London: University of Washington Press, 1982).

53. Young, *Writing and Rewriting the Holocaust.*

54. Feldman, *Above the Death Pits, Beneath the Flag.*

55. Carol Ann Kidron, "In Pursuit of Jewish Paradigms of Memory: Constituting Carriers of Jewish Memory in a Support Group for Children of Holocaust Survivors," *Dapim: Studies on the Holocaust* 23 (2009): 7–43.

56. Kidron, "Toward an Ethnography of Silence," 5–27.

57. Kidron, "In Pursuit of Jewish Paradigms of Memory," 7–43.

58. Kidron, "Toward an Ethnography of Silence," 5–27.

59. Pierre Nora, "Between Memory and History," *Representations* 26 (1989): 7–25.

60. Kidron, "Children of Twilight."

61. Ronit Lentin, *Israel and the Daughters of the Shoa: Re-occupying the Territories of Silence* (New York: Berghahn Books, 2000); Rachel Hughes, "Nationalism and Genocide at the Tuol Sleng Museum of Genocide Crimes," in *Contested Pasts: The Politics of Memory,* ed. Katherine Hodgkin and Susanna Radstone (New York: Routledge, 2003), 175–207.

62. Langford, "Gifts Intercepted," 681–711.

63. Ibid.

64. Fassin, "Humanitarian Politics of Testimony," 531–58.

65. Alexander, "Toward a Theory of Cultural Trauma," 1–30.

66. Alex Argenti-Pillen, "The Discourse on Trauma in Non-Western Cultural Contexts: Contributions of an Ethnographic Method," in *International Handbook of Human Response to Trauma,* ed. A.Y. Shalev, R. Yehuda, and A. C. McFarlane (New York: Kluwer Academic Publishers, 2000), 87–102; M. B. Eggerman and K. Panter-Brick, "Suffering Hope and Entrapment: Resilience and Cultural Values in Afghanistan," *Social Science and Medicine* 71 (2010): 71–83.

67. Asad, "Agency and Pain," 43.

68. Hinton, *Why Did They Kill.*

69. Lila Abu-Lughod, "Writing against Culture," in *Recapturing Anthropology: Working in the Present,* ed. Richard G. Fox (Santa Fe: School of American Research Press, 1991), 137–62.

70. Fassin, "Humanitarian Politics of Testimony," 531–58.

Bibliography

Abu-Lughod, Lila. "Writing against Culture." In *Recapturing Anthropology: Working in the Present,* ed. Richard G. Fox, 137–62. Santa Fe, NM: School of American Research Press, 1991.

Alexander, Jeffrey C. "Toward a Theory of Cultural Trauma." In *Cultural Trauma and Collective Identity,* ed. Jeffrey C. Alexander, Ron Eyerman, Bernhard Geisen, Niel Smelser, and Piotr Sztompka, 1–30. Berkeley: University of California Press, 2004.

Altounian, Janine. "Putting into Words, Putting to Rest and Putting Aside the Ancestors: How an Analysand Who Was Heir to the Armenian Genocide of 1915 Worked Through Mourning." *International Journal of Psychoanalysis* 80, no. 3 (1999): 439–48.

Argenti, Nicholas, and Katharina Schramm, eds. *Remembering Violence: Anthropological Perspectives on Intergenerational Transmission.* New York: Berghahn Books, 2009.

Argenti-Pillen, Alex. "The Discourse on Trauma in Non-Western Cultural Contexts: Contributions of an Ethnographic Method." In *International Handbook of Human Response to Trauma*, ed. Arye Y. Shalev, Rachel Yehuda, and Alexander C. McFarlane, 87–102. New York: Kluwer Academic Publishers, 2000.

Asad, Talal. "Agency and Pain: An Exploration." *Culture and Religion* 1 no. 1 (2002): 29–60.

Barocas, Harvey A., and Carol Barocas. "Manifestations of Concentration Camp Effects on the Second Generation." *American Journal of Psychiatry* 130, no. 7 (1973): 820–21.

Bar-On, Dan. "Israeli and German Students Encounter the Holocaust through a Group Process: 'Working Through' and 'Partial Relevance.'" *International Journal of Group Tensions* 22, no. 2 (1992): 81–118.

Beck, Ulrich, and Natan Sznaider. "Unpacking Cosmopolitanism for the Social Sciences: A Research Agenda." *British Journal of Sociology* 61 (2010): 381–403.

Berger, Allan L. *Children of Job: American Second-Generation Witnesses to the Holocaust.* Albany, NY: SUNY Press, 1997.

Danieli, Yael. "Introduction: History and Conceptual Foundations." In *International Handbook of Multigenerational Legacies of Trauma*, ed. Yael Danieli, 1–17. New York: Plenum, 1998.

American Psychiatric Association. *Diagnostic and Statistical Manual of Mental Disorders (DSM-IV).* Washington DC: American Psychiatric Association, 1994.

Eggerman, Mark B., and Katherine Panter-Brick. "Suffering Hope and Entrapment: Resilience and Cultural Values in Afghanistan." *Social Science and Medicine* 71 (2010): 71–83.

Fassin, Didier. "Humanitarian Politics of Testimony: Subjectification through Trauma in the Israeli-Palestinian Conflict." *Cultural Anthropology* 23 (2009): 531–58.

Feldman, Jackie. *Above the Death Pits, Beneath the Flag: Youth Voyages to Holocaust Poland and Israeli National Identity.* New York: Berghahn Books, 2008.

Gingrich, Andre, and Richard G. Fox. *Anthropology by Comparison.* New York: Routledge, 2002.

Halbwachs, Maurice. *The Collective Memory.* New York: Harper, 1980.

Hayden, Robert M. "Moral Vision and Impaired Insight." *Current Anthropology* 48 (2007): 105–31.

Herman, Judith L. *Trauma and Recovery.* New York: Basic Books, 1992.

Hinton, Alex L. *Why Did They Kill: Cambodia in the Shadow of Genocide.* Berkeley: University of California Press, 2004.

———. "Truth Representation and Politics of Memory after Genocide." In *People of Virtue: Reconfiguring Religion, Power, and Moral Order in Cambodia*, ed. Alexandra Kent and David P. Chandler, 62–84. Copenhagen: Nordic Inst of Asian Studies, 2008.

Hinton, Devon, Dara Chhean, Vuth Pich, Khin Um, Jeanne M. Fama, and Mark H. Pollack. "Neck-Focused Panic Attack among Cambodian Refugees, a Logistic and Linear and Regression Analysis." *Journal of Anxiety Disorders* 20 (2006): 119–38.

Huang, Larke N. "Southeast Asian Refugee Children and Adolescents." In *Children of Color: Psychological Interventions with Culturally Diverse Youth*, ed. Jewelle T. Gibbs and Larke N. Huang, 264–304. San Francisco: Jossey-Bass, 1998.

Hughes, Rachel "Nationalism and Genocide at the Tuol Sleng Museum of Genocide Crimes." In *Contested Pasts: The Politics of Memory*, ed. Katharine Hodgkin and Susanna Radstone, 175–207. New York: Routledge, 2003.

Ida, Donna, and Pahoua Young. "Southeast Asian Children and Adolescents." In *Children of Color: Psychological Interventions with Culturally Diverse Youth*, ed. Jewelle T. Gibbs and Larke N. Huang, 265–95. San Francisco: Jossey-Bass, 2003.

Kidron, Carol A. "Children of Twilight: Deconstructing the Passage from Silence to Voice of Second and Third Generation Holocaust Descendants within the Private and Public Spheres in Israel." PhD dissertation, Hebrew University, 2005.

———. "In Pursuit of Jewish Paradigms of Memory: Constituting Carriers of Jewish Memory in a Support Group for Children of Holocaust Survivors." *Dapim: Studies on the Holocaust* 23 (2009): 7–43.

———. "Silent Legacies of Trauma: A Comparative Study of Cambodian Canadian and Israeli Holocaust Trauma Descendant Memory Work." In *Remembering Violence: Anthropological Perspectives on Intergenerational Transmission*, ed. Nicholas Argenti and Katharina Schramm, 185–220. New York: Berghahn Books, 2009.

———. "Surviving the Distant Past: A Case Study of the Cultural Construction of Trauma Descendant Identity." *Ethos* 31, no. 4 (2003): 1–32.

———. "Toward an Ethnography of Silence: The Lived Presence of the Past in the Everyday Lives of Holocaust Trauma Descendants in Israel." *Current Anthropology* 50 (2009): 5–27.

Kiernan, Ben. *The Pol Pot Regime: Race, Power and Genocide in Cambodia under the Khmer Rouge*. New Haven, CT: Yale University Press, 1996.

Kinzie, J. David, Ronald. H. Frederickson, Rath Ben, Jenelle. Fleck, and William. Karls. "Post-Traumatic Stress Disorder among Survivors of Cambodian Concentration Camps." *American Journal of Psychiatry* 141, no. 5 (1984): 645–50.

Kirmayer, Laurence J. "Failures of Imagination: The Refugees Narrative in Psychiatry." *Anthropology and Medicine* 10 (2003): 167–86.

Kwon, Seok A. "Ethnic Community Organizations: Fostering Cultural Identity among Cambodian and Mien Youth." Paper for Project on South Asians and Visibility in Education. 2006.

Lambek, Michael, and Paul Antze. "Introduction: Forecasting Memory." In *Tense Past: Cultural Essays in Trauma and Memory*, ed. Paul Antze and Michael Lambek, xi–xxxviii. New York: Routledge, 1996.

Langford, Jean. "Gifts Intercepted: Biopolitics and Spirit Debt." *Cultural Anthropology* 24 (2009): 681–711.

Ledgerwood, Judy, May M. Ebihara, and Carol Mortland. "Introduction." In *Cambodian Culture since 1975: Homeland and Exile*, ed. May. M. Ebihara, Carol. A. Mortland, and Judy Ledgerwood, 1–26. Ithaca, NY: Cornell University Press, 1994.

Lentin, Ronit. *Israel and the Daughters of the Shoa: Re-occupying the Territories of Silence*. New York: Berghahn Books, 2000.

Levy, Daniel, and Natan Sznaider. "Memory Unbound: The Holocaust Formation of Cosmopolitan Memory." *European Journal of Social Theory* 5 (2002): 87–105.

Mckinney, Kelly. "'Breaking the Conspiracy of Silence': Testimony, Traumatic Memory and Psychotherapy with Survivors of Political Violence." *Ethos* 35 (2007): 265–99.

Munyas, Burcu. "Cambodian Youth: Transmitting (His)tories of Genocide to Second and Third Generation in Cambodia." *Journal of Genocide Studies* 10 (2008): 413–39.

Nora, Pierre. "Between Memory and History." *Representations* 26 (1989): 7–25.

Quigley, John B. "Introduction." In *Genocide in Cambodia: Documents from the Trial of Pol Pot and Leng Say*, ed. Howard J. De Nike, John Quigley, and Keneth J. Robinson, 1–18. Philadelphia: University of Pennsylvania Press, 2000.

Rothberg, Michael *Multidirectional Memory: Remembering the Holocaust in the Age of Decolinzation*. Stanford, CA: Stanford University Press, 2009.

Rousseau, Cecile, Aline Drapeau, and Robert Platt. "Family Trauma and its Association with Emotional and Behavioral Problems and Social Adjustment in Adolescent Cambodian Refugees." *Child Abuse and Neglect* 23, no. 12 (1999): 1263–273.

Rousseau, Cecile, Maria Morales, and Patricia Foxen. "Going Home: Giving Voice to Memory Strategies of Young Mayan Refugees who Returned to Gutamala as a Community." *Culture, Medicine and Psychiatry* 25 (2001): 135–68.

Rubin, Audrey, and Lorna Rhodes. "Narrative and the Intergenerational Transmission of Trauma among Cambodian Refugees." In *Perspectives in Cross-Cultural Psychiatry*, ed. Anna M. Georgiopoulos and Jerrold F. Rosenbaum, 157–78. Philadelphia: Lippincott Williams & Wilkins, 2005.

Sagi-Schwartz, Avraham, Marinus H. Van IJzendoorn, Klaus E. Grossmann, Tirtsa Joels, Karin Grossmann, Miri Scharf, Nina Koren-Karie, and Sarit Alkalay. "Attachment and Traumatic Stress in Female Holocaust Child Survivors and Their Daughters." *American Journal of Psychiatry* 160, no. 6 (2003): 1086–92.

Smith-Hefner, Nancy J. "Ethnicity and the Force of Faith: Christian Conversion among Khmer Refugees." *Anthropological Quarterly* 67 (1994): 24–37.

Stevens, Christine A. "Perspectives on the Meaning of Symptoms among Cambodian Refugees." *Journal of Sociology* 37, no. 1 (2001): 81–98.

Waterston, Alisse, and Barbara Rylko-Bauer. "Out of the Shadows of History and Memory: Personal Family Narratives in Ethnographies of Rediscovery." *American Ethnologist* 33 (2006): 397–412.

Wessels, Michael G., and Alison Strang. "Religion as Resource and Risk in N. Boothby." In *World Turned Upside Down: Social Ecological Approaches to Children in War*, ed. A Strang and Michael G. Wessels, 199–222. Bloomfield, CT: Kumarian Press, 2008.

Yerushalmi, Yosef H. *Zakhor-Jewish History and Jewish Memory.* Seattle and London: University of Washington Press, 1982.

Young, James E. *Writing and Rewriting the Holocaust: Narrative and the Consequences of Interpretation.* Bloomington: Indiana University Press, 1988.

Young, Katherine G. "The Memory of the Flesh: The Family Body in Somatic Psychology." *Body and Society* 8 (2002): 25–47.

Zilberfein, Felice. "Children of Holocaust Survivors: Separation Obstacles, Attachments and Anxiety." In *A Global Perspective on Working with Holocaust Survivors and the Second Generation*, ed. J. Lemberger, 413–22. Jerusalem: JDC-Brookdale Institute of Gerontology and Human Development, 1995.

CHAPTER 9

Genres of Identification
Holocaust Testimony and Postcolonial Witness

LOUISE BETHLEHEM

Writing in 1950, Aimé Césaire would use the pages of his *Discourse on Colonialism* to make a shocking proposition. In the immediate shadow of the Nazi genocide, Césaire would forcefully assert that Europe is unforgiving of Hitler not for "the *crime* in itself, *the crime against man*, it is not *the humiliation of man as such*, it is the crime against the white man, the humiliation of the white man, and the fact that he applied to Europe colonialist procedures which until then had been reserved exclusively for the Arabs of Algeria, the coolies of India and the blacks of Africa."[1] This impassioned denunciation of European humanism serves as one point of departure for considering how the Holocaust abuts other genocidal histories, including the predatory swathes of the European colonialisms. I invoke Césaire here not merely because his gesture is hospitable to contemporary constructions of Holocaust memory that resist its identitarian appropriations at a time when Holocaust memory is itself being globalized—one of the themes that the present volume addresses. Rather, the historicity of his utterance has different lessons to disclose. For Césaire, as a writer and politician who helped to constitute the trajectory of *Négritude* as the intellectual concomitant of anticolonial resistance, the mobilization of what he terms "Hitlerism" is subordinated to the urgent political priorities of decolonization. Indeed, the very appellation "Hitlerism" seems anomalous as we hear it here long after the fact of its enunciation. It suggests that the Holocaust, for Césaire, had not yet acceded to its construction in the guise with which we currently associate the term, this particular term—catachresis, strenuous synecdoche, and signifier of radical evil at one and the same time. Yet there is still

---

Notes for this section begin on page 185.

more that can be revealed here. To apprehend Césaire without the sediment of retrospect, without anachrony, is to agree with Michael Rothberg's assessment: "[T]he emergence of the collective memory of the Nazi genocide in the 1950s and 1960s takes place in a punctual dialogue with ongoing processes of decolonization and civil rights struggle and their modes of coming to terms with colonialism, slavery, and racism."[2]

Césaire is indeed pivotal to the important intellectual project that Rothberg initiates as "multidirectional memory" in the title of his 2009 volume.[3] This is no coincidence. Rothberg's paradigm of multidirectional memory sees "the emergence of Holocaust memory and the unfolding of decolonization as overlapping and not separate processes," as he writes elsewhere.[4] Multidirectional memory contests identitarian constructions of collective memory that foreclose the distance between past and present in a manner that "excludes elements of alterity and forms of commonality with others."[5] "Ultimately," Rothberg declares, "memory is not a zero-sum game."[6] His volume thus offers a powerful antidote to the "ugly contest[s] of comparative victimization" that suffuse the cultural politics of our times.[7]

The present chapter is in many ways predicated on Rothberg's intervention—one whose disciplinary consequences for postcolonial cultural studies and literary theory, on the one hand, and for Holocaust studies, on the other, I certainly endorse.[8] I share his suggestion that "the ordinarily unacknowledged history of cross-referencing that characterizes the period of decolonization continues to this day and constitutes a precondition of contemporary discourse," particularly insofar as Rothberg goes on to suggest that the "virulence" of competitive memory discourses has to do "partly with the rhetorical and cultural *intimacy* of seemingly opposed traditions of remembrance."[9] My own concerns in this chapter will be different, however. I will orient myself less to the history of cross-referencing, whose contours and consequences Rothberg so admirably sketches, than to the strange intimacies of (dis)avowal that obtain between Holocaust studies and postcolonial theory, heirs to the thickened temporality that Rothberg condenses as "Auschwitz and Algeria" in one memorable syntagma.[10] Legatees of this shared moment, however, the two paradigms also crucially partake of the competition between these two configurations of memory.

The foundational text for the emergence of postcolonial theory as a disciplinary paradigm is, of course, Edward Said's *Orientalism* (1978).[11] Said's insistence on the materiality of a set of discourses held famously to constitute the world they purport merely to describe in accordance with the racialized logic of the unremitting binary—Occident versus Orient—performs what Walter Benjamin might have recognized as the work of historical materialism. In its disaggregation of "civilization," on the one hand, and "race," on the other, postcolonial theory has articulated some of the major ethical and epistemological, historical and historiographic implications of Benjamin's well-known pronouncement: "There is no document of civilization that is not simultaneously a document of barbarism."[12] For Said, whose analysis is presaged on Foucault's notion of discourse, this is literally the case. Subsequent elaborations of postcolonial theory will insist, in a manner congruent with the later Foucault, that race is the biopolitical signifier that renders the "civilizing mission" literally murderous, thus returning discourse to a fateful intersection with the materiality of bodies over which it holds dominion.[13]

Well before its articulation by Foucault, this structural determinant of what Achille Mbembe has termed "necropolitics" would have been familiar to Aimé Césaire, Frantz Fanon, and Hannah Arendt.[14] "African colonial possessions," Arendt writes in *The Origins of Totalitarianism,* "became the most fertile soil for the flowering of the Nazi elite."[15] The trajectory to be emphasized is causal rather than merely chronological, as Arendt's anatomy of racism seeks to demonstrate. The necropolitical mobilization of race is common to the Nazi genocide and to the genocidal irruptions that periodically characterized colonialism, as certain postcolonial theorists would reiterate in fidelity, variously, to Foucault or to the intellectuals who shaped the era of decolonization.[16] To arrogate the causality of genocide to racism, as the biopolitical tack requires, rather than to a more rarefied dynamic of anti-Semitism, is a gesture that itself sets this trajectory within postcolonial theory in opposition to the historiographic trajectory emerging from Jewish—and particularly hegemonic Israeli—constructions of the Holocaust. Moreover, the narrative of anti-Semitism cannot, in the latter variant, be disentangled from the authorizing tropes of Israeli nationhood. It is here, with reference to the very grounds of the conflict between Israel and the Palestinian people, that postcolonialism will play its most adversarial role with respect to post-Holocaust identitarian claims of Israeli Jews and diasporic Zionists. Said's "Zionism from the Standpoint of Its Victims" is obviously the landmark text here.[17]

Yet for all that the Jewish body remains, by and large, unmourned in the canonical texts of postcolonial theory, the Holocaust has, I seek to argue, made an engagement with the ascendancy of witness compelling for postcolonialism precisely because it too *comes after;* it too inhabits the traumatic belatedness of catastrophe. Precisely this shared habitation undergirds the theoretical humanities in a general sense, as Robert Eaglestone observes: "[P]ostmodernism—understood as poststructuralism, a still developing tradition of post-phenomenological philosophy—is a response to the Holocaust."[18] Although I would not like to dissociate postcolonialism (in some of its variants) from poststructuralism in the genealogy that Eaglestone constructs, my own concerns here will be narrower. The fact that postcolonial studies inhabits a particular temporality of the aftermath, I suggest, opens postcolonial discourse in its nascent institutionalization during the late 1970s and 1980s to cultural tropes of witnessing that first arose in the specific context of the institutionalization of Holocaust memory, but that have been generalized beyond this context. The *performance* of witness, I will claim, is encoded in certain canonical texts of postcolonial theory as an unacknowledged substrate, present in excess of its analysis of testimonial practice oriented to the peculiar deformations occasioned by the rendering of subaltern histories in the colonial archive. My emphasis here thus falls not so much on the construction of the aftermath that Rothberg parses as the state of being *nach Auschwitz,* that is to say, *after* but also crucially *oriented toward* the Holocaust, and simultaneously but differently the state of being *après l'Algérie.*[19] Rather, I will focus on forms of witnessing that emerge as the *currency* of the aftermath, where currency is understood in a dual sense: equally as that which sediments and standardizes value, and as that which limns the Holocaust between the lines of contemporary academic discourse.

I will begin to substantiate these claims by revisiting Césaire's *Discourse on Colonialism* in order to exhume the forms of identification available to him during the period immediately after the Nazi genocide. I will trace the manner in which he routes his denunciation of colonialism through a rhetoric that memorializes its victims. I will then contrast Césaire's grammar of memorialization with the gestures, the genres, of identification mobilized by the contemporary postcolonial philosopher Gayatri Chakravorty Spivak, contextualizing her interventions with respect to the consolidation of the Jewish survivor as construct. I will explore the disjunctive dissemination of this construct in its unlikely postcolonial haunt, but will also treat Spivak's aporetic reprise of testimony in light of the debate on the ethics of witness that Holocaust studies inaugurates.

Cities That Evaporate at the Edge of the Sword

Césaire's *Discourse on Colonialism,* first published in 1950 and republished in *Présence Africaine* in 1955, is, as I have already noted, significant for its claim that the Nazi genocide is essentially bound up with the history of colonialism. The violence that Europe wreaks revisits those who disavow it, he emphasizes. Before the Europeans were "victims" of the "supreme barbarism" of Nazism, Césaire insists, "they were its accomplices."[20] Let us return to the claim with which I opened this chapter:

> [I]t would be worthwhile to study clinically, in detail the steps taken by Hitler and Hitlerism and to reveal to the very distinguished, very humanistic, very Christian bourgeois of the twentieth century that without his being aware of it, he has a Hitler inside him, that Hitler *inhabits* him, that Hitler is his *demon,* that if he rails against him, he is being inconsistent and that, at bottom, what he cannot forgive Hitler for is not *crime* in itself, *the crime against man,* it is not *the humiliation of man as such,* it is the crime against the white man, the humiliation of the white man, and the fact that he applied to Europe colonialist procedures which until then had been reserved exclusively for the Arabs of Algeria, the coolies of India and the blacks of Africa.[21]

Césaire's evocation of Hitler as a monstrous synecdoche, indeed, as a synecdoche for the monstrous, puts on display for us one register in which it was possible, five years after the end of World War II, to apprehend the murderous excesses of the Nazi regime, in advance of such catachreses as "Holocaust" or "Shoah." It is telling for what it cannot yet say, at least not in the terms with which we are familiar. The most significant omission is, of course, that of the Jew. Note that Césaire figures the Nazi genocide as a "crime against the white man." The elision of the Jews as a direct referent here constitutes a disavowal that crucially misrecognizes the distance between the denigration, literally, of the Jew in Nazi ideology, and the category of whiteness—in the brutalizing Aryan construction of the latter.[22] This misrecognition is partly a consequence of the structural underpinnings of Césaire's philosophy of history. The *Discourse* radicalizes the matter of European complicity by virtue of its thesis of the *choc en retour*, the "reverse shock," that figures Nazism as the return of a specifically colonial form of the repressed.[23] The Jews are assimilated to a crisis *within Europe* consequent on the corrosion that colonial violence inevitably trails. "[N]o one colonizes with impunity," Césaire asserts.[24] As symptoms of this crisis, the Jews are not yet positioned in relations of alterity with respect to European whiteness.

It is only subsequently, as Césaire recalibrates his position with reference to the events of decolonization, on the one hand, and Stalinism, on the other, that the Jews will accede to a particular history, theorized within the general context of racism. Rothberg notes significant shifts in Césaire's position between the first publication of the *Discourse* in 1950 and the *Lettre à Maurice Thorez*, published in 1956—a text that announces his break with the French Communist Party. Césaire's repudiation of communism as a man of color, Rothberg argues, uses anti-Semitism to name "the problem of particularities that the party cannot subsume."[25] Rothberg finds further evidence of the altered vector of Césaire's position on anti-Semitism in the ironic reference to the work of French ethnographer Roger Caillois, whose racism Césaire denounces in the revised 1955 edition of the *Discourse* in the following satirical manner: "M. Caillois gives immediate proof [of the superiority of the West] by concluding that no one should be exterminated. With him the Negroes are sure that they will not be lynched; the Jews, that they will not feed new bonfires."[26]

It is worth noting, however, that the trope *itself* does not yet commit Césaire to the historicizing thrust of the 1956 text. The emplacement of blacks and Jews in relations of equivalence is not always sufficient repudiation of anti-Semitism, as an investigation of the history of this particular topos shows. Similar parallelisms are, in fact, relatively common in the discourse of African American civil rights activists in the United States during the 1930s. Harold Brackman speaks of W. E. B. Du Bois's "residual insensitivity to Jewish sensibilities" in an editorial that Du Bois published in *The Crisis* in September 1933.[27] "Nothing has filled us with such unholy glee as Hitler and the Nordics," writes Du Bois. "When the only 'inferior' peoples were 'niggers,' it was hard to get the attention of the *New York Times* for little matters of race, lynchings and mobs. But now that the damned include the owner of the *Times,* moral indignation is perking up."[28] "A cruel irony of the 1930s," Brackman notes, "was how often African-American anger at white people's stubborn blindness to the analogy between anti-Semitic barbarism abroad and racism at home came to be directed against anti-Hitler protests for allegedly distracting attention from antiblack racism or even against Jews for somehow deserving anti-Jewish animus."[29] Reduced to a counter in a black economy of identification, the invocation of the figure of the Jew actually occludes rather than promotes an analysis of the historical contours of anti-Semitism or of its murderous implementation by the Nazi regime.

Césaire manifests a similar tendency at times, using the trope of the Jew to stage an equivalence that is also equivocation. His *Notebook of a Return to the Native Land* (*Cahier d'un retour au pays natal*), first published in 1939 and twice revised in 1947 and 1956, mobilizes the Jew thus:

> To go away
> As there are hyena-men and panther-men,
> I would be a jew-man
> A Kaffir-man
> A Hindu-man-from-Calcutta
> A Harlem-man-who-doesn't-vote
>
> the famine-man, the insult-man, the torture-man you can grab
> anytime, beat up, kill—no joke, kill—without having to account
> to anyone, without having to make excuses to anyone
> a jew-man
> a pogrom-man[30]

The "jew-man" figured as "pogrom-man" fails to coincide with the Jew as the historical victim not of pogrom but of genocide or incipient genocide. For Césaire has different priorities. The relations of equivalence to which Jewish victimhood is subordinated in the *Notebook* are cognate with Césaire's analysis in his *Discourse on Colonialism,* namely, that racialized violence, across its individual manifestations, denudes the public sphere of accountability—denudes it, in fact, of all politics except for the necropolitics of domination. The victims of Nazi racism and colonial racism whom Césaire enumerates are each subordinated to the master narrative, *the master's narrative,* of impunity: "without having to account/to anyone, without having to make excuses to anyone," as the *Notebook* asserts.[31] The figure of the Jew is not (yet) invested with a form of victimhood that is irreducibly tied to the Holocaust, nor is the latter understood to be unique in itself.

The *Discourse on Colonialism* will insist on staging a different primal scene of suffering instead. Césaire continues to route his theme—"that no one colonizes with impunity"—through a litany of colonial massacres. "[B]y no means," he assures us,

> because I take a morbid delight in them, but because I think that these heads of men, these collections of ears, these burned houses, these Gothic invasions, this

steaming blood, these cities that evaporate at the edge of the sword, are not to be so easily disposed of. They prove that colonization, I repeat, dehumanizes even the most civilized man; that colonial activity, colonial enterprise, colonial conquest, which is based on contempt for the native and justified by that contempt, inevitably tends to change him who undertakes it.[32]

The cumulative elaboration of atrocity allows Césaire to stage a form of hyperbolic mourning whose excess serves as the displaced mimesis of the excessive violence of colonialism. "[S]hould I have cast back into the shadows of oblivion," he asks in response to the criticism of an imagined interlocutor,

> the memorable feat of arms of General Gérard and kept silent about the capture of Ambike, a city which, to tell the truth, had never dreamed of defending itself: "The native riflemen had orders to kill only the men, but no one restrained them; intoxicated by the smell of blood, they spared not one woman, not one child.... At the end of the afternoon, the heat caused a light mist to arise: it was the blood of the five thousand victims, the ghost of the city, evaporating in the setting sun."[33]

Césaire's strenuous efforts to memorialize those he mourns seem labored in retrospect, precisely to the extent that the "traumatic sublime" in Dominick LaCapra's sense is depersonalized.[34] There is as yet no cathexis in place that might take the exemplarity of the Jewish survivor as *the model of its desire*. Not even the trope of "the Jew" is capable of instigating such an itinerary, as its irruptions demonstrate. Hyperbole turns Césaire's mourning work back on itself, rendering it intransitive or "melancholic" in the familiar Freudian inflection.[35] Melancholic hyperbole does the work of a depersonalized identification with the dead at a time when the inception of a crisis that we might stenographically evoke through the toponyms Madagascar, Indochina, Algeria speaks to the ongoing need to commemorate those killed resisting French imperialism.[36] Yet for all that it is depersonalized, Césaire's melancholic rhetoric gestures toward the enfolding of the victims of colonial aggression within the orbit of that political relation that Judith Butler would come to designate as a "grievable life."[37]

The Cry of the Survivor

Césaire's purchase over the affect of atrocity founders, I have been suggesting, precisely because identification—as a mark of the genre Eli Wiesel catachrestically terms "testimony"—has not yet been routinized through the category of the Jewish survivor.[38] My recourse to the terms "testimony" and "identification" is indebted to the particular inflection that the literary theorist Robert Eaglestone gives them in his 2004 study *The Holocaust and the Postmodern,* which tracks central debates concerning the Holocaust in the field of literature, historiography, and philosophy.[39] Affect is crucial to the manner in which Eaglestone recuperates Wiesel's own particular "hyperbole."[40] Eaglestone ties his claims to the manner in which Holocaust testimony, as a genre reworked in a specifically post-1945 modality, is read. Its affect, he argues, is of a particular kind. While narrative texts and other forms of representation produce affect through generating identification, "the grasping, or comprehending, of another's experience as one's own by 'putting one's self in their place'" says Eaglestone, or through "taking the other as oneself," it is precisely here that the specificity of Holocaust narrative arises.[41] For Holocaust testimony disallows the very purchase that identification offers, given the ethical consequences of the "incomprehension" that attaches to the genocide on the part of those who experienced it.[42] It disallows identification, moreover, because it ruptures the very codes of referentiality itself.[43] It is in its disruption of identification, then, that Holocaust testimony becomes something new; it becomes the site of an "aporia" in Jacques Derrida's sense.[44] Instead of the seizure of the other, Eaglestone offers his readers the caesura of a certain version of *literariness,* deeply indebted to Viktor Shklovsky's notion of estrangement, in order to render a certain construction of testimony compatible with the ethics of Holocaust memory.[45]

Identification is, however, not only an ineluctable component of narrative, as Eaglestone repeatedly asserts.[46] Affect, more broadly speaking, must also be given a constitutive role in structuring social relations. Sarah Ahmed has recently taught us that affect is performative. Emotions "do things," in Ahmed's account: "[T]hey align individuals with communities—or bodily space with social space—through the very intensity of their attachments."[47] Ahmed argues that the circulation of emotions between "bodies and signs" plays a role in the demarcation of individual as well as collective identity.[48] For Eaglestone also, identification is part of the armature of identity construction, although he does not fully articulate the trajectory that makes identification "central not only in aesthetics but also politics."[49] But to tie identification to processes of identity construction and, I would add, to processes of interpellation is to recognize that topoi of identification circulate widely in culture, in a variety of media, including texts—and circulate to different effect. It is not merely that "Holocaust fiction is, in Edward Said's terms, 'wordly,'" as Eaglestone writes.[50] Identifications *themselves* possess a form of worldliness. Acts of identification with Holocaust testimony proceed, proceed perforce, proceed despite interdiction—as Eaglestone rightly concedes—because they *are* worldly.[51] Identification must, in other words, itself be historicized. It must be historicized, moreover, against the background of the ascendancy of the construct of the Jewish survivor, since the forms of *assimilative* identification or surrogacy against which Eaglestone and others caution us, all the way back to Primo Levi, derive their present cultural purchase as well as the affective contracts they set in motion, I suggest, from the adjacent category of the survivor-as-witness.

The claim that the emergence of the survivor—as cultural construct rather than as human subject—postdates the liberation of the Nazi camps is not, of course, a new one. In an exemplary work of historicization, the cultural sociologist Jeffrey C. Alexander shows that identification with Jewish survivors of the

Nazi genocide did not take place in the immediate postwar period, when the "Holocaust" was still subsumed under another category—that of "atrocity": "For an audience to be traumatized by an experience which they themselves do not directly share, symbolic extension and psychological identification are required. This did not occur." Instead, Alexander observes, the survivors "could just as well have been from Mars, or from Hell. The identities and characters of these Jewish survivors rarely were personalized through interviews or individualized through biographical sketches."[52] Over time, Alexander argues, the genocide of the Jews of Europe was recoded as tragedy—the term, for him, takes on a dramaturgical, indeed Aristotelian, cast. "In the new tragic understanding of the Jewish mass murder," writes Alexander, "suffering, not progress, became the telos toward which the narrative was aimed."[53] Suffering, as telos, requires a personalization of the genocide. It must be located within the circumference of a biography. Alexander treats the English translation and stage dramatizations and film adaptations of Anne Frank's *Diary* in the United States, dating to 1952, 1955, and 1959, respectively, as the "prototype of [the] personalizing genre," but sees the reception of such narratives as eventually contributing to the erasure of the specificity of the genocide of the Jews given that the Holocaust undergoes a process of "symbolic extension" that eventually allows it to stand as the preeminent signifier of radical or "engorged evil."[54]

Equally pivotal in the personalization of suffering is the Eichmann trial (1961), although we should immediately observe that what will be at stake is a delineation of the specificity of *Jewish* suffering in a highly determinate political context. In Anette Wieviorka's influential analysis, the trial authorizes the admission of the Holocaust into the public sphere under the sign of the sovereignty of the Jewish state. Crucially, for Wieviorka, the trial confers on the survivors

> the social identity of survivors because society now recognized them as such.... At the heart of this newly recognized identity of survivor was a new function, to be the bearer of history. With the Eichmann trial, the witness becomes an embodiment of memory (*un homme-mémoire*), attesting to the past and to the continuing presence of the past. Concurrently, the genocide comes to be defined as a succession of individual experiences with which the public is supposed to identify.[55]

Proceeding from such claims, we might state that the body of the survivor, imagined in its sedimentation as the amanuensis of the genocidal violence it endured, secures the supposedly unmediated referentiality of history precisely because it was the locus of reduction to the "bare life" of the camps in Giorgio Agamben's schema[56]—or to *zoë* in Arendt's.[57] Indeed, the authenticity of the survivor drives the pedagogical intent of the Eichmann trial.[58] But the testimonial exchange that restores the survivor to *bios*, precisely by conferring upon her the capacity to narrate, whether it occurs in a legal, therapeutic, or documentary context, is never reducible to the referentiality of what is narrated alone. The survivor does not speak until *spoken for*, by the various agendas that would do her justice—therapeutic, nationalist, or universalizing. When the survivor's speech is valorized for its authenticity, and when, in turn, that authenticity is seen as generating powerful emotion on the part of the survivor's addressee—a power that Geoffrey Hartman ascribes to it when he holds the "immediacy of ... first-person accounts" to "[burn] through the 'cold-storage' of history," for instance, we begin to perceive a certain excess that attaches to testimony under this construction.[59] The survivor's address must become compelling for its addressee as the corollary of the survivor's *individuation,* her irreducible biography. The survivor is, in other words, *constructed in a transitive modality.* Identification on the part of the addressee now becomes the *affective supplement to facticity* that must be present in order to safeguard the performative dimensions of the testimonial exchange—that is to say, the conditions of its ethical and emotional intelligibility.

Given the ascendancy of this transitive and performative configuration of the survivor for what Wieviorka has termed "the era of the witness,"[60] it becomes possible for the media scholar John Durham Peters to adduce "the cry of the survivor" in constructing a typology of witness that encompasses, *tout court,* a tellingly reconfigured intersection of law, theology, and atrocity: "The third, most recent, source [for the notion of witness] dates from the Second World War: the witness as a survivor of hell, prototypically but not exclusively the Holocaust or *Shoah....* The procedures of the courtroom, the pain of the martyr and the cry of the survivor cast light on basic questions such as what it means to watch, to narrate or to be present at an event."[61] The survivor is well on the way to becoming part of our cultural armature: an authorizing trope for increasingly codified forms of identification.

Haunted by Slight Ghosts

Initially, at least, postcolonial theory seems indifferent to the forms of cathexis authorized by the survivor. As a political, historiographic, and literary theoretical intervention, postcolonial theory disrupts Europe's production of the racialized other as a foil for its self-consolidating subjecthood and sovereignty.[62] To the extent that its program necessarily crosses the archive, indeed, the literal archives, of colonialism, postcolonial theory must elaborate a methodology for transcribing the traces of the figure whom we know as the "subaltern" in a manner that counters an effacement always already predicated upon the disciplinary construction of history in the West.[63] For Spivak, the exemplarity of the *subaltern*—and *not,* it is almost superfluous to add, the *survivor*—grounds a form of historiographic critique proper to postcolonialism and adequate to its political and ethical aspirations. Let us now intersect Spivak as she crosses the historiographic revisions of Hayden White and, more particularly, Dominick

LaCapra in their respective attempts to perform history after the so-called linguistic turn.

Where LaCapra, a key thinker in Holocaust studies, draws upon Freudian psychoanalysis to propose a "transferential" relation between "practices in the past and historical accounts of them," Spivak is concerned with pointing to a certain slippage within the model of transference that LaCapra deploys.[64] This slippage, Spivak claims, is redolent of LaCapra's "desire"—the desire of the academic intellectual for power; for the consolatory "fiction" (LaCapra's term) of a "*self-consolidating* other."[65] Spivak repudiates the category of the "cure" (in quotes in the original) that she takes to be manifested here by LaCapra's transferential model. Her disagreement with LaCapra culminates with her marking the site of his desire.[66] But now, Spivak abruptly introduces a trajectory of desire—or better still, of identification—all her own, as she reverts to a historical figure, the Rani of Sirmur, the subject of an earlier study and one of the two women upon whom the chapter pivots.[67] "I should have liked to establish a transferential relationship with the Rani of Sirmur,"[68] Spivak suddenly interjects without prior warning—referring to this woman's brief striation of the archive as "a king's wife and a weaker vessel, on the chessboard of the Great Game"—or so Spivak somewhat caustically observes elsewhere.[69] "I should have liked to establish a transferential relationship with the Rani of Sirmur," let us reiterate in Spivak's name, and allow her to continue: "I pray instead to be haunted by her slight ghost, bypassing the arrogance of the cure."[70]

It is crucial to my intent to underscore the type of affective performance that Spivak's rhetoric sets in motion. It is a trope of identification that emerges into visibility here, no less. However, it is also very much to my point that we register its simultaneous disavowal of an assimilative rapport with—or an *incorporation*, one might say, of—the victim. Instead, Spivak will pursue a properly *uncanny* identification in the Freudian sense,[71] as she elaborates the progress of a pilgrimage of sorts that brings her to the Rani's former palace, where the woman, this *particular* woman (Gulani or perhaps Gulari, the record vacillates in naming her) will continue to elude Spivak as the subject/object of knowledge.[72] "As I approached her house after a long series of detective maneuvers, I was miming the route of an unknowing, a progressive différance, an 'experience' of how I could not know her."[73] Despite this pilgrimage, Spivak is strict in keeping her distance from the illusion of continuity between the archive—equally textual and material in this case—and its contemporary interlocutors. To do otherwise would be to reduplicate the orientation for which she criticizes LaCapra.[74] So the archive becomes the site of an *interdiction*, we might say, where the tenuous possibility of exchange cannot precipitate a therapeutic resolution of historical trauma, along the model of Shoshana Felman and Dori Laub.[75] Instead, Spivak will claim that "the epistemic story of imperialism is the story of a series of interruptions, a repeated tearing of time that cannot be sutured."[76]

Spivak's substitution of "[h]aunting for transference, the unconsciousness as interruption," pace LaCapra, proceeds in accordance with the strict protocols of her hallmark intervention in "Can the Subaltern Speak."[77] It remains central to my pedagogical intent to insist that *this* text be read as demarcating the lines of an epistemological fracture, a properly Derridean aporia condensed in and as the body of the sati, rather than as an entry in the identity politics of subalternity—whether we construe the subaltern woman as silent, silenced, or eloquent. Spivak is herself quite explicit about this. Noting that the archival records stage only the trace of the sati's prior interpellation by British imperial discourse, on the one hand, and refusing to defer to Hindu religious authority, on the other hand, she cautions us: "One never encounters the testimony of the women's voice-consciousness.... Faced with the dialectially interlocking sentences that are constructible as 'White men are saving brown women from brown men' and 'The women wanted to die,' the postcolonial woman intellectual asks the question of a simple semiosis—What does this mean?—and begins to plot a history."[78]

My insistence on the aporetic status of the sati intersects Spivak's idiosyncratic coda to her discussion of the colonial archive in "Can the Subaltern Speak," where she devotes the last part of the article to the enigma of the death of a young woman, Bhubaneswari Bhaduri, whose suicide in 1926 constitutes an oblique form of writing-as-resistance, or speech-across-death in Spivak's interpretation. Spivak suggests that we consider the suicide as "an unemphatic, ad hoc, subaltern rewriting of the social text of *sati*-suicide," but also insists on our apprehension of Bhaduri's silencing in a familial context to which Spivak is privy.[79] The relay that has Bhaduri approximate the enigmatic figure of the Rani or the sati uses the domestic context to trope on the properly deconstructive problematic that Spivak brings to bear on the status of the colonial archive. Spivak makes this point quite clear in a retrospective commentary on the readings and misreadings that have become attached to her use of Bhubaneswari Bhaduri's death:

> The woman to whom Bhubaneswari wrote the letter that was forgotten was my mother's mother. The woman who told me the story was my mother. The woman who refused to understand what she has said was my first cousin.... She was quite like me in education, and yet it made no difference. She could not hear this woman who had tried with her suicide using menstruation, that dirty secret, to erase the axioms that endorsed sati. Sati in the piece was *not* given as a generalizable example of the subaltern not speaking, or rather not being able to speak—trying to, but not succeeding in being heard.[80]

The anecdote holds out the promise of narrative consolation despite Spivak's problematization of this very possibility. However, its duality is even more pronounced than this. For the narrative of Bhubaneswari Bhaduri courts its own status as Derridean supplement: seemingly extraneous yet integral to Spivak's intent.[81] But its supplementarity is mitigated, in a sense, if we choose to reframe the recourse to Bhaduri across her various appearances in "Can the Subaltern Speak" and *A Critique of Postcolonial Reason*. The reinscription of a family context allows us to renegotiate the dimensions of *witness* that operate here. Spivak reworks the colonial subject's relation to the past as the structural appropriation of social history by transforming it into the occasion for a much more *private act of mourning*.[82] Not historiography, then; not a delineation of the all-too-familiar incisions of the epistemic violence of colonialism; or not only these things. Spivak's relation to Bhaduri offers us, in fact, an exemplary instance of postmemory.

Marianne Hirsch developed the notion of postmemory with specific relation to first- and second-generation Holocaust survivors, although she does indicate its more general applications.[83] For Hirsch, postmemory is a facet of "intergenerational identification" frequently but not exclusively derived from familial contexts. It is a "belated" form of memory "mediated not through recollection but through representation, projection, and creation—often based on silence rather than speech, on the invisible rather than the visible."[84] The pertinence of postmemory for Spivak is crucial to my argument. What intervenes between the curiously impersonal and hyperbolic mourning work that Césaire offers us and the minutely calibrated familial reprise of sati/suicide in Spivak is, I would suggest, *the consolidation of the genre of testimony after the advent of the individuated survivor-witness.*

Now to read Spivak through her desiring retrieval of a series of dead women is to reposition her intervention as a form of mournful performance. It is also to open postcolonial theory up to a defamiliarization attendant on agreeing to see it as animated, at least in part, by cultural tropes of witness that are deeply tied to the ascendancy of Holocaust memory. Both postcolonial theory and Holocaust studies have something to gain from closer investigation of this intersection. Postcolonial ethics needs to engage more fully with its indebtedness to Holocaust memory, not only out of consideration for historical accountability[85]—but also because it has yet to come fully to terms with its own testimonial agendas. At the same time, Spivak's rehearsal of *aporetic* witness in the face of an archive that refuses to be rendered transparent will become increasingly salient, I suggest, over and above the formidable *ethicity* that it performs for us as we outlive the presence of the Holocaust survivors among us.[86]

Haunting disrupts. By analogy with Spivak's consistent refusal of the theorist's appropriation of alterity in the production of a "self-consolidating other,"[87] we might see her various invocations of dead women as foregrounding an unsettling ethics, an ethics of dispropriation that takes the self as its haunt.[88] Far from being allowed to assume the status of a surrogate victim in the pursuit of entitlement, the self is *undone* in this model, once, twice, many times over. By grief, certainly.[89] But also by language. The irredeemable loss of Spivak's objects of identification—these dead women—is an integral part of this story: "Indeed, it is only in their death that they enter a narrative *for us,* they become figurable."⁹⁰ The self who desires here can desire *only after narration,* only as its consequence. The identifications that Spivak stages are nothing if not mediated. They are entertained, moreover, in order to underscore questions attendant on precisely literary and archival mediation.

As the agent of a certain form of testimonial intervention, Spivak is answerable also to the materiality of the body, in the sense that no corpse is reducible to another. Thus, Bhubaneswari Bhaduri does not *stand in for* the women whose names are "grotesquely mistranscribed" in the police record of the East India Company, as if in some instrumental calculus of substitution.⁹¹ What is at stake is not metaphorical substitution but metonymic relay in relation to a determinate source (or sources) of patriarchal and colonial violence. Exhumed as a function of narration, the women whom Spivak invokes become *envoys of the disjunctive transmission of affect*. We are fully in the realm of an engagement with the past that repudiates the spurious intimacy of proxy witness or "assimilation." What the narration cannot, however, afford to do away with in contexts such as these is its debt to embodiment—to the *life and death* of these women—that persists over and above their mobilization for theory. Signification is answerable to corporeality once more. I take this to be one of the fundamental ethical precepts of witnessing.

The relationality of witness that Spivak enacts here gestures toward a form of politics that can be retrieved from traumatic identifications, over and above the recognizably high modernist injunctions to ethics that emerge from, for instance, Eaglestone's circumscription of testimony-as-disidentification. I take the notion of relationality from the work of Judith Butler in *Precarious Life* (2004), cognizant like Butler of the fact that relationality returns us to the political. Relationality returns us, moreover, to the political as a site of vulnerability where the duty to mourn, or the possibility of mourning, is incipient. Butler reminds us that "[each] of us is constituted politically in part by virtue of the social vulnerability of our bodies—as a site of desire and physical vulnerability, as a site of a publicity at once assertive and exposed. Loss and vulnerability seem to follow from our being socially constituted bodies, attached to others, at risk of losing those attachments, exposed to others, at risk of violence by virtue of that exposure."⁹² That vulnerability unto death, which has historically overdetermined the social constitution of the body interpellated as Jewish under Nazism or as black under colonialism, is an important component of what Holocaust studies and postcolonial theory have to teach us, across disciplinary divides. But indiscriminate identification with such vulnerability, in the first-person singular, occludes precisely the singularity of the changing historical contingencies to which Holocaust studies and postcolonial theory, at their best, have respectively devoted themselves. To rehearse the understanding that *I am vulnerable because you have been vulnerable* may devolve into the banal justification of anticipatory or retaliatory violence—the "never again" rhetoric of Israeli state violence, bolstered by its invocation of the "six million," for instance. This is not the identification with which I seek to conclude. Rather, I propose that we track our identifications as slender portents of our *capacity for relationality* upon which empathy is presaged. *Always here, wherever I am and wherever I look, closest to home.*[93] The genres of traumatic identification are not yet manifestos of the various political projects that our collective renegotiations of the condition of *exposure* to vulnerability would entail. They do, however, constitute one form of prelude to *living on* in the aftermath.

Notes

My thanks to Amos Goldberg and Haim Hazan for creating and sustaining the intellectual community that made this intervention possible. I would also like to acknowledge the support of the Van Leer Jerusalem Institute. This chapter is dedicated to the memory of Oren Gani (17 October 1950–4 November 2010) in whose company I first began to explore the ideas presented here.

1. Aimé Césaire, *Discourse on Colonialism,* trans. Joan Pinkam (New York: Monthly Review Press 1950), 14, emphasis in original.

2. Michael Rothberg, *Multidirectional Memory: Remembering the Holocaust in the Age of Decolonization* (Stanford, CA: Stanford University Press, 2009), 22.

3. Ibid.

4. Michael Rothberg, "Between Auschwitz and Algeria: Multidirectional Memory and the Counterpublic Witness," *Critical Inquiry* 33 (2006): 160.

5. Rothberg, *Multidirectional Memory,* 5.

6. Ibid., 11.

7. Ibid., 7.

8. For further explorations of these implications, see Michael Rothberg, "W.E.B. Du Bois in Warsaw: Holocaust Memory and the Color Line, 1949–1952," *The Yale Journal of Criticism* 14, no. 1 (2001): 186–87; Michael Rothberg, "The Work of Testimony in the Age of Decolonization: *Chronicle of a Summer,* Cinema Verité, and the Emergence of the Holocaust Survivor," PMLA 119, no. 5 (2004): 1232–34; Rothberg, "Between Auschwitz and Algeria," 159–62; Max Silverman, "Interconnected Histories: Holocaust and Empire in the Cultural Imaginary," *French Studies* 62, no. 4 (2008): 418.

9. Rothberg, *Multidirectional Memory,* 7.

10. Rothberg, "Between Auschwitz and Algeria," 158.

11. Edward Said, *Orientalism* (New York: Pantheon, 1978).

12. Walter Benjamin, *Illuminations: Essays and Reflections,* trans. Harry Zohn, intro. by Hannah Arendt (New York: Schocken Books,1969), 256.

13. For the notion of biopolitics, see Michel Foucault, *The History of Sexuality,* vol. 1, trans. Robert Hurley (New York: Vintage, 1978), 149; Michel Foucault, "The Politics of Health in the Eighteenth Century," in *Power/Knowledge,* ed. Colin Gordon (New York: Pantheon, 1980), 166–82; for an investigation of the relation between biopower and race, see Michel Foucault, *Society Must Be Defended,* trans. David Macey (London: Penguin, 2003), 239–63.

14. Achille Mbembe, "Necropolitics," trans. Libby Meintjies, *Public Culture* 15, no. 1 (2003): 11–40.

15. Hannah Arendt, *The Origins of Totalitarianism* (Cleveland, OH and New York: World, 1968), 206.

16. See Achille Mbembe, "Aesthetics of Superfluity," *Public Culture* 16, no. 3 (2004): 373–405; Paul Gilroy, *Between Camps: Race, Identity and Nationalism at the End of the Colour Line* (London: Penguin, 2000); Paul Gilroy, "Race and the Right to Be Human," in *After Empire: Melancholia or Convivial Culture* (London: Routledge, 2004), 31–63.

17. Edward Said, "Zionism from the Standpoint of Its Victims," *Social Text* 1 (1979): 7–58. For an important exception to this polarization, see Homi Bhabha's beautiful reprise of Walter Benjamin in Bhabha's "Unpacking My Library Again," *The Journal of the Mid-West Modern Language Association* 28, no. 1 (1995): 5–18. Here Bhabha explores both Jewish and postcolonial concerns in a careful reading of the figures of the Jewish maidservants in Kasuo Ishiguro's novel *The Remains of the Day*.

18. Robert Eaglestone, *The Holocaust and the Postmodern* (Oxford: Oxford University Press, 2004), 2.

19. For a highly nuanced teasing out of the notion of *nach Auschwitz*, see Michael Rothberg on Theodor Adorno, *Traumatic Realism: The Demands of Holocaust Representation* (Minneapolis: University of Minnesota Press, 2000), 280.

20. Césaire, *Discourse on Colonialism*, 14.

21. Ibid., emphasis in original.

22. Rothberg makes a related point regarding Fanon's use of Césaire: "[T]he white man terrorized by Nazism is not precisely the same white man as the one responsible for colonialism." *Multidirectional Memory*, 93.

23. Césaire, *Discourse on Colonialism*, 14. For a persuasive reading of this motif, see also Rothberg, *Multidirectional Memory*, 23, 80–100. A form of dialectical interchange between Arendt and Césaire is central to the first section of Rothberg's book. Rothberg has Césaire estrange the occluded Eurocentrism of Arendt's critique of European humanism, at the same time as he foregrounds the fractured temporality that invests Césaire's and Arendt's respective arguments concerning the etiology of the Nazi genocide in colonialism, with their properly traumatic freight. Paul Gilroy takes up this conjunction between Arendt and Césaire somewhat differently in the context of an examination of the category of race. *Between Camps*, 54–68.

24. Césaire, *Discourse on Colonialism*, 17.

25. Rothberg, *Multidirectional Memory*, 99.

26. Césaire, *Discourse on Colonialism*, 55; see also Rothberg, *Multidirectional Memory*, 100.

27. Harold Brackman, "'A Calamity Almost Beyond Comprehension': Nazi Anti-Semitism and the Holocaust in the Thought of W. E. B. Du Bois," *American Jewish History* 88, no. 1 (2000): 53–93.

28. Cited in Brackman, "'A Calamity Almost Beyond Comprehension,'" 59.

29. Brackman, "'A Calamity Almost Beyond Comprehension,'" 59–60; see also pages 60–61. After 1933, Brackman notes here, Du Bois would never again "invidiously [comment] at the expense of Hitler's Jewish victims in order to criticize American racism" ("'A Calamity Almost Beyond Comprehension,'" 60). Brackman traces the evolution of Du Bois's thought concerning anti-Semitism and the Holocaust, while Rothberg treats Du Bois's postwar responses to the Warsaw ghetto: Michal Rothberg, "W.E.B. Du Bois in Warsaw," reprinted in Rothberg, *Multidirectional Memory*, 111–34.

30. Aimé Césaire, *Notebook of a Return to the Native Land*, in *Aimé Césaire: The Collected Poetry*, trans. Clayton Eshleman and Annette Smith (Berkeley: University of California Press, 1983), 43. The translation is taken from the 1956 version of the *Cahier*, as Mara De Genarro notes in her "Fighting 'Humanism' on Its Own Terms," *Differences: A Journal of Feminist Cultural Studies* 14, no. (2003), 71. Césaire's oeuvre has been the topic of a themed issue of *Research in African Literatures* 14, no. 1 (2010), edited by H. Adlai Murdoch.

31. Césaire, *Notebook of a Return to the Native Land*, 43.

32. Césaire, *Discourse on Colonialism*, 17, 19–20.

33. Ibid., 19, ellipsis in original.

34. Dominick LaCapra, *History in Transit: Experience, Identity, Critical Theory* (Ithaca, NY: Cornell University Press, 2004), 123.

35. Sigmund Freud, "Mourning and Melancholia," in *The Standard Edition of the Complete Psychological Works of Sigmund Freud*, vol. 14, ed. J. Strachey (London: Hogarth Press and the Institute of Psychoanalysis, 2001), 239–58.

36. Rothberg notes the link between the memory of the Nazi genocide and forms of testimony that shaped anticolonial witness in the Algerian War in the work of figures such as historian Pierre Vidal-Naquet and Fanon's associate, André Mandouze, such that a discursive context emerged where "the association of torture, truth, testimony, and resistance underwrote a link between the Algerian War and Nazi atrocities." *Multidirectional Memory,* 194, 195.

37. Judith Butler, *Precarious Life: The Powers of Mourning and Violence* (London and New York: Verso, 2004); Judith Butler, *Frames of War: When Is Life Grievable?* (London: Verso, 2009).

38. The Holocaust, announces Wiesel, invents "a new literature, that of testimony." See Elie Wiesel, *Dimensions of the Holocaust* (Evanston, IL: Northwestern University Press, 1990), 7.

39. Eaglestone, *The Holocaust and the Postmodern.*

40. The term "hyperbole" is Eaglestone's, ibid., 16.

41. Ibid., 16, 29.

42. Ibid., 19.

43. Ibid., 17. Eaglestone seems to vacillate between the suggestion that the Holocaust fractures epistemological purchase for the victim herself in giving rise to various forms of "incomprehension" (16–19) and the suggestion that identification falters in the synapse between victim/survivor and reader. Elsewhere in the same volume, he writes: "Many forms of prose writing encourage identification and while testimony cannot but do this, it at the same time aims to prohibit identification, on epistemological grounds (a reader really cannot become, or become identified, with the narrator of a testimony: any such identification is an illusion) and on ethical grounds (a reader should not become identified with a narrator of a testimony, as it reduces and 'normalizes' or consumes the otherness of the narrator's experience and the illusion that such an identification creates is possibly pernicious)" (42–43). Note that testimony is being used here with specific reference to Holocaust memoir, and that Eaglestone derives his authority from Primo Levi's interdiction of identification through "assimilation" as well as similar statements in the writings of Charlotte Delbo and Jorge Semprun (Levi's word). See Primo Levi, *The Drowned and the Saved,* trans. Raymond Rosenthal (London: Abacus, 1989), 128; Eaglestone, *The Holocaust and the Postmodern,* 17, 22. In a related manner, Eaglestone cites Dominick LaCapra's admonitions against "the constitution of the self as surrogate victim" and Michael André Bernstein's trenchant critique of "witness by adoption." See Dominick LaCapra, *Writing History, Writing Trauma* (London: Johns Hopkins University Press 2001), 219; Eaglestone, *The Holocaust and the Postmodern,* 35–36; Michael André Bernstein, "Unspeakable No More: Nazi Genocide and Its Self-Appointed 'Witnesses by Adoption,'" *Times Literary Supplement,* 3 March 2000, 7–8.

44. Eaglestone, *The Holocaust and the Postmodern,* 23. See Jacques Derrida, *Aporias,* trans. Thomas Dutoit (Stanford, CA: Stanford University Press, 1993).

45. For estrangement, see Viktor Shklovsky, "Art as Technique," in *Literary Theory: An Anthology,* ed. Julie Rivkin and Michael Ryan (Oxford: Basil Blackwell, 2000), 15–21.

46. See Eaglestone: "[I]dentification happens, despite a wish for them [*sic*] not to happen, because of basic assumptions about narratives and reading, because we expect identification to happen when we read prose narratives." *The Holocaust and the Postmodern,* 23. See also the following assertion in the same volume: "Despite the impossibility of understanding, and the admonitions made against identifying with the victims, Holocaust testimonies are read and the readers do identify with narrators and other characters, precisely because that is what they expect to do in reading" (37).

47. Sarah Ahmed, "Affective Economies," *Social Text* 22, no. 2 (2004): 119.

48. Ibid., 117.

49. Eaglestone, *The Holocaust and the Postmodern,* 5.

50. Ibid., 107. For worldliness, see Edward Said, *Culture and Imperialism* (New York: Vintage, 1994).

51. See Eaglestone, *The Holocaust and the Postmodern,* 23. For my own part, I am pointedly aware of the extent to which identification *takes place* in the context of the Israeli occupation of Palestine as the crucial political imperative of post-1967 Zionist nationalism. Make no mistake,

however. The imperative to identify with the victims of atrocity is a privileged component of the constitution of a wide variety of moral communities at the present time. The nation-state, this particular nation-state—Israel—figures as one among a host of others.

52. Jeffrey C. Alexander, "On the Social Construction of Moral Universals: The 'Holocaust' from War Crime to Trauma Drama," *European Journal of Social Theory* 5, no. 1 (2002): 8.

53. Ibid., 30.

54. See ibid., 35, 29, 44.

55. Anette Wieviorka, "The Witness in History," trans. Jared Stark, *Poetics Today* 27, no. 2 (2006): 391. But see Michael Rothberg for a dissenting reading that contests the exclusivity of the Eichmann trial, repositioning the emergence of the survivor in relation to the Algerian War. *Multidirectional Memory*, 175–98.

56. Giorgio Agamben, *Homo Sacer: Sovereign Power and Bare Life*, trans. D. Heller-Roazen (New York: Zone Books, 1998).

57. Hannah Arendt, *The Human Condition* (Chicago: University of Chicago Press, 1958). I develop a different version of this argument in dialogue with the claims of Tom Cohen, J. Hillis Miller, and Barbara Cohen in my analysis of the embodiment of the witness who testifies before the South African Truth and Reconciliation Commission. See Louise Bethlehem, *Skin Tight: Apartheid Literary Culture and Its Aftermath* (Leiden and Pretoria, 2006), 84; Tom Cohen, J. Hillis Miller, and Barbara Cohen, "A 'Materiality without Matter'?," in *Material Events: Paul de Man and the Afterlife of Theory*, ed. Tom Cohen, Barbara Cohen, J. Hillis Miller, and Andrzej Warminski (Minneapolis and London, University of Minnesota Press 2001), viii. For a discussion of the "apparently phonocentric deployment of a self-present body" in video testimony and *cinéma vérité*, see Rothberg, *Mulitdirectional Memory*, 189.

58. See Wieviorka, "The Witness in History," 389–91.

59. Geoffrey Hartman, "Learning from Survivors: The Yale Testimony Project," in *The Longest Shadow: In the Aftermath of the Holocaust* (Bloomington: Indiana University Press, 1996), 138.

60. Anette Wieviorka, *The Era of the Witness*, trans. Jared Stark (Ithaca, NY: Cornell University Press, 2006).

61. John Durham Peters, "Witnessing," *Media, Culture & Society* 23 (2001): 708–9.

62. See, e.g., Gayatri Chakravorty Spivak, *A Critique of Postcolonial Reason: Toward a History of the Vanishing Present* (Cambridge, MA: Harvard University Press, 1999), 199–200, 205.

63. Gayatri Chakravorty Spivak's "Can the Subaltern Speak?," in *Marxism and the Interpretation of Culture*, ed. Cary Nelson and Lawrence Grossberg (Urbana: University of Illinois Press, 1988), 271–313, is the classic source here. For further elaborations of these concerns, see Dipesh Chakrabarty on the discipline of history, "Postcoloniality and the Artifice of History: Who Speaks for Indian Pasts?" in *The New Historicism Reader*, ed. H. Aram Veeser (New York and London: Routledge, 1994), 342–69. See also Spivak, *A Critique of Postcolonial Reason*, 300: "The task of recovering a (sexually) subaltern subject is lost in an institutional textuality at the archaic origin."

64. Dominick LaCapra, *Rethinking Intellectual History: Texts, Contexts, Language* (Ithaca, NY: Cornell University Press, 1983), 72–73.

65. Spivak, *A Critique of Postcolonial Reason*, 206–7, emphasis in original.

66. Ibid., 207.

67. "This chapter," Spivak writes, "is two stories about the informant in history." *A Critique of Postcolonial Reason*, 198. It reworks two previous contributions, "The Rani of Sirmur: An Essay in Reading the Archives," *History and Theory* 24, no. 3 (1985), 247–72, and the generative "Can the Subaltern Speak" to which I have already referred. The latter essay has recently been revisited by a number of eminent scholars, including Spivak herself, in Rosalind C. Morris's recent edited volume *Can the Subaltern Speak: Reflections on the History of an Idea* (New York: Columbia University Press, 2010). We will come to the second informant, Bhubaneswari Bhaduri, slightly later in this discussion.

68. Spivak, *A Critique of Postcolonial Reason*, 207.

69. Ibid., 231.

70. Ibid., 207.

71. Sigmund Freud, "The Uncanny," in *The Standard Edition of the Complete Psychological Works of Sigmund Freud,* vol. 17, ed. J. Strachey (London: Vintage, Hogarth Press, and the Institute of Psychoanalysis, 2001), 217–52.

72. Spivak, *A Critique of Postcolonial Reason,* 231.

73. Ibid., 241.

74. Ibid., 208.

75. Shoshana Felman and Dori Laub, *Testimony: Crises of Witnessing in Literature, Psychoanalysis and History* (London: Routledge, 1992).

76. Spivak, *A Critique of Postcolonial Reason,* 208.

77. Ibid., 209. See also Spivak, "Can the Subaltern Speak."

78. Spivak, "Can the Subaltern Speak," 297.

79. Ibid., 308. See also Gayatri Chakravorty Spivak, "In Response: Looking Back, Looking Forward," in *Can the Subaltern Speak: Reflections on the History of an Idea,* ed. Rosalind C. Morris (New York: Columbia University Press, 2010), 227–36.

80. Spivak, "In Response," 228.

81. Jacques Derrida, *Of Grammatology,* trans. Gayatri Chakravorty Spivak (Baltimore, MD: Johns Hopkins University Press, 1976).

82. Compare David Lloyd: "In the case of colonialism, the relation to the past is strictly not a relation to one's own past but to a social history and its material and institutional effects." "Colonial Trauma/Postcolonial Recovery?," *Interventions* 2, no. 2 (2000): 216.

83. See Marianne Hirsch, *Family Frames: Photography, Narrative and Postmemory* (Cambridge, MA: Harvard University Press, 1997); Marianne Hirsch, "Surviving Images: Holocaust Photographs and the Work of Postmemory," *The Yale Journal of Criticism* 14, no. 1 (2001): 5–37.

84. Hirsch, "Surviving Images," 9.

85. See Rothberg, "W.E.B. Du Bois in Warsaw," 186.

86. I use Paul de Man's term "ethicity" to throw into relief the passage through discursivity of Spivak's resolute engagement with ethics. For de Man, "Ethics (or one should say, ethicity) is a discursive mode among others." *Allegories of Reading: Figural language in Rousseau, Nietzsche, Rilke, and Proust* (New Haven, CT, and London: Yale University Press, 1979), 206. Spivak's searingly lucid "Ethics and Politics in Tagore, Coetzee, and Certain Scenes of Teaching," *Diacritics* 32, nos. 3–4 (2002): 17–31, depicts more concrete interpersonal engagements in situations of pedagogy in rural India, for instance.

87. Spivak, *A Critique of Postcolonial Reason,* 207.

88. For the notion of dispropriation, see Thomas Keenan, *Fables of Responsibility: Aberrations and Predicaments in Ethics and Politics* (Stanford, CA: Stanford University Press, 1997); see also Mark Sanders's review of Keenan, "Reading Lessons," *Diacritics* 29, no. 3 (1999): 3–20.

89. In her *Precarious Lives,* Judith Butler gives this account of dispropriation by grief: "Freud reminded us that when we lose someone, we do not always know what it is *in* that person that has been lost. So when one loses, one is faced with something enigmatic: something is hiding in the loss, something is lost within the recesses of loss" (21–22). Mourning, she argues, makes the self inscrutable. "On one level, I think I have lost 'you' only to discover that 'I' have gone missing as well. At another level, perhaps what I have lost 'in' you, that for which I have no ready vocabulary, is a relationality that is composed neither exclusively of myself nor you, but is to be conceived as *the tie* by which those terms are differentiated and related" (22). This article was concluded in deference to just such an experience of dispropriation, one associated with the death of the man to whose memory I have dedicated it, Oren Gani.

90. Spivak, *A Critique of Postcolonial Reason,* 245.

91. Ibid., 287.

92. Butler, *Precarious Life,* 20.

93. It is no coincidence that I take this phrase from Derrida's dedication of *Specters of Marx* to the assassinated leader of the South African Communist Party, Chris Hani. "*One name for another, a part for the whole: the historic violence of Apartheid can always be treated as a metonymy. In its past as well as in its present. By diverse paths … one can always decipher through its singularity so many other*

kinds of violence going on in the world. At once part, cause, effect, example, what is happening there translates what takes place here, always here, wherever one is and wherever one looks, closest to home." Jacques Derrida, *Specters of Marx: The State of the Debt, the Work of Mourning, & the New International,* trans. Peggy Kamuf (New York and London: Routledge, 1994), xvi, italics in original. That this citation inscribes my own particular trajectory of desire, as a displaced South African long resident in Israel, should be taken as given.

Bibliography

Agamben, Giorgio. *Homo Sacer: Sovereign Power and Bare Life.* Translated by D. Heller-Roazen. New York: Zone Books, 1998.
Ahmed, Sarah. "Affective Economies." *Social Text* 22, no. 2 (2004): 117–39.
Alexander, Jeffrey C. "On the Social Construction of Moral Universals: The 'Holocaust' from War Crime to Trauma Drama." *European Journal of Social Theory* 5, no. 1 (2002): 5–85.
Arendt, Hannah. *The Human Condition.* Chicago: University of Chicago Press, 1958.
———. *The Origins of Totalitarianism.* Cleveland, OH and New York: World, 1968.
Benjamin, Walter. *Illuminations: Essays and Reflections.* Translated by Harry Zohn. Introduction by Hannah Arendt. New York: Schocken Books, 1969.
Bethlehem, Louise. *Skin Tight: Apartheid Literary Culture and Its Aftermath.* Leiden: Brill; Pretoria: Unisa Press, 2006.
Bernstein, Michael André. "Unspeakable No More: Nazi Genocide and Its Self-Appointed 'Witnesses by Adoption.'" *Times Literary Supplement,* 3 March 2000, 7–8.
Bhabha, Homi K. "Unpacking My Library Again." *The Journal of the Mid-West Modern Language Association* 28, no. 1 (1995): 5–18.
Brackman, Harold. "'A Calamity Almost Beyond Comprehension': Nazi Anti-Semitism and the Holocaust in the Thought of W. E. B. Du Bois." *American Jewish History* 88, no. 1 (2000): 53–93.
Butler, Judith. *Frames of War: When Is Life Grievable?* London: Verso, 2009.
———. *Precarious Life: The Powers of Mourning and Violence.* London and New York: Verso, 2004.
Césaire, Aimé. *Discourse on Colonialism.* Translated by Joan Pinkam. New York: Monthly Review Press, 1950.
———. *Notebook of a Return to the Native Land.* In *Aimé Césaire: The Collected Poetry,* trans. Clayton Eshleman and Annette Smith, 32–85. Berkeley: University of California Press, 1983.
Chakrabarty, Dipesh. "Postcoloniality and the Artifice of History: Who Speaks for Indian Pasts?" In *The New Historicism Reader,* ed. H. Aram Veeser, 342–69. New York and London: Routledge, 1994.
Cohen, Tom, J. Hillis Miller, and Barbara Cohen. "A 'Materiality without Matter'?" In *Material Events: Paul de Man and the Afterlife of Theory,* ed. Tom Cohen, Barbara Cohen, J. Hillis Miller, and Andrzej Warminski, vii–xxv. Minneapolis and London: University of Minnesota Press, 2001.
De Genarro, Mara. "Fighting 'Humanism' on Its Own Terms." *Differences: A Journal of Feminist Cultural Studies* 14, no. 1 (2003): 53–73.
de Man, Paul. *Allegories of Reading: Figural language in Rousseau, Nietzsche, Rilke, and Proust.* New Haven, CT, and London: Yale University Press, 1979.
Derrida, Jacques. *Aporias.* Translated by Thomas Dutoit. Stanford, CA: Stanford University Press, 1993.
———. *Of Grammatology.* Translated by Gayatri Chakravorty Spivak. Baltimore, MD: Johns Hopkins University Press, 1976.
———. *Specters of Marx: The State of the Debt, the Work of Mourning, & the New International.* Translated by Peggy Kamuf. New York and London: Routledge, 1994.
Eaglestone, Robert. *The Holocaust and the Postmodern.* Oxford: Oxford University Press, 2004.

Felman, Shoshana, and Dori Laub. *Testimony: Crises of Witnessing in Literature, Psychoanalysis and History*. London: Routledge, 1992.
Foucault, Michel. *The History of Sexuality*. Vol. 1. Translated by Robert Hurley. New York: Vintage, 1978.
———. "The Politics of Health in the Eighteenth Century." In *Power/Knowledge*, ed. Colin Gordon, 166–82. New York: Pantheon, 1980.
———. *Society Must Be Defended*. Translated by David Macey. London: Penguin Books, 2002.
Freud, Sigmund. "Mourning and Melancholia." In *The Standard Edition of the Complete Psychological Works of Sigmund Freud*, vol. 14, translated under the general editorship of J. Strachey, in collaboration with A. Freud, assisted by A. Strachey and A. Tyson, 239–58. London: Vintage, Hogarth Press, and the Institute of Psychoanalysis, 2001.
———. "The Uncanny." In *The Standard Edition of the Complete Psychological Works of Sigmund Freud*, vol. 17, translated under the general editorship of J. Strachey, in collaboration with A. Freud, assisted by A. Strachey and A. Tyson, 217–52. London: Vintage, Hogarth Press, and the Institute of Psychoanalysis, 2001.
Gilroy, Paul. *Between Camps: Race, Identity and Nationalism at the End of the Colour Line*. London: Penguin, 2000.
———. "Race and the Right to Be Human." In *After Empire: Melancholia or Convivial Culture*, 31–63. London: Routledge, 2004.
Hartman, Geoffrey. "Learning from Survivors: The Yale Testimony Project." In *The Longest Shadow: In the Aftermath of the Holocaust*, 133–50. Bloomington: Indiana University Press, 1996.
Hirsch, Marianne. *Family Frames: Photography, Narrative and Postmemory*. Cambridge, MA: Harvard University Press, 1997.
———. "Surviving Images: Holocaust Photographs and the Work of Postmemory." *The Yale Journal of Criticism* 14, no. 1 (2001): 5–37.
Keenan, Thomas. *Fables of Responsibility: Aberrations and Predicaments in Ethics and Politics*. Stanford, CA: Stanford University Press, 1997.
LaCapra, Dominick. *History in Transit: Experience, Identity, Critical Theory*. Ithaca, NY: Cornell University Press, 2004.
———. *Rethinking Intellectual History: Texts, Contexts, Language*. Ithaca, NY: Cornell University Press, 1983.
———. *Writing History, Writing Trauma*. London: Johns Hopkins University Press, 2001.
Levi, Primo. *The Drowned and the Saved*. Translated by Raymond Rosenthal. London: Abacus, 1989.
Lloyd, David. "Colonial Trauma/Postcolonial Recovery?" *Interventions* 2, no. 2 (2000): 212–28.
Mbembe, Achille. "Aesthetics of Superfluity." *Public Culture* 16, no. 3 (2004): 373–405.
———. 2003. "Necropolitics." Translated by Libby Meintjies. *Public Culture* 15, no. 1 (2003): 11–40.
Morris, Rosalind C., ed. *Can the Subaltern Speak? Reflections on the History of an Idea*. New York: Columbia University Press, 2010.
Murdoch, H. Adlai, ed. "Aimé Césaire, 1913–2008: Poet, Politician, Cultural Statesman." Special issue, *Research in African Literatures* 41, no.1 (2010).
Peters, John Durham. "Witnessing." *Media, Culture & Society* 23 (2001): 707–23.
Rothberg, Michael. "Between Auschwitz and Algeria: Multidirectional Memory and the Counterpublic Witness." *Critical Inquiry* 33 (2006): 158–84.
———. *Multidirectional Memory: Remembering the Holocaust in the Age of Decolonization*. Stanford, CA: Stanford University Press, 2009.
———. *Traumatic Realism: The Demands of Holocaust Representation*. Minneapolis: University of Minnesota Press, 2000.
———. "W.E.B. Du Bois in Warsaw: Holocaust Memory and the Color Line, 1949–1952." *The Yale Journal of Criticism* 14, no. 1 (2001): 169–89.
———. "The Work of Testimony in the Age of Decolonization: *Chronicle of a Summer*, Cinema Verité, and the Emergence of the Holocaust Survivor," *PMLA* 119, no. 5 (2004): 1231–46.

Said, Edward W. *Culture and Imperialism.* New York: Vintage, 1994.

———. *Orientalism.* New York: Pantheon, 1978.

———. "Zionism from the Standpoint of Its Victims." *Social Text* 1 (1979): 7–58.

Sanders, Mark. "Reading Lessons." *Diacritics* 29, no. 3 (1999): 3–20.

Shklovsky, Viktor. "Art as Technique." In *Literary Theory: An Anthology,* ed. Julie Rivkin and Michael Ryan, 15–21. Oxford: Basil Blackwell, 2000.

Silverman, Max. "Interconnected Histories: Holocaust and Empire in the Cultural Imaginary." *French Studies* 62, no. 4 (2008): 417–28.

Spivak, Gayatri Chakravorty. "Can the Subaltern Speak?" In *Marxism and the Interpretation of Culture,* ed. Cary Nelson and Lawrence Grossberg, 271–313. Urbana: University of Illinois Press, 1988.

———. *A Critique of Postcolonial Reason: Toward a History of the Vanishing Present.* Cambridge, MA: Harvard University Press, 1999.

———. "Ethics and Politics in Tagore, Coetzee, and Certain Scenes of Teaching." *Diacritics* 32, nos. 3–4 (2002): 17–31.

———. "In Response: Looking Back, Looking Forward." In *Can the Subaltern Speak: Reflections on the History of an Idea,* ed. Rosalind C. Morris, 227–36. New York: Columbia University Press, 2010.

———. "The Rani of Sirmur: An Essay in Reading the Archives." *History and Theory* 24, no. 3 (1985): 247–72.

Wiesel, Elie. *Dimensions of the Holocaust.* Evanston, IL: Northwestern University Press, 1990.

Wieviorka, Anette. *The Era of the Witness.* Translated by Jared Stark. Ithaca, NY: Cornell University Press, 2006.

———. "The Witness in History." Translated by Jared Stark. *Poetics Today* 27, no. 2 (2006): 385–97.

CHAPTER 10

Commemorating the Twentieth Century
The Holocaust and Nonviolent Struggle in Global Discourse

Tamar Katriel

Introduction

Speaking on the occasion of the first International Day of Non-Violence, Sonia Gandhi, who, as representative of India, was the moving spirit behind its inclusion in the UN ceremonial calendar in 2007, said: "Looking back, if the 20th century was the most bloody in human history, it was also the century where nonviolence saw its greatest triumphs, cutting across the boundaries of continents and faiths."[1] This statement joins a common tendency to assess the twentieth century in moral terms, playing Gandhi's nonviolent struggle and its hopeful spirit against the legacy of despair generated by the century's horrors and atrocities epitomized in the Holocaust.

The present chapter concretizes Sonia Gandhi's exercise in juxtaposition by exploring UN initiatives to commemorate the Holocaust and the Gandhian legacy of nonviolence on a global scale. It does so by addressing some of the commemorative-discursive dynamics associated with the establishment of two international days recently added to the UN ceremonial calendar: the International Day of Commemoration in Memory of the Victims of the Holocaust (International Holocaust Remembrance Day), which was inaugurated on 27 January 2006, the day marking the liberation of Auschwitz-Birkenau by Soviet troops in 1945; and the International Day of Non-Violence, which was inaugurated on 2 October 2007, the day marking Mahatma Gandhi's *jayanti,* or day of birth, in 1869.

Notes for this section begin on page 207.

The Holocaust and Gandhi's nonviolent struggle are distinctive and unrelated chapters in the complex historical legacy of the twentieth century. Yet, as I will argue, their position in the UN annual event cycle makes them part of an evolving global commemorative matrix that is associated with the emergence of what Daniel Levy and Natan Sznaider call a "cosmopolitan memory" culture.[2] Within cosmopolitan memory, localized atrocities become de- and reterritorialized from their original contexts through transnationally mediated processes of commemoration, generating new transcultural trajectories underwritten by "universal values that are emotionally engaging, that descend from the level of pure abstract philosophy, and into the emotions of people's everyday lives."[3] As an international arena fundamentally dominated by the logic of the territorially bounded nation-state, the transnational platform of the UN brings out the local-global nexus that has shaped the memory of pivotal twentieth-century events. It furthermore invites attention to the current scholarly concern with cosmopolitan memory, which Jessica Rapson refers to as the "transcultural turn" in memory studies,[4] as well as to the role of epideictic rhetoric—the rhetoric of praise and blame—in the ceremonial production of a globalized moral community in today's world.[5]

The addition of the two international days discussed in this chapter to the UN ceremonial calendar during the first decade of the new millennium exemplifies how crucial chapters in world history can be mobilized in constructing a collective memory that transcends national borders without obliterating them. The choice to build a global memory culture around these two days signals a preoccupation with the role of human violence—buttressed by the advent of technological progress—in international affairs. These international days promote concern with violence in different ways: the International Holocaust Remembrance Day acknowledges the extremities to which the human disposition toward violence can go, sounding a darkly cautionary note that invokes a commitment to eradicating such violence ("Never again!"); the International Day of Non-Violence celebrates the possibility of overcoming violence by using an inspirational idiom of emulation that promotes an alternative form of human struggle ("In the spirit of ..."). Highlighting the inclusion of these two days in the UN ceremonial calendar is not intended to invoke a problem-solution framework, but rather to propose that the cautionary note and the sense of hopeful struggle respectively cultivated by them represent alternative response strategies to the excesses of modernity, as will be elaborated below.

As we shall see in attending to the public proclamations made by various UN nation-states in discussing the establishment of these international days, the promotion of a shared human ethical sensibility through invoking memories of nonviolence and genocide went hand in hand with the reterritorialization and politicization of these memories. Therefore, the mobilization of the memory of the Holocaust and of Gandhi's struggle points to the possibility of cultivating a cosmopolitan memory culture grounded in the legacy of modernity at the beginning of the twenty-first century, but also to what appear to be the limitations of such a project.

As was argued by Zygmunt Bauman, the Holocaust epitomizes the over-rationalized, industrialized, and militarized social order associated with modernity that has the distinctive brand of Nazi horror.[6] The industrial character of Nazi atrocities distinguished them from other forms of violence, which were attributed to the "barbarism" of premodern times or of wars in non-Western countries, those untouched by the European Enlightenment. The figure of Mahatma Gandhi—the "Half Naked Fakir," as Churchill disdainfully described him[7]—represents, in its own way, a partial rejection of Western modernism as epitomized by the excesses of industrialized urbanism and its destructive effects on human lives. Gandhi's legacy of respect for traditional village ways, his vision of a spiritualized politics animated by a creed of nonviolence, as well as his deep suspicion of modern technology, whose capacities he nevertheless mobilized to great effect in the service of his political campaign, are all part of his legacy. In fact, Gandhi responded to the excesses of modernity long before they found their expression in the extremity of Nazi violence. The disillusionment with the spirit of modernity—as represented in Western civilization's discontents—is thus deeply embedded, though in different ways, in these two international days.

Drawing upon Levy and Sznaider's discussion of the process of the cosmopolitanization of Holocaust memory, I focus on the case of the UN ceremonial calendar as an internationally recognized official instrument designed to create a transnational memory culture. Indeed, the establishment of this ceremonial calendar of international days is one of a number of international mechanisms that have evolved over the past decades through which an "international community" can be imagined. Another such mechanism is the transnational "town twinning" arrangement explored by Jessica Rapson's aforementioned study of the transcultural turn in memory studies that focuses on the mobilization of the memory of the Czech town of Lidice and its razing by the Nazis.

The memory-making processes activated by these two mnemonic mechanisms are very different, ranging from the centralized, all-inclusiveness of UN international days to the direct locale-to-locale arrangements associated with town twinning. In both cases, too, high-profile collective memory projects (Holocaust memory first and foremost) are reconfigured in such a way as to invoke the possibility of a transnational memory culture against the background of local and political interests. While Levy and Sznaider propose that the spatio-temporal disengagement of cosmopolitan memory creates an arena in which its global potential can promote an empathetic understanding of the suffering of cultural others, other scholars have foregrounded the crucial role of the local in "glocalized" memory spheres.[8] The present analysis of the introduction of two international days into the UN calendar is therefore hoped to contribute to the scholarly discussion of the notion of "cosmopolitan memory" (as one aspect of the more general notion of "cosmopolitanism"⁹) by highlighting the many ways in which the emergence of cosmopolitan memory—and particularly the campaigns promoting it—remain rooted in local visions, interests, and power relations even when they are played out on the international stage of the UN floor.

Thus, via their inclusion in the UN ceremonial calendar, the cultural memory of the Nazi brand of rationalized atrocity as a failure of modern societies and the cultural memory of nonviolent struggle as a triumph over imperialism and Western colonialism become vehicles for the cultivation of a cosmopolitan moral sensibility. As will be shown, however, even while it responds to the excesses of modernity, the fact that this project was grounded in the tradition of Western liberalism did not escape generally supportive members of the international community, and did not go unchallenged on the UN floor.

UN International Days

The two international days discussed here are part of a broad and diverse motley of UN observances that have become integral to the UN calendar as designated days, weeks, years, and decades. Most of them are established by the UN General Assembly and some by specialized UN agencies. The purpose and spirit of these observances are presented on the UN website as follows:

> United Nations observances are used to contribute to the achievement of the purposes of the UN Charter and promote awareness of and action upon, important political, social, cultural, humanitarian or human rights issues. Celebrate with us United Nations days, weeks, years, and decades such as the International Day of Peace, or the International Year of Youth at your local community. Spread the word, United Nations it's your world!¹⁰

The first international day—Human Rights Day—was launched in 1950. Other days thematizing and celebrating abstract social values—such as peace, human solidarity, democracy, and world press freedom—were added over time. Some UN days celebrate particular segments of the world population, such as children, women, or youth. Other UN days celebrate aspects of human intellectual and spiritual legacy, such as philosophy, poetry, and world languages (e.g., English, Russian, Spanish, French, and Arabic). Yet other UN days highlight cherished (and often endangered) aspects of the natural environment (e.g., mountains, water, or oceans). Some of these observances are purely celebratory; others combine a celebratory with a cautionary note—upholding a particular good or value while pointing to its endangerment. Some such days are devoted to high-profile existential predicaments, which require world attention and global efforts. These include health conditions such as World Autism Awareness Day, or sociopolitical ills such as International Anti-Corruption Day. There are, in addition, a few UN days that are explicitly commemorative, such as the Day of Remembrance of the Victims of the Rwanda Genocide, which comes closest in spirit to the International Holocaust Remembrance Day. There is a day that is named after a particular historical figure—Nelson Mandela International Day, established in 2009, which is thematically related to the International Day of Non-Violence.[11]

The two international days that form the topic of my inquiry are thus part of a transnational field of discourse in which existential threats and shared values and struggles are intertwined and played against each other. These UN days are often promoted by particular players on the global stage, for example, a nation that seeks to uphold a specific heritage or cultural memory or to draw attention to particular concerns. Yet their adoption is possible only to the extent that they thematize issues that resonate with the agendas of UN member states more broadly. Fundamental issues of survival and morality are thus prime candidates for such thematization, even though the universalizing claims in which they are rooted make them vulnerable to critiques of Western liberalism in the transnational arena.

The claims to universal relevance associated with the addition of a locally sponsored contemporary theme to the UN commemorative calendar of international days entail a spatial and temporal reorientation. The shifting spatiality of memory as it crosses and transcends national borders and its shifting temporality across generational lines are both linked to the increasing reliance on mass mediation in the transmission of cultural memories in the contemporary world. Localized cultural memories, whose initial import and meanings attach to particular times and places, are transmuted and augmented through processes of deterritorialization and temporal expansion as they move beyond a single generational memory and become part of a transnational commemorative idiom.

The spatiotemporal matrix of memory is reconfigured with the process of rendering memory cosmopolitan on UN international days, as on other occasions. Levy and Sznaider address the spatial dimension of this process in discussing the de- and reterritorialization of memory in relation to the pivotal role of the Holocaust in the emergence of cosmopolitan memory. They point out that "while 'national memory' is determined by identity that is produced within clearly defined borders, 'cosmopolitan memory' is characterized by shifting boundaries and a process of de-territorialization."[12] They further argue that Holocaust memory has been increasingly constructed as a transnational narrative of a troubled European past, while the ritual idioms developed around its commemoration have been shaped by locally inflected interests and concerns in each of the three commemorative cultures they examined—Germany, the United States, and Israel.

The temporal trajectory of collective memory relates to the precariousness of intergenerational transmission and narrative continuity as they become increasingly mass mediated. Alison Landsberg has addressed this issue in her exploration of "the possibility of a responsible mass cultural transmission of memory."[13] In exploring this possibility, which is realized in intimate and repetitive exposure to powerful media images and sounds, she speaks of "prosthetic memories," that is, "memories that circulate publicly, are not organically based, but are nevertheless experienced with one's own body—by means of a wide range of cultural technologies—and as such become part of one's personal archive of experience, informing not only one's subjectivity, but one's relationship to the present and future tenses."[14]

The conjunction of shifts in the spatiality and temporality of collective memory in contemporary life gives rise to the design of ambitious and tension-filled projects of "commemorative memory"[15] that involve diffuse, global audiences in search of an encompassing public idiom that can demarcate a transnational sphere of shared purpose and sentiment. Ultimately, the language and symbolism of official commemorative occasions are hoped to become part of individuals' archives of personally meaningful experiences so that globally circulating commemorative images can seep into people's personal "noncommemorative" memories as well.[16]

UN-designated international days provide a prominent example of such top-down, globally oriented cultural formations. Largely declarative in nature, these international days are significant gestures in a concerted attempt to set up a transnational symbolic order. They establish a ceremonial calendar that provides occasions for the statement of visions and goals,[17] as well as for the cultivation of pedagogically oriented epideictic discourses of praise and condemnation at a transnational scale, thereby linking together a strife-filled world into an "international community" through a shared ceremonial and commemorative idiom.[18]

The distinctive range of meanings and values held up for affirmation in and through the discourses generated by each UN international day, as well as the cultural politics associated with its insertion into the global arena, deserve detailed consideration. Since my concern here is with the goals served by the establishment of these ceremonial days rather than with the actual effects of this mnemonic mechanism, my discussion will focus on the negotiations surrounding their introduction into the UN ceremonial calendar rather than addressing issues of implementation. Thus, by juxtaposing the discourses surrounding two international days anchored in the memory of the twentieth century, I hope to shed some light on the discursive construction of a cosmopolitan, value-laden commemorative memory in present times and the power politics associated with it. The extent to which these orchestrated efforts by international agents affect national and regional agendas, shaping what Raymond Williams has referred to as the "structures of feeling,"[19] in particular times and places, remains an open question.

As noted, in contemporary global memory culture the Holocaust serves as an emblem for what Jeffrey C. Alexander has termed a "sacred evil."[20] By contrast, Gandhi's idealized image as the apostle of nonviolence concretizes a positive and hopeful human vision. The commemorative projects signaled by these two international days constitute a move toward cultivating new cultural arenas—at international, national, and local scales—in and through which the projection and reaffirmation of more specific, globally shared moral values and sentiments can take place. Both projects straddle the national and the global in another sense as well. They were both promoted by particular nation-states (Israel and India, respectively) in the hope of elevating highly significant images and stories pertaining to their particular national pasts onto the global scene. Yet these two international days differ radically in the rhetorical strategies they employ—the commemoration of Holocaust memory consists mainly of narratives and images of confronting human atrocity, whereas the story of Gandhi's nonviolent struggle sets up an alternative model of a hope-filled struggle.

As we shall see, whereas these two international days both gained overwhelming approval by UN member states, the launching of the day commemorating the victims of the Holocaust, unlike the launching of the International Day of Non-Violence, gave rise to open controversy on the UN floor. In what follows, I will recapture the discourses surrounding the launching of these two occasions, drawing mainly on the pool of institutional and journalistic materials circulating in cyberspace, but also on participant observation in public events that inaugurated the International Day of Non-Violence in India.[21] In so doing, I will reflect upon their shared functions as well as the distinctive tonalities attending them.

International Holocaust Remembrance Day

On 1 November 2005, in a resolution cosponsored by 104 member states, the UN General Assembly designated 27 January—the anniversary of the liberation of the Auschwitz-Birkenau Nazi death camp sixty years earlier—as an International Day of Commemoration in Memory of the Victims of the Holocaust.[22] The particular day chosen was already marked as a Holocaust commemoration day in Germany since 1996. Following a resolution taken by the participants in the Stockholm International Forum on Holocaust Education held on that date a year earlier, many other European countries instituted this commemorative date since 2001. As a result of this resolution, the special international task force that was formed by the UN to encourage the establishment of ceremonies of various kinds (such as a special annual General Assembly meeting on 27 January) set out to mobilize both governments and civil societies around the world for the purpose of generating locally significant commemorative events as part of the emerging cosmopolitan tradition of UN-sponsored Holocaust commemoration.

The UN resolution to launch the International Holocaust Remembrance Day reaffirmed the historical link between World War II and the founding of the United Nations as an international institution that signaled a new chapter in the annals of international relations. The vision statement accompanying this move foregrounded the simultaneously retrospective and prospective meaning of Holocaust memory by declaring that "the Holocaust, which resulted in the murder of one third of the Jewish people, along with countless members of other minorities, will forever be a warning to all people of the dangers of hatred, bigotry, racism and prejudice." It further urged member states "to develop educational programs that will inculcate future generations with the lessons of the Holocaust in order to help prevent future acts of genocide."[23]

The memory of the Holocaust was thus invoked as a token of the failure of humanity. The historical specificity of 27 January became mobilized toward a general statement about the human capacity for evil as part of a future-oriented, universalized cautionary tale. Yet this universalistic framing of Holocaust memory was challenged by the representatives of some UN member states, notably non-European ones, who at times mobilized its memory in voicing their non-Western construction of cosmopolitanism. To begin with, the very initiative to institute this UN day was nation-centered rather than universalistic in its motivation. The Israeli Ministry of Foreign Affairs officials, the institutional initiators of this move, considered this UN resolution as a political response to Holocaust denial and as a contribution to Jewish Israeli regional politics. Thus, in a speech delivered at a special meeting on 26 January 2006 in the Knesset (Israeli parliament) on the occasion of the first International Holocaust Remembrance Day, Roni Adam, the Israeli official who led the diplomatic campaign in favor of instituting the International Holocaust Remembrance Day, described its goals in explicitly political terms, as designed "to promote a Jewish and Israeli narrative in the UN, to counter the Palestinian narrative that is very dominant in the UN."[24]

Other member states too interpreted the launching of the International Holocaust Remembrance Day in local/political rather than universalistic terms. Indeed, while all speakers at the high-profile General Assembly meeting affirmed the universal relevance of the Holocaust, many of them also gave voice to particularized historical positionings vis-à-vis its memory. The Israeli representative, Dan Gillerman, expressing his people's gratitude for the establishment of this day, constructed this initiative as a gesture extended by the international community toward the Jewish people. Others chose to see this day as standing for all victims of Nazism, including the Sinti and Roma, for example, whose representatives were invited to attend the UN International Holocaust Remembrance Day ceremony in subsequent years. The Austrian representative took upon his nation a measure of culpability as he joined others in asserting the global significance of the Holocaust, but also used the occasion to express national remorse, saying "we feel the pain of realizing that far too many Austrians took part in this greatest of all crimes."[25]

On the other hand, quite a number of representatives, mainly from nations that had no direct association with Holocaust history, interpreted the universal relevance assigned to the International Holocaust Remembrance Day as a call to highlight other atrocities and genocides such as those witnessed in the Balkans, Rwanda, and South America. Not denying the centrality and import of the Holocaust, they set it in a wider canvass of human violence and suffering. In so doing, they voiced a position that resonates with Craig Calhoun's critique of the concept of universalist cosmopolitanism,[26] which argues that it is grounded in the universalization of Western signifiers, thereby pointing to the power relations embedded in the precedence given to atrocities perpetrated on European soil.

Thus, the Brazilian representative further historicized the discussion by voicing a postcolonial critique shared by other speakers as well. He pointed out that neither the word "genocide" nor the international legal apparatus for handling genocides existed before the Holocaust, and therefore "massacres prior to that tragedy could not be properly judged, and their perpetrators could not be punished, including crimes committed against the indigenous peoples of the Americas during the colonial period, along with the practice of slavery."[27] The representative of the Republic of Korea similarly mentioned the Korean victims' great suffering during World War II, and stressed the recurrence of genocides in our contemporary world "from Srebrenica to Kigali to Darfur."[28]

The Jordanian representative gave the discussion an even more blatantly political inflection. Pointing to European nations' culpability during the Holocaust, he spoke of it as "a crime of the most colossal proportions," directly calling on the nations responsible for it to atone for their tarnished past by supporting the International Criminal Court and thus ensuring that genocide can be made truly unthinkable in the future. In a final, thinly veiled comment directed at the state of Israel, he complained that "'never again' was also sometimes used as a form of moral justification for the implementation of some policies, the effect of which was the continued domination of one people over the other."[29] Along a similar political vein, the Venezuelan representative inserted his own tune, calling on the international community to remember Hiroshima and Nagasaki, adding that "since 1945, the United States and other nations had participated in systematic genocides against the peoples of Asia, Africa and Latin America, which must be collectively remembered."[30] These speakers all supported the resolution to internationalize the Holocaust Remembrance Day, but in taking it in directions not originally intended, they exposed the vulnerability (if not the hypocrisy) of the power arrangements in which they considered this move to be embedded.

Thus, in this inaugural discussion—whether the uniqueness of the Holocaust was acknowledged or not—its memory was held to promote a progressive narrative rooted in the spirit of the Enlightenment, whereby the memory of dark historical moments can give rise to a quest for the improvement of mankind. A similar quest underwrites the International Day of Non-Violence. However, it does so, as noted, through a very different strategy of modeling and emulation, holding up the image of Mahatma Gandhi as an emblem of the potential promise of nonviolent struggles in the cause of freedom and justice.

The International Day of Non-Violence

The choice of Gandhi's day of birth to mark the International Day of Non-Violence links this day directly to the Mahatma's historical figure and to the legacy of nonviolent struggle associated with him. This UN day too weaves together a universalist interpretation of human potential—for good rather than evil—with the particular national circumstances of the Indian anticolonial struggle. Thus, even though the Gandhian legacy is contested within Indian society—with questions concerning the effectiveness of this form of struggle and critiques of Gandhi's actual positions on central social issues such as race, caste, and gender[31]—it is nevertheless promoted as an all-encompassing ideal by the Indian state, an ideal they consciously share with the West.

That the UN proposal to commemorate the legacy of nonviolence via Gandhi's figure did not generate the same kind of politicized objections by member states on the UN floor as was the case in debating the resolution concerning the International Holocaust Remembrance Day may reflect the relative ease of rallying behind positive rather than negative symbols, which is also probably why the rhetoric of praise has been so much more central in studies of the epideictic genre.[32] But it also attests to the extent to which Mahatma Gandhi has been mythologized around the world. In his own day and posthumously, he was venerated as a unique blend of effective political leader and saintly figure.[33]

As in the case of the International Holocaust Remembrance Day, the resolution designating 2 October as the International Day of Non-Violence, which was introduced at the United Nations General Assembly by Anand Sharma, the Indian minister of state for external affairs, on 15 June 2007, created a linkage between the principles formulated in the charter of the United Nations and the spirit of Gandhian idealism, stating that "nonviolence, tolerance, full respect for all human rights and fundamental freedoms for all, democracy, development, mutual understanding and respect for diversity, are interlinked and mutually reinforcing."[34]

The International Day of Non-Violence was inaugurated on the same day both in New Delhi and at the sixty-second session of the UN General Assembly informal plenary meeting in New York on 2 October 2007.[35] It was my good fortune to be in New Delhi on that day, attend the highly festive inauguration event, and follow the considerable publicity it received in the public arena. The daily papers were filled with Gandhi's image in various familiar postures and with resonant Gandhian sayings, many of which appeared in large ads sponsored by public organizations, including government ministries. Gandhian images and pronouncements were also lavishly posted in the streets surrounding the upscale venue where the inauguration day ceremony took place. The audience that congregated in the huge convention hall included cabinet members, foreign diplomats, representatives of the local and international press, and groups of well-behaved school children who—rhetorically cast in the role of emblems of the future—were directly addressed by some of the speakers.

Standing next to a large portrait of Gandhi, garlanded in traditional Indian fashion, Dr. Manmohan Singh, India's prime minister at the time, spoke to the audience in the convention hall, as well as to the Indian nation and the world at large in a live broadcast of the ceremony. Dr. Singh foregrounded the local roots of Gandhi's life and philosophy, yet also stressed the universal appeal of Gandhi's legacy. Not unlike the Israeli UN ambassador mentioned earlier, he reappropriated Gandhi's memory by expressing India's gratitude for the UN's recognition of the Mahatma's global relevance, saying: "We in India have observed this day for decades as a day of prayer and thanksgiving.... We are grateful to the world community for declaring this auspicious day as the International Day of Non-Violence. Mahatma Gandhi's message was not just for India.... It is a message for all times, for all societies, for all peoples."[36]

Dr. Singh's address, like so many other speeches made on similar occasions, eulogized Gandhi's saintliness even while stressing his impact on worldly affairs through the national and social struggles he led. It mentioned the way Gandhi inspired great leaders such as Martin Luther King Jr. and Nelson Mandela through the personal example of his life and the practical cadence of his beliefs. The prime minister went on to underscore the contemporary relevance of Gandhi's message, saying that "[i]t is more important today than ever before since nations across the world continue to grapple with the threat of conflict, violence and terrorism. For as long as there is temptation to resort to violence in the human mind, the Mahatma's message of nonviolence will tug at our hearts."[37]

Thus, while recognizing the temptation to resort to violence in the human mind—a much milder version of the dark vision of human nature promoted in the discourse surrounding the International Holocaust Remembrance Day—the celebration of Gandhi's legacy is mainly an affirmation of an alternative human possibility grounded in the rejection of violence. It is a vision that celebrates the positive values encapsulated in such keywords as those explicitly mentioned by Dr. Singh—truth, equality, tolerance, transparency, and self-respect. Indeed, the positive note surrounding the commemoration of Gandhi's legacy was also clearly evident in the parallel inauguration of the first International Day of Non-Violence at the UN General Assembly, which hosted as main speakers UN Secretary-General Ban Ki-moon, who declared Mahatma

Gandhi to be his personal hero, and Sonia Gandhi, who spoke for the people of India.

The UN secretary-general followed the tack of linking the day's event to the history of the UN, saying:

> The United Nations was created in the hope that humanity could not only end wars, it could eventually make them unnecessary. The founders hoped that our Organization could help stop violence by spreading a culture of peace, promoting tolerance and advancing human dignity. These same ideals sum up the legacy of Mahatma Gandhi, whose birthday we celebrate today.[38]

Ban Ki-moon also reiterated the urgency of Gandhi's vision in today's world and concluded by expressing the pedagogical hope implicit in the international day format and the recognition that the goals it promotes have not been attained: "May this Day help spread Mahatma Gandhi's message to an ever wider audience, and hasten a time when every day is a day without violence."[39]

Defining the tribute to the Mahatma as "a collective homage of the world community to one of the greatest men of all time, an homage that rises above politics and speaks to all humankind,"[40] Sonia Gandhi too thanked the assembly in the name of the people of India for their support. She noted that nonviolence as a strategy of human struggle has been overshadowed by violence, as is indicated by the fact that for nonviolence "there is no proactive word ... in almost any language. It has not been regarded as a concept in itself, but simply the negation of something else."[41] Therefore, nonviolence has been misinterpreted as weakness, whereas, in fact, "to practice it in its true spirit demands strict discipline of mind: the courage to face aggression, the moral conviction to stay the course, and the strength to do so without harboring any malice towards the opponent."[42] Highlighting the great contribution of individuals and movements all over the world that continue to develop nonviolent ways to overcome oppression and discrimination in the service of democracy, she thus linked the invocation of Gandhi's life and message to an affirmation of the human potential for goodness.

The establishment of the International Day of Non-Violence thus reflected the idealized image of Gandhi and his legacy as it was constructed in the West over the past century and strategically promoted by the Indian state. The hagiographic discourse garlanding Gandhi's image is closely linked to the modern West's yearnings for a way out of its own legacy of oppression and violence as represented by its relentless competitive capitalism, exploitative economic formations, postcolonial legacies, and militaristic ethos.[43] In Western-based global memory culture, the legacy of nonviolent struggle is pinned onto the exoticized, dehistoricized image of Gandhi as a cultural "other" whose narrative of *satyagraha* (truth force) is vaguely anchored in Hindu tradition (especially Jainism).[44] Indeed, Gandhi's legacy of nonviolence is often linked to other cultural icons of "otherness": Martin Luther King Jr., Nelson Mandela, and the Dalai Lama, all well-recognized icons of nonviolence on the world stage. The Western influences that Gandhi himself readily acknowledged (e.g., Tolstoy, Ruskin, Thoreau, Emerson) have been sidelined or completely erased from popular memory. In addition to the Western theoretical roots credited in Gandhi's writings, one could well argue that he appropriated and further valorized strategies of nonviolent resistance that had not only been theorized in the West but also exercised in the labor, feminist, and pacifist struggles that abounded during his formative years, turning nonviolent struggle into a fully elaborated creed.[45]

The transnational flow of ideas that shaped the emergence of this creed as a globally recognized cultural alternative remains underacknowledged in UN commemorative discourse, as it does in many popular discussions of Gandhi's life and legacy. Stripped of its concrete historical precedents and entanglements, this legacy has been turned into a progressive parable of future promise rooted in the human capacity for hope that is traced to a mythical East untarnished by Western modernity and its discontents.

Through a series of events such as conferences, commemorative meetings, exhibitions, multifaith prayers, pedagogical encounters, the dedication of monuments, and the launching of books and commemorative stamps, a widely shared ceremonial discourse of nonviolence has taken shape. Claims about the growing relevance of the vision this discourse promotes are voiced on the International Day of Non-Violence around the globe. At times it even seeps into the heart of the political arena. Thus, on 2 October 2008, the image of the Mahatma was politically mobilized in a speech made for the occasion of the International Day of Non-Violence by then presidential hopeful Barack Obama, who joined the international chorus while appropriating Gandhi's words for his own needs:

> Gandhi's significance is universal. Countless people around the world have been touched by his spirit and example.... His portrait hangs in my office to remind me that real change will not come from Washington—it will, when the people, united, bring it to Washington. This is a pivotal election. This is our time for change.... Let us all rededicate ourselves, every day from now until November 4th, and beyond, to living Gandhi's call to be the change we wish to see in the world.[46]

Beyond such occasional calls, as the International Day of Non-Violence is embraced in various parts of the world, locally inflected ceremonial gestures are emerging to mark its significance. By now, a budding celebratory discourse of nonviolence has been tenuously infused into the global cultural scene, invoking a vision of a world in which not only genocide is unthinkable, but also one in which lesser evils may be peacefully and effectively overcome.

Concluding Remarks

The United Nations, through its influential organizational bodies and wide-ranging institutional networks around the globe, is becoming a shaping force in the production of a cosmopolitan memory culture. The International Holocaust Remembrance Day and the International Day of Non-Violence are just two nodes in the intricate UN ceremonial calendar, which provides occasions for the elaboration of epideictic discourses that delineate the contours of virtue and sin, good and evil, in the life of nations and in the transnational arenas tenuously constructed by their coming together. In joining these days into a budding transnational memory culture designed to transcend generational lines as well as national borders, the spatiality and temporality of national memories are reconfigured. The globalized pedagogy that emerges from these epideictic occasions employs strategies of de and reterritorialization as well as intergenerational transmission in various forms and venues.

Thus, within UN-sponsored memory culture, the Holocaust and Gandhi's nonviolent struggle are mobilized to anchor a cosmopolitan memory culture, serving as polar reference points around which fundamental parameters of a universal moral compass can be negotiated. Their commemorations become occasions for the discussion of other atrocities as well (such as colonialism or slavery) or other possibilities of human struggle (such as denuclearization or solidarity campaigns). As a deliberately designed cultural formation, each of these UN days invites rhetorical interventions of a particular expressive range, allowing for the dissemination of both traditional and new performative genres.

The designation of international days is an attempt to promote engagement with transnational themes so as to construct an "international community" that is nevertheless grounded in the territorial logic of nation-states that are encouraged to develop their own celebratory idioms. The public occasions thereby designated range from the global scale of abstracted messages floating through international media channels to the micro scale of locally established ritualized events in home communities.

Thus, in mining the West's conscience for its culpability in the Holocaust and projecting a rarified vision of modern saintliness on Gandhi's image and legacy, the two international days discussed here complement and reinforce each other's value messages, depicting a world in which both human cruelty and indifference as well as human greatness of spirit are concretely imaginable options. The sobriety associated with the recognition of evil, as well as the tenacity of the human drive to combat it in nonviolent ways, both suggest that a globally shared moral compass, however tenuous, is within reach. The dark vision attending the memory of the Holocaust and the sense of hope attending the Gandhian legacy both contribute to a universal vision of a future that demands—and is worth—struggling for. Such a vision has been gradually emerging out of the UN-sponsored memory projects whose launching was discussed here. With time, it may eventually generate "prosthetic memories" through which these days become personally significant invocations of a credible moral order in a world riddled with uncertainties.

Notes

Helpful comments by the editors and Oren Livio and Oren Meyers on an earlier version of this chapter are gratefully acknowledged.

1. Sonia Gandhi, chairperson, United Progressive Alliance, on the occasion of the first observance of the International Day of Non-Violence at the sixty-second session of the UN General Assembly informal plenary meeting on 2 October 2007.

2. Daniel Levy and Natan Sznaider, "Memory Unbound: The Holocaust and the Formation of Cosmopolitan Memory," *European Journal of Social Theory* 5, no. 1 (2002): 87–106.

3. Daniel Levy and Natan Sznaider, *The Holocaust and Memory in the Global Age*, trans. A. Oksiloff (Philadelphia: Temple University Press 2006), 3.

4. Jessica Rapson, "Mobilising Lidice: Cosmopolitan Memory between Theory and Practice," *Culture, Theory and Critique* 53, no. 2 (2012): 131.

5. For the classical notion of epideictic rhetoric, see Aristotle, *On Rhetoric*, trans. George A. Kennedy (Oxford: Oxford University Press, 1991); Gerald A. Hauser, "Aristotle on Epideictic: The Formation of Public Morality," *Rhetoric Society Quarterly* 29, no. 1 (1999): 5–23.

6. Zygmunt Bauman, *Modernity and the Holocaust* (Cambridge: Polity Press, 1989).

7. Martin Gilbert, *Winston Churchill 1922–1939*, vol. 5 (London, 1976), 390.

8. See, e.g., Jessica Rapson, "Mobilising Lidice"; Stephen Welch and Ruth Wittlinger, "The Resilience of the Nation State: Cosmopolitanism, Holocaust Memory and German Identity," *German Politics and Society* 29, no. 3 (2011): 38–54; Catherine Goetze, "The Particularism of Cosmopolitanism," *Global Society* 27, no. 1(2013): 91–114.

9. Ulrich Beck and Natan Sznaider, "Unpacking Cosmopolitanism for the Social Sciences: A Research Agenda," in "The *BJS*: Shaping Sociology over 60 Years," special issue, *British Journal of Sociology* 61, no. 1 (2010): 381–403.

10. On UN Observances, see http://visit.un.org/wcm/content/site/visitors/lang/en/home/plan/calendar (accessed 21 January 2013).

11. A list of UN international days can be found at http://www.un.org/en/events/observances/days.shtml (accessed 21 January 2013).

12. Daniel Levy and Natan Sznaider, *The Holocaust and Memory*, 10.

13. Alison Landsberg, "America, the Holocaust, and the Mass Culture of Memory: Towards a Radical Politics of Empathy," *New German Critique* 71 (1997): 64.

14. Ibid., 66.

15. Michael Schudson, "Lives, Laws, and Language: Commemorative versus Non-commemorative Forms of Effective Public Memory," *The Communication Review* 2, no. 1 (1997): 3–17.

16. Ibid.

17. On the symbolic role of calendars and calendrical occasions, see Eviatar Zerubavel, *Hidden Rhythms: Schedules and Calendars in Social Life* (Chicago: The Chicago University Press, 1981), 70–100.

18. The discursive construction of the category of "international community" has been noted in studies dealing with contemporary political discourse, in particular in the context of the "war on terror." See, e.g., Norman Fairclough, "Blair's Contribution to Elaborating a 'New Doctrine of International Community,'" in *The Soft Power of War*, ed. Lilie Chouliaraki (Amsterdam: John Benjamins, 2007), 39–60.

19. Raymond Williams, *Marxism and Literature* (Oxford: Oxford University Press, 1977).

20. Jeffrey C. Alexander, "On the Social Construction of Moral Universals: The Holocaust from War Crime to Trauma Drama," *European Journal of Social Theory* 5, no. 1 (2002): 5–85.

21. For a methodological discussion relating to the use of Web materials in discourse analytic research of this type, see Gerlinde Mautner, "Time to Get Wired: Using Web-Based Corpora in Critical Discourse Analysis," *Discourse & Society* 16, no. 6 (2005): 809–28.

22. Let me note that my parents were among the 7,650 inmates found in the camp by the Red Army on 27 January 1945. They met after liberation, and never failed to mark 27 January in the intimacy of our home as far back as I can remember.

23. Resolution adopted by the General Assembly on the Holocaust Remembrance (A/RES/60/7, 1 November 2005), http://www.un.org/holocaustremembrance/docs/res607.shtml (accessed 21 January 2013).

24. Protocol no. 287 of the meeting of the Parliamentary Committee for Aliyah, Absorption and Diaspora, sixteenth Knesset, fourth session, 26 January 2006.

25. UN Department of Public Information, News and Media Division, New York, sixtieth General Assembly plenary forty-second meeting (AM), GA/10413, "General Assembly Decides to Designate 27 January as Annual International Day of Commemoration to Honor Holocaust Victims," http://www.un.org/News/Press/docs/2005/ga10413.doc.htm (accessed 21 January 2013).

26. Craig Calhoun, "The Class Consciousness of Frequent Travelers: Toward a Critique of Actually Existing Cosmopolitanism," *Journal of Ethnic and Migration Studies* 101, no. 4 (2002): 869–97; Craig Calhoun, "Cosmopolitanism in the Modern Social Imaginary," *Daedalus* 137, no. 3 (2008): 105–14.

27. See General Assembly discussion (ft. 25) http://www.un.org/News/Press/docs/2005/ga10413.doc (accessed 21 January 2013).

28. Ibid.

29. Ibid.

30. Ibid.

31. See A. Raghumaraju, ed., *Debating Gandhi* (New Delhi, 2006); S. S. Gill, *Gandhi: A Sublime Failure* (New Delhi: Oxford University Press, 2001).

32. For a discussion of the different affordances and consequences of the epideictic of praise versus the epideictic of blame, see Elizabeth Church, *Epideictic Without the Praise: A Heuristic Analysis for Rhetoric of Blame* (PhD diss., Bowling Green State University, 2010).

33. See James F. Hopgood, ed., *The Making of Saints: Contesting Sacred Ground* (Tuscaloosa, AL: University Alabama Press, 2005).

34. "Introduction of the Draft Resolution on 'International Day of Non-Violence' by Mr. Anand Sharma, Minister of State for External Affairs at the United Nations General Assembly on June 15, 2007," http://www.topicalphilately.com/Gandhi/PDF/UN percent20India percent20I DoNV.pdf (accessed 21 January 2013).

35. United Nations General Assembly, sixty-first session, agenda item 44, Culture of Peace, 31 May 2007 (A/61/L.62), 1.

36. "PM's Address on International Day of Non-Violence," New Delhi, 2 October 2007, http://pmindia.nic.in/content_print.php?nodeid=569&nodetype=2 (accessed 21 January 2013).

37. Ibid.

38. UN Department of Public Information, News and Media Division, New York, SG/SM/11199, OBV/654, 2 October 2007, "Secretary-General, In Remarks to Non-Violence Day Observance, Calls Mahatma Gandhi His Personal Hero as He Recalls Early Diplomatic Career in India," http://www.un.org/News/Press/docs/2007/sgsm11199.doc.htm (accessed 21 January 2013).

39. Ibid.

40. "Statement by H.E. Mrs. Sonia Gandhi, Chairperson, United Progressive Alliance, On the Occasion of the First Observance of the International Day of Nonviolence at the 62nd Session of the UN General Assembly Informal Plenary Meeting on 2 October, 2007," http://www.un.int/india/2007/ind1345.pdf (accessed 21 January, 2013).

41. Ibid.

42. Ibid.

43. See Jonathan Schell, *Unconquerable World: Why Peaceful Protest Is Stronger than War* (London: Penguin Books, 2004).

44. Mohandas K. Gandhi, *Non-Violent Resistance (Satyagraha)* (1961; repr., Mineola, NY: Dover Publications, 2001). On the impact of the Gandhian legacy of nonviolence in the West, see

Sean Scalmer, *Gandhi in the West: The Mahatma and the Rise of Radical Protest* (Cambridge: Cambridge University Press, 2011).

    45. Mohandas K. Gandhi, *Hind Swaraj and Other Writings,* ed. Anthony J. Parel (1910; repr., Cambridge: Cambridge University Press, 1997).

    46. Obama's statement was circulated on the Web in October 2008. It was fully reproduced in an article published on 13 October 2008 on the website of the World Institute for Asian Studies: Daya Gamage, "Barack Obama Commemorates Mahatma Gandhi," *Asian Tribune* 10, no. 7 (2008), http://www.asiantribune.com/node/13681 (accessed 21 January 2013).

Bibliography

Alexander, Jeffrey C. "On the Social Construction of Moral Universals: The Holocaust From War Crime to Trauma Drama." *European Journal of Social Theory* 5, no. 1 (2002): 5–85.

Aristotle. *On Rhetoric.* Translated by George A. Kennedy. Oxford: Oxford University Press, 1991.

Bauman, Zygmunt. *Modernity and the Holocaust.* Cambridge: Polity Press, 1989.

Beck, Ulrich, and Natan Sznaider. "Unpacking Cosmopolitanism for the Social Sciences: A Research Agenda." In "The *BJS*: Shaping Sociology over 60 Years," special issue, *British Journal of Sociology* 61, no. 1 (2010): 381–403.

Calhoun, Craig. "The Class Consciousness of Frequent Travelers: Toward a Critique of Actually Existing Cosmopolitanism." *Journal of Ethnic and Migration Studies* 101, no. 4 (2002): 869–97.

———. "Cosmopolitanism in the Modern Social Imaginary." *Daedalus* 137, no. 3 (2008): 105–14.

Church, Elizabeth. *Epideictic Without the Praise: A Heuristic Analysis for Rhetoric of Blame.* PhD dissertation, Bowling Green State University, 2010.

Fairclough, Norman. "Blair's Contribution to Elaborating a 'New Doctrine of International Community.'" In *The Soft Power of War,* ed. Lilie Chouliaraki, 39–60. Amsterdam: John Benjamins, 2007.

Gamage, Daya. "Barack Obama Commemorates Mahatma Gandhi." *Asian Tribune* 10, no. 7 (2008). http://www.asiantribune.com/node/13681 (accessed 21 January 2013).

Gandhi, Mohandas K. *Hind Swaraj and Other Writings.* Edited by Anthony J. Parel. Cambridge: Cambridge University Press, 1997. First published 1910.

———. *Non-Violent Resistance (Satyagraha).* Mineola, NY: Dover Publications, 2001. First published 1961.

Gilbert, Martin. *Winston Churchill 1922–1939.* Vol. 5. London: William Heinemann Ltd, 1976.

Gill, S. S. *Gandhi: A Sublime Failure.* New Delhi: Rupa & Company, 2001.

Goetze, Catherine. "The Particularism of Cosmopolitanism." *Global Society* 27, no. 1 (2013): 91–114.

Hauser, Gerald A. "Aristotle on Epideictic: The Formation of Public Morality." *Rhetoric Society Quarterly* 29, no. 1 (1999): 5–23.

Hopgood, James F., ed. *The Making of Saints: Contesting Sacred Ground.* Tuscaloosa: University Alabama Press, 2005.

Landsberg, Alison. "America, the Holocaust, and the Mass Culture of Memory: Towards a Radical Politics of Empathy." *New German Critique* 71 (1997): 63–86.

Levy, Daniel, and Natan Sznaider. *The Holocaust and Memory in the Global Age.* Philadelphia: Temple University Press, 2006.

———. "Memory Unbound: The Holocaust and the Formation of Cosmopolitan Memory." *European Journal of Social Theory* 5, no. 1 (2002): 87–106.

Mautner, Gerlinde. "Time to Get Wired: Using Web-Based Corpora in Critical Discourse Analysis." *Discourse & Society* 16, no. 6 (2005): 809–28.

Raghumaraju, A., ed. *Debating Gandhi.* New Delhi: Oxford University Press, 2006.

Rapson, Jessica. "Mobilising Lidice: Cosmopolitan Memory between Theory and Practice." *Culture, Theory and Critique* 53, no. 2 (2012): 129–45.

Scalmer, Sean. *Gandhi in the West: The Mahatma and the Rise of Radical Protest.* Cambridge: Cambridge University Press, 2011.
Schell, Jonathan. *Unconquerable World: Why Peaceful Protest Is Stronger than War.* London: Penguin Books, 2004.
Schudson, Michael. "Lives, Laws, and Language: Commemorative versus Non-commemorative Forms of Effective Public Memory." *The Communication Review* 2, no. 1 (1997): 3–17.
Welch, Stephen E., and Ruth Wittlinger. "The Resilience of the Nation State: Cosmopolitanism, Holocaust Memory and German Identity." *German Politics and Society* 29, no. 3 (2011): 38–54.
Williams, Raymond. *Marxism and Literature.* Oxford : Oxford University Press, 1977.
Zerubavel, Eviatar. *Hidden Rhythms: Schedules and Calendars in Social Life.* Chicago: The University of Chicago Press, 1981.

CHAPTER 11

Rethinking the Politics of the Past
Multidirectional Memory in the Archives of Implication

MICHAEL ROTHBERG

The Multidirectional Paradigm

What happens when different histories of extreme violence confront each other in the public sphere? Does the remembrance of one event erase others from view? When memories of colonialism, slavery, and the Holocaust bump up against each other in contemporary multicultural societies, must a competition of victims ensue? Such problems of remembrance, justice, and comparison have preoccupied me over the last several years and have served as the impetus for the ongoing exploration of what I call "multidirectional memory." In my book *Multidirectional Memory: Remembering the Holocaust in the Age of Decolonization* and elsewhere, I have focused on a series of exemplary sites of tension involving remembrance of the Nazi genocide of European Jews in order to offer an alternative framework for thinking about and confronting the recent and ongoing "memory wars."[1]

Many discussions of collective memory today remain trapped in the logic of the zero-sum game, a logic in which evocation of one group's history is said to block other groups' histories from view and that I call "competitive memory." According to this understanding, memories crowd each other out of the public sphere—for example, too much emphasis on the Holocaust is said to marginalize other traumas or, inversely, adoption of Holocaust rhetoric to speak of those other traumas is said to relativize or even deny the Holocaust's uniqueness. The literary critic Walter Benn Michaels presents a sharp version of this argument in a typically provocative discussion of the United States Holocaust Memorial Museum. Evoking the perspective of African Americans, whom he suggests are frustrated by the absence of commemoration of their traumatic history on the Mall in Washington DC, Michaels asks if "commemoration of the Nazi murder of the Jews on the Mall [might not] in fact [be] another kind of Holocaust denial."[2] It is not difficult to understand the frustration of individuals and groups who feel, often justly, that their histories have been marginalized by the mainstream. The problem with Michaels's account lies not in the feelings he describes, but rather in the logic he ascribes to the workings of public memory. Michaels assumes that both memory and the public sphere are defined by a logic of scarcity: in this familiar scenario, an excess of Holocaust memory is deemed responsible for the dearth of remembrance of slavery and the lack of acknowledgment of the ongoing forms of racism suffered by African Americans. Although few people would put the matter in such controversial terms, many other commentators, both inside and outside the academy, share the understanding of collective memory articulated by Michaels. But are such conflicts of memory best described as a zero-sum competition over scarce resources? Is the problem really the presence of Holocaust memory, or does the source of injustice in fact lie elsewhere? Could it even be the case that memory of the Holocaust can sometimes be a vehicle for redressing the deficits in recognition of other histories, such as those of slavery and American racism? After all, even Michaels himself uses a reference to the Nazi genocide to bring dramatic attention to "another kind of Holocaust," and public concern with other traumatic histories has hardly seemed to wane as the Holocaust has achieved greater cultural centrality. Indeed, instead of obeying the logic of the zero-sum game, memory discourses seem to spiral and proliferate, even—perhaps especially—in conflicts about the past of the sort to which Michaels draws our attention.

With the concept of multidirectional memory, I seek to address the omnipresence of memory conflict in order to offer a novel way of thinking about the presence of the past in multicultural societies. Over the course of several years of research on different national contexts I have come to see that collective memories of different histories—such as those of slavery, the Holocaust, and colonialism—are not so easily separable from each other. I have discovered not only that memory of the Holocaust has served as a vehicle through which other histories of suffering have been articulated, but also something even more surprising: the emergence of Holocaust memory itself was from the start inflected by histories that at first glance might seem to have little to do with it. The very period during which an international public learned about the extent of Nazi destruction and slowly started to come to terms with it was also the era of decolonization—a time when the world order was shifting radically due to the onset of the Cold War and the collapse of the European colonial system. Until very recently, historians and cultural critics have almost entirely ignored this conjunction of world-historical events. But by focusing on the unlikely pairing of Holocaust memory and decolonization, I have been able to offer new accounts of both the postwar period and the workings of memory.

Besides targeting the problem of zero-sum thinking and bringing together histories that are usually kept separate, my research questions another one of the cornerstones of the memory wars, namely, the taken-for-granted link between collective memory and group identity—the direct line that seems to bind, for example, Jewish memory and Jewish identity and to differentiate them clearly from African American memory and African American identity. As my research reveals, however, memory of the Holocaust is not simply a form of Jewish memory, just as memory of slavery or colonialism is not limited to the victims or descendants of slavery and colonialism. Instead, by leaving behind the zero-sum presuppositions of the competitive model of memory, I have unearthed a dialogic process in which diverse historical experiences provide each other with hybrid vocabularies of remembrance. Not separation and competition best describe the relation between Holocaust memory and the memory of other events, but echoing and creative adaptation. In the place of competitive memory, then, I propose a theory of *multidirectional memory* that redescribes the public sphere as a field of contestation where memories interact productively and in unexpected ways. By making visible an intellectual and artistic countertradition that refuses the dominant zero-sum game and instead links memories of Nazi genocide, colonialism, and slavery, I reveal how the public articulation of collective memory by marginalized and oppositional social groups can provide resources for other groups to articulate their own claims for recognition and justice.

Shifting our perspective from competitive to multidirectional memory affords us new insight into cultural memory in the post-1945 world. From Hannah Arendt's writings on imperialism and totalitarianism and Aimé Césaire's link between colonialism and genocide in his polemical *Discourse on Colonialism* to the "Caribbean" novels of the Polish-French-Jewish writer André Schwarz-Bart and the "Jewish" novels of Caribbean-born, British (now US-based) novelist Caryl Phillips, there has always been a resonance between Holocaust memory and decolonization—even if it has rarely been acknowledged. This multidirectional countertradition is dispersed globally, if unevenly, and often coalesces around particular events or conflicts, such as the partition of India (see, e.g., Anita Desai's novel *Baumgartner's Bombay*). As I demonstrate in the second half of *Multidirectional Memory*, the Algerian War of Independence represents a particularly dense period of intersection between Holocaust memory and decolonization in France and, indeed, globally. French practices of torture and detention and the presence of large numbers of former resistance fighters and deportees in the anticolonial resistance, as well as in the army and police force themselves, ensured that the rise of attention to the Nazi genocide in the late 1950s and early 1960s took place against the backdrop of—and in dialogue with—an ongoing hot war of decolonization.

Bringing together histories of Nazi genocide and colonialism entails at least a double defamiliarization: by reading Holocaust memory in light of decolonization and decolonization in light of Holocaust memory, we obtain a new understanding of post–World War II social and cultural transformations as transnational processes that cannot be limited by our usual methodological containers such as the nation or ethnocultural identity. Drawing attention to intermediate zones of overlap, asymmetry, and potential solidarity, the ethics and politics of multidirectional memory provide an alternative to visions based either on identitarian particularism or abstract universalism, but the tracking of multidirectional memory does not necessarily provide easy answers to ethical and political quandaries.

My focus in *Multidirectional Memory* was primarily on constructing an archive of transnational militant and minority articulations of the past—forms of "minor transnationalism," to cite Françoise Lionnet and Shu-mei Shih's term.[3] Clearly, however, not all forms of multidirectional memory are militant or emerge from minoritized locations, so here I want to pursue a somewhat different archive, which we might call an "archive of implication." I use the deliberately open-ended term "implication" in order to gather together various modes of historical relation that do not necessarily fall under the more direct forms of participation associated with traumatic events such as victimization and perpetration. Such "implicated" modes of relation would encompass bystanders, beneficiaries, latecomers of the postmemory generation, and others connected "prosthetically" to pasts they did not directly experience.[4] These subject positions move us away from overt questions of guilt and innocence and leave us in a more complex and uncertain moral and ethical terrain—a terrain in which many of us live most of the time. These kinds of cases were not completely absent from my book (for instance, see the discussions of *The Stone Face* and *Caché*), but remained somewhat in the background. For the purposes of this chapter, I want to explore how multidirectional memory works in cases of complicity or responsibility where the subjects of remembrance are ethically implicated, however ambiguously, in the realms of a dominant or even perpetrator culture, without themselves being perpetrators.

I take as my examples the late German-born, Britain-based writer W. G. Sebald and the still active British/Israeli visual artist Alan Schechner. While in his novel *Austerlitz* Sebald uses a sublime aesthetic to link the irrecuperable losses of the Holocaust to a network of colonial violence in Africa and elsewhere, Schechner juxtaposes a famous image of the Holocaust with a "mirror" image depicting the Israeli occupation of Palestinian lands. In their different ways, both Sebald and Schechner might seem at first to stage scenes of identification with individualized victims or victim groups via historical analogy. Yet, although such practices of analogization between different histories of violence court the risks of identification—appropriation and the banalization of evils— the multidirectional practices of both Sebald and Schechner ultimately open onto complex scenarios of solidarity and historical responsibility in the face of complicity. The glue that binds together different histories in the works under consideration here is not identification but rather a less appropriative form of relation: implication.

The Multidirectional Sublime

W. G. Sebald's 2001 prose fiction *Austerlitz* concludes with a surprising literary and geographical detour—surprising even for a text whose narrative ranges widely through transnational terrain and whose very fabric emerges from a dense web of explicit and implicit intertextual reference. In the final pages of the novel, the unnamed narrator returns to Breendonk, the Belgian fortress used by the Nazis as a prison camp and the site of Jean Améry's torture, among many others. Sitting beside the moat, the narrator takes out a book given to him by his interlocutor throughout the novel, Jacques Austerlitz, a Prague-born Jew who had been sent on a *Kindertransport* to Britain, where he grew up without any memory of his origins or any knowledge of his parents' fate. The book the narrator receives from Austerlitz is a memoir by Dan Jacobson, a real British writer and critic identified as a colleague of the fictional Austerlitz. Jacobson's book, easily identifiable as the 1998 *Heshel's Kingdom,* recounts, as the narrator of *Austerlitz* explains, "the author's search for his grandfather Rabbi Yisrael Yehoshua Melamed, known as Heshel," and the world he occupied. When Heshel died of a heart attack at age fifty-three just after World War I, his widow—Jacobson's grandmother—decided "to emigrate with her nine children from Lithuania to South Africa," where Jacobson grew up in the mining town of Kimberley.[5] That fortuitous emigration saved this branch of the family from near certain death in the genocide that was not yet on the horizon, but the rest of the family, along with 95 percent of all Lithuanian Jews, would be murdered some twenty years later.

Via the textual detour of *Heshel's Kingdom*—Dan Jacobson's story of a failed attempt to reconstruct a now disappeared Eastern European Jewish lifeworld—a South African diamond mine comes to provide one of the final and definitive images of Sebald's novel, an image I will ultimately link to Kant's notion of the sublime.[6] Sebald's narrator reports that:

> Most of the mines, so I read as I sat there opposite the fortifications of Breendonk, were already disused at the time, including the two largest, the Kimberley and De Beers mines, and since they were not fenced off anyone who liked could venture to the edge of those vast pits and look down to a depth of several thousand feet. Jacobson writes that it was truly terrifying to see such emptiness open up a foot away from firm ground, to realize that there was no transition, only this dividing line, with ordinary life on one side and its unimaginable opposite on the other. The chasm into which no ray of light could penetrate was Jacobson's image of the vanished past of his family and his people which, as he knows, can never be brought

up from those depths again. On his travels in Lithuania, Jacobson finds scarcely any trace of his forebears, only signs everywhere of the annihilation from which Heshel's weak heart had preserved his immediate family when it stopped beating.[7]

Sebald's evocation of the "vast pits" of Kimberley and De Beers seems to take part in an established critical discourse characterizing the mine as an "anti-aesthetic abyss," a site that frustrates representation and thus the possibility of remembrance by dragging it into a kind of "black hole."[8] As such, it stands as the polar opposite of the Proustian trigger of involuntary memory, the madeleine, or more directly in *Austerlitz,* the "uneven paving of the Sporkova" in Prague where Austerlitz attempts to reexperience his childhood, even if the most he can say is that it is "*as if* I had already been this way before and memories were revealing themselves to me not by means of any mental effort but through my senses."[9] Evoking an image of absence, forgetting, nontransition, and historical rupture, the South African mine comes to figure the failure of the character Austerlitz's project: the attempt to recapture lost time, specifically his own childhood before the Holocaust, his mother's death in the camps, and his vanished father. Although Austerlitz discovers traces and fragments of the past, his memory quest ends, like Jacobson's, without his being able to cross the "dividing line" into the dark chasm left behind by annihilation.

In figuring the mine as a site of oblivion, Sebald seems to stay true to Jacobson's intentions. At the end of the prologue to *Heshel's Kingdom,* which Sebald incorporates partially through paraphrase and silent quotation, Jacobson imagines an infinitely deep mine in which a tossed stone would never hit bottom, his ultimate image of the failure of memory: "That is what the past is like: echoless and bottomless. Only its shallowest levels, those closest to us, have recognizable colors and forms. So we fix our gaze there. Below them is darkness that gives back nothing."[10] Like Austerlitz's parents, Jacobson's grandfather, as well as the Lithuanian Jewish lifeworld he inhabited, "remains hidden still, and always will do so. His secrets are enclosed in time past like the pattern inside an uncut agate stone: not just beyond amendment or erasure, but unknowable too."[11] The model of memory shared by Jacobson, Jacques Austerlitz, and Sebald's narrator and embodied in both the mine and the "uncut agate stone" (a metonymy of the diamond mine, perhaps) seems to approximate what Ann Rigney has called the "original plenitude and subsequent loss model": "Following this 'plenitude and loss' model, ... memory is conceptualized on the one hand in terms of an original 'storehouse' and, on the other hand, as something that is always imperfect and diminishing, a matter of chronic frustration because always falling short of total recall."[12]

To be sure, the histories recounted in these texts are histories of radical loss. Yet, I want to suggest, a different model of memory also coexists in the novel *Austerlitz,* and even to a certain extent in Jacobson's memoir. In order to locate this model, we need to differentiate between the experience of Jacques Austerlitz, the character, and the experience of reading *Austerlitz,* the book, a difference with potential significance for thinking about cultural memory. We need to attend not only to what the novel *says*—its enigmatic tale of a frustrated quest for the past—but also to what it *does*, for what it does, as the passage invoking Jacobson makes clear, involves the creation of new forms of memory via intertextuality and a metonymical narrative technique, even at sites of emptiness and forgetting. Such an alternative model, which I would describe as performative because of its attention to the productivity of what the text *does*, also turns out to be multidirectional, because such processes of reconstruction always involve temporal and spatial displacements and thus new layerings and constellations of time and place.[13]

In imaginatively moving in its final pages from Belgium to South Africa and then on to Lithuania, where the narrator recounts Jacobson's discussion of the Nazis' murder of thirty thousand people at Fort IX outside of Kaunas, Lithuania, *Austerlitz* completes its transnational textual circumnavigation of sites of racialized violence. This circumnavigation begins—the closing reference to Africa reminds us—with indirect invocations of the terrors of Belgian colonialism in the Congo. In Antwerp for the first time in the late 1960s, the novel's narrator experiences an imaginative confusion between the city's zoo—and particularly the Nocturama—and its "fantastical" train station: he remembers thinking that the train station "ought to have cages for lions and leopards let into its marble niches ... just as some zoos, conversely, have little railway trains in which you can, so to speak, travel to the farthest corners of the earth."[14] Previously, the narrator tells us, he "had taken in only vaguely" the façade of the station, but "[n]ow ... I saw how far the station constructed under the patronage of King Leopold II exceeded its purely utilitarian function, and I marveled at the verdigris covered Negro boy who, for a century now, has sat upon his dromedary on an oriel turret to the left of the station façade, a monument to the world of the animals and native peoples of the African continent, alone against the Flemish sky."[15] The ironic juxtaposition of "animals and native peoples" in proximity to King Leopold II and the narrator's confusion of the spaces of the railroad and zoo create a constellation of associations that calls up multiple forms of violence without making explicit reference to any of them. We have no warrant to conclude that in these passages from the beginning and end of *Austerlitz* Sebald is equating Nazi genocide, Leopold's Congo massacre, South African apartheid, more ordinary forms of colonial expansion and exploitation, and the treatment of nonhuman animals. But the text's metonymic mode of narration and its layered intertextuality do produce a haunting sense of the fragile copresence of histories somehow connected. Even Jacobson, while explicitly stating that all has been lost of his ancestors' lives and holding to a notion of the Holocaust's uniqueness, uses South Africa as a point of reference for establishing "analogies and distinctions" during his trip to Lithuania.[16] While the dead cannot be resurrected in their plenitude, more can be found than the image of the dark abyss implies; but what is brought back always involves a detour through multidirectional terrain. Because the text juxtaposes different histories without equating them, multidirectionality becomes a self-conscious way of remembering the past without suggesting that memory's figures can substitute for what has been lost or resurrect the disappeared in their full presence.

Significantly, the multidirectional connections evoked in *Austerlitz* turn on disturbed acts of seeing: from the "terrifying" stare into the bottomless emptiness of the mine to the "confusion" of the Nocturama and the train station that occurs, the narrator tells us, perhaps as "the result of the sun's sinking behind the city rooftops just as I entered the room."[17] Such a context of perturbed vision marks another appearance of the South African mine in Sebald's previous novel, *The Rings of Saturn,* where it is also accompanied by a scratchy and faded image, presumably of such a mine, and juxtaposed with histories of empire and Nazi genocide.[18] The crises of vision and representation staged in both *Austerlitz* and *The Rings of Saturn* around the mine and in relation to other sites of violence rupture a harmonious aesthetic vision, but the mine does not thereby become a purely antiaesthetic site. Rather, this crisis bears a strong resemblance to Kant's notion of the sublime, an aesthetic experience that "does violence to our imagination" and is marked by an initial perceptual "bewilderment" and "feeling of . . . inadequacy."[19] In Kant's account, when we are confronted with a sublime site—such as the "Big Hole" of the Kimberley mine—a contradictory process takes place characterized by simultaneous feelings of "displeasure" and "pleasure":[20]

> The mind feels itself moved in the representation of the sublime in nature, while in the aesthetic judgment on the beautiful in nature it is in calm contemplation. This movement (especially in its inception) may be compared to a vibration, i.e., to a rapidly alternating repulsion from and attraction to one and the same object. What is excessive for the imagination ... is as it were an *abyss,* in which it fears to lose itself, yet for reason's idea of the supersensible to produce such an effort of the imagination is not excessive but lawful, hence it is precisely as attractive as it was repulsive for mere sensibility.[21]

In Kant's account, the imagination faces an "abyss" that it fears accessing, but reason helps it to overcome this terror and to proceed nonetheless with its "effort," thus demonstrating reason's own "preeminence."[22]

While I have attempted to map out a related double movement of the blockage and opening of memory in the confrontation with the mine, the feeling of reason's superiority promised to us by Kant in the experience of the sublime does not describe well that confrontation with the terror of mass violence evoked by Sebald. Rather, the dark events of the twentieth century (as well as earlier periods) recounted insistently by Sebald across his oeuvre demonstrate the dangers intrinsic to the alleged superiority of reason and enlightenment. For instance, in its frequent passages discussing architectural modernity, *Austerlitz* tracks the absurd dialectic of security and destruction epitomized by the fortress. Visiting Fort Breendonk for the first time, a Nazi torture camp and the site where he will later sit reading Jacobson's book, the narrator "could make out no architectural plan, for its projections and indentations kept shifting, so far exceeding my comprehension that in the end I found myself unable to connect it with anything shaped by human civilization."[23] In passages such as these—and there are many—*Austerlitz* reveals a dialectic of enlightenment in which a seemingly "rational structure" (here, the fort) takes on the form of an "alien and crab-like creature" (the narrator's description of Breendonk) and the function of housing torturers and genocidal killers.[24] Although the narrator claims to be unable to connect Breendonk with any other human-made artifacts, in fact the narrative insistently performs just such connections, as I have attempted to show in tracing out a few of the many networks of association and intertextuality that constitute the very texture of Sebald's narrative.

These networks come together in what I would call a "multidirectional sublime."[25] In Sebald's multidirectional sublime, reason does not triumph where imagination fails. Rather, cultural memory regenerates itself at the site of historical loss; it does so not by fetishistically disavowing loss, but by inscribing loss in transnational and transcultural networks of association. These transversal forms of association create new memories even while marking those sites of loss, figured here by the South African mine, as irrecuperable. This sublime tension between unmappable loss and seemingly unending transcultural circuits of historical and memorial excess characterizes Sebald's aesthetic in *Austerlitz* and elsewhere.

Although defined by a restless transnationalism, the multidirectional sublime in *Austerlitz* is not an abstract cosmopolitanism that disregards its own situatedness. To the contrary, the text's sublime tension between loss and excess suggests something about the *implicated* subject position from which Sebald writes, that of the second-generation non-Jewish German. In an astute essay on post-Holocaust German authorship, the critic Julia Hell has tracked how crises of vision haunt a number of texts by male authors. As she puts it, "This is a literature that investigates the very conditions of possibility of post-Shoah culture in Germany by revolving obsessively around that which cannot be seen, can no longer be seen, could never be seen, but which still determines both German culture and its subjects." Although she does not discuss *Austerlitz,* Hell situates Sebald squarely in this tradition that "produces fascinating texts that conjure up powerful images produced by the vertigo of the male gaze—images that are always already reaching their vanishing point."[26] In *Austerlitz*—as in *The Rings of Saturn*—the South African mine comes to figure that vanishing point. In other words, I would argue, Sebald's answer to the dilemma of post-Holocaust authorship—the haunting force of a determinant history that cannot be perceived directly—is the multidirectional sublime: a detour around the void that does not turn away from implication and responsibility, but disperses them into more extensive networks of association in order to negotiate a new ethics of the gaze. This gaze is, in Hell's words, "neither voyeuristically aligned with the perpetrators of genocide, nor lost in unproblematized identifications."[27] In *Austerlitz,* the multidirectional sublime operates *horizontally*: the narrator's and narrative's lateral movements establish networks of complicity and connection while forgoing the *vertical* descent into the depths that might signal identification with either perpetrators or victims of genocide. As a mode of coming to terms with the recent German past, Sebald embraces implication against identification.

Between Occupation and Genocide

In constructing a multidirectional sublime, Sebald attempts to process what Gabriele Schwab would call the "haunting legacies" of growing up as a descendant of perpetrators. Engaging the traces of trauma passed down on the side of the victims (through the intertextual adaptation of Jacobson's text) as well as the traces of other histories of perpetration (through references to colonialism in Africa), Sebald's texts use the South African mine as a site for exploring "the paradox of writings from the crypt": the fact that the very "cryptic" sites that are sealed off from memory are the sites that carry traces of the violent past.[28] By activating the mine as knot of absent memory, Sebald maintains the hold of past violence on the present without allowing past losses to be too quickly "overcome" and "repaired." Yet his focus on an *abandoned* mine also implicitly situates violence itself in an earlier moment. That is, the haunting legacies live on, but present-day violence is largely missing from Sebald's account. In *Austerlitz,* at least, Sebald thus largely avoids a question that Schwab situates at the heart of attempts to confront transgenerational trauma: "How do we deal with a haunting past while simultaneously acting in the present, with its ongoing violence?"[29]

Nowhere is Schwab's question more relevant than in the context of the endemic Israeli-Palestinian conflict, in which, for better or worse, present-day violence is inextricable from the shadows cast by the Holocaust and by the Palestinian dispossession of 1948. Consider, for example, the barrage of memory conflict that accompanied Israel's December 2008–January 2009 offensive against Gaza, an assault that in three weeks killed fourteen hundred Palestinians, many of them civilians, and destroyed vast amounts of public infrastructure in a Gaza Strip already weakened by blockade. Thirteen Israelis were also killed during the conflict, ten soldiers (four as the result of friendly fire) and three civilians from southern Israeli towns that came under Palestinian rocket fire. The UN Fact Finding Mission that studied the conflict—headed by the respected Jewish South African jurist Richard Goldstone—found that violations of international humanitarian law had been committed by both sides, but the mission's 575-page report made it abundantly clear how asymmetrical those crimes were in their human impact.[30] The Gaza moment produced a proliferation of controversial Holocaust references and analogies that filtered the contemporary conflict through a historical matrix, from Caryl Churchill's *Seven Jewish Children: A Play for Gaza* (2009)—which in nine short minutes traced a harrowing genealogy from Nazi-occupied Europe to Israeli-occupied Palestine—to the case of the radical American sociology professor who sent an email to his undergraduate students just as the Israeli campaign was ending in which he declared that "Gaza is Israel's Warsaw."[31]

That same professorial email—which prompted a poorly handled and ultimately aborted campus inquiry—also included a photo essay taken from the website of well-known Israel critic and political scientist Norman Finkelstein, which, in the sociology professor's words, presented "parallel images of Nazis and Israelis."[32] This photo essay from the website of Finkelstein, who is the son of Holocaust survivors, circulated widely in the immediate aftermath of the Gaza crisis of early 2009. It begins with the title "Deutschland Uber Alles" and the explanatory subheading "THE GRANDCHILDREN OF HOLOCAUST SURVIVORS FROM WORLD WAR II ARE DOING TO THE PALESTINIANS EXACTLY WHAT WAS DONE TO THEM BY NAZI GERMANY." A vertical strip of images follows, with black-and-white photographs depicting Nazis and Jews on the left side of the page and color images of Israelis and Palestinians on the right. The images range from scenes of the construction of fences, walls, and camps, to depictions of prisoners behind barbed wire, confrontations of soldiers and civilians, and gruesome images of corpses. The images in each of the six sections of the photo essay abut each other without any gap. The lack of space between either the vertical or horizontal axes creates a continuous strip of images and suggests that the histories at stake blur into each other without remainder. While the histories of the Holocaust and Israel/Palestine are certainly proximate, both in terms of historical sequencing and psychic consequences for Israelis and Palestinians, Finkelstein's montage of images translates proximity into equation: the histories are depicted as both identical and strictly identified with each other. There is a long history of such equations, which have been used by all sides in the conflict, starting with the very years of World War II. But must the juxtaposition of these two histories always foster further conflict and competition, as the photo essay inevitably does?

A work by contemporary visual artist Alan Schechner suggests that it is possible to confront both haunting legacies and ongoing violence without either cutting the past off from the present or subsuming the present in a matrix defined uniquely by the past. When a practice of implication, analogy, and resemblance replaces identification, equation, and antithesis, new possibilities for recognizing complicity and responsibility and for forging solidarity can emerge.[33] Two of the images that appear in the Finkelstein photo essay reappear to different effect in the British/Israeli Schechner's *The Legacy of Abused Children: From Poland to Palestine*, a 2003 digitally altered photograph and DVD projection. The Finkelstein photo essay concludes by juxtaposing the frequently reproduced, Nazi-taken photograph of a boy in the Warsaw ghetto with his hands up—perhaps the most famous image from the Holocaust—with two photographs of Palestinian boys confronted by Israeli soldiers.[34] The message of the photo essay's juxtaposition is that the images can substitute for each other without remainder. In Schechner's work, these photographs are no longer simply juxtaposed, but set into motion. In the DVD projection, the camera zooms in on the Warsaw photograph to reveal that the boy, whose hands are empty in the original Stroop Report image, is holding a photograph. As the camera gets closer, it becomes clear that this is a photograph of a Palestinian boy, who has apparently wet his pants in fear, being carried away by soldiers. As the camera zooms in on this image, it becomes clear that the Palestinian boy is himself now holding a photograph as well: none other than the photo of the Warsaw boy.

In folding these two highly charged images into each other, Schechner could easily be described as using a strategy of equation similar to Finkelstein's. In his own account of the piece, he confirms this reading, but also adds nuance to this discourse by suggesting that it is not an equation of events that interests him, but rather the psychological condition of victimhood. As he writes,

> Whilst I have no interest in comparing the two events (The Holocaust and the Intifada) to see which was the most horrific ... I am interested in exploring the very real links between them.... In this project I am using the theory that abused children, unless treated, often become abusers themselves. By applying this to the current situation in Israel/Palestine where both Israelis and Palestinians are victims who replicate and repeat the abuse they have suffered[,] the possibility for constructing solutions to this terrible conflict become[s] more real.[35]

While offering, like the Finkelstein photo essay, a genealogical explanation for the current conflict—that is, one based on a sense that today's horrors are built on yesterday's victimization and passed on from generation to generation—Schechner reverses the affective charge from antagonistic competition to empathy. That is, the Finkelstein photo essay turns past victims into the ancestors of today's perpetrators and tends to blur the distinction between those past victims and today's perpetrators: "The grandchildren of Holocaust survivors ... are doing to the Palestinians *exactly* what was done to *them*" (emphasis added). Key here is not only the blatantly ahistorical "exactly," but also the ambiguous pronoun "them," which erases the distinction between the generations. Schechner, in contrast, might be seen to transfer the Holocaust suffering of the past onto *both* Israelis and Palestinians, who are portrayed in his comments equally as victims. If that were the case, then the work would seem to imply that solidarity *requires* a logic of equation, a requirement that stands in tension with the work's obvious desire to reach across differences. While preferable to competitive discourses, this vision would also risk downplaying historical heterogeneity, with uncertain effects for political mobilization and moral vision. In Iris Marion Young's terms, its promotion of "symmetrical reciprocity" would project a too simplistic vision of the world that reproduces the failure of recognition it sets out to oppose.[36]

However, if one reading of *The Legacy of Abused Children* suggests that it uses equation to promote a too-easy solidarity, a rereading of the work also suggests another possibility premised on the logic of implication instead of identification. Through its self-consciously manipulated form, *Legacy* undermines deterministic genealogical explanations that present an endless cycle of reciprocal violence and reproduce notions of two victim peoples. The digitally manipulated photographs ironize "realist" accounts of causality. Hence, even though the endless loop of the video suggests the circular nature of violence, it also subverts all claims to the morally justified originary position of victim that frequently justifies violence—and certainly does so in the Israeli case, where Holocaust memory has been mobilized for just this purpose.[37]

The particular nature of the photographic manipulation is also crucial in distinguishing *Legacy* from the photo essay: in placing a photograph in each boy's hand, Schechner transforms an image of absolute innocence and abject powerlessness into one of solidarity, defiance, and constrained agency.[38] If Finkelstein's photo essay seems to involve a logic of identification in which Holocaust imagery is appropriated for present-day purposes, this rereading of *The Legacy of Abused Children* suggests that analogy need not function in this way. We are not called to identify with the children's suffering as if it were our own or to see one form of suffering as identical with the other; rather, we are privy to a scene of commonality across and despite difference that is meant to move us, as the images themselves move. In deconstructing the claims to origin that underlie much of the rhetoric of the Israeli-Palestinian conflict (in terms of land claims and suffering), it offers the possibility that analogy can become part of a depropriative and transformative work of memory in which the juxtaposition of different histories reorganizes understanding of both. In opening up a potentially differentiated solidarity, Schechner's work begins to imagine the outlines of a new conception of justice—one in which transcultural comparison does not simply produce commensurability out of difference, but reconfigures the elements it brings together by revealing how they are *implicated* in each other.

Finkelstein and many others on both sides of the Israeli-Palestinian conflict who invoke the Holocaust attempt to reestablish a *known* frame in order to stake a claim in resolving the dispute or obtaining justice. The Nazi genocide is conventionally thought to exceed all "normal" conceptions of justice and to estrange familiar categories such as "guilt," "punishment," and even "the human." Yet, invocations of the genocide in the context of the Israeli-Palestinian conflict tend to reference the Holocaust as the bearer of shared norms of human rights and clear-cut moral distinctions.[39] In scenarios of equation, not only is the past anachronistically rewritten from the vantage point of a very different present (a rewriting that characterizes many acts of memory), but, as a result, the present loses its potential as a locus of novelty. That is, regardless of the complexities of the Nazi genocide as a historical phenomenon, the images of the genocide that circulate in the present reduce it—as well as the contemporary cases to which it is analogized—to a stereotypical scenario of good and evil, innocence and absolute power. A discourse based on clear-cut visions of victims and perpetrators or of innocence and guilt evacuates the political sphere of complexity and reduces it to a morality tale.

By juxtaposing the two images in a dynamic relation, by contrast, Schechner—who has served in the Israeli army—suggests the need to explore the mutual implication of subject positions and rival claims for justice. Even in the case of genocide, a seemingly exceptional situation of polarized innocence and guilt, the most thoughtful responses have been forced to reflect on uncomfortable questions of complicity and ambivalence in the "gray zones" created by extremist political movements.[40] As Susannah Radstone has argued in relation to the photo of the Warsaw ghetto boy, we need strategies of rereading the image that "wor[k] against the grain of identifications with 'pure' victimhood ... by undercutting the sense of an absolute distinction between 'good' and 'evil' and by proffering, or even foregrounding potential identifications with perpetration as well as with victimhood."[41] While there most certainly are victims to be acknowledged and perpetrators to be held responsible, a discourse that turns on absolutes of innocence and guilt can only anchor an absolutist, perhaps even apocalyptic politics. Schechner's *The Legacy of Abused Children* creates a multidirectional link between the Nazi genocide and the Israeli occupation, but it does so neither by collapsing the present into the past nor by a polemical equation of differently situated acts of violence. Rather, like Sebald, Schechner shows that the legacies of the past continue to haunt the contemporary moment; they continue to interpellate us without providing secure grounds for identification. But Schechner also takes a step beyond Sebald and reveals that confronting those legacies necessitates grappling with persistent, present-day violence that implicates us all.

Coda: Decentering Holocaust Memory

Ultimately, the goal of a radical democratic politics of multidirectional memory today is not only to move beyond discourses of equation or hierarchy, but also to displace the reductive, absolutist understanding of the Holocaust as a code for "good and evil" from the center of global memory politics. This task is time and place specific and demands a new vision of justice; critical intervention today is necessarily different from what it was, say, in the 1950s, when Holocaust memory was not yet as central to moral discourses. Today, even critical invocations of the Holocaust under the sign of equation keep in place Israel's most potent legitimating symbol: a narrative genealogy of ultimate victimization coupled with absolute innocence. The displacement called for today does not entail a removal of Holocaust memory from the public sphere, but rather a decentering of its abstract and reified form. Resources for such a decentering can be found in the archive of multidirectional memory. Decentering, in turn, does not mean relativization of the historical facts of the Nazi genocide. The persistence of Holocaust denial suggests that in certain arenas memory of the Holocaust can still play a progressive role.[42] But working through the implications and particularities of genocides needs to be separated from a discursive sacralization of the Holocaust that legitimates a politics of absolutism. Such a sacralization has become so powerful and simultaneously so empty of meaning that it seems to exert a magnetic force even on those who seek to oppose the politics it legitimates.

But it need not be so. In addition to earlier figures such as those, like Aimé Césaire, Charlotte Delbo, and W. E. B. Du Bois, who were central to *Multidirectional Memory,* and contemporary figures such as Sebald and Schechner, we can also take inspiration from the most prominent spokesperson from the Palestinian diaspora, the late Edward Said. Said repeatedly refused "morally to equate mass extermination with mass dispossession" and challenged Palestinians to recognize the specificity of the Holocaust.[43] He also frequently made reference to Palestinians as "the victims of the victims."[44] While this formulation sounds at first like a pure example of equation and symmetry, I do not think he was suggesting that victimization leads inevitably to further identical forms of victimization. Rather, Said meant that Israelis and Palestinians have been brought together by the contingencies of history, by logics only partly in their control. They occupy a shared, yet divided place—both a geographical territory and a geography of memory. This place is not, today, a site of symmetry and peace—it is a site of asymmetry and violence. Transforming that condition will take more than the work of multidirectional memory, but without changing the way we think about the past, it will be difficult to imagine an alternative future.

Notes

1. See Michael Rothberg, *Multidirectional Memory: Remembering the Holocaust in the Age of Decolonization* (Stanford, CA: Stanford University Press, 2009).

2. Walter Benn Michaels, "Plots Against America: Neoliberalism and Antiracism," *American Literary History* 18, no. 2 (Summer 2006): 289–90. See also my response, "Against Zero-Sum Logic: A Response to Walter Benn Michaels," *American Literary History* 18, no. 2 (Summer 2006): 303–11. Michaels's passage can be found in almost identical form in *The Trouble With Diversity: How We Learned to Love Identity and Ignore Inequality* (New York: Metropolitan Books, 2006), 55–56.

3. See Françoise Lionnet and Shu-mei Shih, eds., *Minor Transnationalism* (Durham, NC: Duke University Press, 2005).

4. For "prosthetic" and "postmemorial" approaches to the past that are akin to the multidirectional paradigm sketched here, see Alison Landsberg, *Prosthetic Memory: The Transformation of American Remembrance in the Age of Mass Culture* (New York: Columbia University Press, 2004); Marianne Hirsch, *Family Frames: Photography, Narrative, and Postmemory* (Cambridge, MA: Harvard

University Press, 1997); Marianne Hirsch, "The Generation of Postmemory," *Poetics Today* 29, no. 1 (2008): 103–28.

5. W. G. Sebald, *Austerlitz*, trans. Anthea Bell (New York: Modern Library, 2001), 296–97.

6. In the voluminous and rapidly expanding literature on Sebald, only a very small number of critics has considered the significance of Jacobson's text or of the South African mine in Sebald's work, and none has made it central to their reading of the novel or of Sebald's oeuvre. For the exceptions, see Stephen Clingman, *The Grammar of Identity: Transnational Fiction and the Nature of the Boundary* (New York: Oxford University Press, 2009), 203–4; Richard Crownshaw, "Reconsidering Postmemory: Photography, the Archive, and Post-Holocaust memory in W.G. Sebald's *Austerlitz*," *Mosaic* 37, no. 4 (2004): 215–36, esp. 234–35; Judith Ryan, "Fulgurations: Sebald and Surrealism," *Germanic Review* 82, no. 3 (2007): 227–49, esp. 244–46. While I have learned from all of these critics, none of them pursues the same network of associations I highlight here.

7. Sebald, *Austerlitz*, 297.

8. "To many thinkers, coal mining represents an anti-aesthetic abyss, an impossible challenge to conventional notions of beauty and art." William Thesing, "Introduction," in *Caverns of Night: Coal Mines in Art, Literature, and Film*, ed. William Thesing (Columbia: University of South Carolina Press, 2000), xiii.

9. Sebald, *Austerlitz*, 150, emphasis added.

10. Dan Jacobson, *Heshel's Kingdom* (Evanston, IL: Northwestern University Press, 1998), xi.

11. Sebald, *Austerlitz*, 99.

12. Ann Rigney, "Plenitude, Scarcity and the Circulation of Cultural Memory," *Journal of European Studies* 35, no. 1 (2005): 12.

13. This performative model is also close to the alternative Rigney offers to the "plenitude and loss" model: "a social-constructivist model that takes as its starting point the idea that memories of a shared past are collectively constructed and reconstructed in the present rather than resurrected from the past" ("Plenitude," 14). Indeed, in a personal communication, Rigney told me that she also now prefers to talk of performativity rather than social constructivism.

14. Sebald, *Austerlitz*, 6.

15. Ibid., 5–6.

16. Jacobson, *Heshel's Kingdom*, 151; cf. 143, 228–30.

17. Sebald, *Austerlitz*, 6.

18. W. G. Sebald, *The Rings of Saturn*, trans. Michael Hulse (New York: New Directions Press, 1998), 90–92.

19. Immanuel Kant, *Critique of the Power of Judgment*, ed. Paul Guyer, trans. Paul Guyer and Eric Matthews (New York: Cambridge University Press, 2000), 136.

20. Ibid., 141.

21. Ibid., 141–42, emphasis added.

22. Ibid., 142.

23. Sebald, *Austerlitz*, 20.

24. Ibid., 22.

25. The multidirectional sublime is a version of the historical sublime. See Ann Rigney's discussion of the historical sublime in *Imperfect Histories: The Elusive Past and the Legacy of Romantic Historicism* (Ithaca, NY: Cornell University Press, 2001), esp. 114–20.

26. As Hell also claims, such literature emerges from "an aesthetic project driven by the craving for the visible," but for which "visual mastery does not exist ... because this subject of the gaze is itself the object of another gaze," frequently a Jewish gaze imagined as accusatory. The possibility that Sebald (or his narrators) is haunted by an accusatory Jewish gaze deserves further discussion, which would go beyond the bounds of this chapter. See Julia Hell, "Eyes Wide Shut: German Post-Holocaust Authorship," *New German Critique* 88 (Winter 2003): 35–36.

27. Ibid., 34.

28. On the legacies of perpetration and the figure of the crypt, see Gabriele Schwab, *Haunting Legacies: Violent Histories and Transgenerational Trauma* (New York: Columbia University Press,

2010). For Schwab's brief discussion of *Austerlitz*, which focuses on the eponymous Jewish protagonist and not the non-Jewish narrator, see pp. 49–51.

29. Ibid., 2.

30. *Human Rights in Palestine and Other Occupied Arab Territories: Report of the United Nations Fact Finding Mission on the Gaza Conflict* (United Nations Human Rights Council, 15 September 2009). In a strange turnaround (and after enormous international and local pressure), Goldstone has backed away from certain aspects of the report—even though its main findings remain incontestable.

31. For an extended discussion of the case of the American sociology professor, see Michael Rothberg, "From Gaza to Warsaw: Mapping Multidirectional Memory," in *"Transcultural Negotiations of Holocaust Memory," special issue, Criticism* 53, no. 4 (2011): 523–48.

32. Although the photo essay is not signed by Finkelstein, it can be found on his "official" website: http://www.normanfinkelstein.com/deutschland-uber-alles/.

33. Kaja Silverman defines analogy as distinct from identity and antithesis: "An analogy brings two or more things together on the basis of their lesser or greater resemblance.... [T]hese couplings neutralize the two principles by means of which we are accustomed to think: identity and antithesis." See Kaja Silverman, *Flesh of My Flesh* (Stanford, CA: Stanford University Press, 2009), 173.

34. On the Warsaw Ghetto boy, see Richard Raskin, *A Child at Gunpoint: A Case Study in the Life of Photo* (Aarhus: Aarhus University Press, 2004); Frédéric Rousseau, *L'enfant juif de Varsovie: Histoire d'une photographie* (Paris: Seuil, 2009); Marianne Hirsch, "Nazi Photographs in Post-Holocaust Art" and "Projected Memory: Holocaust Photographs in Personal and Public Fantasy," in *Acts of Memory: Cultural Recall in the Present*, ed. Mieke Bal, Jonathan Crewe, and Leo Spitzer (Hanover, NH: Dartmouth University Press, 1999), 3–23.

35. Cited from Alan Schechner's website, www.dottycommies.com (accessed 28 August 2009). This same piece has also been incorporated into a collaborative performance called DIALOG, created with the Palestinian artist Rana Bishara. On DIALOG, see Alessandro Imperato, "The Dialogics of Chocolate: A Silent DIALOG on Israeli-Palestinian Politics," in *Global and Local Art Histories*, ed. Celina Jeffries and Gregory Minissale (Cambridge: Cambridge Scholars, 2007), 283–97. On *Legacy*, see Richard Raskin, *A Child at Gunpoint*; Adrian Parr, "Deterritorialising the Holocaust," in *Deleuze and the Contemporary World*, ed. Ian Buchanan and Adrian Parr (Edinburgh: Edinburgh University Press, 2006), 125–45. Lutz Koepnick includes a brief but excellent discussion of Schechner in "Photographs and Memories," *South Central Review* 21, no. 1 (2004): 94–129. Koepnick also discusses a different work—the well-known and controversial *It's the Real Thing (Self Portrait at Buchenwald)*, which, although it also uses digital manipulation and references Holocaust memory, is otherwise quite different from *Legacy*. Koepnick writes, "What Schechner's self portrait seeks to exhibit is the failure of the photographic image not only to record reality reliably and to authenticate memory, but also to address the shocks and ruptures associated with traumatic experience" (96). *Legacy*, in contrast, seeks to refunction photography so that it can once again confront traumatic experience, although not in a mode that privileges authenticity.

36. See Iris Marion Young, *Intersecting Voices: Dilemmas of Gender, Political Philosophy, and Public Policy* (Princeton, NJ: Princeton University Press, 1997), 38–59.

37. In setting the two images into motion, Schechner's work might be understood to take part in what Ariella Azoulay calls the "civil contract of photography." In a passage that resonates with this artwork, Azoulay writes, "The photograph bears the seal of the photographic event, and reconstructing this event requires more than just identifying what is shown in the photograph. One needs to stop looking at the photograph and instead start watching it. The verb 'to watch' is usually used for regarding phenomena or moving pictures. It entails dimensions of time and movement that need to be reinscribed in the interpretation of the still photographic image. When and where the subject of the photograph is a person who has suffered some form of injury, a viewing of the photograph that reconstructs the photographic situation and allows a reading of the injury inflicted on others becomes a civic skill, not an exercise in aesthetic appreciation. This

skill is activated the moment one grasps that citizenship is not merely a status, a good, or a piece of private property possessed by the citizen, but rather a tool of a struggle or an obligation to others to struggle against injuries inflicted on those others, citizen and noncitizen alike—others who are governed along with the spectator." See Ariella Azoulay, *The Civil Contract of Photography* (New York: Zone Books, 2008), 14.

38. As Richard Raskin writes, "Schechner presents the two children as calling out to the viewer that each of them protests against the suffering inflicted on the other" (*A Child at Gunpoint*, 167).

39. This point is made nicely in a different context by Sarah De Mul. See her "The Holocaust as a Paradigm for the Congo Atrocities: Adam Hochschild's *King Leopold's Ghost*," in "Transcultural Negotiations of Holocaust Memory," special issue, *Criticism* 53, no. 4 (2011): 587–606.

40. Primo Levi inaugurated thinking about the "gray zone" in an essay of that name from his last collection, *The Drowned and the Saved* (New York: Vintage, 1989).

41. Susannah Radstone, "Social Bonds and Psychical Order: Testimonies," *Cultural Values* 5, no. 1 (January 2001): 65. Radstone also makes productive use of Levi's conception of the "gray zone."

42. Joseph Massad has provocatively argued that Holocaust deniers in the Arab world are "objectively" Zionists, because their irrational insistence on negating an incontrovertible historical fact implicitly and inadvertently pays tribute to the logic by which the fact of the Holocaust justifies the establishment of a Jewish state on Palestinian land. See Joseph Massad, "Semites and Anti-Semites, That Is the Question," *Al-Ahram Weekly On-Line*, no. 720 (9–15 December 2004). http://weekly.ahram.org.eg/2004/720/op63.htm (accessed 24 June 2009).

43. Edward Said, *The End of the Peace Process: Oslo and After* (New York: Vintage, 2001), 208. On Said, Jewishness, and Holocaust memory, see Gil Z. Hochberg, "Edward Said: 'The Last Jewish Intellectual': On Identity, Alterity, and the Politics of Memory," *Social Text* 24, no. 2 (2006): 47–65.

44. David Barsamian and Edward Said, *Culture and Resistance: Conversation with Edward Said* (Cambridge, MA: South End Press, 2003), 147.

Bibliography

Azoulay, Ariella. *The Civil Contract of Photography.* New York: Zone Books, 2008.
Barsamian, David, and Edward Said. *Culture and Resistance: Conversation with Edward Said.* Cambridge, MA: South End Press, 2003.
Clingman, Stephen. *The Grammar of Identity: Transnational Fiction and the Nature of the Boundary.* New York: Oxford University Press, 2009.
Crownshaw, Richard. "Reconsidering Postmemory: Photography, the Archive, and Post-Holocaust memory in W.G. Sebald's *Austerlitz*." *Mosaic* 37, no. 4 (2004): 215–36.
De Mul, Sarah. "The Holocaust as a Paradigm for the Congo Atrocities: Adam Hochschild's *King Leopold's Ghost*." In "Transcultural Negotiations of Holocaust Memory," special issue, *Criticism* 53, no. 4 (2011): 587–606.
Hell, Julia. "Eyes Wide Shut: German Post-Holocaust Authorship." *New German Critique* 88 (Winter 2003): 9–36.
Hirsch, Marianne. *Family Frames: Photography, Narrative, and Postmemory.* Cambridge, MA: Harvard University Press, 1997.
———. "The Generation of Postmemory." *Poetics Today* 29, no. 1 (2008): 103–28.
———. "Nazi Photographs in Post-Holocaust Art" and "Projected Memory: Holocaust Photographs in Personal and Public Fantasy." In *Acts of Memory: Cultural Recall in the Present,* ed. Mieke Bal, Jonathan Crewe, and Leo Spitzer, 3–23. Hanover: Dartmouth University Press, 1999.

Hochberg, Gil Z. "Edward Said: 'The Last Jewish Intellectual': On Identity, Alterity, and the Politics of Memory." *Social Text* 24, no. 2 (2006): 47–65.

Human Rights in Palestine and Other Occupied Arab Territories: Report of the United Nations Fact Finding Mission on the Gaza Conflict. United Nations Human Rights Council, 15 September 2009.

Imperato, Alessandro. "The Dialogics of Chocolate: A Silent DIALOG on Israeli-Palestinian Politics." In *Global and Local Art Histories,* ed. Celina Jeffries and Gregory Minissale, 283–97. Cambridge: Cambridge Scholars, 2007.

Jacobson, Dan. *Heshel's Kingdom.* Evanston, IL: Northwestern University Press, 1998.

Kant, Immanuel. *Critique of the Power of Judgment.* Edited by Paul Guyer. Translated by Paul Guyer and Eric Matthews. New York: Cambridge University Press, 2000.

Koepnick, Lutz. "Photographs and Memories." *South Central Review* 21, no. 1 (2004): 94–129.

Landsberg, Alison. *Prosthetic Memory: The Transformation of American Remembrance in the Age of Mass Culture.* New York: Columbia University Press, 2004.

Levi, Primo. *The Drowned and the Saved.* New York: Vintage, 1989.

Lionnet, Françoise, and Shu-mei Shih, eds. *Minor Transnationalism.* Durham, NC: Duke University Press, 2005.

Massad, Joseph. "Semites and Anti-Semites, That Is the Question." *Al-Ahram Weekly On-Line,* no. 720 (9–15 December 2004). http://weekly.ahram.org.eg/2004/720/op63.htm (accessed 24 June 2009).

Michaels, Walter Benn. "Plots Against America: Neoliberalism and Antiracism." *American Literary History* 18, no. 2 (Summer 2006): 288–302.

———. *The Trouble With Diversity: How We Learned to Love Identity and Ignore Inequality.* New York: Metropolitan Books, 2006.

Parr, Adrian. "Deterritorialising the Holocaust." In *Deleuze and the Contemporary World,* ed. Ian Buchanan and Adrian Parr, 125–45. Edinburgh: Edinburgh University Press, 2006.

Radstone, Susannah. "Social Bonds and Psychical Order: Testimonies." *Cultural Values* 5, no. 1 (January 2001): 59–78.

Raskin, Richard. *A Child at Gunpoint: A Case Study in the Life of Photo.* Aarhus: Aarhus University Press, 2004.

Rigney, Ann. *Imperfect Histories: The Elusive Past and the Legacy of Romantic Historicism.* Ithaca, NY: Cornell University Press, 2001.

———. "Plenitude, Scarcity and the Circulation of Cultural Memory." *Journal of European Studies* 35, no. 1 (2005): 11–28.

Rothberg, Michael. "Against Zero-Sum Logic: A Response to Walter Benn Michaels." *American Literary History* 18, no. 2 (Summer 2006): 303–11.

———. "From Gaza to Warsaw: Mapping Multidirectional Memory." In "Transcultural Negotiations of Holocaust Memory," special issue, *Criticism* 53, no. 4 (2011): 523–48.

———. *Multidirectional Memory: Remembering the Holocaust in the Age of Decolonization.* Stanford, CA: Stanford University Press, 2009.

Rousseau, Frédéric. *L'enfant juif de Varsovie: Histoire d'une photographie.* Paris: Seuil, 2009.

Ryan, Judith. "Fulgurations: Sebald and Surrealism." *Germanic Review* 82, no. 3 (2007): 227–49.

Said, Edward. *The End of the Peace Process: Oslo and After.* New York: Vintage, 2001.

Schwab, Gabriele. *Haunting Legacies: Violent Histories and Transgenerational Trauma.* New York: Columbia University Press, 2010.

Sebald, W. G. *Austerlitz.* Translated by Anthea Bell. New York: Modern Library, 2001.

———. *The Rings of Saturn.* Translated by Michael Hulse. New York: New Directions, 1998.

Silverman, Kaja. *Flesh of My Flesh.* Stanford, CA: Stanford University Press, 2009.

Thesing, William. "Introduction." In *Caverns of Night: Coal Mines in Art, Literature, and Film,* ed. William Thesing. Xi–xxii. Columbia: University of South Carolina Press, 2000.

Young, Iris Marion. *Intersecting Voices: Dilemmas of Gender, Political Philosophy, and Public Policy.* Princeton, NJ: Princeton University Press, 1997.

Section IV

THE POETICS OF THE GLOBAL EVENT
A Critical View

CHAPTER 12

Pain and Pleasure in Poetic Representations of the Holocaust

RINA DUDAI

Little by little my eyes became accustomed to the dark in the new video art section at the Metropolitan Museum in New York.[1] I perceived the flickering figure projected on two adjacent screens like a pair of wide-open eyes staring at me. The voices emanating from the two screens were monotonous and dry, as if delivering a harrowing testimony out of Claude Lanzmann's *Shoah*. Something compelled me to watch it, not knowing yet what the film was about. A number of people were bearing witness. Yet, this could not be another testimonial film on the Holocaust, I said to myself, for among the characters in the exhibited film were young and old, dark and fair-skinned people, who could not be easily associated with the familiar profile of Holocaust survivors. By now I was quite curious. These people spoke alternately in Polish and English, with heavy Polish accents. Could this be yet another Holocaust testimony? Or am I being deceived by some curious phenomenon? The video art I was watching was *Spielberg's List*,[2] by Omer Fast.[3]

In 2003 Fast traveled to Krakow, the Polish city that ten years earlier, in 1993, had served as the setting for Steven Spielberg's film *Schindler's List*. In his video Fast interviewed the Polish extras who had played Jews and Nazis in Spielberg's film and who, by *acting* the atrocity, witnessed it as a second-order experience.

What grabbed me during this unexpected viewing of Omer Fast's film has to do with the position of the witness carrying the memory of the trauma of the Holocaust as a second- and even third-order experience. For neither I, as an accidental viewer of Fast's film, nor the extras who took part in Steven Spiel-

---

Notes for this section begin on page 260.

berg's film had gone through the horrific experience of the Holocaust, and yet, from the moment we were exposed to it by means of artistic media, we became carriers of a different type of memory, which differs from the historical declarative memory of the Holocaust. A poetic text that copes with the memory of this difficult experience creates a highly charged encounter between the real experience and the viewers who perceive this experience through its lens. In such an encounter, I contend, a fierce and complex emotion arises, combining pain with aesthetic pleasure. This powerful and complex emotion, so I would like to argue, enthralls a great variety of audiences and enables it to exist in the arena of a global collective memory, even among people who have not directly experienced the events.

In his article "On the Social Construction of Moral Universals: The 'Holocaust' from War Crime to Trauma Drama,"[4] Jeffrey C. Alexander wonders how a particular historical event like the Holocaust, an event marked by racial and ethnic hatred, turns into a symbol of general human suffering and an opportunity for critical examination of contemporary global conflicts: "Now free floating rather than situated—universal rather than particular—this traumatic event vividly 'lives' in the memories of contemporaries whose parents and grandparents never felt themselves even remotely related to it."[5] Alexander further argues that for a public to sense a trauma that it did not experience, two things are required: a symbolic addition, along with psychological identification with the event. Alexander speaks of an *interpretive grid*[6] through which all the facts concerning the trauma are emotionally, cognitively, and morally mediated. Alexander points out two types of narrative that allow this symbolic process to occur: the progressive and the tragic. The first is a narrative of redemption, in which the trauma that was produced by the social evil of Nazism is defeated by excising evil, thus turning it into something of the past and creating a new world that is devoid of such evil forces. Borrowing from literary theory, Alexander then continues the developmental trajectory of the symbolization by replacing the progressive narrative with the tragic one. This narrative enables a symbolic extension that serves as a bridge to the universal understanding of evil. Rather than allocating attention to a forward-looking construction, based on the illusion of removing evil, as presented in the progressive narrative, the tragic narrative addresses itself to recognizing the nature of evil without resolving it. This literary symbolic extension creates opportunities to observe trauma by means of emotional identification of the experience with the suffering victim. Specifically, Alexander addresses Aristotle's concept of catharsis, which requires the spectator of a tragedy drama to identify with the characters, experience their suffering, and learn about the real reasons for their deaths.[7] We seek catharsis, Alexander claims, because our identification with the tragic narrative compels us to confront the forces of evil and darkness within ourselves too, not only in others. We pity the victims of the trauma and identify with them and with their bitter fate. But the identification with the victims and empathy toward them is not what turns the experience of trauma in tragedy into something meaningful, as much as the centrality of ethical responsibility that it implies.

In this chapter I seek to apply Alexander's interpretive grid to probe the emotional dimension of the traumatic experience of the Holocaust in representations of this memory. I will ask what kind of emotion arises in spectators in an encounter with evil mediated through poetic language, and what is so appealing to such diverse audiences that it enables the global dissemination of this memory? Does Aristotelian catharsis always take place, and can this explain the global receptiveness to the Holocaust?

I would like to draw attention to another type of emotion that does not stem from catharsis, a complex of compassion and dread, but rather of pain and pleasure. The welter of contradictory emotions that arises in response to earth-shattering events is not a trivial matter. In his *Poetics* Aristotle was the first to formulate the complex of cathartic feelings of compassion and dread. On the other hand, the emotional complex that involves feelings of pleasure and pain was first described by Plato in his *Laws*[8] and in the dialogue *Philebus,* where Socrates speaks of an experience in which "[p]ains and pleasures exist side by side; opposite as they are, we experience them simultaneously, one beside the other."[9]

In the course of history, this emotional complex system received different elaborations, especially in the context of extreme experiences, that of the sublime, for example. In the current chapter I will attempt to explain the appearance of pain and pleasure arising in the spectators who encounter poetic texts that deal with the Holocaust, which many researchers have characterized as exhibiting features of the negative sublime. I would like to propose an explanation that will connect this distinctive feature of representation of the Holocaust—the negative sublime—with the feeling of *delight* of which Edmund Burke[10] speaks while referring to the sublime, alongside the psychic phenomenon of *jouissance,* as described by Lacan[11] and Barthes.[12] By establishing this connection, I hope to argue that within the feelings that arise from the poetic representation of the Holocaust experience, another unconscious experience is activated, which "invites" the spectator to dwell in it. This is an intrinsic experience of taking pleasure in pain, and it goes far beyond the identification with the suffering of others. It is this association, between the representation of the memory of trauma—most conspicuously expressed in the negative sublime—and taking pleasure in pain through the revelation of *delight* and *jouissance,* that can impact a great many audiences and has the potential to explain the Holocaust's global dissemination.[13] In the ensuing discussion, I will examine how the paradoxical feelings of pain and pleasure receive their cultural-developmental embodiment in a variety of poetic devices, which I shall illustrate through the example of Steven Spielberg's *Schindler's List* and Omer Fast's video art installation *Spielberg's List*. Finally, I will address the question of the emotions arising in the act of spectatorship of artistic representations of the Holocaust—pain and pleasure—as well as the ensuing ethical stance.

Delight: Experiencing the Sublime from Pain to Pleasure

Philosophers,[14] literary critics,[15] historians,[16] and psychologists[17] all address the presence of a sense of *excess* with respect to memory materials related to the Holocaust. At the heart of this experience something always remains in excess that is obscure, undecipherable, and unrepresentable. The singularity of the event, the problems of representation occasioned by its magnitude, and the subject's position vis-à-vis this magnitude, manifested in his or her inability to comprehend and contain it, all raise the possibility of addressing the event of the Holocaust in terms of *the negative sublime*.[18]

All the scholars who have dealt with the sublime agree that the main power of the sublime lies in its tremendous emotional effect on the addressee.[19] Throughout the history of the discussion of the sublime, a number of them have probed deeply into the paradox of pain and pleasure that arises in the face of the sublime.

In his essay on philosophical inquiry,[20] Edmund Burke was the first to focus profoundly on the essence of this emotional experience. The sublime, in his view, is the reason for the most intense feeling that the psyche can endure. This emotion breaks out from the irrational and disharmonic dimension of the experience of the sublime, but most of all, it arouses a sense of existence:

> Whatever is fitted in any sort to excite the ideas of pain, and danger, that is to say, whatever is in any sort terrible, or is conversant about terrible objects, or operates in a manner analogous to terror, is a source of the sublime.... When danger or pain press too near, they are incapable of giving any delight, and are simply terrible; but at certain distances and with certain modifications they may be, and they are delightful, as we every day experience.[21]

Burke argues here that from a certain distance, which enables one to remain protected from the destructive orbit of the sublime, one may experience a type of pain that can also cause delight. This delight arises from the recognition of a sense of existence, despite the proximity of death. Burke speaks here of an aesthetic distance that allows the processing of emotion and prevents being swept away and drawn into an experience of terror and dread. What produces this distance is a kind of aesthetic refinement, which allows the experience to be experienced from the inside and the outside simultaneously, as both pain and pleasure.

Several years later, Immanuel Kant[22] described the sublime as a tremendous, infinite, and incommensurable being, which cannot be grasped or contained by the senses or faculties of the imagination. Kant, like Burke, saw the sublime as a phenomenon in which pain and pleasure appear as a mix of emotions that arise as a result of contending with the sublime:

> Burke, who deserves to be called the foremost author in this method of treatment, deduces, on these lines, 'that the feeling of the sublime is grounded on the impulse towards self-preservation and on *fear*, i.e. on a pain, which, since it does not go the

length of disordering the bodily parts, calls forth movements which, as they clear the vessels, whether fine or gross, of a dangerous and troublesome encumbrance, are capable of producing delight; not pleasure but a sort of delightful horror, a sort of tranquility tinged with terror'.[23]

However, in distinction from Burke's static conception—the freezing of psychic activity in the face of the sublime—Kant's conception of this emotional experience is dynamic—feeling in motion. The movement of the psyche arises from a situation of distress and pain, in which the sensorium and the imagination break down and are not capable of adequately representing the sublime. The inability of these sensory and perceptual systems to represent the sublime causes the psyche to turn to the rational system, which alone is capable of containing the sublime in an abstract and generalized way. The confrontation with terror, according to Kant, forces us to muster all of our resources of being, while revealing powers we did not know we had. When the senses and imagination fail to represent the phenomenon, the psyche manages to represent it through a rational idea. The pleasure embedded in the sublime, according to Kant, results from the victory of the rational mind over the senses and the imagination. This is a decisive victory in light of the failure of these systems to contend with the sublime. The movement that Kant presents, therefore, is a unidirectional movement, in which one system fails and the other systems redeems the psyche from this failure and distress.

We can thus see that both Burke and Kant describe the complex feeling of pain and pleasure sensed in experiencing the sublime as following a *linear trajectory,* beginning with the intense arousal of a sense of distress and pain through the engendering of a sense of delight deriving from a powerful sense of being, despite the threat of terror embedded in the nature of the sublime.[24]

The revival of the aesthetics of the sublime in recent years is attributed to Lyotard,[25] who responds to the Kantian sublime on the one hand and to the postmodern condition and the role of the avant-garde artist on the other. Lyotard has dwelled on the limits of human capacity to accord presence to the sublime. Yet his focus on this lack of ability, while returning to Burke's point of departure, is more complex. For Lyotard, the sublime marks the boundaries of human understanding, and this is the aspect he wishes to emphasize in connection with the postmodern world. The limits of understanding are a result of an incessant vacillation between different capacities, including the capacity for rational thought. This vacillation testifies to the desire to grasp reality and understand it, which ultimately remains unsatisfied. Lyotard denies the possibility of understanding the sublime totally. Total comprehension, in his view, leads to terror. His philosophy assigns a special place for silence. Silence is testimony to inevitable gaps in our understanding, gaps that should be respected rather than bridged. For him, Auschwitz is this type of gap for which silence is the only fitting response, and therefore it can be characterized as a case of the sublime. Lyotard's aesthetic of the sublime thus seeks to signify that which cannot be represented due to its recognition of the painful experience of a damaged reality: "The postmodern would be ... that which searches for new presentations, not in order to enjoy them but in order to impart a stronger sense of the un-presentable."[26] Lyotard's philosophical move decouples the immediate linear connection between pain and pleasure. He seeks to define a space of suspension, suspension in pain, through which he hopes to attain a never-ending series of new linguistic representations for the experience of the sublime, forever admitting their inadequacy to fill the semiotic-emotional gap.

The subject's experience of shock, pain, and terror serves as the common denominator to all the critics' conceptualizations of the sublime throughout the history of its development. If these philosophers differ from one another, it is in the value they attribute to this intense emotional experience. Longinus sees the intense emotions, produced through the sublime oratory, as having a linguistic practical value, which is enlisted as a ploy to persuade the subject. Burke, on the other hand, relates the value of this intense emotion to the sense of existence in the world and to survival. By arousing the sense of delight originating in pain, contends Burke, the sensitivity to the world and the sense of being are enhanced. Kant accords this emotion a rational value, emanating from the impulse of reason to understand unexplained natural phenomena. Finally, Lyotard views this emotion as having a moral value, as it is the cause of sensing the limits of human capacity.

Jouissance: The Cycle of Pain and Pleasure

As we have seen, for Lyotard, the sublime is an extreme experience rooted in the actual reality of terror, which is accompanied by an intense feeling seeking for its new representation in language.[27] Lyotard uses his concept of the *differend* to conceptualize this semiotic take on the sublime:

> In the *differend,* something "asks" to be put into phrases, and suffers from the wrong of not being able to be put into phrases right away. This is when the human beings who thought they could use language as an instrument of communication learn through the feeling of pain which accompanies silence and of pleasure which accompanies the invention of a new idiom, that they are summoned by language, not to augment to their profit the quality of information existing idioms, but to recognize that what remains to be phrased exceeds what they can presently phrase, and that they must be allowed to institute idioms which do not yet exist.[28]

The source of the feeling of pleasure and pain is the melancholy experience of the failure of representation, the awareness of the unbridgeable gap between the experience and its representation. Something will always remain in excess, which is incapable of being represented, but becomes thoroughly and powerfully present through its absence. The trajectory of the relationship between pain and pleasure is described here as following a circular route, guided by the insistent, almost desperate repetition of the attempt to represent the very excess which is by definition inconceivable and unrepresentable. This structure brings to mind the psychic phenomenon of which Lacan speaks—*jouissance*—which he distinguishes from the pleasure principle. Freud's pleasure principle tends toward release of tension and homeostasis. As opposed to this, Lacan's *jouissance* resides beyond the pleasure principle, and is tied to the real and to repetition.[29] *Jouissance* is the excess, the superfluity that is never satisfied, because something always escapes representation. In Evans's glossary of Lacanian terms, he defines *jouissance* as follows:

> In 1960 Lacan developed his classic opposition between *jouissance* and pleasure. The pleasure principle functions as a limit to enjoyment. At the same time, the subject constantly attempts to go beyond the pleasure principle. However, the result of transgressing the pleasure principle is not more pleasure, but pain, and this painful pleasure Lacan calls Jouissance; jouissance is suffering.[30]

Lacan speaks of *jouissance* in the same breath he speaks of the symptom. The symptom, which generally causes suffering, and is therefore to be removed, insistently retains its hold on the subject and does not permit its removal. At the level of consciousness the subject recognizes the pain that his symptom causes him, but at the unconscious level he does not allow himself and is not ready to be released of it. Thus it appears, from Lacan's teaching, that the stubborn retention of a symptom that causes pain is simultaneous evidence of the marker of taking pleasure in pain. The symptom, says Jacques-Alain Miller,[31] is stubborn and takes hold of the subject because of the unconscious quality of the pleasure; hence, it is defined as *jouissance*. The relentless retention of the pleasure from the painful symptom negates the possibility of processing it and traps the subject in a melancholy state, which has no end.

In his book *The Pleasure of the Text*,[32] Roland Barthes develops Lacan's concept of *jouissance* not as a psychological phenomenon, but rather as a textual phenomenon to which the reader responds. Barthes distinguishes between two types of text: texts that arouse pleasure, and texts that arouse *jouissance*. A text that arouses pleasure is a text that does not transgress its boundaries and produces a relaxed or comfortable effect as it is being read. However, a text that produces *jouissance* imposes a sense of loss and disturbance on the reader: "With the writer of bliss[33] (and his reader) begins the untenable text, the impossible text. This text is outside pleasure, outside criticism … [it] affirms the void of bliss."[34]

As opposed to Lacan's *jouissance,* which is an unconscious experience of one's encounter with the world, *jouissance* according to Barthes is a conscious psychic experience of one's encounter with the text. Following his conceptualization, a text will produce *jouissance* when an experience of writing or reading disabuses the writer or reader of his illusions and of the false ideologies that shape his world. The experience of writing/reading confronts the subject with the chaotic world of the "real," which cannot be represented. The *jouissance* text, according to Barthes, is experienced in a conscious and informed manner, and produces a melancholic understanding of the repeated failure to represent the broken, uncertain world.[35]

I would now like to place the Lacanian intrapersonal conceptualization of *jouissance* in an interpersonal space. When the source of the Lacanian *jouissance* is the gazing at the suffering of others out of compulsive and unconscious identification with the other, the distinction, as well as the psychological distance between self and other, disappears. The resulting effect is a kind of fascination through pleasure and pain. Gazing at suffering by means of a *jouissance* text, according to Barthes, produces a new type of spectatorship, which involves a dimension of empathic attention coupled with critical insights. This is what LaCapra calls "the empathic unsettlement."[36] This kind of emotion does not allow the closure of discourse, which subverts harmonization and elation. LaCapra searches for the stylistic influences that produce "empathic unsettlement," which he counterposes to the experience of the reappearance of trauma as unconscious *jouissance*.[37]

Analysis of Steven Spielberg's *Schindler's List* and Omer Fast's *Spielberg's List*

Since every work of art is informed by the dynamic of exposure to a deep sense of pain, and to the aesthetic delight that allows pain to be contained, I shall attempt to investigate what sort of emotion arises in spectators who view works of art that specifically cope with representing the experience of the Holocaust. I will thus address the question of the kinds of trajectories that can be drawn out between pain and pleasure in these works.

The case I select to analyze these questions is the Schindler affair, a historical event documented by authentic witnesses. On the basis of this historical event, Hollywood director Steven Spielberg produced the film *Schindler's List* in 1993. Ten years later, in 2003, video artist Omer Fast created the film *Spielberg's List*. My focus will be the comparative inquiry into the trajectories of movement between pleasure and pain in both these works. My discussion will show that *Schindler's List* by Spielberg marks an apparently linear trajectory in which movement progresses from pain to pleasure. The feeling that is generated in the spectators as a result of this movement is *delight*. Fast's *Spielberg's List* establishes a viewpoint onto *Schindler's List* through the testimonies of the extras, who were present on the film set. Fast reads Spielberg's work through the lens of a multidirectional, polyphonic, and fragmented style as well as a circular narrative structure. Fast exposes the nature of the unconscious Lacanian *jouissance* that is embedded in the deep layers of Spielberg's film. Fast's video artwork deconstructs Spielberg's film and causes the spectators of Fast's work to follow his lead and view Spielberg's film through a critical and rational lens. Fast's work, in this sense, follows Barthes's version of conscious and reflexive *jouissance*.

Schindler's List by **Steven Spielberg**

Schindler's List by Steven Spielberg is a dramatized account of the true story of Oskar Schindler, a German businessman who saved the lives of more than one thousand Polish Jews during the Holocaust by employing them in his factories. The film, based on the novel *Schindler's Ark*[38] by Thomas Keneally, stars Liam Neeson as Schindler, Ralph Fiennes as SS officer Amon Göth, and Ben Kingsley as Schindler's accountant Itzhak Stern. The film was both a box office success and the recipient of seven Academy Awards.[39] The film has penetrated historical consciousness on a global scale and has transformed the image of the Holocaust as perceived by millions of people all over the world.[40] This globalized phenomenon provides an arena for observing and analyzing the interaction between the feelings of pain and pleasure associated with the global representation of the Holocaust.

In his book *Popular Culture and the Shaping of Holocaust Memory in America*,[41] Alan Mintz points to the power of works of popular culture to illuminate and disseminate awareness of the Holocaust in American public discourse. In his analysis he points to three central matters, which according to him cause the work to be imprinted in American consciousness: (1) the power of the individual to change historical events; (2) the expiation of Christian guilt by presenting Schindler as a rescuer of the Jews; and (3) the ability to create superior entertainment forms.[42] In the ensuing discussion, I will attempt to elaborate on the last point, and to examine, on the textual level, what is the source of the enchantment that the film provokes at the emotional level.

The opening of Spielberg's film fixes on the screen an authoritative narrator who knows the historical event, dominates its narrative, and guides it from crisis to redemption. In Spielberg's opening the transition is from color to black-and-white photography and from the smoke of the Shabbat candle to the smoke of the train images. From the very first opening scene of the film, Spielberg relies on visual icons. On the one hand, these icons, such as the ceremony of candle lighting before the Shabbat, represent the historical continuum of Jewish existence, but on the other, they stand for death and annihilation. As the spectators watch the candles melt away, to be immediately replaced by the smoke of a train, a crude double icon is activated: the train is a visual representation of the vehicle that transported the Jews to the death camps, and the candles' smoke fusing into the train's smoke evokes the crematoria's smoke at Auschwitz. The use of these basic and familiar images at the beginning of the movie—embedded in the context of a story of genocide—creates an immediate connection with profound emotions. In another scene, which depicts the deportees moving over the bridge into the ghetto (figure 12.1), the camera pans from the anonymous crowd, to the family, and then to a single Jewish child (figure 12.2). In depicting the march on the bridge in such a style, Spielberg intensifies an emotional situation that is already charged in and of itself.

Figure 12.1. Spielberg's *Schindler's List*: deportees moving over the bridge into the ghetto (DVD still)

The next scene I will focus on is the scene in which three events co-occur simultaneously and alternately: (1) the meeting of Amon Göth, the Nazi commander of the notoriously cruel Płaszów camp, with Helen Hirsch, a Jewish prisoner, in the villa's basement; (2) Oskar Schindler's birthday party in the first floor of the villa; and (3) the wedding celebration of a Jewish couple in the Płaszów forced labor camp. Much has been written about the scene with Amon Göth and Helen Hirsch as a scene representing monstrous evil: the character of the Nazi;[43] the sensationalist mix of sex and violence;[44] and especially the pornographic depiction of the woman's body.[45] But until now little attention has been paid to the triptych-like composition of the three interwoven events—a

Figure 12.2. Spielberg's *Schindler's List*: the camera pans from the anonymous crowd on the bridge to a single Jewish child (DVD still)

composition that acts upon the spectators and brings about a particular arousal of pleasure and pain.

This triple scene is powerfully described, as in each scene a certain intense event creates aesthetic interaction with the parallel scenes. In this narrative, Amon Göth goes out, in the classic tradition of stalag literature, to search for Helen Hirsch, the beautiful and helpless Jewess, and finds her in the wine cellar. The encounter takes on an erotic character, climaxing in his confession that he has feelings for her. Thus, Amon Göth becomes caught in a conflict that resonates pathetically with Shylock's speech in the *Merchant of Venice*:

> Hath not a Jew eyes? Hath not a Jew hands, organs
> Dimensions, senses, affections, passions?[46]

In Spielberg's film, Amon Göth says to Helen Hirsch:

> Is this face a rat?
> Are these the eyes of a rat?
> Hath not a Jew eyes?
> I feel for you, Helen.
> No, I don't think so.
> You are a Jewish bitch.
> You nearly talked me into it. Didn't you?

In the sixteenth-century Shakespearean drama *The Merchant of Venice,* Shylock is presented in a moving monologue through which he attempts to shatter the anti-Semitic stereotype of the miserly, conniving, interest-lending Jews, which excludes him from the family of Man. In his monologue, Shylock presents his universal human characteristics in order to undermine and overcome this exclusion. In Spielberg's film, the one who utters this monologue is not the Jewess Helen Hirsh but the Nazi Amon Göth, who attempts to convince himself that there is nothing evil about Helen's Jewishness, but immediately retracts and rebounds with an aggressive counterreaction by beating and abusing her.

Through juxtaposition, the two other parallel scenes illustrate and enhance both differences and similarities with the basement scene centering on Amon Göth. The birthday scene in honor of Schindler and the marriage scene in the Płaszów camp substitute for the basement by way of opposition, because both are parties thrown to celebrate an event: a birthday and a wedding. While Helen Hirsch is the object of cruelty in the basement, the other women, the birthday party singer and the camp's bride, are blessed by moments of happiness in their lives. But despite the glaring opposition between sorrow and joy and between pain and pleasure, Spielberg uses poetic devices to create aesthetic links between the three scenes. The three events are merged so that the image from one scene that is substituted by an image from a different event continues creating a graphic movement in the image track and a sonic movement in the soundtrack. In this manner, the synecdochic shot—in the visual track—of a caressing hand and kiss moves smoothly from scene to scene. The accompanying camera movement, stroking Helen Hirsch's body from top to bottom (figure 12.3), continues by dissolving into the next birthday scene (figure 12.4), where the singer's hand strokes Schindler, then back to the Helen Hirsch scene (figure 12.5), and to the Schindler scene again (figure 12.6).

Similarly, the kiss that Amon Göth is about to give Helen Hirsch is substituted by the actual kiss of the Jewish couple in the wedding. The same movement is effected in the audio track, where the sounds of clinking glasses at the birthday party and of a breaking light bulb (as a substitute for the ceremonial breaking of a glass) at the wedding are blended into the sounds of shattered glass when the cupboard is thrown at Helen in the cellar; this cacophony of

Figure 12.3. Spielberg's *Schindler's List*: Amon Göth with Ellen in the cellar (DVD still)

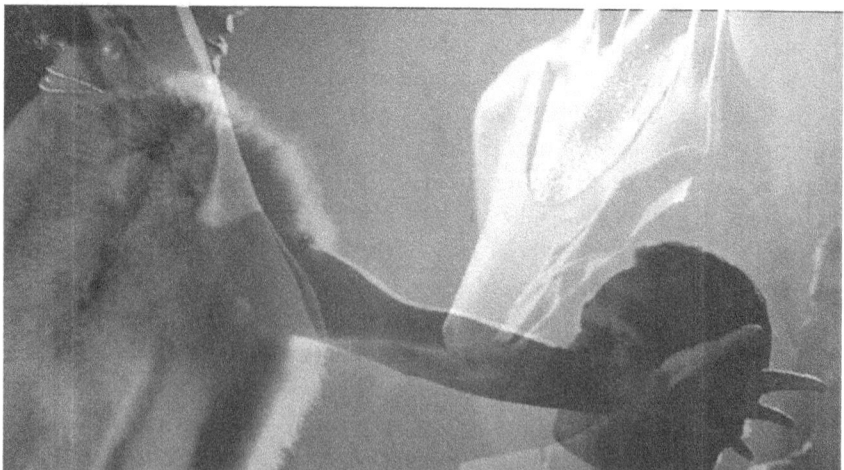

Figure 12.4. Spielberg's *Schindler's List*: the singer with Schindler on the first floor (DVD still)

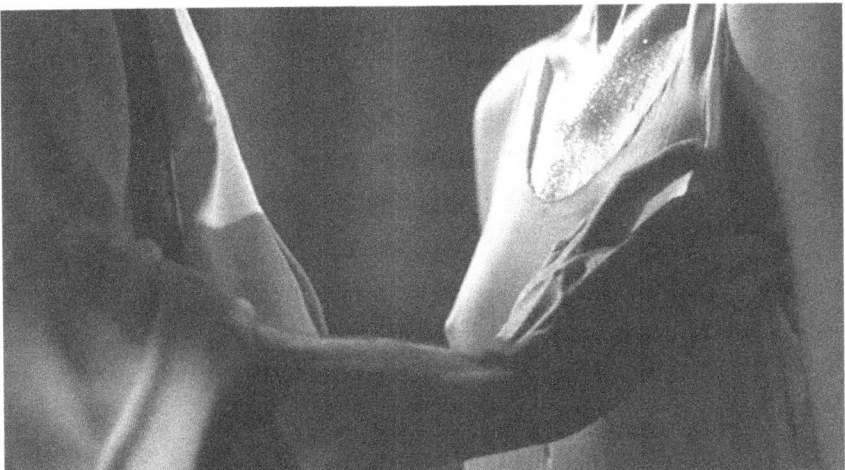

Figure 12.5. Spielberg's *Schindler's List*: Amon Göth with Ellen again in the cellar (DVD still)

Figure 12.6. Spielberg's *Schindler's List*: the singer with Schindler again on the first floor (DVD still)

sounds is next overlaid with the blows and violent abuse that Amon Göth hurls at Helen Hirsch. The quick substitution of images creates a powerful effect of heightened emotion, which is comprised mainly of violence and sex, pain and pleasure.

Another scene exemplifies Spielberg's daring at exposing the core of the trauma to all: the scenes photographed in the gas showers, which become water showers. Here women are seen stripping naked, their hair is shorn, and they are rushed into the gas chamber at Auschwitz. When the doors are locked behind them, the camera approaches a small round porthole, through which the camera voyeuristically portrays the scene in the gas chamber. The door's porthole thus becomes a site from which one has a restricted glimpse into the heart of darkness. But Spielberg does not stop here, crossing the boundary of the door to enter into the space that no person has ever trespassed. The light has gone out, the women are screaming. The camera, in close-up, captures their desperate cries for help.[47] The camera climbs up to the showers, where suddenly water emerges instead of gas, and the faucets are bathed in the luminous gleam of an allegedly sacred aura (figure 12.7).

The screams are replaced by cries of glee, which augur the beginning of redemption. The combination of the women's naked bodies, the sacred luminous light on the shower heads as the water bursts forth from them instead of the gas that was dreadfully anticipated, and the redemptive ending of extrication from death are all embodied in captivating visual images that enchant the spectators and cause them to take pleasure in the horrific sensation of sex and violence.

The characters in the shower scene experience the rush of water as a miracle that partakes of the ecstatic. The lighting creates a halo of light that surrounds the stream of gushing water from the showerheads and thus underscores the religious dimension of the moment. The use of cinematic-poetic devices to represent the ecstatic endows the entry into the heart of darkness with a sacral quality that transforms the secular. In the religious world, according to Garry Leonard,[48] a sense of excess can only be understood by means of a sense that there must be something "beyond," which cannot be understood in terms of the secular world. In a nonreligious world, devices of rhetorical and figurative representation of the Holocaust may become substitutes for the creation of redemptive religious experiences.

The film's final scene emphasizes its "happy end."[49] The soundtrack plays "Jerusalem of Gold" while in the background the liberation march is replaced

Figure 12.7. Spielberg's *Schindler's List*: the gas chamber turns into a shower (DVD still)

by a march of people belonging to a different time and place, the time of pilgrimage to Schindler's grave, when the image switches from black and white back to color. Evil is bound to be punished: Amon Göth is sentenced to hanging, while respects are paid to the righteous Schindler by the survivors, who go up to his grave and place a rock on his gravestone. The end of the film fits its narrative structure—a narrative of extrication, redemption, and rescue. The worthy are victorious, the evil are eradicated. Alan Mintz, as I mentioned above, views the narrative of rescue as one of the most important themes that determined the widespread reception of *Schindler's List*. American viewers, so he argues, could accept that story of the real fate of most of Europe's Jews. Rescue narratives, says Mintz, following Langer, have the chance of containing the difficulty and recognizing the fate of the six million who perished. *Schindler's List* creates this possibility of acceptance.[50]

Kitsch: Spielberg's Main Style

A number of scholars of history, literature, and cinema note the similarities between the style employed in *Schindler's List* and the style known as kitsch. "It leads to moments approaching Holocaust Kitsch," says Hartman, in relation to the film.[51] Hartman is here referring especially to the shower scene and the movie's ending. LaCapra also addresses the movie's final scene, which almost reminds him of "the Yellow Brick Road" on which the survivors advance and, in a certain sense, redeem their past.[52] Indeed, even from the few scenes I have described here it is evident that the film contains the conditions for producing kitsch.

One can wonder what the kitsch has to do with mediating such a terrible event as the Holocaust. In his book *Kitsch and Art,* Tomas Kulka[53] characterizes three constitutive conditions for the creation of kitsch: (1) the choice of objects or themes is especially charged with intense emotion;[54] (2) the objects or themes are immediately and effortlessly recognized;[55] and (3) kitsch does not enrich our repository of associations in respect to the themes and objects described.[56] As for the first condition, according to Kulka, kitsch is heavily charged with emotion on the one hand, but is devoid of reflexivity on the other. The dimension of emotionality is increased by an endless stream of words, rhythms, and images that create excess and a sense of being overwhelmed. These excesses arouse intense feelings that enthrall the audience or readership.[57] According to the second principle, kitsch does not risk taking an avant-garde stance or adopting a style that is not universally acceptable. It comes into being only after innovation has become canonical and fossilized. Thus, literary kitsch does not require interpretation, since it is virtually transparent. Its language is simple and the style is especially conventional. Kitsch always appeals to the broadest common denominator, and it is always utterly clear: nothing is left for the imagination.[58] According to the third condition, kitsch does not enrich our repository of associations in respect to the described themes and objects, nor does it exploit the artistic possibilities of developing the structure or modes of expression innovatively. Kitsch hews close to stereotype. The subject must be presented in a standard and schematic fashion, with no individuality.[59] Kitsch does not enhance our sensitivity, nor does it help us "to make more refined distinction and discriminations. Kitsch often obstructs real emotions ... it provides a simulacrum of the emotion that erodes and degrades the capacity to feel that emotion."[60] Milan Kundera[61] views kitsch as the style whose role is to affirm existence. The feeling aroused by kitsch must be the kind of feeling in which the masses can participate. Therefore, kitsch must be founded on elementary images, which are engraved in mass memory. The true role of kitsch, he argues, is to be a "folding screen set up to curtain off death."[62]

It would seem that Spielberg's movie meets all of these three conditions, and that its kitschy qualities may very well explain its global success and popularity. However, kitsch may not be the most appropriate style with which to depict extreme states of trauma, where this folding screen is blown open and the attempt to cover up reality with an aesthetic of deception is fractured. It is difficult not to wonder why Spielberg chose to describe situations of trauma, which involved a constant confrontation with the dread of death—situations that illustrate the limits of representation—through a style whose principal feature is its acceptance and affirmation of what exists. The trauma of the Holocaust, as argued earlier, requires a unique language, a language that will make space for that which cannot be spoken of. In this sense, kitsch fails to represent the trauma, and it operates as counterfeit rhetoric. So what is it in kitsch that, counter to our intuition, makes it so frequently present aside negative sublime texts?[63]

In *Kitsch and Death,* Friedländer has already demonstrated that kitsch and death cannot be reconciled.[64] Analyzing Nazi texts shows, in his opinion, that the purpose of joining kitsch to death is to arouse a simplistic romantic thrill,[65] to create a ritual, ceremonial atmosphere around death,[66] and thus to become a more effective barrier with which to hide the past.[67] In Friedländer's view, kitsch has a hypnotic dimension[68] that is a product of its excess, and that ultimately protects from anxiety vis-à-vis the apocalyptic reality that is experienced in actuality. Succumbing to the enchantment of the seductive and relaxing power of kitsch can thus push anxiety away and allow it to be forgotten.[69]

Friedländer, however, makes a distinction between common kitsch and elevated kitsch.[70] Elevated kitsch relates to scenes of death and to rituals of sacrifice, and belongs to the world of apocalyptic imagery. According to Friedländer, the use of elevated kitsch creates ethical problems, especially due to its power to arouse fascination.[71] Following Friedländer, my premise is that kitsch serves here as a stylistic mechanism that seduces while simultaneously enabling the creation of a screen that masks the pain of trauma and acts as a type of narcotic, allowing one to experience pleasure in pain while at the same time denying it.

On the surface, *Schindler's List* is a story of delight. The film leads the audience from a state of pain and distress to a state of release and redemption. The kitsch style of the work preserves the aesthetic distance required for delight, and the spectator is placed at a distance that preserves his or her own physical space without threatening him. But is this how things really are? Do Spielberg's poetic devices, his kitsch style, and the linear structure that leads to release and redemption truly create the aesthetic distance that allows the spectator to observe the phenomenon and examine it from a reflective and rational point of view? Is this style and structure appropriate for representing a type of experience that is mostly comprised of helplessness, the dissolution of the self, and a basic lack of exit? What is the role of kitsch in this work, and what is its effect on the audience? I contend that kitsch serves here to intensify feeling and to fix upon pleasure as part of a defense mechanism that allows the denial of anxiety in the face of horror. The work of kitsch becomes a mere form of mass entertainment, which ultimately, despite having made a place for itself in global consciousness, also achieves an opposite result. The presentation of horror as a pleasurable and exciting spectacle that works magic or sorcery on the spectator sucks him into the lawless realm of pornographic pleasure from pain, without the possibility of extrication or of applying a critical reading to the text. Indulgence in this pleasure of horror might be, in effect, the experience of an unconscious *jouissance* that is embedded deep in the permutation of kitsch and death.

The power of kitsch is thus twofold—a double-edged sword. On the one hand, it captures the attention of the spectator, magnetizes, and seduces him, but at the same time, because of the structure of which I previously spoke (stereotypical, clichéd, utterly familiar and uninnovative), it turns the spectator's gaze into an opaque gaze that is trapped in a circle of enchantment, a gaze that does not clearly see the thing itself and is captive in a system of displacements that gradually lose their connection to the original. One artist who reads Spielberg's work in a critical way, who exposes the manifestation of the kitsch and its influence on the spectators, the unconscious *jouissance* in Lacan's terms, is Omer Fast in his video art creation *Spielberg's List*.

Spielberg's List by Omer Fast

From the very beginning of Omer Fast's video work we have entered into a discursive world in which the point of reference is not reality but a cinematic creation: Spielberg's film. Fast presents on the right-hand screen a contemporary view of the train station in Krakow of 2003, while on the left-hand screen he plays Spielberg's movie as seen on a TV screen (figure 12.8).

This movie within a movie gradually becomes distorted and blurred, culminating in an abrupt termination. This opening borrows materials from Spiel-

Figure 12.8. Fast's *Spielberg's List*: the train station in Krakow in 2003 on the right, and the opening sequence of Spielberg's *Schindler's List* movie on the left (DVD still)

berg's film and integrates them in a contemporary, split, and distributed world, with no discrete beginning and end.

Later, Fast follows the activation of memory, as the extras who participated in Spielberg's film reconstruct that experience from the moment they were selected as actors until the end of the filming process. From the outset, the spectator is thrown into the state of uncertainty and hesitancy of whether he is observing a real situation or the re-creation of producing Spielberg's film. This hesitancy stems from the fact that the extras are now witnesses who are describing from their own memory of what they went through. In recounting their experiences, the border between reality and fiction is blurred. For instance, when they discuss the selection they went through to see whether they would be chosen to play Jews or German Nazis, they say:

> And we stood in line for the conscription. We were terribly cold, we stood for a long time.... A few people at a time went inside. And in there was a jury that selected—they would choose or they sent away. They were looking for Semitic types—you know? To me—it seems that I was chosen according to type because I had black hair at the time and they told me to show my profile. When I turned and showed my profile—they said yes.

In an interview with Mr. Less, a tourist guide in Krakov, an even graver reality is reflected, when the interviewee describes the tourist industry that developed in the city of Krakow following the shooting of Spielberg's film:

> Why we do it? In fact we were forced to do it. We were forced by the tourists. Mainly American tourists. Just after the premiere of this film in New York (…) visited us the first American tourists. With New York Times in their hands (…) Because in the New York Times there was a very big article… In the end of Decenber, 93… (…) and they ask: 'where is this? where is this?… from New York Times… many pictures… many pictures were from the film… and real pictures. But they did not distinguish between the real and - for example - decoration for the film (…) then after two three weeks, because people asked the same, the same… we decided to print something: general information for tourists. We printed it as a guide book. And we hired a mini bus. We educated three of our guides in a special way but from the beginning our idea was… not only a so called 'Schindler List

Tour' (...) From the beginning of our tours we placed in the historical context. It means, it means a history of Krakow Jews (...) But in fact all tourists that visited us to now—in fact to now... they see Krakow through the eyes of Mr. Spielberg.

From the words of Mr. Less we can see that the industry of tourist pilgrimage to Holocaust sites meets the tourist's needs to live the memory of the Holocaust via the imaginary account of Spielberg more than via historic reality. In spite of the attempt of the guides to integrate the memory of the disaster into its historical context, the tourists seem to prefer to live the beauty of death by Spielberg's film.

Fast uses two screens. The use of this artistic device is not arbitrary. Each screen can be taken to mimic one of our eyes. In our visual system, we normally receive information via each of our eyes separately. It is important to note that the information conveyed via each of the eyes is a bit different than that conveyed via the other eye. But in spite of this we do not see two different pictures. The information from each eye merges at higher levels of brain processing to yield a coherent percept. This percept is then further processed to yield a unified representation of reality. This phenomenon is called binocular vision.[72]

Metaphorically speaking, Fast exposes here a process of which we are mostly unaware in daily life. By using the device of two screens, side by side, showing a different, yet related, image in each, Fast dissects the representation, bringing it back to the reduced stage at which the information is not yet coherent. In this way he exposes the "noisy" iconic input and the process of merging and interpreting it at higher levels of perceptual processing. The use of two screens serves the issue of splitting the authoritative narrator and demoting the monolithic representation of reality. In order to illustrate this artistic device, I will focus on a leitmotif that runs through Fast's film: the pictures of the bridge connecting the two parts of Krakow, on which the Jews of Krakow passed on their way to the ghetto in 1941.

Fast begins with a picture of the contemporary bridge that is created by juxtaposing the two screens (figure 12.9).

Figure 12.9. Fast's *Spielberg's List*: the contemporary bridge, created by juxtaposing the two screens (DVD still)

After a while, in which the unified picture seems to become fixed, Fast starts dismantling the percept, and the picture of the bridge on the left screen changes its angle and approaches us until we detect a figure in red under the bridge (figures 12.10 and 12.11).

Figure 12.10. Fast's *Spielberg's List*: the bridge on the left screen starts to change its angle and approach the viewer (DVD still)

Figure 12.11. Fast's *Spielberg's List*: on the left screen the figure in red under the bridge (DVD still)

Now, on the right screen, we see half of the bridge from a moderate distance, and at the same time the figure under the bridge appears in proximity to the viewer. In this manner Fast's screen eyes represent to an extreme a dissonance in which one eye sees an object proximally and the other distantly. At this point the information in both screen-eyes has not yet been merged.

Fast echoes in speech and picture the bridge on which three events were taking place: in 1941, in 1993, and in 2003. In the next example we first see duplication of the segment of marching on the bridge from Spielberg's film. This segment is blurred at first, but sharpens gradually (figure 12.12).

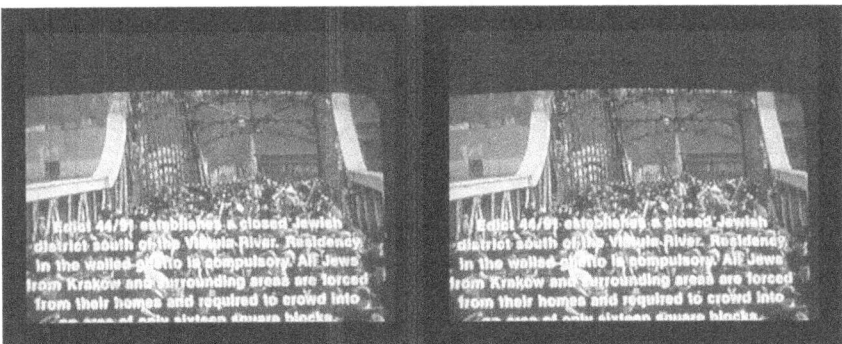

Figure 12.12. Fast's *Spielberg's List*: two screens: showing a segment from Schindler's list: people marching on the bridge (DVD still)

When the two pictures sharpen, they move away from each other into the distance and are transformed into arbitrary cuts to pictures of the contemporary bridge at different times of the day (sunrise and sunset) on the two screens. Instead of taking the path of kitsch, Fast chooses to expose the world of the simulacra in which the tourists follow Spielberg's film. The tourist guide recounts how the film was shot in the direction opposite to that of the real historic march, in order to preserve the setup and avoid catching the modern city in the frame. Yet, Fast's narrative authority is still kept fragmented, as he dismantles the image of the bridge by shooting from inside the tourist van and double it by the two screens(figure 12.13).

Figure 12.13. Fast's *Spielberg's List*: the fragmented bridge seen from the tourist's van (DVD still)

On top of this, another split is provided by creating a discrepancy at the level of the subtitles, the level of translation.[73]

BLACK SYNCH: SEQUENCE FROM SCHINDLER'S LIST SHOWING BRIDGE (00121224) SYNCH: SHOT OF BRIDGE, FRONT, *DAWN, STILL DARK*	BLACK SYNCH: SEQUENCE FROM SCHINDLER'S LIST SHOWING BRIDGE (00121224) SYNCH: SHOT OF BRIDGE, FRONT, *MORNING* SHOT OF BRIDGE IN *EVENING* FROM FAR TOUR GUIDE: OFF CAMERA And now we'll be crossing the bridge which was used by… by Jewish people when they were moving from Kazimierz to the Ghetto…
SYNCH: TOUR GUIDE, INSIDE VAN (english) (00130726) And *afterwards* it was used in the film—in Spielberg's… In Schindler's list <Oh with the wagons—people *pushing* the wagons…> Yeah, yeah, yeah, yeah. And also… But you know after the film they were *seeing* it the other way around … The people were coming back to Kazimierz—because the area has been so *mythologized*… So you know—*it seems like*—fifty years later they *are* coming back. <So this is a *copy* of the bridge that was there?> Yes—this is—this is the bridge.	SYNCH: TOUR GUIDE, INSIDE VAN (english) (00130726) And *also* it was used in the film—in Spielberg's… In Schindler's list <Oh with the wagons—people *pulling* the wagons…> Yeah, yeah, yeah, yeah. And also… But you know in the film they were *filming* it the other way around … The people were coming back to Kazimierz—because the area has been so *modernized*… So you know—*it feels like*—fifty years later they *were* coming back. <So this is *actually* the bridge that was there?> Yes—this is—this is the bridge.

In editing the footage for his two-screen installation, Fast made a crucial intervention. Working with a Polish translator, he was made aware of the translation options in the interviews he had conducted. Reflecting on this, he decided to play identical footage on each screen but to subtitle them with slightly different texts.[74]

By using the bridge motif I demonstrated how Fast represents reality via a polyphonic vision, with its multiple faces and discrepancies. At a certain stage, this polyphonic vision reorganizes into coherent interpretations, those of the extras. An additional route to representing the polyphonic reality in Fast's film is by listening to the testimonies of the extras. The extras give testimonies of a second order, and in spite of the fact that all took part in the same experience—acting in Spielberg's movie—they converted their personal experiences into different impressions. I will now proceed to analyze some testimonies of the extras. One such testimony is that of Yatsek (figure 12.14).

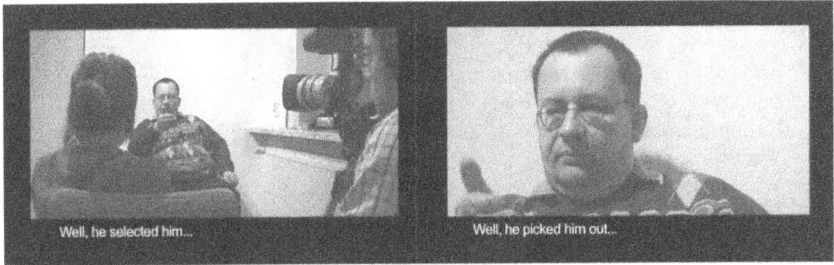

Figure 12.14. Fast's *Spielberg's List*: second-order testimony with camera (DVD still)

In this example, Yatsek wishes to relate to the historical reality by referring to the list of victims. His testimony emphasizes his strong bond to the authentic background of Spielberg's movie. He says that he was mostly impressed by the original lists that Spielberg had and by the accurate advice provided to the director by the real victims of the story in order to make sure events were not invented. Note, however, that even here a simulacrum is concealed, as Yatsek refers to the copy of the list as if it were the real list.

The second testimony is that of Nina, who presents an emotional stand that mixes the reality of the imagery—the actors who played the protagonists in Spielberg's movie—with the historical reality—the protagonists in the real event. Here, Fast's layers of looking add up to a disturbing conclusion: the gaze can even repress the site of genocide and turn it into something magical, sublime. The extra Nina expresses this most eloquently. After describing the brutality of the counterfeit camp, she sighs:[75]

> Well—barracks like any barracks [...]
> The whole place was surrounded by barbed-wire
> *Beautiful scenery* where there are cliffs all around.
> And on top -
> Walking all around...
> Nazis with dogs
> So that no one would escape from the camp.
> *These are beautiful scenes for me.*
> Because all of this is in a valley.
> In a quarry—where these barracks were built.
> So there are cliffs.
> With grass above.
> And on top...
> Nazis walking all the time—watching from above.
> Because there were escapes from the camps.
> *It looked very beautiful.*

In Nina's testimony one can detect fascination with evil in her repeated uttering of the word "beautiful." In the following segment, Nina mentions in one breath both Schindler and Amon Göth, the camp commander who shot his victims indiscriminately, and the actors Liam Neeson and Ralph Fiennes. At the same time, she expresses pride in the opportunity she had to play alongside these actors[76]:

> And so this roll-call was taking place and Schindler was walking with Amon Göth
> So Liam Neeson and that other one…
> Ralph Fiennes…
> With these riding-whips
> Walking beautifully—you know—like real Germans.
> For me—it was a beautiful view.

Finally, the third testimony is that of Theophol, an old blind man. He lives in the world of the simulacra, and he considers the movie setup of the concentration camp to be the historical reality:[77]

> Even when I wasn't an extra but I had some free time…
> I would go with the dog for a walk to the top of the Kopiec Krakusa…
> And I watched how they tortured these people…
> These Jews…
> In this camp…
> In these camps.
> (off camera) But when did this happen, sir?
> Well, it was when he was making the film.
> When he was making the film.
> A film in a camp in Auschwitz.
> I have a photograph from this camp.

An elderly man remembers looking at the work camp on his walks, but we are not sure if it is the real camp, which still exists as a ruin, or the film set, which Spielberg left behind. The act of looking—whether at a camp or at the movie's set—creates its own history, accumulative, constitutive, forgetful, and repressive.[78] Note again that this old man, according to Fast, was blind.

Fast thus disassembles the act of vision and exposes the implicit processes that bring vision into the awareness of the viewer, from the falling of the visual stimulus on each of the two eyes, through the reorganization of the information, culminating in its translation and interpretation. The narrative that he proposes attempts to unveil, in a reductionist manner, the processes by which the impressions of trauma are perceived. Using two screens, he ends up proposing a polyphonic narrative, which is followed only at a later stage by individualistic interpretations.

In his installation *Spielberg's List,* it is Fast who exposes the unconscious *jouissance* hidden beneath the surface of Spielberg's work. The poetic devices in Fast's text expose the sensationalism, the seduction, and the kitsch by emptying them out (see, e.g., the tourists' guide and Nina's testimony). These devices create a new space from within which things can be examined by the spectators more critically. Fast seeks to jump over the hurdle of sensationalism without getting trapped in it; he seeks to transgress Spielberg's monolithic, authoritative structure. The fragmented counterpathetic style employed at different levels of the text allows both the seductive trap of kitsch and the linear redemptive narrative structure to become visible through a polyphonic representation of reality.

Polyphony—Fast's stylistic choice—instantiates itself beginning with the perceptual level, with the very choice to use two screens, which concretely represents binocular vision, as explained above, through the cognitive level, with the very presentation of the translational dissonance, to the affective level, through the presentation of different voices of witnesses—second-order witnesses to the trauma. Fast attempts to expose a circular narrative, a narrative without beginning, middle, or end, an attempt at a reflexive and a conscious poetic expression.

Aesthetic Representation vis-à-vis the Ethical Representation of the Holocaust Experience in a Global Era

Poetic texts coping with traumatic experience impose a state of loss on the reader and mark traces of the ruptured reality. The poetic text, in this case, is the space in which traumatic experience can be revived to a degree that permits processing. The poetic text relocates the trauma to a protected arena and creates checks and balances that permit expressing the worst-of-all while containing the pain of the experience without being engulfed and overwhelmed by it. In a poetic text, the experience is assumed to retain some of the uncontrolled, terrible essence and pain of the trauma, yet at the same time it creates an aesthetic and manageable distance from reality and thus engenders pleasure. Similar to rites, ceremonies, and psychotherapy, literary works can expose the most intimidating events yet observe them from a safe distance. As in the myth of Perseus and the Gorgon Medusa, whoever stared at the monster was petrified, but whoever used a mirror survived.

How can gazing at the trauma of the Holocaust through the artist's aesthetic grid also turn the aesthetic representation into an ethical stance? Santner[79] discusses the fetishistic narrative that traps the audience in the magnetic sorcery of the Holocaust experience, but suggests searching for a way to arrive at a symbolic generalization that will enable the reconstitution of the fragmented identity of the traumatic self. He sees the main challenge in finding the countermove that attempts to suppress the trauma, that is, to work through it. LaCapra,[80] for example, warns against being enchanted by the excess of the Holocaust and proposes a moderated, somewhat reflexive and self-critical response. In respect to critical work vis-à-vis primary memory, which is experiential and subjective in nature, LaCapra further argues that such work, which is performed by the second-degree witness (such as the historian), is not meant to be a complete empathic documentation, which revivifies the other's trauma with complete intensity, but rather a restrained and subdued register of the trauma. This is what the process of working through requires: a subdued or reduced transmission of the traumatic nature of the event, and not its full revivification, that is, its acting out.[81] E. Ann Kaplan[82] proposes a three-phased model in which witnessing is the most fitting genre for working through trauma. Kaplan studies the creation of what she calls a *culture of trauma*, in which she differentiates between three possible emotional reactions to images of disasters: one reaction experiences trauma as a secondary or vicarious trauma, an experience in which the observer is empathically overwhelmed; a second reaction is one that she calls *empty empathy,* a reaction created by sentimental representation that arouses in the spectators nothing more than a voyeuristic view of the life of an individual in war, and does not provoke any subsequent thought about the war in a broader context of ethics, human rights, and other philosophical issues. A third reaction is what she calls the *ethics of witnessing,* which attempts to pose an alternative to the first two reactions. Kaplan proposes that the ethics of witnessing is a process that ought to begin with empathy, but the representation of the object of trauma should lead from this initial feeling to the broader context of active participation against injustice. The ethics of witnessing allows, in her view, for a broader understanding of the meaning of what was inflicted upon the victim.

Adorno's famous dictum in respect to poetry after Auschwitz was, "To write poetry after Auschwitz is barbaric."[83] Although Adorno revised this statement several times in the course of his life, the original statement remains engraved in global consciousness, and it raises a serious question: Does art beautify and aestheticize violence, and by so doing, does it trivialize and mask the pain and terrible loss that it attempts to represent? Or can art become a source of vitality in response to disaster—a place to give expression to suffering and to construct a community that responds to disaster ethically and responsibly?[84]

Adorno's argument against the attempt to represent the Holocaust becomes even more incisive in respect to visual representations. According to Levy and Rothberg, the prohibition against making "a graven image" is a modern taboo that arises from the danger of producing pleasure and beauty from the visual representation of extreme pain.[85] Susan Sontag also worries about the passionate interest that descriptions of horror arouse. Pictures of repulsive things, she argues, may ignite an attraction.[86] Baudrillard views the contemporary apocalyptic genre as an entertainment that combines horror with distraction.[87] Attraction to—and enchantment by—the catastrophe of the Holocaust, and *not* the anxiety caused by it, is what I wish to mark as the source of Lacan's unconscious *jouissance*. This kind of *jouissance* signifies the symptom of entrapment in the experience of the Holocaust death world without the ability to avoid this trap.

Conclusion

Spielberg's film *Schindler's List* is considered one of the most important cultural products to date that have blazed the way for the acceptance of the Holocaust as part of a global consciousness. The film had an extremely significant impact on global public discourse, due to its success in bringing the story of the victims of the Holocaust in a tolerable and accessible way to the awareness of millions of people. As such, it is certainly a most worthy accomplishment. At the same time, it seems pertinent to raise a few challenging questions concerning the qualities of mediations of Holocaust representations for future generations.

Is it possible to arrive at global awareness of the Holocaust without using contrivances that manipulate our centers of pleasure and pain? When attempting to sear the public consciousness at a global level, is there no alternative but to use the contrivances of kitsch, melodrama, and sensation in order to arouse the emotion that combines pain and pleasure? Works of art do search for ways to circumvent these limits and create a different discourse that can cope with the challenges of representation, warn against enchantment by Holocaust excess, and propose a moderate response and a certain degree of reflexive self-critique. In the global era, with its reliance on media and technology, it is tempting to digitally reproduce disasters and consume them as an entertainment opiate. But a work of art that contends with the representation of disaster and atrocity must also deal with these dilemmas.

By analyzing the test case of the Schindler affair, I have tried to unveil two types of trajectories in the interactions between pleasure and pain in reference to the issue of the negative sublime—the Holocaust. Spielberg's *Schindler's List* is an example of a global narrative that is based on elements of fascination with evil that ostensibly operates like delight, but actually draws the viewer into a state of *jouissance* without leaving space for critical thinking or processing. Omer Fast's *Spielberg's List* represents a polyphonic dialogue with reality, by means of its own dialogue with Spielberg's movie. In his video art installation, Fast seeks to lay bare the entire gamut of emotions involved when people are enthralled by evil.

In treating the emotional dimension of these works, I have tried to show that prior to an explicit ethical interrogation, in which we locate within every representation of the Holocaust or any other genocide the warning signal of the next disaster and the potential for change and reparation, it is important to critically examine the way in which the poetic text mediates our memory, and especially the emotional effects that activate and manipulate us as spectators. In the global era, kitsch is a leading "sales promoter" of the Holocaust, which activates the psychic phenomenon of *jouissance*, making it accessible to the masses at the price of emptying out the ethical challenges it poses. The power of kitsch lies in its ability to stimulate basic emotions, seduce its consumers, and aestheticize horror and terror to the point of pleasure.

Notes

I wish to thank Zahava Caspi, Rachel Heiblum, Carol Kidron, Ronit Peleg, Nitza Pereman Drori, Gissi Sarig, and Pnina Shirav for reading a draft of this chapter and for their illuminating remarks. I am grateful for the insightful discussions that were held throughout the two-year research forum "Ethics and Practices of Holocaust Memory in the Global Era" at the Van Leer Jerusalem Institute, 2007–8. I wish to thank Amos Goldberg and Chaim Hazan for their stimulating and insightful leadership, as well as all of the members of this unique group. I would also like to thank Kibbutzim College for supporting me financially and technologically. I am most grateful to Orly Golan and Miri Shor.

1. In 2007.
2. Omer Fast, 65-minute, two-channel color video installation (2003).
3. Omer Fast, born in Jerusalem and currently living in Berlin, is considered one of the most innovative video artists working today.
4. Jeffrey C. Alexander, "On the Social Construction of Moral Universal: The 'Holocaust' from War crime to Trauma Drama," *European Journal of Social Theory* 5, no. 1 (2002).
5. Ibid., 6.
6. Ibid., 10.
7. Ibid., 31.
8. Plato, *Laws*, Translated by Alfred, E. Taylor. In *The Collected Dialogues of Plato*, ed. Edith Hamilton and Huntington Crairns, (Princeton, NJ: Princeton University Press, 1987), 1319. See also Duncan Large, "On the Genealogy of Moral Pleasure," *German Life and Letters* 62, no. 3 (2009): 245–51.
9. Plato, *Philebus*, trans. R. Hckforth, in *The Collected Dialogues of Plato*, 1121.
10. Edmund Burke, *A Philosophical Enquiry* (1757; repr., Oxford: Oxford University Press, 1990), 34–37.
11. Jacques Lacan. *The Seminar*, book 7, *The Ethics of Psychoanalysis, 1959–1960*, trans. Dennis Porter (London: Routledge, 1992), 184.
12. Roland Barthes, *The Pleasure of the Text*, trans. Richard Miller (1973; repr., New York: Hill and Wang, 1999).
13. My discussion will not address the voices of the survivors, but the poetic representations of these voices, as elaborated in different styles. I will examine the effects of these representations on those who did not experience the Holocaust except through the mediation of a poetic text. I will focus only on the psychological aspect, and not on political-historical aspects, in order to investigate how this topic is mediated globally.
14. See, e.g., Jean-François Lyotard, *The Differend: Phrases in Dispute*, trans. Georges Van Den Abbeele (1983; repr., Minneapolis: University of Minnesota Press, 1988), 56–57.
15. See, e.g., Geoffrey H. Hartman, *The Longest Shadow* (1996; repr., Palgrave Macmillan, 2002), 4.
16. See, e.g., Saul Friedländer, ed., *Probing the Limits of Representation* (Cambridge, MA: Harvard University Press, 1992), 5.
17. See, e.g., Cathy Caruth, *Unclaimed Experience* (Baltimore, MD and London: Johns Hopkins University Press, 1996), 56.
18. See, e.g., Lang Berl, *Act and Idea in the Nazi Genocide* (Chicago: University of Chicago Press, 1990), 161; Peter Haidu, "The Dialectics of Unspeakability: Language, Silence, and the Narratives of Desubjectification," in *Probing the Limits of Representation*, ed. Saul Friedländer (Cambridge, MA: Harvard University Press, 1992), 283–84; Dominick LaCapra, *Representing the Holocaust: History, Theory, Trauma* (1994; repr., Ithaca, NY: Cornell University Press, 1996), 105; Dominick LaCapra, *History and Memory after Auschwitz* (Ithaca, NY: Cornell University Press, 1998), 38.
19. S. H. Monk, *The Sublime* (Ann Arbor: University of Michigan Press, 1960), 19.
20. Burke, *A Philosophical Enquiry*.
21. Ibid., 36–37.

22. Immanuel Kant, *Observations on the Feeling of the Beautiful and the Sublime,* trans. J. T. Goldthwait (1763; repr., Los Angeles: University of California Press, 1991); Immanuel Kant, *The Critique of Judgement,* trans. J. Meredith (1790; repr., Oxford: Clarendon Press, 1952).

23. Kant, *The Critique of Judgement,* 130–31.

24. Monk, *The Sublime,* 52–54.

25. Jean-François Lyotard, *Lessons on the Analytic of the Sublime,* trans. E. Rottenberg (1991; repr., Stanford, CA: Stanford University Press, 1994).

26. Jean-François Lyotard, "The Postmodern Condition: A Report on Knowledge," trans. Geoff Bennington and Brian Massumi, *Theory and History of Literature* 10 (1993): 81.

27. Ibid., 11–13.

28. Lyotard, *The Differend,* 13.

29. Alain Vanier, *Lacan* [in Hebrew], trans. Amos Squverer (2000; repr., Tel Aviv: Resling, 2003), 101.

30. Dylan Evans, *An Introductory Dictionary of Lacanian Psychoanalysis* (1996; repr., London and New York: Routledge, 2007), 91.

31. Jacques-Alain Miller, *The Lacanian Symptom* [in Hebrew], trans. and ed. Ernesto Piechotka (1986–87; repr., Tel Aviv: Resling, 2010), 29.

32. Roland Barthes, *The Pleasure of the Text,* trans. Richard Miller (1973; repr., New York: Hill and Wang, 1999).

33. The English text uses the term "bliss" for *jouissance.* For the original, see Roland Barthes, *Le plaisir du texte* (Paris: Edition du Seuil, 1973), 36.

34. Barthes, *The Pleasure of the Text,* 22.

35. See also Zahava Caspi's discussion of Hanoch Levin in Zahava Caspi, *Those Who Sit In the Dark* [in Hebrew] (Jerusalem: Keter, 2005), 183.

36. Dominick LaCapra, *Writing History, Writing Trauma* (Baltimore, MD: Johns Hopkins University Press, 2001), xi, 78–109.

37. Ibid., 112.

38. Tomas Keneally, *Schindler's Ark* (London: Serpentine, 1982).

39. See http://www.imdb.com/title/tt0108052/awards?ref_=tt_ql_4.

40. Yosefa Loshitzky, ed., *Spielberg's Holocaust* (Bloomington and Indianapolis: Indiana University Press, 1997), 7, 14n7.

41. Alan Mintz, *Popular Culture and the Shaping of Holocaust Memory in America* (Seattle and London: University of Washington Press, 2001).

42. Ibid., 153–55.

43. Caroline, J.S. Picart, and David. A. Frank, *Frames of Evil: The Holocaust as Horror in American Film* (Carbondale: Southern Illinois University Press, 2006), 37–38, 61–65.

44. Mintz, *Poular Culture,* 143.

45. Horowitz, Sara R. "But Is It Good for the Jews? Spielberg's Schindler and the Aesthetics of Atrocity" In Loshitzky, *Spielberg's Holocaust,* 127.

46. William Shakespeare, *The Merchant of Venice,* Shakespeare Complete Works (Oxford: Oxford University Press, 1965), act 3, scene 2.

47. To this should be added the gendered issues of voyeurism of the victimized female body, in Sarah Horowitz's "But Is It Good for the Jews?," in *Spielberg's Holocaust,* ed. Yosefa Loshitzky, 128, as well as Omer Bartov's discussion of the sadomasochistic elements of soft porn. Omer Bartov, *Murder in Our Midst* (Oxford: Oxford University Press, 1996), 170–71.

48. Leonard Garry, "Tears of Joy: Hollywood Melodrama, Ecstasy, and Restoring Meta-Narratives of Transcendence in Modernity," *University of Toronto Quarterly* 79, no. 2 (2010): 819–37.

49. On the "happy end," see also Bartov, *Murder in Our Midst,* 168–69; Gertrud Koch, "Against All Odds or the Will to Survive: Moral Conclusions from Narrative Closure," *History and Memory* 9 (1997): 393–491.

50. Mintz, *Popular Culture,* 151–54.

51. Geoffrey H. Hartman, "The Cinema Animal," in *Spielberg's Holocaust,* ed. Yosefa Loshitzky (Bloomington and Indianapolis: Indiana University Press, 1997), 62.

52. LaCapra, *Writing History,* 176–77.
53. Thomas Kulka, *Kitsch and Art* (University Park: Pennsylvania State University Press, 1996), 95, 97.
54. Ibid., 28.
55. Ibid., 33.
56. Ibid., 37.
57. Ibid., 27.
58. Ibid.
59. Ibid., 37.
60. Robert Nozick, "On Kitsch," in *Kitsch and Art,* by Thomas Kulka (University Park: Pennsylvania State University Press, 1996), 99.
61. Milan Kundera, *Nesnesitelna Lehkost Byti,* trans. Ruth Bondi (1984; repr., Tel Aviv: Zmora, Bitan, 1985).
62. Ibid., 184. All translations are the author's.
63. Challenging these questions in a discussion about Ka-Tzetnik, see Rina Dudai, "Modes of Coping with Trauma in the Holocaust Literature (A. Appelfeld, Ka.Tzetnik, P. Levi) [in Hebrew]" (PhD diss., Hebrew University, 2000), 143–45. See also, in reference to melodrama, Amos Goldberg, "The Victim's Voice and Melodramatic Aesthetics in History," *History and Theory* 48 (2009): 220–37.
64. Saul Friedländer, *Reflections of Nazism: An Essay on Kitsch and Death* (New York: Harper and Row, 1984).
65. Ibid., 39.
66. Ibid., 43.
67. Ibid., 97.
68. Ibid., 50.
69. Ibid., 123.
70. Saul Friedländer, "Preface to a Symposium: Kitsch and the Apocalyptic Imagination," *Salmagundi,* nos. 85–86 (1990): 201–6.
71. Ibid., 206.
72. Binocular vision is the ability to maintain visual focus on an object with both eyes, creating a single visual image. Having two eyes confers advantages because it gives a wider field of view. For example, a human has a horizontal field of view of approximately 200 degrees with two eyes, but only 160 degrees with one. Also, two eyes produce stereopsis, in which the two eyes' different positions on the head give precise depth perception. Such binocular vision is usually accompanied by singleness of vision or binocular fusion, in which a single image is seen despite each eye's having its own image of any object (http://en.wikipedia.org/wiki/Binocular_vision). Dis-functional forms of binocular vision—like doubling, blurring, shifting parallax, strabismus—would be appropriate metaphors for elaborating this claim.
73. Cited from Fast's manuscript "Spielberg's List", 2003, Personal communication. Differences in translation are marked by RD in italics.
74. Mark Godfrey, "Omer Fast," VOX, 2007, http://www.centrevox.ca/en/exposition/omer-fast-2/ 17.3-28.4.2007.
75. Cited from Fast's manuscript "Spielberg's List", 2003, Personal communication.
76. Ibid.
77. Ibid.
78. Jennifer Allen, "Showings of Video Installations by Omer Fast: Critical Essay," Art Torrents, 2003, http://arttorrents.blogspot.com/2008/03/omer-fast-omer-fast-demo-disk-extracts.html.
79. Eric L. Santner, "History beyond the Pleasure Principle: Some Thoughts on the Representation of Trauma," in *Probing the Limits of Representation,* ed. Saul Friedländer (Cambridge, MA: Harvard University Press, 1992), 147, 152.
80. LaCapra, *History and Memory After Auschwitz,* 1–20.

81. Ibid., 21; for *jouissance,* see also LaCapra, *Writing History,* 58, 80; for empathic unsettlement, see 78–109.

82. E. Ann Kaplan, "Global Trauma and Public Feelings: Viewing Images of Catastrophe," *Consumption Markets & Culture* 11, no. 1 (2008): 3–24.

83. Theodor W. Adorno, "Meditations on Metaphysics," in *Negative Dialectics,* trans. E. B. Ashton (New York: Seabury Press, 1973), cited in Neil Levi and Michael Rothberg, eds., *The Holocaust: Theoretical Readings* (New Brunswick, NJ: Rutgers University Press, 2003), 281.

84. Ibid., 275.

85. Levi and Rothberg, *The Holocaust,* 371.

86. Susan Sontag, *Regarding the Pain of Others* (New York: Picador, 2003); see also Bartov, *Murder in Our Midst.* Bartov "hopes to point toward new paths of inquiry" (117).

87. Jean Baudrillard, *L'échange symbolique et la mort* Paris: Gallimard, 1976.

Bibliography

Adorno, Theodor W. "Meditations on Metaphysics." In *Negative Dialectics,* trans. E. B. Ashton. New York: Seabury Press, 1973. First published 1966.

Alexander, Jeffrey C. "On the Social Construction of Moral Universal: The 'Holocaust' from War Crime to Trauma Drama." *European Journal of Social Theory* 5, no. 1 (2002): 5–85.

Allen, Jennifer. "Showings of Video Installations by Omer Fast: Critical Essay." Art Torrents, 2003. http://arttorrents.blogspot.com/2008/03/omer-fast-omer-fast-demo-disk-extracts.html.

Barthes, Roland. *The Pleasure of the Text.* Translated by Richard Miller. New York: Hill and Wang, 1999. First published 1973.

Bartov, Omer. *Murder in Our Midst.* Oxford: Oxford University Press, 1996.

Baudrillard, Jean. *L'échange symbolique et la mort.* Paris: Gallimard, 1976.

Berl, Lang. *Act and Idea in the Nazi Genocide.* Chicago: University of Chicago Press, 1990.

Burke, Edmund. *A Philosophical Enquiry.* Oxford: Oxford University Press, 1990. First published 1757.

Caruth, Cathy. *Unclaimed Experience.* Baltimore, MD and London: Johns Hopkins University Press, 1996.

Caspi, Zahava. *Those Who Sit In the Dark* [in Hebrew]. Jerusalem: Keter, 2005.

Dudai, Rina. "Modes of Coping with Trauma in the Holocaust Literature (A. Appelfeld, Ka. Tzetnik, P. Levi)" [in Hebrew]. PhD dissertation, Hebrew University, 2000.

Evans, Dylan. *An Introductory Dictionary of Lacanian Psychoanalysis.* London and New York: Routledge, 2007. First published 1996.

Ezrahi, Sidra DeKoven. *Mirroring Evil.* New Brunswick, NJ: Rutgers University Press, 2002.

Friedländer, Saul. "Preface to a Symposium: Kitsch and the Apocalyptic Imagination." *Salmagundi,* nos. 85–86 (1990): 201–6.

———. *Reflections of Nazism: An Essay on Kitsch and Death.* New York: Harper and Row, 1984.

———, ed. *Probing the Limits of Representation.* Cambridge, MA: Harvard University Press, 1992.

Garry, Leonard. "Tears of Joy: Hollywood Melodrama, Ecstasy, and Restoring Meta-Narratives of Transcendence in Modernity." *University of Toronto Quarterly* 79, no. 2 (2010): 819–37.

Godfrey, Mark. "Omer Fast." VOX, 2007. http://www.centrevox.ca/en/exposition/omer-fast-2/ 17.3-28.4.2007.

Goldberg, Amos. "The Victim's Voice and Melodramatic Aesthetics in History." *History and Theory* 48 (2009): 220–37.

Haidu, Peter. "The Dialectics of Unspeakability: Language, Silence, and the Narratives of Desubjectification." In *Probing the Limits of Representation,* ed. Saul Friedländer, 277–99. Cambridge, MA: Harvard University Press, 1992.

Hartman, Geoffrey H. "The Cinema Animal." In *Spielberg's Holocaust*, ed. Yosefa Loshitzky 61–76. Bloomington and Indianapolis: Indiana University Press, 1997.

———. *The Longest Shadow.* New York: Palgrave Macmillan, 2002. First published 1996.

Horowitz, Sara R. "But Is It Good for the Jews? Spielberg's Schindler and the Aesthetics of Atrocity" In *Spielberg's Holocaust*, ed. Yosefa Loshitzky 119-139. Bloomington and Indianapolis: Indiana University Press, 1997.

Kant, Immanuel. *The Critique of Judgement.* Translated by James. C. Meredith. Oxford: Clarendon Press, 1952. First published 1790.

———. *Observations on the Feeling of the Beautiful and the Sublime.* Translated by J. T. Goldthwait. Los Angeles: University of California Press, 1991). First published 1763.

Kaplan, E. Ann. "Global Trauma and Public Feelings: Viewing Images of Catastrophe." *Consumption Markets & Culture* 11, no. 1 (2008): 3–24.

Keneally, Tomas. *Schindler's Ark.* London: Serpentine, 1982.

Koch, Gertrud. "Against All Odds or the Will to Survive: Moral Conclusions from Narrative Closure." *History and Memory* 9 (1997): 393–491.

Kulka, Thomas. *Kitsch and Art.* University Park: Pennsylvania State University Press, 1996.

Kundera, Milan. *Nesnesitelna Lehkost Byti.* Translated by Ruth Bondi. Tel Aviv: Zmora, Bitan 1985. First published 1984.

Lacan, Jacques. *The Seminar.* Book 7, *The Ethics of Psychoanalysis, 1959–1960.* Translated by Dennis Porter. London: Routledge, 1992.

LaCapra, Dominick. *History and Memory after Auschwitz.* Ithaca, NY: Cornell University Press, 1998.

———. *Representing the Holocaust: History, Theory, Trauma.* Ithaca, NY: Cornell University Press, 1996. First published 1994.

———. *Writing History, Writing Trauma.* Baltimore, MD: Johns Hopkins University Press, 2001.

Large, Duncan. "On the Genealogy of Moral Pleasure." *German Life and Letters* 62, no. 3 (2009): 245–51.

Levi, Neil, and Michael Rothberg, eds. *The Holocaust: Theoretical Readings.* New Brunswick, NJ: Rutgers University Press, 2003.

Loshitzky, Yosefa, ed. *Spielberg's Holocaust.* Bloomington and Indianapolis: Indiana University Press, 1997.

Lyotard, Jean-François. *The Differend: Phrases in Dispute.* Translated by Georges Van Den Abbeele. Minneapolis: University of Minnesota Press, 1988. First published 1983.

———. *Lessons on the Analytic of the Sublime.* Translated by Elizabeth, Rottenberg. Stanford, CA: Stanford University Press, 1994. First published 1991.

———. "Answering the Question: What Is Postmodernism?" Translated by Regis Durand. In "The Postmodern Condition: A Report on Knowledge." Translated by Geoff Bennington and Brian Massumi. *Theory and History of Literature* 10 (1993): 71–82. First published 1979.

Miller, Jacques-Alain. *The Lacanian Symptom* [in Hebrew]. Translated and edited by Ernesto Piechotka. Tel Aviv: Resling, 2010. First published 1986–87.

Mintz, Alan. *Popular Culture and the Shaping of Holocaust Memory in America.* Seattle and London: University of Washington Press, 2001.

Monk, Samuel H. *The Sublime.* Ann Arbor: University of Michigan Press, 1960.

Nozick, Robert. "On Kitsch." In *Kitsch and Art,* by Thomas Kulka. University Park: Pennsylvania State University Press, 1996.

Caroline, J.S. Picart, and David. A. Frank. *Frames of Evil: The Holocaust as Horror in American Film.* Carbondale: Southern Illinois University Press, 2006.

Plato. *Laws.* Translated by Alfred, E. Taylor. In *The Collected Dialogues of Plato,* ed. Edith Hamilton and Huntington Crairns. 1225–513, Princeton, NJ: Princeton University Press, 1987.

———. *Philebus.* Translated by Reginald, Hckforth. In *The Collected Dialogues of Plato,* ed. Edith Hamilton and Huntington Crairns. 1086–150, Princeton, NJ: Princeton University Press, 1987.

Santner, Eric L. "History beyond the Pleasure Principle: Some Thoughts on the Representation of Trauma." In *Probing the Limits of Representation,* ed. Saul Friedländer, 143–54. Cambridge, MA: Harvard University Press, 1992.
Shakespeare, William. *The Merchant of Venice.* Shakespeare Complete Works. Oxford: Oxford University Press, 1965.
Sontag, Susan. *Regarding the Pain of Others.* New York: Picador, 2003.
Vanier, Alain. *Lacan* [in Hebrew]. Translated by Amos Squverer. Tel Aviv: Resling, 2003. First published 2000.

Filmography

Omer, Fast. *Spielberg's List.* Germany, 2003.
Spielberg, Steven. *Schindler's List.* Universal Pictures, 1993.

CHAPTER 13

Auschwitz

George Tabori's Short Joke

SHULAMITH LEV-ALADGEM

The discourse of the Holocaust, like any discourse, is dynamic and transformative. The growing distance from the historical moment accelerates this process, which is currently generating new and contested Holocaust narratives. This ongoing making of meaning out of the term "Holocaust" is also due to its explosive evocative power, encapsulating the incommensurate and ultimate cruelty. The discursive appropriation of the Holocaust has expanded lately, taking a new global direction that focuses on new forms of suffering and genocides. This new ethics and practice of the Holocaust constitutes it as a supervalue appropriated worldwide for self and communal identity formation, as well as for symbolic and material claims. This global turn in the Holocaust discourse has stimulated dispute and negation, especially by those Jews who feel that their absolute monopoly over the Holocaust, perceived as fixed and justified forever, has been brutally appropriated. However, as theater scholar Vivian Patraka indicates, "If Jews crave the historical specificity of the Holocaust then to follow one path of that logic is to create relationships. Connecting the Holocaust with other struggles and other points of oppression may make it less possible to view it as an isolated and therefore nonrepeatable event."[1] Following this stand, which perceives the globalization of the discourse of the Holocaust not as opposed to the original historical event and its major Jewish bearers but as an important, actual, and relevant extension of it, I present George Tabori, the Jewish cosmopolitan dramatist who had pursued this logic even before the formation of the global discourse of the Holocaust. I thus perceive Tabori's contribution to this volume as a vivid example of how the symbolic-artistic sphere

Notes for this section begin on page 280.

sometimes precedes and initiates the public sphere. I focus here on the drama and theater of George Tabori, who from the early 1970s until his death in 2007 dared to break the taboo of the good Jewish victims versus the bad German perpetrators in order to alert people to the danger of framing the Holocaust as a one-off atrocity. He thereby reinscribed the memory of the Holocaust as a macroparadigm by which to expose the suffering and cruelty created and imposed by individuals and groups throughout the world. The drama of Tabori, as I present it here, was and in many ways still is radically avant-garde in comparison to the leading documentary and commemorative genres of Holocaust drama, and undoubtedly contributed to paving the way to the new forms of Holocaust drama that are sporadically appearing today in Israel and elsewhere. Theater, as the old cliché goes, holds up a mirror to reality. Although I believe that drama and theater should be respected and treated as important sociohistorical documents, I nevertheless negate theater as solely a representation of reality. The singularity of theater lies not in mirroring or affirming the accepted discourse. Theater has the potential to create through its artistic language and special energies that text that has hitherto not been part of the discourse and might otherwise never be. This "as-if" text nonetheless succeeds in arousing and agitating our suppressed reflexivity regarding all those complexities that the "as-is" public discourse circumvents and excludes, either explicitly or implicitly. Tabori's plays and performances are an outstanding example of such a theater, by means of which he courageously and provocatively problematized the "sacred cow" of the Holocaust, and hence can be seen as a precursor and messenger of the contemporary global political applications of the memory of the Holocaust.

Representation, Reiteration, and Accountability

Representation, as Patraka indicates, is a hot issue in itself even before connecting it to the Holocaust. Its complexity is a result of its dual nature as both a process and an object. As a process, "a doing," representation presupposes that there is a fixed norm, event, practice, or discourse that can be translated through reiteration. As an object, "a thing done," representation seeks to substantiate what is believed to be fixed. But since nothing in society and culture is static, and since reiteration is a ritualized repetition with the potential to generate something new,[2] representation is an elusive and tricky system. Reiteration in or by theater/performance intensifies the intricate tension between the doing and the thing done or between the performative and performance. Moreover, as Elin Diamond indicates, performance is the site in which "concealed or dissimulated conventions might be investigated."[3] When performativity materializes as performance in that risky and dangerous negotiation between a doing (a reiteration of norms) and a thing done (discursive conventions that frame our interpretation), between someone's body and the conventions of embodiment, "we have access to cultural meanings and critique."[4] Thus, theater/performance reinforces and empowers the generative, innovative, and creative potential of reiteration. As I will demonstrate below, Tabori provides us with such exceptional and original reiterations of the Holocaust, without any intention of producing documentary theater or realistic drama. It was from his drive to open up the memory of the Holocaust to new directions, cultural meanings, and critiques that Tabori confronted Theodor Adorno's reservations in regard to representing the Holocaust. "To write about Auschwitz is an imperative," stated Tabori. "One must overcome it somehow."[5]

Discussing the issue of representing the Holocaust in theater/performance, Patraka suggests that the delicate balance between the doing and the thing done in performance generally becomes highly complex in performances representing the Holocaust. She directs our attention to the absoluteness and the excessive power of the thing done (all the particular discursive categories, conventions, genres, and practices in relation to the Holocaust) that "weighs heavily on any doing in the Holocaust performative."[6] Consequently, she adds that this extra burden claims an added dimension of accountability that artists who wish to touch upon the Holocaust must undertake.[7]

Accountability has recently become a prominent ethical and political concept that serves the new needs, values, and expectations of the international community. The common denominator of the various definitions points to the obligation of an individual, an institution, or an organization to accept responsibility for its actions—to account for them, and to present their outcomes.[8] While accountability is a buzzword whose meaning everyone intuitively knows, not one of the definitions specifically explains it. Nevertheless, it should be emphasized that accountability means more than just responsibility, in the sense that one has to accept unconditional responsibility by promising oneself and others to provide specific results and consequences.[9] Whether this contribution improves and deepens our understanding of accountability or not, its applicability to theater/performance is in any case even more problematic, since what kinds of account (specific report?) can/should an artist deliver? And to whom exactly? If Patraka's appropriation of the term for theater is not literal but symbolic, why does she find accountability more proper than commitment—the concept that was formulated by the counterculture artists of the 1960s and 1970s, who claimed that artists should take social, political, and moral responsibility for their art?

Patraka does not provide a clear answer. She explains accountability as not being reverentiality and also not "what is and is not allowed to be shown, by whom and to whom,"[10] but rather as "the responsibility of all the writers who write for the present, in the present, for the living, but who also must write to and for the dead."[11] Patraka's thesis on the imbalance between the thing done and the doing in theatrical representation, and its heavy burden on the artists, offers an important contribution to the issue of representation and the Holocaust. Seeking a "hard" term by which to articulate the responsibility of artists to the history and memory of the Holocaust, she may have found accountability as the most expressive, but her explanation of precisely what this accountability means is somewhat light and too general. Patraka fails to take a direct look at this burden, and thus does not capture what it truly means and contains. Does she refrain from such an act because of the threat of (Holocaust) accountability to scholars as well? This burden, as I see it, is not the memory of the dead or the historical event itself, but the ongoing struggle over the one, single, proper, and rightful code by which to represent it. Patraka indeed hints at this problem by using the loaded and demanding term "accountability," but fails to identify all those taboos that are still incorporated within this accountability, and demands that the artists hold on to them.

It is exactly this kind of accountability for the Holocaust that Tabori absolutely negated. "There are taboos that must be broken or they will continue to choke us," he wrote in the late 1960s,[12] and indeed he had no interest in fidelity to the precise historical reality of the Holocaust and its factual truth, nor to the original victims or the survivors. Tabori saw his accountability as solely to the art of theater, or in his own humorous words, to "[s]tage, bed and books."[13] Theater for Tabori had a socioaesthetic role as a vehicle for agency, as a special visceral experience that engages the audience bodily and stimulates them to interpret the performance in such a way as to shake up their fundamental values, beliefs, and hopes. Tabori's accountability was to the aesthetic-political potential of theater to interrupt and disturb the habitual by means of estrangement (defamiliarization). He took this artistic principal to its limits by reconstructing Holocaust components into a blasphemous collage in the attempt to produce a cruel shock effect that would propel the audience into a new perception of the Holocaust. In the late 1960s, when he began to write and direct his Holocaust dramas, the prevalent artistic approach followed the social approach, producing plays that depicted the suffering and anguish of the Jewish victims at the hands of the brutal and monstrous German perpetrators. Tabori broke this sacred narrative, which guarded and still forcefully guards the closed boundaries of the local-particular discourse of the Holocaust. For him, such a presentation signified nonaccountability: "It would be an insult to the dead to beg for sympathy.... The event is beyond tears."[14] The traditional, particular approach to the Holocaust, which proclaims, "It will never happen to *us* again," is a dangerous, deceptive, and irresponsible stand. The only way, Tabori believed, to be truly accountable for the Holocaust was to reiterate it as a root metaphor of the human personal and collective ability to cause suffering to others. Tabori's metaphor delivers the warning: "What should we all do that it will never happen again to anyone?"

The Mythical Seed: Synoptic Notes

Performances on the Holocaust generally adopt one of three generic modes of representation (or a combination of these): the realistic/melodramatic and the documentary drama genres were mostly featured from the post–World War II years through the 1970s. Since the 1980s, however, a third genre has come into existence, one that deliberately merges the factual with the fictional, and is identified by Freddie Rokem as the fantastic.[15] This is not a sequential development from one genre to the other, since, as Rokem clearly indicates in all the three modes, "the first-person testimony of the survivor is the rhetorical kernel on which these performances are based."[16] He also notes that the integration of fantastic elements into the documentary and realistic styles has a similar aim: "Some kind of aestheticization of the narrative is necessary in order to tell what has really happened."[17] Choice of genre as Frederic Jameson indicates, is always political,[18] and indeed Tabori is still an exceptional artist who rejected the imperative of the first-person testimony and fully appropriated the fantastic mode. He provided his own one-of-a-kind horrific fantasy, which despite being seemingly real in using concrete Jewish and German characters, was never intended to reiterate what had really happened. Tabori is still an outstanding representative of the fantastic endeavor, whose personal biography is no less fantastic than that of his theater. A Jew, born in Budapest in 1914, his father, an eminent journalist and writer, was murdered in Auschwitz, while he himself managed to escape to London, where he worked as a journalist and in the British Secret Service. He wandered through several countries, including Israel, until reaching the United States, where he spent more than twenty years, writing film scripts for Hollywood, translating Brecht into English, and writing plays that were not particularly successful. Surprisingly, or maybe not, things began to change for the better when he moved back to Germany in the 1970s and started writing and directing his Holocaust corpus: in *Cannibals* (1969), the inmates of a concentration camp who accidentally kill Puffi, one of their companions, have to choose among eating bits of his flesh, starving to death, or perishing in the gas chamber. They eventually cook and eat Puffi in order to survive, but shortly after, they themselves are cooked in the ovens or gassed. Tabori's interest is in human behavior in liminal and acute circumstances. The inmates, a heterogeneous group, not necessarily all Jews, are trapped in a human-made hell, in which some of them nonetheless manage to retain their humanity. In *My Mother Courage* (1979), Tabori counters Brecht's *Mother Courage and Her Children*. He represents, or maybe invents, his own mother Elsa's strangely amazing escape from Auschwitz. She, an ordinary Jewish housewife, manages to save herself by simply approaching the German commander and commenting that her arrest was a mistake since she had a protective pass issued by the Swedish Red Cross but had forgotten it at home. She is released and then finds herself seated on a train facing that same German officer, who is a murderer but also her savior. *The Voyeur* (1982) is Tabori's inverted version of Dreyfus. Here the sentenced Jew is a former inmate from Dachau and now a tycoon from Harlem. He realizes that being a victim himself has not stopped him from abusing the black minority in his neighborhood and, like Oedipus, he blinds himself. Tabori's *Jubilee* (1983) was commissioned by the city of Bochum to mark the fiftieth anniversary of the National Socialists' rise to power in Germany. In a cemetery on the banks of the Rhine, the ghosts of the dead victims of the Third Reich are constantly disturbed by the hostility and brutality of Jurgen, the young neo-Nazi. In *Mein Kampf* (1987), Shlomo-Herzl, a poor Jewish intellectual, pleads with Mother Death to save Hitler's life, and will thus be responsible for the Holocaust. *Weissman and Red Face* (1990) is about a duel between a Jew and a Native American to see who has suffered most. The Jew wins the duel but dies from a heart attack. *Goldberg Variations* (1991) is a bizarre biblical Holocaust theater in which a famous dictatorial theater director, Mr. I, helped by his assistant, Goldberg, his loyal Jewish scapegoat, rehearses his tragic-satiric version of Genesis; and *The Ballad of the Vienna Schnitzel* (1996) is a play about eight top chefs who stuff a Jewish restaurant critic with schnitzels.[19]

Although the above constitute no more than synoptic notes, they nevertheless reveal Tabori's main method of reiteration. He selects various fragments of the history and memory of the Holocaust, dismantles them, mixes them with other canonic pieces of Western culture, and then replays them as a new incommensurable text. The Holocaust for Tabori is thus the mythical seed, the primary, basic element that triggers the creative process of the play. Eli Rozik, in its book *The Elements of Play Analysis,* points out that in contrast to the literary analysis of a play, the theatrical method focuses on the relationship between the play and the audience, which foregrounds theater as a communal institution.[20] As such, the fictional world that the play substantiates is not an accidental assemblage of characters and actions, but a well-organized, multilayered structure. The first layer is the mythical layer, the raw, basic narrative material of the theatrical experience, which relates to suppressed impulses. This primal stuff arouses fear and anxiety, since it breaks taboos and resists accepted values. Aristotle, in his *Poetics,* indicates that the proper material for tragedy is that which represents the breaking of taboos, such as murder within the family and incest, as in *Oedipus*. Drawing on Aristotle and Freud, Rozik highlights the theater as a communal institution that facilitates confrontation with social taboos. Tabori, in a very original and disturbing way, signifies the Holocaust as the modern, collective mythical source that even Aristotle could not have imagined. Thus, by employing the thing done of the Holocaust as the mythical, explosive seed, Tabori liberates himself from the heavy burden of the thing done and commits himself absolutely (becomes accountable) to the doing: he reiterates the Holocaust as the most inclusive and total symbolic tool for human self and collective reflexivity.

In 1992, after twenty years of an illustrious career in Germany, Tabori was awarded the distinguished Buchner Prize and was voted the best German playwright of our time. This occurred despite, or perhaps because of, the fantastic fusion between his own life and his theater: he who had written in *Jubilee* that "criminals are wont to return to the scene of the crime, so are, occasionally, the victims," practiced what he preached.[21] He reconnected his own life to those of the Germans in order to live through the leitmotif of his drama and theater, which calls for a bond between the persecutor and the persecuted in order to fight against the potential for cruelty embedded in each of us.

Such a problematic and risky doing required a unique, innovative artistry. Tabori's method of reiteration is encapsulated in his macabre, horrific, and yet witty and amazing linguistic interpretation of Auschwitz, of which he dared to say: "Auschwitz is the shorter German joke" (*witz*).[22] Thus, Tabori defined himself as "a playwright of catastrophes"[23] and not of the Holocaust, which implies his relation, even if implicitly, to the new global discourse of the Holocaust.

Tabori's theater, I therefore suggest, is a theater of atrocious jokes that compounds the "theater of catastrophes," which fantastically reiterates Auschwitz—the catastrophe of all catastrophes—as a new text of a total stage catastrophe. Tabori's "theater of catastrophes" is thus a singular elaboration of Antonin Artaud's "theater of cruelty."[24]

Theater of Catastrophes as a Theater of Cruelty

Artaud, a French poet, playwright, and director who spent large parts of his life in mental institutions, has become mostly renowned as the author of a revolutionary dramatic theory in the early 1930s, published in 1938 under the title *The Theatre and Its Double*. After his death in 1948, he became the prophet of the avant-garde, experimental theater of the 1960s and 1970s and has since inspired new generations of theater practitioners.[25] Artaud's vision of theater in general and his idea of the "theater of cruelty" in particular deserve a long discussion in themselves. Within the framework of this chapter, however, I will touch upon them only to the extent that is necessary for my discussion.

Artaud had attended a Balinese theater performance in Paris in 1931 that immensely impressed him with its unique combination of stylized, precise symbolic gestures and resonance of deep violence. This experience led him to his formulation of the "theater of cruelty," based on the insight that "the essence of theatre is found neither in the narration of an event, nor in the discussion of a hypothesis with an audience nor in the representation of life as it appears from the outside … [but] when we discover that theatrical reality is instantaneous, not an illustration of life but something linked to life only by analogy."[26] This expressive analogy, by no means realistic or documentary, must uproot the audience from the triviality of daily life and propel it into a ritualistic, spiritually shocking event. The visceral onslaught on the nerves and senses of the audience should attack them at the very core of their unconscious, horrendous, dark, and evil desires. Theater is the medium of staged cruelty, in the sense of staged violence, danger, and extremity, by which it exposes the evil, the savagery, and the cannibalism of humanity. "It is upon this idea of extreme action, pushed beyond all limits that theatre must be rebuilt," Artaud contends,[27] and adds that this cruelty is not the fault of theater, but of life.[28] Tabori, in his Holocaust theater, as already apparent from the discussion above, strove to capture this idea of total theater, imprinted with terror and cruelty, executing drastic actions pushed to the limit. Artaud himself never provided precise instructions on how to practice this "cruelty" on stage. "This cruelty," he said, "is not sadistic or bloody, at least not exclusively so";[29] but he also stated that "this cruelty will be bloody if need to be."[30] What is more important to our discussion here, and pinpoints the link between Artaud and Tabori, is Artaud's insistence that "practicing cruelty involves a higher determination to which the executer-tormentor is also subject."[31] In Tabori's theater, as I have noted above, this is the chief motif and taboo-breaking idea. The Jew is not the only and ultimate executed, the German is not the absolute executer, and the distance between them is not as great as it might seem. In *Jubilee* Tabori asserts: "Criminals are wont to return to the scene of the crime, so are, occasionally, the victims,"[32] and "You don't love me because I am a little Nazi. But in fact you don't love me because you love too much. Because you resemble me, because inside you too there is a little Nazi, exactly as in all the others around here."[33]

However, unlike Tabori, Artaud envisioned the "theater of cruelty" as a beneficial, cathartic experience. "Evil will eventually be reduced but only at the final moment when all forms are on the point of return to chaos."[34] The staged cruelty was intended to encounter the audience with the evil in order to be released from it. It is therefore here that Artaud saw the symbolic analogy between the "theater of cruelty" and the plague, as both destructive and transforming forces that finally heal humanity. Artaud's perception was that a colossal abscess, ethical as much as social, had been drained by the plague. And the "theater of cruelty," like the plague, was collectively made to drain abscesses.[35] At the beginning of the 1930s Artaud appropriated the plague, the historical event, as a hypermetaphor of an all-consuming disaster and crisis. After Auschwitz, Tabori did not need the plague. He had a better historical event (the Holocaust) to appropriate as the supermetaphor for human evil. For Artaud the plague purges, "brings whatever would have been noxious, hidden, and festering to the surface ... and expels it. Theatre can do likewise. It stimulates the dark, unindulged passions, the abnormal feelings ... and by expelling them at one remove, in performance, cleanses the performer and the spectator alike in its collective experience."[36] For Tabori, however, neither Auschwitz nor the theater can heal the human evil. Tabori's staged cruelty constitutes an apparatus for problematizing the discourse of the Holocaust and thus reinforcing the effect of agitation, embarrassment, and dissonance on the audience.

Artaud advocated a physical, sensual, ritual-like theater based on a synesthetic corporal language of images, sounds, and ritualized violent movements of the performers, who like inspired ghosts radiate affective power and jar the spectators into a heightened state of consciousness. The shock effect of the performance impels the audience to become aware of the evil, violence, and cruelty of life, but at the same time purges them of these negative elements.[37]

For Tabori, this advocation was only partially appropriate. His theater indeed strives to bond performers and spectators into an extreme visceral experience, yet never by means of pathos or serious ritualistic enactments. Tabori's "theater of catastrophes" is a unique combination of Artaud's "theater of cruelty" and Brecht's "theater of *verfremdung* [defamiliarization]" that engenders unexpected theatrical and metatheatrical landscapes of nightmarish yet funny, witty, and sardonic performances. Tabori's staged cruelty is a reiteration that obliterates the boundaries between life and art, past and present, historical facts and legendary myths, between the profane and the sacred, the psychological and sociological, the rational and the arbitrary, the local and the global, and above all, between the executioners and the executed.

Bertold Brecht employed Viktor Shklovski's aesthetic theory of alienation/defamiliarization for his Marxist dramatic theory, *verfremdung*, which is usually identified as the V-effect or the A-effect. Shklovski considered the aesthetic quality of the language of poetry to derive from its defamiliarizing means, which estranges the familiar and makes "the stone stony."[38] "By tearing the object out of its habitual context …, the poet … forces us into heightened awareness of things and their *sensory* texture."[39] Brecht, who believed that the effect of catharsis appeases the audience and fosters their complicity with the hegemonic social order, elaborated defamiliarization into the V-effect as the chief cognitive function of his epic, noncathartic theater. The V-effect aimed to improve the audience's knowledge of the social order by means of devices that decontexualized the familiar and thus stimulated the audience into reconsidering it and getting to know it better. Brecht believed that cognition promotes social criticism that in turn instigates social change.[40]

Tabori created his noncathartic theater of cruelty by adopting both Shklovski's and Brecht's methods of defamiliarization: by drawing the attention of the audience to the sensory texture and effect of the language of the theater in general and its own staged cruelty, Tabori provides a here-and-now locus of an alternative remembrance and memory construction of the Holocaust. "True remembrance," says Tabori, "is possible only through sensual remembrance. It is impossible to confront the past without sensing it again in one's skin, nose, tongue, buttocks and stomach."[41] For example, in *Cannibals,* there are episodes of vomiting, defecation, and urination in addition to other scenes in which the actors grapple, embrace, crawl, freeze in fear, and bend over in exhaustion, frailty, and vulnerability. They gesticulate eating noisily, chew, munch, lick their lips, belch, grab imaginary bits of liver, growl and bark like dogs, sibilate, moan, sing, tell jokes, imitate the burbling of water, and produce the hissing sound of the gas oozing from the showers.[42] These corporeal activities primarily draw attention to the aesthetic faculties of the theater to make "the stone stony,"[43] that is, to constitute a signifier that not only stands for the catastrophe of Auschwitz but, more than that, creates an immediate present, symbolic cruelty, which breaks through "one's skin, nose, tongue, buttocks and stomach."[44] This bodily experiential mnemonic apparatus is not, however, intended to stimulate empathy and emotionalism for the horrendous historical events. In *My Mother Courage,* Son says: "Yes, yes, there is nothing like blowing up the metaphor until it explodes."[45] In other words, the aesthetic effect of defamiliarization is intended to foster its cognitive effect, by means of which one should reconsider Auschwitz beyond its habitual conception and capture it as a basic, mythic grand metaphor of new human catastrophes that still continue to happen after Auschwitz. This is the visceral and cognitive effect that Tabori anticipated from his theater and was committed and accountable to create. It is out of this impetus that *Cannibals* was staged on a bare platform "with only a rack of bunks, a winding metal staircase, and an oven with its coarse-looking pipe jutting out,"[46] while only two of the inmates wore the striped camp uniform and all the others were attired in ordinary shabby clothing.[47] Another example is the staging of *Jubilee*. In this play, which was written to mark the fiftieth anniversary of the National Socialists' rise to power in Germany, Tabori's intention was to warn that evil still circulates: "The same old story. Here we go again. Thirty-four years of democracy and again the same thing. Another jubilee. Where did we make a mistake?"[48] Tabori staged this play in an avant-garde approach, in the theater foyer, which was covered with mounds of earth, tombstones, and foliage. A grave mound was raised outside the building as well, extending the inner space in order to signal the bond between the past and the present, theater and life. Through the large windowpanes the audience and the passersby could see each other, while the traffic and the ongoing activities in the street became part of the performance text. The climax of this staging was when Jurgen, the young neo-Nazi, arrived by car in front of the theater building and entered the playing area.[49]

    A prevalent defamiliarizing device in Tabori's drama and theater is that of the stylized, evocative mock and perverse rituals of sacrifice/feast, with no lamb as a surrogate, without salvation or redemption. In *Cannibals* it is the meal of the cooked human body of Puffi. In *Jubilee* it is a loaf of bread, the Jewish Sabbath challah, that Arnold, the specter of a victim, gets from the specter of his murdered father and shares with the other specters of victims of the National Socialist terror regime. In *Mein Kampf* it is Mitzi, the chicken, dismembered, cooked, and eaten while Shlomo-Herzl pronounces Kaddish, the Jewish prayer for the dead. In all these scenes, Tabori employs essential cultural components that are repeated from the magic rites (the totem meal) of the Jewish (Passover) and Christian (Communion) liturgy. He reiterates these sacred rituals in a carnivalesque and subversive manner, which produces discrepant fragments of mock, pastiche-like rituals that interplay curiously between frivolity and horror. These new forms of hybridized, incredible, macabre, and profane rituals deliver Tabori's catastrophic jokes, such as in *My Mother Courage*: "Auschwitz—a Jewish bakery";[50] in *Jubilee*: "Just last week I read that in Auschwitz they had baked bread and not fathers";[51] and in *Mein Kampf*: "One who starts burning chickens will eventually burn human beings as well."[52]

An additional device is that of intertextual allusions, which Tabori appropriates in order to move from ordinary communication to metacommunication, and contrasts levels of style and intellectual significance, evoking ultimate confusion between appearance and reality, and between role, character, and performer. Tabori's drama is loaded with intertextuality and allusions to the Old and New Testaments, the Talmud, Shakespeare, Kafka, Beckett, Dostoyevsky, Brecht, and German legends and myths. On the one hand, the text revives and brings to mind canonical pieces from the Western cultural heritage, including those of the Holocaust. On the other hand, the pastiche-like[53] reiteration of these source texts, and the wild, explosive style with which Tabori interlaces them, disturb our usual collective perception of these grand works of culture and arouse a reflexive rethinking of our cherished heritage, including the narrative of the Holocaust.

Mein Kampf is a keen example of this endeavor. Premiered in Vienna in 1987, and Tabori's most performed play, *Mein Kampf* is a theological, deliberately distorted farce, which shows the encounter of Shlomo-Herzl, the Jew, with the young Hitler in a seedy hotel. The accumulation of inverted vast and diverse intertextuality creates a counternarrative in which both Shlomo-Herzl (a combination of Shlomo [Solomon], the biblical king and poet, and Herzl, the father of modern Israel) and Hitler are parts of a chimerical phantasmagoria in which Shlomo-Herzl is the would-be author of a book by the name of *Mein Kampf*, and the one who encourages Hitler to become a politician and gives him the mustachioed Führer look, brushes his hair, buttons him up, and lends him his own winter coat. Hitler is represented as a Jewish relative of Shlomo-Herzl, a descendant of the Tishler family, whose name was misspelled by the city council. Moreover, it is Shlomo who saves Hitler from Mother Death, confessing: "You somehow seem familiar to me."[54] "I love you. How can I prove it? You do not exactly deserve love, but nevertheless, at this moment, when you are sitting here with wet eyes, I love you."[55] This hypothetical exercise, enabled by theater, reiterates history in a way that intentionally cuts the distance between victim and victimizer and places the responsibility for evil (the future Holocaust) on the victim (Shlomo-Herzl). This radical outlook, which, as I have discussed above, is Tabori's principal endeavor, is further intensified by role playing and role reversal, such as in *Jubilee,* when Helmut, the homosexual, plays a Nazi officer who is the father of Jurgen, the young neo-Nazi, while Jurgen plays the German prosecutor, who tortures the father-officer for being too soft. Another example of role playing is in *Mein Kampf,* when Lubcowitz, the Jewish cook, plays God and Shlomo-Herzl plays Moses. This device is manifested more extensively in *My Mother Courage.* The play, which is Tabori's counter to Brecht's play *Mother Courage and Her Children,* features five characters who, as in a parable, have no proper names but are identified by their typical social roles: Son, Mother, German, Officer, and Lover. The play ostensibly focuses on the miraculous escape of Tabori's mother from Auschwitz, but Tabori has no interest in delivering a moral from this case, or of accusing the Germans. Rather, it is a self-referential play that confronts the validity of narrative/discourse in general and that of the Holocaust in particular. Thus, Son and Mother play the roles of Tabori and his mother Elsa and also exchange roles with the other, "bad" characters. Son tells his mother's salvation story while sitting next to her. Occasionally, Mother interrupts her son's legendary storytelling in order to correct him and provides her own somewhat dry versions. Moreover, Son himself digresses from the central narrative, introducing his own associations back and forth in time. These contextual comments about the pleasant weather and the comfortable everyday life in Vienna during the arrest of Mother, as well as the fragmentation of the story by means of role playing, defamiliarize the miraculous salvation story and present instead an inverted fable. Thus, the spectators' attention is deliberately drawn to the aside, to additional pieces of the story, such as in the case when Son drifts away, describing the warm sunny weather and the peaceful atmosphere in the street that continues in spite of the sudden arrest of Mother: "This is how in those days Jews and non-Jews faced the catastrophe—indifferently; there was no place for panic or resistance."[56] Mother adds shortly after: "Murder begins when the grief no longer wets your underwear or your eyes."[57] The constant peaceful acceptance of evil, which has not changed despite Auschwitz, is what mostly bothers Tabori. In *The Voyeur,* Dreyfuss, the Jewish survivor who became a heartless abuser of his black neighbors in Harlem, says in a moment of recognition: "What is a good man? A good man is a man who has pangs of conscience," without which "we will become scum."[58] The climax of *My Mother Courage,* Tabori's flawed fable, occurs in the train, when Mother is sitting in front of Officer—her savior, the German commander, who has just sent another train full of Jews to Auschwitz. For a second their blue eyes meet, and Mother feels embraced, as if their bodies have become one. This brief eye contact, which blurs the boundaries between the persecutor and the persecuted, encapsulates Tabori's main idea, as Mother says: "Be careful not to look into the eyes of your enemy, my dear, since you might stop hating him."[59]

Tabori's drama and theater are not structured as a logical and orderly development of scenes, but as a complex, fragmented collage, creating a cumulative effect of one intensive episode after the other, biting, terrifying, sticking in the throat, and yet peculiarly humorous.[60] The effect of Tabori's "theater of catastrophes" is hard to verbalize; one has to experience it through the performance itself. Nevertheless, at the end of *Mein Kampf* Tabori articulates the essence of his theater through the character of Lubcowitz, the Jewish cook who likes to play God: "Think that in each joke there is a little Holocaust, for example: Two thieves hanged on a cross, one asks: does it hurt? The other says: 'only when I laugh.'"[61]

Conclusion

George Tabori was an outstanding representative of European cosmopolitanism, which began in the late nineteenth and early twentieth centuries. He was born in Budapest one month before the outbreak of World War I, into an assimilated Jewish family of four generations of writers and intellectuals. He received a broad-based education reflecting liberalism, humanism, and the European high culture. As a loyal agent of liberal cosmopolitanism, he lived and worked as a journalist in Berlin, London, and the Balkans, and even spent a year in Israel. This career saved him from the death that his father and most of his family were sentenced to by the Nazi regime. Tabori thus experienced in full the collapse of the promises of liberal cosmopolitanism. His personal and ideological breakdown awoke his consciousness to the realization of what his character, Uncle, says in *Cannibals*: "You do not become a Jew, you are reminded of being one."[62] This awareness, nonetheless, did not move him to become accountable to the particular, mainly Jewish, approach to the construction of the memory of the Holocaust. On the contrary, after living for twenty years in the United States he chose to challenge his Jewishness precisely in Germany, with the intention of using theater as a laboratory from which to confront Auschwitz in an avant-garde approach that in many ways is still radical and exceptional. He perceived the role of the Jew, as a (literal or metaphoric) survivor, to be to appropriate the Holocaust for the benefit of all humanity, by providing an inclusive, pertinent significance for the horrendous historical event. Tabori's emphasis on the presentness of the historical past of the Holocaust generated a singular corpus of drama and theater that paved the way for new modes of theatrical representation of the Holocaust. His advocating that Jews, although the main target of the Nazi mass annihilation, have no monopoly on suffering (*The Voyeur*) echoes clearly in theater productions such as *The Third Generation*. This is a current (2011) joint production by Israel's national theater, Habimah, and Berlin's Schaubühne, and focuses on third-generation Israelis, Palestinians, and Germans. The production, directed by Yaeli Ronen and based on personal materials molded through a workshop process, confronts the intricate problem of what it means to be Israeli, German, or Palestinian in the third generation after the Holocaust.

Tabori, who died in 2007, was not only the predecessor of a new genre of Holocaust theater, but also of the new global cosmopolitanism that has appropriated the Holocaust as a collective signifier, which obtains different meanings within different national and ethnic communities. For Tabori, the contemporary connections and comparisons between the Holocaust and other genocides, injustices, and human suffering are crucial, since his theater strives to refute the idea that the Holocaust was a one-time deviation that only the Germans could have perpetrated. Tabori asserts that the Holocaust is not the private property of this or that particular group of survivors. For him Auschwitz was indeed the most terrible human laboratory in the history of civilization; but, unfortunately, its defeat did not result in any change in the nature of human evil. Human evil is still ongoing and manifesting itself in new ways. Tabori suggests this, for example, in *Weissman and Red Face,* when "Weissman wonders if there were also Jews who participated in the Buffalo slaughter; tries in vain to recall an example of minority brotherhood, let's say, between the Hyseyoks [a Native American tribe] and his own people [the Jews]."[63] Another example is Dreyfuss, the protagonist of the play *The Voyeur,* who as a survivor of Dachau should have accepted his black neighbors in Harlem with empathy, but treats them instead in the opposite, evil way.

The old liberal European who experienced the disintegration of his own cosmopolitanism thus welcomes the new global cosmopolitanism of the twenty-first century, but at the same time provides it with an important contribution. In order not to crash tragically once again, the new cosmopolitanism should be constantly self-reflexive and self-critical, since the new victims too have no monopoly on the Holocaust either. In *The Voyeur* Tabori says through Dreyfuss: "From where do you take for yourself the credit to think that if your skin color is black you have the permission to mock others? ... You do not have a monopoly on suffering."[64]

The drama and theater of Tabori thus remain highly significant and relevant for both the old, particular, and the new, global, discourse of the Holocaust. From Tabori's point of view, both the persecutors and the persecuted (no matter who they are, when and where) should always be held accountable for their actions. He therefore creates a bond between the two, which is clearly manifested in *Jubilee*: "Criminals are wont to return to the scene of the crime, so are, occasionally, the victims." The bond between Jurgen, the neo-Nazi, and the ghosts of the dead victims is obsessive, heightened by the constant role reversal that Tabori demands of them. The accumulation of all these devices into a "deep play" intends at the end to demand of all of us, as individuals, as communities, as nations, and as the global village, to acknowledge the "Nazi" or, in its wider sense, the human evil that has not yet diminished. It is our choice, however, whether and when to let the beast out; and this is a daily, demanding choice that interweaves the personal with the political, the national, and the global.

Tabori is not popular in Israel. It is obvious why. I, as the only daughter of two Holocaust survivors, can perfectly understand this. And I respect it. However, precisely because I am a second-generation Holocaust survivor, living in Israel, caught within terrible and complex social and political mazes, I find it crucial to follow what I have discovered through this research, and enter into the "deep play" of role reversal with Jurgen: "You don't love me. You don't love me because I am a little Nazi. But in fact you don't love me because you love too much. Because you resemble me, because inside you too there is a little Nazi, exactly as in all the others around here."[65]

Notes

This research was supported by The Israel Science Foundation (grant No. 435/10)

1. Vivian Patraka, *Spectacular Suffering: Theatre, Fascism, and the Holocaust* (Indianapolis: Indiana University Press, 1999), 4.
2. Judith Butler, "Performative Acts and Gender Constitution: An Essay in Phenomenology and Feminist Theory," in *Performing Feminisms: Feminist Critical Theory and Theatre,* ed. Sue-Ellen Case (Baltimore, MD: Hopkins University Press, 1990); Judith Butler, *Bodies that Matters: On the Discursive Limits of Sex* (New York: Routledge, 1993).
3. Elin Diamond, "Introduction," in *Performance and Cultural Politics,* ed. Elin Diamond (New York; Routledge 1996), 1–12.
4. Ibid., 5.
5. Anat Feinberg, *Embodies Memory: The Theatre of George Tabori* (Iowa City: University of Iowa Press, 1999), 99.
6. Patraka, *Spectacular Suffering,* 7.
7. Ibid.
8. Kathy Fitzpatrick and Carolyn Bronstein, eds. *Ethics in Public Relations: Responsibility Advocacy* (London: Sage, 2006).
9. Thomas Birins, "Responsibility and Accountability," in *Ethics in Public Relations: Responsibility Advocacy,* ed. Kathy Fitzpatrick and Carolyn Bronstein (London: Sage, 2006), 19-38.
10. Patraka, *Spectacular Suffering,* 8.
11. Ibid.
12. Anat Feinberg, "The Taboos Must Be Broken: George Tabori's Mourning Work in Jubilaum," in *Staging the Holocaust: The Shoah in Drama and Performance,* ed. Claude Schumacher (Cambridge: Cambridge University Press, 1998), 267.
13. Ibid.
14. Feinberg, *Embodies Memory,* 237.
15. Freddie Rokem, "On the Fantastic in Holocaust Performances," in *Staging the Holocaust: The Shoah in Drama and Performance,* ed. Claude Schumacher (Cambridge: Cambridge University Press, 1998).
16. Ibid., 41.
17. Ibid., 43.
18. Frederic Jameson, *The Political Unconscious: Narrative as a Socially Symbolic Act* (New York: Cornell University Press 1981).
19. Gad Kaynar and Shimon Levi, "Introduction" [in Hebrew], in *George Tabori: Plays,* ed. Gad Kaynar and Shimon Levi (Tel Aviv: Assaph 2004), 7–22; Feinberg, "The Taboos Must Be Broken"; Jack Zipes, "George Tabori and the Jewish Question," *Theater* 29, no. 2 (1999): 98–107.

20. Eli Rosik, *The Elements of Play Analysis* (Tel Aviv; Or Am, 1992) [in Hebrew].
21. George Tabori, *Jubilee*, translated to Hebrew by Tom Levi, in *George Tabori: Plays*, ed. Gad Kaynar and Shimon Levi [in Hebrew] (Tel Aviv: Assaph, 2004), 160, 178. All translations from Hebrew to English are the author's.
22. Feinberg, *Embodies Memory*, 231.
23. Kaynar and Levi, "Introduction," 14.
24. Antonin Artuad, *The Theatre and Its Double* (1958; repr., London: John Calder, 1970).
25. George E. Wellwarth, *The Theatre of Protest and Paradox* (New York: New York University Press, 1965).
26. Jerzi Grotowski, *Toward a Poor Theatre* (New York: Simon and Schuster, 1968), 117–25.
27. Artuad, *The Theatre and Its Double*, 85.
28. Ibid., 31.
29. Ibid., 79.
30. Ibid., 81.
31. Ibid., 80.
32. George Tabori, *Jubilee*, translated to Hebrew by Tom Levi, in *George Tabori: Plays*, ed. Gad Kaynar and Shimon Levi [in Hebrew] (Tel Aviv: Assaph, 2004), 160, 178.
33. Ibid., 172–73.
34. Antonin Artuad, *Collected Works*, vol. 4 (London: John Calder, 1974), 79.
35. Artuad, *The Theatre and Its Double*, 21–22.
36. Albert Bermel, *Artaud's Theatre of Cruelty* (New York: Taplinger, 1977), 18–19.
37. Stephen Barber, *Artaud: The Screaming Body* (London: Creation Books, 2007); Will H. Rockett, *Devouring Whirlwind: Terror and Transcendence in the Cinema of Cruelty* (New York: Greenwood Press, 1988).
38. Victor Shklovski, *Russian Formalist Criticism* (Lincoln; University of Nebraska Press, 1965), 12.
39. Victor Erlich, *Russian Formalism* (London: Muton, 1965), 177, emphasis added.
40. John Willett, ed. and trans., *Brecht on Theatre: The Development of an Aesthetic* (New York: Hill and Wang, 1987); Eli Rosik, "Defamiliarization in Theatre," in *Bertold Brecht: Performance and Philosophy*, ed. Gad Kaynar and Linda Ben-Zvi (Tel Aviv: Assaph, 2005).
41. Feinberg, "The Taboos Must Be Broken," 270.
42. Feinberg, *Embodies Memory*, 201–2.
43. Shklovski, *Russian Formalist Criticism*, 12.
44. Feinberg, "The Taboos Must Be Broken," 270.
45. George Tabori, *My Mother Courage*, translated to Hebrew by Rivka Meschulach, in *George Tabori: Plays*, ed. Gad Kaynar and Shimon Levi [in Hebrew] (Tel Aviv: Assaph, 2004), 73.
46. Feinberg, *Embodies Memory*, 201.
47. Ibid.
48. George Tabori, *Jubilee*, translated to Hebrew by Tom Levi, in *George Tabori: Plays*, ed. Gad Kaynar and Shimon Levi [in Hebrew] (Tel Aviv: Assaph, 2004), 166.
49. Feinberg, *Embodies Memory*, 238.
50. George Tabori, *My Mother Courage*, translated to Hebrew by Rivka Meschulach, in *George Tabori: Plays*, ed. Gad Kaynar and Shimon Levi [in Hebrew] (Tel Aviv: Assaph, 2004), 64.
51. George Tabori, *Jubilee*, translated to Hebrew by Tom Levi, in *George Tabori: Plays*, ed. Gad Kaynar and Shimon Levi [in Hebrew] (Tel Aviv: Assaph, 2004), 192.
52. George Tabori, *Mein Kampf*, translated to Hebrew by Simon Levi, in *George Tabori: Plays*, ed. Gad Kaynar and Shimon Levi [in Hebrew] (Tel Aviv: Assaph, 2004), 246.
53. Hans-Peter Bayerdorfer, "'Born Losers Comparing Notes': Bible Quotation and Drama Construction in George Tabori's Plays," in *Theatre and the Holy Scripts*, ed. Shimon Levi (Brighton, UK: Sussex Academic Press, 1999).
54. George Tabori, *Mein Kampf*, translated to Hebrew by Simon Levi, in *George Tabori: Plays*, ed. Gad Kaynar and Shimon Levi [in Hebrew] (Tel Aviv: Assaph, 2004), 204.
55. Ibid., 231.

56. George Tabori, *My Mother Courage*, translated to Hebrew by Rivka Meschulach, in *George Tabori: Plays*, ed. Gad Kaynar and Shimon Levi [in Hebrew] (Tel Aviv: Assaph, 2004), 61.
57. Ibid., 83.
58. Ibid., 100.
59. Ibid., 81.
60. Feinberg, "The Taboos Must Be Broken."
61. George Tabori, *Mein Kampf*, translated to Hebrew by Simon Levi, in *George Tabori: Plays*, ed. Gad Kaynar and Shimon Levi [in Hebrew] (Tel Aviv: Assaph, 2004), 248.
62. Feinberg, "The Taboos Must Be Broken," 13.
63. Kaynar and Levi, "Introduction," 27.
64. Ibid., 119.
65. Ibid., 172–73.

Bibliography

Artuad, Antonin. *Collected Works*. Vol. 4. London: John Calder, 1974.

———. *The Theatre and Its Double*. London: John Calder, 1970. First published 1958.

Barber, Stephen. *Artaud: The Screaming Body*. London: Creation Books, 2007.

Bayerdorfer, Hans-Peter. "'Born Losers Comparing Notes': Bible Quotation and Drama Construction in George Tabori's Plays." In *Theatre and the Holy Scripts*, ed. Shimon Levi, 82–98, Brighton, UK: Sussex Academic Press, 1999.

Bermel, Albert. *Artaud's Theatre of Cruelty*. New York: Taplinger, 1977.

Birins, Thomas. "Responsibility and Accountability." In *Ethics in Public Relations: Responsibility Advocacy*, ed. Kathy Fitzpatrick and Carolyn Bronstein, 19–38, London: Sage, 2006.

Butler, Judith. *Bodies that Matters: On the Discursive Limits of Sex*. New York: Routledge, 1993.

———. "Performative Acts and Gender Constitution: An Essay in Phenomenology and Feminist Theory." In *Performing Feminisms: Feminist Critical Theory and Theatre*, ed. Sue-Ellen Case, 270–82, Baltimore, MD: Johns Hopkins University Press, 1990.

Diamond, Elin. "Introduction." In *Performance and Cultural Politics*, ed. Elin Diamond, 1–12, New York: Routledge, 1996.

Erlich, Victor. *Russian Formalism*. London: Mouton, 1965.

Feinberg, Anat. *Embodies Memory: The Theatre of George Tabori*. Iowa City: University of Iowa Press, 1999.

———. "The Taboos Must Be Broken: George Tabori's Mourning Work in Jubilaum." In *Staging the Holocaust: The Shoah in Drama and Performance*, ed. Claude Schumacher, 267–80, Cambridge: Cambridge University Press, 1998.

Fitzpatrick, Kathy, and Bronstein Carolyn, eds. *Ethics in Public Relations: Responsibility Advocacy*. London: Sage, 2006.

Grotowski, Jerzi. *Toward a Poor Theatre*. New York: Simon and Schuster, 1968.

Jameson, Frederic. *The Political Unconscious: Narrative as a Socially Symbolic Act*. Ithaca, NY: Cornell University Press, 1981.

Kaynar, Gad, and Levi Shimon. "Introduction" [in Hebrew]. In *George Tabori: Plays*, ed. Gad Kaynar and Shimon Levi, 7–22, Tel Aviv: Assaph, 2004 [in Hebrew].

Patraka, Vivian. *Spectacular Suffering: Theatre, Fascism, and the Holocaust*. Bloomington and Indianapolis: Indiana University Press, 1999.

Rockett, Will H. *Devouring Whirlwind: Terror and Transcendence in the Cinema of Cruelty*. New York: Greenwood Press, 1988.

Rokem, Freddie. "On the Fantastic in Holocaust Performances." In *Staging the Holocaust: The Shoah in Drama and Performance*, ed. Claude Schumacher, 40–52, Cambridge: Cambridge University Press, 1998.

Rosik, Eli. "Defamiliarization in Theatre." In *Bertold Brecht: Performance and Philosophy,* ed. Gad Kaynar and Linda Ben-Zvi, 69–82, Tel Aviv: Assaph, 2005.

———. *The Elements of Play Analysis.* Tel Aviv: Or-Am, 1992 [in Hebrew].

Shklovski, Victor. *Russian Formalist Criticism.* Lincoln: University of Nebraska Press, 1965.

Wellwarth, George E. *The Theatre of Protest and Paradox.* New York: New York University Press, 1965.

Willett, John, ed. and trans. *Brecht on Theatre: The Development of an Aesthetic.* New York: Hill and Wang, 1987.

Zipes, Jack. "George Tabori and the Jewish Question." *Theater* 29, no. 2 (1999): 98–107.

CHAPTER 14

The Law of Dispersion
A Reading of W. G. Sebald's Prose

JAKOB HESSING

In recent years, W. G. Sebald has become one of the most widely discussed authors of contemporary German literature. It was not in Germany, however, that his fiction at first began to gain critical acclaim, but abroad. His reputation spread in the Anglo-Saxon world and throughout Europe before it reached the country of his origin. Already in the 1990s, and increasingly so after his death, Sebald's books were translated into many languages, and in 2001 his last novel, *Austerlitz,* came out almost simultaneously in German and in English.

Is Sebald's rising fame a phenomenon of the age of globalization? Is it due to the fact that the Holocaust, one of his major themes, has become an issue of global interest, or is it perhaps the other way around? Have the universal subjects of his writing—the flow of time, memory and disaster, trauma and melancholy—endowed the Holocaust with a global attraction it usually does not hold?

Writing about the Holocaust, Sebald invariably presents us with a German narrator and his Jewish counterpart. Both the German and the Jew, however, live in exile, and this configuration gives his Holocaust texts their unmistakable countenance. In this chapter I shall attempt to show that the shock of exile lies at the core of his prose, and that it is part and parcel of a long process of which our age of globalization is the outcome. Sebald's texts confront us with some aspects of this process, preparing the ground for a homelessness that is both ubiquitous and universal.

Notes for this section begin on page 294.

Sebald's Reading of Döblin

Born in 1944 in a Bavarian village, W. G. Sebald grew up among adults who never spoke about the war or the Holocaust. It was only when he came to Manchester in the mid-1960s that he made himself familiar with the facts of recent German history.[1] Unlike his fellow students of the 1960s, he did not join the revolution against the elder generation; instead, he decided to leave Germany and to settle in England, where he taught German and European literature at the University of East Anglia until his untimely death in 2001.

Sebald did not participate in the riots at German universities in 1968, but there are obvious traces of the students' movement to be found in his early academic work. In England he wrote his doctoral thesis on the German Jewish writer Alfred Döblin, and the published version of 1980 shows both the influence of left-wing literary criticism in contemporary Germany and Sebald's own, quite unorthodox, way to read Döblin's oeuvre.[2]

Revolting against academic tradition in Germany, young scholars in the 1970s began to analyze the literature of their country in what they called a "materialistic" manner. For all too long, the educated German bourgeois, the *Bildungsbürger,* had tried to keep literature, and culture in general, away from the socioeconomic sphere—a spiritual haven untouched, as it were, by political reality. This was the rule at German universities until far into the 1960s, but the postwar generation refused to uphold the division between what the Germans called *Geist* and public reality. They wanted to understand the catastrophe of their country and take a closer look at how German literature related to German history.[3]

Sebald too adopts this critical view of German literature. "The present study," he writes about his doctoral thesis, defining his approach, "wishes to provide a materialistic analysis of the unstable relationship between fiction and myth, as well as literature and society, in Döblin's oeuvre, in which the ideological dilemma of the author becomes evident."[4] He notes that Döblin tends to blame evolution or nature, rather than human action, for the failures of society;[5] that his penchant for socialism is wishful thinking, not a viable political stance;[6] that he prefers messianic, or apocalyptic, imagery to social analysis and reflection;[7] and that his writings contain a pathological eroticism, and a worship of violence, typical of German bourgeoisie in its decline.[8]

These and other findings clearly show the influence of literary criticism as it developed in West Germany in the wake of the students' movement. And yet, there is a difference. In one way or another, the "materialistic" view of literature was shaped by the doctrines of Marxism that interpreted history as a sequence of struggles between social classes. This made it difficult for the young scholars of the so-called New Left to find a place for the many Jews, and their particular fate, in modern German literature and culture. They saw National Socialism as the epitome of capitalistic imperialism, and the Holocaust made no sense to them, because it had no "materialistic" logic to it. Most of them even turned a strangely blind eye to the fact that their teachers—Theodor W. Adorno, Herbert Marcuse, the late Walter Benjamin—were German Jews deeply affected by Hitler's policy.[9]

W. G. Sebald, on the other hand, had an entirely different feeling for the plight of European Jews in the twentieth century. It is no accident that he chose Alfred Döblin for his doctoral thesis. He was a writer of Jewish origin who later converted to Catholicism, and as Sebald wrote about him: "Döblin's attitude towards assimilation, a decisive factor in the development of many Jewish-German writers, was always ambivalent, if not to say opportunistic. [German] philology does not have to know a thing about these matters, and in all its attempts to read Döblin it has so far made a point of avoiding the issue."[10]

Because of its biological implications, the term "assimilation" is not used anymore and has been replaced by "acculturation," but surely it is a link in the process of alienation, which turns Sebald's world into a place of exile. Döblin exchanges his original identity for something else, and in certain instances, his ambivalence toward this act of transformation reaches the point of self-hatred. Sebald quotes him as saying: "Let the Jews grow rich in the West, and they will soon be exterminated,"[11] and he comments: "After such words, it is difficult to consider Döblin as one of those outstanding representatives of German speaking Jewry who—like Freud, Kafka, or Benjamin—consciously tried to live the risky dialectics of Jewish-German existence.... Instead, he seems to belong to the majority of those who felt that they should disown the Jewish tradition in the same measure in which they reaped success in the contemporary cultural scene."[12]

There is an implied criticism here of German Jews who were ready to betray their origins for short-term success in their cultural environment, but there is more to it. The success of German Jews in the generation before Hitler's rise to power was not only short-termed, it was also ill-fated, and in pointing out the pathology underlying their "assimilation," Sebald was well aware of the unfolding tragedy. In his early career he studied this tragedy as a scholar, uncovering the destruction of identities in Alfred Döblin and other German Jewish authors.[13] Later, when he began to write his prose, he went one step further. His narrative did not merely uncover the process of destruction; it also tried to reconstruct what had been lost.

From Academics to Poetics: Sebald's Homecoming

Sebald's academic, and even more so his fictional, writings leave little doubt that it was the shock at learning about the Nazi past of his country, and the need to come to grips with it in an individual and thoroughly personal way, that influenced his decision to stay abroad. One collection of his scholarly essays is entitled *Unheimliche Heimat* (Sinister Homeland).[14] Among the authors he discusses in this book we find Joseph Roth, Hermann Broch, and Jean Améry, three Austrian Jews driven from their homeland and, in the last resort, to their death. It was another Austrian Jew, Sigmund Freud, who pointed out the semantic connection between *unheimlich,* sinister, and *Heim,* home. An experience in the past—something one has known "at home"—has since been repressed, but then it returns in a different guise and becomes *unheimlich.* Behind a seemingly unfamiliar appearance a long-forgotten familiarity crops up, and the process can be traced in W. G. Sebald's own life as well. His studies confronted him with the past of his country, and behind the atrocities—*das Unheimliche*—he recognized the silence that was kept in his village when he was a child. Realizing what was hidden "at home," he decided to leave.

Most of the essays collected in *Unheimliche Heimat* were written in the 1980s, the decade in which Sebald gradually moved from academic research to creative writing. Bearing the signs of this transition, they are studies in exile, mostly about German Jewish authors who, for various reasons, leave behind what they consider to be their home and must inevitably realize that it is lost forever. Outlining the law of dispersion and the psychic mechanisms that are released by it, Sebald unfolds his major theme and makes us aware of the constant uprooting that went into the making of our globalized world.

Unheimliche Heimat appeared in 1991, and in the following year Sebald published *Die Ausgewanderten,* a volume of four stories about people who, at various times in the twentieth century, left their country and never found a new home.[15] The book established his worldwide reputation as a writer of fiction, and its English translation was published under the title *The Emigrants.*[16] There is an obvious affinity between Sebald's academic work and his prose. As a scholar, he analyzed the impact of disaster recorded in German, and German Jewish, literature of the nineteenth and twentieth centuries; as a writer, he now went on to replace the authors he had studied with fictitious characters whose existence was molded by that very same disaster. Partly based on real persons he had met, Sebald constructed their lives around the marks of memory and oblivion.

The story concluding *The Emigrants* is about a painter whom Sebald calls Max Ferber.[17] Growing up as a Jewish boy in Munich, he was sent to England in 1939, and after the war he began to work in a studio near the old, abandoned port of Manchester. The German narrator, who at the time also lives in this city, describes Ferber's single-minded occupation at the easel. He seemingly creates and destroys his paintings at the same time:

> He drew with vigorous abandon, frequently going through half a dozen of his willow-wood charcoal sticks in the shortest of time; and that process of drawing and shading on the thick, leathery paper, as well as the concomitant business of constantly erasing what he had drawn with a woolen rag already heavy with charcoal, really amounted to nothing but a steady production of dust, which never

ceased except at night. Time and again, at the end of a working day, I marvelled to see that Ferber, with the few lines and shadows that had escaped annihilation, had created a portrait of great vividness.[18]

Ferber labors under the shock of a separation that he has never been able to overcome. In 1939 he left his parents behind, in the early 1940s they were murdered by the Nazis, and as a painter he is desperately trying to recover the images of the past. Yet nothing materializes, and all he seems to achieve is "a steady production of dust." Ferber's art may thus perhaps be seen as a performative act—the horror looming behind the images he cannot create is constantly reproduced as a metaphor for his dead parents.

But there is another, quite tangible remnant of the world that Ferber was forced to leave behind. The German narrator first met him in the 1960s, and only much later, during their second meeting in the early 1990s, Ferber tells him the story of his long-drawn-out separation from home. Every fortnight he received a letter from his parents, but as time went by,

> The correspondence became more of a chore, and when the letters stopped coming, in November 1941, I was relieved at first, in a way that now strikes me as quite terrible. Only gradually did it dawn on me that I would never again be able to write home; in fact, to tell the truth, I do not know if I have really grasped it to this day. But it now seems to me that the course of my life, down to the tiniest detail, was ordained not only by the deportation of my parents but also by the delay with which the news of their death reached me, news I could not believe at first and the meaning of which only sank in by degrees.[19]

In vain he tried to get away from the tragedy in his past, and many years earlier, when he first came to Manchester, he had hoped to begin a new chapter in his life. But soon he found out that he was wrong:

> Manchester reminded me of everything I was trying to forget. Manchester is an immigrant city, and for a hundred and fifty years, leaving aside the poor Irish, the immigrants were chiefly Germans and Jews, manual workers, tradesmen, freelancers, retailers and wholesalers, watchmakers, hatters, cabinet-makers, umbrella makers, tailors ... with names like Leibrand, Wohlgemuth, Herzmann, Gottschalk, Adler, Engels, Landeshut, Frank, Zirndorf.... Throughout the nineteenth century, the German and Jewish influence was stronger in Manchester than in any other European city; and so, although I had intended to move in the opposite direction, when I arrived in Manchester I had come home, in a sense.[20]

Yet coming home, it turns out, is really going into exile again and again. The law of dispersion is effective everywhere, and the names of Germans and Jews remind him of the place he comes from. As they take leave of one another, Ferber hands a package to the narrator. It is a last message from home, which he received after the war—the manuscript of a memoir written by his mother shortly before her deportation. In it she tells her son of the life she has lived in Germany. Like many of her ancestors, she was born in the village of Steinach— "a third of whose inhabitants were Jews long resident there, at least as far back as the late seventeenth century"[21]—and life had a natural flow in the days of her childhood. But as she was growing up, her father, a horse dealer, was getting rich, and this, in the end, made all the difference in her life.

> If I think back nowadays to our childhood in Steinach ..., it often seems as if it were still going on, right into the lines I am now writing. But in reality, as I know only too well, childhood ended in January 1905 when the house and fields at Steinach were auctioned off and we moved into a three-storey house in Kissingen.... The contract Papa had won as a supplier and provisioner to the army, which he proudly mentioned whenever he had a chance, had doubtless been the decisive factor in giving up farming, moving from backwater Steinach, and finally establishing a position in middle-class life. At that time I was almost sixteen, and believed that a completely new world, even lovelier than that of childhood, would be revealed to me in Kissingen. In some respects that was really how it was, but in others the Kissingen years ... seem in retrospect to have marked the first step on a path that grew narrower day by day and led inevitably to the point I have now arrived at.[22]

These rather extensive quotations are presented here in order to show how Sebald turns his scholarship into the art of narration. A piece of social history is transmitted not by objective facts, but by subjective feelings that seem to be oddly out of place. Ferber cannot accept the death of his parents, and the information somehow never reaches him, turning his life into a limbo beyond time. Going to Manchester he wishes to leave his painful memories behind, but in the city of Germans and Jews they catch up with him. Past and present come together in his life as they do in his mother's consciousness, who in 1941 remembers the end of her childhood as though it were the beginning of a long decline. "If I think back to our childhood in Steinach," she writes on the verge of her death, "it often seems as if it were still going on, right into the lines I am now writing." She tells her son how his grandfather left his farm, becoming rich as a provisioner to the army, and W. G. Sebald, the scholar of materialism, now transforms it all into a flow of feelings, of long, meandering sentences in which the sense of history and the sense of death merge into one another.

The years pass by, the artist Max Ferber keeps turning his paintings into dust—and yet, as the narrator notes, it is a "portrait of great vividness" that appears "at the end of a working day." Hidden within the art of the painter, Sebald puts his own poetics in a nutshell for us. Like Ferber, he wishes to draw his characters in a landscape of death, which he constantly peruses, and *The Emigrants* contain a number of them. The physician Dr. Selwyn,[23] the schoolteacher Paul Bereyter,[24] Sebald's fictitious great-uncle Ambros Adelwarth:[25] in one way or another, they all commit suicide, but before they do so, Sebald engraves their portraits onto our memory.

Sebald's Journey beyond Time

The subject of a man in search of his parents reappears in *Austerlitz*,[26] Sebald's last novel, which was published in 2001, shortly before the car accident in which he lost his life. Like Max Ferber, Jacques Austerlitz was sent from Nazi-occupied Europe to England when he was a child; his parents too were murdered in the Holocaust; and neither Ferber nor Austerlitz succeed in their desperate search for a lost identity. At various points the stories of the painter and of Austerlitz correspond with one another, and here I wish to show how ten years after *The Emigrants,* some of these points are taken up again on a more profound level.

Ferber's studio is situated near the old docks of Manchester, and Sebald goes out of his way to describe the desolation of the place. In the nineteenth century, the city was the world capital of industrialism, and although it was some forty miles away from the coast, canals were built to provide it with a port. In the twentieth century all this came to an end, the area fell into irreparable dilapidation, and Ferber chooses this scenery of ruins as the background for his attempts to come to grips with the rubble of his own life.

On the face of it, this is another piece of history. In her memoir, Ferber's mother tells the story of a farmer rising into the middle class, a social improvement that turns out to be a tragedy. In the description of Manchester, the scope seems to be even wider. Sebald gives us the name of the tragedy—the industrial revolution—but he now leaves behind the attitude of his early academic work. He has no scholarly interest in the facts of the past any more; he is in search of an emotional truth that no materialistic point of view can provide.

Ruins loom large in *Austerlitz* too. Sebald, like Walter Benjamin, views the history of modernity as a *Katastrophengeschichte,* a history of disaster, but in his last novel he does not choose an artist for his protagonist. Jacques Austerlitz is a historian of architecture, and his way to reach out for the past is different from Max Ferber's. The landscape of ruins, in which the painter created his portraits out of dust, now becomes the object of intellectual analysis.

Again, as in the story about Ferber, the German narrator approaches his Jewish counterpart and writes down what he is told by him. He meets him for the first time in the second half of the 1960s, in the entrance hall of Antwerp's main railway station, where Austerlitz is preoccupied with taking pictures and making notes about the architectural details of the building. In the ensuing conversation he introduces him to his professional work, and at the same time he brings up a central issue that will gradually unfold in the novel. It was appropriate, Austerlitz explains,

> that in Antwerp Station the elevated level from which the gods looked down on visitors to the Roman Pantheon should display, in hierarchical order, the deities of the nineteenth century—mining, industry, transport, trade, and capital.... And Time, said Austerlitz, represented by the hands and dial of the clock, reigns supreme among these emblems. The clock is placed ... just where the image of the emperor stood in the Pantheon in a line directly prolonged from the portal; as governor of a new omnipotence it was set even above the royal coat of arms and the motto *Endracht maakt macht.*[27]

This new omnipotence of time is linked directly to the invention of the railway. "In fact, said Austerlitz, until the railway timetables were synchronized the clocks of Lille and Liège did not keep the same time as the clocks of Ghent and Antwerp, and not until they were all standardized around the middle of the nineteenth century did time truly reign supreme."[28] On the face of it, this is a rational deduction from empirical evidence, and in the 1960s Austerlitz seems to present the results of what we would nowadays call a cultural study. Sebald, however, does not wish to convey the historical facts, but rather the sense of an all-embracing process of alienation underneath the modern concept of time. Spreading across the entire planet, it has turned the earth into a place of global exile, and many things fall into place here: at the end of the nineteenth century, the railway station at Antwerp was built in order to support the colonial ambitions of Belgium;[29] universal time, an instrument of industrial imperialism, gradually took control of all individuals; and Austerlitz, without knowing it yet when he first met the narrator, was its ultimate victim.

After their first meeting in Antwerp, Austerlitz and the narrator stay in touch for a while, and then, as in the story about Max Ferber, there is a long interruption. Many years later, in 1996, they meet again in London and take a walk through the Royal Observatory at Greenwich.[30] The once powerful British Empire put itself at the center of the world there by arbitrarily establishing the prime meridian at Greenwich. Time was constructed to serve the rulers, and Austerlitz does not hide his scorn. It was, he says, "by far the most artificial of all our inventions, and in being bound to the planet turning on its own axis was no less arbitrary than would be, say, a calculation based on the growth of trees."[31] A solar day is anything but a precise measurement, he goes on to say, and then he makes a confession:

> In fact, said Austerlitz, I have never owned a clock of any kind, a bedside alarm or a pocket watch, let alone a wristwatch. A clock has always struck me as something ridiculous, a thoroughly mendacious object, perhaps I have always resisted the power of time out of some internal compulsion which I myself have never understood, keeping myself apart from so-called current events in the hope, as I now think, said Austerlitz, that time will not pass away, that I can turn back and go behind it, and there I shall find everything as it once was, or more precisely I shall find that all moments of time have co-existed simultaneously, in which case none of what history tells us would be true, past events have not yet occurred but are waiting to do so at the moment when we think of them.[32]

The historian of architecture wishes to do away with history. Austerlitz, just as Max Ferber in the earlier story, lives in a limbo beyond time. A few months after their visit to Greenwich the narrator comes to London again, and Austerlitz tells him how in recent years he became disgusted with the notes he had been taking down for decades. One evening he had taken them all out into his garden and buried them in the ground. It was a decisive moment in the life of Jacques Austerlitz. Putting an end to his architectural studies was tantamount to a total change in his existence, and in the wake of his fateful decision he became extremely restless.

"It was then, after my work of destruction in the garden," Austerlitz says, "that I began my nocturnal wanderings through London, to escape the insomnia which increasingly tormented me."[33] Although he had given up his profession, he clung to the habit of recounting the building history of the city, but now he was interested in the living, and the dead, who were uprooted while London was expanding. "Around 1860 and 1870," he says, "before work on the construction of the two northeast terminals began, [London's] poverty-stricken quarters were forcibly cleared and vast quantities of soil, together with the bones buried in them, were dug up and removed, so that the railway lines ... could be brought to the outskirts of the City."[34]

The law of dispersion is merciless, and not even the dead stand in its way. For a whole year, before he broke down in the summer of 1992, Austerlitz walked through London at night, and the railway lines were the traces he seemed to follow. Again and again, they led him to one particular spot. "Liverpool Street Station, to which I was always drawn back on my night journeys," Austerlitz says, "was one of the darkest and most sinister places in London, a kind of entrance to the underworld, as it has often been described."[35] At the end of the 1980s work was begun to rebuild the old station, and Austerlitz, at that time still interested in architectural history, visited the site quite often. Later, however, he kept coming back to it for a different reason. "Whenever I got out at Liverpool Street Station," he says, "I would stay there at least a couple of hours, sitting on the bench with other passengers ..., or standing somewhere, leaning on a handrail and feeling that constant wrenching inside me, a kind of heartache which, as I was beginning to sense, was caused by the vortex of past time."[36]

And indeed, it was a long-forgotten memory that finally awakened in this sinister place. It was at Liverpool Street Station where Austerlitz arrived when he came to England as a four-year-old boy, and it was from here that two strange people took him to Wales to raise him as their foster child. Here he ultimately lost, and forgot, his parents, and from here, more than half a century later, he would finally start on his long journey into the past. Liverpool Street Station is the pivotal point of the drama of memory and oblivion played out in the novel.[37]

Sebald gives an extensive description of the moment in which this new awareness comes about. On a Sunday morning after one of his nocturnal walks, Austerlitz stepped behind a builders' fence into the Ladies' Waiting Room—a part of the historic station that was erected in the Victorian age—and all of a sudden he found himself engulfed by the past: he saw a little boy sitting on a bench and a married couple coming to meet him. "In fact I felt, said Austerlitz, that the waiting room where I stood as if dazzled contained all the hours of my past life, all the suppressed and extinguished fears and wishes I had ever entertained."[38] A few months before, in the Royal Observatory at Greenwich, he had expressed his hope that time would not pass away and that he would be able to go behind it, but already years ago, at Liverpool Street Station in 1992, he had experienced precisely this. Now he tells the narrator about it, adding a comment concerning the place where it had happened to him: "I remember, said Austerlitz, that ... I could not stop wondering whether it was a ruin or a building that I had entered. Both ideas were right in a way at the time, since the new station was literally rising from the ruins of the old Liverpool Street."[39] A railway station, the *locus classicus* of modernity at which Austerlitz and the narrator met in the beginning of the novel, turns into a scenery of ruins like the one in which the painter Max Ferber is groping for images of the past. Time reigns supreme in these stations, but at a singular moment, when one such station is simultaneously destroyed and resurrected, time opens up, and the past rushes in. Liverpool Street Station is a sinister place, *unheimlich* in more than one sense: it is here that the horrors of his childhood come back to Austerlitz; and it is here that his old home was replaced by a new home, that his foster parents cut him off from his biological parents.[40]

The unexpected revelation of his past existence came as a second shock to Jacques Austerlitz, and in the summer of 1992 he suffered a mental breakdown of which he remembered nothing. In 1993, however, things seemed to pick up. He found his way to Prague, the city where he was born and raised as a child; he traced his mother all the way to Terezín, to the threshold of death from which she never returned, and finally the narrator met him in Paris once more, where he had gone in search of his father, who disappeared in France during World War II.

Austerlitz's journey into the past had reached a dead end, and it came too late to make a difference in his lonely, unhappy life. "In fact I felt," he says about his revelation in the Ladies' Waiting Room, "as if the black and white diamond pattern of the stone slabs beneath my feet were the board on which the endgame would be played, and it covered the entire plane of time."[41] He would soon go on his journey to the place where he was born, but at the same time Austerlitz was near the end already. "[W]hen I saw the boy sitting on the bench," he sums up his epiphany, "I became aware, through my dull bemusement, of the destructive effect on me of my desolation through all those past years, and a terrible weariness overcame me at the idea that I had never really been alive, or was only now being born, almost on the eve of my death."[42]

Both Max Ferber and Jacques Austerlitz survived the Holocaust in which they lost their parents, but are they really survivors? Their lives were saved and lost again, and in the shadow of their past they go through very similar motions. They meet a German and confide in him, and at the end of their stories they leave something at his disposal. Ferber hands him the memoir of his mother, and Austerlitz, at their last meeting in Paris, gives him the key to his house in London. "I could stay there whenever I liked, he said, and study the black and white photographs which, one day, would be all that was left of his life."[43] The law of dispersion has driven these men beyond the point of no return, and W. G. Sebald brings to us the voices of the dead.

Notes

1. See Maya Jaggi, "The Last Word," *Guardian*, 21 December 2001, http://www.theguardian.com/education/2001/dec/21/artsandhumanities.highereducation (accessed 16 December 2014). This was Sebald's last interview before his untimely death in a car accident.
2. Winfried Georg Sebald, *Der Mythus der Zerstörung im Werk Döblins* (Stuttgart: Ernst Klett 1980).
3. See Jan Berg et al., eds., *Sozialgeschichte der deutschen Literatur von 1918 bis zur Gegenwart* (Frankfurt: Fischer Taschenbuch Verlag, 1981), 1.
4. "Die vorliegende Arbeit versteht sich als eine materialistische Untersuchung des instabilen Verhältnisses von Fiktion und Mythus sowie von Literatur und Gesellschaft im Werk Döblins, in welchem das ideologische Dilemma des Autors sichtbar wird." Sebald, *Der Mythus der Zerstörung im Werk Döblins*, introductory note (no pagination). All translations are the author's.
5. Ibid., 18, 101, 113, 115.
6. Ibid., 27.
7. Ibid., 47, 53, 68, 93.
8. Ibid., 125, 134ff.
9. The insensitivity of the New Left to any Jewish perspective is obvious in its hostility toward Israel after the Six-Day War in June 1967. German students almost immediately sided with the Arabs and compared the Israelis to the Nazis. Cf. Martin W. Kloke, *Israel und die deutsche Linke: Zur Geschichte eines schwierigen Verhältnisses* (Frankfurt: Haag + Herchen, 1990).
10. "Döblins Haltung zur Frage der Assimilation, die sich als der entscheidende Faktor in der Entwicklung zahlreicher jüdisch-deutscher Schriftsteller erwies, blieb Zeit seines Lebens ambivalent, um nicht zu sagen opportunistisch. Die Philologie, die um derlei Dinge nicht Bescheid zu wissen braucht, hat in all ihren Ansätzen zur Interpretation Döblins diesen Punkt bislang geflissentlich übergangen." Sebald, *Der Mythus der Zerstörung im Werk Döblins*, 73.
11. "[M]an lasse die Juden im Westen reich werden und sie werden bald ausgerottet sein." Ibid., 74.
12. "Es hält schwer, Döblin nach solchen Äußerungen noch zur Reihe der hervorragenden Repräsentanten der deutschsprachigen Judenheit zu rechnen, die wie Freud, Kafka oder Benjamin die riskante Dialektik einer jüdisch-deutschen Existenz … bewußt durchzustehen versuchten. Er hat wohl eher zu der Mehrzahl jener gehört, die die jüdische Tradition in eben dem Maße glaubten verleugnen zu müssen, in dem sie im zeitgenössischen Kulturbetrieb reüssierten." Ibid.
13. In his earlier master's thesis on the German Jewish playwright Carl Sternheim, both the criticism and the sense of tragedy are even more pronounced. Cf. Winfried Georg Sebald, *Carl Sternheim: Kritiker und Opfer der Wilhelminischen Ära* (Stuttgart: Kohlhammer, 1969).
14. W. G. Sebald, *Unheimliche Heimat: Essays zur österreichischen Literatur* (Salzburg: Residenz Verlag, 1991).
15. W. G. Sebald, *Die Ausgewanderten* (Frankfurt: Eichborn, 1992).
16. W. G. Sebald, *The Emigrants*, trans. Michael Hulse (London: Harvill Press, 1996).
17. Ibid., 149–237; in the original German, the painter was called Max Aurach, but the name was too close to one of Sebald's models, the painter Frank Auerbach, who was living in London, and in the English edition he therefore changed the name.
18. Ibid., 161–62.
19. Ibid., 190–91.
20. Ibid., 191–92.

21. Ibid., 193.
22. Ibid., 207–8.
23. Ibid., 1–23.
24. Ibid., 25–63.
25. Ibid., 65–145.
26. W. G. Sebald, *Austerlitz* (Munich: Carl Hanser, 2001).
27. The quotes are taken from the American edition of W. G. Sebald, *Austerlitz,* trans. Anthea Bell (New York: Random House, 2001), 10–12.
28. Ibid., 12.
29. Ibid., 9.
30. Ibid., 98ff.
31. Ibid., 100.
32. Ibid., 101.
33. Ibid., 126.
34. Ibid., 132.
35. Ibid., 127–28.
36. Ibid., 128–29.
37. In later years too, Austerlitz seemed to return quite often to Liverpool Street. In 1996, his reunion with the narrator took place in the bar of the Great Eastern Hotel near the station; cf. ibid., 39.
38. Ibid., 136.
39. Ibid., 135–36.
40. It is not surprising that Austerlitz's childhood in the house of the Calvinist preacher Emyr Elias and his wife is almost unbearably harsh.
41. *Austerlitz,* 136.
42. Ibid., 137.
43. Ibid., 293.

Bibliography

Berg, Jan, Hartmut Böhme, Walter Fähnders, Jan Hans, Heinz-B. Heller, Joachim Hintze, Helga Karrenbrock, Peter Schütze, Jürgen C. Thöming, and Peter Zimmermann, eds. *Sozialgeschichte der deutschen Literatur von 1918 bis zur Gegenwart.* Frankfurt: Fischer Taschenbuch Verlag, 1981.

Catling, Jo, and Richard Hibbitt, eds. *Saturn's Moons: W. G. Sebald—A Handbook.* London: Legenda, 2011. – The book contains the most extensive primary and secondary bibliographies concerning Sebald.

Jaggi, Maya. "The Last Word." *Guardian,* 21 December 2001. http://www.theguardian.com/education/2001/dec/21/artsandhumanities.highereducation (accessed 16 December 2014).

Kloke, Martin W. *Israel und die deutsche Linke: Zur Geschichte eines schwierigen Verhältnisses.* Frankfurt: Haag + Herchen, 1990.

Sebald, W. G. *Die Ausgewanderten.* Frankfurt: Eichborn, 1992. Published in English as *The Emigrants,* trans. Michael Hulse. London: Harvill Press, 1996.

———. *Austerlitz.* Munich: Carl Hanser, 2001. Published in English as *Austerlitz,* trans. Anthea Bell. New York: Random House, 2001.

———. *Unheimliche Heimat: Essays zur österreichischen Literatur.* Salzburg: Residenz Verlag, 1991.

Sebald, Winfried Georg. *Carl Sternheim: Kritiker und Opfer der Wilhelminischen Ära.* Stuttgart: Kohlhammer, 1969.

———. *Der Mythus der Zerstörung im Werk Döblins.* Stuttgart: Ernst Klett, 1980.

CHAPTER 15

Holocaust Envy
Globalization of the Holocaust in Israeli Discourse

BATYA SHIMONY

During the past two decades Holocaust discourse has been globalized, crossing borders of nationalities and territories. With its prevalence, the Holocaust gains increasingly powerful and desired symbolic values. One of the central aspects of the process is the ongoing detachment of Holocaust organizing terminology from the concrete events that established its meaning, changing it into generalized, universal values enabling global identification. The predominant Holocaust discourse, in itself a founding myth, evolves gradually into identity formation discourse, highly desired for its victimhood. The status of the victim constitutes a central stratum in establishing private or collective identities as, on the one hand, it generates empathy and identification, while on the other, it legitimizes various actions.

The appropriation of Holocaust terminology and its leverage into symbolic capital is demonstrated in various writings in the literary, cultural, and political discourse of the Western world. Clear expression of such process appears in Binjamin Wilkomirski's *Fragments*,[1] apparently shreds of memories as a child during the Holocaust. A statement on the book cover notifies the reader that the writer's repressed memories were restored to consciousness through psychoanalysis. Years later, as is well-known, the memoirs were revealed to be a fabrication, and the writer, Bruno Grosjean, was not even Jewish.

Laurence Langer in his research suggests that the Grosjean action issued from an "impulse to create a more sympathetic image of his orphaned self than the true story of illegitimacy and abandonment."[2] Langer accepts Grosjean's need to create an alternative image for himself, though he disapproves of its

---

Notes for this section begin on page 311.

appropriation and presents the writing as a misuse of the Holocaust. Beyond the ethical questions, the example reveals the Holocaust as a strong and impactful resource that gained the writer temporary worldwide acceptance. While Grosjean's book was written out of an identity crisis, similar use of the Holocaust and its terminology appears among ethnic groups who experienced catastrophes and wish to shape their story through concepts from the Holocaust narrative. Some follow the practice implicitly, like Toni Morrison, who begins *Beloved*[3] with the motto "Sixty million and more," suggesting the number of slave trade victims while at the same implying the Jewish Holocaust. The novel presents a powerful description of a tormented black female slave who escaped slavery, but her life was affected and haunted by the past in ways reminiscent of Holocaust survivor traumas. Undoubtedly, the motto refers to the Jewish Holocaust, and the book reveals the disruptive consequences of atrocities on moral systems and judgmental abilities.[4]

The symbolic capital of the Holocaust narrative functions as such mainly among groups confronting political and cultural struggles. One such example is the Turks, the largest minority living within Germany and struggling for political and cultural status within the hegemonic system. In an article titled "We Don't Want to Be the Jews of Tomorrow," the writers present the strategy of the Turkish immigrants as based on Jewish organizational models and on Holocaust rhetoric, which includes creating a comparison between the racism toward the Turks and neo-Nazi ideology. "Accusing Germans of anti-Turkish Racism per se is only partly effective. Rhetorically far more effective is to associate Turkish concerns with those of the Jews. This strategy compels Germans to listen to Turkish intellectuals, because on this point, the German environment is vulnerable."[5]

The writers present the appropriation of the Holocaust narrative by the Turkish community in a number of cases. One of them was the response of the Turkish community to the publication of an anti-Turkish cartoon in the German *Stern* in 2004. The cartoon presents "a heavily mustached man crawling through a cat hole fixed in a door captioned 'European Union,' trying to gain entry into Europe"[6] and a Turkish flag on the suitcase indicating explicitly the man's origins. The publication raised an uproar within the Turkish community, and one of its eminent members, in a response to the magazine, compared the cartoon to Nazi (anti-Semitic) caricatures, its only difference being that "here in the *Stern,* the nose was replaced by the mustache."[7] Additional replication of the Jewish Holocaust narrative appears in commemoration ceremonies performed following skinheads' arson on homes and the killing of Turkish immigrants in Möln and other cities in Germany. The writers point to the similarity between the ceremonies of the Turkish community and the commemoration of the *Kristallnacht*.[8]

The Israeli-Palestinian conflict presents an additional case of such utilization. Israeli researchers make note of the immense usage of the Holocaust narrative aimed at inciting worldwide public opinion for the Palestinian cause to generate action.[9] Litvak and Webman examine Holocaust discourse within the Arab world and observe its affect on the Palestinian Nakba narrative. The appropriation is based on the Palestinian view of themselves as "victims of victims," the primary casualties "since the immigration to Palestine emerged as the solution for the displaced Jews in Europe"[10] and led to the Palestinian displacement and status as refugees. Having discerned the symbolic capital of "victimhood" in Western discourse, the Palestinians create an analogy between the Holocaust and their catastrophe to emphasize the Palestinians' status as victims: "Therefore, they have preserved the refugee camps as a visible presentation of victimhood."[11] The tendency to create analogies between the Holocaust and the Nakba is evidently expressed in Ghasan Abdallah's statement after two visits to Yad Vashem: "he couldn't but feel a sense of 'déjà vu,' realizing the resemblance between the images exhibited and what happened to the Palestinians. The dehumanization of the enemy, especially the victim, is the same, just 'change the word "Arab" in Israel with "Jewish" in Germany,' the 'yellow star' with the orange identity card or the special car-plate number."[12]

The examples show the extensive use of Holocaust terminology and illustrate the depth of the global consciousness regarding Holocaust discourse and its political and cultural application. Parallel to these worldwide processes, similar changes are identifiable within Israeli discourse, where the memory and the use of the Holocaust forms a highly sensitive issue. This chapter will point to the impact of Holocaust discourse on one of the huge minority groups in Jewish Israeli society—the Mizrahim. In my discussion of the literary works of Mizrahi writers, I will present the means of internalization of the Holocaust and its use as a model for collective identity formation from the viewpoint of "Holocaust envy" and, at the same, through feelings of pain and defiance.

Israeli Mizrahim and the Holocaust

Since the massive immigration during the establishing years of the state, Israeli society has been divided into two dominant groups—Ashkenazim, from European countries, and Mizrahim, from Arab countries, North Africa, and even Greece.[13] The Ashkenazim, who initiated the Mizrahim into the state, viewed their culture as inferior, primitive, and backward and displayed arrogance clearly bearing signs of a colonial attitude.[14] In consequence, socioeconomic and cultural tension evolved between the groups, manifested in social inequality and a sense of persisting exclusion experienced by the first generation of Mizrahim and their descendants.

The secular Israeli, the Sabra, created by Ashkenazim from the first waves of the aliyot,[15] became the dominant identity, and Mizrahi immigrants of the 1950s were required to conform in defining their place within the new culture.

During the initial years of the state, their Arab culture was denied and suppressed by the absorbing group.

The gap and tension between the groups is discernable in Holocaust discourse within Israeli society. Until about the 1980s the Mizrahim were absent from the public and historic Holocaust consciousness, which viewed the trauma as singular to the Jews of Europe, thus generating the Mizrahim's alienation from Holocaust discourse. Until about the 1960s the Mizrahim viewed the Holocaust Remembrance Day as the Ashkenazi Day of Mourning. Balfour Hakak writes in the preface to the pamphlet *Shoah BaMizrah* (Holocaust in the East): "The guide of a street gang said that when he approached the gang on the Holocaust Remembrance Day, he heard whispers: 'Guys, we have to be sad today. The leader has the Holocaust Day today.'"[16] The short phrase contains some of the blatant aspects of the relationship between the Mizrahim and Ashkenazim: though the text does not mention the ethnic identity of the characters, those familiar with Israeli society would distinguish the guide as Ashkenazi and the boys as Mizrahim.[17] The attitude of the gang to the Holocaust Remembrance Day demonstrates both alienation as well as empathy. On the one hand, alienation toward those identified with that day, the Ashkenazim, who are viewed as the oppressing and dominant group, and on the other, empathy toward the guide, who belongs to the dominant group but has personal relationships with the members of the gang.

The majority of Mizrahi Jews did not experience the Holocaust; however, the stories of Mizrahim who did experience persecution by the Nazis were excluded from the national narrative. The exclusion is apparent in regard to the Jews from Greece, of whom approximately 90 percent perished, mainly in Auschwitz. The story of the Jews of Greece during the Holocaust was unheard until the mid-1980s despite the intense activity of the survivors and the descendants who wished to raise it to public awareness.[18] Similarly, the story of the Jews of North Africa who suffered the atrocities of the Nazis did not penetrate Holocaust consciousness in Israel until recently.[19] Shimon Adaf[20] points to the preclusion of the Mizrahim from the collective Israeli identity:

> The new myth is a nightmare—the Holocaust of European Jews. The perfect cross for the perfect victim, the cruelty that is demonstrated is none other than self defense. In this way he is able to wipe out all the problems that bother him, including the nagging question—what about the sectors within society who fought for many years for their identity, and were expelled from the collective myth. What about the population segments that are not gathered within the flock due to their genetic lineage?[21]

Hanna Yablonka, a Holocaust researcher, studied the change in the role of the Mizrahim within Israeli Holocaust discourse since its first years, in the mid-1940s, to recent times. Yablonka primarily concludes that the inclusion of the Mizrahim within Holocaust discourse was an established process issuing from the need to create national unity. The Holocaust commemoration, during the first years until the mid-1960s, was done mainly by a few leading figures from the survivors who had exerted special efforts to commemorate their own original communities.[22] Consequently, the stories of survivors from the Mizrahi group, Greeks and North Africans, were totally absent from the Holocaust discourse.[23] The Six-Day War (1967) was followed by a reconsideration of the Holocaust as constituting the Israeli collective social consciousness. Subsequently, the memory of the Holocaust was leveraged to unite the Israeli consciousness. This process reached its peak during the mid-1980s with the institutional recognition that the Jews of North Africa also experienced the Nazi persecution.[24]

The educational authorities, realizing the consequential damages to Israeli society in the alienation of the Mizrahim from the memory of the Holocaust, took vigorous actions to alter the perception and turn that same memory into a means of unity. Intensive actions included additional programs at schools and the presentation of the Holocaust as a collectively significant event. All Jews were considered potential victims. These means assisted educators to raise a sense of identification among the Mizrahi students, who felt until that point that the Holocaust had no relevance to them. The success of this process can be seen in a study conducted by Yair Auron in 2008. In this research, he examined the connection between the identity of the participants, Jewish students, and events in Jewish and Israeli history. In response to the question, "Should all Jews see themselves as Holocaust survivors?" students of Mizrahi origin expressed the greatest degree of affirmation.[25]

The results are hardly surprising in view of the centrality of the Holocaust in the construction of the secular Israeli identity since the 1960s. During the first two decades of the state, the status of survivor was a source of embarrassment, scrutinized by the Israeli arrogant and judgmental view. The attitude changed later on, and the survivors came to be viewed as heroes of a new kind, precisely *due* to their survival. The Six-Day War and the preceding existential anxiety marked a new stage in the Israeli consciousness, Yablonka writes: "The Holocaust was engraved in the Israeli genetic code to the point that every-day events started to be evaluated according to it and in relation to its existential strengths."[26] With time, the memory of the Holocaust and its status within Israeli society gained power and precedence, and from a historical catastrophe of massive atrocity it evolved into a symbolic resource. According to Kimmerling, "The survivors' individual and collective stigma has been removed, since the 'entire nation' was supposed to consider itself as a Holocaust survivor.... Moreover, to be a Holocaust survivor or a survivor's relative or the 'second generation' of the Holocaust victims ... has turned into a source of prestige and strength in Israeli society."[27]

The status of the Holocaust as a privileging, symbolic capital brought about an interesting, prevalent phenomenon among the Mizrahim, which I refer to as "Holocaust envy."[28] The association to Freud's "penis envy" is not coincidental. The concept describes a central process in a female child's development and separation from the mother figure.[29] The penis/phallus represents the father, and in accordance with Lacanian theory stands for the symbolic order and the dominant sociocultural identity. The function of the theory is clearly metaphoric, indicative of the centrality of the Holocaust in Israeli identity and experience, a status parallel to that of the phallus within psychoanalytic theory. In order to be a part of the symbolic order, Mizrahim are required to separate from the mother figure—the original Mizrahi culture associated with femininity[30]—and identify with the father figure—the Zionist secular order.

The association with psychoanalytic theory is of significance since it highlights the primordial instinctual system present within the human mind. To follow Mitchell and Black: "Psychoanalysis is not only a professional and scientific discipline *within* our culture, but a form of thought, an approach to human experience, that has become *constitutive* of our culture and pervades the way we have come to experience ourselves and our minds."[31] Nevertheless, the phenomenon should be viewed as part of the Israeli sociological structure, where various ethnic groups are positioned in accordance with the ultimate justifying factor of Israeli existence—the Holocaust. Closer association with the Holocaust and its values acquires a group higher status and legitimacy within Israeli society.[32] Since the 1980s onward, Israeli society has been persistently seeking powerful and effective means of identification with the Holocaust to create a collective, national experience. One such effective means has been journeys to Poland by groups of young people who undergo an intensive introduction to the extermination camps and aspects of victimization. Jackie Feldman, an anthropologist, interprets the journeys as a modern pilgrimage aimed at enhancement of Holocaust memory as central to the civil ethos of the younger generation. The participants come in close contact with the camp victims and emerge as triumphant survivors remaking aliyah to Israel. The intensive replication of the Holocaust survivors' experience and the eyewitnesses' return to Israel reinforces the narrative of a strong state as the ultimate response to the Holocaust.[33]

The Holocaust in Mizrahi Literature

The review and discussion presented will refer to the literary corpus of three generations, by social definition, of Mizrahi authors, whose literature reflects the Mizrahi experience. The first generation of writers arrived from North African and Arab countries during the founding years of the state and experienced the "melting pot" and absorption policy. The group includes writers who came from Iraq as young men, having undergone a process of sociocultural identity formation: Sammy Michael (born in 1926), Shimon Balas (1930), and Eli Amir (1937). The writers' corpus extends over decades and therefore was influenced by the ongoing political, cultural, and social changes within Israeli society, which finds expression in their formation of the memory of the Holocaust. The second generation of writers referred to in this chapter came to Israel at an earlier age, a fact that had considerable influence on their perception. The group referred to here as the "interim generation," situated between the first and second generations, includes the writers Yitzhak Gormezano-Goren (1941, Egypt), Herzl and Balfour Hakak (1948, Iraq), and Haim Sabato (1952, Egypt).[34] The interim generation's writing was affected by their early immigration and initiation into Israeli society. The second generation includes writers born in Israel during the 1960s, who mainly grew up in peripheral small towns where they absorbed a sense of marginalization and exclusion related to their Mizrahi origins.

Yablonka observes in regard to the first generation, and especially Sammy Michael and Eli Amir, that they "tend to include the Holocaust in their novels while expressing deep empathy towards the survivors;"[35] "the members of the Mizrahi Judaism internalized the lessons of the Holocaust along with the depth of the mourning that their parents' generation expressed and upon their encounter with the Israeli society where they were raised and educated, and which was still a society of an hegemonic story."[36] However, the fissures in the hegemonic presentation of the immigrants' acceptance and the Holocaust narrative are obvious in the earliest works of the Mizrahi writers; most of them did not identify with the establishment discourse and expressed disappointment about their cultural rejection.[37] The identification with Holocaust survivors, according to Yablonka, stemmed from a sense of shared fate with the survivors, a mutual feeling of being underprivileged, as opposed to the veteran Israelis. However, this sense of identification was not shared by all immigrant writers, and a few held different views.

The earliest example of the opposed point of view appears in Shimon Balas's book *The Ma'abara* (The Immigrant Camp),[38] the first to recount the story of Iraqi immigrants' absorption into Israel from their personal point of view. The Holocaust concept is mentioned in a conversation between two immigrants discussing the meaning of the word "Ma'abara," a name given to the transient settlements during the 1950s:

> It seems to me that since the Babylonian Exile, no calamity had happened to the Aram-Naharayim Jewry that was as terrible as the Holocaust that happened to it in our time. The entire ancient and civilized Jewry was destroyed and dispersed in deserted and neglected areas called Ma'abarot. The name that they called these immigrant camps was just as tragic as the immigrants' fate. I asked why these camps were called Ma'abarot, and I was told that they served as a transition phase towards full absorption in Israel. I searched for this word in the Bible and I found it in the Book of Samuel.... [I found] a verse on Jonathan who went through the "ma'abarot" where "one rock is on one side and another rock is on the other side." This is a Ma'abara! One rock here and one rock there. Go ahead and break some rocks! Isn't this exile?[39]

The application may be dismissed by attributing to the speakers a conventional and unintentional use of the word intended to convey the sense of total devastation experienced by the immigrants. The assumption that Balas's choice of words may be accidental seems improbable, taking into consideration the time of writing, the 1960s. The period is marked by highly significant events, among them the trial of Eichmann and the testimonies of the survivors, which placed the Holocaust at the center of Israeli public consciousness. Moreover, the rest of the excerpt illustrates the importance Balas attributes to words and the meaning contained within. The writer's classification of the experience of Jews from Iraq as a "Holocaust" preempts by one generation the extremely critical views expressed by the second generation of Mizrahim, who explicitly compare their oppression by the dominant class to genocide and the Holocaust.

An interesting change of views regarding the status of the Holocaust and its survivors within Israeli society is present in Sammy Michael's writing. The writer, who came to Israel in 1949, presented in his first book, *Shavim VeShavim Yoter* (All Men Are Equal—But Some Are More),[40] a harsh criticism of the Mizrahim's absorption. The novel describes the hardships experienced by David and his family after coming from Iraq, and these are grounded against a socially charged environment given to tensions between the two groups—Mizrahim and Ashkenazim. Except, one group he is unable to categorize; they are special, different and segregated, engulfed in sanctity—the Holocaust survivors.

The Holocaust survivors are first mentioned when Shaul, David's brother, brings food for his parents from the military base. The father asks where the food is from, and the son says:

> Look, here we all say "vuz-vuz." It is like a curse. It is even an expression of hatred. But I am stuck in the military camp with forty of them in one room. Ten of them were born here: these people start getting ready at four o'clock, they sit on the bus and leave … but the others do not rush anywhere. They are "vuz-vuzim" as well, but they turn around in their beds in the large shack, they smoke, they stare at the ceiling … they have nowhere to go. Their families were slaughtered. Before you arrived here, I was like one of them—but *I* had some hope to meet my family one day. *They are* just lying there, dreaming dead dreams. When they heard that *you came*—all of them got together to help … by shoving something into my bag, before my arrival at the Ma'abara, they gave a slice of bread for their dead dreams.[41]

Further into the story, David loses his parents and sister in a fire that consumes their tent. Later he enlists in the army and arrives at his brother's station base, where he comes in close contact with these survivers that engender compassion: "I liked the guy. He was a person who did not belong to any race—neither Sephardic nor Ashkenazi. In the classification system that I had adopted at the Ma'abara, there was no place for *this kind of people*. The enormous suffering that they had gone through purified their souls."[42] Within the reality of categorization, he has difficulties in determining their place among the groups undergoing identity and control struggles.

Michael's later novel, *Mayim Noshkim LeMayim* (Water Kissing Water),[43] presents a different view. The story, taking place during the 1950s, presents the tense relationship between Mizrahi immigrants and Ashkenazi society. The figure of a Holocaust survivor, Tibi Nemet, is a good friend of Yosef, the main protagonist. However, the description in the novel includes slight criticism, not directed against the survivor but referring to a wider discourse, which at the time had become highly significant in Israeli society and affected the two dominant groups—the Mizrahim and Ashkenazim. At the beginning of the novel, the narrator describes Yosef and Tibi spending leisure hours on the beach. They had been friends since their military service: "The military camp was their home. They stayed there on Saturdays and holidays too. Their friendship was one of uprooted people who had no kin."[44] At this point the differences between the refugee and the immigrant are blurred; they share the same status. However, later on, it is Tibi who gains some preference. When they search for a place to sit, Yosef tries to find out whether the place is available. "Since the day he arrived at Israel, he tried to avoid sitting on a vacant seat before making sure that it is not intended for someone else. In comparison, Tibi Nemet was determined to immigrate to the homeland owed to him by humanity and history."[45] Yosef's caution marks the difference between the two. The alterations illustrate the changes in the level of awareness between the first and second novels after thirty years, the time span between the two novels. The first novel shows deep empathy with the fate of the survivors who had lost their families in the Holocaust, while the last book emphasizes the privileged status of Tibi Nemet as a Holocaust survivor in Israeli society. The emphasis had shifted from the personal-emotive to the national-social aspect. With time the Holocaust had gained symbolic and cultural status and turned into a classifying resource. Consequently, *Mayim Noshkim LeMayim* presents the survivors through the viewpoint of political awareness rather than emotional empathy. The retrospective view used in describing the events and the renewed understanding of the power relationships in Israel allow Michael to shape the survivors' image in the context of the privileges gained through the Holocaust, privileges that facilitate their acceptance into Israeli society rather than function in the context of the suffering they had endured. The Holocaust survivors are now perceived as those who have been entitled to an "admission ticket" into Israeli society due to their suffering, a "ticket" that was denied to the Mizrahi immigrants.

The depiction of the first generation of writers was done from a point of view of people with a defined personality, as they arrived here as adults. Their writing contains a dual attitude toward the Holocaust and its survivors, an approach that gained focalization and expansion as with time the prestigious status of the Holocaust in the politics of Israeli identities became more evident. However, the writing of the interim generation of writers, such as Balfour Hakak (1948) and Haim Sabato (1952), reveals a naïve standpoint in distinction to the complex perception of the first generation of writers. These writers present profound identification with the Holocaust and accept beyond criticism the preferred status of the direct and indirect survivors. The acceptance issues from several reasons, among them their initiation into Israeli society at an early age, which spared them the hardships of absorption;[46] they also came from families with a high degree of Zionist consciousness, minimizing the extent of their objection to the exclusive policy of the authorities.[47] *Shoah BaMizrah,* edited by Hakak,[48] expresses the status of the Holocaust as a desired symbolic capital for the Zionist Mizrahi youngsters. Hakak complains in the introduction that the story of the Holocaust is associated only with the annihilation of European Jews, while the Mizrahi Jews were excluded from the narrative. The writing offers an alternative historical narrative through which the Mizrahi Jews would become a legitimate part of the Holocaust heritage.

The main goal of Hakak's pamphlet was educational, to present a range of literary works that would help teachers impart the heritage of the Mizrahi Holocaust, to correct the national narrative and stress the common fate of Jews. The essence of the pamphlet is the symbolic adaptation of the Farhud events in the Zionist narrative gist. Farhud (violent dispossession) refers to the riots and killings carried out against the Jewish population of Baghdad, Iraq, on 1–2 June 1941 during the Jewish holiday of Shavuot, the result of pro-Nazi, anti-Semitic incitement. In two days 179 Jews were killed, approximately two thousand people were injured, and property was looted. The pamphlet includes stories, poems, and testimonies describing the massacre and its outcome and serves as a memorial to the tragic event. The date noted in the introduction is symbolic: "Shavuot 5741, 40th anniversary of the Babylonian Holocaust." The use of the concept of "Holocaust" is intentional, to present the Farhud as an additional disaster in the series of calamities carried out by the Nazis and their accomplices. He stresses: "The process preceding the annihilation of Jews was the same in the Christian as well as the Islam countries: Jews were not protected, and were humiliated. We all share the Holocaust experience. Its meaning is the same for all of us: we are the members of a persecuted nation, being in danger of annihilation throughout history."[49]

Undoubtedly the Jews of Bagdad went through a traumatic period during the two days of violent rioting. However, the formulation of the Farhud story as part of the historical narrative of the Holocaust is a later interpretation, originating in the high status of the Holocaust and its survivors in Israeli society. Other scholars and researchers among Iraq's expatriates do not participate in this Zionist structuring of the story. Shenhav mentions the singularity and the relatively modest scope of the massacre in comparison to the Holocaust. Still, in Zionist historiography the events function as a watershed in the history of Iraqi Jews and as a part of the Holocaust: "The invocation of the Holocaust analogy is not accidental. It reflects the deep desire of the Arab Jews to be admitted to the Israeli civil religious, in which the Holocaust plays a crucial role."[50] Sasson Somekh claims that Iraqi expatriates' organizations emphasize the Zionist activity and the Farhud to the point that they appear to be "the essence of the Jewish-Iraqi experience, and thus they tend to forget and wipe out hundreds of years of close connections and cultural prosperity."[51] While the first generation of immigrants from Iraq limit the intensity of the Farhud events and its significance within the overall relationship with their Muslim neighbors, others from the intermediate generation seek connection with the Holocaust through the Farhud.

Haim Sabato's writing also exhibits intense empathy with the Holocaust.[52] In his book *From the Four Winds*,[53] he returns to his childhood days at Beit Mazmil, a neighborhood in Jerusalem, and to his friendship with the influential Hungarian Holocaust survivor, Moshe Farkash. The story was written from a delayed perspective, which was supposed to create a time gap between the childhood experiences, the time of the events, and adulthood, when he looks back in retrospective from distance and percipience. However, the gap does not materialize. Weiss notes in a review of the novel:

> The power of this book stems from the multi-focused story that it brings. The story is about what had happened to a child, but it is told by an adult looking back nostalgically at his childhood and the experiences he had at the Ma'abara that had shaped his personality. In addition, the inter-cultural axis serves in this case as an important literary tool. The child's Egyptian background forms a unique point of view on the culture, which is the center of this novel—the Ashkenazi culture. Despite his privileged descent, which he mentions quite frequently, the child studies at Ashkenazi institutions, and the majority of the characters that are meaningful for him in this novel, are of Ashkenazi descent.[54]

Farkash considers Sabato, the narrator, his spiritual son. He grants Sabato his most precious memories—the story of his painful childhood, and of his parents' death, and the poems written for him by his mother. These childhood memories contain enormous emotional value for Farkash. He requests Sabato to tell the story when his children are older, and Sabato follows his wish. However, Sabato has to erase his own heritage and self-awareness to tell Farkash's story. He mentions his background and describes his ethnic group, but these descriptions are lifeless and pale. Weiss adds: "The narrator describes his own group very poorly, in a traditional and orientalistic way: all of them are religious Jews who maintain a traditional community structure and hierarchy, without the sense of an actual devastation following the traumatic immigration experience that they had gone through."[55]

On the other hand, the Eastern European Jewish shtetl, as conveyed by Farkash, materialized in the consciousness of Sabato. After Farkash's death, Yossi, his son, comes to study at the yeshiva managed by Sabato, who welcomes him and recalls:

> Images passed quickly before my eyes. The main street in the town of Hajdubeserman, in the sunlight and shade of the acacia and chestnut trees. Farkash had painted this picture for me. … [H]ere was Rabbi Joseph Farkash hurrying at dawn to the *beit midrash* with Tractate *Bava Metzia* under his arm. Today he would prove to the

rabbi the validity of his interpretation of the passage.... Or there was the little boy, Moishele Farkash, riding his bike on the narrow streets of the village called Szerep. ... Or there was the Hungarian policeman who lashed out at him at the gathering point next to the town square in Budapest, tearing his mother's letters and throwing them in the fire before his eyes, while he hid his small volume of Tractate *Bava Metzia* in his clothing. And the whole time he was saying to me, "I am entrusting you with this charge."[56]

Farkash extends his patronage to the narrator and considers him his own son, owner of his spiritual heritage, while the narrator's own family and cultural world are made irrelevant and hardly mentioned in the novel. After Farkash's death, the situation is changed, and Sabato takes up the role of the father who protects the orphaned son, Yossi. This moment expresses the narrator's total identification with Farkash; he lives his memories and cultural heritage as if they were his own. He can actually see the pictures, the small town and Farkash's father. Applying the free indirect speech technique, he is able to penetrate Farkash's consciousness and live his thoughts. He can see Farkash beaten up by the officer. The heritage of Farkash's suffering is poured into his blood and flows into his consciousness. In comparison, the life of his own community, the ones close to him, is left out of the story, diminished, almost as if their lives had never been lived.[57]

Mimicry and the Grotesque in the Holocaust Representations

Beginning from the mid-1990s significant change took place in the adaptation of the Holocaust consciousness within the young Mizrahi prose. The voices of authors with common biographical characteristics evolved almost simultaneously into the saturated Holocaust discourse. All of them were born in the 1960s, and were the sons of immigrants from Arab countries and North Africa who had spent their adolescent years in small towns or neighborhoods of new immigrants. The similarity is also manifested in the poetic shaping of their works. The events take place in the peripheral areas of Israel, in poor neighborhoods where the new immigrants were settled, and these turned over years into centers of social negligence, crime, and distress. The stories are set in the present—the 1990s of the twentieth century. A repetitive plot motif of physical and conscious transformation is experienced by the Mizrahi characters within their surroundings, a change that allows them, apparently, to complete the lack in their identity—the biographical relation to the Holocaust. Fundamental differences exist between the writing of the second generation and the literature of the interim generation. The latter is naïve and lacking criticism, while the texts of the third group, the second generation, involves an act of mimicry, at times grotesque, holding to a potentially undermining and ambivalent position similar to the concept of postcolonial mimicry.[58]

The examples presented demonstrate this point. The novel *Pere Atzil* (Noble Savage) by Dudu Busi[59] describes Yom-Tov, an Iraqi painter from the HaTikva neighborhood, a marginal neighborhood in Tel Aviv, who becomes addicted to the Holocaust. He paints obsessively realistic paintings of the Holocaust and while doing so experiences physical and spiritual transformations. He is convinced that in a previous life he was a tailor in Warsaw who was murdered by the Nazis. Out of total identification he barely eats, wears striped pajamas that give him the appearance of a prisoner, and shaves his head. Yom-Tov's son observes him with concern:

> This Iraqi got himself completely into the character of the Polish Yom-Tov Isaakovsky. During the period of creating his Holocaust paintings he committed himself to a stringent diet in order to feel the consuming hunger suffered by Yom-Tov Isaakovsky in the Warsaw Ghetto…. The man lost fifteen kilograms…. In the beginning of his working day he used to light six memorial candles … then worked for hours while his portable stereophonic tape-recorder was playing sad Yiddish tunes. Sometimes, in the middle of work, he would burst into tears over the misfortunes of his virtual family members who perished.[60]

Later on the son describes the striped pajamas with the yellow badge worn by his father and his shaved head like the heads of the prisoners in the camps. Toward the end of the story the father tries to inhale gas and explains to his son: "True, this is not cyclone, but somehow I had to experience the feeling that they had in their last moments. I just had to!"[61]

A similar motif of transformation recurs in *Avaryan Tzatzua* (Petty Hoodlum) by Kobi Oz,[62] which takes place in Jaffa and recounts the story of a street gang led by Nir Damti, a hooligan raised by his grandfather Morris Betito. The grandfather, an elderly man who came to Israel from North Africa in the 1950s, has strange dreams about himself as a small child in Buchenwald. One morning he wakes up with a blue number tattooed on his arm. While talking with a beggar woman on the street, he finds out that the identity of her late husband has returned to life through his living self, and the tattooed number on his arm and the memories from the concentration camp are her husband's.

The ambivalent transformative narrative appears also in Yossi Avni's writing. The Holocaust and its influence on his identity have a keynote presence throughout his entire work, and are expressed intensively in his novels. His first novel, *Doda Farhuma Lo Hayta Zona* (Auntie Farhuma Wasn't a Whore After All),[63] an autobiographical novel, reveals the complex processes that shaped his contradictory identity: "A Mizrahi guy, devout patriot and gay. I accepted my being unusual as taken for granted."[64] These elements of identity are controlled by an intense Holocaust experience that shapes his life. In the opening phrase of the novel, "On the day that Eichmann was hanged, I was circumcised," he marks his identity through two formative events, one from a national perspective and the other from a Jewish perspective. The reference to the circumcision, a transformative ritual, implies that the Holocaust is engraved in the flesh of the protagonist.

From this point on, the protagonist internalizes the heritage of Jewish suffering. His connection to the Holocaust intensifies as he grows, moving from emotional yearning to obsessive studying of the atrocities. As a seven-year-old child he reads piles of books from the forbidden shelves in the public library, books commemorating communities that perished and describing stories of cruel deaths. He becomes an expert on the subject of the Holocaust and connects with subtle threads small matters, incidents from his personal life, with Holocaust-related events. Thus, the secret number he chooses for his bank account is the blue number tattooed on the arm of the neighborhood grocer's wife, and while having sex he listens to the song "Lulinke Mine Feygele," a well-known Yiddish song about the Holocaust. The perception of himself as a survivor is expressed explicitly when he tells his new German comrade: "Don't mess with me, I'm a Holocaust survivor."[65]

Avni returns to the 1950s, to his childhood in a poor neighborhood of Mizrahi immigrants, hardly surviving and holding to superstitions. The narrator describes his parents, immigrants from Afghanistan and Persia who are trying to cope with their new life, in a manner that is both grotesque and pathetic. Several Holocaust survivors live in the neighborhood right next to the Mizrahi immigrants. There is a certain similarity between Avni's and Sabato's novels; both go back to the formative years of the state of Israel and describe the Ma'abarot populated with Mizrahi immigrants and Holocaust refugees, who are presented as haunted spirits, provoking fear, and in both novels the story is from the point of view of a Mizrahi child who experiences the Holocaust in an intensified way. However, in addition to the similarities there is conspicuous difference reflected in the tone used by the narrator. In Sabato's novel, we witnessed a nostalgic return, free of criticism and totally devotional, while Avni describes a grotesque world. He is highly affected by the Holocaust and expands into the theme so it becomes a second nature. However, the presentation of the survivors is not only through empathy. They are described in a grotesque, threatening, and ugly manner. The characters are called by obscene names related to sex and bodily excretions. The local shopkeeper, for example, is called Zona (prostitute) Kusman (the word *kus* is slang for vagina). Moreover, Avni expresses the castration experienced by the Mizrahim in the encounter with the Ashkenazim, mainly in the painful and angered formation of his mother's total subservience in her encounters with the Ashkenazi establishment and culture. Her weeping and pain are burned in his soul to an extent that "they engraved in it black digits of a private concentration camp."[66]

These few examples demonstrate the gap between the naïve imitation that we saw among the interim generation authors and the critical grotesque mimicry presented here. The critical position is created through the narrative framework of time and place, which is of supreme importance. Anchoring the story in the Israeli "here and now" is a decision of political significance. People are still living in these poor neighborhoods, even after fifty years of the state of Israel, and they still feel marginalized and rejected. The stories are consequently derived from an extreme crisis of social identity, which is experienced by the characters against the background of the hegemonic Israel. For Oz, the transformation experienced by the grandfather, his becoming a survivor, takes place against the background of his grandchild Nir's fight with the representatives of the social elite—the street gang leader attempting to reform him, and Henrietta, the leader's mother and a Holocaust survivor, attempting to civilize Nir and his gang by donating a library and books to their club. Nir, who strongly objects to the attempts to make him civilized, reacts with the most basic means available to him—his physical secretions. In one of the toughest parts, immediately following the library donation, he smears his feces on Henrietta's golden car, draws a swastika on it, and writes the word "Nazi." The grotesque description of the events and the clear social background express the dual and conflicting positions in regard to the memory of the Holocaust and its status within Israeli society. On the one hand, there is a mimicking envy expressing a strong desire to be *like* the survivors, in their place and in their situation. On the other, there is aggressive rejection of the object of envy and a wish to inflict pain, due to a profound understanding that the Mizrahi consciousness was castrated by the ruling social class through the Holocaust fixation.

Summary

The marked awareness of the Holocaust in the protagonists of Mizrahi origin, in the Israeli reality preceding 2000, marks a new and different phase in the discussion of Holocaust literature. The writing of the second generation (both direct and indirect descendants) of Ashkenazim that has been researched so far brings forth a variety of means to deal with this hard subject.[67] Examples include the documentation of trauma experienced by the parents or stories of journeys to the parents' hometowns. Authors who are not the children of Holocaust survivors do not offer a contemporary experience of the Holocaust, Instead, they return to the area of actual memory—the concentration camps, the time of war, and the tragic past—which is sometimes both fantastic and grotesque.[68] David Grossman's book *See Under: Love* (1984) is a clear example of such writing.[69]

The starting point of the Mizrahi second generation is not historical, sentimental, or documentary, but rather political. The chronotopic context of the stories—the time and space of the Israeli here and now—is critical. The Holocaust does not function in this writing as a historical event, but rather as symbolic capital. Therefore, the Holocaust images applied are overused, banal;

such are the hunger, the number on the arm, and the drawings in *Noble Savage* showing "[n]aked victims in the gas chambers, Jewish prisoners at forced work, hands coming out of the train cabins and mountains of human skeletons."[70] There is no attempt to show the Holocaust from a new and unknown angle or to shock, but rather to intentionally use the familiar, the "banal Holocaust," in order to divert the discussion to a different arena—to the rupture in the consciousness of Mizrahi identity in Israel.

The grotesque mimicry of the character of the victim has a double role. It reflects an ambivalent position in regard to the status of the Holocaust in Israeli society. On the one hand, it is a pathetic result of "Holocaust envy" indicating a strong desire to engrave the missing gene into the DNA of Mizrahi identity in order to be affiliated with the superior group that possesses the legitimacy in Israeli society. On the other, the very same act conceals protest and criticism, the main point being the tough question: "Do we have to go through a Holocaust to gain recognition in Israeli society?" Shaul Bibi[71] describes in the picturesque language he uses at one of the alternative Holocaust ceremonies the kind of Holocaust delusions that he had experienced after taking drugs: "I saw myself burning while eating a Torah book ... *look what you have done to my consciousness* ... I have to imagine myself as an old man being burnt."[72]

The coercion of the Holocaust memory as a narrative that organizes the identity of the Mizrahim is revealed in their literary work as a violent act, the price of which is the loss of ethnic group identity. Shlomo Deshen, a sociologist, states: "By imposing the perception of the Holocaust centrality on someone for whom it is not natural—the majority of Mizrahi Jews—it is possible to distort their identity and history."[73] If in the past, the Mizrahim felt that "their pain suffocated our pain,"[74] now, approximately sixty years after the Holocaust, the shattered consciousness finally finds a disturbing reflection through literature, an expression that can no longer be overlooked.

Notes

1. Binjamin Wilkomirski, *Fragments: Memories of a Waretime Childhood,* trans. Carol Brown Janeway (New York: Schocken Books, 1996).

2. Laurence L. Langer, *Using and Abusing the Holocaust* (Bloomington: Indiana University Press, 2006), 63.

3. Toni Morrison, *Beloved* (London: Pan Books, 1988).

4. Another interesting symbolic usage of the Holocaust is by the African Hebrew Israelite Nation of Jerusalem. The religious minority lives as a close community based on the Torah in southern Israel. Close to the Holocaust Remembrance Day they wear a yellow star, with the word "Jude" in the center replaced by a rowboat, a symbol in the memory of black slaves. (This information is eyewitness testimony provided by Prof. Yossi Yona.)

5. Gokce Yurdakul and Michal Y. Bodemann, "'We Don't Want To Be the Jews of Tomorrow': Jews and Turks in Germany after 9/11," *German Politics and Society* 24, no. 2 (2006): 45.

6. Ibid., 44.

7. Ibid.

8. Ibid., 52–53.

9. Linn Ruth and Ilan Gur Ze'ev, "Holocaust as Metaphor: Arab and Israeli Use of the Same Symbol," *Metaphor and Symbolic Activity* 11, no. 3 (1996): 195–206.

10. Meir Litvak and Esther Webman, *From Empathy to Denial: Arabs Responses to the Holocaust* (New York: Columbia University Press, 2009), 313.

11. Ibid., 316.

12. Ibid. For an opposing view of the Palestinian discourse of the Nakba, see Achcar Gilbert, *The Arabs and the Holocaust: The Arab-Israeli War of Narratives* (New York: Metropolitan Books, 2010).

13. The status of Greek Jews in this context is complex. Greece is part of Europe, but many of the Jewish community who lived in Greece before the Holocaust arrived there following their expulsion from Spain. Significantly, they are perceived by the Israeli public as part of the Mizrahim group. The term "Mizrahim" has been discussed in several important studies. Yehouda Shenhav claims the Arab Jews had to get rid of the Arab characteristics of their identity in the encounter with Zionism in order to be a part of the Israeli national collective. Since Judaism was the only feature that created a distinction between them and the Arabs, they had to be religious. In this sense, religion was a means to recruit the Mizrahim into national Judaism, meaning into Zionism. But, at the same time, religion was the ethnic signifier of the Mizrahim versus secular Israelis (which were in fact the Ashkenazim). Yehouda Shenhav, *The Arab Jews: A Postcolonial Reading of Nationalism, Religion, and Ethnicity* (Stanford, CA: Stanford University Press, 2006). See also Sami Shalom Chetrit, *Intra-Jewish Conflict in Israel: White Jews, Black Jews* (London: Routledge, 2009).

14. Ella Shohat, "Sepharadim in Israel: Zionism from the Standpoint of its Jewish Victims," *Social Text* 19, no. 20 (1988): 1–35; Hannan Hever, Yehuda Shenhav, and Pnina Motzafi-Haller, eds., *Mizrahim be' Israel* (Jerusalem: Van Leer Jerusalem Institute, 2002); Batya Shimony, *Al Saf Hageula, Sipur Hama'abara Dor Rishon Vesheni* (Or Yehuda: Dvir, 2008).

15. Oz Almog, *The Sabra: The Creation of the New Jew* (Berkeley: University of California Press, 2000).

16. Balfour Hakak, *Shoa'h BaMizrah* (Jerusalem: Ministry of Education, 1981), 1. All translations are the author's.

17. A "street gang" refers to a group of Mizrahi adolescents of Israel's social peripheral class who need to be socialized and educated in order to prevent involvement in crime.

18. This activity was manifested in the establishment of the Institute for the Study of Saloniki Jewry, which was intended to serve as a major branch for the advancement of documentation and commemoration of the history of the community members. An annual booklet called *Lo Nishkah* (We Shall Not Forget) was also produced by the survivors' children, telling their story. The booklet has been published for twenty years since the beginning of the 1980s.

19. There has been research activity on the subject in recent years. See, e.g., Hannah Yablonka, *Harchek MeHamesila, HaMizrahim VeHashoah* (Tel Aviv: Yedioth Achronoth, 2008); Robert Satloff, *Among the Righteous: Lost Stories from the Holocaust's Long Reach into Arab Lands* (New York: PublicAffairs 2006). It is worth noting the studies of Haim Saadoun and his unique initiative to hold a research workshop in the United States Holocaust Memorial Museum in 2009. The participants were scholars from Israel, the United States, and North Africa, and the workshop dealt with North African Jews in World War II. The recognition is also manifested on the political level—in recent years it was decided to correct a historic injustice and give money to the camp survivors of Libya and Tunis.

20. A poet and author born in Sderot (a small town in southern Israel).

21. Shimon Adaf, "Hashoah Berei Hasifrut Hamizrahit," *Yedioth Achronoth,* 19 April 2004.

22. For example, Zvia Lubetkin, Yitzhak Zukerman, Zvi Shaner, and Sarah Shaner-Nishmit, who were among the founders of Kibbutz Lohamei HaGetaot (Ghetto Fighters). Yablonka, *Harchek MeHamesila,* 85. Abba Kovner was one of the founders of Moreshet (Heritage) Organization, which was intended to coordinate the documentation (ibid., 87).

23. Ibid., 85–99.

24. Ibid., 100–29.
25. Yair Auron, *Zehuyot Israeliyot* (Tel Aviv: Resling, 2010), 190.
26. Yablonka, *Harchek MeHamesila,* 102.
27. Baruch Kimmerling, *Mehagrim, Mityashvim, Yelidim* (Tel Aviv: Am Oved, 2004), 299.
28. The concept of "Holocaust envy" was proposed by Prof. Haim Hazan during a study workshop on Holocaust and globalization (Van Leer Jerusalem Institute, 2008–9).
29. Contemporary feminist researchers object to Freud's basic assumptions of phallocentricity, and to the definition of femininity as the absence of something. However, the centrality of the Freudian and Lacanian theories in Western culture is not dubious and is widely expressed in the literature.
30. Many studies deal with the gendered aspect of Zionism and the Mizrahi tradition—Zionism is perceived as masculine and the Mizrahi tradition is perceived as feminine. See, e.g., Dror Mishani, *Bechol HaInyan Hamizrahi yesh Eize Absurd* (Tel Aviv: Am Oved, 2006); Michael Gluzman, *Haguf Hazioni: Leumiyut, Migdar Veminiyut* (Tel Aviv: Hakibutz Hameuchd, 2007).
31. Stephen A. Mitchell and Margaret J. Black, *Freud and Beyond: A History of Modern Psychoanalytic Thought* (New York: Basic Books, 1995), 18–19.
32. One can see this in different cases: in Roberman's study about Jewish Russian veterans who fought in World War II, she demonstrates how they shape their Israeli identity by the infiltration of a new narrative of heroism that extends the conservative narrative of the Holocaust. Sveta Roberman, *Zikaron Bahagira, Chayaley Hatzava H'adom BeYisrael* (Jerusalem: Magnes, 2005).
33. Jackie Feldman, *Above the Death Pits, Beneath the Flag: Youth Voyages to Poland and the Performance of Israeli National Identity* (New York and Oxford: Berghahn Books, 2008). The journeys raised an extensive debate in Israel. Some opposing arguments were heard; one relevant to this chapter is the social distortion caused by the high cost of the journeys. As a result, only students who come from well-to-do families can go on the journeys. Clearly, there is a strong correlation in Israeli society between low socioeconomic status and Mizrahi origins. The Mizrahi students are excluded once again from the Israeli hegemonic narrative of the Holocaust. Yablonka, *Harchek MeHamesila,* 180–85, describes the efforts made by the mayor of Beit-She'an (a northern Israeli small town, most of its residents of Mizrahi origins) to send the students there to Poland. Due to lack of budget he sent the students on a short and concentrated journey of fourteen hours. This example shows the enormous significance the Mizrahim attribute to the experience of the Holocaust as a bridge into Israeli society.
34. These authors arrived to Israel at the ages of ten, two, and five, respectively.
35. Yablonka, *Harchek MeHamesila,* 274.
36. Ibid., 276–77.
37. Shimony, *Al Saf Hageula.*
38. Shimon Balas, *Hama'abara* (Tel Aviv: Am Oved, 1964).
39. Ibid., 51.
40. Sammy Michael, *Shavim VeShavim Yoter* (Tel Aviv: Bustan, 1974).
41. Ibid., 39, highlighted as in the original.
42. Ibid., 146, highlighted as in the original.
43. Sammy Michael, *Mayim Noshkim LeMayim* (Tel Aviv: Am Oved, 2001).
44. Ibid., 12.
45. Ibid., 14.
46. One of the reactions that I frequently encountered while working on Ma'abarot literature was that whoever experienced the Ma'abara period as a child remembers it as a positive experience. However, in many other cases, the critical awareness in regard to immigration to Israel developed during these children's adolescence.
47. Kimmerling claims that "in fact, in the beginning, very few immigrants from the Islam countries, who were the main object for the required change [modernization and Westernization], saw it as an oppressive and immoral act. In the first generation, the protest and objection were mainly sporadic and random." Kimmerling, *Mehagrim, Mityashvim, Yelidim,* 294.
48. Hakak, *Shoa'h BaMizrah.*

49. Ibid., 1.

50. Shenhav, *The Arab Jews,* 141.

51. Sasson Somekh, *Baghdad, Etmol* (Tel Aviv: Hakibutz Hameuchad, 2003), 12. Satloff studied the effect of World War II on the Arab arena; he claims that he chose not to include the Farhud events within the drama of the Holocaust: "The Germans certainly inspired the local actors and even delivered them some material support, but neither the Germans nor their other European partners were pivotal players in the Iraqi drama." He concludes: "I consider it more appropriate to view it as one—perhaps the worst—of the periodic spasms of violence by Arabs against Jews . . . rather than as part of the European-spawned campaign to persecute and annihilate Jews that eventually came to be known as the Holocaust." Satloff, *Among the Righteous,* 25.

52. Sabato wrote a lament in memory of the Holocaust that is recited on the ninth day of Av. It is probably the only lament written by a Mizrahi author about the Holocaust. The lament "How the verdict was made and sealed on my brothers" is mentioned in the book *From the Four Winds* and is brought in it in full.

53. Haim Sabato, *From the Four Winds,* trans. Yaacob Dweck (New Milford, CT: Toby Press, 2010).

54. Haim Weiss, "And I Saw the Way Those Wicked Evildoers Treated My Compatriots," *Haaretz,* 19 February 2008.

55. Ibid.

56. Sabato, *From the Four Winds,* 127–28.

57. This phenomenon is evident in additional cultural activities, such as naïve mimicry representations at alternative Holocaust ceremonies conducted in the past few years in Tel Aviv. At these events people who are perceived as "others" in regard to the Holocaust story can express themselves—the Mizrahim, the Orthodox, Jews from Ethiopia, and even Israeli Arabs. Yablonka describes the performance of Shimi Ron, a musician of Yemenite descent, of the song "The Small Town Is Burning": "Ron is about forty years old. He sings with devotion as if this was 'his song,' as Blau [one of the ceremony organizers] says. The most interesting thing is that Ron, who usually sings with the 'throaty' H and A as the Yemenite pronunciation, felt this time that he should 'clean up' these sounds. This is a very significant act from the cultural and emotional points of view." Yablonka, *Harchek MeHamesila,* 287. Another example is the actor Shai Kadimi, of Moroccan descent, who portrayed a Holocaust survivor named Mania and "turned into a medium" (ibid., 288). The audience was convinced that the actor really was a Holocaust survivor. Similar to Sabato, total identification is prominent here, as when the two artists, Ron and Kadimi, remove the Mizrahi characteristics from their bodies (the Yemenite pronunciation, the physical appearance of a young Mizrahi man) to instill a different substance.

58. Homi K. Bhabha, "Of Mimicry and Man: The Ambivalence of Colonial Discourse," in *The Location of Culture* (New York: Routledge, 1994), 121–31.

59. Dudu Busi, *Pere Atzil* (Jerusalem: Keter, 2003). Busi was born in Israel to parents who immigrated from Persia and Yemen; he grew up in the HaTikva neighborhood.

60. Ibid., 43.

61. Ibid., 269.

62. Kobi Oz, *Avaryan Tzatzua* (Tel Aviv: Keshet, 2002). Oz was born in Israel in 1969 to parents who immigrated from Tunisia. He grew up in Sderot, a small town in southern Israel.

63. Yossi Avni, *Doda Farhuma Lo Hayta Zona* (Tel Aviv: Am Oved, 2002).

64. Ibid., 139.

65. Ibid., 241.

66. Ibid., 214.

67. Iris Milner, *Kirey Avar: Biographya, Zehut Vezikaron besifrut Hador Hasheni* (Tel Aviv: Am Oved, 2003); Avner Holzman, "Nosei Ha'shoah Basiporet Haisraelit, Gal Chadash," *Dappim Lemechkar Besifrut* 10 (1996–97): 131–58.

68. In *The White Hotel* Thomas attempts to reconstruct the experience of the death of a young woman at Babi-Yar. Parts of the novel are written in a clearly grotesque manner. One phrase that is supposedly quoted from a letter from Freud to his friend points to the relation to

Rabelais and his carnival world: "If you can look beyond the gross expressions ..., you may find passages to enjoy. I speak as one who knows your Rabelaisian temperament." D. M. Thomas, *The White Hotel* (New York: Viking Press, 1981), 14. However, the chapter where the storyteller penetrates the fear of death at Babi-Yar does not include any grotesque elements.

69. David Grossman, *See Under: Love,* trans. Betsy Rosenberg (New York: Farrar, Straus, and Giroux, 1989).
70. Busi, *Pere Atzil,* 42.
71. A Mizrahi journalist and activist.
72. Yablonka, *Harchek MeHamesila,* 288, emphasis mine.
73. Shlomo Deshen, "Ivut Shel Zehut," *Haaretz,* 26 August 1998.
74. Yablonka, *Harchek MeHamesila,* 282.

Bibliography

Adaf, Shimon. "Hashoah Berei Hasifrut Hamizrahit." *Yedioth Achronoth,* 19 April 2004.
Almog, Oz. *The Sabra: The Creation of the New Jew.* Berkeley: University of California Press, 2000.
Auron, Yair. *Zehuyot Israeliyot.* Tel Aviv: Resling, 2010.
Avni, Yossi. *Doda Farhuma Lo Hayta Zona.* Tel Aviv: Am Oved, 2002.
Balas, Shimon. *Hama'abara.* Tel Aviv: Am Oved, 1964.
Bhabha, Homi K. "Of Mimicry and Man: The Ambivalence of Colonial Discourse," in *The Location of Culture,* 121–31. New York: Routledge, 1994.
Busi, Dudu. *Pere Atzil.* Jerusalem: Keter, 2003.
Chetrit, Sami Shalom. *Intra-Jewish Conflict in Israel: White Jews, Black Jews.* London: Routledge, 2009.
Deshen, Shlomo. "Ivut Shel Zehut." *Haaretz,* 26 August 1998.
Feldman, Jackie. *Above the Death Pits, Beneath the Flag: Youth Voyages to Poland and the Performance of Israeli National Identity.* New York and Oxford: Berghahn Books, 2008.
Gilbert, Achcar. *The Arabs and the Holocaust: The Arab-Israeli War of Narratives.* New York: Metropolitan Books, 2010.
Gluzman, Michael. *Haguf Hazioni: Leumiyut, Migdar Veminiyut.* Tel Aviv: Hakibutz Hameuchd, 2007.
Grossman, David. *See Under: Love.* Translated by Betsy Rosenberg. New York: Farrar, Straus, and Giroux, 1989.
Hakak, Balfour. *Shoah BaMizrah.* Jerusalem: Ministry of Education, 1981.
Hever, Hannan, Yehuda Shenhav, and Pnina Motzafi-Haller, eds. *Mizrahim be' Israel.* Jerusalem: Van Leer Jerusalem Institute, 2002.
Holzman, Avner. "Nosei Ha'shoah Basiporet Haisraelit, Gal Chadash." *Dappim Lemechkar Besifrut* 10 (1996–97): 131–58.
Kimmerling, Baruch. *Mehagrim, Mityashvim, Yelidim.* Tel Aviv: Am Oved, 2004.
Langer, Laurence L. *Using and Abusing the Holocaust.* Bloomington: Indiana University Press, 2006.
Litvak, Meir, and Esther Webman. *From Empathy to Denial: Arabs Responses to the Holocaust.* New York: Columbia University Press, 2009.
Michael, Sammy. *Shavim VeShavim Yoter.* Tel Aviv: Bustan, 1974.
———. *Mayim Noshkim LeMayim.* Tel Aviv: Am Oved, 2001.
Milner, Iris. *Kirey Avar: Biographya, Zehut Vezikaron besifrut Hador Hasheni.* Tel Aviv: Am Oved, 2003.
Mishani, Dror. *Bechol HaInyan Hamizrahi yesh Eize Absurd.* Tel Aviv: Am Oved, 2006.
Mitchell, Stephen A., and Margaret J. Black. *Freud and Beyond: A History of Modern Psychoanalytic Thought.* New York: Basic Books, 1995.
Morrison, Toni. *Beloved.* London: Pan Books, 1988.
Oz, Kobi. *Avaryan Tzatzua.* Tel Aviv: Keshet, 2002.

Roberman, Sveta. *Zikaron Bahagira, Chayaley Hatzava H'adom BeYisrael*. Jerusalem: Magnes, 2005.
Ruth, Linn, and Ilan Gur Ze'ev. "Holocaust as Metaphor: Arab and Israeli Use of the Same Symbol." *Metaphor and Symbolic Activity* 11, no. 3 (1996): 195–206.
Sabato, Haim. *From the Four Winds*. Translated by Yaacob Dweck. New Milford, CT: Toby Press, 2010.
Satloff, Robert. *Among the Righteous: Lost Stories from the Holocaust's Long Reach into Arab Lands*. New York: PublicAffairs, 2006.
Shenhav, Yehouda. *The Arab Jews: A Postcolonial Reading of Nationalism, Religion, and Ethnicity*. Stanford, CA: Stanford University Press, 2006.
Shimony, Batya. *Al Saf Hageula, Sipur Hama'abara Dor Rishon Vesheni*. Or Yehuda: Dvir, 2008.
Shohat, Ella. "Sepharadim in Israel: Zionism from the Standpoint of its Jewish Victims." *Social Text* 19, no. 20 (1988): 1–35.
Somekh, Sasson. *Baghdad, Etmol*. Tel Aviv: Hakibutz Hameuchad, 2003.
Thomas, D.M. (Donald Michael). *The White Hotel*. New York: Viking Press, 1981.
Weiss, Haim. "And I Saw the Way Those Wicked Evildoers Treated My Compatriots." *Haaretz*, 19 February 2008.
Wilkomirski, Binjamin. 1996. *Fragments: Memories of a Wartime Childhood*. Translated by Carol Brown Janeway. New York: Schcken Books, 1996.
Yablonka, Hanna. *Harchek MeHamesila, HaMizrahim VeHashoah*. Tel Aviv: Yedioth Achronoth, 2008.
Yurdakul, Gokce, and Michal Y. Bodemann. "'We Don't Want To Be the Jews of Tomorrow': Jews and Turks in Germany after 9/11." *German Politics and Society* 24, no. 2 (2006): 44–67.

Section V
CLOSURE

CHAPTER 16

Messages from a Present Past
The Kristallnacht *as Symbolic Turning Point in Nazi Rule*

EMANUEL MARX

Introduction

The events of the *Kristallnacht* have been studied in depth by three generations of scholars. This does not mean that they are fully understood, if only because no amount of study can ever exhaust a complex theme. Besides, the new materials that are continually coming to light require revisions or even new interpretations. Thus, the symbolic aspect of the pogrom was first pointed out by Loewenberg,[1] forty years after the event. He called it a national "ritual of degradation" threatening the Jews of Germany with annihilation. The other messages, and especially the insidious threats directed at the seemingly privileged "Aryan" Germans, have gone almost unnoticed and will be discussed in the following pages. Both sets of messages turn *Kristallnacht* into a symbolic cue for things to come, and in Confino's locution, "a foundational past."[2]

The pogrom touched me personally: in the night between 9 and 10 November the Nazi mobs destroyed both the synagogue and the Jewish school that I attended in my hometown, Munich. On the morning of 10 November policemen arrested my father. He was sent to Dachau concentration camp and released after two months, a broken man. I was at the time eleven years old, and the events had such a profound impact on me that for many years I could not bear to think about them. It took seventy years for the childhood trauma to resolve to the point that I could accept an invitation by Haim Hazan and Amos Goldberg to join their research group on the Holocaust and globalization at the Van Leer Jerusalem Institute. In that scholarly framework I hoped to study

---

Notes for this section begin on page 336.

the pogrom from a safe distance. Since I began the study about eight years ago, however, it has pervaded my thoughts. I worked on it compulsively for long periods, often at the expense of my other research interests.

Much of the time I was an apprentice; I acquainted myself with the voluminous literature and almost drowned in an ocean of information. However, the more I immersed myself in the literature, the more perplexed I became. I found that the scholarly community rapidly accumulated large quantities of data, but then hesitated to interpret and integrate them in a larger picture. I also noticed that the professional literature occasionally ignored the findings of reputable scholars. This should not have surprised me, as I had encountered a deep-seated resistance to new ideas in my own profession. As students we were trained to follow the ethnographic material wherever it led, and to reassess data and revise explanations in an unending dialectical process,[3] but then found that original ideas were hard to publish, and when published—not necessarily adopted by colleagues. Here are three striking examples of such elision in the literature on the Nazi era.

The historian Wilhelm Treue published in 1955 the only surviving copy of Hitler's policy paper (*Denkschrift*) of August 1936 on the Four-Year Plan, in which the dictator explicitly proposed a "final solution [*endgültige Lösung*] to the German problem" by setting up a colonial empire in Eastern Europe.[4] The project drove Germany into a war that caused the death of over eleven million Germans. Most scholars (excepting Tooze)[5] pay little attention to the fact that this first "final solution" concerned the lives of proper "Aryan" Germans, and that Hitler gave the phrase a precise and deadly meaning.

The investigative journalist Ernst Klee showed in 1985 that the Nazi scheme to murder institutionalized handicapped Germans began in 1936 (and perhaps as early as 1933).[6] By 1939 the so-called euthanasia project had grown into a compact organization that had developed efficient methods of murder, including gas chambers. While most historians are familiar with Klee's study, they still date the beginning of the euthanasia scheme to the invasion of Poland in September 1939 and thus fail to notice that it first targeted German victims.

The historian Christian Streit showed in 1978 that during the assault on Soviet Russia in 1941 the Nazi armies and security forces systematically eliminated 3.3 million Soviet prisoners of war as part of a grand project to clear Eastern Europe for German colonization.[7] The death camps of Auschwitz-Birkenau and Lublin-Majdanek were constructed to expedite the murders and to reduce the emotional strain on the executors. When the tide of war turned in August 1941 and the supply of Soviet prisoners of war stopped, Himmler provided Jewish victims in order to keep the extermination machinery running. Despite the facts, some historians, especially in Israel, still believe that the Nazis targeted Jews as their major victims from the day they rose to power and that they constructed the infamous death camps especially for them.

There seems to be a system to this forgetfulness. In Germany, many historians hesitated for years to face the fundamental truth that not just the army, SS, and police personnel perpetrated the Nazi atrocities, but that millions of other Germans participated in or approved of them. That some of the perpetrators were colleagues and friends, who resumed a respectable life and work routine in postwar Germany, made it even harder for them to explore the Nazi past. The heated arguments about the authorship of the Holocaust that divided German historians from 1986 onward was itself the outcome of the successor states' attempts to return to normalcy and reintegrate millions of Germans who had participated in, approved of, or feigned ignorance of the Nazi murders. It narrowed the focus of scholarly attention to a limited set of perpetrators, namely, the Nazi leadership and its military and police organizations. In the desire to return to normalcy, and "draw a ... line under the Nazi past,"[8] some German historians lost sight of the endless number and variety of Nazi victims and the large number of German organizations and individuals (and their non-German helpers) who were involved in the implementation of the Holocaust. Nor was it a coincidence that they also forgot the millions of Germans who became victims of Nazism. While Hans Fallada's posthumous novel *Every Man Dies Alone* (2009) truthfully portrays the misery of the German people during the war years, it has yet to inspire historical research.[9]

Israeli Holocaust research too is still hampered by its close links with the state. For political and economic reasons, researchers insist that there was one Jewish Holocaust that dwarfs all other genocides. They know of the Nazi murder campaigns against handicapped patients, Gypsies, and Soviet prisoners of war, but nevertheless believe that the Jewish Holocaust is unique. While some scholars have critiqued this failing,[10] others, like Yehuda Bauer, dean of Israeli Holocaust scholars, still believe that the Holocaust is different: only in this case "Nazi racial antisemitic ideology was the central factor in the development toward the Holocaust," and while "pragmatic considerations were central with all other genocides ... [w]ith the Holocaust, pragmatic considerations were marginal."[11] Both German and Israeli scholars possess all the materials for constructing a fully contextualized account of the Nazi period. There is hope that independent-minded and innovative scholars in both countries will before long achieve important breakthroughs.

When the evidence forced me to swim against both the German and the Israeli currents, I knew that my work would raise the hackles of some historians. Perhaps I should have desisted, for most of the insights gained in eight years of work on the Nazi regime now seem to me almost self-evident (and are therefore probably correct). On the other hand, I feel that the great questions have eluded me: I still have only tentative notions how the Nazi regime operated and why it sacrificed millions of victims. My continuing efforts to obtain better answers may fail, but I am duty-bound to play my part in recovering the memories of the Holocaust. While my childhood trauma provides the driving force behind this study, my anthropological training gives it direction. I am well aware that most of the significant research on the Holocaust has been and will be done by historians. However, I believe that anthropologists can add novel viewpoints and offer new insights.

Messages of the *Kristallnacht*

This chapter treats the *Kristallnacht* pogrom of 9–10 November 1938 as a staged violent event that the Nazi regime used, as customary at organized mass events, to deliver important messages to diverse audiences. The event cast a sudden beam of light on the Nazi regime's core project: to prepare the German people for total war against neighboring countries. The immediate aim of war was to acquire a colonial empire in Eastern Europe, and the long-term target was to raise Germany to the pinnacle of world power. The Nazis intended to use the wealth of the Jews to help finance the rearmament program during the first stage and then rely on the resources of the conquered countries. The various messages that the Nazi leadership conveyed during the pogrom pertained to four interconnected themes.

First, it gave notice to the world that the regime's Jewish policies were changing. In its first five years in power the Nazi regime pursued two contradictory policies: it sought to expel the Jews, but also used them as convenient whipping boys in its continuous efforts to discipline and control the German population. It curtailed the civil rights of Jews and restricted their economic activities in order to drive them out, and at the same time put many fiscal and bureaucratic obstacles in the path of those who wished to emigrate. By the end of 1936, however, the Nazi leaders realized that they fully controlled the German population, and thus no longer needed the Jews as warning examples. Göring, the supreme leader of Germany's rearmament program, in particular, sought the right moment to introduce a more radical Jewish policy, one that would contribute to a solution of the chronic economic troubles of the rearmament project. He believed that by tapping new external resources through territorial expansion and internal resources—by dispossessing the Jews—the state would be able to continue its forced rearmament. As a result of territorial gains large Jewish communities would come under Nazi sway. Even the Jews who had fled Germany would once again become German subjects. Göring recognized that the opportunities to expropriate Jews would soon grow apace. He decided, therefore, no longer to press for emigration, and instead first to despoil the Jews and then to dispose of them in an as yet undefined manner. The new situation had the direst consequences: it radicalized the relentless process of exclusion of German Jews while turning them into captive victims. It became clear that the process would end with the physical elimination of the Jews and, furthermore, that the Nazis would also target other groups for exploitation and elimination.

Second, the event marked a turning point in the relations between Germany and the world. The Nazis had made the consolidation of a greater Germany and the acquisition of a colonial empire a major political aim. In the first years in power, Hitler had meticulously prepared the territorial exploits and calculated the risks, "always leaving open the possibility of an immediate climbdown in the event of genuine resistance."[12] After each conquest he reassured the world that he would refrain from further territorial demands. This time matters were different. Hitler decided to come out in the open. In the annual speech to the party stalwarts on 8 November 1938 he announced that Germany would become a world power. On the same day Himmler spoke to the assembled SS leaders. He went somewhat further than Hitler and promised them that the Führer would create a "Greater Germanic Empire [*Grossgermanisches Imperium*] … the greatest empire [*Reich*] ever established by mankind."[13] A variant of this theme animated the messages the Nazis sent out in the *Kristallnacht*. They wanted the world to know that they were now powerful enough not to care what it thought of them. From now on they would pursue their foremost political project, the founding of a colonial empire in Eastern Europe, accompanied by the displacement of the Slav and other non-Aryan peoples, and follow it up, perhaps in another generation, with a bid for world domination.[14] Nothing, and certainly no moral qualms or diplomatic considerations, would be allowed to stand in the way of their ambitions. To this end the Nazi militias (SA) and other party organizations performed the riots quite blatantly and brutally, all over the country and even in the city centers, to the accompaniment of burning synagogues, vandalized shops, and tortured men and women.

Third, the Nazis signaled to the German public that the party had almost completed its infiltration and subjugation of the state, and that the party and its affiliated security organizations now ruled supreme and were above the law. The pogrom was executed mainly by the Nazi Party and the SA, assisted in some places during the first hours by the SS and Hitler Youth.[15] Ordinary citizens too joined the rioters. While these men and women engaged in arson and torture, the police and fire brigades were ordered to stand idly by, so that the members of the public would clearly perceive who was in charge and who was doing the dirty work. The bystanders were given to understand that the Nazis would not stop there, and were out to take over the remaining branches of government, and not least the rampaging SA storm troopers.

Fourth, it signaled to the Germans who were still considered "Aryans" that the Nazis were likely to treat them just as they were now treating their Jewish compatriots, just as they had in recent years dealt with political opponents and with other weak and vulnerable groups of Germans. The Nazi leaders were demonstrating on the Jews how "we exterminate all criminals in our law-abiding state: with fire and sword."[16] Anyone who cared to listen realized that the threat was directed at him, her, and every German. The Nazi leaders' efforts to enslave and intimidate the seemingly privileged Aryan citizens had largely succeeded. The Nazi regime had forged an unbreakable bond with the citizens, who rapidly lost control of their own destinies. The regime had come to supervise and regulate the citizens' lives to the point where they could permit or order them to commit excesses, without fear of losing control or being censured by the man in the street. Hundreds of ordinary citizens willingly joined the SA details in the acts of destruction and pillage[17] or participated in the pogrom as curious onlookers, thus becoming accessories to the crimes.

The Nazi state would soon drop all remaining moral restraints, and deploy or destroy the Aryan citizens at will. They were already being treated as undifferentiated members of the nation (*Volksgenossen*) and not as individual persons. The party's numerous organizations, whether dedicated to social welfare, sports, labor, national aggrandizement, or warfare, brought them into line, indoctrinated, and strictly supervised them. If their rulers considered it opportune, they too could be declared enemies of the state, just like their fellow citizens, the Communists, Socialists, SA leadership, Jews, Gypsies, institutionalized handicapped persons, vagrants, homosexuals, and leaders of Christian churches. If the common people managed to stay in line, the regime would in due course treat them as expendable cannon fodder or replaceable units of production, and move them around according to its imagined priorities. Men would eventually be sent to fight in the various war zones, as disciplined soldiers and more or less consenting mass murderers, and many of them would lose life and limb. Women would be exploited as workers and mothers of successive generations of soldiers and workers. If these men and women ever ceased to work, fight, and bleed for their Nazi masters, they would lose the right to live.

The events unfolded in three phases, beginning with the pogrom night of 9–10 November, when Nazi storm troopers and mobs burned down over a thousand synagogues all over Germany and Austria[18] and destroyed "at least 7,500 Jewish-owned shops ... out of a total of no more than 9,000 altogether."[19] They also murdered ninety-one Jews.[20] Not one of the murderers and arsonists was arrested, for the public prosecutors had been instructed to reserve the jails for the use of the Gestapo,[21] and orders issued by Nazi authorities were above the law.

The second phase started on 10 November and continued for a week, during which the police arrested between thirty and forty thousand Jewish men,[22] that is, every fourth Jewish man in greater Germany. The men were hauled to Dachau, Buchenwald, and Sachsenhausen concentration camps. They were kept in custody for up to three months, during which the SS killed over five thousand of them.[23] Those who survived the SS treatment were released in small batches and advised to leave Germany immediately.[24]

The third phase began on 12 November, when the Nazi leaders decided that the time had come to fully expropriate the Jews. As the operation had been prepared in the preceding months, they could act quickly: on 21 November they ordered all Jewish taxpayers to pay the state 20 percent of their assets, to the amount of one billion reichsmarks.[25] These impositions were rapidly followed by other decrees designed to pauperize German Jews.

With the hindsight of seventy years, I understand that the *Kristallnacht* marked a symbolic turning point in the transformation of Nazi Germany into a lawless tyranny that precipitated a succession of wars and mass murders. In another way too it was a unique event: it was the only time during their twelve-year rule that Nazi leaders resorted to nationwide street mobilization. The Argentine political activist Miguel Bonasso has characterized street mobilizations in his country as events where "years of history are compressed, and where one sees history turning a page to start a new chapter."[26] This observation is true for the *Kristallnacht*: it brought into the open a new turn in the Nazi regime. The party leaders had spent many months preparing the pogrom, but the massive participation of the Nazi rank and file, joined by members of the public, transformed it into a rising of the people. The participants in such mass mobilizations enjoy a sense of freedom and unity that may well run out of control.[27] Therefore, the Nazi leaders hesitated before permitting even such a centrally organized surge of "popular" violence. What led them finally to grant permission was the shortage of funds for the state's rearmament program, which could be supplied by money extorted from Jews. In the pogrom the Nazi Party asserted its ownership of the Jews against other contestants, such as the SS. At the same time, the active and vicarious participants in the pogrom were invited, and even required, to enjoy the suffering and death of others and thus still their own fear of disorder, violence, and death.[28]

The pogrom was also a major public ritual staged by the Nazi Party machine, whose performers addressed a cluster of symbolic messages to several audiences. The messages concerned four main issues, all of which would eventually reappear in the various "final solutions" to the Nazi state's imaginary geopolitical, eugenic, and racial problems.

A New Jewish Policy

An attentive reading of German literature shows that hatred of the Jews has long been deeply engrained in German nationalist thought. The Jew was the paradigmatic other, against whom the diverse inhabitants of the German states could consolidate their German identity. This did not prevent Jews from gradually entering most occupations, especially from the mid-nineteenth century onward, and becoming patriotic Germans.[29]

This kind of ethnic prejudice was irrelevant for the Nazi leaders. They did not wish to draw national boundaries but to supersede them. Therefore, they postulated the absolute superiority of Germany and the Germans to all other nations. They linked nationalism with race and blood and divided human beings into ranked ethnic groups according to their capacity to fight. At the apex of the hierarchy stood a putative Aryan race, whose most advanced representatives were the descendants of the Germanic tribes of the Roman Empire. They had, however, no desire to develop a scientific theory of race. A vulgar social Darwinism that emphasized the survival of the fittest was sufficient for their requirements, as they simply wanted to apply the tried methods of selection and weeding of plant and animal breeders to the production of a purebred, physically sound, and spiritually committed Germanic race of soldiers.[30] The purification of Germany of inferior and polluted races became a basic tenet of belief, which they preached tirelessly.[31] They categorized a host of human groups—among them Socialists, Communists, Slavs, Gypsies, Africans, and Asians, as well as homosexuals, asocial and work-shy individuals, and mentally and physically handicapped persons—as impure and unfit to live side by side with proper Germans. In the war years, the Nazis extended the list further, until it included all those persons who were thought to oppose the regime. By then they also knew how to deal with them: those whose lives were unfit to live or who were useless eaters could be routinely killed.

Yet even these practical ideologies were quite unstable and changeable, for the Nazis were not primarily interested in intellectual debate. They were keen on action, especially the bureaucratic exercise of every conceivable kind of massive coercion. Volkov perceptively observes that the unending torrent of "verbal aggression was not a substitute for action, but its preparation."[32] Spoken and printed words were there to enable, justify, and explain actions ranging from organized violence against interior enemies to rearmament and military conquest of inferior peoples, from draconic exclusionary laws to violent persecution and genocide. The regime's wide-ranging propaganda activities served to entrench and justify its rule; the media supplied arguments and preached ideologies that deftly fitted the requirements of the moment.

The Jews of Germany occupied a special place in Nazi racial ranking. The Nazis considered the Jews a mongrel race, too diversified and individuated to fit into a martial hierarchy. Evans puts it in a nutshell: in the Nazi view the Jews were "a race of parasites that could only live by subverting other peoples, above all ... the Aryans."[33] Thus, the Jews became candidates for exclusion and derision, who could be set up as warning examples to the "Aryan" population.

The SS leaders, in particular, set themselves up as the official arbiters of racial purity, and continually sought to extend the margins of pollution caused by the presence of Jews. They categorized persons with ever-smaller doses of Jewish blood as Jews of mixed descent (*Mischlinge*), to the point where a mere drop of Jewish blood could pollute the blood stream of the national body. Himmler himself ardently believed that a candidate for the SS who had even a single Jewish ancestor eight generations removed was unfit to join the organization.[34] However, Hitler left the issue of where to draw the line undecided, insisting at the same time that only he was entitled to decide on it,[35] thus causing an estimated one hundred thousand Christian Germans with Jewish ancestors to fear continually for their lives.[36]

The Jewish Germans were mentally unprepared for Nazi rule. They had sunk deep roots in German society and only strove to become fully absorbed in it. The imposed segregation went against all they wanted in life. Even while the Nazi state rejected them, most Jews, including the Zionists, found it hard to struggle free of their attachment to the German nation and its "culture."[37] While many Jews emigrated, among them most of the wealthier ones, others held stubbornly to the belief that better times were in store. Those who did not have the means or the opportunity to leave the country, as well as the mixed breeds, who hoped to be treated as akin to Germans, were content with waiting for better days. Thus, the insightful diaries of Victor Klemperer reveal that throughout the war years the Jewish academic and his Christian wife hoped that things could at any moment change for the better.[38]

There were two reasons why the Jews could not clearly perceive the looming danger. First, up to the *Kristallnacht* the Nazis did not pursue a consistent anti-Jewish policy. In their public speeches the Nazi leaders always linked the Jews with both the essential and the current enemies of the state. They personified some of the most powerful social forces in the world, such as American capitalism, European socialism, and Soviet communism, as well as the struggling Weimar democracy.[39] The gallery of archenemies was so large and impressive that the Jews considered themselves too insignificant a target.

Second, there were lulls in the Nazi state's agenda of terror against the Jews. Thus, it appears that between 1933 and 1937 the Nazi leaders attended to the "Jewish question" only sporadically. Through most of the year of 1933 the Nazis were busy subjugating the Communist, Social Democratic and People's parties and forcibly "coordinating" (*gleichschalten*) the civil service, as well as the universities, the farmers, and all the nationwide professional and cultural associations. During that period, writes Evans, "The [Nazi] terror was comprehensive in scope, affecting anyone who expressed dissent in public, from whatever direction, against deviants, vagrants, nonconformists of every kind."[40] Yet that was a year in which the Jews enjoyed a partial respite from Nazi terror. While the Nazi state tolerated and instigated sporadic localized violent assaults on Jews, it concentrated its efforts on imposing on them numerous legal and administrative restrictions.

Only toward the end of 1937 did the Nazi regime develop a radical new Jewish policy. They issued a series of anti-Jewish laws and regulations[41] and simultaneously promoted a vicious anti-Jewish publicity campaign. It culminated in a pronouncement by the Nazi Party's supreme judge that "the National Socialist has recognized [that] the Jew is not a human."[42] Tal justly comments that such statements presented the Jew as "an object [that] could be used in any way for any purpose." It became ever more evident that the Nazis were intent on expelling all Jews from Germany. Many Jews did not heed these warning shots; only the *Kristallnacht* brought them to a full awareness of the situation.

The inconsistencies in Nazi practice were guided by pragmatic considerations. Even the "Final Solution to the Jewish Question" had a checkered history, and was driven by the Nazis' desire for living space in the East, as well as by perceived political, economic, and military contingencies and departmental rivalries, and not simply by an implacable hatred of the Jews.

Three "Final Solutions"

A German Ministry of External Affairs circular issued in January 1939 called 1938 "the year of destiny" (*Schicksalsjahr*), for it prepared the way for the "realization of the Greater German idea and also got closer to a solution of the Jewish problem."[43] Both ideas were dear to the Nazi leaders, but their foremost concern was to establish a colonial empire in Eastern Europe that would provide food for Germany's citizens and raw materials for its factories. The quest for a colonial empire had been central to Hitler's political program since his early struggles, and he referred to it time and again in his *Mein Kampf*.[44] At his very first meeting with the army and navy command after his accession to power, on 2 February 1933, Hitler spoke about "the conquest of new living space in the East, and its resolute [*rücksichtlos*] Germanization."[45] However, only in August 1936 did he put down his thoughts on the matter in a "policy paper" (*Denkschrift*). In this unique document he expressly proposed a "final solution" (*endgültige Lösung*) to Germany's lack of colonies. A Four-Year Plan of rearmament would prepare the German economy and army for a colonial war in Eastern Europe.[46] This was a very significant moment, for as Hitler later remarked, "I prepare policy papers only on the most fundamental issues, such as the Four-Year Plan in its day or last year's War in the East."[47] Hitler and his minions pursued this original "final solution" forcefully and tenaciously until the end of his life.

Hitler immediately translated his ideas into practice by appointing the efficient and unscrupulous Göring as head of an all-powerful Four-Year Plan administration whose sole task was the rearmament of Germany. A planning unit for the colonization of Eastern Europe was set up in the National Bureau for Regional Planning (Reichsstelle für Raumordnung) attached to Hitler's chancellery, and Konrad Meyer, a professor of agriculture, became its referent for regional planning, including the colonization of Eastern Europe.

In 1939 Himmler, in his newly acquired role as Commissioner for the Strengthening of German Nationhood (Reichskommissar für die Festigung deutschen Volkstums, abbreviated RKF) in occupied Eastern Europe invited Meyer to transfer to that organization's department for Planning and Soil (Planung und Boden), where his team developed from 1940 to 1942 several versions of a radical plan of colonization, dubbed "Generalplan Ost" or "Gesamtplan Ost."[48] Early versions of the plans provided for the settlement of 3.4 million Germans in the annexed parts of occupied Poland, while a similar number of Poles, as well as all the Jews, were to be deported to eastern Poland.[49] The planning usually lagged behind the new realities on the ground created by the rapidly advancing German forces. Especially Himmler's agents in the occupied regions, the police "task forces" (*Einsatzgruppen*), implemented the plans as they saw fit. Thus, in the wake of the occupation of Poland in September 1939, task forces committed mass murders of Poles and Jews in order to "pacify" the country and to make room for German settlers in the regions annexed by Germany. The successful execution of the massacres and evacuations, and the only partially successful attempts to settle ethnic Germans (*Volksdeutsche*) in the empty spaces, underlay the regime's decision to conduct the war against the Soviet Union too as a "war of annihilation" in order to release even larger areas for German colonists.[50]

Merely a month after the *Kristallnacht,* the Nazis decided on another "final solution," that of the approximately thirty thousand Gypsies of Germany. The wagon camps and hamlets of these semi-itinerant people were dispersed throughout the German states. For centuries they had been treated suspiciously by fellow citizens and harassed by the local gendarmes. On 8 December 1938 Himmler issued a decree that heralded a "Final Solution to the Gypsy Problem" (*endgültige Lösung der Zigeunerfrage*).[51] The decree required Gypsies to register and undergo medical tests and restricted their freedom of movement. It regulated and standardized the old supervisory policies and cleared the way for the future annihilation of Gypsies by sterilization, pauperization, and incarceration in slave labor and death camps. The treatment meted out to Gypsies was to become one of three prototypes of extermination that fed into the "Final Solution to the Jewish Question." The two other prototypes were, of course, the unpublicized and secretive annihilation of mentally and physically handicapped Germans begun in 1936, which became the testing ground for advanced methods of murder,[52] and the mass executions of Polish civilians and soldiers in 1939–40 by army and police task forces.[53]

While hatred of the Jews had deep roots in Nazi ideology, until 1937 the Nazi leaders had only rough ideas for a possible "solution to the Jewish problem." Basically, they desired the total emigration of Jewish Germans, to render the country free of Jews (*judenrein*).[54] The continued harassment of Jews by legislative and administrative means had caused many of them to emigrate, so that between 1933 and 1938 Germany's Jewish population of five hundred thousand had declined to just over two hundred thousand.[55] The *Kristallnacht* marked a turning point: it announced a new policy that had been in the making for a year. Jews would not be pressed to emigrate; instead, they would be robbed of their property and deported to the East. This new course was precipitated by the occupation of Austria and Czechoslovakia's Sudeten region in 1938, when the Nazi leaders acquired many new Jewish citizens. Once again they were burdened with about five hundred thousand Jews. They reasoned that there was no point in expelling Jews to countries that would sooner or later fall prey to Germany's drive to conquer the rest of Europe. Indeed, as a result of the conquests, the number of Jews under German hegemony rose by 1941 to almost eleven million.[56]

Yet one looks in vain for a policy statement by a Nazi leader on a "Final Solution to the Jewish Question." Rather, it seemed to grow out of the colonial project and the changing fortunes of war, on the one hand, and the power struggles between the SS hierarchy and other sectors of the Nazi Party, on the other.

Degrading and Annihilating Aryan Germans

The *Kristallnacht* showed, among other things, that the Nazi leaders had assumed full control of the German population, and had lost all shame before their own people. The Nazis had always believed that violence is the ultimate form of power, that the state holds a monopoly on violence, and that its authority is ultimately upheld by the perpetual threat of violence. They had always employed violence to achieve their aims, and had never hesitated to kill real and imagined opponents, whether Aryan or non-Aryan. In the first two years in power they had presented the violent events perpetrated by the SA, or against the SA, as necessary acts of state, designed to bolster security. As they became used to ruling the country, the Nazi leaders became coy about SA mob rule. While they continued to abet violent acts or condoned them after the event, they did not support the ransacking mobs openly. They construed such acts of political violence as isolated local events, carried out by unruly elements.

The ultimate aim of the state's mounting violence against the Jews, as distinct from the no less violent persecution of other segments of the population, such as the opponents of the regime, was not so much to rid the country of the Jews as it was meant to subject the rest of the population to party rule.[57] It was to instill terror in every individual citizen and cause him or her to feel vulnerable and powerless, exposed to arbitrary interventions by the state. He was to live under constant fear that the fate of the Jews would befall him or anyone else who dared oppose the party and its leaders.

The Nazi leaders also demonstrated that the law of the country had been suspended. In the *Kristallnacht* the fire brigades were instructed to watch that the flames of the burning synagogues did not spread to adjacent buildings, the police were ordered to stand aside while Jewish shops were being looted, and the district attorneys were instructed "to make no investigations regarding the ... actions against Jews."[58] The killers and arsonists were, on principle, not brought to justice. On the contrary, the lawlessness of the *Kristallnacht* was in the following months systematically extended and regularized, and from the invasion of Poland onward turned into massive murder campaigns by the SS and police mobile task forces (*Einsatzgruppen*). A new principle of "legality" was instituted: officials who carried out the leader's orders of the moment were assured of impunity. They could get away with murder, as long as they "worked towards the Führer,"[59] and were coordinated with the party and the SS. In Bauer's words, "the Nazis wanted to put an anti-normative norm, the Party's free-floating and arbitrary rule that the Führer's wish was the law, in place of any norm, even one laid down through Nazi laws—they did not want to be fettered by any legal restraints."[60]

In a celebrated article, Garfinkel introduced the concept of "ceremonies of degradation" as rituals that seek to "bring about the destruction of the person being denounced."[61] The *Kristallnacht* has been interpreted by Loewenberg as a national "ritual of degradation."[62] He argues persuasively that the Nazi leadership used the "first pogrom in Germany since the Middle Ages" to further degrade the Jews.[63] While that is undeniably true, I believe that the Nazi leadership's chief intention was to humiliate, discipline, and incriminate the "Aryan" Germans. The Jews had for years been systematically delegitimized and economically segregated, and were to be exposed to even worse excesses. But in the course of the *Kristallnacht* the Nazi storm troopers were not so much after the Jews, and therefore committed only sporadic murders and atrocities.[64] Their main target was to incriminate those Germans who had hitherto stood aside. The bystanders who were provoked to actively participate in the pogrom became thereby accomplices of a criminal leadership. They joined the storm troopers and drowned eventual pangs of conscience in their rowdy company. They threw all morality to the winds, wantonly destroyed property, looted valuables, and taunted and tortured their victims. The memories of shameful deeds committed against fellow citizens turned them into accomplices of the Nazi storm troopers, and stigmatized them in the eyes of their fellow citizens. By means of the pogrom the Nazis reaffirmed their intent to treat "true" Germans as brutally as the other victims of the regime; they would mobilize and move them at their whim, exploit them as ruthlessly, and punish them as draconically as the non-Aryans.

Subsidiary targets were the Christian churches. Goebbels well knew that his insistent demand to burn down all the synagogues in the country was misplaced, as it was directed at the Jews as a religious community and not as a race. Yet he wanted the flames of the burning synagogues to rise high and "see a blood-red [glare] on the sky."[65] He intended this as a warning signal to the churches that their turn would come soon. Only a few churchmen spoke out against the pogrom, like the priest who said that "the temple which was burnt down is also the House of God," but they all understood its message.[66] To reinforce the message the National Socialist Teachers' Association decided on the following day that German schools would no longer provide Christian religious education.[67]

Ordinary people were afraid to criticize their leaders, and almost incapable of offering any organized opposition. They dared not protest against the assaults on Jews in the course of the *Kristallnacht,* and only complained about "the unnecessary destruction of property." Yet one perceptive observer notes that many bystanders were filled with shame. "Even fears to become the next victim of persecution were present."[68] Even those who were merely passive onlookers became accessories to the crime, because they dared not raise their voices in protest. Overnight the citizens of Germany had become a guilt-ridden people.

Several hours after the pogrom a self-satisfied Hitler spoke at a press conference, at which he subjected the assembled German journalists to their own ritual of degradation. He repeatedly reminded them that the press "serves as an instrument of the leadership" and that "it is necessary that especially the press blindly believes in the principle: the leadership acts right!"[69] Its role would now be "gradually to convert the German people psychologically, and slowly make it clear to them, that there are things which, when they cannot be implemented with peaceful means, must be implemented by means of violence."[70] While Hitler did not mention the *Kristallnacht* in his speech, he made it abundantly clear that it played a role in the mental conditioning of the German people for mass murder and war.

The Nazi leaders knew, of course, that they had fully subjugated and terrorized the German population. Most Germans had been forced to join numerous Nazi organizations, which controlled members' bodies and minds and involved them in a frantic routine of community service. They were also supervised at home by local party representatives (*Blockleiter*), whose duty was to know them intimately and denounce them on the slightest provocation to the Gestapo.[71] In a speech on 2 December 1938, Hitler made no bones about this comprehensive system of control: "After [German] youths have entered our organizations at age ten and there experienced ... some fresh air, ... [we] place them immediately in the Labor Front, the SA or SS.... And then the army [*Wehrmacht*] takes them over for further treatment.... They will never be free again, for the rest of their lives."[72]

These preoccupations left German men and women little time to cater to their individual needs, including the maintenance of social networks. The result was that "at no time in its history were the German people so fragmented and segmented as under the conditions of the National Socialist 'folk community.'"[73] Thus, Germans became obedient, and often willing, instruments of the leadership's policies.

The *Kristallnacht* was preceded by five major Nazi projects for disciplining the German people. They were all first tried out on Germans and only later applied widely and indiscriminately to additional populations. These were the murder of rivals within the Nazi party, the murder of institutionalized handicapped Germans, the concentration camps set up from 1933 onward, the Nuremberg laws of 1935, and the forcible relocation of populations begun in 1938.

Within a year of Hitler's assumption of power the membership of the SA, the Nazi Party's uniformed militia, increased ninefold to 4.5 million men.[74] It had already incorporated numerous paramilitary organizations, and was arming itself and threatening to become a rival to the regular army. Its leader, Ernst Röhm, and his associates negotiated with Hitler for a greater share in power. In order to pacify the regular army and to eliminate the competition, Hitler ordered the SS on 30 June 1934 to arrest and execute between 150 and 200 leaders of the SA and some other suspected opponents of his regime.[75] The SS, true to its motto "Your honor consists of loyalty" (*deine Ehre heisst Treue*), had proven its blind devotion to the leader.[76] Hitler richly rewarded it for its services. While it had for some years been a segment of the SA, he now elevated it to the status of a separate organization and entrusted it with securing the regime. He also promoted all the members of the murder squads in rank. None of them was ever taken to court, a practice that soon became the norm in Nazi Germany.

The organized massacre of Germans thus became an acceptable norm, which facilitated its repetition in the *Kristallnacht*. During that night Hitler allowed the SA to terrorize and slaughter innocent Germans of the Jewish denomination. Was this another "night of long knives," in which the SA avenged the victims of the 1934 executions on other Germans? Göring's aside to Heydrich at the 12 November meeting, "I wish you had killed two hundred Jews and not destroyed such property,"[77] is presumably a slip of tongue that hints at the two hundred victims in 1934 and indicates that he made the mental connection between the two events. While the *Kristallnacht* pogrom was the last nationwide public appearance of the SA, mass murders of Germans, followed by the murder of non-Germans, became from that point onward an integral element of central planning, with the SS and police acting as chief executioners and the army as active accomplices.

The battle of German eugenists against mentally and physically disabled persons has a history that goes back to the beginning of the twentieth century. The Nazis adopted eugenic doctrines at an early stage. In 1929 Hitler proclaimed in a speech to the party congress that if a million children were born annually in Germany, and seven to eight hundred thousand of the weakest persons were at the same time put to death (*beseitigt*), this would ultimately amount to an increase in power.[78] As soon as the Nazis assumed power, they began to implement the doctrine: in July 1933 they introduced a Law for the Prevention of Genetically Sick Issue (Gesetz zur Verhütung erbkranken Nachwuchses) that would permit them to forcibly sterilize a wide range of racially inferior persons.[79] Hitler's demand that "whoever is not physically and mentally sound and worthy should not perpetuate his suffering in the body of his child" was now expanded to include any German incapable of "earning his living in orderly employment, or to fit in socially."[80] The project was to sterilize one hundred thousand out of an estimated three hundred thousand inmates of care institutions. By 1936 the Nazi leaders thought that the project was advancing too slowly, and gradually shifted the emphasis from sterilization of physically and mentally handicapped patients to systematic murder of patients who did not contribute to the economy. They first put to death Jewish patients,[81] and then others who were incapable of work.[82] In early 1939 the Nazi leaders believed that the coming war would require the elimination of the disabled and provide the opportunity to speed up the killing process. An enlarged euthanasia project that was to murder an unspecified number of children and one hundred thousand adults was planned in Hitler's chancellery. The murder of children began secretly in the children's wards of some thirty German hospitals in August 1939,[83] and the murder of adults shortly after the invasion of Poland, with Hitler's secret authorization.[84] The medical staff on the project tested various methods of killing, such as withholding food, administering lethal injections, and, for the first time, murdering groups of victims in gas chambers.[85] By 1941 approximately five thousand children and ninety thousand adults had been killed. Most of the victims in the killing centers that were spread all over Germany had caring relatives who made some feeble protests. These eventually moved a few church leaders to denounce the adult killings publicly. These calls had some effect, for Hitler ordered in August 1941 to stop the operation officially, and to continue it under a new name in the East.[86] However, executions of handicapped adults and children continued even on German home territory up to the end of the war, and after.[87]

The concentration camps were established in 1933 for the disciplining of enemies of the state. At the time the enemies were mostly Germans who had, for one reason or another, fallen foul of the Nazi rulers. From 1938 onward the camp system expanded rapidly, and during the war years the branches set up in occupied territories were used for the internment and extermination of a wide range of people categorized as enemies. In January 1945 the camps held 714,000 prisoners.[88]

The number of Germans among camp inmates too rose until the demise of the regime. From 1938 onward Germans were interned on the flimsiest pretext. They only needed to be denounced as deviants from social, political, mental, or bodily norms to be sent to concentration camps, forced labor camps, and even to their death. On 18 July 1940 the Ministry of the Interior gave the screw another turn when it issued guidelines for eliminating healthy but "asocial" elements of the German population.[89]

The racial legislation adopted by the Reichstag at the Nuremberg Nazi Party rally in September 1935 appeared, on the face of it, to be directed at the Jews. In reality, it had since 1933 been applied to the members of the SS. New recruits, and their brides, had to provide documentary proof that no drop of alien blood had entered the veins of their ancestors from the year 1800 onward.[90] The 1935 law applied the SS regulations to the rest of the population.[91] The "Ancestry Proof [*Ahnennachweis*] [became] a document that now formed the essential prerequisite for a career in the civil service or indeed virtually any other kind of job."⁹² During the course of the war the SS used the rules on "homecoming" Germans (*Volksdeutsche*) with the same stringency.⁹³

The first people to be forcibly "relocated" by the SS were the inhabitants of eight Aryan Austrian villages. The Army needed their land for training purposes, and the SS Race and Settlement Bureau (Rasse- und Siedlungshauptamt, abbreviated RuSHA) acted as contractor of the evacuation. In July 1938 it proudly reported that the SS had "carried out the project precisely, punctually and smoothly."⁹⁴ The same methods were later applied in the resettlement of Germans in the East and the deportations of Poles, Jews, and others.

The Nazis' incessant total war of annihilation was, of course, the most callous and destructive form of sacrificing German lives. The German army had by the end of the war lost 5.3 million men, half of whom, 2.7 million men, fell in the war against the Soviet Union.⁹⁵ Tragically, the lives of millions of German soldiers could have been saved if the German leaders had ended the war in August 1941, when they momentarily realized that they could not win it. Around 95 percent of the German victims died from August 1941 onward.⁹⁶ In addition to the casualties it suffered in battle, the German army also executed at least 21,000 of its soldiers, often on the flimsiest of pretexts.⁹⁷ According to an authoritative study of the German prisoners of war, over 11 million German soldiers became prisoners of the Allies in the course of the war.⁹⁸ When the war ended there were about 8.7 million German prisoners in Allied custody, of whom all but 500,000 were released by January 1949.⁹⁹ The Germans remaining at home did not fare well either; during the later war years they went short of food and shelter, and were exposed to massive air raids in which almost half a million persons perished. Their suffering culminated in the first postwar years, when Soviet Russia expelled to the west about 11.8 million Germans, an operation that was preceded by the deportation of half a million ethnic Germans to the Russian interior.¹⁰⁰ An estimated one to two million of the deportees lost their lives in the expulsions.¹⁰¹

The harvest of death and desolation left behind by the Nazi regime is horrendous. A grand total of nearly eight million Germans lost their lives in the war, including approximately eight hundred thousand "Aryan" Germans murdered by the Nazi regime on various grounds. No less terrible was the uprooting of whole populations by the war: over eight million German prisoners of war returned in the first four postwar years to a country in ruins, and ten million penniless Germans deported by the Soviet authorities descended in the decade after the war on the two German successor states. This concatenation of disasters affected every German household, village, and town and turned the Germans into a peace-loving society. The suffering did not end Germany's imperial and racial ambitions, but kept them in abeyance for at least two generations.

Finally, the German Jews became anathema to the Nazis precisely because many of them were freethinking Germans from whose ranks emerged the intellectual giants who irrevocably changed their world and ours. Hitler and his associates had read, or at least knew about, the writings of Marx, Heine, Einstein, and Freud and thought from the outset that their liberating ideas were detrimental to the regimented uniform warrior nation they were creating. The influence of these ideas was, however, inescapable, as is curiously evidenced by the name of the Nazi Party: both "socialist" and "workers" in the name National Socialist German Workers' Party are ultimately derived from Marxist thought. The Nazis brainwashed Germans day and night in order to find and destroy such liberating thoughts. By first expelling and then killing the apparently gifted German Jews, the Nazis hoped to curtail their "demonic" intellectual hold on the German-speaking world and to prevent the budding of a new generation of intellectual giants. When the Nazi leaders realized in August 1941 that in spite of their efforts the friends of the Jews were winning the war, they resigned themselves to preventing a future war by eradicating all European Jews. Thus, the Holocaust became a major German war aim.

Acknowledgments

My obligations are many. Being a novice to Holocaust research, I completely depended on the profound studies of three generations of historians of Nazi Germany and the Holocaust, and learned to appreciate and admire their accumulated wisdom and insight. Their writings on the *Kristallnacht* and its aftermath gave me the impetus to take a fresh anthropological look at the data.

The lively and often profound discussions of the study group on the Holocaust and globalization at the Van Leer Jerusalem Institute led by Haim Hazan and Amos Goldberg have helped me immensely. I am deeply grateful to Haim Hazan for encouraging me to work out my first impressionistic thoughts on the *Kristallnacht*. I gratefully acknowledge the important comments of Roni Be'er-Marx, Amos Goldberg, Christian Hartmann, Esther Hertzog, Peter Loewenberg, Dalia Marx, Shimon Maoz, Herta Nöbauer, Kathy and Klaus Riechel, Jacqueline Rose, Vivien Rose, Bernhard Streck, and Richard P. Werbner. I am obliged to the Yad Vashem library for giving me access to its extensive resources.

Notes

1. Peter Loewenberg, "The Kristallnacht as a Public Degradation Ritual," *Leo Baeck Institute Year Book* 32 (1987): 313.

2. Alon Confino, *Foundational Pasts: The Holocaust as a Foundational Understanding* (Cambridge: Cambridge University Press, 2011).

3. Haim Hazan and Esther Hertzog, "Introduction: Towards a Nomadic Turn in Anthropology," in *Serendipity in Anthropological Research: The Nomadic Turn,* ed. Haim Hazan and Esther Hertzog (Farnham, UK: Ashgate, 2012), 1–3.

4. Wilhelm Treue, "Hitlers Denkschrift zum Vierjahresplan 1936," *Vierteljahrshefte für Zeitgeschichte* 3, no. 2 (1955): 184–210.

5. Adam Tooze, *The Wages of Destruction: The Making and Breaking of the Nazi Economy* (London: Penguin, 2007).

6. Ernst Klee, *"Euthanasie" im NS-Staat: Die "Vernichtung lebensunwerten Lebens"* (Frankfurt: Fischer Taschenbuch Verlag, 1985).

7. Christian Streit, *Keine Kameraden: Die Wehrmacht und die sowjetischen Kriegsgefangenen 1941–1945* (Stuttgart: Deutsche Verlags-Anstalt, 1978).

8. Ian Kershaw, *Hitler, the Germans, and the Final Solution* (Jerusalem and New Haven, CT: Yad Vashem and Yale University Press, 2008), 314.

9. Hans Fallada, *Every Man Dies Alone* (New York: Melville House, 2009).

10. Daniel Blatman, "Shoah Studies: A Lesson in Ossification" [in Hebrew], *Haaretz*, 19 April 2013.

11. Yehuda Bauer, *Rethinking the Holocaust* (New Haven, CT: Yale University Press, 2002), 42, 47.

12. Klaus Hildebrand, *The Foreign Policy of the Third Reich* (London: Batsford, 1973), 28.

13. Andreas Hillgruber, *Hitlers Strategie: Politik und Kriegführung 1940–1941*, 2nd ed. (Munich: Bernard and Graefe, 1982), 64. All translations are the author's.

14. Hildebrand, *Foreign Policy*, 76; Hillgruber, *Hitlers Strategie*, 717–18.

15. Anselm Faust, ed., *Die Kristallnacht im Rheinland: Dokumente zum Judenpogrom im November 1938* (Düsseldorf: Schwann, 1987), 110–12.

16. Ulrich Herbert, "Von der 'Reichskristallnacht' zum 'Holocaust': Der 9. November und das Ende des 'Radauantisemitismus,'" in *Arbeit, Volkstum, Weltanschauung: Über Fremde und Deutsche im 20. Jahrhundert* (Frankfurt: Fischer Taschenbuch Verlag, 1995), 75, quoting the SS organ Das Schwarze Korps of 24 November 1938.

17. Wolfgang Benz, "Der Rückfall in die Barbarei: Bericht über den Pogrom," in *Der Judenpogrom 1938: Von der "Reichskristallnacht" zum Völkermord*, ed. Walter H. Pehle (Frankfurt: Fischer Taschenbuch Verlag, 1988), 37; Wolf-Arno Kropat, *Kristallnacht in Hessen: Der Judenpogrom vom November 1938—eine Dokumentation* (Wiesbaden: Kommission für die Geschichte der Juden in Hessen, 1988), 72–74.

18. Richard J. Evans, *The Third Reich in Power* (New York: Penguin, 2006), 584; however, see Saul Friedländer, *Nazi Germany and the Jews*, vol. 1, *The Years of Persecution, 1933–1939* (New York: Harper Perennial, 1998), 276, and numerous other writers, who rely on Heydrich's report of 267 wrecked synagogues.

19. Evans, *The Third Reich in Power*, 585.

20. Leni Yahil, *The Holocaust: The Fate of European Jewry, 1932–1945* (New York: Oxford University Press, 1991), 111.

21. Lionel Kochan, *Pogrom: 10 November 1938* (London: Deutsch, 1957), 58.

22. Andreas Heusler and Tobias Weger, *"Kristallnacht": Gewalt gegen die Münchner Juden im November 1938* (Munich: Stadtarchiv München and Buchendorfer Verlag, 1998), 122, report thirty to sixty thousand arrests; however, Nikolaus Wachsmann, "The Dynamics of Destruction: The Development of the Concentration Camps, 1933–1945," in *Concentration Camps in Nazi Germany: The New Histories*, ed. Jane Caplan and Nikolaus Wachsmannn (London: Routledge, 2010), 25, reports only twenty-six thousand arrests.

23. Martin Gilbert, *Kristallnacht: Prelude to Destruction* (London: Harper Collins, 2006), 183.

24. Fritz Goldschmidt, "My Life in Germany: Before and After the 30th of January 1933" (London: unpublished, 1941), 44–45; Beate Meyer, *Tödliche Gratwanderung: Die Reichsvereinigung der Juden in Deutschland zwischen Hoffnung, Zwang, Selbstbehauptung und Verstrickung (1939–1945)* (Göttingen: Wallstein, 2011), 47.

25. Emil Carlebach, "'Reichskristallnacht,'" in *Reichspogromnacht: Vergangenheitsbewältigung aus jüdischer Sicht*, ed. Micha Brumlik and Petra Kunik (Frankfurt: Brandes & Apsel, 1988), 21–24; Evans, *The Third Reich in Power*, 595.

26. Antonius C. G. M. Robben, *Political Violence and Trauma in Argentina* (Philadelphia: University of Pennsylvania Press, 2005), x, quoting Miguel Bonasso, *Recuerdo de la muerte* (Mexico City: Ediciones Era, 1984), 361.

27. Robben, *Political Violence and Trauma in Argentina*, 62.

28. Israel W. Charny, "A Contribution to the Psychology of Genocide: Sacrificing Others to the Death We Fear Ourselves," *Israel Yearbook of Human Rights* 10 (1980): 99.

29. Shulamit Volkov, *Germans, Jews, and Antisemites: Trials in Emancipation* (New York: Cambridge University Press, 2006), chaps. 9–11; Shelley Baranowski, *Nazi Empire: German Colonialism and Imperialism from Bismarck to Hitler* (New York: Cambridge University Press, 2011), 27.

30. Susanne Heim, ed., *Research for Autarky: The Contribution of Scientists to Nazi Rule in Germany* (Berlin: Max-Planck-Gesellschaft zur Förderung der Wissenschaft 2001), 11.

31. Isabel Heinemann, *"Rasse, Siedlung, deutsches Blut": Das Rasse- und Siedlungshauptamt der SS und die rassepolitische Neuordnung Europas* (Göttingen: Wallstein, 2003), 21–24.

32. Shulamit Volkov, "Kontinuität und Diskontinuität im deutschen Antisemitismus 1878–1945," *Vierteljahrshefte für Zeitgeschichte* 33, no. 2 (1985): 242.

33. Richard J. Evans, *The Coming of the Third Reich* (London: Penguin, 2004), 174.

34. Heinemann, *"Rasse, Siedlung, deutsches Blut,"* 553.

35. Christian Gerlach, *Krieg, Ernährung, Völkermord: Forschungen zur deutschen Vernichtungspolitik im Zweiten Weltkrieg* (Hamburg: Hamburger Edition, 1998), 114.

36. Ibid., xxix.

37. Yahil, *The Holocaust*, 31–32.

38. Victor Klemperer, *I Will Bear Witness: The Diaries of Victor Klemperer, 1933–1941* (New York: Modern Library, 1999).

39. Christopher R. Browning, *The Origins of the Final Solution: The Evolution of Nazi Jewish Policy, September 1939–March 1942* (Lincoln and Jerusalem: University of Nebraska Press and Yad Vashem, 2004), 432; Toby Thacker, *Joseph Goebbels: Life and Death* (Basingstoke, UK: Palgrave Macmillan, 2010), 66.

40. Evans, *The Coming of the Third Reich*, 381; see also Michael Wildt, *An Uncompromising Generation: The Nazi Leadership of the Reich Security Main Office* (Madison: University of Wisconsin Press, 2009), 130.

41. Avraham Barkai, "'Schicksalsjahr 1938': Kontinuität und Verschärfung der wirtschaftlichen Ausplünderung der deutschen Juden," in *Das Unrechtsregime: Internationale Forschung über den Nationalsozialismus*, ed. Ursula Büttner (Hamburg: Christians, 1986), 2:47–59; Peter Longerich, *Holocaust: The Nazi Persecution and Murder of the Jews* (Oxford: Oxford University Press, 2010), 100.

42. Uriel Tal, *Religion, Politics and Ideology in the Third Reich: Selected Essays* (London: Routledge, 2004), 70–71.

43. Kochan, *Pogrom*, 15–16; Barkai, "'Schicksalsjahr 1938,'" 45.

44. Adolf Hitler, *Mein Kampf* (Munich: Eher-Verlag, 1925); in a paper first published in 1939 the Nazi ethnologist Reche brings together the relevant passages from Hitler's book. See Otto Reche, "Leitsätze zur bevölkerungspolitischen Sicherung des deutschen Ostens," in *Der "Generalplan Ost": Hauptlinien der nationalsozialistischen Planungs- und Vernichtungspolitik*, ed. Mechtild Rössler and Sabine Schleiermacher (Berlin: Akademie Verlag, 1993), 351–55.

45. Thilo Vogelsang, "Neue Dokumente zur Geschichte der Reichswehr 1930–1933," *Vierteljahrshefte für Zeitgeschichte* 2, no. 4 (1954): 435.

46. Treue, "Hitlers Denkschrift zum Vierjahresplan 1936," 206, 210.

47. Ibid., 184, quotes Hitler's table talk of 13–14 October 1941; see Omer Bartov, "Operation Barbarossa and the Origins of the Final Solution," in *The Final Solution: Origins and Implementation*, ed. David Cesarani (London: Routledge, 1996), 119–36. In "As it really was," (*Yad Vashem Studies* 34, 2006): 349 Bartov discusses Hitler's reluctance to commit himself in writing.

48. Mechtild Rössler and Sabine Schleiermacher, "Der 'Generalplan Ost' und die 'Modernität' der Grossraumordnung: Eine Einführung," in *Der "Generalplan Ost": Hauptlinien der nationalsozialistischen Planungs- und Vernichtungspolitik*, ed. Mechtild Rössler and Sabine Schleiermacher

(Berlin: Akademie Verlag, 1993), 7–19, particularly 8–10; Irene Stoehr, "Von Max Sering zu Konrad Meyer—ein 'machtergreifender' Generationswechsel in der Agrar- und Siedlungswissenschaft," in *Autarkie und Ostexpansion: Pflanzenzucht und Agrarforschung im Nationalsozialismus,* ed. Susanne Heim (Göttingen: Wallstein, 2002), 79.

49. Heinemann, *"Rasse, Siedlung, deutsches Blut,"* 192–94.

50. Jürgen Förster, "The Relation between Operation Barbarossa as an Ideological War of Extermination and the Final Solution," in *The Final Solution: Origins and Implementation,* ed. David Cesarani (London: Routledge, 1996), 89.

51. Friedländer, *The Years of Persecution, 1933–1939,* 204–5; Guenter Lewy, *The Nazi Persecution of the Gypsies* (New York: Oxford University Press, 2000), 52; Michael Zimmermann, *Rassenutopie und Genozid: Die nationalsozialistische "Lösung der Zigeunerfrage"* (Hamburg: Christians, 1996), 370; Evans, *The Third Reich in Power,* 27.

52. Henry Friedlander, "Euthanasia and the Final Solution," in *The Final Solution: Origins and Implementation,* ed. David Cesarani (London: Routledge, 1996), 52.

53. Phillip T. Rutherford, *Prelude to the Final Solution: The Nazi Program for Deporting Ethnic Poles, 1939–1941* (Lawrence: University Press of Kansas, 2007), chap. 4.

54. Hans Safrian, *Eichmann's Men* (New York and Washington DC: Cambridge University Press and United States Holocaust Memorial Museum, 2010), 18.

55. Evans, *The Third Reich in Power,* 599.

56. Götz Aly, "'Jewish Resettlement': Reflections on the Political Prehistory of the Holocaust," in *National Socialist Extermination Policies: Contemporary German Perspectives and Controversies,* ed. Ulrich Herbert (New York: Berghahn, 2000), 58.

57. Kurt Pätzold, "Judenverfolgung auf dem Kriegspfad: Vom Pogrom zum Kriegsbeginn," in *Der Krieg vor dem Krieg: Ökonomik und Politik der "friedlichen" Aggressionen Deutschlands 1938/1939,* ed. Werner Röhr, Brigitte Berlekamp, and Karl Heinz Roth (Hamburg: VSA-Verlag, 2001), 194; Peter Longerich, *"Davon haben wir nichts gewusst!" Die Deutschen und die Judenverfolgung 1933–1945* (Munich: Pantheon, 2007), 77.

58. Uwe Dietrich Adam, "How Spontaneous Was the Pogrom?," in *November 1938: From "Reichskristallnacht" to Genocide,* ed. Walter H. Pehle (New York: Berg, 1991), 79.

59. Kershaw, *Hitler,* 29.

60. Bauer, *Rethinking the Holocaust,* 84; Richard Overy, *The Dictators: Hitler's Germany and Stalin's Russia* (London: Penguin, 2005), 294.

61. Harold Garfinkel, "Conditions of Successful Degradation Ceremonies," *American Journal of Sociology* 61, no. 5 (1956): 421.

62. Loewenberg, "Kristallnacht," 313.

63. Friedländer, *The Years of Persecution, 1933–1939,* 277; the argument is taken up by Peter Fritzsche, *Life and Death in the Third Reich* (Cambridge, MA: Harvard University Press, 2008), 136, and Wolfgang Benz, "Exclusion as a Stage in Persecution: The Jewish Situation in Germany, 1933–1941," in *Nazi Europe and the Final Solution,* ed. David Bankier and Israel Gutman (Jerusalem and New York: Yad Vashem and Berghahn, 2009), 40–52, especially 49.

64. Alan E. Steinweis, *Kristallnacht 1938* (Cambridge, MA: Belknap Press of Harvard University Press, 2009), chap. 4.

65. Friedländer, *The Years of Persecution, 1933–1939,* 272.

66. Ibid., 297; Steinweis, *Kristallnacht 1938,* 125.

67. Friedländer, *The Years of Persecution, 1933–1939,* 298.

68. Longerich, *"Davon haben wir nichts gewusst!,"* 136.

69. Wilhelm Treue, "Rede Hitlers vor der deutschen Presse (10. November 1938)," *Vierteljahrshefte für Zeitgeschichte* 6, no. 2 (1958): 185, 189.

70. Ibid., 182; Steinweis, *Kristallnacht 1938,* 103.

71. Detlef Schmiechen-Ackermann, "Der 'Blockwart': Die unteren Parteifunktionäre im nationalsozialistischen Terror- und Überwachungsapparat," *Vierteljahrshefte für Zeitgeschichte* 48, no. 4 (2000): 584.

72. Michael H. Kater, *Hitler Youth* (Cambridge, MA: Harvard University Press, 2004), 37.

73. Hans Mommsen, "What Did the Germans Know About the Genocide of the Jews?," in *November 1938: From "Reichskristallnacht" to Genocide,* ed. Walter H. Pehle (New York: Berg, 1991), 187.

74. Peter Longerich, *Heinrich Himmler* (Oxford: Oxford University Press, 2012), 170–71.

75. Ibid., 170–74; Heinz Höhne, *Mordsache Röhm: Hitlers Durchbruch zur Alleinherrschaft 1933–1934* (Reinbek: Rowohlt, 1984). Höhne identifies eighty-five victims by name.

76. Longerich, *Heinrich Himmler,* 118.

77. Friedländer, *The Years of Persecution, 1933–1939,* 281.

78. Klee, *"Euthanasie" im NS-Staat,* 31–32.

79. Ibid., 36–37.

80. Ibid., 37–38.

81. Marianne Hühn, "Rassenideologie wird Gesetz," in *Totgeschwiegen 1933–1945: Zur Geschichte der Wittenauer Heilstätten, seit 1957 Karl-Bonhoeffer-Nervenklinik,* 2nd ed., ed. Arbeitsgruppe zur Erforschung der Geschichte der Karl-Bonhoeffer-Nervenklinik (Berlin: Edition Hentrich, 1989), 93.

82. Klee, *"Euthanasie" im NS-Staat,* 66–75; Ernst Klee, ed., *Dokumente zur "Euthanasie"* (Frankfurt: Fischer Taschenbuch Verlag, 2007), 62.

83. Martina Krüger, "Kinderfachabteilung Wiesengrund: Die Tötung behinderter Kinder in Wittenau," in *Totgeschwiegen 1933–1945: Zur Geschichte der Wittenauer Heilstätten, seit 1957 Karl-Bonhoeffer-Nervenklinik,* 2nd ed., ed. Arbeitsgruppe zur Erforschung der Geschichte der Karl-Bonhoeffer-Nervenklinik (Berlin: Edition Hentrich, 1989), 152.

84. Klee, *Dokumente zur "Euthanasie,"* 85.

85. Klee, *"Euthanasie" im NS-Staat,* 109ff; Yahil, *The Holocaust,* 308–9; Friedländer, *The Years of Persecution, 1933–1939,* 87; Longerich, *Heinrich Himmler,* 446, reports that on 12 December 1939 Himmler attended an execution of nursing home patients in a gas chamber.

86. Friedländer, *The Years of Persecution, 1933–1939,* 111.

87. Klee, *"Euthanasie" im NS-Staat,* 446–53; Raul Hilberg, *The Destruction of the European Jews,* 3rd ed., 3 vols. (New Haven, CT: Yale University Press, 2003), 930–32.

88. Wachsmann, "The Dynamics of Destruction," 32–33.

89. Bauer, *Rethinking the Holocaust,* 34.

90. Heinemann, *"Rasse, Siedlung, deutsches Blut,"* 50–60.

91. Longerich, *"Davon haben wir nichts gewusst!,"* 94.

92. Evans, *The Third Reich in Power,* 546; Fritzsche, *Life and Death in the Third Reich,* 76–82.

93. Heinemann, *"Rasse, Siedlung, deutsches Blut,"* 232ff.

94. Ibid., 121.

95. Rüdiger Overmans, *Deutsche militärische Verluste im Zweiten Weltkrieg* (Munich: Oldenbourg, 2000), 255; Christian Hartmann, *Unternehmen Barbarossa: Der deutsche Krieg im Osten 1941–1945* (Munich: C.H. Beck, 2011), 116.

96. Overmans, *Deutsche militärische Verluste,* 238–39.

97. Bartov, "Operation Barbarossa," 122–23; Richard J. Evans, *The Third Reich at War* (New York: Penguin, 2009), 502; Ian Kershaw, *The End: The Defiance and Destruction of Hitler's Germany, 1944–45* (New York: Penguin, 2011), 220.

98. Werner Ratza, "Anzahl und Arbeitsleistungen der deutschen Kriegsgefangenen," in *Die deutschen Kriegsgefangenen des Zweiten Weltkrieges: Eine Zusammenfassung,* ed. Erich Maschke (Bielefeld: Gieseking, 1974), 191.

99. Hartmann, *Unternehmen Barbarossa,* 119; Evans, *The Third Reich at War,* 682–83, refers to 4.7 million prisoners.

100. Andreas Hillgruber, *Zweierlei Untergang: Die Zerschlagung des Deutschen Reiches und das Ende des europäischen Judentums* (Berlin: Siedler, 1986), 34–35.

101. Hartmann, *Unternehmen Barbarossa,* 120.

Bibliography

Adam, Uwe Dietrich. "How Spontaneous Was the Pogrom?" In *November 1938: From "Reichskristallnacht" to Genocide,* ed. Walter H. Pehle, 73–94. New York: Berg, 1991.

Aly, Götz. "'Jewish Resettlement': Reflections on the Political Prehistory of the Holocaust." In *National Socialist Extermination Policies: Contemporary German Perspectives and Controversies,* ed. Ulrich Herbert, 53–82. New York: Berghahn Books, 2000.

Baranowski, Shelley. *Nazi Empire: German Colonialism and Imperialism from Bismarck to Hitler.* New York: Cambridge University Press, 2011.

Barkai, Avraham. "'Schicksalsjahr 1938': Kontinuität und Verschärfung der wirtschaftlichen Ausplünderung der deutschen Juden." In *Das Unrechtsregime: Internationale Forschung über den Nationalsozialismus,* ed. Ursula Büttner, vol. 2, 45–68. Hamburg: Christians, 1986.

Bartov, Omer. "As it Really Was." *Yad Vashem Studies* 34 (2006): 339–53.

——. "Operation Barbarossa and the Origins of the Final Solution." In *The Final Solution: Origins and Implementation,* ed. David Cesarani, 119–36. London: Routledge, 1996.

Bauer, Yehuda. *Rethinking the Holocaust.* New Haven, CT: Yale University Press, 2002.

Benz, Wolfgang. "Der Rückfall in die Barbarei: Bericht über den Pogrom." In *Der Judenpogrom 1938: Von der "Reichskristallnacht" zum Völkermord,* ed. Walter H. Pehle, 13–51. Frankfurt: Fischer Taschenbuch Verlag, 1988.

——. "Exclusion as a Stage in Persecution: The Jewish Situation in Germany, 1933–1941." In *Nazi Europe and the Final Solution,* ed. David Bankier and Israel Gutman, 40–52. Jerusalem and New York: Yad Vashem and Berghahn, 2009.

Blatman, Daniel. "Shoah Studies: A Lesson in Ossification" [in Hebrew]. *Haaretz,* 19 April 2013.

Bonasso, Miguel. *Recuerdo de la muerte.* Mexico City: Ediciones Era, 1984.

Browning, Christopher R. *The Origins of the Final Solution: The Evolution of Nazi Jewish Policy, September 1939–March 1942.* Lincoln and Jerusalem: University of Nebraska Press and Yad Vashem, 2004.

Carlebach, Emil. "'Reichskristallnacht.'" In *Reichspogromnacht: Vergangenheitsbewältigung aus jüdischer Sicht,* ed. Micha Brumlik and Petra Kunik, 21–26. Frankfurt: Brandes & Apsel, 1988.

Charny, Israel W. "A Contribution to the Psychology of Genocide: Sacrificing Others to the Death We Fear Ourselves." *Israel Yearbook of Human Rights* 10 (1980): 90–108.

Confino, Alon. *Foundational Pasts: The Holocaust as a Foundational Understanding.* Cambridge: Cambridge University Press, 2011.

Evans, Richard J. *The Coming of the Third Reich.* London: Penguin, 2004.

——. *The Third Reich in Power.* New York: Penguin, 2006.

——. *The Third Reich at War.* New York: Penguin, 2009.

Fallada, Hans. *Every Man Dies Alone.* New York: Melville House, 2009. Published in German in 1947.

Faust, Anselm, ed. *Die Kristallnacht im Rheinland: Dokumente zum Judenpogrom im November 1938.* Düsseldorf: Schwann, 1987.

Förster, Jürgen. "The Relation between Operation Barbarossa as an Ideological War of Extermination and the Final Solution." In *The Final Solution: Origins and Implementation,* ed. David Cesarani, 85–102. London: Routledge, 1996.

Friedlander, Henry. "Euthanasia and the Final Solution." In *The Final Solution: Origins and Implementation,* ed. David Cesarani, 51–61. London: Routledge, 1996.

Friedländer, Saul. *Nazi Germany and the Jews.* Vol. 1, *The Years of Persecution, 1933–1939.* New York: Harper Perennial, 1998.

Fritzsche, Peter. *Life and Death in the Third Reich.* Cambridge, MA: Harvard University Press, 2008.

Garfinkel, Harold. "Conditions of Successful Degradation Ceremonies." *American Journal of Sociology* 61, no. 5 (1956): 420–24.

Gerlach, Christian. *Krieg, Ernährung, Völkermord: Forschungen zur deutschen Vernichtungspolitik im Zweiten Weltkrieg.* Hamburg: Hamburger Edition, 1998.

Gilbert, Martin. *Kristallnacht: Prelude to Destruction*. London: Harper Collins, 2006.
Goldschmidt, Fritz. "My Life in Germany: Before and After the 30th of January 1933." London, 1941. Unpublished document held by grandson Bob Goldsmith.
Hartmann, Christian. *Unternehmen Barbarossa: Der deutsche Krieg im Osten 1941–1945*. Munich: C.H. Beck, 2011.
Hazan, Haim, and Esther Hertzog. "Introduction: Towards a Nomadic Turn in Anthropology." In *Serendipity in Anthropological Research: The Nomadic Turn*, ed. Haim Hazan and Esther Hertzog, 1–11. Farnham, UK: Ashgate, 2012.
Heim, Susanne, ed. *Research for Autarky: The Contribution of Scientists to Nazi Rule in Germany*. Berlin: Max-Planck-Gesellschaft zur Förderung der Wissenschaft, 2001.
Heinemann, Isabel. *"Rasse, Siedlung, deutsches Blut": Das Rasse- und Siedlungshauptamt der SS und die rassepolitische Neuordnung Europas*. Göttingen: Wallstein, 2003
Herbert, Ulrich. "Von der 'Reichskristallnacht' zum 'Holocaust': Der 9. November und das Ende des ´Radauantisemitismus.'" In *Arbeit, Volkstum, Weltanschauung: Über Fremde und Deutsche im 20. Jahrhundert*, 59–77. Frankfurt: Fischer Taschenbuch Verlag, 1995.
Heusler, Andreas, and Tobias Weger, *"Kristallnacht": Gewalt gegen die Münchner Juden im November 1938*. Munich: Stadtarchiv München and Buchendorfer Verlag, 1998.
Hilberg, Raul. *The Destruction of the European Jews*. 3rd ed. 3 vols. New Haven, CT: Yale University Press, 2003.
Hildebrand, Klaus. *The Foreign Policy of the Third Reich*. London: Batsford, 1973.
Hillgruber, Andreas. *Hitlers Strategie: Politik und Kriegführung 1940–1941*. 2nd ed. Munich: Bernard and Graefe, 1982.
———. *Zweierlei Untergang: Die Zerschlagung des Deutschen Reiches und das Ende des europäischen Judentums*. Berlin: Siedler, 1986.
Hitler, Adolf. *Mein Kampf*. Munich: Eher-Verlag, 1925.
Höhne, Heinz. *Mordsache Röhm: Hitlers Durchbruch zur Alleinherrschaft 1933–1934*. Reinbek: Rowohlt, 1984.
Hühn, Marianne. "Rassenideologie wird Gesetz." In *Totgeschwiegen 1933–1945: Zur Geschichte der Wittenauer Heilstätten, seit 1957 Karl-Bonhoeffer-Nervenklinik*, 2nd ed., ed. Arbeitsgruppe zur Erforschung der Geschichte der Karl-Bonhoeffer-Nervenklinik, 93–103. Berlin: Edition Hentrich, 1989.
Kater, Michael H. *Hitler Youth*. Cambridge, MA: Harvard University Press, 2004.
Kershaw, Ian. *The End: The Defiance and Destruction of Hitler's Germany, 1944–45*. New York: Penguin, 2011.
———. *Hitler, the Germans, and the Final Solution*. Jerusalem and New Haven, CT: Yad Vashem and Yale University Press, 2008.
Klee, Ernst. *"Euthanasie" im NS-Staat: Die "Vernichtung lebensunwerten Lebens."* Frankfurt: Fischer Taschenbuch Verlag, 1985.
———, ed. *Dokumente zur "Euthanasie."* Frankfurt: Fischer Taschenbuch Verlag, 2007.
Klemperer, Victor. *I Will Bear Witness: The Diaries of Victor Klemperer, 1933–1941*. New York: Modern Library, 1999.
Kochan, Lionel. *Pogrom: 10 November 1938*. London: Deutsch, 1957.
Kropat, Wolf-Arno. *Kristallnacht in Hessen: Der Judenpogrom vom November 1938—eine Dokumentation*. Wiesbaden: Kommission für die Geschichte der Juden in Hessen, 1988.
Krüger, Martina. "Kinderfachabteilung Wiesengrund: Die Tötung behinderter Kinder in Wittenau." In *Totgeschwiegen 1933–1945: Zur Geschichte der Wittenauer Heilstätten, seit 1957 Karl-Bonhoeffer-Nervenklinik*, 2nd ed., ed. Arbeitsgruppe zur Erforschung der Geschichte der Karl-Bonhoeffer-Nervenklinik, 151–76. Berlin: Edition Hentrich, 1989.
Lewy, Guenter. *The Nazi Persecution of the Gypsies*. New York: Oxford University Press, 2000.
Loewenberg, Peter. "The Kristallnacht as a Public Degradation Ritual." *Leo Baeck Institute Year Book* 32 (1987): 309–23.
Longerich, Peter. *"Davon haben wir nichts gewusst!" Die Deutschen und die Judenverfolgung 1933–1945*. Munich: Pantheon, 2007.

———. *Holocaust: The Nazi Persecution and Murder of the Jews.* Oxford: Oxford University Press, 2010.

———. *Heinrich Himmler.* Oxford: Oxford University Press, 2012.

Mommsen, Hans. "What Did the Germans Know About the Genocide of the Jews?" In *November 1938: From "Reichskristallnacht" to Genocide,* ed. Walter H. Pehle, 176–200. New York: Berg, 1991.

Overmans, Rüdiger. *Deutsche militärische Verluste im Zweiten Weltkrieg.* Munich: Oldenbourg, 2000.

Overy, Richard. *The Dictators: Hitler's Germany and Stalin's Russia.* London: Penguin, 2005.

Pätzold, Kurt. "Judenverfolgung auf dem Kriegspfad: Vom Pogrom zum Kriegsbeginn." In *Der Krieg vor dem Krieg: Ökonomik und Politik der "friedlichen" Aggressionen Deutschlands 1938/1939,* ed. Werner Röhr, Brigitte Berlekamp, and Karl Heinz Roth, 188–208. Hamburg: VSA-Verlag, 2001.

Ratza, Werner. "Anzahl und Arbeitsleistungen der deutschen Kriegsgefangenen." In *Die deutschen Kriegsgefangenen des Zweiten Weltkrieges: Eine Zusammenfassung,* ed. Erich Maschke, 185–230. Bielefeld: Gieseking, 1974.

Reche, Otto. "Leitsätze zur bevölkerungspolitischen Sicherung des deutschen Ostens." In *Der "Generalplan Ost": Hauptlinien der nationalsozialistischen Planungs- und Vernichtungspolitik,* ed. Mechtild Rössler and Sabine Schleiermacher, 351–55. Berlin: Akademie Verlag, 1993. First published 1939.

Robben, Antonius C. G. M. *Political Violence and Trauma in Argentina.* Philadelphia: University of Pennsylvania Press, 2005.

Rössler, Mechtild, and Sabine Schleiermacher. "Der 'Generalplan Ost' und die 'Modernität' der Grossraumordnung: Eine Einführung." In *Der "Generalplan Ost": Hauptlinien der nationalsozialistischen Planungs- und Vernichtungspolitik,* ed. Mechtild Rössler and Sabine Schleiermacher, 7–19. Berlin: Akademie Verlag, 1993.

Rutherford, Phillip T. *Prelude to the Final Solution: The Nazi Program for Deporting Ethnic Poles, 1939–1941.* Lawrence: University Press of Kansas, 2007.

Safrian, Hans. *Eichmann's Men.* New York and Washington DC: Cambridge University Press and United States Holocaust Memorial Museum, 2010.

Schmiechen-Ackermann, Detlef. "Der 'Blockwart': Die unteren Parteifunktionäre im nationalsozialistischen Terror- und Überwachungsapparat." *Vierteljahrshefte für Zeitgeschichte* 48, no. 4 (2000): 575–602.

Steinweis, Alan E. *Kristallnacht 1938.* Cambridge, MA: Belknap Press of Harvard University Press, 2009.

Stoehr, Irene. "Von Max Sering zu Konrad Meyer—ein 'machtergreifender' Generationswechsel in der Agrar- und Siedlungswissenschaft." In *Autarkie und Ostexpansion: Pflanzenzucht und Agrarforschung im Nationalsozialismus,* ed. Susanne Heim, 57–90. Göttingen: Wallstein, 2002.

Streit, Christian. *Keine Kameraden: Die Wehrmacht und die sowjetischen Kriegsgefangenen 1941–1945.* Stuttgart: Deutsche Verlags-Anstalt, 1978.

Tal, Uriel. *Religion, Politics and Ideology in the Third Reich: Selected Essays.* London: Routledge, 2004.

Thacker, Toby. *Joseph Goebbels: Life and Death.* Basingstoke, UK: Palgrave Macmillan, 2010.

Tooze, Adam. *The Wages of Destruction: The Making and Breaking of the Nazi Economy.* London: Penguin, 2007.

Treue, Wilhelm. "Hitlers Denkschrift zum Vierjahresplan 1936." *Vierteljahrshefte für Zeitgeschichte* 3, no. 2 (1955): 184–210.

———. "Rede Hitlers vor der deutschen Presse (10. November 1938)." *Vierteljahrshefte für Zeitgeschichte* 6, no. 2 (1958): 175–91.

Vogelsang, Thilo. "Neue Dokumente zur Geschichte der Reichswehr 1930–1933." *Vierteljahrshefte für Zeitgeschichte* 2, no. 4 (1954): 397–436.

Volkov, Shulamit. *Germans, Jews, and Antisemites: Trials in Emancipation.* New York: Cambridge University Press, 2006.

———. "Kontinuität und Diskontinuität im deutschen Antisemitismus 1878–1945." *Vierteljahrshefte für Zeitgeschichte* 33, no. 2 (1985): 221–43.

Wachsmann, Nikolaus. "The Dynamics of Destruction: The Development of the Concentration Camps, 1933–1945." In *Concentration Camps in Nazi Germany: The New Histories,* ed. Jane Caplan and Nikolaus Wachsmannn, 17–43. London: Routledge, 2010.

Wildt, Michael. *An Uncompromising Generation: The Nazi Leadership of the Reich Security Main Office.* Madison: University of Wisconsin Press, 2009.

Yahil, Leni. *The Holocaust: The Fate of European Jewry, 1932–1945.* New York: Oxford University Press, 1991.

Zimmermann, Michael. *Rassenutopie und Genozid: Die nationalsozialistische "Lösung der Zigeunerfrage."* Hamburg: Christians, 1996.

CHAPTER 17

A Personal Postscript

Sidra DeKoven Ezrahi

It has become commonplace to claim that what we used to think of as "global"—in politics, culture, and ethics—is actually "glocal," that even the most widespread, "universal" of values are inflected in specific tongues, mores, and national if not tribal claims. My own journey as scholar and citizen of two countries—the United States and Israel—began in what I thought was a "value-free," that is, "global," "Western" space and migrated into a practice self-consciously informed by the specifics of time and place.

But my journey was not unique; this book is a testament to the courage of many people who have faced the deep ethical challenges underlying the politics of Holocaust representation generally and Israeli politics more specifically.

What began for a few of us in the 1970s as a series of scattered scholarly intuitions regarding the fictional, dramatic, and poetic accounts of writers who had survived Nazi Europe was channeled, with time, into nuanced conversations about what Saul Friedländer would felicitously call the "limits of representation."[1] In the beginning, or so it seemed, there were no limits, but rather floating essences, "graves in the air" (Paul Celan[2]), "the transparent wake of the past" (Dan Pagis[3]), unbound by any gravitational pull. My earliest work, which culminated in *By Words Alone* (1980[4]), was an attempt to diagram a typology of Holocaust literature premised on generic moves (from documentary fiction to myth) and on the notion that texts written by so many refugees in so many borrowed languages and venues represented a kind of global—or what we would then have called transnational, transcultural—conglomerate of dismembered parts. This was, I suppose, an un-self-conscious corollary of the idea, in vogue

Notes for this section begin on page 351.

for a time after Ka-Tzetnik (Yehiel Dinur)'s collapse during his testimony at the Eichmann trial, that Auschwitz—and Jewish Europe, for that matter—was "another planet" that had exploded and sent meteors, traces of both its material existence and its total destruction, into perpetual orbit. Ka-Tzetnik's "message," however, had political ramifications that took many years to fathom.

Spatial metaphors soon came to dominate the theoretical conversation. What had appeared as random detritus of cosmic particles or a global museum of the artifacts of dead cultures would congeal in the critical discourse as a few iconic geographical or geological points of reference. At first this allowed all of us who lived "after" to erect barriers between us and that time and place. Theodor Adorno in the late 1950s and 1960s offered the fragile boundaries demarcating the barbaric from the civilized; Jean-François Lyotard in the mid-1970s evoked the earthquake that had swallowed up the instruments of measurement as well as the objects to be measured.[5] Slowly, however, we returned to that "other planet," revisited Paul Celan's airy graves and Pagis's transparent wake as spatial metaphors of the radiating effects of total destruction. "Was geschah?" asks Celan. "Der Stein trat aus dem Berge / Wer erwachte? Du und ich" (What happened? The rock detached from the mountain / Who awoke? You and I).[6] What became clear and urgent by the 1980s was that we had all been touched by meteoric dust, by the earthquake's aftershocks and the rock's debris. Levi's "gray zone" of contamination, where "you and I" abide, was, then, at the outer limits of our own sphere—just this side of the "black hole" that had been introduced by physicists in the late 1960s as the site at which all matter and all meaning are annihilated.[7] The "gray zone" was that murky place where postwar poetic, philosophical, ethical, and political acts were performed.

Within a generation after the end of World War II, each country had begun to re-member and to ground these remnants of the traumatic past in its own narratives. And moving one's critical platform from a transnational to a local context meant, naturally, acknowledging particular boundaries of discourse. Focusing on Israel, I began to explore cultural events and texts, including highly experimental and counterhegemonic narratives written in the 1960s by three Hebrew writers who were not survivors of the war (though two of them had been born in Europe): S. Y. Agnon's hitherto largely overlooked novella *Kisui hadam* (Covering the Blood; published posthumously in 1975 but written in the early 1960s), Yehuda Amichai's *Lo me-akhshav ve-lo mi-kan* (*Not of This Time, Not of This Place*, 1963), and Yoram Kaniuk's *Adam ben kelev* (*Adam Resurrected*, 1969).[8] Each of these fictional narratives was set in an Israel whose primary reference was a remote and undeciphered site of trauma but whose far-reaching effects constituted a covering up, a bifurcation, or an upending of all inherited systems of meaning and representation. The strong-arm edicts by officials in the educational and political sectors trying, during those first decades after the creation of the state, to sublate the Shoah into a dialectic that eventuated in Israel's birth appear in retrospect as manipulative and obtuse. They were, nonetheless, part of a desperate attempt to create alternative frameworks of meaning and to keep the unburied ghosts from hijacking the entire enterprise. Each in their own way, writers began to explore this terrain. Even Dan Pagis's poetry, which had seemed on first reading to epitomize the unfettered, "global" status of a material culture no longer anchored in time or place, revealed itself as quietly but obstinately engaged with the cultural and political forces in Israel that kept trying to contain it.[9]

By the time David Grossman's *See Under: Love* appeared (1986),[10] the trauma had been passed to the second generation and the unknowable site was referred to as "over there" (*eretz sham*).[11] The primary reference, by then, was Israel, and the contested legacy of the Shoah had become one component in a robust culture of protest against sacred cows and moral complacency, especially with regard to Jewish treatment of the Palestinians both within Israel and under occupation. The most shocking discovery to have emerged from *See Under: Love* was what Momik, the Israeli protagonist and son of survivors, called the LNIY (the Little Nazi in You, *ha-Nazi ha-katan she-be-tokhekha*). Grossman had, it seems, identified the bacillus that infected not only the survivors and their progeny but the entire body politic; whether that bacillus would inoculate us all against the plague of racism and persecution of the other in our midst or actually bring on the plague remained to be seen.

If the drama was internal to Israeli political culture, the ethical standards were becoming insistently universal. This was capped in the early 1990s by the Arab Jewish Akko Theater's production *Arbeit Macht Frei*. The public scandals precipitated by many of these cultural events testified to the fact that acts of trespass were being performed regularly across normative borders demarcating both the languages and the ethics of representation. No longer insulated from accountability, the local had indeed become glocal.

Parallel trajectories were being constructed in other countries, including Germany, Poland, France, Italy, and the United States. Simultaneously, local cultural venues were becoming global frames of reference: largely through the explosion of media technologies, audiences worldwide came to be engaged in what might otherwise have remained parochial cultural events. The medium of film and its expanding channels of distribution began both to standardize the modes of representation and to expand moral debates beyond specific communities. The two most powerful—and antithetical—expressions of this are Claude Lanzmann's *Shoah* (1985)[12] and Roberto Benigni's *Life Is Beautiful* (1997).[13] Much has been written on both these films; I am alluding to them here as the two poles of a representational and ethical polarity that persists to this day—between the legacy of revenge and the legacy of reconciliation and empathy. When at the end of Lanzmann's movie, Antek Zuckermann, the adulated hero of the Warsaw ghetto uprising, says, "If you could lick my heart, it would poison you," he is passing on the baton to the directors of the films *Defiance* (Zwick, 2008) and *Inglourious Basterds* (Tarantino, 2009)[14]—and to the settlers in the West Bank who declare that any withdrawal from territories captured in the Six-Day War would be "withdrawal to the crematoria."[15] When, on the other hand, little Joshua emerges from his hiding place in a generic concentration camp, is rescued by American soldiers, and reunites with his mother, Benigni is passing on the baton to all those whose vision of the future is as open-ended and poignant as an Italian landscape and a mother's embrace. If the naïveté at the heart of Benigni's fiction appears more fanciful—less "real"—than the cynicism that undergirds Lanzmann's opus, the languages of representation performed in these two films nonetheless enable two antithetical political trajectories.

Neither Lanzmann's *Shoah* nor Benigni's *Life Is Beautiful,* I am arguing, is a representation of life and death in the ghettos and camps so much as a cornerstone of a very divergent vision of the future. The sanctification and ossification of memory—Lanzmann's "centripetal" gaze directed unblinkingly at the gas chambers—privileges the avenging forces and handicaps genuine ethical struggles in the present. One factor that contributed to the fetishization of the concentrationary universe was the physical inaccessibility not only of Auschwitz and Treblinka, but also of alternate sites of memory in Central and Eastern Europe. The "centripetal" forces—the train tracks leading inexorably to Treblinka as they punctuate Lanzmann's film and victim testimony limited mainly to the survivors of the *Sonderkommando* who operated the gas chambers—are especially powerful and primordial when located in a remote and relentlessly menacing landscape.

But the centripetal thrust toward a mythicized terminus, which gives rise to historical absolutes, avenging spirits, and apocalyptic politics, is counteracted by the "centrifugal" impulses that originate when one turns one's back on Auschwitz and substitutes other points of departure—both into the past and into an open-ended future. From the early 1990s, with access to formerly occluded places in Eastern Europe and to the historical data in archives newly opened to scholarly scrutiny, the cultural and theoretical focus could move to myriad sites where historical dramas were—or might have been—enacted, and one could begin to argue for an alternative aesthetics and ethics of representation—and for alternative legacies that could generate alternative political cultures.[16]

Genre matters. If the "centripetal" impulse finds its generic expression in tragedy (specifically revenge tragedy), the "centrifugal" impulse, we come to understand, is inherently comic. Here again *Life Is Beautiful* forms the paradigmatic counterpart to Lanzmann's *Shoah*. In Israel the culture of comic sacrilege that stretched from the early 1980s to the mid-1990s fed the conviction that *laughter after* ... , like *poetry after* ... , is an act of faith in the time/place we call "after."[17] Drawing on classical Jewish sources that codified life-affirming, culturally constitutive responses to cataclysm, including the comic version of Jewish messianism as endlessly deferred promise, one could argue that the reinstatement of laughter after Auschwitz is not the infidelity of a comic representation *of* the Shoah but a reinstatement of faith *in a post-Shoah* universe.

The comic impulse is both the most local in its apparatus—Benigni's Guido and his son Joshua walking down the streets of Arezzo bantering about spiders and Visigoths—and the most universal in its moral lexicon. It is grounded in the tragic worldview and employs the most artificial of dramatic conventions to set itself free: "[T]he playwright," writes Scott Shershow on comedy's conclusion as tragedy *manqué,* "may also draw our attention to the ropes and pulleys of the *deus ex machina* and, indulging us with a beneficent vision of fate, may at the same time suggest 'this is not the way it would happen.' ... The happy ending magnifies the world with its infinite sense of the possible, and diminishes it with its ironic sense of the impossible."[18]

Comedy as the art of the impossible possible, history-as-it-should-have-been, drives the Hebrew novel *Eyen erekh: Ahava* (*See Under: Love,* 1986), the German novel *Jakob der Lügner* (*Jakob the Liar,* Jurek Becker, 1969; film version, 1974),[19] and the French Romanian film *Train de Vie* (*Train of Life,* Radu Mihaileaunu, 1998),[20] as well as Benigni's Italian film *La vita è bella* (*Life Is Beautiful,* 1997). Elements of comedy and the grotesque appear also in the narrative and stage versions of Kaniuk's *Adam Resurrected* (*Adam ben kelev*) and in the Akko Theater's production *Arbeit Macht Frei*.[21] The facts themselves, "history" as "what hurts," in Frederick Jameson's memorable phrase,[22] is the "given" against which each of these comedies is enacted. Each employs some degree of magic or magical thinking to both undermine history's successes and challenge the ways memory has been nationalized. And those comic novels and films that go out into the world through the medium of translation or theater distribution also carry snippets of a "Jewish conversation," however mediated it may be, traces of the comic impulse that made its way from biblical and Talmudic counterhistories through the Jewish fictions of Eastern Europe and the Yiddish stage, into the radical innocence of that Jew-*ish* "clown-turned-prophet," Charlie Chaplin, followed by his disciple, Roberto Benigni.

But from our perch in the middle of the second decade of the third millennium, the comic impulse seems to be in eclipse. In the long aftermath of the murder of Yitzhak Rabin and what may have been the murder of the peace process itself, Israel appears to have succumbed to a climate of vendetta and mythic projections—forward and backward. In a country that has become more isolated politically while maintaining global economic ambitions, the evidence grows for what philosopher Adi Ophir calls a culture of infinite loss (*ovdan ein-sofi*),[23] the "melancholy" that Amos Goldberg invokes in the spirit of Freud, or Lacan's "Imaginary" in its manifestation as identity politics.[24] Geographical coordinates are reintroduced as absolute references, though this time not as metaphors but as arbiters of the Real: Auschwitz once again becomes the dominant center of global reference, a kind of negative axis mundi that leads straight to that other absolute, the Temple Mount in Jerusalem. The settlers' strident cry that withdrawal from territories captured in the Six-Day War would be "withdrawal to the crematoria" is reified in a cult of sacred sites and sacrificial space.

The protest culture in post-1967 Israel, characterized by acts of trespass (between us and them, now and then, here and there), was predicated on boundaries ("limits")—on a polity that aspired to both geopolitical and temporal boundaries. Since the assassination of Yitzhak Rabin in 1995, those boundaries have been all but erased, and the centripetal pull of the sacred center has replaced a centrifugal culture of empathy, comic projection, and reconciliation. Sacred stories have been conflated with sacred shrines to produce a toxic narrative in which the Shoah plays an increasing role.

As boundaries are erased, so is distance. Without the blessed recognition of our own existential distance from that time and place, we are all victims; without the sense of history's contingencies, we are all Isaac waiting to be sacrificed. For Jews haunted by unburied martyrs from Europe and intoxicated by new proximity to the sacred center, a continuum stretches from the biblical topos of the *akeda* (the binding of Isaac, Genesis 22) through Auschwitz (back) to the Temple Mount in Jerusalem, where the *akeda* "happened"—an arc that is also a circle. In this circle, which radiates out concentrically to endless, borderless vistas, there are only two alternatives: to sacrifice or to be sacrificed. Jacques Derrida, in his reading of the *akeda* and the other sacrificial stories that converge on Jerusalem, gives us the tools and the courage to explore this terrain.[25] The stony gaze at the ruins of Auschwitz, "holy" in its awfulness, is conflated with the proprietary—and idolatrous—gaze at the ruins of the original site of holiness, the Temple of Solomon. It is not in the ruins themselves, but in the gaze that cannot embrace the future that the danger lies.

This fixed gaze is, needless to say, deaf to the cosmopolitan, late modernist, and postmodernist discourses that inform most of the chapters in this book and gain their inspiration from what Carolyn Dean, following Martha Nussbaum[26] and Dominick LaCapra,[27] calls the "fragility of empathy."[28] In relinquishing, along with Ronit Peleg, the "beautiful death" that undergirds so much philosophy and so much political cataclysm,[29] I find comfort in returning to (of all things) a *fundamentalist,* comic reading of Isaac's story: replete with the biblical equivalent of ropes and pulleys, deus ex machina appears to abort the sacrifice embedded in the tragic structure. A glocal politics of contemporary Jerusalem would, similarly, free us from the centripetal force field that keeps us in the deadly embrace of the Temple Mount and Yad Vashem. The *akeda* as comedy can, indeed, only be retrieved by turning *away* from two thousand years of misreading the Bible and forty-four years of gazing at dead stones instead of human faces.

Notes

1. Saul Friedländer, *Probing the Limits of Representation*. Cambridge, MA: Harvard University Press, 1992.
2. Paul Celan, "Todesfuge," *Selected Poems and Prose of Paul Celan*. Translated by John Felstiner. New York: W. W. Norton, 2001, 30–33.
3. Dan Pagis, "Point of Departure," *Points of Departure*. Translated by Stephen Mitchell. Philadelphia: Jewish Publication Society, 1982, 41.
4. Sidra DeKoven Ezrahi, *By Words Alone: The Holocaust in Literature*. Chicago: University of Chicago Press, 1980. Paperback, 1982.
5. Readings of both Adorno and Lyotard have become far more nuanced than when they were first encountered. T. W. Adorno, "Cultural Criticism and Society" [in German]. Translated by Samuel and Shierry Weber. In *Prisms*. London: Nevills Spearman, 1967. Jean-François Lyotard, *The Différend: Phrases in Dispute*. Translated by Georges Van Den Abbeele. Minneapolis: University of Minnesota Press, 1988. Published in French as *Le différend* in 1983.
6. Paul Celan, *Selected Poems and Prose of Paul Celan,* trans. John Felstiner (New York: W. W. Norton, 2001), 186–87. I have modified Felstiner's translation somewhat.
7. The term "black hole" was evidently first publicly used by John Wheeler during a lecture in 1967. http://en.wikipedia.org/wiki/Black_hole. *The Black Hole of Auschwitz* (Cambridge: Polity Press, 2005) is the English translation (and exegetical appropriation) of a posthumously published book of Levi's essays, entitled in the original *L'asimmetria e la vita: Articoli e saggi 1955–1987* (Torino: Einaudi, 1997). There are, of course, lively debates over Levi's legacy, especially in light of the temptation to read his suicide back into his writing. In *Booking Passage,* I suggest a very different, more "centrifugal" reading of both Levi and Celan. Sidra DeKoven Ezrahi, *Booking Passage: Exile and Homecoming in the Modern Jewish Imagination* (Berkeley: University of California Press, 2000), 141–56.
8. S. Y. Agnon, *Kisui hadam o bad be-vad* [Covering the blood]. In *Lifnim min ha-homa*, 51–104. Jerusalem: Schocken, 1975.; Yehuda Amichai, *Not of This Time, Not of This Place*. Translated by Shlomo Katz. New York: Harper & Row, 1968. Published in Hebrew as *Lo me-akhshav ve-lo mikan* in 1968; Yoram Kaniuk, *Adam Resurrected*. Translated by Seymour Simckes. New York: Grove Press, 2000. Published in Hebrew as *Adam ben kelev* in 1969.
9. Dan. *Points of Departure.* Passim.
10. David Grossman, *See Under: Love.* Translated by Betsy Rosenberg. New York: Farrar, Straus and Giroux, 1989. Published in Hebrew as *Eyen erekh: ahava* in 1986.
11. Ibid., p. 50.
12. Claude Lanzmann, dir. *Shoah.* New Yorker Films, 1985.
13. Roberto Benigni, dir. *La vita é bella*. Cecchi Gori Group, 1997. Released by Miramax Films in the United States as *Life Is Beautiful* in 1999.
14. Edward Zwick, dir. *Defiance.* Paramount Vantage, 2008; Quentin Tarantino, dir. *Inglourious Basterds.* Universal Pictures, 2009.
15. See Idith Zertal, *Israel's Holocaust and the Politics of Nationhood,* trans. Chaya Galai (Cambridge: Cambridge University Press, 2005), 184–208.
16. Radical acts of counterhistorical imagination take place in the work of Albert Camus, Jaroslaw Rymkiewicz, and Jurek Becker, among others (Albert Camus, *The Fall*. Translated by Justin O'Brien. In *The Plague, The Fall, Exile and the Kingdom and Selected Essays*. New York: Everyman's Library, 2004. Published in French as *La chute* in 1956; Jaroslaw Rymkiewicz, *Final Station: Umschlagplatz*. Translated by Nina Taylor. Farrar Straus & Giroux, 1994. Published in Polish in 1992; Jurek Becker, *Jacob the Liar.* Translated by Leila Vennewitz. New York: Arcade, 1996. Published in German as *Jakob der Lügner* in 1969.) See Eric Santner, *Stranded Objects: Mourning, Memory and Film in Postwar Germany* (Ithaca, NY: Cornell University Press, 1993); see on the above Sidra DeKoven Ezrahi, "Representing Auschwitz," *History and Memory* 7, no. 2 (Winter 1996): 121–54.

17. This, of course, echoes Adorno's much-misappropriated statement that "to write poetry after Auschwitz is barbaric." On this see, among others, Michael Rothberg, *Traumatic Realism: The Demands of Holocaust Representation* (Minneapolis: University of Minnesota Press, 2000); Sidra DeKoven Ezrahi, "Acts of Impersonation: Barbaric Space as Theatre," in *Mirroring Evil: Nazi Imagery, Recent Art* (exhibition and catalog), ed. and curated by Norman L. Kleeblatt (New York: Jewish Museum; New Brunswick, NJ: Rutgers University Press, 2001): 17–38; Sidra DeKoven Ezrahi, "After Such Knowledge, What Laughter?," in "Holocaust and Interpretation," special issue, *Yale Journal of Criticism* 14, no. 1 (2001): 287–317.

18. Scott Shershow. *Laughing Matters: The Paradox of Comedy.* Amherst: University of Massachusetts Press, 1986, 20.

19. Jurek Becker, *Jacob the Liar.* Translated by Leila Vennewitz. New York: Arcade, 1996. Published in German as *Jakob der Lügner* in 1969.

20. Radu Mihaileaunu, dir. *Train de Vie.* 1998.

21. Dudi Ma'ayan, dir. *Arbeit Macht Frei.* Akko Theater, 1991–94.

22. Frederick Jameson, "On Interpretation: Literature as a Socially Symbolic Act." In *The Jameson Reader*, ed. Michael Hardt and Kathi Weeks. Oxford: Blackwell, 2000, 56.

23. Adi Ophir. *Avodat ha-hoveh.* Tel Aviv: Ha-kibbutz hameuhad, 2002, 12–50.

24. See Amos Goldberg, "Ethics, Identity, and Antifundamental Fundamentalism," this volume; also Goldberg, "The 'Jewish Narrative' in the Yad Vashem Global Museum." *Journal of Genocide Research* 14, no. 2 (2012): 187–213.

25. Jacques Derrida. *The Gift of Death.* Translated by David Wills. Chicago: University of Chicago Press, 1995. Published in French as *Donner la mort* in 1992. See Sidra DeKoven Ezrahi, "From Auschwitz to the Temple Mount," in *After Testimony: The Ethics and Aesthetics of Holocaust Narrative for the Future*, ed. Jakob Lothe, Susan Rubin Suleiman, and James Phelan (Columbus: Ohio State University Press, 2012), 291–313.

26. Martha Nussbaum. "Compassion: The Basic Social Emotion." *Social Philosophy and Policy* 1 (Winter 1996): 27–58.

27. Dominick LaCapra, *Writing History, Writing Trauma.* Baltimore, MD: Johns Hopkins University Press, 2000.

28. Carolyn Dean. *The Fragility of Empathy after the Holocaust.* Ithaca, NY: Cornell University Press, 2004.

29. See Ronit Peleg, "'After Auschwitz,'" this volume.

Bibliography

Adorno, T. W. "Cultural Criticism and Society" [in German]. Translated by Samuel and Shierry Weber. In *Prisms.* London: Nevills Spearman, 1967.

Agnon, Shmuel Yosef. Y. *Kisui hadam o bad be-vad* [Covering the blood]. In *Lifnim min ha-homa*, 51–104. Jerusalem: Schocken, 1975.

Amichai, Yehuda. *Not of This Time, Not of This Place.* Translated by Shlomo Katz. New York: Harper & Row, 1968. Published in Hebrew as *Lo me-akhshav ve-lo mi-kan* in 1968.

Becker, Jurek. *Jacob the Liar.* Translated by Leila Vennewitz. New York: Arcade, 1996. Published in German as *Jakob der Lügner* in 1969.

Benigni, Roberto, dir. *La vita é bella.* Cecchi Gori Group, 1997. Released by Miramax Films in the United States as *Life Is Beautiful* in 1999.

Camus, Albert. *The Fall.* Translated by Justin O'Brien. In *The Plague, The Fall, Exile and the Kingdom and Selected Essays.* New York: Everyman's Library, 2004. Published in French as *La chute* in 1956.

Celan, Paul. *Selected Poems and Prose of Paul Celan.* Translated by John Felstiner. New York: W. W. Norton, 2001.

Dean, Carolyn. *The Fragility of Empathy after the Holocaust.* Ithaca, NY: Cornell University Press, 2004.

Derrida, Jacques. *The Gift of Death*. Translated by David Wills. Chicago: University of Chicago Press, 1995. Published in French as *Donner la mort* in 1992.

Ezrahi, Sidra DeKoven. "Acts of Impersonation: Barbaric Space as Theatre." In *Mirroring Evil: Nazi Imagery, Recent Art* (exhibition and catalog), ed. and curated by Norman L. Kleeblatt. New York: Jewish Museum; New Brunswick, NJ: Rutgers University Press, 2001.

———. "After Such Knowledge, What Laughter?" In "Holocaust and Interpretation," special issue, *Yale Journal of Criticism* 14, no. 1 (2001): 287–317.

———. *Booking Passage: Exile and Homecoming in the Modern Jewish Imagination*. Berkeley: University of California Press, 2000.

———. *By Words Alone: The Holocaust in Literature*. Chicago: University of Chicago Press, 1980.

———. "From Auschwitz to the Temple Mount." In *After Testimony: The Ethics and Aesthetics of Holocaust Narrative for the Future*, ed. Jakob Lothe, Susan Rubin Suleiman, and James Phelan, 291–313. Columbus: Ohio State University Press, 2012.

———. "Representing Auschwitz." *History and Memory* 7, no. 2 (Winter 1996): 121–54.

Friedländer, Saul. *Probing the Limits of Representation*. Cambridge, MA: Harvard University Press, 1992.

Goldberg, Amos. "The 'Jewish Narrative' in the Yad Vashem Global Museum." *Journal of Genocide Research* 14, no. 2 (2012): 187–213.

Grossman, David. *See Under: Love*. Translated by Betsy Rosenberg. New York: Farrar, Straus and Giroux, 1989. Published in Hebrew as *Eyen erekh: Ahava* in 1986.

Jameson, Frederick. "On Interpretation: Literature as a Socially Symbolic Act." In *The Jameson Reader*, ed. Michael Hardt and Kathi Weeks. Oxford: Blackwell, 2000.

Kaniuk, Yoram. *Adam Resurrected*. Translated by Seymour Simckes. New York: Grove Press, 2000. Published in Hebrew as *Adam ben kelev* in 1969.

LaCapra, Dominick. *Writing History, Writing Trauma*. Baltimore, MD: Johns Hopkins University Press, 2000.

Lanzmann, Claude, dir. *Shoah*. New Yorker Films, 1985.

Levi, Primo. *L'asimmetria e la vita: Articoli e saggi 1955–1987*. Torino: Einaudi, 1997.

———. *The Black Hole of Auschwitz*. Edited by Marco Belpoliti. Translated by Sharon Wood. Cambridge: Polity Press, 2005.

———. "The Gray Zone." Translated by Raymond Rosenthal. In *The Drowned and the Saved*, 22–51. London: Michael Joseph, 1988. Published in Italian as *I sommersi e i salvati* in 1986.

Lyotard, Jean-François. *The Differend: Phrases in Dispute*. Translated by Georges Van Den Abbeele. Minneapolis: University of Minnesota Press, 1988. Published in French as *Le différend* in 1983.

Ma'ayan, Dudi, dir. *Arbeit Macht Frei*. Akko Theater, 1991–94.

Mihaileaunu, Radu, dir. *Train de Vie*. United States: Paramount Productions, 1998.

Nussbaum, Martha. "Compassion: The Basic Social Emotion." *Social Philosophy and Policy* 1 (Winter 1996): 27–58.

Ophir, Adi. *Avodat ha-hoveh*. Tel Aviv: Ha-kibbutz hameuhad, 2002.

Pagis, Dan. *Points of Departure*. Translated by Stephen Mitchell. Philadelphia: Jewish Publication Society, 1982.

Rothberg, Michael. *Traumatic Realism: The Demands of Holocaust Representation*. Minneapolis: University of Minnesota Press, 2000.

Rymkiewicz, Jaroslav. *Final Station: Umschlagplatz*. Translated by Nina Taylor. Farrar Straus & Giroux, 1994. Published in Polish in 1992.

Santner, Eric. *Stranded Objects: Mourning, Memory and Film in Postwar Germany*. Ithaca, NY: Cornell University Press, 1993.

Shershow, Scott. *Laughing Matters: The Paradox of Comedy*. Amherst: University of Massachusetts Press, 1986.

Tarantino, Quentin, dir. *Inglourious Basterds*. Universal Pictures, 2009.

Zertal, Idith. *Israel's Holocaust and the Politics of Nationhood*. Translated by Chaya Galai. Cambridge: Cambridge University Press, 2005. Published in Hebrew as *Ha-uma ve- ha- mavet* in 2002.

Zwick, Edward, dir. *Defiance*. Paramount Vantage, 2008.

Contributors

Louise Bethlehem is a senior lecturer in the English Department and the former chair of the Program in Cultural Studies at the Hebrew University of Jerusalem. Her book, *Skin Tight: Apartheid Literary Culture and Its Aftermath* (Unisa Press and Brill, 2006), was published in Hebrew translation in 2011. She has coedited six volumes in South African literature, African studies, and cultural studies, including most recently a special issue of *Critical Arts* with Ashleigh Harris, entitled "Unruly Pedagogies, Migratory Interventions: Unsettling Cultural Studies" (2012). In 2013, Louise Bethlehem was awarded the European Research Council Consolidators' Grant for a five-year project entitled "Apartheid—The Global Itinerary: South African Cultural Formations in Transnational Circulation 1948–1990."

Alon Confino is a professor of history at the University of Virginia and Ben-Gurion University, Israel. His recent books are *Foundational Pasts: The Holocaust as Historical Understanding* (Cambridge University Press, 2012) and *A World Without Jews: The Nazi Imagination from Persecution to Genocide* (Yale University Press, 2014).

Rina Dudai is a senior lecturer in literature at the Kibbutzim College, Tel Aviv. In her studies she focuses on intersections among literature, cinema, and psychoanalysis. She studies coping with trauma, with a special emphasis on the representation of the memory of trauma in psychological and poetic contexts. She has published several articles on Holocaust trauma as it is represented in poetic language by Primo Levi, Aharon Appelfeld, Ka-Tzetnik, Dan Pagis, and Ida Fink in literary work, and by Michael Heneke and Ari Folman in film.

Sidra DeKoven Ezrahi is professor emerita of comparative literature at the Hebrew University of Jerusalem. She is the author *of By Words Alone: The Ho-*

locaust in Literature (1980), which was a finalist for the National Jewish Book Award, and *Booking Passage: Exile and Homecoming in the Modern Jewish Imagination* (2000), which was a finalist for the Koret Jewish Book Award. Her work ranges from explorations of literary and cultural representations of the Holocaust to studies of Jewish configurations of exile and homecoming. Ezrahi has been a featured speaker at the Chicago Humanities Festival (2005) and the Jewish Arts Festival in New York (2006). In 2007 she was awarded a Guggenheim fellowship for her project on "Jerusalem and the Poetics of Return."

Michal Givoni teaches in the Department of Politics and Government at Ben-Gurion University of the Negev. She specializes in contemporary political theory, and her work focuses on the history, ethics, and politics of humanitarianism and on ethical witnessing in the twentieth century.

Amos Goldberg is a senior lecturer in Holocaust studies at the Hebrew University of Jerusalem. His major fields of research are cultural history of the Jews in the Holocaust, Holocaust historiography, and Holocaust memory in a global world. Among his publications is his recent book in Hebrew *Trauma in First Person: Diary Writing during the Holocaust* (2012). His coedited book with Bashir Bashir, *The Nakba and the Holocaust: Memory, Identity and Jewish-Arab Partnership*, will come out in Hebrew in 2015.

Haim Hazan (PhD) is a professor of social anthropology at Tel Aviv University and an author of numerous articles and books, including: *The Limbo People: A Study of the Constitution of the Time Universe among the Aged*; *Managing Change in Old Age: A Paradoxical Community*; *Old Age: Constructions and Deconstructions*; *From First Principles: An Experiment in Aging*; *Simulated Dreams: Israeli Youth and Virtual Zionism*; and *Serendipity in Anthropological Research: The Nomadic Turn*. He is the former director of the Tel Aviv University Herczeg Institute on Aging and a current codirector of the Tel Aviv University Minerva Center for the Study of the End of Life.

Jakob Hessing, born in 1944, is professor emeritus of German literature at the Hebrew University, Jerusalem. He has written numerous publications in the field of German Jewish literature, incluing books on Else Lasker-Schüler, Sigmund Freud, and Heinrich Heine.

Tamar Katriel is a professor of communication at the University of Haifa, Israel. Her research areas are the ethnography of communication, discourse studies, and museum ethnography. She is author of *Talking Straight* (1986); *Communal Webs* (1991); *Performing the Past* (1997); *Dialogic Moments* (2004); a collection of essays in Hebrew, *Key Words* (1999); and a range of articles in journals and book chapters.

Carol A. Kidron is senior lecturer in the Department of Sociology and Anthropology at the University of Haifa, Israel. Kidron has undertaken ethnographic work with Holocaust descendants in Israel and children of Cambodian genocide survivors in Cambodia and in Canada. Her research interests include personal, communal, and collective Holocaust and genocide commemoration, and the way in which therapeutic discourse and particularly trauma constructs have informed contemporary subjectivities. Kidron's publications include: "Toward an Ethnography of Silence: The Lived Presence of the Past in the Everyday Life of Holocaust Trauma Survivors and Their Descendants in Israel" (*Current Anthropology,* 2009), "Embracing the Lived Memory of Genocide: Holocaust Survivor and Descendant Renegade Memory-Work at the 'House of Being'" (*American Ethnologist,* 2010), and "Alterity and the Particular Limits of Universalism: Comparing Jewish-Israeli Holocaust and Canadian-Cambodian Genocide Legacies" (*Current Anthropology,* 2012).

Shulmith Lev-Aladgem (PhD) is a professor of theatre studies, chair of the Theatre Arts Department at Tel Aviv University, a lecturer, researcher, and community-based theater practitioner. She is also a trained actress who uses her acting experience in both her research and teaching. Lev-Aladgem's main interests include play theory, performance studies, and cultural studies and their relation to community-based theater, political theater, alternative theater, educational drama, drama therapy, and feminist theater. Her research on these subjects has been published in numerous leading periodicals in the United States, Europe, and Israel. She has published two books to date: *Theatre in Co-Communities: Articulating Power* (Palgrave Macmillan, 2010) and *Standing Front Stage: Resistance, Celebration and Subversion in Community-Based Theatre* (Haifa University Press and Pardes, 2010) (in Hebrew).

Emanuel Marx, a social anthropologist, is professor emeritus at Tel Aviv University. He has done fieldwork among Bedouin in the Negev, Israel; a new town in Galilee, Israel; Bedouin in South Sinai, Egypt; and Palestinian refugee camps in the occupied West Bank and Gaza. His main research interests are the politics and economics of pastoral nomads, changing conditions in refugee camps, the social organization of prehistoric man, and the connection between state bureaucracies and violence.

Peter Novick (26 July 1934–17 February 2012) was a history professor at the University of Chicago. He was best known for writing *That Noble Dream: The "Objectivity Question" and the American Historical Profession* (Cambridge University Press, 1988) and *The Holocaust in American Life* (Houghton Mifflin, 1999).

Ronit Peleg is a lecturer of continental political philosophy in the Department of Political Sciences at Tel Aviv University and in the Department of

Political Sciences at The Hebrew University. Her dissertation, entitled "Language and Morality: *The Differend* by Jean-François Lyotard," was written at the Cohn Institute of the History and Philosophy of Sciences and Ideas at Tel Aviv University. Ronit is cofounder and chair of the Seminar of Continental Philosophy, which takes place in the public sphere of the city of Tel Aviv annually since 2006. Her book on Jean-François Lyotard will be published by Resling in 2016.

Nigel Rapport is a professor of anthropological and philosophical studies at the University of St. Andrews, Scotland, where he is founding director of the Centre for Cosmopolitan Studies. He has also held the Canada Research Chair in Globalization, Citizenship and Justice at Concordia University of Montreal. He has been elected a fellow of the Royal Society of Edinburgh. His research interests include social theory, phenomenology, identity and individuality, community, conversation analysis, and links between anthropology and literature and philosophy. Nigel Rapport's recent books include: *Of Orderlies and Men: Hospital Porters Achieving Wellness at Work* (Carolina Academic Press, 2008); *Anyone: The Cosmopolitan Subject of Anthropology* (Berghahn Books, 2012); and, as editor, *Human Nature as Capacity: Transcending Discourse and Classification* (Berghahn Books, 2010).

Michael Rothberg is a professor of English and head of the Department of English at the University of Illinois at Urbana-Champaign, where he is also director of the Holocaust, Genocide, and Memory Studies Initiative. His latest book is *Multidirectional Memory: Remembering the Holocaust in the Age of Decolonization* (2009), published by Stanford University Press in their Cultural Memory in the Present series. He is also the author of *Traumatic Realism: The Demands of Holocaust Representation* (2000), and has coedited *The Holocaust: Theoretical Readings* (2003) and special issues of the journals *Criticism, Interventions, Occasion,* and *Yale French Studies.* Currently he is completing *The Implicated Subject: Beyond Victims and Perpetrators.*

Batya Shimony (PhD) is a senior lecturer in the Hebrew Literature Department at Ben-Gurion University of the Negev and at Achva Academic College, Israel. Her research interest is Mizrahi literature in its various aspects: identity, perception of the Holocaust, gender, immigration, and more. She has published numerous articles in these areas, such as "On 'Holocaust Envy' in Mizrahi Literature," in *Dapim: Studies on the Holocaust,* volume 25 (2011). She is the author of *On the Threshold of Redemption: The Story of the Ma'abara, First and Second Generation* (Dvir, 2008) (in Hebrew).

Index

A

Abdallah, Ghasan, 298
Abraham's sacrifice, 88, 91
absolute eradication, model of, 77
accountability, 267–9
A Critique of Postcolonial Reason, 183
Adam, Roni, 200
Adenauer, Konrad, 12
Adorno, Theodor, 70, 71, 73, 104, 258, 286
    "after Auschwitz," 70–94
    beautiful death, 79
    boundaries (barbaric and civilized), 346
    concepts, morals, 71
    fearing death, 79
    loss of creativity, 104, 258
    model of absolute eradication, 77
A Farewell to Arms, 111
African-Americans
    discrimination against, 175–6
    memory, 212
Agamben, Giorgio, 39, 139
Ahmadinejad, Mahmoud, 5, 115
Ahmed, Sarah, 178
Alexander, Jeffrey C., 178, 179, 198, 234, 235
American Historical Review, 64
American Israeli Public Affairs Committee (AIPAC), 53
American memory, 7, 51
Amir, Eli, 301
Ancestry Proof document, 334
Annan, Kofi, 3
annihilation of Aryan Germans, 330–6
anthropology, 32–4
    Claude Lévi-Strauss, 107
    savagery, 34–6
antifundamentalism (Western), 19–21
anti-Semitism, 15, 17, 132
apologies, demands for, 12
Arendt, Hannah, 135, 173
Aristotle, 234, 235
Armenian genocide, 20
art, 39
Artaud, 272, 273
artifacts of World War II, 109
Aryans, 323, 324, 326
    annihilation of Aryan Germans, 330–6
    as closed community of names, 78
    "final solution," 77
Ashkenazim, 298, 299
atavistic tribalism, 32
Aufhebung, 75, 79, 80, 86, 90
Auschwitz, 34, 266–80
    "after Auschwitz," 70–94
    experience of visiting, 114
    ignoring consequences of, 83
    outlines of philosophical-ethical discourse, 87–93
    as personal history, 112
    Primo Levy's experience at, 31
    reactions to, 86
    role as global shrine, 5
    symbolic meaning of, 61
    tours, 112
Austerlitz, 215–20, 284. *See also* Sebald, W. G.
authorization, process of, 82

autonomy, 101
Avaryan Tzatzua (Petty Hoodlum), 308
Avni, Yossi, 308, 309

B
Bakshi, Roni, 66
Balas, Shimon, 301, 302
Balkenende, Jan Pieter, 3
Barkan, Elazar, 12, 20
Barthes, Roland, 239
Bauman, Zygmunt, 195
beautiful death, 76. *See also* speculative death
  detachment from, 80
  lack of possibility of, 77
  moral of, 82
  permanent danger of, 83
  as political model of the West, 78
Beck, Ulrich, 4
Beloved, 297
Benigni, Roberto, 347, 348, 349
Benjamin, Walter, 286
Bernstein, Michael, 103
Bhaduri, Bhubaneswari, 182, 184
Biafra, Nigeria, 127–30
Bildungsbürger, 285
Black Book of Communism, 13
blacks, 212. *See also* African-Americans
Blanchot, Maurice
  argument against beautiful death, 80
  disasters, 87
  philosophy of, 71, 72, 74
  productivity of death, 75
bodies (physical), 99
  experience of, 109–13
  separation of, 100
Bonasso, Miguel, 325
Boyarin, Jonathan, 17
Brackman, Harold, 175
Brauman, Rony, 131, 133, 135
Buddhism, 154
Burke, Edmund, 58
  freezing of psychic activity, 236, 237
  reflections on the French Revolution, 59, 62
  negative sublime of the Holocaust, 235
Busi, Dudu, 308
Butler, Judith, 184
By Words Alone, 345

C
Calhoun, Craig, 201
Callois, Roger, 175
Cambodia, 132, 133. *See also* Khmer Rouge
  descendent genocide legacies, 150–2
Cannibals, 270, 274
Celan, Paul, 346
Césaire, Aimé, 171, 174, 176, 213, 225
Charcot, Jean-Martin, 109
Chaunu, Pierre, 62
China, 56
  symbolic manual of Holocaust, 65
Chriac, Jacques, 13
Christianity, 107
Churchill, Caryl, 221
Churchill, Winston, 195
coexistence, 34
Cold War, beginning of, 12
collaboration, 135
collective memory, 5, 47
  postcolonial witnessing, 172
  shifts in, 198
colonialism, 212
  history of, 174–7
  oppression, 33
colonization, plan for, 329
commemoration, 156–61. *See also* testimonies
  ceremonies, 34
  genocide, 146 (*see also* cosmopolitan memory)
  Twentieth century, 193–6 (*see also* Twentieth century commemoration)
commemorative memory, 198
Communism, 134
community
  membership in, 78
  of seeing, 122 (*see also* witnessing)
compensation claims, 11, 12
concentration camps, 64, 100, 310
  ambiguity of life in, 104
  Auschwitz (see Auschwitz)
  establishment of, 334
  existence in, 102
  Kristallnacht (see Kristallnacht)
Confino, Alon, 47
Consoni, Manuela, 16
contradictions, humanity of, 101–4
core memory, 61

cosmopolitan memory, 7, 103, 113–15, 146. *See also* Levy, Daniel; Sznaider, Natan
   commemoration, 146
   culture of, 194, 206
   emergence of, 7, 194, 195, 197
   promotion of understanding, 195
Courtois, Stèphane, 13
creation myths, 107
The Crisis, 175
culture, 31
   attacks on respect for individual, 101
   changes in, 345–251
   confrontations, 37–8
   limitations of, 33
   of trauma, 258

D
dafamiliarization, 274
Darquier, Louis, 132
Dean, Carolyn, 350
death, 75. *See also* speculative death
   called Auschwitz, 76 (*see also* Auschwitz)
   fear of, 79
   Plato's view of, 84
   Western thought of, 77
decentering Holocaust memory, 224–5
decolonization, 172, 173, 212, 213
Delbo, Charlotte, 60, 225
delight, 235, 236–8
denial (Holocaust), 5
   cover-ups, 39
   memory (*see* memory)
   outlawing, 15
   taboo of denial in Europe, 62
deportation of Jews (France), 13
Derrida, Jacques, 71, 84, 178
   economics of life and death, 75, 76
   silences, 87
Dershowitz, Alan, 18
descendent legacies, 150–2. *See also* testimonies
   Cambodian Canadian, 153–4
   Cambodian descendants in Cambodia, 154–6
   Jewish Israeli, 152–3
dialectics, speculative, 71
Diamond, Elin, 267
The Diary of a Young Girl, 179

dichotomy paradox, 106
The Differend, 71, 80, 88. *See also* Lyotard, Jean-François
differend, concept of, 238
Diner, Dan, 33
Dinur, Yehiel, 35, 346
disasters
   "after Auschwitz," 74 (*see also* Auschwitz)
   containment of, 72
   history of, 290
   Holocaust envy, 298
   Maurice Blanchot, 87
   moral philosophy responses to, 71
   philosophy's responsibility to, 86
   silences that surround, 87
discourse, 39
   "after Auschwitz," 72
   construction of pronoun "we," 76
   identity, 10–11
   legal-ethical-political, 9–10
   legitimating republican, 81
   outlines of philosophical-ethical, 87–93
   surveillance properties of, 32
Discourse on Colonialism, 171, 174, 213
discrimination, 33
dispersion, law of, 284–94
Döblin, Alfred, 285–6
Doctors Without Borders, 124, 125, 127. *See also* humanitarian witnessing
documentaries, 272
Doda Farhuma Lo Hayta Zona (Auntie Farhuma Wasn't a Whore After All), 308
Don Quixote, 101
Du Bois, W. E. B., 175, 225
Dwork, Debórah, 20

E
Eaglestone, Robert, 173, 177
Eckel, Jan, 7
Eichmann, Adolf
   hanging of, 308
   trial of, 35, 179, 303, 346
Eichmann in Jerusalem, 135
elevating death, 80 (*see also Aufhebung*)
Eliot, T. S., 107–8
The Emigrants, 287
empty empathy, 258
Enlai, Zhou, 58
Enmmanuelli, Xavier, 130

envy (Holocaust), 296–311
eradication
    of collective names ("Jews"), 78
    model of absolute, 77
Eternal Treblinka: Our Treatment of Animals and the Holocaust, 40
ethical responsibility, 91
ethics, 8–9
    accountability, 267–9
    of "after Auschwitz," 71
    versus identity, 11–14
    of poetic representations, 257–8
    of witnessing, 134, 258
Ethiopia, 135, 136
ethnic cleansing, 33, 63
eugenic doctrines, 333
Europe, taboo of denial in, 62
European Enlightenment, 115
Every Man Dies Alone, 321
exiles, 115
expression, freedom of, 102

F

fact-based truth, 130–4
Fallada, Hans, 321
Fassin, Didier, 126, 146
Fast, Omer, 233, 249–57
Fateless, 100, 102, 104. See also Kertesz, Imre
Faurisson, Robert, 132
Felman, Shoshana, 122, 139, 181
Ferber, Max, 287, 288, 289, 291, 292
film, 52. See also poetic representations
final death, 78. See also beautiful death
"final solution," 77, 79, 320
    Kristallnacht, 328–30
Finkelstein, Norman, 221–4
foundational events, 59, 60
"Four Quartets," 107–8
Fragments, 296
France
    anti-Semitism in, 17
    deportation of Jews from, 13
    Marxism in, 133–4
    The Origins of Contemporary France, 62
Franco-Algerian war, 60
Frank, Anne, 179
Freiman, Moshe, 66
French Communist Party, 132
French Revolution, 8, 16

association of Holocaust with, 63–5
    global memory of, 58
    symbolic manuals, 58
Friedländer, Saul, 20, 21
Friedman, Thomas, 49
From the Four Winds, 306

G

Gandhi, Mahatma, 193, 198, 203, 204
Gandhi, Sonia, 193, 204
Gaza Strip
    infrastructure of, 220
    Israeli withdrawal from (2005), 65
    Sharon's plan of disengagement from, 17
genocide, 62, 63, 137, 212
    commemoration, 146. See also cosmopolitan memory
    Khmer Rouge, 131–2
    multidirectional memory, 220–4
Germany, 48, 49. See also Nazis; Nazism
    behavior of, 50
ghettos, 121
"gift of death" *(donner la mort)*, 83
"given death," 84
"giving death to myself" *(se-donner la mort)*, 84
globalization
    ability to change memory, 57
    construction of otherness, 36–7
    dilemma of, 30–2
    of memory, 3–8
global semiotics, 146–7, 161–3. See also testimonies; trauma
    burden of memory, 148
    descendent legacies, 150–2
    testimonies and commemorations, 156–61
    testimonies of genocide witnesses, 149–50
    trauma theories, 147
    traumatic legacies, 152–6
Goebbels, Joseph, 63
Goldberg, Amos, 319
Goldstone, Richard, 220
Göring, Hermann, 322, 328
Göth, Amon, 242–5, 256. See also *Schindler's List*
Grosjean, Bruno, 296
groups, constitution of, 71
Gypsies, 324, 326, 329

H

Hacking, Ian, 32
Hakak, Balfour, 299, 304, 305
Hartman, Geoffrey, 180
Hazan, Haim, 319
Hegel, G.W., 75
Hegelian speculative thinking, 71, 72
   detachment from, 73
   final breakdown of, 74–87
hegemonic roles of memory, 59, 60
hegemony, 57
Hell, Julia, 219
Hemingway, Ernest, 111
Hesel's Kingdom, 215–16
Hirsch, Helen, 242–4. *See also Schindler's List*
Hirsch, Marianne, 183
history
   of disasters, 290
   of Germany, 285
Hitler, Adolph, 63, 322–3
   Kristallnacht (*see* Kristallnacht)
   postcolonial witnessing, 171
   system of control, 332
   as viewed in *Discourse on Colonialism,* 174–7
Hollywood, 52
Holocaust
   as concepts, 109
   envy, 296–311
   as global trope, 103
   memory, 48 (*see also* memory)
   as tragedy, 104–6
Holocaust (American TV series), 132
The Holocaust and Memory in the Global Age, 6
The Holocaust and the Postmodern, 177
Holocaust Museum (Washington D.C.), 34, 212
homo sacer, Agambenian concept of, 36
hostages, 92, 93
humanitarian witnessing, 121–7
   direct presence, 130–4
   seizing of speech, 127–30
   speaking out, 134–9
humanity, 31
human rights, 6, 63
   Holocaust as metaphor for, 18
   Palestinians, 19
Human Rights Day, 196
Hungary, anti-Semitism in, 17
Hutu refugee camps, 137, 138
Hyslop, Beatrice, 64

I

identification, 177–80
identity, 8–9
   discourse, 10–11
   ethics *versus,* 11–14
If This Is a Man, 31, 104
intellectual trends, 60
international commemoration, 194
International Committee of the Red Cross (ICRC), 121, 125, 127
International Day of Non-Violence, 193, 199, 202–5
International Holocaust Remembrance Alliance (IHRA), 7
International Holocaust Remembrance Day, 6, 19, 194, 199–202
interpretation, 99
interpretive grids, 234, 235
Iran, 5
Irving, Andrew, 109
Islam, 18
Israel, 49
   American support for, 51
   behavior of, 50
Isreali Mizrahim, 298–301
Isreali-Palestinian conflict, 220, 297

J

Jacobson, Dan, 215–16
Jewish Israeli descendent legacies, 152–3
Jewish Museum (Berlin), 5
Jewishness, 103
Jewish policies, Kristallnacht, 325–8
jouissance, 235, 238–40, 249, 256
Journal of Modern History, 64
Jubilee, 273

K

Kafka, Franz, 102, 296
Kant, Immanuel, 236, 237
Kaplan, E. Ann, 258
Katastrophengeschichte (a history of disaster), 290
Katriel, Tamar, 19
Ka-Tzetnik. *See* Dinur, Yehiel
Keneally, Thomas, 241
Kertesz, Imre, 100, 102, 104, 105, 106–9, 113–15

Khmer Rouge, 131–2, 161–3
    atrocities of, 132
    descendent genocide legacies, 150–2
    reconciliation with, 149
    trials of, 155
Kierkegaard, Soren, 102
King, Jr., Martin Luther, 203
kitsch, 247–9
Klee, Ernst, 320
Klemperer, Victor, 64
Kouchner, Bernard, 128, 134
Köves, György, 104, 106–9. *See also* Kertesz, Imre
Krakow, Poland, 111, 233, 249–57
Kristallnacht, 319–36
    annihilation of Aryan Germans, 330–6
    "final solution," 328–30
    Jewish policies, 325–8
    messages of, 322–5
Kristallnacht, 297
Kundera, Milan, 101, 102, 115
Kurasawa, Fuyuki, 126
Kwaßniewsk, Aleksander, 3

L

LaCapra, Dominick, 10, 177, 181, 350
    empathic unsettlement, 240
Landsberg, Alison, 197
Langer, Laurence, 296
Lanzmann, Claude, 112, 233, 347
    interview of Maurice Rossel, 121–3
Laub, Dori, 139, 181
Law for the Prevention of Genetically Sick Issue (1933), 333
law of dispersion, 284–94
Laws, 235. *See also* Plato
Leach, Edmund, 107
legacies, 152–6, 161–3. *See also* narratives
    accessing, 149
    Cambodian Canadian descendants, 153–4
    Cambodian descendants in Cambodia, 154–6
    descendants, 150–2
    Jewish Israeli descendants, 152–3
The Legacy of Abused Children: From Poland to Palestine, 221–3
legitimization of the pronoun "we," 81
Les temps modernes, 121
levée en masse (mass conscription), 58

Levi, Primo, 31, 104, 115, 178
Levinas, Emmanuel, 71
Lévi-Strauss, Claude, 107
Levy, Daniel, 6, 7, 12, 57, 146
    argument for human rights, 126
    hegemonic roles of memory, 59
    political consequences of memory, 15
    Twentieth century commemoration, 194, 195, 197
Liberté Sans Frontières, 137
Life is Beautiful, 347, 348, 349
linguistic analysis, 82, 89. *See also* Lyotard, Jean-François
Lionnet, Françoise, 214
listening, exercise of, 87, 88, 90, 92
literature, 39
    German, 285
    Mizrahi, 301–7
Lithuania, 13
Litvak, Meir, 298
Loewenberg, Peter, 319
Lyotard, Jean-François, 60, 71, 139, 346
    on "beautiful death," 76
    ethical thought, 93, 94
    legitimating republican discourse, 81, 82
    moral obligation, 73
    outline of ethical discourse, 87
    phases of obligation, 78
    understanding of sublime, 237

M

The Ma'abara (The Immigrant Camp), 302
Macdonald, Dwight, 104
magical death, 74
Maier, Charles, 16, 20
Malhuret, Claude, 131, 132, 133
Mandela, Nelson, 203
Marcuse, Herbert, 286
Marx, Karl, 112
Marxism in France, 133–4
mass conscription *(levée en masse),* 58
Matar, Ruth, 66
Mayim Noshkim LeMayim (Water Kissing Water), 304
meaning-making. *See* global semiotics
Mearsheimer, John, 53
Médecins Sans Frontières (MSF), 124, 125, 127. *See also* humanitarian witnessing

mediation, 80
Mein Kampf, 275, 276, 277, 278, 328
membership, test of, 94
memory, 99
    collective, 5, 47
    commemorative, 198
    core memory of Holocaust, 61
    cosmopolitan, 7, 113–15 (*see also* cosmopolitan memory)
    distribution of, 48
    of French Revolution. *See* French Revolution
    globalization of, 3–8
    hegemonic roles of, 59
    molded by global issues, 61
    multidirectional, 172
    of perpetrators, 57
    political consequences of, 15–19
    universalization of, 19, 100
    of victims, 57
    wars, 211
Michael, Sammy, 301, 303, 304
Michaels, Benn, 212, 213
Miller, Jacques-Alain, 239
Ministry of External Affairs (Germany), 328
Mintz, Alan, 241
Mizrahi literature, 301–7
Mizrahim (Isreali), 298–301
mnemonics, 48, 52, 195
mob rule, 330
model of absolute eradication, 77
modernity, 4, 32
Moisel, Claudia, 7
morality, 31, 224, 331
    as candidate for thematization, 197
    public discourse about, 56
    of witnessing, 125
morals, 61
    "after Auschwitz," 70–94
    beautiful death, 82
    evaluation, 87
    obligation, 73, 85, 93
    responses to disasters, 71
Morrison, Toni, 297
Moses, A. Dirk, 18
Mother Courage and Her Children, 270
multidirectional memory, 172, 211–20
    decentering memory, 224–5
    between occupation and genocide, 220–4

Multidirectional Memory: Remembering the Holocaust in the Age of Decolonization, 211
museums, 3, 5
    commemorative practices of, 48
    Yad Vashem. *See* Yad Vashem
Musil, Robert, 48
My Mother Courage, 270, 275, 276, 277

N

Nancy, Jean-Luc, 78, 84
narratives. *See also* testimonies
    French Revolution and Holocaust, 59
    placing memory in, 59
    Twentieth century, 14–15
Nazis
    "bad guys" narrative, 14
    genocide (*see* genocide)
    history of colonialism, 174–7
    Kristallnacht, 319–36
    rearmament program (Germany), 322
Nazism, 9
    association of French Revolution with, 63
    collaboration, 13
    negation of, 50
Negative Dialectics, 71. *See also* Adorno, Theodor
Neveh Dekalim, 66
noble savages, 35
nonbeautiful death, 79, 86. *See also* beautiful death
    contamination of, 83
nonviolence, message of, 203
Nora, Pierre, 5, 47, 128
normative laws, 91
Notebook of a Return to the Native Land, 176
Novik, Peter, 7, 8
Nuremberg Trials, 9
Nussbaum, Martha, 350

O

Obama, Barack, 53, 205
occupation, multidirectional memory, 220–4
Ofir, Adi, 10
Open, The, 39
Orientalism, 172

The Origins of Contemporary France, 62. See also Taine, Hippolyte
The Origins of Totalitarianism, 173
otherness, 9, 10, 15, 36–7
outlines of philosophical-ethical discourse, 87–93
Oz, Kobi, 308

P

pain, description of, 237
Palestinians
    human rights violations, 19
    oppression of, 18
Patraka, Vivian, 266, 268
Patterson, Charles, 40
Peleg, Ronit, 140
perception, 99
Pere Atzil (Noble Savage), 308
performances, 270–2
perpetuators beyond Nazi army/SS, 321
Peters, John Durham, 180
Philebus, 235
philosophical-ethical discourse, outlines of, 87–93
philosophy, 70. See also morals
photo essays, 221–4
Plato, 76
    Laws, 235
    view of death, 84
pleasure, description of, 237
The Pleasure of the Text, 239
poetic representations, 233–6, 347
    delight, 236–8
    ethics of, 257–8
    jouissance, 238–40
    Schindler's List, 240–9
    Spielberg's List, 249–57
poetry as symbolism, 107–8
Poland, 13
political disasters, 137
political responsibility, 91
political trends, 60
political "we," 93. See also Auschwitz
politics, 8–9, 211–20
Poole, Ross, 14
Popular Culture and the Shaping of Holocaust Memory in America, 241
postcolonial witnessing, 171–4
    ethics, 183
    history of colonialism, 174–7
    survivor testimonies, 177–80

    visibility of, 180–5
post-traumatic stress disorder (PTSD), 147, 148–50, 155
postwar Germany, 49. See also Germany
Precarious Life, 184
Probing the Limits of Representation, 20
propaganda, 63, 123
public declaration of importance, 4
purification of Germany, 326

R

Rabin, Yitzhak, 17
racial discrimination, 33, 175–6
Radstone, Susannah, 224
Raffarin, Jean-Pierre, 3
Rapson, Jessica, 194, 195
reach of memory, 47
rearmament program (Germany), 322
recollection, 99
reconciliation, 87
Redfield, Peter, 134
Reflections on the Revolution in France, 59. See also Burke, Edmund
refugee camps, 133, 137
reiteration, 267–9
relocation, 332. See also Kristallnacht
reparation, 20
representations, 267–9
    mimicry and the grotesque in, 307–10
restitution, 12
The Rings of Saturn, 218. See also Sebald, W. G.
Robertson, Ronald, 6
Rokem, Freddie, 270
Roman Catholicism, 108
Rosenfeld, Alvin, 7
Rossel, Maurice, 121–3
Rothberg, Michael, 125, 172
Rousso, Henry, 132, 136
Russia, assault on, 320
Rwanda, 137

S

Sabato, Haim, 304, 306, 309
sacrifice, economics of, 84
Said, Edward, 172, 173, 178, 225
Santayana, George, 112
savagery (anthropology), 34–6
Schechner, Alan, 214, 221, 222
Schindler's Ark, 241

Schindler's List, 112, 233, 240–9. *See also* Spielberg, Steven
Schlegel, Friedrich, 60
Schwab, Gabriele, 220
Sebald, W. G., 113, 214–20, 284
    Austerlitz, 289–94
    decision to stay abroad and homecoming, 286–9
    reading of Döblin, 285–6
Seven Jewish Children: A Play for Gaza (2009), 221
Sharon, Ariel, 3, 17, 65
Shavim VeShavim Yoter (All Men Are Equal—But Some Are More), 303
Shih, Shu-mei, 214
Shklovsky, Viktor, 178, 274
Shoah, 112, 121, 122, 180, 233, 348. *See also* Lanzmann, Claude; witnessing
Shoah BaMizrah, 299, 305
silence
    concerning disasters, 87, 88
    politics of, 149
Silencing the Past: Power and the Production of History, 33
Singer, Bashevis, 40
Singh, Manmohan, 203
Six-Day War, 66, 300, 348
Socrates, 235
Sonderkommando, survivors of, 348
Soussan, Judith, 130
Soyinka, Wole, 14, 15
speculative death, 72, 73, 74
Spielberg, Steven, 112, 233
Spielberg's List, 233, 249–57
Spirit's journey, 89
Spivak, Gayatri Chakravorty, 173, 180, 181, 184
Stockholm Holocaust Conference (2000), 51
Strauss, Leo, 103
Streit, Christian, 320
sublime, experience of, 236
survivor testimonies. *See* testimonies
symbolic manuals, 57
    Auschwitz, 61
    duplication of events, 62
    French Revolution, 58
    hegemonic roles of memory, 59, 60
    meaning and use, 65–7
symbolism, 16. *See also* global semiotics; museums
    Kristallnacht, 319–36
    limits of, 106–9
    use of, 66
symbols, 99
    elusiveness of, 100
    narrative genealogy, 224
Sznaider, Natan, 6, 7, 12, 57, 146
    argument for human rights, 126
    hegemonic roles of memory, 59
    political consequences of memory, 15
    Twentieth century commemoration, 194, 195, 197

T

taboo of denial in Europe, 62
Tabori, George, 266–78
Taine, Hippolyte, 62
television, 52
Temple Mount, 350
testimonies, 156–61
    Cambodian Canadian descendent, 157–8
    Cambodian descendants in Cambodia, 158–61
    of genocide witnesses, 149–50
    global semiotics of, 146–7
    Jewish Israeli descendants, 156–7
    MSF-France, 138 (*see also* witnessing)
    postcolonial witnessing, 177–80
theater of cruelty, 272–8
The Theatre and Its Double, 272
theocracy, 102
therapeutic practices, 36
Theravada Buddhism, 154
Theresienstadt, Rossel's visit to, 121–3
Third Reich, 92. *See also* Nazis
Tonus, 128, 131
Torpey, John, 12, 20
tours of Auschwitz, 112
tragedy, Auschwitz as, 104–6
transitions, "after Auschwitz," 86
trauma
    burden of memory, 148
    culture of, 258
    descendent legacies, 150–2
    global semiotics of, 146–7
    post-traumatic stress disorder (PTSD), 147–8
    suppression of, 257
    theories, 147

traumatic legacies, 152–6
    Cambodian Canadian descendants, 153–4
    Cambodian descendants in Cambodia, 154–6
    Jewish Israeli descendants, 152–3
trends
    emergence of memory in, 59
    intellectual, 60
    political, 60
Treue, Wilhelm, 320
Trouillot, Michel-Rolph, 33
Tuol Sleng, 158
Turkish community, 297
Twentieth century commemoration, 193–6
    International Day of Non-Violence, 202–5
    International Holocaust Remembrance Day, 199–202
    UN international days, 196–9

U

uncivilized spaces, 37–8
    Holocaust as an, 39–40
UN Genocide Convention, 126
Unheimliche Heimat (Sinister Homeland), 353
United Nations (UN), 3
    international days, 196–9
United States Holocaust Memorial Museum, 5
Universal Declaration of Human Rights, 126
universal domain (anthropology), 33
Universalisierung des Holocaust?, 7
universalism, 52
universalization of memory, 19, 100
UN Resolution 60/7 (2005), 6
Un vivant qui passe (A Visitor from the Living), 122, 123

V

Vallaey, Ann, 130
Valley of Communities, 66. *See also* Yad Vashem

Van Leer Jerusalem Institute, 319
Van Pelt, Robert Jan, 20
V-effect, 274
verfremdung (defamiliarization), 274
victims, identification with, 16–17
Vinchy syndrome, 136
violence of colonialism, 177
Voice
    ethics of, 92, 93
    sacrifice to, 88, 89, 91
The Voyeur, 271

W

Walt, Steve, 53
Webman, Esther, 298
Western antifundamentalism, 19–21
White, Hayden, 180
Whorf, Benjamin Lee, 114
Wiesel, Elie, 18, 52, 177
    influence of, 53
Wieviorka, Anette, 179
Wilkomirski, Binjamin, 296
Williams, Raymond, 198
Wisenthal, Simon, 52
witnessing, 34, 38
    ethics of, 134, 258
    humanitarian, 121–7
    postcolonial (*see* postcolonial witnessing)
Wittgenstein, Ledwig, 101
world order shifts, 212
world-transforming events, 54
World War II artifacts, 109
The Writing of the Disaster, 72. *See also* Blanchot, Maurice

Y

Yablonka, Hanna, 299, 302
Yad Vashem, 3, 5, 15, 16, 66, 350
    Ghasan Abdallah's visit to, 298
"the year of destiny" (*Schicksalsjahr*), 1938, 328
Yom Kippur War, 52

Z

Zionism, 50

www.ingramcontent.com/pod-product-compliance
Lightning Source LLC
Chambersburg PA
CBHW072142100526
44589CB00015B/2044